Goddess Coaching Companion
A Woman's Guide to Magick, Protection and Empowerment
By B. Melusine Mihaltses, C.L.C., M.M., B.M.
ISBN# 978-0-9851384-5-5

Feminine Divine Works
Schertz, Texas, U.S.A.

ISBN#978-0-9851384-5-5

✶✶✶✶✶✶✶✶

Goddess Coaching Companion
A Woman's Guide to Magick, Protection and Empowerment
By B. Melusine Mihaltses
ISBN# 978-0-9851384-5-5

LCCN: 2018942672

GODDESS COACHING COMPANION
A WOMEN'S GUIDE to
MAGICK, PROTECTION AND EMPOWERMENT
B. Melusine Mihaltses, C.L.C., M.M., B.M.

ISBN#978-0-9851384-5-5
Publisher: Feminine Divine Works
Schertz, Texas 78154, U.S.A
©B. Melusine Mihaltses
Year: 2018

Goddess Coaching Companion
a Woman's Guide to Magick, Protection and Empowerment
© 2018 by B. Melusine Mihaltses

Published by:
Feminine Divine Works
P.O.Box 114
Schertz, Texas 78154
Femininedivineworks@gmail.com

©B. Melusine Mihaltses 2018
B. Melusine Mihaltses asserts the moral right to be identified as the author of this work.

Library of Congress Cataloging- in- Publication Data
Mihaltses, B. Melusine, 1970-
      Goddess Coaching Companion
        a Woman's Guide to Magick, Protection and Empowerment

     1. Women Spirituality   2. Goddess Mythology   3.Self-Improvement 4. Metaphysics 5.Life Coaching I. title

Includes bibliographical references
ISBN: 978-0-9851384-5-5
Library of Congress Control Number: 2018942672

Goddess Coaching Companion, a Woman's Guide to Magick, Protection and Empowerment
© 2018 by B. Melusine Mihaltses
All rights reserved. No part of this book may be used, reproduced, nor transmitted in any form or by any means, electronically or mechanically, including photocopying, recording or by any information storage or retrieval system, whatsoever without written permission from Publisher; Feminine Divine Works, except in the case of brief quotations embodied in critical articles and reviews.

Although the author and publisher have made every effort to ensure accuracy and completeness of information contained in this book. We assume no responsibility for errors, inaccuracies, omissions, or any inconsistency herein. Any slights of people, places, or organizations are Unintentional.

First edition
First printing, 2018
Cover Art by: B. Melusine Mihaltses
Text, poetry and photographs all by: B. Melusine Mihaltses
Interior Illustration and Original Art all by: B. Melusine Mihaltses

Printed and bound in the U.S.A.   LCCN: 2018942672

Goddess Coaching Companion
A Woman's Guide to Magick, Protection and Empowerment
By B. Melusine Mihaltses

Feminine Divine Works
Schertz, Texas, U.S.A.

ISBN#978-0-9851384-5-5

Other Books By B. Melusine Mihaltses

Gathering for Goddess,
A Complete Manual for Priestessing Women's Circles
978-0-9851384-4-8

❋❋❋

Living Goddess Spirituality,
A Feminine Divine Priestessing Handbook
978-0-9851384-7-9

❋❋❋

Goddess Grimoire Journal,
A Collection of Simple Prose and Spells
978-0-9851384-3-1

❋❋❋

The Spellcrafting Coach,
A Metaphysical Guide to Revamp your Life
978-0-9851384-0-0

❋❋❋

Major Arcana Goddess Living Tarot,
A Feminine Divine Works Creation
978-0-9851384-8-6

❋❋❋

Feminine Divine Works Intuitive Oracle,
A Powerful Tool for Daily Insight and Inspiration
978-0-9851384-9-3

❋❋❋

Feminine Divine Works Intuitive 70x Oracle Deck

❋❋❋

Goddess Coaching Companion,
A Women's Guide to Magick, Protection and Empowerment
978-0-9851384-5-5

Feminine Divine Works,
Texas, U.S.A.

Dedication

Dedicated to my Children and all of my Teachers....

***

To women who dare...

***

To all of our ancestresses (Goddesses)
whose blood and sacrifice paved the way
for our existence - in gratitude I dedicate this book to you.

***

To all who recognize the privilege of
being in this time and space
and the debt we owe to our
ancestors to carry onward; walking the path,
the continuous Spiral path of her Divine Light,
Love and Evolution.

***

Bless it be to all who recognize the Goddess within...may your journey
bring you magick, protection and empowerment...)O(

****

GODDESS COACHING COMPANION
A WOMEN'S GUIDE to
MAGICK, PROTECTION AND EMPOWERMENT
B. Melusine Mihaltses, C.L.C., M.M., B.M.

ISBN#978-0-9851384-5-5

****

GODDESS COACHING COMPANION
A WOMEN'S GUIDE to
MAGICK, PROTECTION AND EMPOWERMENT
B. Melusine Mihaltses, *C.L.C.*, *M.M.*, *B.M.*
ISBN#978-0-9851384-5-5

TABLE OF CONTENTS

DEDICATION	8
INTRODUCTION	13

I. INTUITION — 19
Theme	20
Tarot	22
Moon	23
Herstory/Affirmation	23
Chakra/Gemstone	24
Gemstone Channeling	25
Animal Protection: The Owl	26
Goddess Empowerment	27

Persephone, Isis, Aradia, Circe, Hekate

Journaling	45
Invocations	46
Magick Rite	47
Altar Photos	48

II. LEADERSHIP — 49
Theme	50
Tarot	51
Moon	51
Herstory/Affirmation	52
Chakra/Gemstone	53
Gemstone Channeling	55
Animal Protection: The Buffalo	56
Goddess Empowerment	57

Amaterasu, Oduduwa, Sif, Oya, Hestia

Journaling	79
Invocations	80
Magick Rite	81
Altar Photos	82

III. CREATION & BIRTH — 83
Theme	84
Tarot	86
Moon	86
Herstory/Affirmation	87
Chakra/Gemstone	88
Gemstone Channeling	89
Animal Protection: The Spider	90
Goddess Empowerment	92

Gaia, Brigit, Saraswati, Olwen, Nu-Kua

Journaling	111
Invocations	112
Magick Rite	113
Altar Photos	114

IV. LOVE & JOY — 115
Theme	116
Tarot	118
Moon	119
Herstory/Affirmation	120
Chakra/Gemstone	121
Gemstone Channeling	122
Animal Protection: The Swan	123
Goddess Empowerment	125

Baubo, Erzulie-Freda, Hathor, Oshun, Aphrodite, Flora

Journaling	141
Invocations	142
Magick Rite	143
Altar Photos	144

V. MOTHER ARCHETYPE — 145
Theme	146
Tarot	147
Moon	148
Herstory/Affirmation	149
Chakra/Gemstone	150
Gemstone Channeling	151
Animal Protection: The Turtle	152
Goddess Empowerment	154

CornMother, Demeter, Yemaya, Kwan-Yin, Maia, Asherah

Journaling	177
Invocations	178
Magick Rite	179
Altar Photos	180

VI. STRENGTH & RAGE — 181
Theme	182
Tarot	183
Moon	184
Herstory/Affirmation	185
Chakra/Gemstone	186
Gemstone Channeling	187
Animal Protection: The Tiger	188
Goddess Empowerment	189

Kali, Pele, Sekhmet, Aine, Ereshkigal

Journaling	205
Invocations	206
Magick Rite	207
Altar Photos	208

(Con't)

VII.	**BODY & HEALTH**	**209**
Theme		210
Tarot		211
Moon		211
Herstory/Affirmation		212
Chakra/Gemstone		213
Gemstone Channeling		214
Animal Protection: The Deer		215
Goddess Empowerment		217
Artemis, Skadi, Uzume, Macha, Sunna		
Journaling		234
Invocations		236
Magick Rite		237
Altar Photos		238
VIII.	**JUSTICE**	**239**
Theme		240
Tarot		240
Moon		241
Herstory/Affirmation		242
Chakra/Gemstone		243
Gemstone Channeling		244
Animal Protection: The Ostrich		245
Goddess Empowerment		246
Ma'at, Rhiannon, Astraea, Tara, Sedna, Themis, Irene		
Journaling		267
Invocations		268
Magick Rite		269
Altar Photos		270
IX.	**SEX, POWER & DEATH**	**271**
Theme		272
Tarot		273
Moon		274
Herstory/Affirmation		275
Chakra/Gemstone		276
Gemstone Channeling		277
Animal Protection: The Snake		278
Goddess Empowerment		281
Lilith, Blodeuwedd, Ishtar, Inanna, Maman Brigitte, Baba Yaga		
Journaling		313
Invocations		314
Magick Rite		315
Altar Photos		316

X.	**AMBITION**	**317**
Theme		318
Tarot		320
Moon		320
Herstory/Affirmation		321
Chakra/Gemstone		322
Gemstone Channeling		323
Animal Protection: The Eagle		324
Goddess Empowerment		325
Durga, Mauve, Freyja, Ix Chel, Nike		
Journaling		348
Invocations		350
Magick Rite		351
Altar Photos		352
XI.	**WORK & PROSPERITY**	**353**
Theme		354
Tarot		355
Moon		355
Herstory/Affirmation		356
Chakra/Gemstone		357
Gemstone Channeling		358
Animal Protection: The Horse		359
Goddess Empowerment		361
Athena, Gefjun, Fortuna, Benten, Tyche, Sri Lakshmi		
Journaling		377
Invocations		379
Magick Rite		381
Altar Photos		382
XII.	**LIBERATION**	**383**
Theme		384
Tarot		386
Moon		387
Herstory/Affirmation		388
Chakra/Gemstone		389
Gemstone Channeling		390
Animal Protection: The Wolf		391
Goddess Empowerment		395
Erzulie-Dantor, Feronia, Shina Tsu Hime, Iris, Hina		
Journaling		411
Invocations		413
Magick Rite		414
Altar Photos		415
XIIII.	**FINAL THOUGHTS**	**417**
***RESOURCES & BIBLIOGRAPHY		421
***AUTHOR INFO		431
***ORDER FORM		434

INTRODUCTION

"There is no force equal to a woman determined to rise..." W.E.B. Dubois

   "Goddess Coaching Companion, a Woman's Guide to Magick, Protection and Empowerment," is an exceptional book for all women to find guidance in their personal spiritual journey. As the title suggest, it is a goddess companion coach, a book that aims to serve women in their personal development as their own personal guidebook. It serves as the reader's personal goddess coach and offers many modalities and tools that we use at **Goddess Empowerment Life Coaching.**

   The author, B. Melusine Mihaltses, has written numerous books on the subject of Goddesses and Spirituality. This latest book is her seventh offering, among an already impressive collection of published books. There are 30 new goddesses introduce in this new book, along with a reintroduction of the 24 goddesses presented in the author's first book, *"Gathering for Goddess, a Complete Manual for Priestessing Woman's Circles,"* and a reintroduction of the 12 goddesses presented in *"Living Goddess Spirituality a Feminine Divine Priestessing Handbook."* In total there are 66 powerfully diverse faces of the Sacred Feminine in the, **"Goddess Coaching Companion."**

You will find an amazing collection of 66, culturally diverse, Goddesses to incorporate into your own spiritual growth along with so many other pertinent tools for your journey. The book is organized into 13 chapters that correlate with the 13 lunations in a year and the 12 astrological zodiac signs, which gives you a chance to work one chapter per month, for a year. Not only do we explore several Goddesses for each chapter but we also delve into totems or animal energies, along with chakra and gemstone studies and the tarot. Each chapter also offers an opportunity to create and document your own rituals and sacred altar. There are also journal prompts to facilitate deeper exploration of our theme for each chapter.

In her previous books, **"Living Goddess Spirituality,"** and" **Gathering for Goddess,"** B. Melusine Mihaltses shares her vast knowledge, as a priestess of the Divine Feminine. She opens the reader's world up to all the many diverse Goddesses and mythologies from across the globe, and their powerful significance in a women's life. These two books are geared towards Woman's Group facilitating; how to priestess and form a woman's Goddess group. These books are an invaluable resource offering all the tools a priestess and an organizer would need to create, teach and sustain a woman's monthly goddess group.

In her book, "**Goddess Grimoire Journal,"** she offers her numerous invocations, art, spell incantations and poetries, all devoted to the Sacred Feminine, and various lunations. In "**The SpellCrafting Coach,"** she offers a rich volume of clear information on numerous ancient spiritual practices that can enhance our own modern day personal spirituality. It is really a rich compendium of a multitude of metaphysical tools and spiritual resources to incorporate into our lives; to change, improve and revamped our world. Among her numerous publications, the author also has created a Major Arcana Goddess Tarot along with a companion colored guidebook and a unique 73 oracle card deck, also with a companion colored guidebook. These two Tarot and Oracle books, illustrate in color, the many unique intuit, goddess artworks, the author has created throughout her own personal Goddess journey. They are yet another addition to the collection of invaluable tools and resouces for those seeking enlightenment and growth.

"Goddess Coaching Companion, a Woman's Guide to Magick, Protection and Empowerment," is yet another important publication that is being offered by this author. Its objective is to offer the reader personal coaching, more specifically, self-coaching, using the modality of Goddess Spirituality. It is not limited in its audience to only Pagan and Goddess women, but intended for all women, regardless of background or spiritual or religious persuasions.

This book addresses personal coaching through Goddess Spirituality. When we encounter an issue or a problem in our lives and we seek outside assistance, we go to a professional who we feel will best help us tackle the problem, much like we call a plumber for a water leakage in our pipes. However, when it is an issue related to personal development our options, regarding who can best assist us, increases substantially, and the options can be very diverse.

When we have a problem and we have to decide where to get help, we consider who and in what package that help will present itself. For example if you have a relationship problem and you go to your local priest, the priest/minister will approach your problem from a Biblical standpoint. He or she might consult the Bible and offer support through Biblical verses. If you have the same problem and you take it to a psychologist or psychiatrist, they will approach your problem through a psychological modality, using patient case studies, medical reference books and even maybe incorporating medicinal support. If you take that same relationship problem and go talk with an Addiction Counseling specialist, they will approach your problem from that modality; using the 12 step guide and exploring the connection with substance abuse, etc.

Goddess Empowerment Life Coaching works in a similar way like most coaches, except our modality is rooted in Goddess and Spirituality. Through Goddess and other metaphysical tools, there is a wealth of resources to offer clients in a coaching session. *"Goddess Coaching Companion,"* is meant to be a personal coaching guidebook for women that are seeking to change and transform their lives or to enhance work that has already begun on a one on one coaching alliance. This book is perfect for women that are seeking to bring into their lives a little bit of magick, protection, and empowerment, as indicative of the title of this book.

"Goddess Coaching Companion, a Woman's Guide to Magick, Protection and Empowerment," highlights special milestones (known as themes) that every woman goes through as she embarks on her spiritual journey. Milestones like; creation, leadership, sexuality, finding our purpose and prosperity, etc... In this way, its structure is almost reminiscent of the Fool's journey in the 22 Major Arcana of the traditional Tarot deck. It is unique in its structure and its offerings, especially as a coaching companion guide for women. Every chapter begins with an introduction of the theme or the milestone, a look at the corresponding tarot and astrological lunation. In every chapter you will find information and an opportunity to work with gemstones, animal energies, affirmations, and chakra portals. And of course every chapter offers the introduction of numerous Goddesses and mythologies that will be relevant to your chapter's themes. It's important to recognize that these Goddesses are multi-dimensional and have a plethora of powerful relevant attributes for us as women to explore. The Goddesses presented here should not be limited to the given chapters and themes. You are encouraged to see the potential of working with these Goddesses not just in the chapters they are introduced in, but also in relation to other themes and chapters throughout this unique book. For example Kwan Yin is introduced in chapter 5, where the theme offered is, "Mother Archetypes." There were numerous Goddesses that could've easily saturated this chapter; however we chose to include six. Kwan Yin, like many other deities presented here could also be revisited in other chapters, like chapter 8, where the theme is Justice. The Mother of Liberation, Tara, is introduced in chapter eight but can clearly be revisited in chapter twelve, where the theme is liberation. These are just a few examples and I hope you will find many more and hopefully these suggestions prove to be helpful to you as you explore this collection of amazing Goddeses.

In this book you will find inspiration to create altars, sacred rites, reflective journaling, and your own form of magick. In essence, *"Goddess Coaching Companion, a Woman's Guide to Magick, Protection and Empowerment,"* delves into various tools that are pertinent to our personal development and spiritual journey as women.

It is a remarkable first step to seek growth, transformation and empowerment, and I commend you for it. It is an effort that will not go unnoticed and you can rest assure that once you're awaken to a path, the Universe continues to bless us with a plethora of opportunities for positive changes, growth and more journeys. It is an honor to meet you at this sacred crossroad. Thank you for allowing me to be a part of your journey through the work we are about to explore together here in this book.
***Many Blessings.)O(

INTRODUCTION OF LUNATION IN THIS BOOK

Part of why the subject of astrology is even being addressed in a book about Goddess coaching is because we cannot underestimate the powerful influence Lunar and planetary aspects have on us; as above so below. It is a common esoteric belief that what is happening above us, around us and in the heavens, all collaborate to have quite a presence and influence in our daily lives. Therefore, when we are endeavoring to make changes in our lives and we are committing to address certain issues, it's important to look at everything around us and within us, to consider the engagement of all resources available to us. I believe Astrology; the moon placements (called lunation) and the planetary transits, can have a powerful effect on us. Our ancestors knew this and both ancient and modern practitioners of the Metaphysical arts, know the great value of studying and harnessing the energy that is prevalent around us, and readily available to all of us.

There are many different aspects I can delve deeper in with regards to astrological signs but for this coaching book, I am going to try to really stay focused on the attributes connected to the lunar transits. We've all heard of horoscopes and most of us know our own sun sign. It is essentially the sign that the sun was in the month you were born. As is evident the sun lingers a little longer in an astrological sign than the moon. The sun travels through each astrologically sign once a month while the moon, however, transits each of the 12 astrological signs every 2 to 3 days. It is not hard to see how its faster moving influence, changes more frequently for us and therefore, we have a chance to utilize this resource with a lot more consistency. Each chapter will have a short introduction about the corresponding lunation for each of our themes.

THEMES: AN OUTLINE OF OUR JOURNEY

Our journey is similar to the Fool's Journey in the Major Arcana of the Tarot, only we're not calling him a Fool. We are calling this character an aspect of our awakened selves. Therefore, here in this book, we see ourselves as creating our spiritual journey and, ultimately, our growth with each theme we encounter in each chapter. Below is a short synopsis of our path.

1. We begin with our **Intuition.** The awakening of are psychic abilities and a desire to uncover the Mysteries of life and death. At this milestone we endeavor to explore our intuitive gifts, connect with our ancestors and spirit guides. We are encouraged to delve into the occult and the metaphysical, to expand our knowledge of the esoteric.

2. The next stage for us brings us to the theme of **Leadership.** We see ourselves, after a period of solitude (The Hermit, The High Priestess, and The Moon) as part of a community. We can now begin to see ourselves in relationship to our greater community and consider how our past experiences and our gifts can be best utilized. We take a moment to consider how we can be of service to humanity. What can we offer our community, how can we be of service to our families and our community? How do we expand our own spiritual growth and evolution through the process of service to others?

3. The next step in our journey brings us to **Birth/Creation.** We reach a point in our expedition where we have a desire to create and give birth to something. The muse begins gnawing at our bellies and the fires of inspiration seek expression. There is something that wants to be born now; something that requires your breath of life. Our powers of manifestation begin to stir in our fired up belly. We start tapping into our own fecundity and feel the gnawing need to connect with our gifts of creation.

4. The Next Step brings us to Chapter 4, where we find **Love & Joy.** At this milestone we may find ourselves asking, what do we love? How do we invite the energy of love in our lives? Where is our passion? What stirs our heart? What brings us joy and awakens our heart to love? How do we choose Love? Here we explore the theme of Love and Joy. All too often we waste too much energy contemplating on all the things we hate not realizing that this is counter productive to our powers of manifestation. Instead, if we focus our energy on love and consistently reflect on the multitude of things that bring us joy, we begin to harnesss our powers of manifestation. We can effect great changes and positive vibrational shifts in our lives, when we start from a place of love and joy.

5. Our journey brings us to the next theme, The **Mother Archetype,** as we enter chapter five. The **Mother Archetype** is honored & explored here and whether it is the mother within us, the mother we hope to be or reflections of the mother who raised us- her power is palpable. The mother archeytype is a critical part of every woman's spiritual journey. As we explore this theme

we delve into healing aspect of the Mother archetype and reflect on the role of motherhood; how we **Nurture** ourselves or how we were nurtured as children?

6. In chapter 6 we encounter the catalyst of **Rage** and its ability to awaken our Inner **Strength.** We consider what is provoking anger within us and how we may utilize this anger to, not self-destruct or destroy but empower. We consider how to transform our anger to recreate landscapes and boundaries and thus, construct new worlds...

7. In chapter seven, we confront our issues with our **Physical body and Our Health.** We learn to tap into the power of our physical bodies and how to form a positive relationship with our earthly form to bring harmony into our lives. At this important milestone we are encouraged to prioritize our physical body, through movement, fitness, self-care and living with mindful presence. We are encouraged to be attentive to our overall wellbeing and prioritize our health.

8. Our next chapter is **Justice.** We reach a point in our journey where we are asked to bring balance into our lives and correct a wrong or bring Justice to something that is unfair. We become our own executioner of Justice and seek balance in our lives.

9. The next chapter brings us to the theme of **Sexuality, Power and Death.** We explore the subject that always seems taboo or too uncomfortable to explore; **Death and Sex**. We encounter the cathartic and empowering energy of sex and explore its connection to our autonomy and Power.

10. The next chapter relates to the discovery of our inner fires of **Ambition** and our ability to **focus** on our desire. We have arrived at a point where we are exploring what it is that we truly want; placing value on the power of our sight and vision. In this chapter we explore our true desire and the many ways we can make efforts to manifest them.

11. In chapter eleven, we arrive at the point where we are ready to **Work and manifest Prosperity**. We're ready to roll up our sleeves and make our dreams a reality. In chapter 11 we are awakened to our desire to put our best work forward to become victorious. We connect with our powers of manifestation to make our way towards success, and great fortune in this world.

12. The last chapter is about the desire for **Freedom and Liberation.** We reach a point in our journey where we have learned a great deal and our growth brings us to this point of liberation. We are ready to carve a path for ourselves that is uniquely ours and build our lives the way we see fit; free of judgment of other people's negative input and secure in who we are. In this chapter, we are awakened to our inherent need to exist in the world free and liberated. We have garnered much strength and our spirit has been fortified by all the previous themes we successfully explored throughout this book. The wheel turns and the cycle begins once more; only now it begins with a harvested set of valuable experiences, the Fool is ready for freedom and new adventures.

13. After this stage, we are reflective in chapter 13. Here we return; we spiral once again, now, only more elevated and enlightened. We may review our journey thus far and perhaps proceed again to chapter one, to the pursuit of our intuitive gifts; developing even greater psychic abilities. It brings us into solitude and a meeting again with the High Priestess. We are reflective in chapter 13, ready to **Spiral forward** into new journeys, with a desire to develop further our gifts.

CHAPTER ONE

"At times you have to leave the city of your comfort and go into the wilderness of your intuition. What you'll discover will be wonderful. What you'll discover is yourself."
Alan Alda

THEME: INTUITION

We begin our journey together by endeavoring to delve into our intuitive gifts. While intuition, particularly a woman's intuition, will become a very obvious theme throughout this book, it is something we will at least in this chapter take a closer look at and commit to further developing.

I think it's important, given the type of work we are about to embark on, to give proper reverence and honor to what will inevitable become a large part of our own growth and evolution. Our intuition can be an invaluable tool for us, as we devote ourselves to growth, empowerment and positive life changes. Admittedly though, it has varying ways of presenting itself to us and sometimes when we least expect it. For example, the fact that this book has found its way into your hands is no coincidence. It is a strong indication that there is some part of you that has begun the search for something more. Intuitively, you've felt the call that has moved and inspired you to search for ways to bring more magick into your life and tap into the powers of manifestation you know, somewhere inside you, you possess.

Personally, I've been there... I've been exactly where you are and I am writing this book because I know what that feels like, and the extraordinary journey it leads to. When your soul starts gently tapping at your intuitive window and you start to feel a type of restlessness that, after a while, you can no longer ignore, things start to happen. And, coincidentally, we begin to notice that life takes on a different hue and all of a sudden everything is communicating with you in some shape or form. The mundane joins the magickal and all of sudden everything has meaning; everything has something to impart to you.

This is how we begin our journey together to explore and develop the theme for this chapter; the first chapter of this book.

When you know how to listen,
everyone is the Guru...Ram Dass

I like to define Intuition, our theme in this chapter, as simply that inner world within ourselves that knows. It is infinite wisdom found deep within our inner body. It is that sacred chasm resource, infinitely connected to source energy and the interwoven tales of our collective ancestry. It has the potential to be a power source of guidance but, as with all skills, it requires acknowledgement, respect, and a concerted effort to study, practice and further develop it.

The "Moon in Pisces" is a perfect place to begin our work because the astrological sign of Pisces tends to be ruled by the element of things we sense but can't quite always put our fingers on. It is the intangible trying to express itself in varying languages; both ancient and modern. Pisces can be seen as the awakener of the spiritual and the effable; the watery realm ruled by Neptune. Here we take our collection of symbols, our hunches and coincidences; our nocturnal dreams and premonitions, and learn to interpret their unique messages to us. It might organically lead us to explore other metaphysical practices like astrology, numerology, chakra work and tarot studies, all in an effort to enhance intuitive gifts. Each chapter in this book will offer us an opportunity to explore these facets in conjunction with our themes.

Lastly, I will say that I find it interesting that oftentimes, as with most things in life, there is a catalyst that appears in our lives that inaugurates this massive shift in our world and brings us to this magickal crossroad. I was fortunate enough to have grown up in a household where my intuitive development was valued and encouraged. At an early age I became quite adept at interpreting symbols, coincidences and dreams. I also learned quite early on how to work with tarot and astrology. However, I can distinctly remember when my desire to connect deeper with my intuition became so strong that it was having a profound effect on everything in my life and, as a result, it brought the right teachers, experiences, books, relationships and specific groups to usher in this new level of intuition.

In this chapter we will explore further our theme with the help of several resources. We will endeavor to connect with the Goddesses, Aradia, Hekate, Persephone, Isis, Circe and the sacred animal energy of the Owl. We will connect with our 6th chakra, the Third Eye chakra, and gemstones that can help better facilitate this connection. We will also look at the corresponding Lunation and a Tarot card that is connected to our theme.

THE HIGH PRIESTESS TAROT CARD

The High Priestess card in the traditional Rider Waite tarot deck is often depicted with an expressionless mysterious woman, sovereignly seated between two pillars. The pillar to her right is black and marked with the letter B and the other pillar, to her left is white and marked with the letter J. The **B** on the black Pillar stands for the word *"Boaz"* which means, negation and the **J** on the white pillar stands for *"Jachin"* which means beginning. It is clear she is seated at the entrance of a temple, which connects her to the sacred place of worship for the Divine. These two pillars or temple columns are often associated with the ancient Temple of Solomon and represent duality.

The High Priestess knows the past, the present and the future. She is the holder of all divine secrets connected to life, death and the spiritual world. It is through our communion with her that we are initiated into the mysteries of the occult. In her hands she holds the Book of Knowledge, which is illustrated as an ancient scroll tucked neatly halfway, underneath her arms. It is indicative of her supreme knowledge, which is not all revealed to the uninitiated.

Depicted with a white cross on her chest, she is dressed in a blue and white robe. Her overflowing garment appears to puddle like a small body of water by her feet. If we look very closely we can also detect a larger body of water behind her. The prevalence of water in the card of the High Priestess not only denotes her intimate connection with the fluid subconscious mind but all the gifts of this sacred element; and again all things related to the Feminine.

It is important to note that there are often two moons represented in this card. Usually the presence of a large crescent Moon can be noted by her feet but also on her crown. On her head she wears a circlet that resembles a Full Moon sandwiched between two crescent moons; it appears to represent her connections to the Cosmos, the Moon the cycles of life, her psychic gifts and her representation of Feminine intuitive powers.

Sometimes she is connected to the Greek Goddess Persephone and if we look behind her, there appears to be a tapestry of pomegranates; yet another esoteric symbol of the Goddess. Remember it is the Goddess, Persephone who eats of this fruit in the underworld. Known as the fruit of the dead, her consumption of this fruits condemned her to Hade's Realm for half of the year. It made Persephone the only Goddess who had dominion over two opposing realms, at different times of the year. She was known as Queen of the underworld for half of the year and the other half; she was known as Goddess of the spring. The pomegranates are yet another sacred symbol seen in this card that connects The High Priestess to the secrets of life and death.

There is something very still and serene about the image of the High Priestess. Her very stillness speaks to us about solid confidence, holding on to what we know, ancient wisdom, quietude and our need to connect with our own intuition in order for her truths to be revealed. She is not animated or aggressive in her approach, unlike the Magician. She will not reveal her secrets so haphazardly. She represents patience and a deep inner wisdom connecting many lifetimes. She is the power of the unconscious world and she holds the knowledge of the mysteries of life.

MOON IN PISCES   WATER/NEPTUNE

THEME: Intuition

PISCES   MUTABLE   WATER   FEMININE   FISH

Pisces is known as the 12th astrological sign in the zodiac. It is considered the last sign in the astrological calendar before the start of the fiery Aries season, which often denotes the start of the Pagan year. This is of great significance to us because it speaks to us about quiet preparations and honoring that magickal period of transition before the start of something new. That pivotal, quiet, reflective moment we observe before anything of significance happens. Ever witness the eerie hush before a storm or the palpable energy in the labor room right before a child is born into this world? Think of an orchestral conductor, her commanding arms, raised tensely, holding silence before the outpouring of sounds rushes in. This is Pisces, this is the last sign of the zodiac, with much more implication than we consciously realize. It is the sacred crossroad and it is the reason why I felt compelled to begin our journey here.

Pisces is a water sign and therefore it should be of no surprise that its symbol is the fish. We can reflect for a moment on the energy and gifts of the fish and its habitat. Considering this watery realm, we can deduce much about Pisces energy. It is slippery, sometimes hard to get a hold of, like a fish, and it has an ebb and flow quality that makes it allergic to definitive lines and boundaries. When you are working with this lunation these are aspects that you want to be fully aware of and, hopefully, make the best use of.

Pisces is also ruled by Neptune, the planet and God of the Oceans. This Neptunian rulership undoubtedly has a powerful influence but when we consider how the moon rules the tides, we can see how watery and potent this lunation can be. It can awaken issues related to boundaries and emotions and offer us interesting nocturnal dreams. It can inspire our artistic and musical gifts and awaken new visions. This lunation can stimulate our intuition and psychic abilities as well. But, Neptune's influence can also make it nebulous, illusive and tricky. Concentration may be harder to achieve and implementing anything that requires meticulous detail will cause strain.

Astrologers often say when the moon is in Pisces, because it is the last sign of the zodiac, it might be a good time to finish up old work, slow down and clean up any loose ends. It can be a great time to engage in a lot of meditations, daydreaming, visualizing and planning. Its watery nature makes it also a good time to delve into your emotions and explore your true feelings; journaling at this time can be quite cathartic and revealing.

*"I feel there are two people inside me –me and my intuition.
If I go against her, she'll screw me every time,
and if I follow her, we get along quite nicely."* Kim Basinger

HERSTORY

She was having many unusual occurrences and coincidences; visions and premonitions that were being proven right. She knew her Grandmother had psychic gifts and spent much of her youth hearing of the many times she was consulted by family members. It never occurred to her that she too might be gifted, since her mother often dismissed "The Arts." But here she was, now feeling a strange shift within. Her dreams were becoming more intense and full of symbols she was still learning to interpret.

She knew something inside of her was shifting and she felt moved to explore what that was. Spirit was calling and it was time for her to explore her intuition and develop her psychic powers…

********Take a moment to document here, or in your journal, your unique story.**

_____

_____

_____

AFFIRMATION

**I forge a solid, trusting, relationship with
my inner knowing by listening.**

**Moments of silence and solitude
invite my inner knowing to speak.**

I Know

**I pause and retreat from the outer world to go within,
for I know all the answers I seek are within me
waiting to be unearthed.
All of my questions have answers and
solutions connected to the sacred thread of my ancestry.**

**I connect to the sacred pool of my ancestors and the Divine…
I drink in the wisdom and knowledge that is
freely offered to me. I only have to ask
to receive what is already deep within me, waiting for consumption…**

CHAKRA & GEMSTONE WORK

6th Chakra **AJNA/THIRD EYE CHAKRA** **COLOR:** Purple/Indigo

Intuition and Psychic realm, Clarity and related to the Mind, Sight, Telepathy, Astral travels.

Mantra: I See

)O(WORKING: Psychic Development Oracles Psychic Development, Divination

GEMSTONE CONNECTION: Amethyst is the well-known stone of Spiritual enlightenment and psychic awareness. It is a violet-purple colored quartz crystal, often used in metaphysical spiritual practices. Used to facilitate trance in meditations, it is also a companion stone for those practicing divination or oracle/tarot readings. Interesting to note, it is reputed to help lessen addictive habits and can help prevent hangovers. Amethyst opens your mental capacities and helps you attain clarity. When placed under your pillow it can also help with insomnia.

GEMSTONE CHANNELING

Find a comfortable place where you can be assured of your privacy, safety and comfort... If you can go outdoors in nature that would be most ideal but any place where you can relax, undisturbed, will be ideal.

You are invited then, to place yourself in a comfortable position; you may sit or lay down. If it is available to you, place in your hands the Amethyst that we are working with today. Take a moment to actually look at your Amethyst. Notice how it feels in your hands. Make note of its various purple hue and the different shapes and images it might create. Hold your crystal up and study it carefully for a few minutes, in silence... Quietly, gaze upon it and make note of any thoughts or visions that immediately start to unfold before you.

When you're ready, you may close your eyes now and begin this short meditation. As with all trance work, we begin with our breath. You are asked to take a deep breath. See this first breath in a purple hue, as if it was the Amethyst itself, transformed into ether. Slowly fill your lungs up now with this purple hue, for 3 seconds and then release it... Counting now at your own pace; breathe, 1, 2, 3, and exhale on 4....and again....breathe in, 1, 2, 3, and exhale on 4. Let's do this one more time and then quietly counting in your head.... Breathe 1, 2, 3, and release on 4. Breathe, trusting in the natural rhythm you have now established, of your relaxed inhalation and exhalation.

Amethyst wishes to impart a special channeled message for you. See this gemstone in your mind's eye. See it shining brightly, embedded upon its dark, fertile, mother earth. Draw nearer to it and ask if it will allow you to pick it up. When permission is granted, gently gather it in your hands. With your mind's eye, gaze upon it; studying its color, its texture, its veins or any other details that captures your eyes.... Ask it to speak to you. (Pause) Visualize now, the top of your head opening like a window. Open yourself up now to any messages that may unfold... You may envision your crown chakra now unveiling a magnetic Amethyst portal, allowing for this **Crystal Transmission** to come through... Continue to breathe and when you can, make note of any messages that are coming through. You may write them here, or in your journals or any other sacred place you wish.

_____
_____
_____

OWL PROTECTION ENERGY

Snowy Owl, Great Horned Owl, Barn Owl, Western Screech Owls, Spotted Owl, Long-Eared Owl, Hoot Owl, Burrowing Owl, Eurasian eagle Owl, Elf Owl, these are just some of the many types of Owls known to us. Across the globe it might surprise you to know that there are at least two hundred sixteen different types of owls that exist today. They are all absolutely gorgeous, some with similar traits and yet with noted subtle differences, too many for us to discuss here. For now, however, we will explore the Owl as a powerful ally and protector in our spiritual journey.

Owls are nocturnal, birds of prey. They are best distinguished by their large piercing eyes and their impeccable night vision. They have the capacity to nearly rotate their heads all the way around, which only supports the concept of the owl as an all seeing predator. Think upon how useful these unique traits might be to someone who is seeking wisdom and knowledge in their own lives. Owl medicine helps us to see and extract hidden secrets. It facilitates our own ability to discern the truth in all situations. They are known as, *"Guardians of Wisdom,"* and can awaken in us Clairvoyant and Clairaudience gifts.

Owls have the proclivity for adventures and absolute freedom. They are also known as solitary beings and you won't find them in groups but rather alone in their sanctuaries, perched, high up on tree tops. They almost become exemplary of what is sometimes required in our own pursuit of enlightenment. They are keen observers of their environment and natural silent fliers in the night. They are able to quietly swoop down on their prey, virtually unnoticed. Their distinguishable hoot heard across the night sky, however, is received as an omen of change and those studying spirituality, would not dismiss its call.

Due to their nocturnal nature, they are naturally affiliated with shadow work and the Moon, thus making them an ideal ally and protector when we are delving into the unknown. Their nocturnal vision almost becomes a distinguished attribute that can help us see beyond the veil of deception and illusion. Owl medicine, for many cultures, helps warn us of impending change and offers deep insight and spiritual guidance.

Across numerous European traditions and folktales, the owl appears to have been the preferred animal for witches to shape-shift into and partake in nocturnal journeys. They served as eyes and spirit teachers to those seeking ethereal wisdom. In Celtic mythology, the owl was a guide for the soul traveling into the underworld. Owl in this tradition became known as the, *"Gatekeeper to the Akashic realm."* The Romans believed Owls helped to ward off evil. In some Native American traditions, Owl is seen as a harbinger of death, whether it was an actual, physical death of someone we knew, or a visit from a deceased loved one. There was a strong correlation between the underworld and the presence of an owl; more specifically, the sound of his haunting hoot, which often signaled a change. For many indigenous cultures, Owl medicine allows us to connect with our deceased loved ones and here we see a strong link between our beloved wide-eye creature and the underworld. For ancient Sumerians, the screeching owl was linked to the Goddess Lilith, who was believed to have owl talons as feet. The piercing, high pitched sound of a screeching owl announced her presence nearby. For most indigenous cultures, the owl is known as the "*night eagle*," a nocturnal version of the highly revered eagle seen in the light of day. The owl is also closely linked with the Athenian Goddess of Wisdom, Athena. In Greek mythology the Goddess of Wisdom and War, was purported to carry an owl on her shoulder as a symbol of her infinite wisdom and foresight. As an animal so often connected to the Goddess of wisdom, Owl medicine awakens in us a desire to acquire knowledge and commune with our spirit guides. It can also stir our hunger for freedom and travel adventures, including astral travel capabilities.

Our awareness of the Universe at large becomes heighten when we connect with the Owl. We become awaken to all the many ways the Universe is speaking to us; via omens, oracles and animal sounds. We learn to value more our sanctuaries and our solitary moments, especially our evening hours. As a "*Guardian of the Underworld,*" the Owl connects us to change that is often linked with a death or a transformation of some sort. Whether we are physically parting with a loved one or psychically saying goodbye to a particular energy.

The Owl as our ally and protector helps us connect to the truth of all matters and strengthens our ability to fly forward, with greater wisdom. If we are open to their gifts, the Owl becomes a great teacher and guide, for esoteric studies and spiritual growth.

THEME WORK SUGGESTIONS

Work with the Pisces moon, symbolized by the Fishes,
and work with The Owl energy and Goddesses offered in this chapter.
You are encouraged to keep a Dream Journal and record your dreams
every morning upon waking up. Explore Metaphysical studies
like: astrology, numerology, SpellCrafting, candle magick, Oracles
and Tarot card usage. Consult a Psychic or connect with a Shaman.
Connect with your Spirit Guides and
create an Ancestral Altar to your deceased loved ones.

GODDESS EMPOWERMENT

PERSEPHONE

Persephone or Proserpine (in Latin) is the Greek Maiden Goddess of Spring and Queen of the Underworld. Persephone has been immortalized as the beloved daughter of the Goddess of the Grain-Demeter. The ancient myths associated with her and her mother, place her as an important integral part of the renowned, Great Eleusinian mysteries.

The name Persephone has been anglicized but to begin our study of this Goddess it's best to first begin etymologically. As a young girl and daughter to her mother, she was first known, most popularly as "Kore", (variations of this name include Koura, Cora, Koure) which translates as *"the Maiden, young girl."* This became almost a sort of nick name when referring to her in Eleusis. Some scholars also claimed that another connotation to this name alludes to *"young bride."* This would mean that right from the start, her name reflects the role and path she would inevitably take.

Many discovered ancient vases and art work of the time, show depictions of her and her name noted as *"Pherophata," "Phersephata"*, and *"Pherephassa."* This would appear to be her accurate, more formal name, as her actual Temple at Eleusis was called, *"Pherephation"*.

The first part of the name Persephone, erroneously is linked with light and if we look at the second part of her anglicized name, *"phone."* It is derivative of *"phonos," "phoneme,"* it roughly means *"to slaughter or sacrifice."* Therefore, upon a closer look at her name, Persephone is normally translated as *"destroyer of the light,"* a rather unusual title for the Spring maiden Goddess but perhaps not so unusual for the Queen of the Underworld.

Upon closer inspection of her more authentic name, *"Pherophata,"* we get a different meaning and a more revealing insight into this ancient deity. Her name takes on a different hue if we consider the meaning of the first half of her ancient name, *"pheros"*, this word roughly means *"to bear, offer, carry, to bring."* Yet the second part of her original name *"phattas"* derived from *"phatos"* means *"the unspeakable, unutterable, incommunicable."* After much research, it would appear then that the name of this Goddess means, *"She who brings or conveys the unspeakable."* Thus, as Queen of the Underworld, the Greeks believed her to be a bringer of the indescribable, of that experience that goes beyond words. She is the "Maiden of the ineffable" and a vastly crucial component of the Eleusinian Rites, which were responsible for teaching initiates, the secrets of life and death.

The Eleusinian mysteries and the Greek myths tightly associated with this epic have forever immortalized, Persephone as the Maiden Goddess of Spring and the Underworld. The ancient writings of the time like; Hesiod's Theogony (c700BCE), Homer's Iliad (written c 750-725BCE) The Odyssey (written c743-713BCE) and the Homeric hymn to Demeter, set in Eleusis,(written around 650-550-BCE) by an unknown author, all have contributed greatly to our knowledge of this Goddess.

As a child, Kore was extremely close to her mother, one of the twelve original Olympian Deities - Goddess of the Grain, Demeter. Her birth came about as a result of typical trickery played by the Gods. In one tale, Zeus turned himself into a Bull and with his sister, fathered Persephone. There is another more obscure myth that comes from Greek scholar, Appolodorus (180-120BCE) it places Persephone as daughter of Zeus and the underworld Goddess River Styx, born already in the realm of Hades, but this version is rarely mentioned and used typically to explain how Persephone becomes the Queen of the Underworld.

Demeter and Persephone had a very close intimately relationship and some speculate that perhaps the Gods, like Aphrodite and Zeus himself, did not completely understand nor approve. In one tale it is Aphrodite who is credited for arousing in Hades desire for his niece.

One day the beloved Kore was out in the flower fields near Enna, with her young virginal cousins, like Artemis, Pallas and numerous other maidens friends like; Galaxyria, Acaste, Calypso etc... She was not alone, as some artistic depictions might lead you to believe. She was actually in great company, plucking an array of beautiful fragrant flowers and engaging in the typical games that young girls play. When behold, the most beautiful flower she had ever seen, captivated her. Some described it as a three-petalled, blue fleur-de-lys, but the Homeric hymn described it as the one hundred bloom, white, sweet Narcissus flower. Enamored by its celestial beauty, the impetuous girl stretched out her arm and reached to pull it out and upon doing so, the earth split open from below her feet, and, abruptly a chariot of black stallions came forth with Hades snatching the young maiden; disappearing from the scene. She let out one yell, but it all happened so fast, no one could claim that they saw or heard anything...no one, except for the all-seeing Sun God, Helios and the Wise Crone- Hekate.

For nine days and nine nights, distraught Demeter searched everywhere for her beloved daughter, but could not find her anywhere. On the tenth day, Hekate comes to her aid, shares what she knows and then takes her to Helios, for further information on the matter. To Demeter's astonishment and devastation, she learns of her daughter's abduction and horrid fate, as Bride of Hades. And to make matters worse, she learns that this arrangement was made and approved, behind her back, by Zeus himself. According to the popularized Greek myth, the despondent and enraged Demeter abandoned her post on Mount Olympus immediately and refused to let anything grow upon the earth until her daughter was returned to her. If humans now lacked the crop to nurture themselves due to Demeter's retaliatory actions, they would surely lack the ability to feed the Gods with proper offerings; and this was a monumental reality for the Olympians to consider. Demeter spent her sad days traveling the earth, in disguised as an old woman and pledged the earth would witness a horrid famine that would destroy both mortals and immortals alike, until she was reunited with her beloved Kore.

Meanwhile, Kore was in the underworld now, as Persephone, Wife to her uncle, Aidoneus Hades. Imagine her confusion and her own lamentation- youthful flowering bright maiden, finding herself in the abysmal dark caverns of the underworld, greeted by the stench of death and the overwhelming sadness of loss souls. On the earth, she was brightness, frivolity, fecundity, growing the flowers and the corn. As a girl she knew love only via her devoted mother. Here, so abruptly, she finds herself in this new realm, alone, in a foreign new role, as wife. The myth tells she would not eat nor drink anything in the underworld, during this time. Yet time went by and upon receiving word from the messenger God, Lord Hermes, that she would be allowed to leave the underworld and return to her mother, she partook of the food of the dead- seeds of the Pomegranate. Some conflicting stories state that she was offered 4-6 pomegranate seeds, by Hades himself and some state that someone else tricked her into taking them, in any case, upon consuming them she was now obligated to this realm. Her heartwarming reunion with her mother was bittersweet, as Demeter learned she would have to sacrifice her daughter to Hades and his underworld, one third of the year, due to the pomegranate seeds the maiden had ingested. During this time, the earth would be barren and cold and Demeter committed herself to forbidding anything to grow upon the earth while she mourned the absence of her daughter. This myth, on the surface, would serve to explain the winter season and the agricultural sacred cycles so important to the Greeks and most civilizations at this time.

Persephone was sometimes depicted holding a torch flame or a sheath of Corn. She is often described as youthful, beautiful, trimmed ankle, bright minded, the one who makes the corn grow, and the one who has sympathy over the dead. One myth even tells of how she was not abducted but rather willingly sacrificed herself to the underworld upon learning of the sadness and confusion plaguing lost souls. She wanted to be their hope and guide. In this case she would be very reminiscent of many sacrificial Deities like Selu, the Native American Corn Goddess. As the Queen of the underworld she mothers and consoles the dead and it is through the entry of her bright aura, that THEIR hope is renewed. She appears supportive and much needed and yet, as can be expected, there are some conflicting tales of Persephone in her role as Queen of the Underworld. Some of the writing of the time makes her almost just as fearsome and mistrustful as her husband, Hades, and this is quite logical when we view unions between Gods in other cultures and other time periods. Consider how typically divine couples begin to share similar attributes. But in her, we see a consistent duality and it is this duality that intrigues me the most about Persephone.

Here is a Goddess who is required to live in two vastly contrasting worlds. Half of the year she is among the living, under the bright sun, amidst the fertile and all that grows. The other half of the year she is in the abysmal darkness among the dead, the hopeless, and the stagnant, hidden away from the brightness of the sun. Yet, when she goes from one realm to another, it is as if she never knew the other... It seems like no trace of darkness follows her when she returns to her mother's arms and her warm, carefree, maiden brilliance seems tempered in the underworld. It appears as if she surrenders herself to whatever realm she is in and locks the door, and perhaps the memories, of the realm she just came from.

Thus, she appears to me to be a patron Goddess for those who walk in two worlds. Witches, psychics, priestesses and seers also intimately know Persephone, as they too are somehow required to live in the mundane world while simultaneously, having extrasensory, spiritual experiences. I reflect on the mother who is answering her toddlers question about the spilt milk, while concurrently seeing the ghost of her deceased father hovering nearby- she is present and answering the call of two opposing realms. In my own life I think of how often I have been active in an intense community ritual, in a trance, floating, priestessing for the Divine and clearly in a completely different space, then at the end of it all, having to ground, pack up my stuff, catch the local bus or subway and travel through a vastly different realm to get back home, after communing, so deeply with the Divine.

Goddess of the twofolds indeed, we all touch upon Persephone at some point in our lives. Initially, I think about those who suffer with schizophrenia, Bi- polar disorder, depression, but perhaps less obvious are those among us who are forced to live in two realms in the exact way Persephone must. I reflect on the multitude of coal miners in our world and how they are required to live and work an inordinate amount of time under the earth, in deep caves, separated from their families and friends and then, when mining season is over, they return to the upper part of the earth's surface, rejoin their families and routines, until they are called back to mine again. I reflect deeply on our Military and how they too touch upon Persephone's journey. Countless of men and women are called to duty and get deployed to places that probably make Hade's realm look like "Candy land." The things that these men and women of service are exposed to when they are deployed in war zone, places like Iraq and Afghanistan, is horribly astounding. Death and its gruesome stench is ever prevalent for the military and while they are in service, they are subject to a world vastly different than the ones they originated from. When their tour of duty is over, somehow they are required to put all those gruesome, bloody war memories behind them and come back to their families and loved ones, assimilate into their respective community and resign themselves to civilian living again....or at least, until they are called back again. This is Persephone's experience. She teaches us how to reconcile living in two opposing realms and as wommin, in particular, with so many roles we are obligated to take on, she is an ideal Goddess to work with.

Persephone, the Maiden, is often seen as part of the well revered Greek trinity, with Demeter as Mother, Hekate as Crone, but upon closer inspection, she is not only a part of the trinity, Persephone herself IS the trinity. For me, Persephone comes across as really embodying the three most important feminine archetypes; Maiden, Mother, Crone. Some might say, she exemplifies four archetypes, the last one being the Queen. When she is Kore, her Mother's daughter, she is the Maiden and when she is in the realm of the dead, she is touching upon the Crone archetype, but also the Mother, as she is compelled to mother the loss souls. As Hade's wife she is called Queen, which is a newly adopted archetype in the 20th century. Upon her return to the fields, she again seems to touch upon the attributes of the Mother archetype in her ability to do exactly as **her** very own mother does, make the Grain grow. She is Kore and while her mother, Demeter, was closely linked with Barley, the Corn, was made to sprout from the earth and grow because of her. As Kore (whose name resembles the word corn)she had the ability to make things grow from above and below the earth.

  I believe Persephone also has much to teach us regarding our relationships with our mother and consequently all wommin. As the first womyn in our lives, our relationship with our mother can have a positive or negative effect on how we relate to all other, future wommin. The Maiden Goddess had a uniquely strong relationship with her mother, but so strong was her mother's love for her that Persephone's whole identity was mostly that of "daughter" and only after Hades enters the picture does she take on another, new role. Yet she vacillated between these two very strong roles as wife and daughter (belonging to her mother then belonging to her husband) and yet, even as daughter she now exemplified the same gifts as her mother. Becoming wife bestowed upon her a Goddesss crown that had only been reserved for her own mother. I think for many of us, who do have trouble with our mothers, it stems from a lot of sources, but certainly not recognizing the thread that runs through both, mother and daughter, can contribute to some strife. When we can't acknowledge or embrace the attributes (good or bad) of our mothers' we fail to see those same attributes inherent in our own selves. And its not just our mother, dare I say, it also includes other wommin as well. When we try to separate ourselves from something or someone that we don't like, it's occasionally because, before us, they are reflecting back, something in us we are unwilling to face. Working with Persephone might help us unearth better ways to interact with our mothers and consequently all wommin and this is yet another reason why she is a wonderful Goddess for our gender to connect with. She would've been another excellent deity to include and explore in various other themes found in this book like the chapter on mothering.

  *The Greek Maiden Goddess, Persephone, is the daughter of Demeter. She is the mystical one who directs the flowers and the corn fields to blossom but also gives light to a most auspiciously dark realm. Her energy is one immersed in the mysteries of life and death. Persephone is she who is Queen, Wife, Daughter, and Mother. She embodies all of these archetypes at once and she is every woman on the face of this earth. Our gender is constantly required to wear a multitude of hats and roles, sometimes even conflicting ones. Yet, we never falter in our ability to comply and execute them flawlessly.

  As someone who is seeking to develop psychic gifts you might find yourself in the beginning straddle between two worlds; learning how to walk the two paths simultaneously. Persephone enters your life to offer you balance and compassion for your own self and the multitude of offices you hold. Persephone's story exemplifies this best, as she was forced to move into contrasting realms and not abandon fully her main characteristics. Walking in multiple worlds and in a multitude of different roles, while we pursue our most cherished wish is quite the challenge but the Goddess Persephone reflects an example we can anchor our faith in. She comes into your life to inaugurate your intuitive gifts and an awareness of the necessity of balance, as we walk in various roles, pursing our life's mission.

ISIS

The ancient Egyptian Goddess, Isis, is a patron Goddess of a multitude of relevant blessings and attributes; she is of particular significance to women. She was worshipped in ancient time as a Goddess of love, fertility, healing, immortality, magick, agricultural blessings and as humanities' savioress. By far one of the earliest most venerated deities recorded in history was the Queen of Heaven, Isis. Her widespread worship and her longevity were partly due to the fact that she was worshipped among the nobility as well as the lower classes. There was an unusual approachability found within Isis that was absent among many other aloof Gods. Her worship spread across numerous lands and she was cherished by all for her great benevolence. She was known then as a Goddess who would fight for your personal cause and her worshippers believed her to be their defender and guardian.

Her worship and myths traveled across various terrains and they were often connected with her consort and twin brother, the God, Osiris. Her myths are so ancient they can be traced back to Pyramid text (late third millennium BCE). According to the ancient texts the Egyptian deities, Isis and Osiris loved each other deeply even while in the womb as twins. Upon their birth they were destined to unify as husband and wife. Their story is one of great significance and illuminates, Isis's great powers.

According to her most famous myth, Osiris had an evil brother name Seth. This brother eventually lures and traps Osiris into a wooden chest/coffin and then tosses it away in the river. This very evil act inaugurates the suffering and deep mourning of the Goddess, Isis. Her myriad of shed tears are often connected with the flooding of the Nile River and consequently the lands fertility and nourishment. In this way we see her great relevance as a Goddess of fecundity and harvest.

The wooden chest/coffin that held the lifeless body of Osiris somehow find its way to Byblos, where it gets hidden inside of a tree. This tree then becomes a pillar for the King's abode but all the while the Goddess, Isis, continues to mourn for her lost consort. She eventually learns of her lover's whereabouts, tells the king her story and he then gives her the chest with Osiris. She takes this chest/coffin, opens it, only to find her lover lifeless and dead. It is at this very pivotal moment in the story that we get a glimpse into the great power of this Egyptian Goddess. For as the story continues, Isis so loved Osiris that she was able to use her magick and her great love for him to revive him and bring him back to life. She revives his genitalia as well, has intercourse with him, and manages to conceive a child with Osiris. Together they have Horus, the Egyptian falcon headed God. Horus then eventually becomes the one to destroy Seth and avenge his father's demise, however not before another tragedy ensues related to Osiris. The wicked Seth manages to kidnap Osiris again only this time he cuts him up into tiny pieces and scatters them across the globe; purposely making it almost impossible for his resurrection. The Goddess Isis however, is no ordinary deity, as is revealed in this tale. She manages to search the globe, successfully retrieve and gather all the pieces of Osiris, except for his genitals. Because she's a Goddess of great power she is thus able to travel to the land of the dead, where eventually she resurrects her beloved consort, long enough for him to pass down his power and knowledge to his son, Horus.

Many of the ancient texts reveal numerous prayers and beautiful invocations to the Queen of Heaven. These eloquent writings depict Isis as a supreme mother deity, as an important Goddess of healing and a patron Goddess of deep love, fertility, magick and sexuality. She is a nurturing Goddess that is so intimately connected with the land and the flowing Nile River that some believe her to be the sacred land itself. She was worshipped then as she is still today as; *Regina*/Queen, *Domina*/Mistress, as *Augusta*/the Glorious

One. Isis is beloved and forever remains; Queen of Sorcery and Magick, Queen of the Pharaohs, Life of the Nile, Protectress and Mother, Queen of Heaven.

ARADIA

Etruscan Goddess of the oppressed; the poor and enslaved and those that lived on the margins and outskirts of society.... those who would later be called witches. Aradia is the Goddess of the Strega, or Stregheria (an Old Italian tradition of witchcraft). Her manifestation is ornately rich with interesting folklore and conflicting stories and yet, she is one of the most important deities for Pagans and modern day Goddess women.

She was known as the daughter of the Roman Moon Goddess Diana. According to Janet and Stewart Farrar's book, *"The Witches' Goddess, the Feminine Principle of Divinity"*, 1987, Phoenix Publishing Inc., Aradia was born out of the tempestuous union between sister and brother, the sun and the moon. Because she attained both of her parent's light bearing attributes, she can be seen as the Maiden who brings enlightenment and magick to her people. In the *"Vangelo, the Gospel of the Witches"*, which is attributed to being conceived by a Florentine hereditary witch named, Maddalena and later published by Charles Godfrey Leland, Diana was the first Goddess in the universe. This Tuscan Stregheria cosmology proselytizes that in the beginning was darkness and this darkness was the Goddess Diana and from her, she divided herself between light and darkness. The light, that was a part of her and that she eventually birthed, was the Sun, known as god of light, Lucifer. He became both brother and son as he was a part of her divided self and a manifestation, born of her.

In this Etruscan folklore, Lucifer was excruciatingly handsome and as the Sun God, he was divinely beautiful. In the Moon Goddess Diana he stirred within her a passion that was a taboo and an overwhelming desire for him. Being her brother and son, this deity of sunlight wanted nothing to do with what she offered and thus, the Sun fled her sight, whenever she was present. This only made her long for him even more. According to one tale, Lucifer owned a very special, beautiful cat, which he loved dearly and kept by his side. It was a known fact that he frequently slept with this cat, as cat owners so often do. One night Diana overtaken by her desire for him, shape-shifted, taking on the form of this cat and it was then, in the night that she was able to seduce her brother, the light, and with him conceived their daughter, Aradia. Aradia is she who beholds the divine heavenly attributes of both her radiant parents. It is from the sun and the moon that magick is born and thus, Aradia is the Goddess of Magick.

As recounted by Janet and Stewart Farrar in their book, *"The Witches' Goddess, the Feminine Principle of Divinity."* The Sun God was enraged to discover this grave deception, but Diana, skilled in the art of enchantment, hummed him a melody that made him succumb to her love. This humming melody was described as reminiscent of the buzzing of bees, an incessant buzzing reverberation that was symbolic of the spinning wheel of life. This spinning would ultimately weave and spin in man's life. From her all beings came to be and she ultimately controlled their destiny.

The myth goes on to tell of how one day the Goddess Diana decided to live upon the earth with mortals and quickly she garnered a great reputation, as people learned of her numerous remarkable abilities. Her powers could no longer be concealed from the world and thus they made her into their Queen. She eventually revealed her true identity and returned to the heavens, to continue chasing after the light, Lucifer, but before leaving the earth she promised to continue to educate humanity on the art of magick and sorcery. Diana looked to her daughter, Aradia, to continue upon the earth, the work that she had started – educating the oppressed and spreading her teachings on witchcraft.

It's important to note that the earth, at this particular time in these folklores, had become a nightmarish, dreadful place for those who were poor, uneducated or of the "wrong class," culture, gender and religion. The climate in Europe, in particular, in Italy at this time, catered to the church and the wealthy. They were brutal and tyrannical against the poor. It was class warfare as the rich brazenly abused and degraded the uneducated and those that lived outside of the city, in the countryside. The powers that be were enforcing all kinds of new laws meant to destroy their existence. It was a tense time in our history as the church and the rich were uniting, asserting more power, de-manding higher taxation, oppressing more people to enslave and rule over them, while demanding that they give up their Gods and replace them with new church saints.

Back in the 1300's, poor peasants were seen as the oppressed class and they were victimized by the wealthy feudal land owners. Sadly they were often desperate, highly impoverished people and when they would finally escape their abusive masters, they often found themselves living like outlaws in the woods, ostracized vagabonds, living like scavengers. These marginalized people thus, became known as the first witches of the Stregheria tradition in Italy.

It should go without saying but if you (like most of our ancestors) lived close to the land, entrenched in your familial tradition, you would certainly have great reverence for the earth and nature, not the papacy. Praying to the spirits of the earth so that your small garden would produce food, or to the rain gods, so that your thirst could be quenched or to the fire sprits to keep your makeshift hearth and home ablaze with warmth, would seem logical. But this very act extracted power away from the growing church and state. Many people were imprisoned, their lands overtaken when they failed to follow new societal rules or pay taxes, and they were treated horribly. A Goddess like Aradia then becomes necessary, almost compulsory as their personal saviouress. And, her gifts of educating people on magick and the craft of the old ways, and thus, how to thrive and rule over oppressors becomes the factor that gives rise to her popularity; given the social conditions of the time period.

As instructed by her mother, the Moon Goddess Diana, Aradia was to teach the oppressed class how to free themselves from enslavement, how to poison and how to enchant. She taught them how to utilize the gift of magick found amidst nature and how to manipulate weather patterns to work and conjure rain, lightning and thunderstorms. Aradia taught how to bind and eradicate enemies and escape their persecution.

For many of us, who follow the traditional threefold and tenfold Wiccan law, we cringe at the thought of exercising or advocating such severe hexing measures but it is very important for us to understand the validity for a Goddess like Aradia, and her teachings, when we consider the social climate of the time.

The discovery of Aradia and this prominent beloved archetype in the pantheon of Goddess Spirituality must be credited to nineteenth century author, Charles Godfrey Leland (1824-1903). He was an American journalist, anthropologist, folklorist, linguist, collector of myths and practices, and even a veteran of three wars. He was educated in Princeton University, continued his studies in Heidelberg, in Munich and then the Sorbonne in Paris. Mr. Leland spent a great deal of time in Europe researching Gypsy lore, magick, mythology and witchcraft. In particular, he spent a vast amount of time in Tuscany researching Italian Folklore. Through his research he came across a woman he named, Maddalena. Maddalena, whose real name might have been Margharita Taluti, was a type of rare witch informant for Mr. Leland, who became close friends with him during this time. Also important to note, he was initiated into *"La Vecchia Religione"* (the Old Religion), which is another term for Italian witchcraft, in 1888, after becoming the first president of the Gypsy-Lore Society. According to Leland, his friend, Maddalena, claimed to be a real hereditary witch and part of an old dying tradition of witchcraft called Stregheria, in Tuscany. He met her in 1886 and according to the legend, it took her nearly eleven years to handwrite and finally submit her documentation of her familial witchcraft practices and folklores, to the author. In this manuscript we learn a great deal about Aradia and the ancient Cult of the Moon Goddess, Diana, as recounted by the hereditary witch.

Mr. Leland, who was by this time already in America, took her manuscript and tried to translate the Italian and decipher her fragmented handwriting as best as he could. It took him two years to finally get this work published but in 1899, his book, *"Aradia-Gospel of the Witches"* was finally published by David Nutt. It remained fairly unknown, until around the 1950's when other writers and practicing occultist unearthed it, recognizing its scholarly importance, at a time when there was an obvious resurgence of interest in witchcraft in the U.S.A. and abroad.

Today some of the beautiful invocations in this little book have become a sort of liturgy for all Wiccans. *"The Charge of the Goddess"* first found in Maddalena's handwriting, appeared in the Gardnerian witch, Raymond Buckland's book, in 1968. Doreen Valiente (1922-1999), another well-known witch during this enlightening revolutionary time period, later adopted it into her own writings. Both, Starhawk and

Z. Budapest have also rendered their own versions of this beloved adopted invocation. Today it continues to be a beautiful expressive prose, often recited and adopted by most Pagans as a part of traditional Wiccan liturgy.

The Goddess Aradia, though initially she was not viewed as a Goddess but rather as an avatar, appears to be very much like the Christian Messiah. Aradia was her mother's messenger. She was imparting magickal wisdom that was to be shared while on Earth, to spread the word and teachings of her mother, the Moon Goddess. In this case she fulfilled the role of a teacher and messenger about Witchcraft to those who were sorely oppressed by the Catholic Church. She becomes, in essence, their heroiness and savioress. In Aradia we see the spirit of the Priestess, the teacher, the messiah and the spirit of the daughter (like Persephone with Demeter) because her identity was so strongly linked into her role as daughter and fulfilling her Mother's worship. Her value comes, when we remember her as a messenger of empowerment through the practice of witchcraft and as a divine messenger of the ancient Moon Goddess, Diana, sharing her mother's traditions and acting as a daughter and Priestess of the Moon

Etruscan Maiden Goddess, she is the Magick woman, the *Strega*, bringing the gifts of sorcery. She comes into your life at this moment to awaken your inner Goddess and liberate your inner, sovereign priestess. She avails herself to whatever we may need her help with and becomes a great source of empowerment and freedom from hopelessness. She is the embodiment of magick; a great teacher and guide. She reminds us that nature is our ally (within us and all around) to protect and heal us; to lend us their infinite wisdom. Her energy comes to offer the opportunity for occult knowledge, lineage, and ancient respected traditions of the Craft. With Aradia, we acquire the empowering practice of magick and the gift of the priestess. It is time to connect with the powers of the moon, and the strength of the night. How do you empower yourself with your spiritual allies, magick and occult knowledge? How do we reverently employ magick and the sacredness of nature to propel ourselves forward?

STREGHERIA

"True Magick is neither black nor white. It is both, because Nature is both, loving and cruel…all at the same time. The only good or bad is in the heart of the Witch. Life gives a balance of its own…" The movie, *"The Craft"*

Although Stregheria shares many similarities to Wicca, it is arguably not a form of Wicca. It prides itself in being a revival of an archaic religion that dates back, probably further than the once presumed fourteenth century. It is an ancient spiritual religion, akin to an early form of Shamanism, steeped in Tuscan cultural history and Italian folklore. Like most archaic religious practices, there are numerous, conflicting stories of its origins, but there is also much that confirms its validity, birth and existence.

Etymologically, *"Stregheria"* is the archaic Italian word for witchcraft. It is sometimes referred to as *"La Vecchia Religione"* which means in English, "The Old Religion". The word, *"Strego,"* means to enchant and in Italy, the word *"Strega,"* refers to a female witch, while the word *"Strogone,"* refers to a male witch. Stregoneria is a common Italian word used now when referring to witchcraft, but you might also find the archaic Italian word, Stregheria, more commonly used.

Two distinctly different authors are attributed for unearthing and devoting further research into this long, almost forgotten hidden religion; Charles Godfrey Leland (August 15th, 1824- March 20th, 1903)and Raven Grimassi (born 1951-). "**Aradia, Gospel of the Witches**" was published by Charles G. Leland in 1899 and in 1994 Raven Grimassi published, "**Ways of the Strega.**" Grimassi later published several more books on the fascinating subject; "***Italian Witchcraft***" in 2000 and in 2001 "***Heridatary Witchcraft.***"

Charles Godfrey Leland claimed that this religion goes back farther than the 14th century, before Pre-Christian times. His writings reveal that this is actually an ancient Etruscan Religion that blended itself with the Tuscan peasant religious practices of the time. Charles Godfrey Leland, among his many professions, was an American writer, anthropologist, Linguist, Folklorist. Educated in Princeton University, he traveled a great deal and in the late 1800's lived in Italy, where he was studying and researching Gypsy and Italian folklores. In Tuscany, he formed a very close, special friendship with a woman by the name of Maddalena and from this relationship he acquired a great deal of knowledge about "La Vecchia Religione..." Maddalena proclaimed to be a Hereditary Witch with a vast knowledge of the ancient witch practices that had been passed down to her by her family. With her as his informant and her own Italian hand writings and documentations (which were later translated), Mr. Leland was able to publish with David Nutt, a small book. He had written numerous books before, but by far the one that gave him notoriety and has survived all these years was, "***Aradia; Gospel of the Witches,***" published in 1899- years after his initial meeting with Maddalena.

The book revealed a number of incantations, spells, practices, incredibly beautiful and eloquent prose and the mythos of Aradia. It presented the Maiden Aradia as daughter of the great ancient moon Goddess, Diana, and told of how she was sent down to Earth, temporarily, as a messenger to teach the art of sorcery to those who were enslaved and oppressed by the wealthy, Feudal lords of the land. Life was very different back then and these spell workings and incantations reveal how necessary magick and the craft was to the hopeless and the poor. It was their only salvation, when Christianity was victimizing and abusing them and Aradia became their personal, spiritual avatar.

According to Raven Grimassi, "Stregheria is the worship of the source of all things through the personification of the Goddess and God." *Raven Grimassi, "Way of the Strega."* Grimassi believed that the Hereditary witch cult of Stregheria became widespread due to a type of Holy Strega (Aradia) and he believed she was not just an archetype, but an actual woman who was documented as living in Tuscany in the fourteenth century, teaching the old ways that had been taught to her, by her family.

Long ago in the Tuscan Hills of a town named Arida, a woman by the name of Aradia di Toscano was born. Some documents claim she was born on August thirteenth in the year 1313. Perhaps this date is given in an effort to connect her even further with witches and the revered thirteen moons in a year or perhaps indeed this is her precise date of birth. According to Grimassi, Aradia traveled from town to town in the Roman and Tuscan hillside to share, among the rustic Italians, her aunt's teachings of the "La Vecchia Religione." At a time when the poor and those that lived outside the margins of "civilized" society, were being oppressed and enslaved by the rich and privileged class, her teachings were the only source of empowerment and hope. It would seem to fit the bill in fulfilling the desperate hunger of an oppressed class.

The people that lived on the hillsides, in far away remote villages, quite far removed from the cosmopolitan city centers, could not relate to the lofty Gods and the growing, oppressive religions, like Catholicism and Christianity. For those who lived so close to their land, whose livelihood was dependent on the benevolence of nature, their reverence and worshipped was relegated to those they were in communion with on a daily basis. Hence, Stregheria with its proselytization of the old ways and the worship of agricultural Gods, elemental Spirits, forest faeries, the Moon and the stars, was a religion they could easily identify with.

Aradia became affectionately known as *"La Bella Pilligrina"* for she traveled far and wide, teaching her family's ancient tradition of Italian witchcraft and as a result Stregheria became wide spread throughout rural villages, the Alban hill region, Etruscan villages, and in particular the towns near Lake Nemi, as some documents of the time period reveals. The city of Benevento as well, became particularly instrumental in flourishing *"La Vecchia Religione"* and was even attributed for later inventing an alcoholic drink, appropriately named by them, *"Strega Liquore."*

According to Raven Grimassi, Aradia became known as the Holy Strega and accumulated quite a following. Consequently, to her devotees, she became known as a highly regarded avatar and the beloved daughter of her mother, the Moon Goddess - Diana. The worship of nature Gods and Goddesses (honoring both polarities of genders) was common; with their Moon Goddess, Diana and her Consort Dianus being the two most highly regarded. There were many others like Herodias, Tana and Tanus and faeries, forest & tree spirits were also venerated.

Similar to Wicca, in their use of enchantments, incantations, amulets, talisman, hexes, poppets, oracles and divinations, theirs was an old tradition. They utilized herbalism, animal magick, fairies, incantations, magick of spell casting, and rituals. They had sky clad (nude) meetings under the full moon in groves or Boschetto (forest) amidst nature - these are all part of the Stregheria tradition. Like Wicca, there are eight holy-days or sabbats traditionally celebrated and they coincide with the change of season and the honored Nature Deities.

Their Rites traditionally focused on the agriculture and fertility of the land, hexes and protection, as well as imbuing everyday objects like Keys, scissors, knives, horseshoes, pearls, gemstones, rocks, trees, salt, clove of garlic, herbs, roots, red ribbons, statues, (to name just a few), with the energy of the Divine. For sacred rites, a High Priestess assisted by her High Priest led the group (coven) and this too is very similar to most Wiccan traditions. They also utilized a Maiden known, in Italian, as *"Dama D'onore"* and the traditional Gate keeper, known in Italian as *"La Guardia."* Altars were normally placed in the highly venerated North Quarter because it was believed to be a place of great power. Their tools of magick were everyday items like feathers, sea shells, and needles, rocks painted with a pentacles, crystals and wood branches as wands. Knives as athame, salt, sand, potions and herbal concoctions, chalice or bowls of water, sometimes candles, bells and offerings of honey, milk, wine, and spirits like "Strega Liquore."

Interesting to note that Hebrew Mysticism in the Middle ages, undoubtedly, had a great influence on Stregheria rites and practices. Masonic Lodges in the 1800's, obviously, borrowed from various traditions, not excluding, *"La Vecchia Religione"*. The notorious protagonist and main contributors to Wiccan Religion; like Gerald Gardner, Doreen Valiente, Dion Fortune, Aleister Crowley are indebted to the teachings of Italian Witchcraft and *"La Vecchia Religione"*. According to Raven Grimassi in his Book "The Holy Strega," Aleister Crowley studied Italian occultism and lived in Italy from 1920-1923. He was attributed to forming the "Abbey of Thelema," with licentious mural paintings of the nature deities like the Horn God, Pan and the Goddess. When the city got word of his Pagan creation, he was booted out of Sicily. Yet another well-known contributor to Wicca, Gerald Gardner, borrowed much from Stregheria and initially had learned a great deal from Aleister Crowley himself. This would explain the coincidental similarities, Wicca and Stregheria share.

Witchcraft has always appealed largely to women, with its message of female empowerment and inherent feminine divinity. It appears more matriarchal than other religious faiths. In major cities, in the fourteenth century, men were the predominant rulers during this time and one can only presume how the practice of Stregheria and the sight of a large group of women gathering for any reason, could've been seen as suspicious, bothersome and possibly a threat to their own patriarchal religions. When Stregheria found itself in danger of being banned and extinct by the patriarch, it needed to transmute itself. According to Raven Grimassi, three witch clans, a Triad, sprung forth in an effort to preserve this ancient religion and safely pass down Aradia's teachings, to future generations. The distinctly three traditions of Tanarra, Jannara, Fanarra, evolved from Aradia's ancient witchcraft teachings.

Fanarra was located mainly in Northern Italy and this was a witch tradition that was considered the keepers of the Earth mysteries. Their form of worship emphasized the land, sacred sites and places and objects found among the earth. They held true that Nature is filled with spirits that inhabits objects and places, making them sacred to witches and at our disposal for powerful magick.

Janarra, was a tradition mainly located in Central Italy and they were believed to be the keepers of the Lunar mysteries. Their form of witchcraft highly regarded the cycles of the moon and the powers inherent in our own connection to the moon. Drawing her down and regular gatherings under the Full moon *Veglione*, (Italian word for full moon rites) was part of their tradition. During this time there was also a common, indigenous belief that the souls of the dead dwelled in the moon awaiting their final resting place and in the Janarra tradition, the moon is honored as the sacred dwelling place of the feminine divine-the Goddess- as was Aradia's initial teachings.

Central Italy also became the home for the Tanarra Tradition, whose emphasis was on the Stellar Mysteries. In 1981, The Aridian Mysteries was born (named after Aradia's birthplace) and it was established in North America. The Aridian tradition is considered a direct extension of the Tanarra, Stellar mysteries. According to Raven Grimassi, it is a tradition dedicated to reviving the archaic teachings of Aradia, the Holy Strega.

There are numerous wonderful books on Italian Witchcraft, *"La Vecchia Religione"* and both the ancient and modern practices of Stregheria. I know that I have only touched the surface of this profoundly, fascinating subject here. To learn more, I encourage you to look into Charles Godfrey Leland's books and the multitude of books written by one of the leading, modern day protagonist of the Stregheria tradition, Raven Grimassi.

CIRCE

Circe is the beautiful, magnetic, ancient Greek Goddess of Sorcery, Magick, Incantation and Herbology. She was gifted with the art of hallucinogenic and the ability to turn men into beasts. Her name comes from the Greek word, "*Kirkoo*," which means to "secure with rings or to bind."

We know much about the Goddess Circe and her beautiful appearance, due to the numerous descriptions in the early writings of the time and the plethora of illustrations and renderings in paintings and sculptures by various talented artists throughout the centuries.

The Goddess Circe was believed to be the daughter of the Titaness, Sun God, Helios and the nymph, Perse (daughter of Oceanus). Other writings indicate that she was probably the daughter of the great Goddess of the Crossroads and Witchcraft, Hecate. She was also the recognized aunt of yet another enchantress in Greek Mythology, Medea. Circe's brother, Aeetes, fathered by Helios, was a God known also for his magical gifts, incantations and Herbology. He was the guardian of the Golden Fleece. Circe had two additional siblings; her sister, named Pasiphae, who became the wife of King Minos, in Crete, and her brother, named Perses.

Her home was noted to be on the island of Aeaea but there were also many islands connected to her Temple and worship. Her mansion on Aeaea was depicted as a magickal fortress, surrounded by all types of wild exotic creatures. It was a place where all was not what it seemed and it was enveloped by her crafted illusions and serviced by her servants.

Circe was mentioned in numerous ancient texts like; *"The Odyssey"* by Homer, *"Theogony"* and *"The Homeric Hymns"* by Hesiod, and *"Metamorphoses"* by Ovid, to name just a few. These early writings established her as the archetypal image of the Witch.

The Odyssey

She is strongly linked with the legend of the Odyssey and the brave, Odysseus and his men. According to the early writings, it was said that Odysseus's ship and his crew ended up on the shore of her Island. For three days and three nights they lay hopeless in total despair, abandoned on the shore. Then Odysseus detected smoke rising from the distance. Cautious, he decided to split his crew into two groups. He stayed behind on guard with one group of men, while sending the other group with Eurylochus to investigate the source of the smoke. Eurylochus and half of his crew ventured out to search the island for life and hopefully bring back much needed help. What they encountered was the alluring Goddess, Circe, and her illusionary magical abode.

The famished men were greeted by the powerful Goddess and her beautiful servants with much feasting and overflowing libations. Naturally, the men enjoyed themselves but, unsuspectedly, while in her abode, they were charmed and spellbound by her powerful potions. Her concoctions turned them into swines and placed them under her arrest in pigsties. After some time had passed, when the men did not return, it concerned Odysseus. Of all the men captivated and charmed by the Goddess, Eurylochus managed to escape and quickly returned to Odysseus to alert him of the shocking news about what had occurred to his crew. Determined to get his men back, Odysseus takes the great risk and ventures alone to make the trip to the home of Circe. But, before reaching Circe, he is visited by the messenger God, Hermes, who warns him and instructs him on how to secure his safety while in the presence of the great enchantress.

Odysseus confronts the Temptress, and following all of Hermes instructions, he manages to safeguard himself and befriend her. They even become lovers. All the men that had been turned into swines were turned back into men, even stronger and more handsome than they were before. According to the legend, their time in Circe's home was so full of revelry and ecstasy that they willing stayed with her, on the island, for a year. As lover and friend, Circe helped Odysseus complete the Odyssey. It is also speculated that together they had numerous offspring during the year they spent together. Some of her known children were Agrios & Latinos, as stated in Hesiod's Theogony, and Telegonos, as mentioned in Homeric Hymns. She was also mother to Nausithous and Phaunos.

The Legend of Picus
One day while out in the woods, the Goddess, Circe, fell madly in love upon catching sight of the handsome, Picus. He was the son of Saturn, according to the writings of Servius, and later became the First King of Latium. Picus was devoted to his wife, the beautiful nymph, Canens, although some writings reveal he was in love with Scylla. There are clearly different renditions of this story but needless to say, they are all reflective of Circe and her gifts as a Sorceress. When her advances to Picus were rejected, she immediately turned him into a woodpecker and her rival, Scylla, was converted into a gruesome looking monster.

The worship of the Goddess Circe extended far beyond the land of Greece but also into Roman territories. She was so beautiful and renowned that there are numerous images rendering her as this breathtaking seductress; with long flowing or braided hair, often holding her wand. Mentioned throughout a plethora of writings from ancient times to Modern literature, she is forever cemented in our collective remembrance as a beautiful enchantress; the quintessential image, created in ancient times and sustained throughout our modern era, of the Witch.

Circe is the powerful Goddess of Sorcery & Magick. She is the patron Goddess for all who seek to know the ancient mysteries of the occult; that includes but is not limited to incantations, transmutation, and Herbology. She is also clearly an expression of the independent, empowered, magick woman, who lives her life by her own rules. What she desires, she passionately endeavors to attain, and she is not shy about employing all of her inherent gifts. She is the awakener of our intuitive abilities and our inner Enchantress.

HEKATE

Goddess of the Crossroads, Hekate is an Ancient chthonic deity of the Moon and the night. Hekate is better known as a Guardian and Triple Goddess of the Crossroads. She is also the Goddess of magick and sorcery and a patron Goddess for women in all stages of life. She is a protector of entrances and homes. Sometimes, she is even seen as a patron Goddess of Childbirth- as this too, is an entry way, of magickal significance, into the world of the living. Ancient Crone Goddess of the Gateway and a beloved deity among practitioners of the Craft, in ancient Greece she was just as significant then, as she remains today among Goddess women.

Her name means *"she who works from afar"* also interpreted as *"she who works her will"* and one of her primary roles was to guide the souls to the underworld. She was the only Goddess who could travel through all realms. Beloved by Zeus, she was given rule over the Underworld, but also the Earth and the Sky. She had a special relationship with Zeus because according to some, she was the only Titan that aided him during the battle of the Olympians against the Titans, but, as with all ancient deities, there are many conflicting stories about her early incarnations.

Some believe this ancient Goddess has origins in Mycenaen Greece, possibly originating in Carians of Anatolia; though she had a very large cult following in Thrace. She is said to have been a native of ancient Thrace. In Asia Minor and Thrace she had numerous followers and a very large cult following among the Eunuchs, her servants. In many Greek homes, while the hearth was Hestia's domain, the entryway was Hekate's and altars with offerings were often dedicated to her here. Offerings to Hekate were also made at cemeteries and at three way fork roads with meat, honey, goat blood or actual black dogs, being sacrificed to her.

Hekate is often depicted with three heads. Sometimes they were the heads of a snake, a dog and or a horse, other depictions portray her with just the heads of three dogs. The sound of barking dogs were said to warn you of her omnipotent presence and she was known to easily shape shift at will, into her beloved totem. Black female dogs, in particular, were sacred to her and were sometimes sacrificed in her name by her devotees. Because black dogs were her sacred animal she, herself, was also sometimes referred to as the "black bitch." The Frog was another animal connected to Hekate because of its ability to cross between two elements.

There are some conflicting stories about Hekate and her birth. She appears to be a Goddess of ancient origins with many myths regarding her manifestation. One theory, found in the Theogony, was that she was a child of the great Mother Earth, Gaia and Uranus or perhaps even a sibling of Zeus. A more accepted genealogy came from other writings by Hesiod who stated that Hekate was the daughter of the Pre-Olympian Titans, Perseus and the Star Goddess, Asteria. The sister of Star Goddess Asteria was the Goddess of Childbirth, Leto. Leto as we know gave birth to the twins; Apollo and Artemis. This would mean that Hekate was a cousin of the Maiden Moon Goddess, Artemis. Here we understand her connection as a Moon Deity and the genealogy that intimately connects her to light, most notably, the Moon's. This would also imply that their Grandmother would have been Phoebe, the ancient Titaness Moon Goddess and their Great Grandmother, the Primordial Earth Goddess- Gaia. In either case, her strong associations to light, in particular moonlight, is very clear.

Not much is known about Hekate's romantic life but we do know she had two daughters. Her union to Phorcys created her daughter, Scylla. With Hermes, the Messenger God of Magick and Science, she unites and gives birth to Circe. Circe later becomes Medea's aunt. Medea, according to the myths of her time, becomes a notoriously powerful Sorceress, Priestess and Queen of the Witches, due to the teachings from her extended family. She later becomes a devoted High priestess of her grandmother, Hekate.

Perhaps, Hekate will forever be most remembered for her involvement with Demeter and Persephone in the legend of the *Great Eleusinian Mysteries*. Remember that it was Hekate who heard the Maiden's cries, when she was abducted by Hades and it was She, who tried to console the despondent mother and offer aid in regaining her beloved daughter. Thus Hekate became known as a Goddess who was very sympathetic to the universal cries of all wommin, most notably those in great distress and in danger. Women abused or mistreated by men received her utmost protection. If called upon, she executed just retribution against those offensive men, when supplications were made by her worshippers. As a Goddess who could travel through all three realms, she was often invoked for safe journeys by those going to unknown, distant lands. In ancient times, she was often called upon by women in the midst of childbirth, a precarious delicate state for most women and as a Goddess of entryway; one can see how her presence would be compulsory for both, death and births alike. As a Goddess of the night, the dark moon and all things mysteries, she became a patron to witches and sorcerers, seeking divine occult knowledge.

Today there is a great resurgence in her cult and her worship remains strong among her growing followers. One trip to the library now will reveal an increase in the amount of books published on the fascinating subject of Hekate and her continuous worship. Her festivals, in which she was honored, were held on August 13th and the 30th of November.

There are many herbs associated with Hekate. Yew berries, Cypress, belladonna, mandrake, hemlock, opium poppy are all linked to the Goddess of the underworld. Not surprising, herbs that were hallucinogen or help alter states of consciousness are all appropriately associated with this ancient Greek Goddess.

*Ancient, immortal Goddess of the Threshold, she rules the night, death, sorcery, witchcraft and the sacred portals that lead to the underworld. She is the venerated archetype of the wise crone. Hekate brings a plate offering with our lineage and ancestry and the importance of our spiritual connection. She is the night wandered and facilitates travels through all the realms. She is the guide through all of life's various thresholds and portal of transformations.

There is much wisdom to unearth in our ancestry and in our past-lives. Hekate guides us through this realm to attain magickal knowledge and our ancestral connections. Hekate endeavors to help you connect to spirit allies and your sacred ancestors for guidance. She awakens in you other realms, other sources for support and other ways of knowing. She awakens you to your sacred role as an ancestress and your intrinsic part of your family's lineage. Ancestresses that you are already…what will you leave behind for your beloved one? This is the time to look closely at who we share this realm with, honor our Spiritual family, and the sacredness of the cycles of life and death.

IN RITUALS TO HEKATE:
1. Call on Hekate during the Dark of the Moon
2. Pay close attention to the dreams you have after working with her.
3. She has been known to speak using her worshippers therefore aspecting with her is fairly easy. Wiccan and Trance Author Diana L. Paxson suggest, protecting your head Chakra with a veil if you do not wish to go into spontaneous trance or spirit possession. To come out of trance work you might try water over your head to help ground you.
4. To symbolize her torches it is best to have two flames/candles at her altars, along with food offerings and her herbs and fragrances….
5. **OFFERINGS**: Eggs, Barley, Garlic, onions, black plums or grapes, honey, Caviar, cedar or sage, myrrh Incense, Retsina Wine or dry Red Wine or berry juice

JOURNALING

Do I trust my inner Guidance?

_____

_____

How do I further develop my psychic/intuitive gifts?

_____

_____

Who are my ancestors? How do I honor my ancestors?

_____

_____

Who are my Spirit Guides?

_____

_____

How do I strengthen my connection to them?

_____

_____

THEME WORK SUGGESTIONS
1. INTUITION

Light a purple candle.
Seek a teacher or a class on a metaphysical subject that interests you. Read a few books on metaphysical subjects, explore which modality you feel more comfortable with. Start recording your nightly dreams in your dream journal.

INVOCATION & POETRY

RECLAIMING MY GIFTS

I stand before the Sacred Ones
And by the Moon, Earth, Water and Sun,
To reclaim my lineage
And Strega gifts
Inaugurate in ritual
This portal shift...

Reclaim my Power,
And singe oppressive ties,
From those pathetic ones,
Who tell and live lies...

I sever what does not serve me well,
And draw the Goddess to hear her tell,
Invoking incantations,
Surrounding me with sight
I break free now,
From all that is NOT Right!!!

Away from harm,
And closer to Love,
I magnetize good fortune,
From below and above.

I honor the Divine
And Her path for me,
By will and word, (this Strega's Wish)

It is Done, So Mote it be!!!!!!

ARADIA: MAGICK & THE PRIESTESS

By the light of the dark
The candles aflame
Reflections are seen through the scented haze.

A glimmer into
What daylight hides,
Lineage- ancestry
Magick from inside.

The strength of the Goddess
The beauty of the Moon,
Sky-clad forms
Illuminating rooms.

I look deep, ever deeper
Through the mirror to find,
A Priestess has returned
From Ancient times.

Daughter of the Moon
Temple of her domain
From the infinite realm
Our journey is the same.

We call you Diana's pearl,
Beloved daughter of the Moon.
Hail to you Aradia,
All Blessings and Gratitude to you!
Hail and Welcome Aradia!

Page 24 from "Goddess Grimoire Journal, a Collection of Simple Prose and Spells" by B. Melusine Mihaltses (Isbn# 9780985138431)

***You are now invited to create your own altar(s) & invocation(s).)O(Blessings!

MAGICK RITES & TOOLS

When preparing to do any form of sacred rite, it's important to first and foremost consider where you can set up your working space. You'll want a space that provides some level of privacy and a place where you'll feel comfortable to set up. If you share your space with others, like family or roommates, please consider what you'll feel comfortable sharing. Traditionally, it's best to protect your altar from the scrutiny and suspicious eyes of cynics. Nothing worse than having skeptics spew negativity or doubt on your work. Enjoy this process and understand you are creating a special place for yourself.

This is your personal page to document your sacred rites and the tools you elected to use.

DECIDE WHERE TO SET UP AN ALTAR

Place an Altar Cloth in the Color of your choice.
Color: _____

GODDESS

Place an image of your Deity.
Goddess: _____
This image can be a Statue, handmade Sculpture or a simple Photo _____

FIRE REPRESENTATION

Place a blessed/charged Candle in the color of your choice.
Candle Type and color: _____

AIR REPRESENTATION

Light your Incense stick.
Incense Scent: _____

WATER REPRESENTATION

Place a Chalice of Water
Water Item: _____

EARTH REPRESENTATION

Place a Potted Plant or Fresh Flowers on your Altar
Add Salt or a plate of Dried Herbs
Herbs: _____
Chosen Gemstone: _____

YOUR WISH

_____

_____

_____

Place a symbol of your desire, if you have one available, and also write your wish out clearly, on a piece of parchment paper, or you can even use a cut up brown paper bag. These are the basics for a very simple altar & rite. Ultimately, your sacred space is only limited by your imagination. You can make your altar & rite as big or as small as you prefer and the addition of other personal items is really up to you.)o(Enjoy!

ALTAR PHOTOS

CHAPTER TWO

*The first responsibility of a leader is to define reality.
The last is to say, Thank you. In between, the leader is a servant..."*
Max DePree

THEME: LEADERSHIP

I have heard it said many times before that Leadership is not for the faint of heart and thus, not everyone is meant to lead. And admittedly, I think it can be quite easy to live an entire life never stepping foot into a leadership role. Yes, we can make our own personal goals, strive to reach them and then, spend the better part of our lives simply preserving them as we initially envisioned them. However, every once in a while, life has a way of brazenly confronting us, challenging our ideals, expanding us and forcing us to take a path we wouldn't ordinarily consider.

We've arrived at a critical point in our spiritual journey where we are asked to consider what it means to serve our community. What does it mean to be a leader and could you possibly step foot into this noteworthy role? It is time to survey our gifts and the experiences we've garnered throughout our lives and consider how they may be of value to our community.

Sometimes we are unexpectedly thrust into a leadership role, especially when there is no one else around to fulfill it. And sometimes leadership simply becomes the natural progression in our journey of mastery. In other words, when we've gained a certain level of knowledge and experience, it becomes only natural to want to share the skills and wisdom we've acquired. In this process of sharing we begin to serve our communities and thus, find ourselves in roles of leadership. Sometimes, this process can become quite organic and other times it is wrought with inner turmoil, resistance and insecurities.

We don't often think we're good enough or ready to take on the role of Leadership but sometimes, it is in our mere desire to serve others that instantaneously cloaks us in the armor of a Leader.

For me, personally, I found myself so many miles away from home, in a brand new state, among a new demographic, and a whole new environment that lacked all the familiar experiences I had garnered from my previous life in my home state. In the absence of all the familiar things and experiences I had worked so hard to learn throughout the years, from my upbringing, I recognized a vacancy and an unfulfilled need in my newly adopted community. I quickly learned that I possessed these rather unique, sought after experiences and knowledge, coming from my esoteric upbringing on the east coast. And, all of a sudden, I felt a strong calling to share what I knew and be of service to anyone wanting my help. This desire, to serve and teach, eventually led me to developed "Grove of the Feminine Divine," my monthly Goddess Group. Unbeknownst to me at the time, this simple act of stepping into a Leadership role would exponentially shape my own spiritual journey, to lead me to where I am today.

As we have done before, in this chapter we will explore further our theme with the help of several resources. We will endeavor to connect with the Goddesses Oya, Sif, Hestia, Odudua, Amaterasu and the sacred animal energy of the Buffalo. We will connect with our 7th chakra, the Crown chakra, and gemstones that can help better facilitate this connection. We will also look at the corresponding Lunation and a Tarot card that is connected to our theme.

THE EMPEROR TAROT CARD

The Emperor Tarot card in traditional tarot decks is represented by a strong, older looking man, dressed in a regal red robe. He is crowned, as the king he apparently is, seated in his throne, with his royal scepter and sword.
The card often speaks of the forceful authoritative energy of the patriarch, but more specifically, it speaks of those who are in position of power and leadership. It is the archetype of those who are actively planning, structuring communities, families and planting their seeds for their legacy to live on, long after they are gone. It is, after all, the duty of every king to guarantee that his law and rulership lives via his heirs. Thus, this might be why we often associate this card with the father. The Emperor card is also connected with Aries, which is the lunation we will be working with in this chapter.

The symbolism and meaning of the Emperor card evokes great strength, long-range vision and determination. The Emperor is able to evaluate situations logically and come up with proper conclusions to benefit the greater good. His stubbornness and determination to protect what is under his domain is quite unmatched. He is equipped with all the skills and wisdom required of any person in a position of leadership. The Emperor card speaks of great maturity and thus, great experience and mastery of control. It is a card of authority, independence, sovereignty and the natural gift of the leader; an ideal card to explore with our theme of Leadership in this chapter.

MOON IN ARIES   FIRE/MARS
THEME: LEADERSHIP

ARIES   CARDINAL   FIRE   MASCULINE   RAM

When the moon is in Aries we have entered a very different platform than when the moon was in watery Pisces. The Moon in, Mars ruled, Aries is very dynamic. It is energetic, ambitious and its influence is known to be aggressive. As a Fire sign and the first sign of the zodiac, it is a natural initiator and thus, a perfect time to begin projects or execute a new goal. Notice how I used the word, execute. Aries as we know is ruled by Mars, and this planet, named after its Deity, is notorious for being a God of War and volatility. It is a natural fighter and fiercely endeavors to win all battles it engages in. Can you see how useful this energy can be if we apply it judiciously in our own personal lives? Consider where you can use more of this assertive energy? What area in your life requires a jolt start to propel you into action and ultimate determination to success?

Moon in Aries wants to initiate and execute, in all battles, victoriously. When we are working with this energy we would do best to apply it to situations or goals that require a great big energetic push to victory.

"My own definition of leadership is; that capacity and the will to rally men and women to a common purpose and the character which inspires confidence..."
General Montgomery

HERSTORY

She had grown so comfortable in her job and for years watched as others moved passed her with every promotion. She knew she had something special to offer and was tired of often being overlooked. She was ready to take on a higher position that was in alignment with her hidden gifts and more in sync with her talents. She was ready to be a leader.

******Take a moment to document here, or in your journal, your unique story.

_____

_____

_____

_____

_____

AFFIRMATION

My life is exemplary of the Divine;
I honor and share what has been given to me.

I Lead

Ten Million and more, Beloved Ancestors,
I stand here today as a recipient of all of their blood and sacrifice.
It is my duty to serve my community and give honor,
through my leadership, to all those who came before me
and paved the way for my existence.

CHAKRA & GEMSTONE WORK

7th Chakra   **SAHASRARA/CROWN CHAKRA**   **COLOR:** White/Clear
Enlightenment, Ascension, Wisdom, Divine connection, integration, receiving Divine insight.

Mantra: I Know
)O(WORKING: Awareness, Insight, Ancestral Work, Knowledge, Spiritual Communication

GEMSTONE CONNECTION: Clear Crystal Quartz has been prized and used since the beginning of time by numerous cultures. Crystals have long been known for their ability to record, store and emit knowledge and energy, and thus, it is a perfect tool for spiritual healing (physical, mental and emotional healing as well). Because clear crystal quartz is alleged to have a similar vibrational quality as humans, it is the ideal stone to work with for spiritual knowledge of our evolving species. It has the ability to transport and impart ancient esoteric knowledge to us, kinesthetically, and our understanding of the world is exponentially expanded by its very presence. It is an invaluable tool for spiritual growth and psychic development. The clear crystal quartz has the ability to amplify and transform our own energy. When we are feeling exhausted or scattered and confused, working with our crystal quartz can help bring us back to alignment and balance our energy. It is also a powerful tool to work with, when doing trance meditations. It allows one to connect with our higher consciousness and can facilitate channelings and communications with spirit guides. It can also be used in conjunction with our divination and oracular practices.

As a purifier, we can transmute almost any negative energy with clear crystals. Clear crystal quartz, in particular, has the unique ability to amplify anything near it, more specifically; it can amplify and purify the attributes of nearby stones. Connected with the element of; air, fire, earth, and water and all the directions from; south, north, east and west, it can be used in conjunction with other stones when working with our chakras. It can also act as a substitute for any gemstone needed in chakra work. For those practicing magic and ritual spells, the use of clear crystal quartz is invaluable. It can enhance the potency of your herbs and spell works. We are able to cleanse, purify and psychically charge any item we wish, by simply pointing our crystal quartz to the object or by letting the object rest upon the clear crystal quartz. This can be anything; from a pendant, a special ring, a sachet or poppet, a wand or a candle, a piece of ribbon or head circlet, a piece of parchment paper or a writing pen etc… etc… Anything that you wish to clear, purify and psychically charged can be done with a clear crystal quartz on hand. It is important to note that clear quartz can help with chronic fatigue, arthritis, fibromyalgia, intestinal problems as well as a number of other ailments and disorders. It is reputed to give off physical and mental stamina and strength. Almost every culture throughout history has valued the clear crystal quartz. The ancient Greeks believed it was actually water from the heavens that was converted into **eternal ice** by the gods. The word crystal to the ancient Greeks was *"krystallos"* which means, ice. For the Australian aboriginals, crystals are closely linked to a substance called *"maban,"* which they believe is where all wise shamans attain their magical powers. Native American tribes and the aborigines used clear crystals to invoke thunderstorms. It is one of the most common minerals found on the face of the earth and it can be found in all types of environments and all types of rocks; sedimentary metamorphic or Igneous. Although found in many areas of the world, it is still mainly attained through Africa, Brazil and the U.S.A.

THEME WORK SUGGESTIONS
2. LEADERSHIP
Light a yellow candle.
Make a list of all of your skills, gifts and a list of all of your experiences. Volunteer with an organization within your community that may use your services or skills. Form an Organization to be of service to others. Gather women in your community and form a monthly gathering.

GEMSTONE CHANNELING

Go to a comfortable place where you can be certain you will not be disturbed for a few minutes and where you'll find some peace and quiet. If you can go outdoors in nature that would be most ideal but any place where you can relax, undisturbed, will be fine.

You are invited, to place yourself in a comfortable position; you may sit or lay down. If it is available to you, place in your hands the Clear Quartz Crystal that we are working with today. Take a moment to connect with your crystal. (Pause) Place it in your hands, how does it feel? (Pause) Study its form and look deeply at any inclusions, foils, or any images that you see within it. Make note of any pictures or visions that come to you throughout this process. (Pause) Hold your crystal up and study it carefully in silence for a few minutes... Quietly, gaze upon it and make note of any thoughts that immediately start to unfold before you.

When you're ready, you may close your eyes now and begin this short meditation. As with all trance work, we begin with our breath. You are asked to take a deep breath, slowly filling your lungs up now. Take a deep breath, envisioning your Clear Quartz Crystal now like vapors, gracefully dancing in and out of your beautiful lungs. Breathe in the Clear Quartz Crystal now....breathe, hold for 3 seconds and then release it... Counting now at your own pace; breathe, 1, 2, 3, and exhale on 4....and again....breathe in, 1, 2, 3, and exhale on 4. Let's do this one more time and then quietly counting in your head.... Breathe 1, 2, 3...release on 4. Breathe, trusting in the natural rhythm you have now established, of your relaxed inhalation and exhalation.

Clear Quartz Crystal wishes to impart a special channeled message just for you. See this gemstone in your mind's eye. See it shining brightly, embedded upon its dark, fertile, mother earth. Draw nearer to it and ask if it will allow you to pick it up. When permission is granted, gently gather it in your hands. With your mind's eye, gaze upon it; studying its clarity; its inclusions and texture. Let your eyes follow its lines and any other details you notice that is capturing your interest..... Ask it to speak to you.

Visualize the top of your head opening like a window. Open yourself up now to any messages that may unfold now... You may envision your own crown chakra now unveiling a magnetic, Clear Quartz Crystal, portal, allowing for this **Crystal Transmission** to come through... Continue to breathe and when you can, make note of any messages that are coming through. You may write them here, or in your journals or any other place you wish.

_____

_____

_____

_____

BUFFALO PROTECTION ENERGY

By virtue of their size alone, the Buffalo becomes a massive, impressive ally and protector in our Spiritual work. When we feel small or defenseless the image of this gargantuan protector can provide a palliative level of comfort. There are a number of descriptive adjectives that come to mind when we think about the Buffalo; powerful, regal, generous, obstinate, courageous, are just some that immediately come to mind.

For Native Americans, the Buffalo/Bison was one of the most important, beloved, sacred animals. According to indigenous tribes, buffalo can show us how we store and release our burdens. The shoulders were considered a sacred power point on our physical bodies and this particular animal carried a large hump around his shoulder. It is thus, a symbol of the responsibility it shoulders for its community; an attribute we can further study and connect with as we develop our own leadership skills.

As a symbol of community and the sacrifices necessary for the protection and nurturance of the whole, the Buffalo becomes almost archetypal. Every part of the Buffalo was put to important use for indigenous tribes. Native Americans would offer prayers of gratitude before and after a buffalo is killed, to honor the spirit of the animal that provided them with meat, shelter and clothing. Indeed every part of the Buffalo was valued and consumed and it becomes clear the Buffalo can help us connect with the element of the earth and our powers of manifestation. It's important to note they are also a potent symbol of survival, as they were on the brink of extinction in America and struggled collectively to survive.

With Buffalo energy we can learn to be more mindful of the sacrifices of life that have allowed us to survive. They connect us with the gift of gratitude for our ancestry and the recognition of the sacrifices offered for the greater good of all. Buffalo teaches us to honor the traditions and resources from the past and the contributions to the wellbeing and prosperity of our community. Interesting to note, when provoked, buffaloes can be unpredictably dangerous. When they feel threatened, they are known to form circles of protection in an effort to protect their community. The female buffaloes are known to form circles around other smaller animals, like calves and the male buffaloes will form circles around the cows. These unusual act of encircling, exemplifies the buffaloes' attributes of respect for all in the community. Their natural instinct is to protect and honor all life forms and in this manner they are invaluable teachers and examples of leadership for us.

Highly revered by numerous cultures, the Buffalo is a powerful symbol of strength, community, generosity, sacrifice, protection, courage and survival. Its overall mammoth size makes it an obvious symbol of strength, protection and courage but what is most interesting to our theme on leadership is the many ways the Buffalo is a potent symbol of generosity, sacrifices and community.

GODDESS EMPOWERMENT

AMATERASU O-MI-KAMI (Ohiru-menomuchi-no-kami)
    Amaterasu, the Japanese Goddess of the Sun, whose name, in some text, is interpreted as meaning, "the *exalted deity which illuminates the Heavens*." Like Athena, she was birthed by her father, according to Japanese scriptures. Prior to the creation of the world, Japanese cosmology declares there were invisible Gods in the Heavens. The first God Izanagi, translates as, *"He who invites"* and the name of the first Goddess, Izanami, translates as, *"She who invites."* According to Japanese legend these two respective male & female deities were the first known Gods and they were called upon to create the island of Japan and its eight nearby islands. They were also called upon to populate the Earth with humans and thus, they united, resulting in the unearthing of *sex and procreation.* Together they created a number of deities, before Amaterasu came to be.
    There are two known stories regarding these Japanese deities. One comes from the Nihongi, an eighth century collection of Japanese myths and legends and the other from the Kojiki (712 C.E.), the oldest of the two. The Nihongi makes Amaterasu first born from white copper mirrors held by her father, Izanagi alone. According to the

writings in the Kojiki, when the Goddess Izanami, gave birth to the God of Fire, she was severely hurt. As can be expected, she was horribly injured during the birthing of this scorching God and consequently, it forced Amaterasu's mother to go into the underworld. Izanami descended into the land of the dead where she began to decay. Her lover, the God Izanagi, was devastated and sought to find his love in the underworld, but when he arrived there, she refused to be visited by him in her putrefying condition and she sends him away. He returned to the land of the living, surprisingly, unharmed, but as was the tradition of this time, he underwent a purification upon his return, by bathing in the streams. In this special purification bath, came forth three Gods; Tsukiyomi, Susano-o and Amaterasu.

According to Japanese Mythology, from the left eye of Izanagi was born the first Deity, the beloved Goddess of the Sun -Amaterasu. From the right eye came forth the second Deity, Tsukiyomi, the God of the Moon. From the unfavorable nose of the God Izanagi, the God Susano-o came forth and he was to rule the Ocean and later the underworld.

Tsukiyomi, is God of the Moon and this God ruled the night. The Goddess Amaterasu, was to rule over the almighty Heavens, as the Goddess of the Sun. Susano-o, as God of the Ocean, was not a pleasant deity and thus, he was not well received. His wicked, untamable, irrepressible, ego centered ways, were viewed as dangerous to a flourishing society. Some feared that the early death of his mother had affected him adversely and he was much too dysfunctional to interact in a stable, proper Japanese society. Fearing his son's unpredictable volatile ways would destroy the Earth, he was soon cast into the underworld to rule this realm and join his missed, beloved mother. Needless to say he had acquired a bad reputation. One legend reveals that he tried to endear his sister prior to going to the underworld. Somehow, he had this idea that if he aligned himself with his adoring, most popular Sister, the Goddess of the Sun, he could improve his status and make himself more appealing to the world.

One day he crawled out of his dark realm to have a word with Amaterasu. Susano-o approached his sister desperately explaining his plight and pleading his case to welcome him in the world. Always benevolent, she agreed to help him in whatever way possible and soon she found herself uniting with her brother. From this union, eight important deities were born. According to Japanese mythology, the Sun Goddess took her brother's sword, broke it into three pieces and chewed them. She then spat it out and thus three Goddesses were born from her. Susano-o, in turned, took five pieces of his sister's jewels. He chewed the jewels and like Amaterasu, he spat it out. Five Gods were born from his action. According to Japanese Lore, these Gods became direct descendants of the royal Imperial Japanese families.

It seemed all was well with Susano-o's initial honorable intentions, but quite quickly he changed his tune and was back to his old irrepressible volatile ways. As one mythology tells it, one day he entered Amaterasu's sacred temple and started haphazardly tossing excrement all over the holy sanctuary, where first fruits were often offered to the Goddess. The final act of vile disrespect took place when according to one Japanese lore; he broke into the sacred palace where all the women were weaving holy garments. The horse was considered a sacred animal to Amaterasu, yet Susano-o, in an act of unfathomable behavior, violently threw a horse unto the priestesses that were weaving. As a direct result of his wretched action one of Amaterasu's beloved priestess was killed. The myth divulges that the blow of the horse killed her, but other myths reveal that she hit her own genitalia and then killed herself after this traumatic event. The symbolic language used in this myth might be a reference to perhaps being raped or sexually assaulted by Susano-o himself and this very act thus resulted in her own suicide.

The Sun Goddess was so outraged at her brother's repulsive disregard of her sacred temple and his defilement of her worship with this vile action. Some believe that perhaps she too was a victim of Susano-o sexual assault and thus, incest, a most vile traumatic incident, would've taken place. Regardless, Amaterasu was clearly distraught beyond measure and so greatly traumatized that she could no longer shine her divine light. She took her despondency and retrieved from the world, burying herself into a cave. Amaterasu withdrew all of her glorious divine light from the world and as a result the Earth stood in darkness. Susano-o's chaos now reign on the Earth and without the Sun Goddess, discord was ever prevalent in the world. At this time, he threatened civilization and the earth's survival with his ego driven, wild untamable ways.

The pantheons of Japanese Gods were needless to say, very concern for the Earth's survival. After sometime they grew desperate and joined to collaborate on a way to disentomb Amaterasu and bring her Divine light back to the world. At first, they brought out the cocks and enticed them to crow, as this was a trusted symbol of dawn. As the sun begins to rise in the mornings, these feather creatures are usually crowing to announce the impending new day. The Gods believed this would surely bring out the Sun Goddess. Next, they hung stringed jewels, sparkling tiny reflections of her light, all around the trees by the cave she had now resigned herself to. They also decorated the trees with cloth streamers all in an effort to entice her to stay. As the mirror was one of her most prized sacred symbol, they also erected a very large, special eight sided mirror for the Goddess to catch her own reflection upon exiting the cave. The last step in their plans to bring back Amaterasu, was calling on the Goddess Ama no Uzume to come to their aid. Uzume adorned herself with plants and bamboo shoots, appearing very much like a frolicsome Spring Maiden. She was encouraged to dance by the other Gods but her dance soon became rather frenetic, lewd and an ecstatic dance where she stripped her clothes off. It caused quite a raucous of laughter and an unexpected loud commotion. From deep within the cave, Amaterasu heard this and it confused her. She had taken her divine light away from the world and, instead of silence and mourning, all she heard now, from outside her cave, was laughter and merriment. This made her very curious. Gingerly, she slid the rock, slightly opening the cave entrance, just enough to get a peak. When she saw her own brilliant reflection caught in that special eight-sided mirror she was mesmerized. Then she came out a little further and caught a glimpse at all those brightly colored jewels hanging from the nearby trees. As she stepped out even further, the Gods quickly moved the boulder to close off the entrance to the cave, forcing Amaterasu to stay out longer and return to her post as Goddess of the Sun.

From this Myth we can extrapolate many facts about this beloved Goddess and her worship. We learn about some of her symbols and appreciate their value. According to Japanese lore, some of these gifts were bestowed to her Grandson, the direct descendant of the Japanese Imperial Family, and thus they take on even greater importance to the culture.

According to Japanese scriptures, to her grandson, Ninigri, she gives him three regalias - divine gifts from the Goddess herself. Amaterasu gives Ninigri the mirror, which she instruct him to assume as the Goddess herself, reflecting truth and light. She gives him the Sword, which was originally an impressive gift from her very own brother, Susano-o. Perhaps, it was seen as a powerful weapon, but we must also remember that she broke and chewed three pieces of the sword and thus three Goddesses were born. Her brother's sword, thus, played an important part in the procreation of important Japanese deities, linking the country to its future leaders. The last gift was the Imperial Jewels. They were seen as symbols of the Goddess- gifts of fertility and agricultural procreation. We must also remember that her brother took five of her jewels, chewed them and spat out Five Gods as a result. Like the Roman Goddess, Diana sends Aradia to Earth as a messenger and Like the Christian Father God sends Jesus to Earth to be the messiah, so too here we have the Divine Mother sending her grandson Ninigri to Earth, to the Japanese people, to continue her laws of order and civilization.

It also becomes very apparent that Amaterasu's withdrawal from the Earth was reminiscent of an actual Solar Eclipse. It can also be linked to the season's natural cyclical rhythm; for the Sun's bright power seems to wane, almost dying during the Autumn/Winter months. Upon the Winter Solstice the Sun is reborn again and slowly regains its full power leading us into Spring and then Summer. The Goddess Ama no Uzume can be seen as a Spring, fertility, Maiden deity drawing the sun's powers out by dancing her licentious dance. Amaterasu thus takes on an important role as an agricultural Goddess, who lends her light to help Japanese crops multiply and prosper. Here she is reminiscent of Demeter the Greek Goddess of the grain.

She also appears like a warrior Goddess, in her intolerance of Susano-o's destructive, sabotaging behavior, which put Japanese Society in great danger, almost destroying Japan. She is therefore seen as Japan's defender and the country's divine protector. Interesting to note, Japan's early name was "Dai Nihon" which literally means "*Great Sun Source*," revealing Amaterasu's strong connection to her birth country.

Throughout history Amaterasu is often seen as a parental, direct ancestor of the Japanese people In school text books there are even references to Amaterasu as a universal deity directly connected to the royal Imperial family. Her divine grandson, Ninigri, married a woman from earth and they had two sons. These two sons find wives and get married as well and have children. One of these children gives birth to a son - Jimmu and He then becomes the first Japanese Emperor. Here we have that important evidence that the Imperial family is directly related to the Great Divine and can justly assert its power over its people.

Amaterasu is one of the few Japanese Goddesses still highly venerated and worshipped today. Her existence reflects a belief in Japan as a divine land with divine people as it is believed that this Sun Goddess is ancestor to all of its people. Thus, she is the ancestral founder and protector of Japan. Shrines were created everywhere in her honor. During colonization many shrines were erected for her expanding worship. The most famous and largest shrine can be seen at The Ise Shrine. Here the sacred, eight sided mirror is reputed to be maintained. At these altars people might worship the Goddess with special ceremonies, invoking her powers of light & order and also with acts of purification. The Sun Goddess, Amaterasu, is seen as holy and pure, and as a reflection of truth, and she inspires her people to live life with the same ideals. It is for this reason why Amaterasu is an ideal deity to include in our chapter on leadership.

*The Japanese Goddess of the Sun; of truth and light, the mirror. She asks you to bring clarity and order into your life. Amidst turbulence and disruptive chaos, she calls you to breathe, regroup and reconnect to your authentic self. Look into the mirror and do not fear your own reflection staring back at you. It will reveal truths that perhaps, you have avoided seeing. She is the mirror and a personification of truth. She will awaken your own self-worth -a vital component for all magick. Do not let situations or other people dim your brilliance. Amaterasu reminds you of your own gifts and your divine light. Stop hiding and shine your light; you are a powerful being!!! Your light is needed within your community but first you are required to recognize and fully embrace your own light.

ODUDUWA

Oduduwa is one of the most mysterious Orishas in Yoruban religion, she is also known also as Odua, Oddua, Odduduwa. This mystery connected to her, especially regarding her gender, is partly due to a number of conflicting folklores and sets of beliefs that require deeper contemplation.

Oduduwa is one of the oldest Orishas in the Yoruba pantheon. She is essentially primordial and like most primeval deities can express itself in ways we as human beings have difficulty comprehending. But, we can start the process of attempting to understand this Orisha by first simply examining her name, as names throughout history have often provided a great deal of information.

In the Yoruba Language "O," which is at the start of many Orisha names, relates to ownership. The middle of her name "*dudu*" means Black. Oduduwa is often translated as, "owner of the black womb" or simply as Black woman. Her name is directly linked with the color black and if there was one physical attribute we can associate with her, it would have to be her beautiful dark ebony skin color. The dark ebony skin tone found among some people of African descent is deemed extraordinary and divinely blessed exclusively by her.

Oduduwa was also known by the name, *Iya Ogbe* and this translates in Yoruba as, "Mother who receives." Aside from the color black, she is deeply connected to all matters related to the womb, unity, love, mothering, fertility, creation, leadership, devotion and community.

As a Primordial being we have to first accept that they do not walk upon the earth like you and I. They tend to be powerful energy forces that we as humans try to reimagine, often in images that make more sense to us. However, the fact is, most primordial energy/Gods can challenge some of our most accepted view of divinity. And thus, the confusion regarding Oduduwa's true gender can be understood but when you examine this Orisha's name, it becomes obvious. It is also well supported by the surviving oracular folklores, from various regions in Africa, that she was indeed the Female Principle, and in direct contrast to her consort, Obatala, who is considered the Male principle.

In Yoruba Mythology, it is believed that both, this male and female; Obatala and Oduduwa, were well contained in the sacred Calabash. Inside this crammed Calabash, Obatala was positioned on top, representing the obvious, the Consciousness and Oduduwa was positioned on the bottom, representing the hidden, the Subconsciousness. She is darkness, receptivity, earth/water, female, while he is light, expansiveness, sky/air, male. Together they behold the mysteries of life and death. They would eventually mate and create evolution; the joining of opposing forces. She is the Black womb and he is the King of the White Cloth. Later on, Oduduwa then gives birth to Aganju (the Land) and she gives birth to Yemoja/Yemaya (the water).

According to Yoruban Cosmology, in the beginning was The Supreme Being, Olodumare, and he decided he wanted to populate and create a universe. He instructed his emissary, Obatala, also known as Orisha-nla, to go down upon the earth and create humanity. Along the way to fulfill his mission, the Orisha Obatala becomes very thirsty. There are some versions of this tale that state he had a pebble placed in his stomach by Eshu to make him unusually thirsty, but in any event, Obatala found himself very parched. He decided to quench his thirst by drinking lots of Palm Wine. He drank so much Palm wine that he became inebriated and eventually passed out in the middle of his mission. When Olodumare noticed he had failed to report back, he sent down the Orisha, Oduduwa, to check up on him. Oduduwa descended and much to her surprise she finds Obatala in a drunken stupor, passed out. With Olodumare's permission she took on Obatala's failed mission and went on to successfully complete the human race. She is attributed for creating mankind.

As a primordial Orisha we know she is linked with the womb and the color black. She was also believed to be blind or possibly only beholding one eye. There is a common folklore that speaks of Obatala ripping her eyes out while they were inside the sacred Calabash during a heated disagreement. It is believed Oduduwa is instructed on Ifa (a system of Divination and an African spiritual tradition or path) by the Orisha, Orunmila. He becomes her chief consultant.

For the people of Yoruba, Oduduwa is ancient. She's primordial; existing at the beginning of time but it is Orunmila, who in his great wisdom, creates Ifa and further develops the Yoruba religion. He becomes Oduduwa's chief counselor and passes down this wealth of esoteric knowledge to her. Therefore, she unquestionably becomes highly instrumental in the expansion of the Yoruban culture and religion. She is the one who takes all of Orunmila's wisdom, and highly developed spiritual systems, and shares it with others; serving her community and birthing a new emperor.

Like the Goddesses Amaterasu and Athena, there appears to be a Divine direct connection between the first Emperor of a region and their patron deity. One can speculate this has happened here for the people of Yoruba because the first Emperor of Yoruba becomes King Oduduwa. This is perhaps another reason why many people confuse this Orisha's gender.

Part of the confusion regarding Oduduwa's gender might be connected to another prominent individual in Yoruba folklore sharing the same name. In the 12th century CE there was a prince who eventually became the First King of Ifa, his name was Oduduwa. There is much confusion about his birth origin but he became the beloved Emperor of Yoruba and it is through his existence that Ifa (spreading) becomes expanded upon.

Because she's primordial, like the Chinese Goddess Nu-Kua or the Greek Goddess, Gaia, she could have easily been included in the chapter exploring the theme of creation. Some would say she's the mother of humanity, after all, she is the one attributed for creating humanity. As the mother of Yemaya/Yemonja, her matriarchal attributes cannot be overstated. She is clearly a pinnacle Mother deity/Orisha and could have also been included in the chapter about Nurturance and Mothers. Like many of the other deities presented throughout this book, there are a multitude of attributes Oduduwa offers us to explore. In this chapter we're looking at her leadership attributes and how they can inspire our own growth. As part of your evolution, you are invited to work with her potent energy to unearth your own inner wisdom, honor your powers of creation, develop your leadership gifts and expand on your community building skills.

ODUDUWA MUSING

*I am excited to present the Orisha, Oduduwa, in this book as I felt a very strong calling by her to be included in this chapter. All week long my eyes have been strangely, itchy, watery and giving me some concerns regarding my vision. And yesterday, I woke up to a red bump, on my right eye lid which swelled up. I can't help but wonder if this is connected to my work with Oduduwa. The dreams I've been having may also be connected to her and I share them here, as personal as they may be, because it sheds light on the subtle way Orishas/Deities and Spirit begin to affect our own personal journeys.

Two nights in a row, I've had very telling dreams. Last night, in this dream, I found myself in an outdoor market, where lots of beautiful, ethnic and African wares were being sold. There were also lots of large religious statuaries and I noted the Yemayas and Virgin Marys in the dream. A proprietor singled me out among the crowd, took me by the hand and walked me to the back area where a curtain was parted so that I may see. It was an old railroad station but it was turned into a river and there was water everywhere. You could even see the old tracks of the railroad under the flowing river water in the dream. They had covered up this old significant railroad station with a man-made lake, lots of water covered the area, and for some reason it was a secret that was being revealed to me. I looked at it, and then left to continue perusing the large religious statuaries throughout the market.

Today, I woke up from another strange detailed dream. I was seated among some people at a very long banquet table. The table was fully set, covered with plates of food offerings. It was literally adorned with lots of different types of rich foods fit for a King. Nearby, I noticed there were lots of very diverse looking people. I happened to notice that nearby, to my right, were a plethora of children, beautiful black skinned children. Lots of joyful, African children, laughing together, preparing their dances. They were rehearsing some dance moves and it was clear there was about to be some type of spiritual rite or Voodoo ceremony taking place soon.

At the banquet table, I was seated before a man and what appeared to be his family. He was speaking to me very passionately, almost fighting his tears, as he talked with me. I can't recall all the details of what we were speaking about (was it unrequited love or some other dramatic situation?) but I do remember very clearly the word; LUCUMI. This word came out of his mouth as clear as can be Lucumi.... and he was fighting the tears as he was making some type of compassionate plead. Our intense interaction was interrupted by what appeared to be a Caucasian man approaching the table...probably my husband. It propelled me to get up from the table and go to the back of the other side of the room, where the candles were set. I searched for my candles and lit one at the altar (it was like a unique waterfall altar). Then I picked up my other candle and started to walk with it, when I noticed, oddly enough, it had a double wick.... I think I eventually lit this candle as well before waking up from this strange dream.

SIF

The beloved Norse Goddess with the long sun-kissed colored hair is known as Sif. Her long golden hair was reminiscent of the wheat, the yellow corn, the harvest she exemplifies. In Old Norse text she was also known as the Swan Maiden because she could easily shape-shift into this form. She is Goddess of abundance, prosperity, self-sacrifice and peace. Consummate wife and mother, she is a symbol of community, family, the clan and the protection of the whole, as oppose to the individual. Sif and her long Golden hair, is often considered the Harvest and the Earth itself. She represents the sacrificing of the individual for the greater good of all and as the guardian of the family she represents the importance of strengthening lineage, family bonds and community.

Sif is worshipped as a fertility deity, connected to the archetype of the Mother and very much like the Greek, Grain Goddess Demeter. She is worshipped as the Earth itself which is reminiscent of Gaia and most Earth fertility deities. But her numerous tales in Norse mythology reveal to me that she is indeed very reminiscent to the Aboriginal Goddesses of the Americas; Selu, Iyatiku and Corn Mother. This will be revealed when we delve further into the numerous examples that depict her role as a sacrificial Harvest Goddess who concerns herself with the wellbeing of her family and maintaining peace and harmony for all.

SIF'S ETYMOLOGY

Perhaps it's best to start with the etymology of her name. The word, "*Sippe,*" in the German language means "*kin*", "*kindred*" and or "*kith*" and the word "*sibling*" comes from the word "*sib*" which is very closely linked to this Norse Goddess. Scholar, Andy Orchard, believes her name means "*relation,*" while scholar, John Lindow, notes the meaning of Sif to be, "*in-law-relationship.*" It becomes clear from numerous sources that her name is intimately linked with the idea of kinsmen, family, relationships and or related via a marriage. And these definitions are corroborated by her well known myths in Norse mythology. More precisely, her name is believed to be the singular form of the plural word "Sifjar," which is an Old Norse word, related to siblings, relations and again…connection via marriage. Some sources define the word "Sifjar" to mean, "to marry" and thus, the name Sif connotes a relationship via marriage and it aptly describes Sif, as she does become a highly venerated Norse Goddess exclusively via her union to the supreme God of Lightning, Thor.

SIF'S ATTRIBUTES

Sif's ancestry is a mystery and sadly not much is known about her origins. We don't know who her mother and father are, nor if she had any brothers or sisters in her mythologies. We don't know where she exactly stemmed from but we can make some inference based on what little has been written about her and those she interacted with in her myths. She was believed to be part of the Elder race of Gods, possibly a part of the Vanir, a second clan of Gods that existed before the Aesir. Vanir concerned themselves with cultivation, fertility, wisdom and prophecy. Sif was viewed as an Asa-Goddess that was later assimilated into the Aesir (newer clan of Gods that concerned themselves with power and wars) due to her marriage to Thor. Hence she is embraced as part of the modern race of Gods. Surprisingly not much is noted in the ancient text of the Viking period about this Goddess, thus what we do know about her comes from a few surviving poems, some fragmentary references to her and the few excerpts that have survived in the Elder Edda, the Prose Edda.

We do know that Sif is worshipped as Thor's wife and this very fact bestows on her a great position of importance among the Aesir Norse Gods, for Thor was highly revered as the beloved son of the King of the Gods, Odin. Thor's mother is the primordial earth mother Goddess, Jord, considered the last evidence of an earth deity who's position was later taken over by Frigga and Freyja, though some would argue that Sif herself was often mixed and amalgamated with these deities and might actually be the best representation of one generation or elder race, bequeathing her divine attributes to the next.

Sif garnered for herself a great position of power as the wife of the Great God of lightning and protection, Thor. He was liken to the Roman God, Jupiter and the Greek God, Zeus. And because marital unions in those days had less to do with romance or great love affairs and more to do with contractual business arrangements in an effort to preserve and strengthen the clan, we can only conjecture the dynamics of their marriage. She is actually his second wife and he is her second husband, as she was previously married to the Giant Orvandil. Interesting to note, this association with Orvandil also connects her even more to the Elder race of Norse Gods, the Vanir.

Sif comes into the union with her Divine second husband already with a child- a son named Ull or Ullr, the God of Snow & Archery. Ullr is associated with Winter, skiing and all things related to snow. His name means "the Magnificent." Known as a God of Archery, he later becomes the perfect consort for the Jotunheim Giantess, Snow Goddess, Skadi. The father of Sif's son is unknown or at least not mentioned in the text of this time period but we do know he is not considered Thor's child. He is not listed as one of Thor's children but Modi (which means Anger or the Brave one) and Magni (which means Might) are indeed listed as Thor's offspring and consequently, Sif's step children. They were conceived with his mistress and enemy of Sif, the giantess, Jarnsaxa, which means, "Iron Sword." Together, the Goddess Sif and her Aesir consort do give birth to one child; their daughter, Thrud (which means "Might"). Thrud becomes the Goddess of Storms and Clouds and one of the Valkyrie.

Our knowledge about the Golden haired Goddess comes from a compilation of the writings in Norse mythology. Deciphering, researching, compiling and putting all the little pieces together helps us get a better look at who Sif is and still remains to be, in the sacred realm of Asgard. It is through the writings found in The Prose Edda, written in the 13th century by Snorri Sturluson (c.1179-1241) and also the Poetic Edda, which is the oldest of the two and is considered a compilation of earlier traditional writings, that we are privileged to get a closer look at Norse deities. Sif is mentioned in both, though not with great frequency. Astonishingly enough, her name is not listed by Snorri Sturluson (c.1179-1241) in the Gylfaginning among the numerous other Norse Gods but her name does appear in numerous other tales. There are a combination of probably four different stories I will mention here that will help us learn, in greater detail about Sif, her lineage, her character, her important gifts and attributes and her vital role within the Norse pantheon. We will look at her presence in the Lokesenna, the book of Gylfaginning, the Skaldskaparmal and the story of the Giant Hrungnir.

SKALDSKAPARMAL

By far the most notable myth revealing a significant amount of information about this Norse Goddess is in the Skaldskaparmal tale in the Prose Edda.

One night while Thor was probably away, his stepbrother, the trickster god, Loki, also known as Loki Laufeyarson, decided to sneak into Sif's bedchamber. While the Goddess slept he crept, ever so sneakily and in his usual manner, and he cut off the beautiful golden hair of the Goddess while she slumbered. Now her beautiful golden long tresses had greater value than one would initially expect. Her hair was symbolic of her fertile powers and succinctly represented her as Goddess of the Harvest. A woman's hair in ancient times represented her powers of fecundity and often measured her beauty. Most ancient text, when describing a Goddess, do not frequently refer to physical bodies but will commonly make reference to the length of her hair, as a measure of her great beauty and fertile powers. And thus Loki, cutting off Sif's golden long hair was considered to be severely offensive; an act of monumental significance and detrimental to the Goddess herself. It was a symbol of her great sovereignty. When Thor returned home and discovered what his stepbrother had done and the pain and heartache it caused his wife, he became outraged. And when he got a hold of Loki, he proceeded to break every single bone of the scoundrel's body. In desperation, Loki begged Thor to spare him and promised he would make amends and rectify the situation.

When released from Thor's deadly grip, Loki then hurriedly arrives at the land of the Svartalheim, one of the nine sacred realms of Norse cosmology and here he connects with the Black dwarves to explain his plight and acquire their help. Some interpretation of the Norse text reveals he connected with dwarves or craftsmen-elves but a more common interpretation states that Loki connected with the sons of Ivaldi in this realm.

The dwarves came to the rescue and handcrafted a magickal wig that would grow hair made out of purely spun gold when placed upon the head of the Goddess, Sif. They truly outdid themselves with this magickal creation but they went even further by also crafting more gifts for the Aesir Gods. The sons of Ivaldi crafted powerful tools of magick for Odin and for Frey. Both Odin's Spear, known as the Gungnir and Frey's magic boat, known as the Skidbladnir, were manifested as an indirect result of Loki's mischievousness deed. Upon their completion, Loki was needless to say very pleased and relieved but... as was his nature he could not leave well enough alone...

On his way back to Thor and the Gods of Asgard, he ran into two more dwarves from the Elf-smith clan of Sidri; Brokk and Eitri. And he started to boast heavily about what had happened and the great successful craftsmanship by the sons of Ivaldi. He showed off their impressive works and questioned the two dwarves before him and their own ability to do better. As was his mischievous nature, he presented an irresistible challenged to the two dwarves. Loki placed a wager with Brokk and Eitri that they could not surpass the artistry, skill and craftsmanship of the sons of Ivaldi. He challenged them with a bet that if they crafted something grandeur and far superior than the sons of Ivaldi had, he would offer them his own head on a platter. Well, this wager excited the Dwarves as they did not care much for Loki and they delighted in the possible conquest. Together they began crafting three additional tools that would prove to be most powerful for the Norse Gods. Loki watched in amazement and in his fear of losing to them, he shape-shifted into a horsefly to pester them while they diligently worked on the divine tools but it didn't stop the clever Dwarves from completing their grand masterpieces. Eventually, they won the competition by crafting; Frey's golden Boar, Gullinbursti, Odin's multiplying ring, Draupnir and Thor's revered Hammer, Mjollnin.

When proudly they presented their work to Loki, he refused to admit defeat and he would not surrender his head to the dwarves as promised, claiming that it was attached to his neck and he never promised his neck along with his head in the wager. The Norse Gods were called upon to decipher who indeed was the winner and when they gave their stamp of approval to Brokk and Eitri, it was Loki who had to eventually pay up. The Gods allowed the Dwarves to sew and shut up Loki's mouth for his chaotic shenanigans and mischievous dealings and while the Dwarves took great pleasure in being declared the winners and finally punishing Loki by sewing up his mouth, it was the Norse Gods who were the ultimate winners, benefitting most by the exquisite magickal creations of the Dwarves.

PROLOGUE OF THE PROSE EDDA -REFERENCE AS A SYBIL

One thing is clear, the cutting off of Sif's locks by Loki resulted in the growth, extension and advancement of the Norse Gods, for her hair being chopped off, acted as a sacrificial rite that resulted in the manifestation of five of the most important Divine gifts and powerful tools of the Gods.

In the Prologue of the Prose Edda by Snori Sturluson, Sif is actually called a seer, a prophetess. She is described as a Sybil and thus someone with the gift of prophecy, powers of Divination and great psychic abilities. And in this prologue we learn of how she and Thor meet for the first time in the realm of Thrace or Thrudheim and then they later marry. Interesting to note, Thrace is the place that some scholars have claim Hekate, the Greek Goddess of the Underworld and Patroness of Witches and Seers, originates from. It is certainly thought-provoking to consider that Sif, with her gifts of prophecy, might have known and orchestrated this important, sacrificial rite in order for the Gods to grow in their powers. Of course, some would argue that many of the Norse Goddesses, like Freyja for example, had these inherent psychic abilities in varying degrees automatically as part of their numerous attributes, but it's interesting to note this ability in the Goddess Sif, paired with her role as a sacrificial harvest deity, who ultimately just seeks to create harmony and family unity.

Some would argue that perhaps the Goddess Sif, being attributed with psychic abilities, knew or had some psychic knowledge and premonition that this would need to occur for the advancement of the Gods. After all, this is her very nature, sacrificing for the greater good of all. These are parts of her known attributes and represented in her long flowing golden hair is the resemblance of the corn harvest. Upon closer inspection it would seem quite obvious that Sif and the cutting off of her long golden hair represents the first harvest pruning so often required in order to facilitate and help proliferate the subsequent harvest. As is her nature, she sacrifices for the harmony and greater good of all and thus her hair, which is so intrinsically a part of her, is shorn, surrendered into the hands of the trickster God Loki, in order that the Norse Gods grow in power and strength. The end result is that the five powerful gifts to the Norse Gods; Frey's golden Boar- Gullinbursti, Odin's ring – Draupnir, Odin's Spear – Gungnir, Frey's magic boat – Skidbladnir and Thor's revered Hammer –Mjollnin, would never had manifested, had it not been for her golden tresses being cut off by Loki's mischievous deed.

LOKASENNA- CHALICE & PEACE MAKER

We get an even better glimpse into the Goddess, Sif, when we look at yet another powerful tale in the Prose Edda, which confirms and supports her established role as a peacemaker. In the Lokasenna, (Stanza 53-54), we meet Loki once again, only this time he arrives at the sacred banquet hall of the Gods to manifest yet another stage of cacophony and mayhem.

Prior to this moment, Loki had been banished by the Gods from the banquet hall for killing a host servant but he now returns with much to say. He stands in the middle of the sacred hall and with much malice and disgust, he begins to accuse the male Gods of being cowards and a fearful bunch. This is Loki's attempt to hit below the belt, so to speak. Then he proceeds to speak of the women present, the Goddesses; referring to them as flirts and "trampish." He even goes as far as making inappropriate claims about the Norse Virgin Chaste Goddess, Gefjion. Clearly in that moment, Loki is being very cantankerous, unstable and quite vulgar to the Norse Gods and in his usual manner, he's creating quite a scene, as he angers the Gods of Asgard. Yet, in the middle of this disruptive mayhem, it is the Goddess Sif who bravely steps forward to confront Loki and attempt to rectify the situation. Holding her sacred crystal chalice in hand, she approaches Loki and offers him the antique mead linked to the powers of her husband, Thor. In her efforts to calm his belligerent heart and bring peace and harmony to the banquet hall, she says to Loki, that as she is being cordial to him he should do likewise with her, but Loki has other plans. She mentions that she is blameless and his insults to the Goddesses do not reflect her own true character, but Loki appears to have some insightful knowledge that he elects to maliciously divulge before all the Gods, as if to try to embarrass her.

> *"Hail to thee, Loki, and take thou here,*
> *The Crystal Cup of Old Mead;*
> *For me at least, alone of the Gods,*
> *Blameless thou knowest to be..."*

Loki drinks down the Antique Mead given to him and afterwards begins to direct all his insults towards Sif, amongst the tribe; insinuating that she has not been as chaste, nor as pure and faithful as she claims. He goes on to reveal that the wife of the great Norse God, Thor, is not so innocent and has actually had intimate relations with him.

Loki in his volatile, mischievous state actually makes the claim of infidelity with almost all the Goddesses throughout Norse mythology, so it is not clear how much truth there is in his statement. However, what is important to note in this poem is that Sif, again, has placed herself willingly in the middle of a very disruptive, uncomfortable and potentially dangerous situation, in her effort to manifest peace and harmony for the greater good of all and to protect the Gods from Loki's insults. Loki was being obnoxious and riling up the Gods in that banquet hall and it is Sif who decides to approach him to calm him down. Yet in the end, she again acts as the sacrificial one, for Loki diverts his attention now unto her and instead of continuing to insult all the Gods present, he turns to deliver his most venomous accusation and insults towards her. She makes herself available to circumvent a potential war and redirects his insults to spare her Divine community.

There is also an important connection between the chalice (cup, goblet and cauldron) regarding Sif, for she is considered the vessel or cornucopia that holds the essence of life. She is the Chalice, the feminine, the Yoni, the receptor and her consort, Thor as the masculine; is the mead, the fertilizer, the semen. In the Lokasenna she is thus, the cup bearer who is essentially offering herself when she offers the Crystal Chalice to Loki, filled with old mead. In this very significant act, she is also standing in her power as true representative of her husband's authority in his absence, which reflects her great sovereignty.

In the Lokasenna, we see a perfect example of her role as a peacemaker, as a Goddess who is looking out for the greater good of her community and as the one who steps forward to offer herself as the chalice; the sacrifice, to help diffuse the already volatile environment that Loki has created. In her efforts to make peace in that banquet hall among her family of deities, she is the one who ends up being trampled on because Loki begins to attack her, making inappropriate claims about her true nature and their past carnal history. It certainly leaves one more intrigued and wondering if there is any truth to Loki's claim, especially when we remember how he entered her bedchamber and cut off her hair in the Skaldskaparmal tale in the Prose Edda but none of this matters more than her consistent role as the one who self – sacrifices for the wellbeing of all.

This tale is yet again another example of how, Sif, in her effort to manifest peace puts herself in the mist of the chaos for the greater good of the Clan. But it's interesting because it turns your attention to yet another possible aspect of hers. And we don't know if there is any truth to Loki's claim but certainly there are other writings in the Prose Edda that alludes to this beautiful Goddess as having many intimate relations apart from her husband, Thor.

GYLFAGINNING

In the Gylfaginning, it is Thor's father, the God Odin, who also makes a claim that Sif is entertaining lovers. In this tale, stanza 48, Odin, in disguise, meets his son and the two begin this sort of bantering, throwing jabs and insults at one another. One of the claims Odin makes, is that Thor's wife is back at home being unfaithful to him. Thor is not moved by this comment and neither does he appear angered or combative. He simply replies by accusing the masked Odin of lying.

We don't know all of the validity of these accusations or even if it merits further investigation. It makes me wonder if this was just a common way to teasingly insult and degrade a Goddess, especially one who was known for her great beauty and discriminatory gifts of inciting desire. But perhaps what becomes most obvious is that not much has been written about the Goddess Sif and this creates a kind of tugging at all hints of her nature, subjecting any mention of her in writings, through rigorous investigation, gravely analyzing every mention of her in ancient text; whether it was small or large, truth or fictional. Consequently, there is not enough written about her and thus every little bit of information we can discern from fragmentary comments, poems and excerpts, becomes weighted with great importance for those seeking to know her best.

It is important to note that marriages were contractual agreements that afforded greater power to tribes for the Norse and it becomes clear that infidelities were probably not such a big issue or concern among the Aesir.

GIANT HRUNGNIR

To say that she is a beautiful Goddess is an understatement, for almost every mentioned of Sif in the writings of the Viking and pre-Viking period reveals her as being exceptionally beautiful.

In the Hymir Poem we see how much she is valued and desired by one of the strongest Jotnar Giants. When the Giant Hrungir, in a drunken stupor, begins to berate the Gods and makes outlandish threats that he is going to destroy the Aesir Gods, he reveals his desires for the two most beautiful deities in all of Norse mythology. In this poem, Hrungir shares aloud his plans to destroy the Gods and take for himself the two most beautiful female deities; Freyja and Sif. This is very indicative of how important these two deities were. Eventually Thor kills off the Giant but it's interesting to note that these two Goddesses, lumped together, were the only two the Jotnar Giant wished to save for himself, as if they were the most valuable prize in all of Asgard. This becomes more intriguing because some scholars have even attempted to claim that both of these Goddesses are really one and the same, due to their many similarities. It is more likely however, that Sif, being from the Elder race of Gods, came before Freyja and while both share in similar attributes, especially their gift of prophecy and their reputed magnanimous great beauty, they are more than likely two different Goddesses that came to us from different periods and tribes, and are now equally embraced as two separate, powerful deities in modern Norse mythology.

SOME ADDITIONAL OBSERVATIONS

Sif is the fertile land; the yellow corn, the wheat, the Harvest. She is the Chalice that holds the essence of life and the mother archetype that protects and unifies the clan. Sif is a prophetess, beautiful beloved wife of Thor and a sacrificial fertility Goddess intrinsically linked with the prosperity and sustenance of her tribe. Like Selu, the indigenous Corn Mother deity of the Americas, there is a striking resemblance in their attributes and roles as Sacrificial Harvest deities, for both were considered representative of the land itself and both... willingly sacrificed themselves in an effort to save or sustain something bigger than the individual. Selu, whose very own body produced the harvest corn, allows her body to be cut up and scattered across the land so that when she is gone her children will survive, thrive and not be extinct from hunger. Sif, in a similar manner, allows her hair, which is the harvest corn itself, to be cut up, shorn, and as a result, the Gods are strengthen and their powers expanded upon, via the new tools they acquired from her sacrificed tresses.

It is through this sacrifice that she must surrender a part of herself, a valuable part of herself for the benefit of the greater good and the clan-which she and Thor are responsible for protecting. Her hair is what helps manifest the Divine gifts; Frey gets the golden Boar (Gullinbursti), the magic boat (Skidbladnir) and Odin gets his Spear (Gungnir), the ring (Draupnir), and Thor gets his Hammer (Mjollnin). Just as it is through the willing offering of Selu's spilt blood across the field, that the land then becomes fertilize to forever feed and sustain her people, in much the same way, Sif, as a prophetess, knows her role is to sacrifice, to strengthen the Norse Gods, facilitate their longevity, for she is their chalice and the fertile land.

Another example of her role as family protector, peace keeper and sacrificial Goddess is the way she takes on the two children (Modi and Magni) of her Husband and his mistress. Under most normal human circumstances, a wife would be conflicted to learn that her husband's mistress was birthing to life two children but Sif is a Goddess whose sole role is to create harmony and wellbeing for the clan and thus, the children of her enemy, Jarnsaxa, are embraced as her own. All are taken in by Sif and gathered, unified as one, to sit amidst the family dinner table. And any antagonistic emotions that would surface as a result of learning about this affair are relinquished for peace and the greater good of the whole family.

I find it titillating that she enters her union with Thor already possessing a child (paternal lineage undocumented) and both, She and Thor, come from starter marriages. Together they have a child, Thrud, but along with the two previously mention step-children; it appears Sif's familial situation is very similar to our Modern day, 21th century blended, nucleus family. In this day and age of unconventional unions, where divorce rates are at record high number and multiple marriages (unions) carry with them the potential for numerous step-children; combining households seems to be the norm. This ancient Norse Goddess is reflecting a modern condition affecting our growing society as a whole today. The grace in which she handles this sacrifice of herself, despite any pain or heartache she may deeply feel, for the benefit of the whole Divine Clan, is exemplary of a Goddess and one we can fully identify with in our modern day era.

*The beautiful Norse Goddess, Sif, is the embodiment of the Harvest. Sif is the sacrificial one, who chooses to act considering the bigger picture and her community. She is less concern with the individual and chooses to align herself with the overall good of the clan. Sif is the one who seeks to formulate peace and harmony among her tribe and will often offer herself up in sacrifice for the peace and greater good of all. This is precisely what makes her an exemplary leader for us to explore in our chapter of leadership. The Goddess Sif willing surrenders parts of herself for the protection and sustenance of her tribe. With her, we are made aware of our leadership role within our community and the sacrifices sometimes required of us for peace, harmony and prosperity. Her beautiful blonde tresses, which resemble the wheat in a Harvest, is cut, pruned, and sacrificed, and this very act blesses the clan with a number of additional, invaluable gifts. Sif is the golden Harvest that must be sacrificed and pruned in order for greater prosperity to eventually ensue and bless the community at large.

OYA-YANSAN, IANSA

Her name means, "Mother of Nine" and in the Yoruban language it means: "She Tore". In Brazil they salute this Goddess with **"EPI, EPA HEYI",** while her Afro -Cuban salute is: **"HEKUA HEY YANSA",** thus, we begin our journey to Oya with this salute...
"EPI, EPA HEYI Oya-Yansa!!!! HEKUA HEY YANSA"

Respectively known as Oya-Yansa, Iansan, Iansa and Yansa, Oya is an Elemental African Goddess, attributed with the gift of bringing sudden drastic change. She is called upon for dramatic transformations and is considered among one of the most powerful Orishas (meaning African Deities) in the Yoruban pantheon.

Oya-Yansa is a Goddess associated with the Niger River, where it is believed she originates from, but one of the most amazing fact about this Goddess is how she permeates numerous cultures and traditions. From African and Yoruban practices, to Brazilian and Candomble, her worship stretches into the Americas and Cuba, touching upon Catholicism, Voodoo and the practice of Santeria. In the Catholic religion, she is associated with Joan of Arc and Lady Candelaria. In Santeria, she is sometimes known as Santa Barbara. In New Orleans, some see her manifested as Maman Brigitte. It becomes quite evident that she is revered and embraced by numerous cultures and various religions and this substantiate her supremacy among the African pantheon.

Often portrayed holding her sword, (her Machete) for she cuts through illusions, she is notoriously known for her abilities to cut through deceit, dishonesty and injustices. She is a force of change and anywhere she is invoked, Oya clears the way for new growth. Like cutting out that which is no longer needed, she amputates that which serves no purpose and extracts the tumor growth to make wave for healing. These are just some of Oya's powerful gifts.

Oya is known to have many attributes, but she is best known as an Elemental Goddess because of her connections to strong winds, earthquakes, roaring fires, omnipotent rainstorms, thunder-filled lightning and the drastic changes that natural disasters impart. As a matter of fact, all the elements (Air, Fire, Water and Earth) seem to be embodied by this all powerful African Goddess. In the howl of a strong wind, you can hear her name... Oya... She stirs and brings the winds of external and internal changes. It is perhaps why she is so easily embodied in the Tarot, Tower card, for she brings about structural changes. Tornadoes, cyclones, earthquakes, hurricane, lightning, rainstorms, thunder, fires etc... all of these Earth/natural disasters fall under her domain and naturally make her one of the most powerful Goddesses and a force to be reckoned with.

This highly revered Orisha was known to have two husbands. Her first husband, Oggun, also known as Oba and Ochun, was later replaced by the warrior God, Chango, who was more suited to her fiery personality. It is often stated in the Orisha lores that she joined him in battles and together they fiercely fought side by side. While Chango is considered the lightning in the midst of heavy rainstorm, it is Oya who is the torrential rain that brings flooding and the thunder and deathly electric bolts that catapults and destroys anything in her sight.

Oya is known to be very protective of her initiates and she is a beloved, patron Goddess for women. In particular, she is very protective of those women in leadership roles. Known as a Goddess of movement, her initiates would often dance, swirling in their long wide sweeping skirts, as they do a dance that can either invite the dead to join in or, with the simple sweep of their hands, keep them at bay. As can be expected from a Fire Goddess, she is known to be very passionate and independent and like most fire Goddesses, angers easily with a fierce temper much like the Volcanic Hawaiian Goddess, Pele. It is therefore of no surprise that she has garnered the reputation for being a warrior Goddess. Yoruban folklore claims she is a Warrior Goddess, who can sometimes even grow a beard, alluding to her great powers and strong, masculine energy. It is said "...She puts on the pants to go into battle..." Again, in this very patriarchal statement, there is a reference to Oya's great powers matching that of a man's' and therefore equal in brute strength.

Oya is also known as Lady of the Cemeteries and in New Orleans, she may sometimes take on the name of Maman Brigitte, as both Goddesses are considered guardians of the dead, cemeteries, skeletons and skulls. These Spirits/Goddesses were to guide the souls of the dead and bring them to the underworld. Like the ancient Goddess Hekate, this aspect of Oya-Yansa is known as a Goddess of Sorcery, Magick, intuition and the psychic arts. Thus, she is also patron Goddess of Witches and beholder of ancient occult knowledge and the Magickal arts. Some of her other numerous titles are Lady of the Masks, as they were sacred to her and Lady of the Market, for she will always find you a good deal when shopping. Her energy is often described as swirling prevalently in the market place; in the midst of haggling, fast talking pitches, fast- paced sale transactions. In the act of procuring the best deal for your money, Oya is ever present. She is also titled as, Lady of the mind, because of her great intellect and shrewd business sense. It is said she can impart genius and great memory or toil with you with the curse of insanity.

According to Yoruban cosmology, she is considered to be one of Yemaja's daughters, although it is best to never invoked them together in rituals, as they have quite a volatile history and some animosity towards each other. Some of this has to do with her philandering husband, Chango, but there are numerous other tales. According to Yoruban Lore, long ago Oya, first ruled over the Ocean and through trickery, the Mother of all the Gods and the sea, Yemaja, managed to trick Oya into relinquishing her Ocean Realm, in exchange for the Cemetery, she now rules over. Thus, this aspect of her as ruler of the cemetery is probably not one fully embraced by Oya, but there are varying opinions on this matter.

Oya is indeed a powerful Goddess and there are many ways to begin working with her energy. Perhaps begin by calling her, on her special day -Wednesdays and incorporate her favorite number -nine. To honor this Goddess, offer her special ritual masks, sharp machetes and swords, and anything made of copper, like pennies and copper cooking pots. Her favorite colors of maroon, purples and reds can also adorn an altar or shrine for her and she will always appreciate jamming, drumming session with lots of frenetic, ecstatic dancing. Beware though, Oya detest smoke, palm kernel oil, ram and pork, but eggplants, grape, wine, gin, rum, kola nuts, roosters, hen, porridge, fruits, fish, anything spicy are all sacred to her and a most appropriate offerings for this powerful Yoruban Goddess.

The Yoruban Orisha, Oya, is the fierce Goddess of storms, thunder, winds and soul-transformations. In her presence, drastic change is inevitable and life will never look the same. She is the fierce flagellation of a whipping tornado, the rumbling desolation of an earthquake, the electric omnipotent thunderstorm and the power to unexpectedly crumble your neatly existing structures. She is the Goddess of Drastic Change. She invites you to take up your role as a leader to boldly stand with all of your gifts and offer them to your community. She may come like the intense windstorms and tornadoes, to sweep that which does not serve you well anymore; maybe she is inspiring you to facilitate global changes. It is only in this severing of the old and outworn, that we get to allow a new life force to take root, grow and manifest -healthier and stronger than before. She comes to sweep away, with her long rainbow colored skirt, its various colors representing nations of all diversity, held together by her power. She awakens in you the courage and strength to welcome your role as a leader.

OYA-YANSA- IANSA- NOTES
- Yoruba African Goddess. Oya means "She tore" in the Yoruba language.
- Goddess of the Niger River
- Worshipped in Africa, Brazil, Cuba, Haiti, New Orleans etc…
- Her name also means "Mother of Nine"…. (She had Egungun and four sets of twins…)
- She is Winds of Change, Structural change, Known as a Weather Goddess
- She destroys Outworn structures, sweeps away debris making room for new growth.
- Goddess of Transformation
- Unpredictable,
- She can be as a gently breeze upon your skin or as destructive as the winds of a hurricane
- Lightning, Torrential rain storms with her tears
- Cyclones, Tornadoes, hurricanes, earthquakes her domain,
- Strong Storms , Fast paced movement,
- Fast paced energy of the marketplace,
- Patron of Woman leadership

- Wild Woman, Amazon,
- Protector of Women
- She is the power of Feminine leadership
- Mistress of Masquerades
- Fiercely independent
- Shrewd Business Woman
- Queen of the Marketplace
- Goddess who Can impart Great intellect /genius or Insanity
- Library/ Den in your house should be dedicated to her
- Speech is her domain
- Her Symbol is the Machete or Sword and she Cuts thru illusions, to get the truth
- She is Justice Seeker
- Fierce Warrior Goddess, fights with Chango her 2nd Husband, 1st husband was Ogun.
- She is known as the one who grows a beard and puts the pants on to go to war.
- As a Goddess of Movement, Loves to Dance and those who she possess do a special dance.
- Like Celtic Goddess Brigit with her association with Fire and water thru her Niger River and thunder and lightning rain.
- Like Athena, She is armed and helmeted to fight injustices and is associated with Wars, Air, intellect, swords.
- Like Hecate affinity to the dead and Sorcery and the magical arts
- Like Maat with her dedication to injustices, exposing deceits and dishonesty
- Like Voodoo Loa, Maman Brigitte, Guardian and Keeper of the Cemetery and the newly dead.
- She is Lady of the Cemetery... She led the spirit of the dead. She can call forth the spirit of the Dead or hold it back.
- Grim Reaper association.
- She was known as the Buffalo before she came to have human form.
- Associated with the Dark Moon and the planet Uranus
- Her day is Wednesday
- Her number is Nine
- Copper is her metal
- Burgundy, Reds, Browns, purples, Burnt orange are her colors
- Eggplants, Plums, chocolates, red wine, roosters, hens, goats, bean fritters, fish, kola nuts,
- Shea Coco Butter, Buffalo Horns, fruits or anything spicy are appropriate offerings,
- Taboos: Smoke, palm kernel oil, ram and Pork.
- Saints associated with her are; Santa Barbara, Catherine, Theresa Dymphna, Joan of Arc, our Lady of Candelaria (whose feast day is like Brigit's -Feb2nd)
- Oya is therefore honored on Feb 2nd but also on her Feast day-December 4th.
- She is said to be the daughter of Yemaja- Yemaja being the mother of all --But you cannot invoke both goddesses together because of a love rivalry. Chango her husband, was like Zeus with infidelity issues and at some point he was a lover of Yemaya and her Sister Oshun, according to some of the oral Yoruban myths.

HEKUA OYA, EPI HEY YANSA!!!

HESTIA

Hestia is the keeper of the Sacred flames on Mount Olympus and was highly respected and regarded as one of the original twelve Olympian Gods/Goddesses. According to numerous ancient writings, first offerings were always offered up to Hestia and her flames were the first lit. She was revered and greatly cherished by all Gods and mortals alike.

Greek Goddess of the Hearth and Home, Hestia is the personification of Hearth Flames. Her Roman counterpart was the Goddess Vesta. She is a Fire Goddess and her name literally means "*heart.*" In Latin, the word is interpreted to mean "*Focus.*" The hearth, in a domicile, was indeed considered to be the focus and heart of all dwellings and thus, she is embraced throughout the ages, as the patron Goddess of Hearth and Home. Her symbol is the infinite, sacred circle and in ancient Greece, a circular Hearth Fire was a place of reverence for this beloved deity.

Not much is known about this ancient Virginal Goddess, but what we DO know, we have learned mostly through her rituals, the Homeric invocations and her worship, documented in the writings of her time. For example; the hearth, in most Greek homes, was considered the center of the home. The architecture of the time reflected its importance as most homes were built around this important entity. One common documented rite that reveals Hestia's importance was the blessing of a newborn. When a baby was first born to a family and the child was five days old, they would walk around their hearth, the center of their home, presenting the child to Hestia for her divine blessings. Afterwards they would commemorate the event by having a huge feast in gratitude for her blessings.

Another documented rite, that has still survived the ages, involves the blessings of newlyweds. It was customary for the mother of the bride to light a torch from her hearth fires and bring that light into the newlyweds' home, to reflect the undying flames of lineage, being passed down from one generation to the next. Here too, Hestia's blessings would be invoked for a happy marital home life. Today this tradition continues only more subtly, via the unity candles incorporated in many marriage ceremonies, as bride and groom light one flame from the joining of their own, two, respective candles.

Hestia was greatly adored as the oldest of the Olympian Gods. She was the first born child of the Goddess Rhea and the God Cronos and thus was the oldest sister to all the Olympian Gods and Goddesses. As a result she was also the beloved Aunt of the second generation of Olympian Gods. Hestia was one of the first Olympian Goddesses on Mount Olympus, but was later replaced, in Greek mythology, with the God of Wine, Dionysus. Sadly, some believe this is reflective of a society that was already starting to undervalue the importance of wisdom, traditions and spiritual enlightenment -attributes Hestia represented and defended.

As Vesta, in Rome, her fires were attended to by the Vestal virgins, who took vows of celibacy as part of their initiations and service to her. They were supposed to be human, living embodiments of Vesta/Hestia herself, who was often depicted as pure and bright, a living flame, and thus the Vestal virgins had strict rules to live by. They were severely punished if they dared deviate from their role as celibate priestesses. Young girls, no older than six, were recruited to Hestia's service and their hair and clothing were unified to create anonymity within the priestess-hood community.

The Goddess Hestia was rarely depicted in female flesh form, but rather as a flame, a spirit, a feeling of warmth and comfort. All of her attributes are deemed helpful for those in leadership roles. Her immortal spirit continues to live on today as she transcends all time and space. As a Virgin Goddess, she was an advocate for wommin's spirituality and was sometimes compared to Sophia, the Gnostic Goddess of Wisdom.

Hestia is synonymous with purity, sincerity, and spiritual devotion. As the oldest of the Virgin Goddesses, Hestia was one of three Deities unaffected by Aphrodite's charms and love enchantments. However, Aphrodite did manage to arouse great love for the beautiful Hestia, in both the God of the Sea, Poseidon and in the Sun God, Apollo. The chaste Goddess refused both of their advances, choosing to dedicate herself to her role as Goddess of the Hearth and vowing to remain pure and unfettered by romantic love liaisons.

She espoused celibacy and valued Spirituality above sensuality and derived great pleasure and satisfaction simply being herself, honored in the home, and being of service to humanity and her Divine family. Many of the myths of the time, are all in an agreement that Zeus was quite supportive and respectful of his older sister, thus he willingly (according to patriarchal writings) gave her the honored place of the hearth in the center of the home, as the ultimate expression of reverence to this Goddess. At Mount Olympus, hers were the first sacred flames lit, always in her honor first and she was given dominion over the entire maintenance of this Divine home. Unlike other virginal deities, she really does appear fully whole unto herself, content with simply being and serving her Olympian family and the whole of humanity with her sacred flames. She was disinterested in the power, drama and notoriety her siblings were incessantly engaged in.

When I think of Hestia I think of calm, tranquility and a deep spiritual love and peace. I think of profound devotion to high ideals and service to our family traditions, our tribe, and our community. With Hestia, I reflect on those things that bring about stability and serenity, as she was never documented being involved in any of the numerous quarrels or disputes between the Gods. Hestia is the comfort and safety of our hearth fire, our core, our heart, our spirit and thus, both our internal and external homes.

Goddess of the Hearth and home, today she is still venerated and tended to with great honor. Hestia still lives on in the flames we tend to - the flames of our hearth found in the core of our homes and the flames we tend to in the core of our spirits and souls. Hestia is the flame that sparks our inner desire to be of service to humanity.

Greek Goddess of the Hearth and one of the beloved twelve Olympians, Hestia is the immortal Maiden Goddess. She is the embodiment of our hearth fires, the flames of our spirit and the core of our very being. Hestia comes to remind you to honor that part of yourself that is in tuned with the Feminine Divine and the archetypal leader. It is Hestia that invites you to tend to your inner flames, for they light the way for others. She arrives with the gifts of old, venerated traditions and honored communal customs that extend our families. With Hestia, it is time to honor your journey and give thanks to all those who have added the invaluable, loving, diverse, golden threads of your strong communal tapestry. She invites you to step up to the plate and begin to create traditions, structures, and communities that will stand the test of time. She is longevity and traditions, afterall. Hestia, in ancient Greece, was the oldest among her Olympian sibbllings. They looked to her for wise counsel and prudent leadership. Let her surviving ancient hearth fires stir and inspire your heart to serve, as she served on Mount Olympus.

THEME WORK SUGGESTIONS
Work with the Aries moon, symbolized by the Ram, and work with The Buffalo energy and the Goddesses presented in this chapter. You are encouraged to Organize Community Activities and Family Gatherings. Look into creating a support Group, facilitating a town talk session or explore other ways you can be of service in your community through volunteerism.

JOURNALING

Define your community and its needs....Ask yourself, who am I within my community?

_____
_____

Are there any leaders (past or present) you look up to and what characteristics do they hold that appeal to you most?

_____
_____

How do you show up in your community?

_____
_____

Ask yourself, what skills or gifts can you offer your family or community?

_____
_____

How do can I serve?

_____
_____

Ask yourself, do I feel I can contribute and make a difference in the world at large?

_____
_____

How will I commit to exercising my leadership skills?

_____

How will I show up in the world at large?

_____

What additional work or skills can I develop now to help me expand in my new leadership role?

_____
_____

INVOCATION & POETRY
QUICK CALL TO OYA
Mother of Nine
Be by my side,
Fierce lightning Mama,
Shaking the sky...

Gyrating fiercely
To the Congo Drums
Remove all the hurt
Until the cleansing is done.

Beloved Orisha,
Hear my desperate call.
I beg you Dear Mama,
Protect me from any fall...

In your heart,
Let me BE tenderly held,
Safely knowing,
With you, I am well.

Place me in your embrace,
Empower my inner space,
Fuel me with your storms,
With you I am reborn!

Hail to your winds,
And your storms of Change,
Gently walk me through
The gifts I now reclaim

Hail to you Oya,
Hail to the Orisha of My Heart
Hail to you Goddess,
Let our Magick now start!

***You are now encouraged to create your own altar(s) & invocation(s).)O(Blessings!

MAGICK RITES & TOOLS

This is your personal page to document your sacred rites and the tools you elected to use.

DECIDE WHERE TO SET UP AN ALTAR
Place an Altar Cloth in the Color of your choice.
Color: _____

GODDESS
Place an image of your Deity.
Goddess: _____
This image can be a Statue, handmade Sculpture or a simple Photo _____

FIRE REPRESENTATION
Place a blessed/charged Candle in the color of your choice.
Candle Type and color: _____

AIR REPRESENTATION
Light your Incense stick.
Incense Scent: _____

WATER REPRESENTATION
Place a Chalice of Water
Water Item: _____

EARTH REPRESENTATION
Place a Potted Plant or Fresh Flowers on your Altar
Add Salt or a plate of Dried Herbs
Herbs: _____
Chosen Gemstone: _____

YOUR WISH
_____
_____
_____

Place a symbol of your desire, if you have one available, and also write your wish out clearly, on a piece of parchment paper, or you can even use a cut up brown paper bag. These are the basics for a very simple altar & rite. Ultimately, your sacred space is only limited by your imagination. You can make your altar & rite as big or as small as you prefer and the addition of other personal items is really up to you.)o(Enjoy!

ALTAR PHOTOS

CHAPTER THREE

"Birth is the sudden opening of a window, through which you look out upon a stupendous prospect. For what has happened? A miracle; you have exchange nothing for the possibility of everything."
William MacNeile Dixon

THEME: CREATION/BIRTH

I am really excited to delve into this chapter's theme of Creation and Birth. As a writer, singer, mother and artist I have an obvious proclivity to this subject. I even, often times, call myself a natural Creatress; acknowledging that my sole life's work is indeed to birth and create. But if we are going to be honest here, I think every human being is inherently a creator; it is simply a matter of exploring and dancing with this aspect of ourselves. For me, every expression of creativity has always resulted in a powerful cathartic process that opened me up to a wellspring of astounding healing and helped me to connect to the Divine.

When we think of creation, we can easily connect it to the sacred act of birthing. Yet, the process of birthing is not an experience limited to the bringing forth of a new human life into the world, nor is it regulated only to women. The magickal course of creation and birthing is quite a powerful experience to both men and women. But surprisingly, it is not always embraced consciously nor examined in great detail. It might even feel irrelevant for those who have very left-brained occupations or for those who have no interest in birthing infants or connecting to their creativity at all. There are some that fear the creative process and have stalwart objections on the subject and, sadly, some that just don't see the value in it. Our journey together here will prove otherwise.

We have arrived at yet another pivotal point in our journey together. Our inner Creatress is strongly asserting her important presence in our lives and there is much value and necessity for her existence. Just look around you and you will see the pervasive hand of the Goddess of creativity; for all things are first and foremost born out of our thoughts and then birthed into some kind of physical manifestation. This is the sacred process of Creativity and it is what makes our world so remarkable.

There is much that seeks to be birthed by your thoughts, your heart and your hands now. It is time to explore this aspect of yourself; you are ready to birth something, and you are ready to tap into the powers of creation. Ask yourself what are you ready to create now?   What do you hope to eventually give birth to?

Getting that initial spark of an idea in our head and letting our imaginations create a picture and roadmap for the manifestation of this idea is essentially the sacred act of creation and birth. It is the same energy that creates forest from tiny planted seeds. It is the same energy that takes our love and desire and transforms it into a new human life. It is the inspiration that dares you to place the first paint stroke on an empty white canvas before it becomes a masterpiece. When we are delving into this theme, we are encompassing the many faces of creation and birth.

As I mentioned before, the process of creation has been an integral part of my daily existence for practically all of my life. As an artist I need not go into the obvious ways Creativity has consumed me my whole life. However, there have been various times throughout my journey when birthing and creativity have ebbed and flowed to reveal its varying levels of potency and magick. The most obvious examples of this have been when I felt ready to start a family of my own and when I finally felt ready to create and birth my first publication. However, because of my vocation, every day I am engaged in the birthing and creative process and as a result I feel as if I touch aspects of the Divine on a daily basis.

As we have done before, in this chapter we will explore further our theme with the help of several resources. We will endeavor to connect with the Goddesses; Gaia, Brigit, Saraswati, Olwen, Nu-kua and the sacred animal energy of the Spider. We will connect with our 5th chakra, the Throat chakra, and gemstones that can help better facilitate this connection. We will also look at the corresponding Lunation and a Tarot card that is connected to our theme.

*"Every day is an opportunity to be creative-the canvas is your mind,
the brushes and colors are your thoughts and feelings,
the panorama is your story, the complete picture
is a work of art called, "my life."
Be careful what you put on the canvas of your mind today it matters..."*
Innerspace

THE EMPRESS TAROT CARD

The Empress card in the traditional Rider Waite tarot deck is often illustrated with a beautiful Harvest Goddess sitting upon her throne. She is depicted amidst nature and all her bright colors of fecundity. The symbol of Venus is clearly evident by her foot, which alerts us of her connection to all things of a Venusian manner; music, the arts, beauty, love, romance , creativity, designing, fine dining and great prosperity, to name just a few. This card is also ruled by the astrological sign of Taurus, which is an earth sign, ruled by Venus.

You will notice she wears her overflowing garment that puddles over the rich green landscape and she basks under the bright yellow sun. It is a beautiful idyllic scene reflecting the beauty and harmony this card represents. Her image clearly speaks to our soul about all that is created by her very presence and all that blooms and grows by her simple touch. She is the personification of conception, gestation and the potent impetus of creation.

The Empress card is the embodiment of creativity and overflowing abundance. She is Gaia, Demeter, Venus, Hambodia and all the fertile Mother Goddesses of Creation.

MOON IN TAURUS   EARTH/VENUS

THEME: Creation/Birth

TAURUS	FIXED	EARTH	FEMININE	BULL

The Moon entering the sun sign of Taurus brings a very earthy, slower paced energy. Unlike the fiery, aggressive energy of the Moon in Aries, Moon in Taurus slows things down. Taurus is ruled by the Bull, so you can imagine this large, slow-moving, nurturing animal, cascading its influence on this lunar transit. One can surmise that anything we begin now, using this energy, might have a heavier, earth-bound, tenacious aspect to it.

Taurus is also ruled by Venus, the planet named after the Roman Goddess of Love & Beauty. It should come as no surprise then that this lunar transit is ideal for anything connected to love, romance, beauty and igniting our general earthly senses. This lunar transit heightens our sensory experiences and wants to delight in our earthly forms. Keep in mind that the planet Venus also rules over prosperity and life's luxuries and thus, when the moon is in Taurus we can employ this energy for anything we feel will add value to our lives.

The combination of Taurus, being an earth sign, and the influence of Venus being a planet of love, beauty and prosperity, lends itself to being a ripe time for creative pursuits. We can best utilize this lunation to connect with Venusian gifts, conceive ideas, birth new ways of creating prosperity and manifest our visions.

> *"An artist paints, dances, draws, writes, designs or*
> *Acts, at the expanding edge of consciousness.*
> *We press into the unknown rather than the known.*
> *This makes life lovely and lively..."*
> *Julia Camaron*

HERSTORY

All of her life she never gave children a second thought and here, all of a sudden, she felt the pangs of creation gnawing at her insides. She felt seeds of creation inside of her multiplying, just waiting to be born. She wanted to have children, yes, but even more... she felt a surge of inspiration and readiness to give birth to so much more in her life; like that new artwork, and that book, and that new song she keeps humming in her head.

She was being summoned by an inexplicable force. She was ready now to birth and feel the pulse of creativity.

********Take a moment to document here, or in your journal, your unique story.**

_____

_____

_____

AFFIRMATION

Every creative expression is a veneration
and prayer to the Divine.

I Create

I tap into Source and all Sacredness of the Divine
when I engage in my own powers of creation.

Every creative work of art I engaged in is an expression of soul healing.

The creative force that so powerfully
manifested me into existence is the same energy
I connect with, when I engage in the creative process.

As children of the Divine, it is our inherent natural gift to create and
proliferate... in the same way our Creatress/Creator does.

"And standing before my collection of art works, I realized that every single work of art
I created was an attempt at my own self-healing..." B. Melusine Mihaltses

CHAKRA & GEMSTONE WORK

5th Chakra   **VISHUDDHA/THROAT CHAKRA**   **COLOR:** Blue/Green
Speaking, Singing, eloquence of speech, speaking your truth, hearing and being heard, Connecting to your creative gifts.
     Mantra: My Voice Is My Power
)O(WORKING: Voice And Creative Expression, Creativity spell

GEMSTONE CONNECTION: Chrysocolla is a beautiful greenish-blue healing stone. It is a coppery gemstone, much like Azurite and Malachite; it will reflect tiny specks of copper within its make-up. It was believed to be, first mined in the legendary mines of King Solomon, in ancient Egypt. During this time it was also considered a special gemstone that imparted great wisdom. Chrysocolla is highly valued by Native Americans and numerous other cultures, across the ages. One story tells us that Cleopatra allegedly carried a piece of Chrysocolla with her, at all times, believing it was necessary to help her with creating innovative strategies, when dealing with opposing diplomatic relations. It is known as a highly creative stone that inspires new ideas and blesses ones throat chakra. The lovely, greenish-blue stone, therefore, becomes a desired gemstone for singers, public speakers and coaches, orators and teachers. It also helps one remain calm in the midst of a chaotic situation and Chrysocolla is known to dispel nervousness; allowing one to remain neutral in the face of instability.

The name comes from the Greek word, which means gold (*chrysos*) and glue (*kola*). In ancient times, smiths used the greenish stone as a type of connecting glue with gold metal jewelry and thus, it attained its name. It has an affinity to Gemini and Taurus and the planets Venus and Mercury.

GEMSTONE CHANNELING

     Go to your comfortable, safe space, where you can have a moment of silence and tranquility. If you can go outdoors in nature that would be most ideal but any place where you can relax, undisturbed, would be fine.

     You are invited now, to place yourself in a meditation position; you may sit or lay down. If it is available to you, place in your hands the Chrysocolla gemstone that we are working with today. Take a moment to actually look at your Chrysocolla gemstone. Make note of its varying blue and green hues. Notice how it feels in the palm of your hands. Is it warm, cold, hard or soft? (Pause) Hold your Chrysocolla gemstone up and study it carefully for a few more minutes, in silence... Quietly, gaze upon it and make note of any thoughts that immediately start to unfold before you.

     When you're ready, you may close your eyes now and begin this short meditation. As with all trance work, we begin with our breath. You are asked to take a deep breath, slowly filling your lungs up now. Breathe in the blue/green hues of your gemstone, as if the Chrysocolla has become part of the ethers. Breathe in its powers of creativity with each inhalation. Slowly take in your deep breath and hold it for 3 seconds and then release it... Counting now at your own pace; breathe, 1, 2, 3, and exhale on 4....and again....breathe in, 1, 2, 3, and exhale on 4. Let's do this one more time and then quietly counting in your head.... Breathe 1, 2, 3...release on 4. Breathe, trusting in the natural rhythm you have now established, of your relaxed inhalation and exhalation.

     Your Chrysocolla gemstone wishes to impart a special channeled message for you. See this blue/greenish gemstone in your mind's eye. See it shining brightly, embedded upon its dark, fertile, mother earth. Draw nearer to it and ask if it will allow you to pick it up. When permission is granted, gently gather it in your hands. With your mind's eye, gaze upon it; studying its color, its texture, its veins or any other details that captures your eyes... What images do you see appearing before you now? What visions are coming to you now through this process? Connect to your Chrysocolla gemstone and ask it to speak to you.(Pause)

     Now envision the top of your head opening like a window. Open yourself up now to any messages that may unfold... (Pause) You may envision your crown chakra now unveiling a magnetic Chrysocolla gemstone portal, allowing for this **Crystal Transmission** to come through... Continue to breathe in and out and let the energy of Chrysocolla travel down from your crown chakra to your throat chakra. Connect to this gemstone as it invigorates your throat chakra, the place of creative expression. Stay with this energy for a few moments and see if any additional messages want to come through for you. When you feel ready, open your eyes, and make note of any messages that have come through. You may document them here or in your personal journal.

_____
_____
_____

SPIDER PROTECTION ENERGY

Spiders are connected with the wheel of life. They are emblematic of our power as weavers and keepers of our own destiny. We weave and create our lives with our own daily thoughts, feelings and actions. For indigenous cultures there was a belief that we are all born with these sacred threads coming out of our crown chakra and when these threads fuse themselves with others, we are creating a powerful tapestry, the web of life.

One of the first things we need to address when speaking about spiders is that they are not insects. Their body consists of two sections, unlike the three parts of an insect, and they have eight legs, unlike the typical six of most bugs. The fact that they have eight legs, (some species even have eight eyes too) and their body seems to form, what looks like the number eight, speaks to us about the symbolism of this number. When we look at the number eight, it forms the symbol of infinity, a highly regard metaphysical emblem that represents the never ending energy of life. It is related to spiral energy which connects everything in the cosmos. The past is always interwoven with the future and we are intrinsically linked with our ancestors and one another. As we walk our individual path, all things are connected and we are all one. Knowledge and wisdom travels to us through these sacred silk-pun threads.

There is magick in our creative life force. The Spider is an ancient symbol reflecting this belief. Just study a spider's web long enough and you will understand what I mean. They are exquisite, and yet here, in this beautifully created work of art, is where life and death takes place. The spider traps, ensnares and eats its prey on this intricate web labyrinth. Life and death are held in this special place. It is also where she will lay her numerous eggs and nurture new life. The creation of such an intricate master piece can sometimes also exhaust a spider to the point of her death. Clearly, life and death are represented in her powerful creative domain. It is not hard to see how a spider's web becomes a powerful symbol of our world and she; an invaluable teacher and guide.

When we study the energy of the Spider we quickly learn what a powerful ally and protector we have available to us, especially as we delve into the subject of creation and birth. Spider medicine awakens our creativity but also our awareness of how influential we all are to one another. We are awakened to our part in the circle of life. We become aware of ourselves in the small center of this ever expanding web and we see how far reaching its effects can be felt.

It is interesting to note most spiders are poisonous and most weave and spin their intricate silk webs to catch their prey. The tarantula, one of the biggest types of spiders, is the only exception. It catches its prey by digging itself under sand, hiding there, and attacking its victim when it senses it nearby. Its mouth is located under her belly and she does not weave webs but spins.

Spiders are a symbol of strong feminine power and assertiveness. The black widow spider, for example, is reputed to kill her male partner after copulating and rendering him weak. Spider medicine represents beauty, strength, unity, balance, gentleness and creativity. It is industrious, loquacious and wise.

Spiders and their important lore have long existed throughout history in numerous cultures. In the Lakota tradition, she is known as Iktomi, the trickster and shape shifter, teaching moral lessons to humanity. In Greece, she was associated with the three Fates, the celestial weavers of our lives. She was also known as Arachne, the woman who dared challenge the Greek Goddess, Athena, in a weaving contest. She lost her human form to become a spider, after boasting that her skills were comparable to the Goddess. In India she was known as Maya, the Goddess of illusion. For most Native Americans, she was known as Grandmother and sometimes just as Spiderwoman.

For ancient cultures, Spider was attributed for creating our alphabet and thus our language. Through the intricate patterns of a spider's web, early humans detected letters and shapes that would later become our language. Thus, the Spider is highly linked with the magick of words and the power of our language. She is the teacher of invocations and spells. She blesses the orator, the poet, the writer and all those that endeavor to weave words in creative ways that can magically affect others. Spider is mother, grandmother, sister energy that inspires us to create and tap into our feminine creative life force. She is a most powerful energy to work with, especially for those in the creative arts.

THEME WORK SUGGESTIONS
Work with the Taurus moon, symbolized by the Bull,
and work with The Spider energy and the
Goddesses offered in this chapter.
Tap into your inner Muse. Make creativity
a priority, you can; paint, sculpt, sing, dance,
compose music, poetry, or write.
Make a Collage or a Vision Boards.
Explore Singing bowls and Recite Hindu Mantras daily.
Consider planting a few seeds and starting a small garden.

GODDESS EMPOWERMENT

"Birthing is the most profound initiation to spirituality a woman can have..."
Robin Lim

GAIA

The name of this chthonic Greek Goddess is a compound word. The first part of her name, "Ge" means land or Earth, in pre-Greek substrate, while the second half, "Aia" refers to, grandmother, and has origins in the Indo-European language.

Primordial Goddess of the Earth, Gaia is maternal archetype, who was the personification of the Earth itself. Gaia whose powers created all living creature and beings on this planet, the sea and the sky. Gaia who was from the beginning, before the existence of Time, for Time was an actual child of hers. She was born from the dark, formlessness of Chaos and wasted no time in producing numerous beings on the Earth. Ancient Greek Goddess Gaia, whose origins and worship has been absorbed by numerous cultures and probably originated from Attica. Even today, Pagans and Non-Pagans alike see the Earth, and all of its intricacies, as Gaia herself, still breathing and living today, thousands of years later.

Gaia Theory and Gaia Hypothesis were documented in 1976 by James Lovelock. Here the Earth's living; producing, self-regulating system is seen as Gaia herself, a living tangible Goddess. On April 22nd we celebrate "Her" via Earth day, which has become her modern day holiday, as we honor the Earth and concern ourselves with its survival and wellbeing.

According to Hesiod's Theogony, in the beginning was dark, formless, open, vast space known as Chaos. There was also desire, known as Eros. From the union between Chaos and Eros our beloved Gaia was born. One can view this delicate beginning described by Hesiod as very similar to the beginning of all life. The vast, dark, empty womb, mysterious and yet so full of potential, un-manifested until Desire comes into play. The joining of the two gives birth to our Primordial Mother Earth and from her all living creatures proceed.

According to the Greek myths, after Gaia manifested herself, she gave birth to her son, Uranus, who soon became her consort. With him, but also via parthenogenesis, she produced a multitude of beings, some monstrous and some Gods and Goddesses and not all anthropomorphic. She gave birth to Nymphs, the Sea, the Sun, Themis, Phoebe, the Cyclopes, One eye giants, Multi headed creatures, Memory (who would birth the Muses), Time, Cronos (who would later birth Zeus) and a multitude more. Her awe striking powers of fertility, procreation and abundance were evident in her ability and desire to populate the grand universe. Unquestionably, she is the raw power of fertility and creation- multiplying herself with and without a partner.

Uranus, as her son and lover, became very jealous, scared and angered at Gaia's obvious powers of creation- birthing and multiplying as continuously as she did. I suppose bearing witness to all those magnificent and monstrous creatures was probably quite intimidating for Uranus. Cunningly and with ulterior motives, he noted her birth canal and decided he would block her sacred passageway, with his own genitals, to prevent any more monstrous offsprings from being born. Daily, Uranus would enter Gaia, causing her much pain and blocking the birth of any further creations from being born. As can be expected, her womb, which served to procreate, grew and grew and expanded with each creation she manifested and retained, inside of her, unable to unleash them. Her fertile womb continued to grow and expand, holding in all of her multitude of creations. With her blocked passageway she keeps them inside, a painful, selfless act to protect them, but eventually she knew she had to devise a plan.

According to one myth, she crafted and constructed a sickle which was to be used specifically on Uranus himself. She called upon her first born, Cronos, and enlisted his help to end her agonizing pain by castrating his very own father. Carefully, Cronos followed his mother's detailed instructions. Upon approaching his father, he held the sickle and chopped off his father's genitals, tossing them into the Sea. From this act, his severed penis brought forth the sea foam Goddess of Love-Aphrodite. It also put an end to Gaia's labor and safely, she was able to release all of her contained children from her crowded womb. She became the grandmother of the first generation of Gods and

Goddesses, and in her, we can see that we too are direct descendants of her lineage and intimately connected to this ancient deity. She is indeed our benevolent immortal, Mother Earth, who has garnered great respect and reverence through-out the ages by all.

Gaia is seen as the Goddess of creation, abundance, multiplicity and fertility. In her ability to create numerous children with and without partnership, we see her autonomy and her wholeness. We can tap into any one of her numerous Goddess gifts but also, we can call upon her as our Great grandmother to guide and protect us, as she's been known to do, for her beloved children of the Earth. She is a living, breathing relevant Goddess that was, is and ever shall be, long after we are gone.
Blessed Gaia, Hail to you Earth Mother!!!!

*Primordial fertile Earth Goddess who is the essence of fertility, proliferation and the powers of creation. Life is full of wonderment and all around us, there are examples of her fertile creative gifts. It is her very nature to proliferate and multiply her sacred creations and she invites you to do the same. It is encouraging and inspiring to know that her primordial gifts are vibrantly within us as well, for her blood courses through every single one of her creations and that includes her earth children- humanity. There is much that we can create in the spirit of the Goddesses of abundance and propagation. She comes into your life at this time and asks you, "How do you create? At this stage in our Goddess journey, the sacred wheel of the year supports our endeavor to multiply and tap into our own powers of fertility; whether they are used for creativity, prosperity, ideas or actual birthing of children. She awakens in you a desire to multiply and manifest your gifts on the earthly planes. She invites you to enjoy the birthing process and tap into the sacred energy of the fertile season and the earth.

BRIGIT

Brigit is the Celtic Goddess of the Forge, The Fiery Goddess of Poetry and Inspiration. She is Goddess of the healing well waters and of the hearth. She is a Goddess of transformations, smithcraft, midwifery and the bard. This beloved agricultural Goddess was known by many names like; Brigit, Brigantia, Brighid, Brigid, Briget, Brid, Bride. Her name means *"the Exalted One"* and Breo-Aigit (another one of her many names) means *"Fiery Arrow."*

One story tells us that Brigit was the wife of the ruler of the Children of Danu, Bres. With him she conceived one son who was tragically killed in battle. She mourned for her beloved son on the battlefield and introduced the Celtic practice of Keening. Caoine or keening, as it is better known, was the act of sorrowful, very audible, weeping and wailing and Brigit is credited for inventing this practice when she herself lost her beloved son.

There is another known tale of Brigit being the wife of Tuirean and with him birthing three boys; Ircharba, Brian, Luchar. These three sons were said to have killed the God Cian, Lugh's father.

There are many myths about Brigit and her life. Some of these tales conflict with one another. For example, in a 10th century text she is described as the daughter of the Daghda, who was the God of the Tuatha de Dannan. In her role for the Catholic Church, as Saint Brighid, she was known to have been the daughter of a Druid, pagan priest, by the name of Dubthach. Some believe she was actually baptized by St. Patrick himself and some early Christian poetry of the time, claimed that she was the beloved, foster mother of Christ himself.

According to one legend, as a young maiden, she feared her father would push her into marriage. To make herself less desirable to romantic suitors, she disfigured herself by making her eyes pop out. Supporting this story is the numerous myths regarding the eyes and Brigit's sacred well waters bringing miraculous healing to people with opthalmological disorders.

This Pagan Celtic Goddess was so beloved by her people that there was great resistance when the Catholic church tried to assert its power to eradicate Paganism across the land. Her shrines and temples were converted to Abbeys and monasteries and she was thus converted to the Christianized, St. Brighid. Her Gifts of transformation were exemplified best in this very act, as her survival all these years has come about because of that transformation. From Pagan deity, she allowed herself to be transformed into the Christianized saint and thus her devotees grew and remained throughout the decades.

At Kildare, her sacred shrine was kept and sustained allegedly, by nineteen vestal virgins tending to her sacred flame in the guise of nuns. Nineteen has thus become known as a special number associated with this Goddess. These sacred Brighid flames had been tended to for over six hundred years, but the Archbishop of Dublin, Henri de Loundes, put out Brigit's divine flames when he feared and suspected these as Pagan rites. Thankfully, in 1993 her sacred Flames were re-lit again by Sister Mary Minchin. Today her undying flames are maintained by the Brigandines, an order of Sisters of Bridget.

Brigit was known to have provided many gifts to her people. She was attributed to inventing whistling as a way to call her friends, after the death of her son. She was credited for inventing Ogham, an ancient form of writing.

Beloved as a Healer, she healed with the waters from her numerous sacred wells. At Kildare there were more than 30 known wells dedicated to her. The largest well is still in use today and famous for bringing all sorts of healing, particularly healing of eye diseases. In her myths there were many known stories of miraculous cures for all sorts of ailments at her numerous sacred wells. It was a common practice to highly decorate these special wells with ribbons and flowers and leave various gift offerings to the Goddess there; like cakes, milk and honey.

Brigit was worshipped as a triple Goddess of healing, inspiration and the forge. Her symbol was the fire, like the sacred fires of creativity and the forge, but her symbol was also of the waters, with her healing sacred wells. Interesting to note how she can rule over two such opposing elements but certainly, a lesson about balance is to be learned here. In this example, she is reminiscent of the Hindu Goddess Saraswati, who also rules over two opposing sacred elements- fire and water.

Brigit was and still is well-known as the muse; inspiring the bard, the poet, the storyteller and the songsters. She was Goddess of the blacksmith, the glasswork creator, the artist, the sculptors, the weaver, the jewelry maker, needle worker and knitter. Brigit is a Goddess for those who use their hands to forge and create, for inherent in these skills, is the sacred act of transformation, which she rules.

This Celtic Goddess, whose sacred trees were the Rowan, Apple, Birch and Willow trees, was closely associated with the sabbat of Imbolc. Oimelc or Imbolc, was also known in its Christianized name as Candlemass, celebrated February the 2nd. Imbolc, means, *"in the Belly"*, a reference to the Earth's potential Spring stirrings in the womb. According to the Carmina Gadelica, the Celtic Goddess, as a snake, would emerge from her wintry hibernation. She would appear slithering from the mountains or a cave, where she had been all winter long. The tale was similar to our modern custom of the male Groundhog announcing the season's status. The snake was seen as a prediction of Spring's arrival, to inform us whether the Goddess will allow Spring to arrive early or let Winter linger on. During this Sabbat, cakes were left out for the Goddess. Loaves of bread and pitchers of milk were often left at the entrances of homes, as offerings, or they were shared with neighbors to attract Brigit's goodwill and better crops for the coming season. The cross plaiting with straws from the harvest was believed to protect the home from fires and bring good luck throughout the year and they were often hung around the home and farms.

Brigit is a Goddess of great transformation, for she takes our pain and transforms them into healing. She takes ideas and transforms them into creative works of arts, like songs, art works, sculptures, poetry, stories. She transforms us at the forge and with her flames forges our soul -as metal works are transformed into smith craft, so is our soul able to metamorphosize and undergo magical transformations with her imput, guidance and blessings.

*Brigit, the Celtic Creativity Goddess of the forge, is our divine healer, the matriarchal nurturer and the sacred "creatrix." Deep in the dark belly of the earth's womb, magick is awakening slowly, unseen by the naked eye but unquestionably forthcoming. All things are born from the hidden, in this deep dark, moist abyss, and it is embodied by the Goddess. Brigit is the Goddess who thaws and warms our winter heart with inspirations to create and express ourselves. She, who also through her bright flames, is able to transform us inside and out, is our beloved matriarch. She offers us the healing gifts found in both fire and water and beckons you to approach her at the sacred well with ribbons of supplications. Brigit enters your life now, asking what needs to burn to ashes, and like the Phoenix, be transmutated so that the power of creation and healing may come. She brings self –transformations, sacred initiations, creative awakenings, and the willingness to begin "the Journey."

SARASWATI

Saraswati is the Hindu Goddess of Learning, Wisdom, Music and Cosmic Knowledge. Saraswati is considered Supreme Knowledge herself. She is Mahavidya (holder of supreme knowledge), Maha-vani (the transcendent word), Smirtishakti (the power of memory), Maha-vidya (transcendent knowledge) and Arya (the noble one). She is the Goddess of the word, education and all Art forms; music, poetry, dance, writing, crafts, science, literature and because of this, she becomes a patron Goddess to students, teachers, scientist and those in the creative arts. Saraswati is also known as Vagishvari (mistress of speech), Jnanashakti (the power of knowledge), Bharati (eloquence). In Japan she is known as the Goddess Benzaiten. Subhaga (the bountiful one who provides immortality), as she is sometimes addressed, is also the Guardian of Truth. She is the representation of Sattua Guba which is; Goodness, Grace, and Purity. Born from Brahma, Saraswati is both daughter and wife of the creator of the universe and thus becomes known as Mother of the Universe.

In Hinduism, She is part of the Feminine Divine Trinity, also known as Trimurti, along with Durga and Lakshmi and she was one of the very first Deities in Hindu mythology addressed and revered as Mother. Long ago, it was believed that Vishnu had three wives that quarreled constantly. Vishnu, enamored by Lakshmi's brilliance, kept her as his wife and gave Ganga to the God Shiva. The Goddess Saraswati was bestowed upon the God Brahma. Her husband, Brahma, was the God of creation, creator of the Universe and she is considered his counterpart. Saraswati is the feminine aspect of the creator and thus, is revered as the Creatrix -overseeing all forms of creations in the Universe. Known also as Satarupa, Savitri Gayatri and Brahmi/Brahmani (related to Brahma), Saraswati, is a Goddess also called upon for Divine protection and spiritual enlightenment.

In Sanskrit, Sara means "*Essence*" and Swa means "*self.*" Saraswati thus literally means; the "*essence of self.*" In Hindu mythology, she is at times referred to as "dhaara-pravaah", a Sanskrit word meaning "The One who flows." This is more likely a reference to her role as a River Deity.

Aryan history presents her, first as the Saraswati River, a river that purifies and nourishes. She was known as the sacred river that imparts the flow of creativity, hence Saraswati becomes known as "*the One who flows.*" Though it does not exist today, it was a mighty river that once flowed from the West-End of the Aravalli Hills into the East-End of the Rann of Kutch, flowing into the Arabian Sea. Ancient text, like the Rig-Vedic Hymns, praise Saraswati, depicting her as a great, powerful river, bursting with energy; a fertile roaring invigorator, with strong flowing movement and able to break down mountains. It is in this sacred work that we get a strong descriptive image of this beloved Hindu Goddess.

As a River deity, Saraswati was associated with fertility, prosperity and the agricultural growth and productivity of her land and thus like the Greek Grain Goddess, Demeter, she becomes very much a Mother Goddess; protective and nurturing of her people.

There are numerous beautiful detailed images of Saraswati, but immediately, in all of them, we note that she is not heavily adorned, with heavy colors and jewels, the way Lakshmi is. Unquestionably, this reveals a strong symbolism, that knowledge is valued and more prominent than earthly riches for this deity. Saraswati's skin is often depicted as luminous white or light yellow. The predominance of the color white is quite evident, as she is often shown wearing a white sari and more often than not, sitting on a white lotus. The color white represents her purity, truth and her supreme knowledge.

Sometimes she is depicted ridding a white swan as her vehicle and this is a symbol of her powers of discrimination. The Swan is a bird with the reputable gift of discrimination, known for its ability to separate milk from water, it represents one of Saraswati's powerful attributes- as she is able to discriminate between the good and the bad, falsehood and truth.   In some depictions we sometimes see a beautiful peacock sitting by her side, gazing up at the Goddess, almost as if it is awaiting her gifts. Peacocks are birds associated with arrogance and pride. Traditionally known as a vain, temperamental, yet beautiful creature, the peacock becomes a symbol of the supreme beauty, possible through her powers of creations, but it also warns against vanities and the preoccupation on external beauties and appearances.

Saraswati is often portrayed with four arms and they reveal some of her most important divine gifts. They are a symbol of her omnipotence and the four human personality elements; mind, intellect, alertness and ego.   Her two front arms, represent her engagement in the physical realm, and they are usually occupied playing the Vina/Lute. Her obvious connection to music and the arts is well represented in this pose. Her two back arms represent her connection to the spiritual realm, as one arm holds a book, the sacred Vedas/scriptures, also known as Pustaka. On her other arm she holds Akshamala, also known as mala or prayer beads.

Saraswati is sometimes worshipped as a purifier, an attribute directly related to her gift with fire; the fires of creativity and those found in our belly. The Navel Center region, sometimes depicted in the color gold, with 64 lotus petals or 64 sun fire flames, is often associated with the Goddess Saraswati. It was considered the center of transformation, the source of energy of creation and here we meet one of Saraswati's attributes as a blood purifier and healing Fire Goddess. In Vedic scripture, sometimes she is referred to as Shonapunya, which is a sankrit word meaning, "one who purified blood." In this case she is reminiscent of the Celtic Fire Goddess Bridgit, who was also closely associated with the elements of water and its purifying fires, both for healing and creativity.

Saraswati's home was believed to be in the state of Kashmir, among the Himalayas. In many parts of the U.S.A. and in India today, Saraswati is still very much loved and revered. There are numerous festivals all across India that honors this beloved, Creatrix, Mother Goddess. In the South, there is the Navaratri, a nine day festival honoring the feminine divine, it celebrates this Great Goddess and there is also the infamous PUJA, a three day Spring Festival in Bengal and North India, which also honors Saraswati annually.

Kalpanashakti (the power of forming ideas), Sarada (giver of essence), and Dhaneshvari (the divinity of wealth) are among some of her other numerous titles. This beloved Goddess was also known as Kamadhenu, which means, *"wish fulfilling cow."* Reflected in this particular title is a deity that nurtures and provides sustenance for her people; much like the Egyptian Goddess Hathor, who was considered the Celestial Bovine for Egyptians.   Interesting to note that Apples, which have always been a symbol of supreme knowledge, are her favorite food and it is customary to leave offerings of honey, water and fruits upon your devotional altars to this iconic matriarchal Hindu Goddess. All Hail and welcome Divine Mother, Goddess Saraswati!

*Venerated as one of the first matriarchal deities mentioned in the ancient sacred text of the Rig Veda, Saraswati is the beloved Hindu Goddess of Wisdom and Sound. She is the Goddess of sacred learning and embodied as the once fertile Saraswati River. She awakens in us our powers creativity, higher learning and the value of our voices. Do not think you are immune to her gifts as the swirling power of creativity has numerous guises to reveal itself. The written word, scriptures and sacred sound are her gifts to us as well and she blesses the writer, the teacher, the songstress, and the artist. When Saraswati appears in our lives we have the ability to create various works of wonder - big and small, they are all of equal value to the Divine. Saraswati asks you, "What are you creating? What artistic projects are you working on? Ask yourself, "How is my unique soul transmitting through my hands and voice? Do I have the spirit of creativity? The Hindu Goddess arrives in your life at this time to awaken artistic offerings of the self to the Great Divine.

OLWEN

The name Olwen is translated to mean, "*Golden Wheel.*" She is the patron Welsh Goddess of the arts and creativity and a benevolent obstacle remover. She overcame numerous obstacles to find her freedom and obtain true love. She is often depicted with bright yellow tresses reminiscent of the sun's rays.

The Goddess, Olwen is also known as "Lady of the White Track," because it was rumored four white trefoils clover blossoms (White Shamrock flowers) would always spring forth wherever her footprints were left. She was also alleged to leave her rings and rays of sunlight wherever she bathed. She was purported to be the Daughter of Goleuddydd and her father was the chief giant Ysbaddaden Penkawr (also known as Giant Hawthorne Tree). He was a gruesome ogre much feared and was determined to keep his beautiful daughter unmarried because his death was imminent upon her marriage, as his fate was foretold. Olwen was breathtakingly beautiful and obviously, many suitors tried and failed, to their detriment, to gain her hand in marriage. The Mabinogion reveals much of what we know about this Welsh Goddess.

She is briefly mentioned in the Mabinogion in relation to King Arthur's cousin, Culhwch. This story is believed to be one of the oldest in the Mabinogion and, although her mention is temporal, it hints at Olwen's true ancient nature. It delves into this great love story between Culhwch and Olwen; the trials and tribulations they faced in their journey towards love. It explores their seemingly impossible union and the 39 inconceivable obstacles her father imposed on Culhwch to prevent their marriage. After much struggle, Culhwch manages to accomplish all 39 tasks by the first of May but the gruesome Ogre still refused to allow this marriage thus averting his own death. Culhwch loved Olwen and was determine to marry her, despite her father. He and the Ogre went into battle, resulting in the decapitation of Ysbaddaden and his death.

Some speculate that upon closer inspection this tale speaks about the struggle between the old and the usurping new order in the world. Olwen and her family lineage represent the old order, the ancient Gods and their rulership, much like the Titans in Greek mythology. Culhwch, King Arthur and their family lineage appear to represent the new order approaching; Christianity slowly asserting itself into the tapestry of this world.

Olwen and Culhwch finally were able to marry on May Day, cementing this day as a special holiday, and the blood of her father was shed as the sacrifice of the old order before the new is manifested. His blood drops are reminiscent of the ripe, dark, Hawthorne Berries ready for plucking and consumption in the spring.

Olwen is the Golden wheel that spins the sun's rays upon the earth. She has rulership over three realms; the earth, the heavens and the underworld. Like Persephone, she too rises from the underworld to inaugurate spring and bring her white flowers track, on May Day. She is the golden wheel that awakens both the sun and the earth to light at this sunny time of the year.

NU-KUA

Nukua, also known as Nu Wa, Nugua, Nu-Gua, Nu Kwa, Nu Kua Shih, Nu Hsi, is the foremother of Humanity in Ancient Chinese mythology.

Nu-Kua is a primordial Chinese Goddess connected with the creation of Humanity and Civilization. She is a half dragon, serpent bodied Goddess, sometimes appearing almost like a melusine or a mermaid due to her half creature and half divine makeup and yet, sometimes depicted in contemporary Chinese art as a beautiful woman. She is also associated with the sky, the heavens, waters, the moon and the earth. She is often depicted as a divine woman with her lower body resembling a snake or a Dragon's tail but she was a known shape-shifter, like many primeval ancient deities. She is worshipped as a fertility Goddess and a patroness of marriages and childbirth. Nu-Kua is the beloved Goddess of Order and Creation, a benevolent matriarchal deity associated with teaching humanity about agriculture, dam building and irrigation and even introducing the art of whistling. She is attributed for inventing the *shenghuang*, a reed-pipe musical wind instrument and the vertical bamboo flute, known as *xiao*. Nu-Kua is a Goddess who helps restore order and clarity amidst chaos and disarray and as many of her Chinese myths will reveal, this matriarchal deity is also venerated as the savioress of the earth and its inhabitants.

What is most interesting to note is that in a culture that has a plethora of male deities and in its contemporary state, so often appearing to be downright patriarchal, here is an ancient female deity, in its midst, held in the highest regard, as the supreme mother of humanity. This Goddess called on me as the perfect deity to present in this chapter, although she could easily be included in a number of other chapters found throughout this book. Nu-Kua's most prominent myths greatly resonated with me in their obvious exaltation and positive depiction of our gender.

While in Christianity, and many other mainstream religions, humanities birth is attributed to a single male God and women are depicted as secondary or as a lesser form of man, in ancient Chinese writings a vastly different depiction can be, thankfully, unearthed.

Nu-Kua's name frequently appears in early records of the Hans Dynasty, most notably the ancient texts of "*Huainanzi*," but also text from the Warring State era, like the "*Shanhaijing*" and the "*Tianwen*" in "*Chuci*." Interesting to note, in the *Tianwen*, her actual insides are credited for nursing and birthing ten spirits that would later spread across the earth's wilderness and become humanity, of course that is only one obscured version of her myth.

According to the ancient text of the second century CE, found in *"Fengsu Tongyi"* (*Popular Customs and Traditions*) Nu-Kua is the foremother and creator of humanity. The early myths explain Chinese cosmology by introducing the belief that in the beginning of time there was simply a cosmic egg. There was chaos, nothing formed; no earth, no sky, no star, no moon, no boundaries set... nothing... just an egg. And in this cosmic egg was a microcosm of chaos and within this contained chaos, a sleeping giant named P'an Ku dwelled, in a tiny embryonic state.

The first part of his name, "P'an", means "coiled up" and "Gu" or "Ku", the second part of his name, refers to "antiquity." Thus this divine being was the old or antiquity curled up, encapsulated in this cosmic egg and it held the promise of our earth's creation, according to Chinese cosmology.

As the years went by, the giant P'an Ku grew and grew within this cosmic egg. He slept, as various myths reveals, for 18,000 years and as he slept he grew bigger and bigger. The sacred egg also grew and expanded to accommodate the growing giant. Amidst this chaos of light and darkness, jumbled and crammed inside this encapsulating egg, the Giant slept, until one day the deafening sounds of chaos woke him up. He stretched out his enormous muscular physical form and the egg, unable to support his out-stretching limbs, cracked and shattered open. Everything that, up until that point, had been held together inside this cosmic egg was now released, surrendered to the nothingness of the formless Universe. All darkness and the light that had been held pinched and strangled by it, was now released with the Giant's birth. All the fragments of light united as they levitated and rose up to create the sky and all the essence of darkness fell down, creating the earth. The giant who was, according to some scholars, around thirty thousand miles large, watched as light and darkness separated before him. He saw the fragments of the shattered egg rise up to create parts of the moon, the sun and the stars. He witnessed the Universe forming itself, as light created the sky and the darkness sunk, creating the earth. And in his fear that the sky would fall unto the earth and chaos would return if they would collapse into each other again, he decided to hold up the sky and hold down the earth to keep them separated. P'an Ku took it upon himself, as the only living being, to banish chaos and preserve order with the sky and the earth separated.

For centuries the giant, P'an Ku held up the sky with his strong muscular form but he then began to age and inevitably grew fatigued. Slowly, he began to lose his strength according to some folklorist. As he got older he started to get weaker and weaker and, exhausted, this impaired his ability to continue holding the sky upward. Eventually the giant died. Now some scholars claim he had held the sky up, long enough, probably over ten thousand years as some sources claim. And being confident that his mission to maintain the sky and earth separated had been accomplished, he then gave himself permission to release it and expire.

Regardless, P'an Ku's exhaustive mission was accomplished but he could not live forever. His death, however, brought about a number of important gifts to the earth. According to Chinese mythology, P'an Ku's body served to become the mountains, the hills and the land. His tangled long hair and beard became the trees and the bushes. His remaining teeth and pieces of his bones sunk down into the earth to become precious metals, gems and minerals. Chinese myths claim that the precious gemstone of Jade, which is highly regarded in Chinese culture, manifested from P'an Ku's decaying bone marrow. His blood flowed as streams and rivers while his veins became the arteries of the earth. His semen became pearls, his sweat and final tears became rain droplets and dew. And P'an Ku's voice became thunder while his very last breath became the winds and the puffy clouds in the sky. In this way, the giant P'anKu was indeed the traditional sacrificial entity whose death created the lush, colorful, fertile earth. This was documented in the third century CE, in "Wuyun Linianji" (*A Chronicle of the Five Circles of Time,*) a compiled book from the Three Kingdoms era.

We must note that P'an Ku is well-regarded and considered one of the "*Three Divine Sovereigns,*" the earliest divine beings highly venerated in ancient Chinese mythology. He is accompanied in this honor by Nu-Kua and Shennong (the Divine Farmer) although other variations include Fu Xi. P'an Ku is first mentioned in the Three Kingdom era and his myths can be found in ancient text of the third century CE; *Sanwu Liji,* "Historical Records of the Three Sovereign Divinities and the Five Gods." He was described in some text as being a giant with a cat's head and his trunk, like that of a serpent. The people of the Henan Province in Central China viewed P'an Ku as divine protector of humanity and executor of the earth. They believed he had horns, as it was a common belief all primordial divine beings in ancient times had horns. He is also depicted with a Dragon's head in the *Wuyun Linianji*.

In some myths P'an Ku is associated with earth-quakes by the people in the Gansu Province of Northwestern China. Here there was a lore that connected him to an ox. In this myth P'an Ku would hold up the heavens but he required additional help keeping the earth below from sinking. It was then that P'an Ku crafted an ox from clay mixed with his own saliva and he breathes life into it and assigns it the duty to maintain the earth. At this time, P'an Ku also crafted a divine rooster to help keep watch over the ox's important duty. Keeping the earth from sinking proved to be too arduous a job for the ox and one day he wanted to take a break and nap. The rooster however, would not let the ox rest, as it firmly upheld P'an Ku's commands and this angered the divine ox. In his anger he shook the earth on his back three times and this explains early earthquakes in ancient Chinese lore.

P'an Ku is still venerated today in many of his temples found in Henan, Guandong, Jiangxi, Zhejiang provinces and the Guangxi Zhuand regions. Henan Province holds his most famous temple on mount P'an Ku and many from distant lands sojourn to gather on his feast day, celebrated on March 3rd of the Lunar calendar.

When P'an Ku eventually expired he left the earth as a beautiful oasis and it was perfect but no one inhabited it, according to most myths. Then from across the sky slithered the half Dragon Goddess, named Nu-Kua. Her birth or origins are unmentioned and unknown, we simply are told that she roamed the heavens and upon P'an Ku's death she descended to find his divine body spread across the earth below. She marveled at the great beauty of the earth and what P'an Ku had accomplished and yet, she felt a twinge of sadness in her isolation and inability to share this great world with anyone. Of course, later we will address another version of this myth where Nu-Kua is not alone at this pivotal time in the myth, but rather, paired with her older brother. But I digress, in her sadness at finding herself alone, Nu-Kua sat by the river banks, where she picked up the accumulating yellow clay and began to shape it into a ball and then into an image like hers, only with legs. She continued to gather the yellow clay and formed numerous human beings in her image to keep her company and banish her loneliness but they were inanimated and they simply stood there as rows upon rows of tiny human clay figurines. She longingly picked one of them up and placed her divine breath upon it. Remarkably the clay statue became animated with her vital breath of life upon it. It gave her great joy to see her statue creations come to life and she derived great pleasure in their laughter as well. She decided to animate all of her clay creations and then started crafting more beings; both male and females.

As time went on, the Goddess Nu-Kua began to get tired and overwhelmed at the thought of how many humans she would have to sculpt by her hands, with the yellow clay, in order to fully populate the earth. She looked at the arched reed near the river (although most myths state she took a cord or a rope) and she dipped it in the mud to complete the human race. Wherever a dripping of the mud fell on the ground, a new animated human being emerged. In this Chinese myth we have an explanation for the two distinct types of people on the earth. Those that are noble and rich were descendants of Nu-Kua's initial hand crafted yellow clay human being and those who were poor peasants were the descendants of the human figures she crafted afterwards with the rope's mud droplets. A rather prejudicial, harsh way of looking at things but revealing that for the Chinese, there are only two types of people; the rich and the poor, those divinely touched and sculpted by the Goddess herself and those that came later as a result of her fatigue, via the mud droplets.

Yet there are other versions to Nu-Kua's myth to consider. There is even a tale that holds an uncanny resemblance to Genesis in the Old Testament of the bible. In this Chinese tale, Nu-Kua is not just attributed for birthing humanity, but for creating all of the creatures upon the earth. The myth claims that on the first day she created chickens and on the second day, she crafted dogs. Then it goes on to state that on the third day she made sheep and then pigs on the fourth day. On day five she created cows and on the sixth day she made horses. Finally on the seventh day she created humanity from the yellow clay by the banks of the river.

The Goddess Nu-Kua resembles the Greek Goddess Gaia in her primordial matriarchal Creatrix abilities. Both are ancient deities credited for populating the earth with its inhabitants. It is also interesting to note another tale linked with Nu-Kua and the seeds of similarities it holds to many other deities from various cultures. Quite often with primordial Goddesses there is a connection between their creation, bloodline and their consorts. With Nu-Kua there is one version of her myth that alludes to her sexual connection to her brother, who becomes her husband, Fu-Xi. And there is some ambiguous concern or guilt she wrestled with concerning procreation with her brother, according to some interpretations of these Chinese old folklores, which is why she begins to impart to humanity the importance of marrying, birthing children and admonishes the practice of incest.

In the ancient Chinese text, "*Duyizhi*" (*A Treatise on Strange Beings and Things*) by Tang dynasty writer, Li Rong (ca.846-974CE) we have a different tale of the Goddess Nu-Kua connecting her to a partner. According to this Chinese folklore,

Nu-Kua was initially not alone on the earth after P'an Ku's death. She was accompanied by her older brother and they lived on the mountain of Kunlun. In this myth they desired each other and wanted to procreate and fill the earth with their children but the shame and guilt of incest caused them much apprehension and distress. Together the siblings prayed to the heavens asking for direction and a clear sign that would grant them permission to unite and procreate. They began to divine by numerous interesting means, for example; the Goddess would run down the mountain and if her brother could catch her, then they were ordained to be married. Another way of divining involved threading a needle successfully from a long distance and yet another test was if the smoke from a fire would gather and unite, then that was a sign that they indeed had divine permission to marry. Although they were given clearance to unite as husband and wife, according to these various myths, the shame was too much for Nu-Kua. As a result, she gathered and weaved grass into a fan to cover her face and thus, this is the Chinese explanation why traditionally brides hold up fans during their nuptial ceremonies.

Her consort Fu-Xi resembles Nu-Kua in his half dragon, half human appearance and when they are depicted together sometimes their Dragon tails are actually intertwined to show their deep intrinsic partnership. He is seen in artistic depictions holding a square to represent the heavens, although some sources say he holds a representation of the round sun, while she often holds a compass in her hands to represent earth or the moon. Together they unify the heavens and the earth.

Fu-Xi is a Chinese God who imparts to humanity the gifts of tending to ones flock, hunting and the art of fishing with a net. He was also known to be a music teacher, inventor of musical instruments and a song composer of a melody known as "Jia Bian." He was credited for the eight tiagrams/diagrams, the Ba Gua, which helped develop the Chinese form of divination known as the, I-Ching. He taught humanity to barbecue food and is attributed for inventing the calendar, matrimony dowries and written characters for documenting life events, instead of the traditional knots on a cord. Fu-Xi also made copper coins and manufactured many tools and objects from metal. While Nu-Kua's main myths always seem to present her alone or single, it is interesting to also make note of who she was inevitably paired with in Chinese Mythology. Writings, particularly in the Hans Dynasty, refer to Nu-Kua and Fu-Xi as the parents of Humanity and the first of the San Huang people. Nu-Kua is also highly revered by the Miao people.

Some folklore reveals that Nu-Kua did not want to spend eternity tending to her clay human figures. And she did not want to continue laboriously hand crafting mud or clay beings. It was becoming much too tedious for her to craft daily and tend to the earth's population. Thus, she taught humanity the importance of joining male and female, ying and yang, to procreate, self-populate and maintain the human race upon the great earth. In this way, Nu-Kua expressed a desire to equip humanity with all the tools they needed to thrive and succeed upon the earth on their own, without her constant watchful eyes. It gave her great joy and satisfaction to empower humanity in this manner and it allowed her to simply enjoy their existence.

Nu-Kua's name itself can be looked at for further insight as some suggest the Goddess contained both male and female essence. The first part of her name "Nu" is translated as "first male" while the second part, "Kua" or "Kwa" denotes a "first female." Perhaps revealing that in this Goddess we see the "ying" and the "yang" uniting and the very first male and female embodied.

HOW SHE BECAME SAVIORESS OF THE WORLD

The earliest mention of the collapsed pillars of the heaven and Nu-Kua saving the earth is found in the early Chinese writing of the "Tianwen." She is also mentioned in the Lunheng (*Critical Essays, written by Wang Chong, ca. 27-100CE*) and "Bu Shiji Sanhuang Benji" (*Biographies of the Three Divine Sovereigns: A Supplement to the Historical records,*" Tang dynasty). According to the text of this period, one day a quarrel ensued between a few of the most powerful deities in Chinese mythology, the details of what they were arguing about are lost to us but according to folklore the quarrel turned into a huge vicious battle. Included in this battle was the Water God named Gong-Gong and the God Zhuanxu (also known as, Zhurong, Di Ku or Shengnong). Some sources refer to Gong-Gong, also known as Kaghui, as a monster so we can only assume he was quite powerful and volatile in Chinese mythology. As the story elucidates Gong-Gong became angered when he feared he was losing the battle and in his volatile anger he proceeded to whack his head against one of the sustaining sacred Pillars of the sky, which was known as Mount Buzhou (meaning, "not full"). Needless to say this resulted in the imbalance and tilting of the sky towards the northwest and consequently the shifting of the earth's axis. With one pillar off course the existing pillars collapsed and the sky could no longer cover the earth. And the earth was said to be unable to hold all things. The "*Huainanzi*" text, however, states that initially all four pillars collapsed but this challenges other sources. Nevertheless, the Chinese nine sacred regions of the world were exposed and in severe jeopardy. Gong-Gong's thoughtless explosive act inaugurated much devastation upon the earth, as it set a chain reaction to numerous catastrophic events. Floods and roaring fires ensued, as well as the strange manifestations of man eating beasts spreading across the earth, threatening humanities existence. The earth was badly plagued with insurmountable chaos and devastation at this time.

The Chinese Goddess, Nu-Kua came to rescue humanity during these monumental calamitous times. Some tales claim she used her very own body, as a half dragon deity, to seal up the torn parts of the sky and this helped stop the flooding that was permeating the various realms. She was also believed to have gathered the ashes of the reeds to help stop this flooding. To this day, some parts of China worship Nu-Kua in an annual Water Splashing Festival that honors her as the one who saved ancient China from the cataclysmic floods. She is a Goddess attributed for the seasons and the rain falling where it is most needed upon the earth.

A more popular myth reveals that Nu-Kua gathered colored rocks (some sources say seven different rocks, others say five) and she melted these colored stones and used them to patch and mend the various holes in the sky that were causing the flooding. She managed to stop the flooding in this manner but the sky could not be fully fixed and remained slightly tilted. This folklore explains the earth's unusual tilted axis and why the sun, the moon and the stars move northwest, while the river in China is said to flow southeast into the Pacific Ocean.

The beloved Goddess Nu-Kua is highly venerated for rescuing humanity and restoring the balance of the earth during this catastrophic time. The earth's cardinal points fell out of alignment when the monster God, Gong-Gong, banged his head on one of the pillars of the sky. Her myths reveal that she helped support the compromised four corners of the sky by utilizing the four cut legs of the sacred giant tortoise and replacing the pillars with these cut turtle legs. She confronted and killed the Black Dragon that was one of the creatures causing much havoc on the earth. Eventually Nu-Kua pacified the numerous hideous creatures that were devouring human being and because of this she became a Goddess recognized for introducing animal domestication. There is another myth that tells of her taming a treacherous giant named King-of-Oxen, at another time, by jamming a rope through his nose. This miraculously allowed her to tame him, as well as many other wild animals she encountered, according to Chinese legends.

When the earth was restored to her peaceful state, Nu-Kua, without seeking accolades, humbly departed to the heavens, where some believe she remains today. Some claim she rode to the heavens seated on a chariot of six winged dragons and yet other creative depictions reveal she was carried off by a thundering chariot containing two winged dragons and two green hornless dragons. A special mattress is reputed to be under her as she travels on her chariot while holding her sacred compass. White dragons are before her and a flying snake is visibly behind her and she is said to be surrounded by the most celestial gilded clouds. Clearly, references of this Goddess in ancient Chinese literature idealize her with much respect and grand adoration and she continues to be worshipped today, especially among women.

Nu-Kua's worship continues in Shexian County and Hebei Province. There is a great Temple dedicated to her, named *"The Palace of Empress Nuwa"* and from February 15th till March 18th, in the Lunar Calendar, festivities take place to honor the Divine mother and great grandmother of humanity. March 15th is notated as Nu-Kua's birthday and thus, this day takes on great significance for the Chinese. She is exalted with singing and dancing on this day, in the hopes that she will bless her worshippers with fertility, good health, happiness, safety and blessing on marriages and children. *"The Temple of Human Ancestors,"* also known as *"Renzu Temple"* or *"Tomb of Tai Hao,"* found in Huaiyang County, Henan Province, celebrates the God Fu-Xi, along with the Goddess Nu-Kua, for a month long. From February 2nd till March 3rd in the Lunar Calendar, women offer the Goddess dances like the *"danhualan"* or the *"danjungtiao."* These are ancient ritual dances for the Goddess Nu-Kua, performed solely by women. At the Renzu Temple, contemporary worshippers might burn incense, paper money, paper architectural buildings to represent ancestral dwellings and offer handmade shoes, lovingly dedicated and ritualistically burned to Nu-Kua.

Clearly Nu-Kua is a beloved Chinese deity that exemplifies women's creative powers and her innate ability to manifest peace and order out of chaos and calamitous situations. For feminist Wiccans, she is a beautiful symbol of matriarchal energy, attributed for humanities birth, and our gender unearths a great source of empowerment in this beloved highly venerated ancient Goddess.

MUSING ON NU-KUA, CHAOS & ORDER AND THE NEED FOR POLYTHEISM

"Chaos is what we've lost touched with. This is why it is given a bad name. It is feared by the dominant archetype of our world, which is Ego, which clenches because its existence is defined in terms of control..." Terence McKenna

As an artist and a mother of three boys and numerous household critters, Nu-Kua is a Goddess that I can easily identify with. Even as I write this and research this highly revered Chinese Goddess I feel her energy, for as mothers we are always called upon to find order amidst chaos.

My home is often subjected to the challenge of maintaining itself organized, most days it suffers from a topsy-turvy, laundry piles waiting by the laundry machines, piles of animated shoes by the entry doorway, dirty dishes gracing our kitchen sink, various children's toys scattered about with every step one tries to take in our home and yet, I am required to thrive and somehow find order amidst this chaos, as well as facilitate my loved ones to do the same. It is in these moments that I sense some of Nu-Kua's important attributes and I am able to connect with this ability to confidently get organized and get things done despite the less than ideal situations and challenges.

Yes, I feel her necessary presence in my life and her great importance for my own sanity and sense of accomplishment. There are things that, as a womyn, I must do, things related to my own personal well-being that sometimes differ and conflict with the things I must do as a mother. Finding time to connect with my spirit, commune with my inner voice, write, paint, meditate and be in stillness feeds my wellbeing as a womyn but goes in complete opposition sometimes to being a mom of rambunctious little ones. Needless to say, finding a moment of serenity and quietude in our household is somewhat challenging but even amidst these obstinate obstacles, it is indeed achieved and I do manage to find those important moments to cultivate inner peace and order.

There is a beauty and order I must create for myself daily amidst chaos and disarray (whether it's physical or mental) and yet, I am also required to create it for others by providing an environment that is safe, clean and conducive to raising healthy children. There are things of beauty and expressiveness that, as an artist, I am passionately obliged to create for my own happiness and wellbeing, just as I imagine the Goddess Nu-Kua felt, as she created that first yellow clay human figure. It made her feel good to create this being in her beautiful image (the mother archetype must create). It also helped her feel less lonely and it made perfect sense to add this, almost necessary, finishing touch to a world that seemed incomplete without it.

As a matriarchal Goddess I find Nu-Kua fascinating, even more fascinating is her part in a cosmology that differs so greatly from what mainstream religion would have you believe. Her role in cosmology greatly contrast the tales found in Genesis; a tale most mainstream religions wholeheartedly accept and believe. Here in this ancient Chinese tale, explaining humanity's birth and the earth's creation, is an empowering tale for our gender, certainly much more empowering than the crippling, degrading explanation of a male god creating man and then creating a woman from the rib of that man. There is no sense of equality in that myth, dare I say, there is no sense of true Divine love in humanity's manifestation in those tales in the bible. There is an obvious perverse domination and distasteful hierarchy that serves only to disempower one gender and thus harm one half of the human race. When you compare the two tales; one deems a male god creating humanity in his image and that was Adam. Then a female was formed by taking of this man's rib. Inherent in this biblical tale is the potentiality for massive injustices, obvious discrimination and a subordinate view of women; a downright cruel view, clothed in divine reasoning of why women should be deemed as the lesser human than man.

Herein this ancient Chinese tale is an explanation of humanity's birth filled with the potentiality for gender equality. We have a loving Goddess, composed of both creature and divine essence, for she is part dragon (a sacred ancient serpent) and part human and she hails from the heavens. She embodies the sacredness of the earth and the sky and yet also the waters and fire in her savioress and creatrix abilities. And she lovingly creates humanity out of sheer love, desiring someone to share the great beauty of the earth - the earth that had been created and passionately maintained by one who was birthed and formed inside of chaos in the sacred cosmic egg, the giant P'an Ku. And after maintaining the sky above and successfully keeping the earth and the sky separated, an act that he does for fear of the destruction of something he finds so precious; our earth, he then finally grows weary and old and dies. He is the sacrifice so commonly recurring in many ancient mythologies regarding humanity and the earth's existence across numerous prominent cultures. It is not from a place of soveignty or a great self-imposed power that the giant creates and sustains the earth but from a place of love. Something beautiful is before him and P'an ku does not want to see it destroyed; he was after all, birthed from its essence. The creation of the universe and humanity is thus beautifully shared by both genders, both male and female, and by all really, for less not forget Nu-Kua is half beast and P'an Ku is a giant, sometimes also depicted as half beast as well. And thus this cosmology includes everyone as being part of the creation of this Universe, not just one male deity as we so often see in other patriarchal religions. It is not one person, nor one ruler, not one god who is attributed for creating the earth and the human race, it is a combination of many who left their divine imprint on us and because of this we are many, in respectively different sizes, colors, shapes, gender, different life paths and titles. We are not one type of people, we are many and this diversity is mirrored for us in this cosmology much more so than in the one presented to us in Christianity. It is this noted fine detail that purports polytheism vs. monotheism.

I must say that here is where the study and connection to the Chinese Goddess Nu-Kua has been the most impactful for me personally, and where I may stray from some established Pagan, Christian and Non-Christian viewpoints. There are many who discovered Paganism after years being indoctrinated into other monotheistic religions and this obstinate belief in *"the One"* has a way of lingering rather subtly into newly adopted religious and spiritual practices. This *"one deity"* concept seeps into our culture's prejudicial practices and seeps into the fibers of our so called melting pot that seems to only want to lump everyone into the same mold, whether that mold is Christianity, Paganism or Americanism etc.. It seems to feed the *"oneness monster"* that is so often threatened and intimidated by anything that stands out in its diversity and its eccentricities. I think the rise of monotheism has brought about a wave of unconscious and conscious prejudicial harm and I can see that issue harboring in many aspects of our lives.

The problem with our nation's intolerance for differences becomes most apparent when we see the epidemic of bullying taking place in schools now a day. From an early age children are indoctrinated into this perverse practice of tearing down and degrading anything or anyone that appears different or dares to assert itself as unique. And the evil of this world is not in our differences, the evil in this world is in our inability to embrace, respect and seek understanding of differences. No… it's much easier to bully people into submission to assimilate, abandon their culture, race, belief, sexual orientation and succumb to social pressures. It's much easier to manipulate, beat down with alienation until they question their very own self -worth and whole purpose to exist… that's the world we've become, a world that fears the unknown, the different, and does not seek to conquer its fear with knowledge but rather, feed it with hate and prejudice and false assumptions.

I think Polytheism supports diversity and honors differences and, dare I say, reveres unconventionalities and this has magnanimously more far reaching implications than we can fathom –it extends into all human and civil rights matters.

I, personally, do not like to impose a "oneness" belief tenet in my spiritual practice; advocating for Polytheism and opting for diversity and great respect and embracing of all cultures. We are indeed all human beings composed of spirit and matter and most cultural myths do unify us as being divinely manifested, but we all come from different parts of the world, with different cultural myths aligned to our ancestral genetic makeup and that's a great thing!!! It is not something to shake off or be admonished for. The Gods of our ancestors are just as indispensably important as the Gods of this new found land and neither needs to be placed on a pedestal at the expense of the other. While some mainstream religions set out to eradicate any cultural religious allegiance people may have, with numerous violent crusades, wars, persecutions and persistent missionaries, a belief in Polytheism renders these practices unnecessary and almost tragic. We have much to learn from one another but the "oneness" concept found in monotheism purports that there is only one way, one culture, one supreme race and one being and one God and one religion, leaving little room for anything else. It is these consistently narrow definitions in our world that are at the root of all forms of prejudice.

We pride ourselves in being a melting a pot of various races and cultures but the operative word is melting pot because you are expected to melt away what makes you, you, and blend into the vanilla-ness of the "ruled over." It allows for the "one" to have full authority to declare what should and shouldn't be accepted. It is irrespective of people's various cultural, ancestral differences and it begs one to assimilate and assimilation is disregard for one's uniqueness and history. Assimilation is the one thing that has destroyed so many beautiful ancient cultures and religions and yet, assimilation, is almost required to herd the sheep, control and manipulate the masses. We've become a nation intolerant of differences, as if differences can and would destroy the very fibers of our nation and yet, difference are not what causes strife and wars, it is our intolerance and prejudice, which is rooted in ignorance, that creates wars and devastations, it is our insistence that everyone be ruled by the "*one theory.*"

Diversity is a positive thing only when we respect and embrace our differences. I think the problem in our society is that a lot of people want to glaze over it and not respectfully acknowledge differences of race, religion, sexuality, culture and class and deceptively lump everyone under preordained stereotypes or categories and if you don't fit that societal criteria you get ostracized. This has the stench of monotheism because we are not so easily classified as the same but to someone who sees this as positive trait, this is a gloriously divine human attribute to be celebrated not a reason to persecute, dominate or destroy. These differences, while they appear like societal chaos, are in fact that sacred kaleidoscopic beauty of our very human divine nature which upon closer inspection has perfect order.

*Nu-Kua is the ancient Chinese Goddess of creation and order. She is attributed for creating the human race out of little clay figurines. It is so empowering to our gender to learn of this rather unique cosmology. Naturally, as the Goddess who created humanity, she is highly revered. Her gifts to us are similar to Gaia's, as one can surmise, and thus Nu-Kua awakens us to our own gifts of creation. Nu-Kua is a powerful sovereign Goddess that is deemed as the Mother of humanity and her presence awakens our own creative gifts. She was also known as humanities' saviouress whose ingenious quick thinking helped save the earth from a cataclysmic disaster. She represents the strength to dive into chaos and create order and peace out of Global disasters. Calamitous events do not need to destroy us but rather can give us an opportunity to display our strength, our creativity and our problem-solving skills; this is yet another one of her powerful messages to us.

JOURNALING

What seeds of creation are waiting to be born?
_____
_____

In what form does my creativity express itself?
_____
_____

How do I feel about other's creations?
_____
_____

Where can I express best my creativity?
_____
_____

What am I ready to give birth to?
_____
_____

THEME WORK SUGGESTIONS
3. CREATION & BIRTH
Light a green candle

Meditate and decide on what it is you wish to birth into the world. Peruse through numerous magazines and clip out images that speak to you about those things you would like to birth now in your life. Create a collage or vision board.

INVOCATION & POETRY

GAIA, A LIVING GODDESS

Living breathing shifting Goddess
Quaking, bursting flowing with life.
You who was since time began,
Live today in all the land.
Look across this wide landscape,
See you in tree roots, water and caves.

See you in mountains
And continents and new formed lands,
See you birthing, creating
With immortal hands.

See you exploding in volcanoes,
And rustling in the breeze,
How can anyone deny
Your sacred energy?

In the animals; wild and tamed
In our food source, you are contained
In every seed and living tree,
You are the pulse in everything.

We are conceived in reflections of you,
Held by the threads of ancestral spool,
You are the womb that holds us at birth,
Nourish our souls and bodies on this Earth.

Living now as in ancient times,
How can anyone not see Earth Mother Divine?
You shift and expand and continue to grow,
Your powers un-weakened by those who just don't know.

Feel her sighs, feel her breath
Feel her hold your earthly form,
Feel her trembles and her strength,
As with seasons she Transforms.

Holder of life, of seeds, of bones,
From you we emerged to make our temples and homes.
Not dead on a cross, but present and alive,
Know her in your body, feel her from inside.

Believer in truths, secure in her powers,
She'll even allow you to worship whom you desire,
But know without question whom she truly is
For you'll meet her in the beginning, as you will in the end.

She is your Mother Divine, the Earth,
Living Goddess who has sustained you since birth,
Requiring nothing but your love and respect
Hail to Gaia,

Hail and Goddess Bless !!!!

Page 41 from "Goddess Grimoire Journal, a Collection of Simple Prose and Spells" by B. Melusine Mihaltses (Isbn# 9780985138431)

WEAVING CREATIVITY

*Spider Weaver,
Weave your Tale,
Spark Creation
Color what is Pale.*

*Stir ideas
That I may Birth,
Weave me into
Mother Earth.*

*Let me Bloom and grow
Like a Flower,
Tap into
My Creative Power.*

*Flow with ease
Into this stage
Paint and write
And fill the Page...*

*Tap into
Thy Fertile Gifts,
I create
And find my Bliss.*

*Sacred Source,
I honor thee,
Bless my
Creativity...*

***You are now invited to create your own altar(s) & invocation(s).
)O(Blessings!

MAGICK RITES & TOOLS

When preparing to do any form of sacred rite, it's important to first and foremost consider where you can set up your working space. You'll want a space that provides some level of privacy and a place where you'll feel comfortable to set up. If you share your space with others, like family or roommates, please consider what you'll feel comfortable sharing. Traditionally, it's best to protect your altar from the scrutiny and suspicious eyes of cynics. Nothing worse than having skeptics spew negativity or doubt on your work. Enjoy this process and understand you are creating a special place for yourself.

This is your personal page to document your sacred rites and the tools you elected to use.

DECIDE WHERE TO SET UP AN ALTAR
Place an Altar Cloth in the Color of your choice.
Color: _____

GODDESS
Place an image of your Deity.
Goddess: _____
This image can be a Statue, handmade Sculpture or a simple Photo _____

FIRE REPRESENTATION
Place a blessed/charged Candle in the color of your choice.
Candle Type and color: _____

AIR REPRESENTATION
Light your Incense stick.
Incense Scent: _____

WATER REPRESENTATION
Place a Chalice of Water
Water Item: _____

EARTH REPRESENTATION
Place a Potted Plant or Fresh Flowers on your Altar
Add Salt or a plate of Dried Herbs
Herbs: _____
Chosen Gemstone: _____

YOUR WISH
_____

_____

_____

Place a symbol of your desire, if you have one available, and also write your wish out clearly, on a piece of parchment paper, or you can even use a cut up brown paper bag. These are the basics for a very simple altar & rite. Ultimately, your sacred space is only limited by your imagination. You can make your altar & rite as big or as small as you prefer and the addition of other personal items is really up to you.)o(Enjoy!

ALTAR PHOTOS

CHAPTER FOUR

"Love makes your soul crawl out from its hiding place…"
Zora Neale Hurston

THEME: LOVE & JOY

Love… how timeless and universal is this powerful emotion? The very word itself can evoke a whirlwind of varying strong feelings. Of course, these feelings are dependent on our own personal life experiences on the subject and the many images we might have developed and linked to it over the years. It may stir a deep longing for something we may feel we are lacking or a surge of warmth, support and sweet comfort we believe is automatically connected to this emotion. We may associate the word love to a mixture of unresolved, conflicting emotions, related to past expressions of love in our life experiences or a sweet remembrance of the taste of what we may have experienced in the past. We may feel our vibrations elevate at the word love, if we are connecting it to the people, places or things that stir our passions, or we may slump vibrationally if we find this emotion illusive and out of our grasp. Whether positive or negative, it is clear that our view of Love; what we love and how we love, can be as varied as the stars in the night sky.

We've reached another important point in our spiritual journey together, where we are called upon to delve into this heart and soul awakening emotion called, love. The desire for love and the exploration of how we love is as universal as time itself. As part of our healing work here, we are being guided to explore our own personal definition of love when it comes to the types of partnerships and romantic relationships we are seeking to cultivate in our lives. But, we are also, first and foremost, encouraged to examine all the things that we associate with love; all the people, places, activities and objects that are donning us in the powerful golden light of love. Love begets love and when we surround ourselves with the things, people or places that awaken love within us, we attract its magick even further.

As part of our process here, it is my hope that we will touch upon one of the most fundamental aspects of love… the Love that we carry for ourselves – self-love. Admittedly, it has been a popular term, perhaps overused in our recent times but its necessity cannot be overstated. Love begets love and the feeling of love that we first cultivate and recognize within our own self is the spark that can light the way to a trillion candles in a seemingly, darkened world.

Our theme for this chapter is the exploration of love and the many aspects connected to it. We are asked to explore what we love and how we find growth and healing in the process of that love. We are also called upon to explore how we cultivate self-love and how we recognize and connect to all the things, activities, people, places that we love.

One final side note I wish to share here, relates to a revelation I received in one of my meditations. I came to the realization that, in my own personal journey, every significant love relationship that had initially poured into my life always came in the midst of unforeseeable trauma and considerable shifts in my life; shifts that perhaps were most significantly initiated by simply my mere choice... Therefore, I feel compelled to begin this chapter by inviting us to first and foremost make a choice....choose love, choose to BE love, choose to be in the realm of happiness and love. It all starts with exploring what brings us joy, what stirs our heart?
What do you love?

As we have done in previous chapters we will explore further our theme with the help of several resources. We will endeavor to connect with the Egyptian Goddess Hathor, the Goddesses Baubo, Aphrodite, Oshun, Flora, Ezulie Freda and the sacred animal energy of the Swan. We will connect with our 4th chakra, the Heart chakra, and gemstones that can help better facilitate this connection. We will also look at the corresponding Lunation and a Tarot card that is connected to our theme.

THE LOVERS TAROT CARD

There is perhaps no greater tarot card in the Major Arcana that stirs such warm feelings of love and celestial blessings. The Lovers card, in traditional tarot deck, is often depicted with a man and a woman and the Archangel Raphael at the center, as the glue of their fated union. It is this divine Archangel that is bringing God's blessings and ordaining this special relationship. It is perhaps what gives this card a powerful celestial connotation that makes its appearance in a spread so distinctive. It is a card with a meaning connected to love and a significant relationship in our lives.

Sometimes in other decks, the Lovers tarot card is illustrated simply with a pair of lovers in an arduous embrace; either way we understand quite quickly that this card is about a powerful romantic relationship. It can signify a marriage, a soulmate union or simply a balanced partnership of great importance.

As our theme in this chapter is connected to love and joy, the Lovers card becomes an ideal tool to work with and further explore our theme. It is also interesting to note that this card is often associated with the astrological sign of Gemini, the same lunation we will be working with in this chapter.

I've often heard it being said that, in the traditional Rider Waite tarot deck, the naked man and woman seen in the Devil tarot card are the same ones found in the Lover's card; only they aren't chain to a dark beast. In the Lover's card, we see this naked couple blessed and in harmony with the Divine. There is a tangible happiness and fruitfulness implied in the illustration, as you will find the addition of the blazing sun behind the Archangel and much green foliage to denote growth and wellbeing.

The card has a message about a significant relationship in our lives but it also speaks of a choice. Sometimes it alludes to a choice between two lovers or between two contrasting things that we love. The presence of three beings in this card can hint to third party situations, however, its message relates to love and a choice linked to that love. A choice needs to be made, especially in regards to an important relationship, but in order to make the right choice one is required to know thyself. The Lovers card tells us we must know what we love, and where our passion truly breathes, in order to come to the right decisions regarding relationships in our lives.

MOON IN GEMINI   AIR/MERCURY

THEME: Love & Joy

GEMINI   MUTABLE   AIR   MASCULINE   THE TWINS

If you ever met a Gemini (Sun Sign) you will understand quite clearly the wildly energetic influence of a lunar transit in Gemini. Its symbol is the Twins thus painting a vivid picture of its duplicitous nature. The Moon in the air sign of Gemini is known to be quick-witted, highly loquacious, curious, and, dare I say, fun. Its Mercurial influence cannot be underestimated and its ability to take on multiple tasks at once can have its juicy advantages for us to consider. As an astrological sign ruled by the planet and trickster deity, Mercury (the God of travel and communication) this lunar transit is ideal for anything related to these aspects. Any goals connected to travel, juggling multiple tasks at once, curiosities, extracurricular activities or anything connected to communication is enhanced by the Moon transiting Gemini.

THEME WORK SUGGESTIONS

Work with the Gemini moon, symbolized by the Twins,
and work with The Swan energy and the Goddesses
presented here.
Daily, work with positive Affirmations.
Create a Gratitude List and expand this list.
Explore a Special Ritual for self-love; enjoy an herbal love bath
made with scented oil and rose petals.
Create a Honey Bottle (recipe offered in this chapter).
Experiment with the Belly Laugh rite.

> *"Love's greatest gift is
> its ability to make everything
> it touches sacred..."*
> *Barbara De Angelis*

HERSTORY

She was raised to follow all rules and stick to routines and the proverbial "to do" list. This pattern of straight and narrow living, of being a good girl, served her well all of her life. She had achieved much thus far and one could assume she had it all. But with all of her accolades and great achievements she never thought she would find herself dissatisfied and lacking in one area of her life… Why the dissatisfaction? Why the deep hunger, as she sat at a full table, a Life, so seemingly rich and fulfilling with offers…

She secretly craved fun and romance. Too many nights alone left her wondering if she was ever meant to feel love, romance, lightness, pleasure, and the enjoyment of the simple things in life….

******Take a moment to document here, or in your journal, your unique story.

_____

_____

_____

_____

AFFIRMATION

I choose love above all things

**The love and beauty I am so fortunate
to see before me
in the universe,
resides within me as well.**

I Love

I am worthy of experiencing great love, joy and beauty

CHAKRA & GEMSTONE WORK

4th Chakra   **ANAHATA/HEART CHAKRA**   **COLOR:** Green/Pink
Love, compassion, trust, relationships and community.
Mantra: I Heal & Love
)O(WORKING: Love/Forgiveness, understanding, patience, endurance, compassion

GEMSTONE CONNECTION: Rose Quartz is probably one of the most well-known gemstones for issues related to our heart and our emotions. It is recognized as a gemstone that helps soothe and heal a broken heart. It is a pink quartz known as the gentle love stone, for its ability to console the heart, remove negativity and heal emotional wounds. It is known to return the wearer to Self-love and can also help attract positive, beneficial friendships. It is reputed for helping the actual heart, circulatory system and reproductive organs. It helps to shift and uplift vibrations and connects us with our true emotions. Rose Quartz has also been used as an elixir to reduce wrinkles on the skin and maintain a youthful appearance. When used in romantic spell workings, it is reputed to bring a higher soul-mate connection.

GEMSTONE CHANNELING

In our busy day to day life, especially as women, it may be quite challenging to find a quiet moment for ourselves. I encourage you now to make a concerted effort to find that place where you will be safe and undisturbed for at least a few minutes to devote to yourself to self-care and healing. The importance and revelatory value of this daily habit cannot be overstated enough. As part of this work you are invited now to find a comfortable place where you can be assured of your privacy, safety and comfort... If you can go outdoors in nature that would be most ideal but any place where you can relax, undisturbed, would be fine.

Place yourself in a comfortable meditative position; you may sit or lay down. If it is available to you, place in your hands the Rose Quartz Crystal that we are working with today. This Rose Quartz Crystal is reputed to possess gentle healing energy and it can awaken us to love in any one of its numerous forms.

Hold this pink colored gemstone in your hands. Consider how it feels upon your skin... Gaze upon its shape and its pink hues. (Pause) Look at this Rose Quartz Crystal more deeply and let your scrutiny unveil all of its precious details. Quietly, continue to study this gemstone and make note of any thoughts or vivid images that immediately start to unfold before you. (Pause) When you're ready, you may close your eyes and begin this short meditation. As with all trance work, we begin with our breath. You are asked now to take a deep cleansing breath; slowly filling your lungs up.... Now let your next breath possess the element of this Rose Quartz Crystal. Feel the pink hue of your Rose Quartz rise into the ethers and inhale this swirl of gentle love. Direct this breath in to your heart chakra, at the center of your chest. (Pause) Stay with this energy for as long as you need to. (Pause)

Continue to breathe and hold this breath for 3 seconds and then release it... Counting now at your own pace; breathe, 1, 2, 3, and exhale on 4....and again....breathe in, 1, 2, 3, and exhale on 4. Let's do this one more time and then quietly counting in your head.... Breathe 1, 2, 3...release on 4. Breathe, trusting in the natural rhythm you have now established, of your relaxed inhalation and exhalation.

Rose Quartz wishes to impart a special channeled message for you about Love and all the things that bring you joy. See this gentle, pink gemstone in your mind's eye. See it shining brightly, embedded upon its dark, fertile, mother earth. Draw nearer to it and ask if it will allow you to pick it up. When permission is granted, gently gather it in your hands. With your mind's eye, gaze upon it again; studying its color, its texture, its cloudy formations and inclusions or any other details that captures your eyes.... Ask it to speak to you.

Now imagine the top of your head opening like a window, this is your crown chakra. Let it become almost like a chalice; receptive and open to any spiritual messages that may be unfolding for you now... You may envision your crown chakra now unveiling a magnetic Rose Quartz Crystal portal allowing for this **Crystal Transmission** to come through... Gently guide this energy of the Rose Quartz Crystal from your crown chakra to your heart, the sacred place of love... (Pause)

Continue to breathe in the loving energy of Rose Quartz. When you are ready, you may begin to open your eyes and gently stretch out a little. As you come out of this meditation, it is a perfect time for you to document any images or messages that came through for you. You may write them here, or in your personal journal.

_____
_____
_____
_____

SWAN PROTECTION ENERGY

As we delve into the subject of love in this chapter, there appears to be no better ally and protector for us, than the Swan. Swans are connected with elegance, beauty, grace and longevity, as they tend to live a long time. They are teachers of patience, empathy and altered states of awareness. They are also linked with magick portals and faery realms. Because the Swan is often seen emerging annually in the spring, when the sun is growing in light, they were believed to usher in the beauty of spring.

Study a Swan in her habitat and you will be immediately entranced by her exceptional beauty and flowing grace. They are typically white, although in Australia they are black, and they have these long elegant necks that almost command our admiration. When they are in the water, they appear to glide seamlessly as if they are on ice. They invoke a feeling of peace and serenity, and speak to us of the importance of grace through movement. Swans are beautiful, powerful birds but do not underestimate them. They can cause much harm to a perceived enemy with the beat of their strong wings and it must be noted they can execute a gnarly bite.

As an aquatic bird, they do not like the heat and prefer cool wetlands or land surrounded by water. They are very territorial and protective of their offspring. Swans usually reach maturity within two to three years and they breed at three to four years of age. Mother swans tend to stay with their young for a long period of time. They are fiercely protective, devoted parents and can live up to twenty years in the wild and fifty years in captivity. It is interesting to note, they are known to mate for life and thus, become a powerful message of love, truth, fidelity and honoring our commitments. White swans, in particular, predict happiness and enduring love. They are seen as harbingers of blessings on our most romantic relationships and thus, they are an ideal animal to connect with at this point in our spiritual journey.

Swans are very social living beings. During migration, they fly together creating a V formation at great heights. Their wings beat slowly and steady; this gives them the endurance needed to reach their destination quickly without tiring. Pacing yourself, therefore, is one of the many gifts swan medicine also offers us.

The Swan also teaches us that there is beauty in all things, even those things we initially don't consider beautiful. Just think back to our beloved childhood fairytale, by Hans Christian Andersen, titled, *"The Ugly Duckling."* It is a message about transformation, inner strength and patience. It is an apropos, sweet message for children transitioning into their teen years and those going from awkward adolescence into adulthood. It serves to remind us that no matter what ugly phase in life you find yourself in, powerful transformation will always begin with the discomfort of an ugly phase before birthing itself into something quite beautiful and remarkable. We are encouraged to unearth and embrace our own inner beauty with the energy of the Swan.

As we explore the subject of love and what brings us joy, the Swan becomes a teacher to help us work with our inner child. Throughout folklores we see swans being connected with the sacred archetype of the maiden. Swans are considered solar beings, connected with the direction of the north and have an affinity to the elements of air, earth, and water. In mythologies from across the globe, they were often perceived as a sacred bridge between the worlds and an awakener of intuitive gifts. Because they have always been connected to music, poetry and the mysteries of songs, they have a strong association to the bard. The skin and feathers of swans were often incorporated into Bardic rites and ceremonial cloaks were decorated with the swan's feathers for added swan blessings.

Working with the energy of Swan we can facilitate travels to other realms, according to ancient Druid beliefs. They related this sacred bird with the festival of Samhain due to its mystical nature. For the Celts, Swan is associated with water deities, healing and the sun. Swans were believed to be shape-shifters that can take the form of humans and they were often associated with music, love, beauty and poetry.

For nearly all Native American traditions, the Swan is associated with the gift of grace. Because it is able to fly even higher than the revered eagle, the Elders believed the swan is a great shamaness, who is able to see, not only this world, but into the next. Here, she is connected to divination and the ability to see into the future. Swan feathers were also used in smudging and healing ceremonies, a practice that still takes place today. In Greek mythology the Swan was the bird associated with the Sun God, Apollo, who one should remember is linked with music and songs. The swan is purported to sing a melody of haunting beauty just before its death, according to Greek legends. She was also known as an emblem for the muses. The Greek Goddess of beauty and love, Aphrodite, was often represented riding on a swan or a goose. Both of these creatures are represented, at times, interchangeably. According to one Greek myth, the God Zeus was alleged to have turned himself into a swan, in order to facilitate sexual relations with Leda. In Hindu mythology there are swan Maidens known as the heavenly nymphs, called Apsaras. The Hindu God, Krishna, became a swan knight in order to copulate with these beautiful swan maidens. We often see the swan with various Hindu deities. She represents breath and spirit in Hindu mythology and is often the sacred vehicle for the beloved matriarchal Goddess of Wisdom, Saraswati.

The Swan is clearly an invaluable being to explore for those in the artistic expression and musical field but also most importantly for those studying mysticism and metaphysics. We connect with the beautiful Swan to discover a powerful ally and guardian as we delve deeper into the subject of all that we love.

GODDESS EMPOWERMENT

BAUBO

Baubo is the bold, Greek Goddess of laughter, joy, and liberated sexuality. According to the Greek philosopher Homer, Baubo was born out of the union of Pan and Echo. Her name is believed to mean, *"belly."* Other interpretation state that her name means, *"old crone."* We can understand this interpretation of her name because during her time, the word crone had a different meaning than it does today. The word crone, back then, was believed to be a Wise mature woman, not the old hag stereotype meaning its become today. Thus Baubo, right from the start, appears to us as the wise matron who has something to teach us regarding our belly.

In mythology, we speculate that Baubo was married to a known Swine herder, as some of the writing of the time allude to this and this was consider quite a profitable occupation. During this time in history, a Swine Herder made a rather good salary and thus it was considered to be a desired vocation for a man. Baubo was believed to have had a son from this union and his name was Eumolpos. Eumolpos literally means *"Sweet Singer"* and often, the writing of the time reveals that many aspiring singers in folklores were notorious for referring to him as their own original Singing teacher, to gain for themselves some credibility.

According to one of the popular, well known Greek lore, Baubo was employed as the nurse to the lame daughter of King Celeus, named Iambe, but the bawdy Goddess will forever be known in mythology as the one who succeeded in breaking through Demeter's sadness and lament. The Goddess Demeter, distraught by the disappearance of her daughter, Persephone, wandered the Earth aimlessly. In disguised, she came upon the King's abode and was welcomed to stay with their family. Everyone in the kingdom tried to cheer up this sorrowful old looking woman, but no one was able to reach her soul. Baubo offered her Barley and started to talk to the Grain Goddess, who at this point was disguised as an old woman. Still to no avail, Baubo was just not able to reach her and Demeter remained sad. In a moment of complete and utter silliness, Baubo lifted up her skirt to Demeter and reveal something that must have been strange and hilarious because it not only shocked Demeter, but also moved her to smile. That initial smile busted into a laughter that somehow helped her recover parts of her old forgotten Divine self. Somehow through this very act of her boisterous belly laughter, Demeter rediscovers her brilliant self, once more. Because of this occurrence, she was able to move to action and eventually return to her post as Goddess of the Grain. Consequently, she was able to return the Earth to its natural cycle, thanks to Baubo.

It is not clear what Baubo revealed under her skirt that made Demeter laugh so greatly, but some text allude to transgender genitalia, or a deformity or just an over exaggerated open vagina, like the Celtic, Shela-na-gig. Throughout history Baubo is often drawn and depicted with this exaggerated genitalia to reflect the sexual freedom she so expressed with Demeter in this tale. Sometimes she is also depicted with her face drawn or painted upon her belly, to reflect her connection to this sacred place in our body.

Unquestionably, Baubo is a Goddess that takes pleasure in bawdiness, friendship and unabashed light in her sexuality. She is the healing power of laughter and light heartedness. She is the Goddess of friendship because of her connection to Demeter and she wields the power of laughter. When she is invoked, she brings joyful mirth, fun, and helps connect us to the powerful healing nature of a good healthy laugh; the kind that emanates first from our core. Cathartic deep laughter that is found in our sacred belly.

"Close friends contribute to our personal growth.
They also contribute to our personal pleasure, making the music sound sweeter,
the wine taste richer, the laughter ring louder because they are there..." Judith Viorst

BAUBO'S GIFT TO US

As with some ancient Deities there are always bound to be conflicting stories about their origins and their myths, Baubo is no exception. However, I would like to focus on Baubo's unquestionable attributes, her importance among the assemblage of Feminine divine deities and most importantly her gifts and relevance for us, as modern day wommin.

Baubo, is known as the Goddess of sexual liberation, bawdiness, a good hearty belly laugh and the healing power of joy, friendship and laughter. These are gifts that transcend time, as laughter has always been deemed magickal and alchemical in its ability to transform severe pain, spiritual malaise and heartache, into something we don't need to collapse from, but, quite possibly, can overcome and actually trascend. It is a widely known occult knowledge that the presence of boisterous laughter can eradicate even the most obstinate negative energy.

There have been numerous scientific studies revealing the positive effects laughter and regular comedic relief has on our serotonin levels and our overall health and well-being. No one can deny the power of a good chuckle when we are feeling less than our best. It is also a well-known fact, among occultist, that laughter is the death of all maladies, awkwardness and even negativity is weakened by a joyful heart. The phenomenon of trolls, psychic vampires, dark entities and malign spirits are weakened and dissipate with the piercing sounds of jovial laughter -especially those of children, who can teach us a thing or two about surrendering to the joys of unabashed silliness and cackles. One of the best ways to raise the vibrations in a home plagued by strife, arguments and darkness, is to create multiple opportunities to laugh in that home. Thus a house warming party full of joviality has become a great customary ritual and an ideal way to bless a home and assure the grumbles will stay far away from the premises. These are just some spiritual remedies Baubo alludes to in her myths. Laughter can indeed heal, elevate and cure all temporarily weakened souls, as it did with Demeter.

The Greek Goddess of the Grain was in severe mourning and had suffered a great lost. Her sole, beloved daughter had been abducted and possibly raped by her own uncle, Hades. The tragedy of such a devastating occurrence appeared to have moved her to the brinks of her own death, as Demeter was no longer recognizable, no longer shone in her effervescence divine brilliance. And in her mourning, she willingly relinquish her duties and her authentic self. The story is very reminiscent of Amaterasu (The Japanese Sun Goddess) in that, both Divine Deities are so traumatized by the tragic occurrences in their respective lives that they surrender to great depression, retreat from their daily duties and their sadness almost seems to engulf, drown and overpower who they really are.

As the myth goes, Demeter was inconsolable and it appeared no one, nor anything, not even the multitude of decadent God offerings, could bring her back. I contemplate on how often unexpected tragedies have a way of traumatizing, shifting us into this dark realm where we too temporarily forget our inherent gifts and abilities to resurrect and regenerate ourselves. Yet as wommin, regenerating ourselves is clearly our domain and it is where we excel.

Everything about us, as wommin, points to this inherent gift and the exposure of our Yoni makes it undeniable because it's such a powerful ancient symbol of our Womynhood and our regenerative powers. In both Uzume's and Baubo's iconic stories, the liberation and exposure of the Yoni results in a necessary, personally transformative Global change. Both Amaterasu and Demeter experience a sort of death and rebirth, an awakening, through this unveiling of the naked Yoni.

We, as wommin, are truly regenerative creatures and Baubo chooses our yoni as the sacred vehicle to remind us of this vastly awe-inspiring detail. The gift of rebirthing and regeneration is ever exemplified in our blood; its monthly cycles, in the way we produce eggs every month and release those unfertilized eggs in our monthly menses. We are example of that power of regeneration in our ability to rebirth new eggs, a month later, and again repeat this same cycle of death and rebirth. Some of us even bleed (menstruate) in conjunction with the appearance of the full or new moon in the heavens and we're able to synchronize our menses together within a group of sisters. Our ability to birth new life within us, if we wish to, is another obvious example of women's ability to regenerate herself over and over again, if she chooses to.

We are regenerative in the way our breasts (as new mothers) knows just the right amount of milk to produce to feed our infants and after breast feeding, hours later, our body is able to reproduce even more milk than before, in order to meet the expanding, nutritional demands of a growing human being. That is the gift of creation and re-creation at its finest.

Our multi orgasmic nature compared to a man's lack thereof, also exemplifies this inherent gift of regeneration. In the way that we, as wommin, can be multi-orgasmic and after pouring out our juices of ecstasy, we can come again and again and again, whilst a man will ejaculate once and lose a great deal of his vital energy and life force in that one expulsion. Hence the reason men are more likely to fall asleep after an orgasm, while a womyn experiences a resurgence of energy.

It is in our very nature to continually regenerate ourselves and unearth our strengths and rebirthing skills, over and over again. The image of our Yoni is a powerful symbol and reminder of this gift. And because of this, birth, death and rebirth are closely linked to our gender's gift.

"Baubo's sudden exposure of her genitalia reminds Demeter (of who she is) that being a woman, having a yoni, gives her the power to endlessly create new life...." (page 61, "The Yoni...." by Rufus C. Camphausen)

I imagine that the sight of a middle aged woman, unexpectedly exposing her genitalia would shock anyone into a fit of laughter. Some speculate that what Baubo exposed was far more than just your average Yoni. There are some that suggest Baubo was a hermaphrodite, containing within her, both male and female genitalia. Still there are others that suggest that Baubo might have just had a very unusual, exaggerated large yoni. One will never really know what exactly Baubo exposed between her legs, but whatever it was, it held the antidote and remedy for Demeter's lament. The act of such an unexpected, some might say, crude gesture, was enough to shock the Goddess OUT of her despondent state and place her back on the road to remembering her authentic self and her divine capabilities. In Baubo's rather exhibitionistic display of her Yoni, she rather beckons the Fertile Grain Goddess to remember her inherent womanly gifts of rebirth, transformation and regeneration found within her own magickal cavernous yoni.

When greatly grieved and saddened, it is dangerous to forget that within us (more specifically our womanhood, our yoni) there is a capacity to regenerate, transform and re-connect with our inner joy; our sacred sanctum and the power of unabashed, belly laughs. These are the gifts of the Goddess Baubo. She introduces us to the healing powers found in our Yoni, our gender and the cathartic magick of laughter. Baubo shows us how our belly laughs, in particular, can move mountains, even those obstinate, self-destructive state of beings, like depression, while directing our attention to one of the most ancient powerful symbol of the Goddess- our Yoni.

*Our immortal friend is found in the cackling, supremely bawdy, ancient Goddess, Baubo. She arrives, like an old dear playmate, bubbling with jubilee and radiating with laughter and naughty jokes. Just when you started to feel the pull of sadness and stress caving in on you, she comes with warmth, jokes, encouragement and sincere friendship. She lightens your load and reminds you of your most precious weapon against feelings of defeat, sadness and depression. It is within you, your gender, your labyrinths and inner caverns, where cathartic treasures are to be found, and Baubo has no inhibitions about revealing this to you. Have you ever looked at yourself, really looked at yourself and marveled with laughter? Do you take pleasure in your existence? Have you ever heard the funny stories of an old friend echoing in your ears after a long, hard stressful day? This is Baubo's gift to you. She awakens you to the transformative powers of laughter. Take the time to laugh; lighten up & allow the cathartic power of friendship an honored place in your life.

ERZULIE FREDA

Erzulie Freda, with her penchant for lounging around, is the Haitian Voodoo loa Spirit, or (most appropriately termed) Mystere of Love and Beauty, like the Greek Goddess of love, Aphrodite. She is the watery, Feminine mystere or Goddess (as I like to use these terms interchangeably) of all things that bring you pleasure, including decadent sweets, jewelry, cosmetics, fragrances, lacy feminine textiles, soft music, and affection. She is the benevolent spirit of sensual pleasures and sweet scents like the Egyptian Goddess, Hathor. Erzulie has also been compared to the Hindu Goddess, Lakshmi, as she is also the Voodoo loa Spirit of luxury, opulence and abundance.

Maitresse Erzulie Freda can be seen as a Goddess of Romantic ideals. She is the beloved feminine supreme archetype in the Haitian Voodoo pantheon and rules over all matters concerning relationships, flirtations, sensuality as well as prosperity, and her worshippers' wellbeing. But she is also known to have another darker side. There are some conflicting stories about her depiction, as some sources claim she was often portrayed, in New Orleans, as a light skin mulatto, sometimes almost white, with long, dark straight hair, while another aspect of her, more specifically, Erzulie Dantor, was depicted as the dark skinned Loa with a scar from her husband, upon her face. The author, Milo Rigaud, in his reputable book, *"Secrets of Voodoo"*, states that Erzulie was considered a very dark skinned Ethiopian and that the notorious, Queen of Sheba, was often identified with her. Because in Voodoo, the bright Sun was the Masculine spirit, known as Damballah/Danbhalah Wedo (also known as Legba), Aida Wedo (his wife), was his opposite, the night, the Moon and the Feminine Spirit, known in Haiti as Erzulie. It would make sense that in Haiti she would be represented as the dark skinned loa while in New Orleans, with the influence of colonialism, a lighter version emerged.

Erzulie is the Mystere of eloquence, refinery, French culture, opulence and good fortune and, as can be expected, a very much beloved, powerful loa for all who practice Voodoo. She is so important to the culture, that she is considered the Heart of Voodoo.

Her catholic counterpart is the Virgin Mary, Mater Dellorosa (suffering Mother) as she is often depicted crying towards the end of Voodoo ceremonies, while in possession of her serviteur. Some believe she cries because she is never quite able to attain enough of what she wants. Others feel that she cries lamenting for those who are hurt by poverty or unrequited love and her tears symbolically take on the pain of the world so that others do not need to cry. In this compassionate role, she begins to resemble the Buddhist Goddess of Human Compassion, Kwan Yin, carrying the weight of human suffering upon her own heart.

Originally, the name Erzulie referred to a river in Benin and her worship comes from the West coast of Africa, but soon it traveled to New Orleans and Haiti and all across the Americas with the advent of slavery. There are many names given to this loa depending on the role that she is fulfilling. She is also known as Ezili and some Haitian literature claim that there are several aspects of this one Spirit such as; the older Grande Erzulie, Erzulie-Mapiangueh, Freda Dahoumin, Negresse Imanou Ladeh, Negresse Miroi-Ze, Erzulie Dantor, to name just a few. Here we will focus on Erzulie Freda as one spirit.

In Voodoo, a loa was seen as a powerful spirit, a mystere, and not as an archetype or Goddess aspects, the way we are accustomed to hearing about in Wicca and other earth based religions. A Voodoo loa, like Erzulie, was revered, honored and seen as an actual living person, who might even live near you and possess the same complex, yet tangible personality as any family member would. These spirits were not ethereal beings up in the sky, but were rather viewed as real, here on earth, and they were appeased and given flattery and various offerings.

Even the practice of Voodoo, in general, utilizes common every day household items and ceremonial rites, are not restricted to just church edifices. In this way the practice of Voodoo is appealing to all kinds of people, regardless of class or financial status.

The name for a Voodoo temple is an Oum'phors and it contains a partly enclosed area in the middle called a peristyle. In the center of the peristyle is the Poteau-mitan, which is a most significant center post that plays an integral part in almost all Voodoo rites. Among its many meanings, it acts like a cosmic axis and connects earth to sky.

Two ways that this Voodoo Loa communicates with "Her" worshippers were through dreams and possession. Possession is when the human body becomes a vessel or container for the loa to act and speak from. It is reminiscent of evocations and aspecting in traditional Wicca and, often time, it is also referred to as "ridding the loa", for indeed, the worshipper appears to be taken on a wild ride, as the mystere incarnates into its worshipper, completely taking over the body and ridding it like a horse. When Erzulie is in full possession of a serviteur (worshipper), they will often speak French, even if they have only spoken in the Creole language all of their life. For this opulent feminine spirit is all about status and class, something that the French culture and language exudes, *that is*, according to popular Haitian belief. It is quite a phenomenon to witness someone who may never even have had a proper education, as is the case for most citizens within impoverish countries, and to see them quite suddenly start speaking in French as a result of a possession. It only serves to confirm that the loa do exist. Along with crying lamentation for the world, you can expect to see her serviteurs dance with sensual movements (girating and slithering their hips) and flirt incessantly with the male gender. It goes without saying that a man possessed by Erzulie Freda is going to express very frilly, feminine mannerism and have eyes only for his gender, therefore uptight heterosexual men might want to steer clear of her, for she is a true lover of men.

Erzulie Freda can also be seen as a spirit of promiscuity. It was quite obvious that she relished and loved men. She enjoyed giving as well as being lavished with affection and was quite skilled at flirting. Her views on women were very different however. As Erzulie Dantor she was defender and very protective of women, but as Erzulie Freda, she was indifferent. Often depicted wearing three rings, which symbolize her three husbands, but interesting to note, her role with them appears to be more of a mistress than sole wife. Her Consorts were; Met Agwe (Lord of the Ocean), Ogou Ferraile (The Bold Warrior), and Damballah (The Wise White Serpent). Yet these three Voodoo loa were heavily invested in other prominent romantic relationships. For example, Agwe was said to have another wife in, La Sirene and, according to some Haitian writings, Damballah really loved Aida Wedo, (The Rainbow Spirit). Erzulie's third husband Ogou, had a strong attraction to Erzulie Dantor, who some considered Erzulie Freda's actual sister and not just an aspect of her.

This strong, iconic, Voodoo Feminine Spirit, is known to be very generous, but extremely demanding, with high expectation from her worshippers. It is not taboo to bargain with this Mystere, but be sure you remember your promise to her, for she will wreak havoc if you forget. When creating a shrine or altar for Erzulie, one is advised to use her favorite colors like baby pink and white. Never offer anything in the color black or red, as red is the color for her warrior sister, Erzulie Dantor.

An offering to Erzulie would not be complete without some kind of bouquet of flowers, like roses, champagne, and sweets; like chocolate, honey and candies. Generously court her and offer Erzulie Freda all the romantic accoutrements you would, to a new love in your life. She wouldn't expect any less from her worshippers. During

Voodoo ceremonies, mirrors (one of her sacred symbols), fine clothing and fancy jewelry was made available to the serviteurs, who would come down with this spirit. At all cost, one is discouraged from exposing her to dust, dirt or any kind of smoke for she detested these things. She loves cleanliness and order, so you would be wise to provide a clean altar for this Voodoo loa. Because she is known to be very jealous, it is also best not to share her altar with the worship of other deities or spirits. It is best not to offend her by having a shrine in her honor, in your bedroom, where intimate relations are expected to take place. Strangely, this might offend her or stir-up her powerful jealous streak. Remember that the loa are real spirits, with strong human-like personalies and that includes some sticky ones like, jealousy and spite. If these demands seem too intimidating, know that it is okay to make the occasional offerings to Erzulie without a permanent, established shrine to her. Also, according to Haitian folklore, you cannot invoke Erzulie without first getting a pass from Legba, for Legba is the door opener to the spirit realm. Connecting with Legba will allow you to worship and invoke any Voodoo loa you choose.

Another way to connect with Erzulie is through her Veve. Veves were sacred symbols drawn to invoke the Voodoo loa spirits and they were usually drawn over the floor with corn flour, spread across the ground or walls in special ceremonies. They were also drawn on doors and painted on ceilings and walls. It is quite a magickal act to re-draw one yourself, as you prepare to work with Erzulie. Redrawing a veve is quite meditative and almost becomes a sacred ritual to honor her, by its very nature. In this very simple act you will begin to feel her energy transpire. Another way to work with Erzulie and invoke her energy is through the common practice of ritual baths called *"Lave tet."* Since she is a spirit that loves fragrances, creating a ritual bath of clean rain water with basil, sugar and rose petals is a wonderful way to purify yourself before beginning a ritual for her, or as a ritual on its own. It is often suggested to bathe beforehand with a French fragranced soap and then create this sacred bath to soak in, while offering flattery to this beloved Voodoo Goddess. When you are finished, allow yourself to air dry.

Voodoo is an oral tradition but also initiatory, as some believe you cannot declare yourself a priestess of a Loa without proper initiation from a Hougan or Mambo. Finally, it is also highly recommended to study, respect and support the Haitian Culture of your chosen Voodoo Loa spirit, to receive the utmost blessings from them. Voodoo is not a textbook religion but rather a spiritual practice that can be understood and appreciated best when, experienced. To benefit and work positively with a spirit requires you to build a respectful, loving relationship, slowly, cautiously and with a sincere commitment. I suppose the same rules apply for any solid relationship, whether human or spiritual. All relationships require time, patience, nurturance and careful cultivation, and above all, love.

Take the time to get to know your loa and if you can, create a shrine for her. Spending time meditating and conversing with Erzulie Freda, daily, can open you up to the beauty of Voodoo and its intricate pantheon. In this way you build a personal relationship with your chosen Loa and will soon be gifted with their message(s).

Make special note, however, that there are times when a Loa spirit will just not be drawn to you. According to Hougan and author, Kenaz Filan, if you have been invoking a spirit for some time, with petitions and offerings and making special shrines while praying to a loa and nothing seems to change for you, perhaps this is not the right loa for you to work with or perhaps, just not the right time for you to connect. Remember the Loa are real, with complex personalities, and they will either genuinely like you and attach themselves to you and your cause, or show no interest... but rest assure you will know when they are at work in your life. Voodoo loa make themselves very well-known and very obviously so, and you will know, without a shadow of a doubt, when you are being blessed by them.

All Hails to you and Welcome Maitresse Erzulie Freda!

*Voodoo Loa of love, beauty, refinement and abundance, she is the embodiment of romance and those delightful luxuries of life. She, who demands nothing but the best, invites you now to hold the same standard for your own life. She awakens in you a desire to pursue prosperity, abundance and all that is juicy and good for you; including the right type of love. What are some of life's luxuries that you are willing to manifest at this time? Is your "Love" bringing you true fulfillment? Are you approaching life from a place of lack or from the rich fertile realm of abundance and appreciation? She enters your life at this time to awaken a desire for the finer things in life and calls you to treat yourself with reverence and love.

THEME WORK SUGGESTIONS
4. LOVE & JOY

Light a Pink candle
Set your altar with objects that you love. Add a bouquet of flowers,
photos of loved ones, special mementoes and a chalice of water.
Create a gratitude list and every morning add something new to it.
Enjoy a special Herbal Bath with salt crystals, dry herbs, blossoms and scented oils. Create a self-love rite in which you work with your beautiful reflection in the mirror.

<u>Create a Honey Bottle:</u> Recipe: On a piece of paper write down what you love or what you hope to manifest in the realm of love. Pour some honey on this piece of paper; add 3 pinches of sugar, a couple of rose petals and dab a bit of scented oil. Place this paper and these items in a glass container. Inside this glass container, with your parchment paper, add sweet red wine and then seal the bottle. Charge this bottle under the Full Moon for a few nights. Then, place this bottle underneath your bed for 3xnights. Afterwards, keep this bottle in a safe place until you have manifested your wish.

HATHOR

Hathor is a Pre-dynastic Goddess, worshipped for over 3,000 years. She is the Egyptian Goddess of Joy, Pleasure, Beauty and Love. Yet Hathor is known by a multitude of other names and titles. As is typical of most ancient deities, Hathor appears to be an important Goddess of many names, duties and significant attributes. The name Hathor means, "House of Horus," perhaps a reference to her role as mother of Horus. Hwt-Hrw, Het-Hor, Het-Hert, Athor-Athyr are just some of the names ascribes to her in the writings of her time period.

She was most commonly known and depicted as the *"Celestial Bovine"*, nurturing all of humanity. Images of her appeared as a beautiful winged Cow with stars over her head and sometimes as a cow on a boat over water, alluding to her connection with the Nile River. This image later developed into a lady with the head of a cow, wearing the illustrious head dress of a pair of horns and a moon or solar disk in the center. Eventually she was depicted with a human head and the ears or horns of a cow, while wearing the Goddess head-dress. As a cow, she represents all of the generous attributes typical of a bovine and was believed to have given birth to the universe, according to one Egyptian cosmology.

Interesting to note, Hathor seems to embody all the elements; earth, fire, air and water. Often depicted as a Sky Goddess, existing before time and called Mistress of the Heavens, she is also the Goddess of Moisture, associated with the inundation of the Nile River. She was seen as a Solar Goddess in her connection to her consort Ra- the Sun God and also in her aspect as the Fiery Lioness, Sekhmet. She is the Goddess of the Moon and the Goddess of the underworld, protecting dead souls and guiding them to the Judgment Hall. Known as Mistress of the Necropolis, she tenderly cared for the dead souls and offered them water, with the branch of her sacred Sycamore tree, as they journey to the underworld.

In ancient times, she was considered the Goddess of Agriculture and, to Egyptians, she was called upon to assure the fertility of the land. Unquestionably, Hathor was a beloved, multifaceted, ancient Deity, greatly revered by both men and women.

Her main Cult was in Dendera, but she had many devotees and followers throughout the world. From Africa (places like modern day Ethiopia, Somalia and Libya) to Semitic West Asia she was highly venerated in ancient times. She is a patron Goddess for wommin and all Feminine aspects of life, but she was also adored and worshipped by many men as well.

Hathor was the protectress of pregnant women and all women at different stages of their lives. From birth to death, she was believed to oversee and be invested in the many stages of a womyn's life. A Goddess of perfumery, cosmetics and jewelry, she was known as Lady of the Malachite and Lady of the Turquoise. Malachite was mined in her Providence of Sinai and thus easily attainable in this region and some of these precious stones had many sacred usage, some were even grinded and used as cosmetics. As a Goddess of cosmetics and beautification, Hathor often adorned her eyes but so did both, priestesses and male priest in Egyptian temples.

The Menat, a multi strand necklace, was her beloved symbol. This was a necklace that was not used for mere adornment but rather was used during special rituals. As a Goddess of Music, the Sistrum was also another sacred symbol of Hathor that was used mainly to bless, ceremonially cleanse and purify a place of worship.

Hathor was believed to be the daughter of Nut, Sky Goddess and Mother of all Gods, and Ra, The Sun God. She was also the wife of the Sun God and given the esteemed titled of the "Eye of Ra." This daughter- wife relationship (similar to the Hindu Goddess Saraswati and the God, Brahma) appears to be a common occurrence among ancient deities of the time.

According to a famous legend, Ra feared his kingdom was coming to an end. He was angered at the Egyptian people and their apparent lack of respect and commitment to him, as their God. He sent his beloved Hathor as the bloodthirsty Sekhmet, to go out to kill off those who appeared to be going against the old ruler. Rather unexpectedly, however, Sekhmet became uncontrollably blood thirsty and was determine to massacre everyone in sight, regardless of their political allegiance.

As Sekhmet, she is an irrepressible force, determined to draw blood, feast and dance on the multitude of corpses. I can't help but see the image of the Hindu Goddess, Kali Ma in this depiction of Sekhmet, but I digress. Ra feared the worse and recognized his impulsive grave error. In a desperate attempt to end Sekhmet's killing spree, he poured red colored beer and tricked the Goddess into drinking it, believing it to be blood.

According to one myth, Sekhmet became so intoxicated after ravenously ingesting all of that beer that she completely passed out and the next day woke up in total contrast, as the sweet, benevolent Hathor once more. In this myth, we see our Egyptian Goddess as the savior of Egyptian people and we also see her association with intoxication. Interesting to note how Sekhmet becomes representative of this fierce dark aspect so often seen in most revered mother archetype, like Hathor. It reflects the double aspect most often exemplified by matriarchal deities. They are sweet, generous and nurturing, yet capable of fierce protection, and severe destruction swiftly, if the situation calls for that energy.

When later, the cult of Isis and Osiris came to Egypt; it changed Hathor's popularity and worship. Many of her aspects and functions were taken over and absorbed by the new Egyptian Goddess, Isis, whose worship spread to Rome, Africa,

some parts of Asia and throughout Europe. Though on the surface they might appear the same, these are two quite distinctly different deities. In the myths of Isis, we learn of her pain, tragedy and grief but with Hathor, such emotions almost seem foreign to her character. In her myths, Hathor is the embodiment of success, happiness, joy, pleasantries and beauty –in complete contrast to her dark aspect as Sekhmet. Hathor is benevolence, pleasure and the pinnacle of Solar brightness-rarely do we hear of any hints of ugliness, nor tragedies in her tales and she has remained a beloved Egyptian Goddess, who bestows joy and pleasure to her worshippers and she continues to be a Feminine deity many wommin can easily connect with in this modern era just as in previous years past.
Hail and Welcome Bovinian Goddess Hathor!!!!!

*Hathor is the Beloved Egyptian Goddess of Pleasure and Love. She is the bringer of beauty, joy and sensual gifts. She is the highly venerated Bovinian Goddess that awakens us to our physical body and the importance of pleasure in our life. Whatever you do in life, make sure it brings you joy and gratification. When it seems as if the vibrant earth is a vision of great delight to all of our senses and we are in a state of titillation and arousal, the Celestial Bovine becomes the ideal Goddess to call upon. Her message to you is to seek joy, harmony and pleasure. She exalts the transformational magick of music, dance, sex and physical adornments. Amidst the doldrums of our obligations and the unavoidable mundane, seek to know and honor the highly cathartic power of ecstasy. She beckons you to delight in all the beauty that is surrounding you from within and from without, across the earth. Seek to know and explore the power of ecstasy!

"For all acts of love and pleasure are my rituals..."
Doreen Valiente, -The Charge of the Goddess

OSHUN

Oshun is the powerful Orisha of sensuality, attraction and the sweet waters of life. Always dressed in shimmering gold and yellows, she rules over all matters of the heart and pleasure. Hers are the gifts of sensual dances, lovemaking, romance and sensual sweet sticky foods, like honey. She is hypnotic swaying hips, shimmering lights, suggestive smiles, cascading waterfalls, verdant ripe fruits and fertile moist lands. She is benevolence and magick, for she was taught the art of Divination by Obatala, as a reward for helping him. As a result, she became the patron Goddess of the art of divination of cowrie shells and a teacher of magick.

According to African folklore, in the beginning there were a few Gods/Orishas sent down to earth to help mankind and establish civilization. In this early tale of Yoruban cosmology, Oshun was present and much needed as a Goddess that rules over waters and love. One of the orishas questioned her value upon the earth and managed to convince the other Orishas that she wasn't as vital to their work upon the earth. Well, Oshun was not one to argue with them, instead she pulled back all of her divine energy and retreated to the moon. There, she lounged without a care in the world in confidence that they would soon see and regret their disrespect of her gifts. Sure enough, when the Orishas found themselves unable to accomplish anything upon the earth without her sweet waters, and vital energy, they were forced to seek her out once more, beg for her forgiveness and bessech her return to the earth. With the intermediary of the God/Orisha Odulomare, she was petitioned to return but she only agreed if they vowed never to devalue or disrespect her again, and so they did.

Another folklore that shows the power of attraction Oshun possesses involves the Orisha, Ogun. Ogun is the God of blacksmith, war, civilization and advances in technology. According to one famous legend, Ogun grew tired and frustrated with humanity and decided he had enough with human follies. Despondently, he departs from civilization and retreats into the wild woods, far away from any human contact. The earth and its inhabitants starts to suffer as a result of his departure and the Orishas are much grieved by what begins to ensue in his absence. Oshun is implored by the Gods to help but her approached to the situation at first appears unconventional for she doesn't resort to brute force or demands. Instead, Oshun simply goes into the wild woods were Ogun is reportedly hiding and in her usual manner, she strolls and dances around the woods with her honey pot, giggling incessantly. She is clearly having some fun and emitting her golden light into the atmosphere. She then dips her curvaceous golden body in a nearby pond and starts to play with her beloved element of water. All along she is totally submersed in her joy and sensuality. Ogun catches a glimpse of her and finds himself instantaneously captivated by her beauty. Intrigued by her overflowing giggles and golden beauty he slowly draws nearer and nearer to her until he is right before her. At that pivotal moment, she is said to have dipped her finger in her honey pot and smeared it seductively upon Ogun's lips. In this very act she eradicates his despondency and any malaise and he is thus returned to humanity. It is her powers of attraction and seduction that mends all situations and this tale reveals her supreme skills of subtle persuasion.

When petitioned appropriately she will bless her devotees with great love, fertility, beauty and all the sweetness desired but cross her and you will soon meet another side to her. Her passionate nature can be expressed in numerous ways and most prefer to see that passion manifested in sweet loving ways not retaliatory or withheld.

Oshun is the beauty and love awakener! She seductively beckons you to care for yourself and invite sensual experiences into your life. She stirs your heart and ignites your inner flames so that you may awaken to passion. She opens your eyes so that you may value romance and finally embrace all the beauty and love surrounding you.

> *"Seduction is more powerful than coercion"*
> Joseph S. Nye Jr., *Soft Power: The Means to Success in World Politics*

APHRODITE

Aphrodite is the Greek Goddess of Love and Beauty, her Roman counterpart was Venus. Aphrodite is one of the oldest and most recognized, powerful deities of our time. Her origins can be traced to the East of Cyprus and Cytheria. She is known as the Goddess of Beauty and Gracefulness. She is cherished as Goddess of Attraction and the iconic, beloved Goddess of love, but more specifically, she is about that instant attraction and she can bring pleasure as well as pangs of love.

Aphrodite doesn't concern herself with consequences for she is the one that arouses desire and great passion, regardless of the situation. She is about physical coupling, infatuations and sexual longings. She is not about the institution or sanctity of marriage but rather that of sexual attraction, first experienced and necessary to maintain within a marriage.

She was sometimes known as the Goddess of the Prostitutes, for here again, in this profession, her powers of seduction and attraction was greatly needed and called upon. Hetairai, as they were called, were not only beautiful, but were highly skilled in music, dancing, art, eloquent speech and the art of seduction -all considered Aphrodite's domain.

Sea foam born, according to one Greek myth, she was born of the severed genitalia of her father, Uranus and this myth clearly supports her role as a Goddess of sexual pleasure - strongly emphasizing her own sexuality. Sometimes her sea foam birth reveals her coming out of a scallop seashell. This again is hinting at her role as a Goddess of Sexuality, as the sea shell highly resembles the form of a female's genitalia. The word scallop in Greek is, "Kteis." In Greek literature this word is also used to describe a woman's yoni.

Golden Aphrodite was often depicted and described as nude or half naked, or dressing, undressing, or being adorned. This called attention to her incredible physical beauty as a sexual Goddess. Often she was depicted with the Three graces: Algaia (*the bright one*), Euphrasy (*the glad one*) and Thaleia (*the abundant one*). They are reflections of Aphrodite herself and they assist her in ornamenting her curvaceous body. The Graces are often employed to help with anointing the Goddess with divine oils, bathing, dressing and adorning her according to the writings of her time. They were always seen happily dancing, acting maiden-like and again emphasizing the flowing elements of the Goddess of Love.

The laughing One, giggling with a smile that would reduce men to babbles, her skills and art in seduction were unmatched by any other being. Aphrodite was the definition of feminine warmth, sweetness and lightheartedness, rarely ever depicted as scornful, sobbing or angry but rather always light and inviting. She was portrayed as the Golden one, whose fragrance lingered long after her absence. Her presence aroused great passion and often as a result, some tricky situations. Some of her many symbols are; honey, semen, gold, sweetness and flowers; like Roses. Sweet smelling fruits like the apple and passion red pomegranate, are also her symbols.

There are two different tales about her birth according to Hesiod and Homer. Homer states that Aphrodite was born out of the union between Zeus and a Sea nymph. The most commonly accepted tale of her manifestation comes from Hesiod's literature. According to Hesiod, Gaia's consort, Uranus, was causing upheaval by not allowing Gaia to give birth to their children. Cronos, one of their sons, sought to come to his mother's aid and took a sickle and cut off his Father's genitalia. The severed Penis was thrown into the Sea, where its semen mixed with the ocean creating foam. Aphrodite emerged from this foam as a fully grown Goddess in all of her curvaceous splendor. In the early Renaissance, the Florentine Artist, Sandro Botticelli (1444-1510), created a masterpiece artwork around 1485, called "*The Birth of Venus*", that will forever encapsulate this moment in Greek Mythology, when newly born Aphrodite came ashore the Island of Cyprus.

She was the only Goddess allowed to choose her own consorts, unlike some of the other Greek Goddesses that were either raped, seduced, abducted or tricked. In mythology there are countless of stories of her amorous conquest and entertaining tales, involving her many dalliances.

She married Hera's son, Hephaestus, the Smith God, deity of craftsmen and the fire of the Forge. They had no children together. She also consorted with, Ares, God of War. This was a known, long term, love affair that resulted in three children. Together they had a daughter Harmonia (*Harmony*), and two sons, Deimos (*Terror*) and Phobos (*Fear*). The boys, according to the writings of the time, were often depicted joining their father in the bloody battlefields. Aphrodite also found a consort in, Hermes, Messenger God, God of science, magick, and trickery. With Hermes, She bore him Hermaphroditus, the Bi-sexual God, who had both sexual characteristics of his parents. Eros, who also had a very mystical birth and who has a number of conflicting tales describing his manifestation, was in later mythology considered Aphrodite's fatherless son. He was also known as "Amor," in Rome and today is depicted as the beloved, celebrated Cupid, exalted during our U.S.A. Valentine day celebrations.

Aphrodite also found lovers in mortal men. She was aroused with great desire upon seeing, Anchises, the Mountain Sid cattle grazer. With him she conceived a child that later would become the founder of Rome, Aeneas. Aphrodite was also completely smitten with Adonis, a youthful handsome hunter, who was later torn to pieces by a wild Boar. According to Greek myths, he was sent to the land of the Dead, but was permitted to return to his beloved Goddess part of the year, as a symbol of returning fertility. The Cult of Adonis performed this sacred rite -commemorating the annual return to Aphrodite in the same way Demeter and Persephone did in the Eleusinian Mysteries.

In the story of Pygmalion, the King of Cyprus creates his ideal woman by carving a large ivory sculpture. Little by little he becomes completely enrapture with his creation and falls in love with this image. During a festival honoring this great Deity he beckons Aphrodite to help him find this ideal woman in the flesh. Aphrodite in turn allows the sculpture to come to life. With one kiss from the king, his work of art comes to life, and the king finds love and marries his ideal woman.

There are also numerous tales involving women being touched and affected by Aphrodite. Throughout the story of Hera and Zeus, we learn of Aphrodite's powerful girdle and its ability to make its wearer irresistible, when Hera lays hands on it. Myrrha was made to fall madly in love with her own father and have relations with him because she neglected her Aphrosinian worship; still another probable cause was because her own mother had boasted that Myrrha was more beautiful than Aphrodite.

In yet another tale, Aphrodite caused Phaedra to have great desire for her own step-son. Uncontrollably, she finds herself in love with her step-son, Hippolytus, because Aphrodite was displeased with the son's disregard for the Goddess of Love. Hippolytus had taken vows of celibacy and devotion to the Virgin Moon Goddess, Artemis. To punish him, Aphrodite created a horrible situation in which Phaedra committed suicide and left a note falsely accusing her step-son of rape. As a result, Poseidon was summoned to kill Hippolytus.

Another interesting tale was that of Psyche. Psyche was considered so beautiful, that she was often revered as a Goddess herself and she had garnered the reputation of often being compared to the Goddess of love. Obviously, this did not sit well with the supreme Goddess of Attraction. Aphrodite created a number of challenges and road block that Psyche, eventually, was able to successfully master and as a result, she received Aphrodite's blessings in her union with her son, Eros.

Aphrodite had many important symbols like the apple and the pomegranate fruit. These fruits are commonly associated with fertility and sexuality. Sweet scents and flowers, in particular; roses and the lily, are also her sacred symbols, again suggesting sexuality and generative sexual organs. She is often depicted with dolphins - a reference to her birth at Sea and perhaps because dolphins were considered sociable, frisky and very friendly, particularly to sea travelers. Doves are associated with her because they coo and are publicly affectionate. Sparrows were said to be her charioteers and they too were her beloved symbol for their wantonness. Their eggs were often eaten as an aphrodisiac in her honor.

Anything gold and shimmering was attributed to her divine essence. Throughout the literature of her time the Goddess of love is often described with these complimentary, golden, demonstrative words. Gold is a metal that is brilliant and does not tarnish and is appropriate for this Cypriot Goddess who seem to exemplify those same qualities.

This immortal brilliant goddess is ever present in romantic and sexual unions but her engrossing spirit is easily detectable in so many other areas in our lives. In our very own creativity we can also encounter Aphrodite's gifts. For as artist, sometimes we find ourselves creating things of beauty and sensuality. When the artist is at work, there is a feeling of enrapture, drive, obsession and the type of attention and focus that most lovers experience for one another at the beginning of a romantic relationship. This is an Aphrosinian experience. In creativity there is great love, cultivations, attraction and engrossment throughout the creative process. A heighten sense of aesthetics is experienced as well as during the creative process...here too; this is Aphrodite's divine essence and gift to us.

Hail to you, captivating Aphrodite!

*Greek Goddess of love, beauty and attraction. Sweet, curvaceous watery Queen, she brings you the power of beauty and attraction and most importantly, the unwavering power of self-love. You say you want a new lover but are you the honey and light, love so often seeks to meld and attach itself with? She is the embodiment of attraction and love, in its many guises. From a gentle stirring, to an all-consuming passion, her Venusian gifts spread into so many different areas in our lives. Even in the passion we might feel towards our goal's fruition, creative projects and its unfolding sacred processes. Here she helps you cultivate your own powers of attraction, to attract whatever your heart truly desires. She invites you to acknowledge your own beauty and your powers of attraction, for these are her domain. Who or what do you ensnare in your life at this time? Where can you cultivate further, your Aphrosinian powers of love and attraction?

FLORA

Flora is the Roman Goddess-Nymph of Flowers and springtime. She was also believed to be of Sabine origins; an old italic tribe, of Apennines pre-dating Rome. In Greece she was known as Chloris, wife of Zephyrus, the westward winds. She was given dominion over the blossoming of flowers.

Goddess of ceremonies, magick, sexuality, nature, the earth and time itself, Flora is the patron Goddess of youth and pleasure. She is a Goddess closely linked with the veneration of Flowers and Beauty. Much like the Egyptian Goddess, Hathor; dancing, sensuality and perfumed floral scents, were an important part of her worship at her temples and annual Festivals.

In ancient times her famous salacious festival was the Floralia. It was held annually, for six days (April 28th through May 3rd) during her sacred month of April. The Floralia, also known as "*Florifertum*," with games known as the "Florales Lundi," started around 238 BCE. It was reputed to be a lively debaucherous, flower festival, dedicated to her worship and held at her sacred temple. It offered numerous opportunities for fun, games, gift-giving, various dances and blessing rites for flowers and crops. It was a time for releasing inhibitions and tapping into Flora's powers of fecundity. Honey and milk offerings were common at this time and there was an air of frivolity and joy. Obviously, an abundance of colorful flowers and floral head wreaths were prevalent at this festival and animals were incorporated into many of the fertility rites. There were countless open air theater performances and pantomimes and of course, lots of brazen nudity, according to the writings of the time.

The Floralia was actually passionately embraced by prostitutes, and the courtesans of local brothels. They saw this annual festival as their very own and venerated, Flora as their patron Goddess.

Flora is also a powerful Goddess of magick; most notably the magick of flowers and floriculture & horticulture studies. According to one Roman legend, it was the Goddess Flora that presented the Roman Goddess Juno, with a most auspicious magickal flower. She provided Juno with an enchanted flower of fecundity that allowed Juno to become pregnant parthenogenesis, that is, without male contribution. Thus, Juno later gives birth to the God of War, Mars.

The Pagan holiday of Beltane still celebrated today and the incorporation of the Maypole were all attributed to her ecstatic, joyful flower festival and the worship of the Roman Goddess, Flora.

When working with the ancient Goddess Flora, she will heighten all of your senses and awaken desire for fun, pleasure and the enjoyment of life. She invites you to abandon your inhibitions and bedeck your beautiful body with her sacred flowers. With her energy, she asks you to prioritize love and sensuality and calls you to admire the beauty found in her myriad of colorful flowers and explore her numerous gifts.

THEME WORK SUGGESTIONS

Laughter Rite: It is simply placing yourself in a cackling, laughing mood. Start a loud hardy belly laugh and just start chuckling. If it helps listen to a comedian or remember a funny experience or a past funny story and simply laugh. Keep laughing really hard and loudly for a few minutes. If you're having trouble, begin with a forced smile and see where it leads you.

JOURNALING

What do I love? What brings me joy?
_____
_____

What activities can I do today to put a smile on my face?
_____
_____

Who are the people around me that support and elevate my vibration?
_____
_____

What makes me laugh?
_____
_____

What stirs my heart in delight?
_____
_____

Do I have love in my life?
_____
_____

Are the right people in my world?
_____
_____

How do I invite my joy in my life?
_____

INVOCATION & POETRY

APPLE LOVE SPELL

Goddess of Love,
I call on you,
Holding two halves
Of your Sacred Fruit.

Offering this altar
With supplications
And flames,
Making invocations
To honor your name.

I am ready now
To taste your gifts;
To know your pleasures,
Ecstasy and bliss...

To draw my Other Half,
And unite like this fruit,
Magnetically join,
The one who is true...

My twin flame & I bond,
We find each other now,
Let the magick of this spell,
Allow our love to be found.

Let the scent of my loins
Stir the cauldron of this spell,
And by my will and word,
Let all go as well

Draw my lover to me,
End the pain of this drought,
Dissolve all the blocks
To let this love sprout

As I sing your (Sacred) name,
May He sing mine,
Merry meet, my Twin Flame,
Heart to Heart, Eye to Eye....)O(

***You are now encouraged to create your own altar(s) & invocation(s).)O(Blessings!

MAGICK RITES & TOOLS

This is your personal page to document your sacred rites and the tools you elected to use.

DECIDE WHERE TO SET UP AN ALTAR
Place an Altar Cloth in the Color of your choice.
Color: _____

GODDESS
Place an image of your Deity.
Goddess: _____
This image can be a Statue, handmade Sculpture or a simple Photo _____

FIRE REPRESENTATION
Place a blessed/charged Candle in the color of your choice.
Candle Type and color: _____

AIR REPRESENTATION
Light your Incense stick.
Incense Scent: _____

WATER REPRESENTATION
Place a Chalice of Water
Water Item: _____

EARTH REPRESENTATION
Place a Potted Plant or Fresh Flowers on your Altar
Add Salt or a plate of Dried Herbs
Herbs: _____
Chosen Gemstone: _____

YOUR WISH
_____

_____

_____

Place a symbol of your desire, if you have one available, and also write your wish out clearly, on a piece of parchment paper, or you can even use a cut up brown paper bag. These are the basics for a very simple altar & rite. Ultimately, your sacred space is only limited by your imagination. You can make your altar & rite as big or as small as you prefer and the addition of other personal items is really up to you.)o(Enjoy!

ALTAR PHOTOS

CHAPTER FIVE

"To describe my Mother would be to write about a hurricane in its perfect power. Or the climbing, falling colors of a rainbow..."
Maya Angelou

THEME: MOTHER ARCHETYPE

What does the word Mother evoke within you? Are you a mother or on the precipices of starting this journey into motherhood? Or maybe you immediately think about your own mother or your own experience as a child being mothered, upon hearing the title of our theme in this chapter.

Utter the words mother and a myriad of images may flood your mind; much like the word Goddess will evoke a plethora of diverse images of the Sacred Feminine from across the globe. There are a myriad of Deities from numerous cultures throughout history that are intimately linked with the Mother archetype, therefore her value in our collective consciousness cannot be overstated. Her significance is also not limited to the female gender, for men too are highly affected by her gifts and her undeniable presence in our world.

The visual images of a Mother in our modern day era will astound you when compared to the limited oppressive views we had of her, years ago. All around the world we see so many beautiful diverse examples of what it means to be a mother and no longer are we bond by one oppressive stereotypical image of motherhood. Mothers nowadays break all forms of outdated, traditional appearances and have become as diverse as women's varying roles in society.

However, there is one aspect of Motherhood I'd like to shine a light unto, as we explore, in this chapter, the theme of Mother and Nurturing. As part of our spiritual work here we arrive at the gates of the Mother Archetype to explore how we interpret and value this role in our world today and more importantly, how we provide for ourselves the gifts of the Mother archetype. That is to say, how do we nurture, teach, guide, protect and mother ourselves; and how do we extend that energy in a healing manner of compassion and forgiveness to ourselves and to others. The exploration of these questions will have a great impact on our spiritual journey as we proceed forward.

In this chapter we have reached a point in our journey where we are being asked to explore the concept of mother and what it may personally mean to you. There are many ways this may present itself in your life; you may even find yourself reflecting on your upbringing and the examples that were set before you about what it means to be the mother. Perhaps you are a mother now contemplating on the affects you have on your own children and the next generation or perhaps you are at a pivotal point endeavoring to become a mother yourself. You are invited to connect with this energy and explore the numerous gifts of the Sacred Mother Archetype.

As we have done before, in this chapter we will explore further our theme with the help of several resources. We will endeavor to connect with the Native American Goddess Corn Mother, Goddesses Ashera, Demeter, Maia, Yemaya, Kuan-Yin and the sacred animal energy of the Turtle. We will connect with our 4th chakra, the Heart chakra, and gemstones that can help better facilitate this connection. We will also look at the corresponding Lunation and a Tarot card that is connected to our theme.

THE HANGED ONE TAROT CARD

Our tarot card for this chapter is, The Hanged One or The Hanged Man, as it is known in most traditional tarot decks. The Hanged One is depicted with a person hanging upside down from a tree. Sometimes known as the Norse God, Odin, or the Christian God, Christ, this character is shown hanging serenely, upside. He/she appears comfortably hanging upside down with no frown or other concerning grimace on his/her expression. He/she is literally comfortably suspended, oftentimes with one leg wrapped up, bond in a rope, hanging from a tree. One leg is bond and the other leg rest at a ninety degree angle behind it. His/her head is also often crowned in a celestial halo, denoting the great spiritual connection of this card.

The Hanged One is a card about surrendering, sacrifices and suspensions. It is also a card about getting a different perspective on a situation since he/she is viewing the world from a non-traditional viewpoint. It brings with it a message about a willing sacrifice for something of a higher ideal. It is connected to the Mother archetype theme of this chapter because so often the role of Mother necessitates a willingness to see the bigger picture and offer a sacrifice that will benefit the whole rather than the parts. There are so many examples of how a mother's willing sacrifice becomes compulsory but the first one that comes to mind is how her own physical body is offered up for the sacred period of gestation, and even long after that, in order to birth and nurture new life into this world.

The Hanged One offers a proclivity to be in this moment of surrendering knowing there is something of greater value in the works that will unfold as a result. The way a spiritualist might fast, renounce material possessions or take a vow of silence in order to receive spiritual enlightenment. In this manner, we are presented with an opportunity to suspend our immediate desires and gratifications to hold out for something of greater significance.

To sacrifice is to make something sacred and holy. The tarot card of the Hanged One represents a pursuit of higher spiritual ideals through the willingness to surrender ego; sacrifices are offered to fulfill or manifest something incalculable in its value. It is just one of many gifts the Mother archetype offers us.

*"The Heart of a Mother is a deep abyss
at the bottom of which you will always find, forgiveness..."* Honore de Balzac

MOON IN CANCER — WATER/MOON

THEME: Mother Archetype

| CANCER | CARDINAL | WATER | FEMININE | THE CRAB |

The Moon entering the astrological sign of Cancer finds itself in its beloved home sign. This is where the Moon's most potent characteristics can be greatly enhanced due to its powerful conglomeration with Cancer. I am speaking of the Moon's characteristics, like the ones related to the Sacred Feminine; intuition, psychic development, channelings and priestessing and connecting to ancestral spirits.

Moon ruled Cancer, is known as a water sign, with its symbol being the hard-shell, side stepping, Crab. It is highly feminine, nurturing, and emotional. In astrology, Cancer is also deeply connected to the mother and all things related to domesticity; our home, our upbringing, our family, our children, and even our pets.

This Lunar transit awakens our intuitive gifts but it may also bring to the surface our deepest suppressed emotions. It is not unusual during this lunation, to hear of people, inexplicably crying or feeling uncomfortably moody and expressing the surge of emotions brought on by the moon, in unpredictable ways.

Cancer Moon can resurrect any issues connected to the mother, family dynamics, and emotional healings. During this lunation we can reflect and consider where in our present day lives to utilize the nurturing quality of this lunar transit. What deep suppressed emotions need to come to the surface from her ebb and flow waves, brought on by the Moon? What area in our lives requires the Mother? Where can we employ the Moon's intuitive gifts and delve deeper into the exploration of our emotions, for clarity and healing.

THEME WORK SUGGESTIONS

Work with the Cancer moon, symbolized by the Crab,
and work with The Turtle energy and the Goddesses shared
in this chapter. Enjoy a day of nurturing and pampering
yourself. Make a trip to the sea or the lake and
spend some time with the element of water.
Write a Letters to communicate to the matriarchs of your family.
If you can, try adopting an animal or even a simple plant.
If you are seeking more experience as a mother, offer Babysitting services
to your local neighbors. Nurture yourself with
good healthy meals. Make your meal time sacred;
cook with positive intention as a form of kitchen-witchery. Spend time Moon-bathing.

*"You have to find a Mother inside yourself. We all do.
Even if we already have a mother, we still have to find this part of ourselves inside..."*

Sue Monk Kidd, The Secret Life of Bees

HERSTORY

She always struggled with the love that she had for her mother and yet, the type of painful and contentious relationship they endured most of their lives. She knew her history and negative relationship with her mother was starting to have an effect on her adult life.

She already had little trust in other women in her environment and she found herself often feeling pessimistic about ever forming good solid, trusting friendships with women.

She knew there were some deeper issues that were linked back to her mother and it was time to work through them. In her heart, she also felt a growing fear she, herself, wouldn't be a good mother to her future children. It felt like the right time to heal her relationship with her mother and consequently, find a way to mother and nurture her own self.

******<u>**Take a moment to document here, or in your journal, your unique story.**</u>

_____

_____

_____

_____

AFFIRMATION

**How would my Divine mother
nurture me? This is
how I will nurture myself**

I Nurture

**Regardless of my upbringing,
I vow now to nurture and mother myself
in a way that is conducive
and supportive to my ultimate wellbeing.**

CHAKRA & GEMSTONE WORK

4th Chakra   **ANAHATA/HEART CHAKRA**   **COLOR:** Green/Pink
Love, compassion, trust, relationships and community.
Mantra: I Love
)O(**WORKING:** Love/Forgiveness, understanding, patience, endurance, compassion

GEMSTONE CONNECTION: Rhodonite is a gemstone found in varying shades of pink with black vein-like patterns. It is a love gemstone that promotes generosity, compassion, altruism, peace and dispels confusion. It is even reputed in helping trauma victims. Rhodonite is connected with the elements of fire and earth, and the planet Mars. It is connected with auditory blessings as well. With the gemstone, rhodonite, we unearth our hidden talents and nurture our gifts.

GEMSTONE CHANNELING

    As part of this important healing work of love and self-care, you are invited now to embark on this meditative journey. Please find a comfortable place where you can be assured of your privacy, safety and comfort... If you can go outdoors in nature that would be most ideal but any place where you can be free of distractions would be fine. It is most important that you are able to offer yourself now, the gift of serenity and relaxation.

    Place yourself in a comfortable meditation position; you may sit or lay down. If it is available to you, place in your hands the Rhodonite gemstone we are working with today. You may hold this mauve/ pink colored gemstone and begin to connect with its energy. Consider how it feels in your hands. Does it feel smooth or rough, cold or warm? Gaze upon its shape and its varying pink hues and notice the black veins that are traditionally associated with this gemstone. (Pause) Look at your Rhodonite more deeply now and let your scrutiny unveil all of its precious details. Rhodonite is connected to our Heart Chakra and it is known to offer much healing, love and guidance. Quietly, continue to study this gemstone and make note of any thoughts or vivid images that immediately start to unfold before you. (Pause) When you're ready, you may close your eyes and begin this short meditation.

    As with all trance work, we begin with our breath. You are asked now to take a deep cleansing breath; slowly filling up your lungs, then exhale.... (Pause) Now let your next breath possess the element of this Rhodonite gemstone you're holding. Envision, if you will, the varying pink shades of this love stone rising vaporously into the ethers. Inhale this unique energy of love and healing. Breathe. (Pause) As you breathe in, direct the energy of your breath, from your crown chakra, all the way down to your chest; where your Heart Chakra is located. Stay with this gentle, loving energy for as long as you need to. (Pause) Continue to breathe and hold this breath for 3 seconds and then release it... Counting now at your own pace; breathe, 1, 2, 3, and exhale on 4....and again....Let's do this one more time and then quietly counting in your head.... Breathe 1, 2, 3...release on 4. Breathe, trusting in the natural rhythm you have now established, of your relaxed inhalation and exhalation.

    Rhodonite gemstone wishes to impart a special channeled message for you about nurturance and the power of love and forgiveness. See this gemstone in your mind's eye. See it as the Heart itself, pulsating with life-force.... Notice it now embedded upon the dark, fertile, mother earth. Draw nearer to it and ask if it will allow you to pick it up. When permission is granted, gently gather it in your hands. With your mind's eye, gaze upon it again; studying its pink color, its traditional black veins and any other details that stand out.... Ask it to speak to you. (Pause)

    Now with your next breath, place your attention on your crown chakra and imagine a lid being open. Allow your head or crown chakra to become almost like a chalice; receptive and open to any spiritual messages meant for you. Envision your crown chakra unveiling a magnetic Rhodonite gemstone portal allowing for this **Crystal Transmission** *to come through... Gently guide this energy of the gemstone, again from your crown chakra, to your Heart Chakra, the place of love, happiness, nurturance and healing... (Pause) If you wish, stay in this sacred space of love, for as long as you need to.*

    When you feel ready, you may open your eyes and prepare to document your experience. As you come out of this meditation, it is a perfect time for you to document any images or messages that came through for you. You may write them down here, or in your personal journal

_____

_____

_____

TURTLE PROTECTION ENERGY

As we continue on this spiritual journey and endeavor now, in this chapter, to connect with the mother, Turtle makes her appearance. Turtles are one of the oldest symbols of the planet and this very fact intimately links them to the Sacred Feminine and our Mother Earth. Turtles are reptiles that breathe air and live, both on land and in water; thus, earth and water are the elements connected with this medicine. Sea turtles, in particular, can successfully navigate under, really deep waters through vibrations and sound waves. It serves to remind us to also connect with vibrations and learn to use, these higher dimensional, modes of communication. Everything around us is vibrating at varying levels and learning this form of communication is simply a matter of practice and awareness when we are connecting to our teacher, the Turtle.

Turtles also have an extraordinary heightened sense of smell and hearing. They have strong jaws but by far their most interesting physical characteristic we can probably all agree on, is the hard shell that covers most of their body. It is essentially their home, carried upon their back. Most importantly, it is their protective hard shield from predators which has kept them from extinction throughout the centuries. It is this very fact that makes Turtle our ideal ally and protector as we plunge deeper into this powerful work.

The Turtle walks slowly upon the earth, never needing to fear predators, for they are securely shielded within their hard shell. It is one of the most vital elements that have helped them survive all these years. Clearly, the turtle is a powerful symbol of longevity and survival, as one of the oldest living creatures on the earth. They can live to be hundreds of years old and they survive not by being the biggest, strongest, loudest or most aggressive, but by being cautious and slow. Turtle medicine thus, speaks to us about the value of slowing down, being cautious of our surroundings and learning when it is in our best interest to retreat within our protective shell.

Another attribute that connects them to the subject of the mother and nurturance is linked with its fecundity. When turtles reproduce, they deposits a multitude of eggs within the earth, letting the sun hatch them naturally into being. Their survival is assured, due also to the sheer volume of eggs they bury within the earth. For indigenous people, turtle is a most powerful teacher and spirit guide. She is a symbol of mother earth, which is infinitely seen as a provider to humanity. In ancient Chinese and Hindu folklore, it is the tortoise that supports and carries the world on its back. Here turtle is the nurturer and the protective celestial Mother of the earth. In Japanese mythology, the mountains were believed to be supported by a divine tortoise. In Greek and Roman mythology, turtle was often linked with the Goddesses of love and beauty, respectively, Venus and Aphrodite. The messenger deities, Hermes and Mercury were also linked with the turtle. In West Africa, the turtle symbolized fertility and was directly connected to female energy. The Turtle, for most indigenous cultures, has always been a symbol of the Sacred Feminine and was closely linked with the element of earth and water.

Turtles eat plants, insects, and fish, and on occasions, even small mammals; making them omnivorous. It's important to note they also have very slow metabolism. In many cultures, Turtle is known as a healer that helps us cultivate a respectful relationship with Mother Earth. It is considered a powerful spirit guide that will help you to acquire ancient wisdom. The energy of turtle is not one of aggression or force, but rather one of peace and defense. Even in indigenous rite, when turtle rattles are produced, and used, they are emblematic of the peace and harmony that is strived for among the tribe. The Turtle is a symbol of peace, patience, self-reliance, nurturance and protection and thus an ideal animal to connect with as we progress in our work. Its energy is slow but it assures steady progress toward reaching our goals. It teaches us to honor the creative source within us and thrive to attain goals through patience, nurturance and perseverance. It also warns us to beware of our surroundings. We are encourage to retreat into our shell, and go within, when we feel unsafe and perceive a threat. In many ways turtle advocates our own self-care and nurturance.

Turtle teaches us to develop our ideas before bringing them out into the light, much like a turtle buries its precious eggs in the sand and allows the sun to slowly hatch the little ones into being. Our creative ideas sometimes need time to be anchored and formed quietly, hidden away from the critical eyes of others. Turtles are connected with incubation, self-paced journeys, strength, gestation periods, and the wisdom of our foremothers. When we find ourselves in need of guidance, connecting quietly to this powerful ally can open us up to her infinite wisdom and counsel.

"Giving birth and being born brings us into the essence of creation, where the human spirit is courageous and bold, and the body, a miracle of wisdom..." Harriette Hartigan

GODDESS EMPOWERMENT

SELU/CORN MOTHER

Corn, or Maize as it is known by most Native Americans, was first developed in Central Mexico over 7,000 years ago. It was not something that grew naturally on its own in the wild but rather needed to be cultivated. According to historians it was started from the wild grass known as teosinte and in the beginning it looked very different from our modern day corn husk. As the Native American Indians migrated, corn began to be introduced to Peruvian culture, further south, as well as further up North, in the Southwest region of the Americas. Eventually its consumption became wildly popular throughout the Americas and when Christopher Columbus returned to Europe, after his expedition, he introduced the comestible to Europeans.

Corn became an imperative source of food for Native Americans, but also a significant part of their daily lives and culture. Various part of the corn was utilized to make sleeping mats, moccasins, ceremonial masks and games and baskets, which helped transporting many different vital items. The ability to feed a whole nation with the grains of corn made it one of the most important staples in aboriginal's diet. Today Corn is no less important than it was 7,000 years ago. Reflect, if you will now, on what our lives would be like without corn.

Today our dependence on corn goes beyond the obvious; bread, cake, tortilla chips, popcorn, corn-muffins, sweet corn on the cob, etc., etc. It might surprise you to know that corn is employed in our aspirins, glue, cosmetics, shoe polish, and in our books as corn starch, as well as our clothing. It is utilized as corn syrup in our soft drinks and often used to feed farm Chickens that provide for our eggs. Corn can be found in the ink that graces our books and newspapers and it's a key ingredient to Ethanol, which is found in automobile fuel. So it becomes clear that Corn is incredibly valuable to the sustenance of a nation today, as it was with its inception.

It is therefore not surprising that corn would receive such veneration from aboriginals. To indigenous cultures that practice animism and saw spirit in all things, one could easily see how something so crucial and important, like corn, can become deified. Studies into these native cultures reveal that it was customary to craft a puppet made of stalks of maize from the first corn husk in a harvest and great care was taken to preserve this puppet or corn dolly (as it was sometimes referred to) in order to guarantee a continuous fertile crop for the year. It was ceremonially dressed in woman's attire and it was well regarded, for the duration of the year, until it was ceremonially burned and replaced with the first corn of the next harvest.

Corn woman appears in numerous indigenous tribes by various names and with a multitude of myths and folklore traditions, intertwined into Native's culture. And because they have been passed down, throughout generations, via oral tradition (through song and dance) we are blessed to have many surviving tales.

Mayan believed humans were actually fashioned out of corn and Penobscot Indians believed Corn mother to be the first mother of her people. The Lakota plains Indians correlated the existence of Corn mother with White Buffalo woman and for the Seneca Indians of the Northeast, they believed in a beautiful Woman who lived high above the mountains as their divine Maize Goddess. The Creeks, in Southeast Americas, viewed Corn Mother as a highly revered Old Woman, while the Zuni people of the Southwestern United States of America had a myth about eight corn maidens. To the Aztec and Mexico, Corn Mother was known as Chicomecoatl, the Goddess of Maize but to the Cherokee nation, she was known as Selu. She was also known as yellow woman and Iyatiku to the Keresan people of Southwest Americas.

In researching and becoming acquainted with many of Corn Mother's various myths, there is a similar thread running through all of them. Inherent in the corn, and the myths related to Selu, are the themes of sacrifice, forgiveness and the cycles of birth, growth, life, death and rebirth. I have elected to elucidate here and share one of the Cherokee tales of Corn Mother, also known as Selu.

Some claim Corn woman was a spirit that was sent down to earth once a year to help the crop grow tall and strong, others tell a different story. Cherokee folklore reveals she was sent down to earth to live and feed the people. In this tale Selu, living on the earth, gave birth to two sons, who apparently were always hungry. Every time they complained of hunger and asked for food, she would instruct them to sit and wait patiently, while she would quickly disappear into a nearby hut and magickally always come back with a basket full of corn. This happened quite often and the boys (while dutifully relishing their meals and plumping up on corn) started to wonder where and how their mother was getting food. One night curiosity got the best of them and they defied their mother's instructions to wait patiently. Instead, on this night, they decide to follow; creep and spy on their mother, as she entered the small hut. What they saw was far beyond compre-hensible for the minds of two small boys and needless to say quite traumatic. Inside the hut, they saw their mother squatting above the basket, producing a multitude of corn from her very own body; filling the basket with their next meal. There are some lore that state Corn Mother produced corn from scabs on her body and some say from her feces. In either case she is essentially producing corn from her very own body and, the boys, in their ignorance and immaturity were completely baffled and disgusted. That night at dinner time, the boys would not eat, they confronted their mother with what they had seen and here again, some myths vary, claiming that the boys, horrified, threaten to tell the entire village. In this Cherokee lore, Corn Mother realizes that her children and her people are now in jeopardy of not being able to provide for themselves and sadly she realizes the sacrifice required of her. She tells her boys that now that they know the truth, they must kill her and drag her body through the fields to ensure that corn will continue to grow and sustain her people. Wherever droplets of her blood spilled, there, corn will grow and now the children will need to feed themselves from this point onward. Some other myths tell another version of this story, claiming that Corn Mother's body had to be cut up into tiny pieces and scattered around the various corners of the world to ensure the survival of corn for the Native American people.

    In this popular folklore of Selu, we meet the universal archetype of the fertile mother and her message of procreation, nourishment, death, rebirth and sacrifice. In her sacrifice, she willingly sheds her body and blood, to save and secure a nation of people and the future generations of Native Americans to come. With her sacrifice, she ensures her children will thrive and not starve to death.

    As a powerful Matrirachal archetype there are many obvious aspects we can explore with Selu. She invites us to explore what it means to be a mother, more specifically what it means to sacrifice as a mother. We are asked to contemplate the legacies we hope to leave behind to our grandchildren and future generations and recognize our part in the tapestry of our great-grandmothers. Deep within Corn Mother we may find yet another gem to consider while working with her. Yes, she is a mother archetype and inherent in this title is the theme of nurturance; whether it is self-nurturance or extended to our creations, but there is also a lesson about balance. Working with Corn Mother might unearth a lesson on cultivating balance in our lives and improving our personal relationships to foods we chose to nurture ourselves with.

    I find that tapping into the energy and lessons of Corn Mother makes perfect sense to me as we work through the theme offered in this chapter but like many other Goddesses with multiple powerful attributes, she can easily be incorporated into various other chapters found in this book. Corn Mother/Selu is also a wonderful deity to work with at Mabon, the second harvest. For most Pagans, honoring Selu at this time of the year seems most appropriate, although I have also called upon her during the first harvest, at Lammas. I find that the holiday of the Autumnal Equinox, presents the theme of equilibrium in our lives, as we stand, in perfect symmetry, between both night and day. It is therefore a good time to reflect on what requires perfect balance in our own lives. Selu also touches upon the issue of food and nourishment, and I can't help but consider how food and our relationship to it, is not always in perfect balance.

Our society struggles greatly with issues related to food. Just perusing through a contemporary woman's magazine I can't help but notice the predominance of malnourished looking, skinny models and then walking outside my door and seeing the unusual amount of unhealthy, obese people. Clearly as a society, we struggle with finding a balance or right relationship with food. We either abuse it (consume too much of it, without regards to its sacred vital role) or we disrespect it and call it the enemy, avoiding it, to fulfill an unreal body image. In either case, food is not being respected, nor approached with the reverence it deserves. Yet, if like indigenous people and our ancestors, we too saw Corn as Goddess, wouldn't our approach to food be vastly different? Wouldn't our relationship to food be immeasurably different than what it appears to be today for millions of people?

As I endeavor to present Corn Woman and her numerous cathartic lessons in this chapter, I also reflect on the lessons she has taught me, as a Goddess womyn, about nourishment, balance and proper alignment with food.

*Selu/Corn Mother is the nurturing sacrificial iconic Corn Goddess, embraced by the myriads of indigenous tribes, across the Americas and abroad. Corn Mother shed her blood so that her people would strive onward and not extinct. She, who willingly sacrificed her very own truncated body so that her people would never hunger again, is the supreme being of compassion. Despite the unappreciative nature of her greedy children and her community, she understood her role and obligation in the larger scheme of life and thus, she awakens the sacrificial Mother within every one of us. She calls to mind your core, your heart-chakra and asks you, "*How do you nurture yourself?*" Step back, if you will, and consider for a moment what sacrifices are required of you? What is in your heart now, that requires sacrifice for the greater good? What symbolizes your sacred blood and where is it being required to pour forth and serve a greater good in your family or even within your community?

DEMETER

Demeter is the Greek Goddess of the Grain, also known as Deo and Chloe. Her Roman counterpart was Ceres. She was the most generous of the Greek Goddesses, representing the bounty of the fertile Earth. She was depicted as warm, altruistic and beautiful, with long luscious golden hair. Wearing a blue robe, wherever she was present, there was divine light and growing crops sprouting abundantly by her feet. Often seen as very matronly in a seated position, her presence brought celestial lights and a most wonderful fragrance, according to the writings of her time. She was responsible for the fruitfulness of nature and the fertility of the Earth. Her gifts to humanity were the harvest and agriculture. Interesting to note, the last part of her name, "meter", translates as Mother, revealing her other significant role as a Maternal Deity. She was a mother Goddess, with a most emblematic role as Persephone's mother.

Demeter was the granddaughter of Uranus and the primordial Earth Goddess - Gaia. She was the second daughter of the Goddess Rhea and the God Cronos. Rhea was mother of the first generation of Olympians and thus she was also mother to Hades (God of the Underworld and Maiden abductor) and Zeus (Husband and Father to Persephone). According to mythology, Demeter's father swallowed up his children and as the second child to her mother, she too was swallowed, then later released and saved by her sibbling.

According to Greek mythology, Demeter married her brother, Zeus, and became his fourth wife before Hera, who was ultimately wife number seven, and the last of Zeus' wives. Her union with Zeus produced their only child, the beautiful maiden, Persephone, also known as Kore.

According to the well-known Eleusian myth so often linked with Demeter, one day Persephone and her maiden friends were out picking flowers. Attracted by a beautiful Narcissus flower, the young girl reached out her arms to pick it and it was then that Hades, God of the underworld, abducted the beautiful Maiden. According to one legend, he opened up the Earth and snatched her up and only two Deities heard her cry; Hekate and Helios. As the myth reveals, for nine days and nine nights, the once brilliant, benevolent Goddess Demeter, now roamed the Earth, sadly searching endlessly for her daughter. It was on the tenth day that Hekate, Goddess of the Crossroads, finally came to Demeter and told her she had indeed heard Persephone's cries. The sympathetic Crone, Hekate, now endeavored to help and console the despondent Goddess.

Upon hearing that the Lord of the Underworld, Hades, had abducted her daughter to become his unwilling bride and that Zeus, could've probably sanctioned this horrid act without her authority, enraged her beyond belief. To add insult to injury, Demeter (who at times, appeared to exist solely for her daughter) was made to feel as if she had no power over this situation and she was suppose to simply accept the abduction and disappearance of her beloved child. Demeter was beyond grief and anger and would not accept this fate. Betrayed and full of grief, she withdrew her divine gifts from the Earth and left Mount Olympus. Inconsolable and terribly distraught, she wandered the Earth, in a stuporous haze of sadness and misery, as if her very soul had been stripped and her inner divine light snuffed completely. Disguised as a very old lady, in dark veils, concealing any hint of her previous Divine golden essence, she traveled throughout the cities and countryside and then came upon the city of Eleusis.

According to the Homeric Hymn, the despondently dark, unrecognizable Demeter found herself sitting by a well, on the outskirts of the city, when four bright maidens, endeavoring to draw water from the well, approached her. Callidice, Cleisidice, Demo, Callithoe were the daughters of Celeus, King of Eleusis and these four maidens approached the old lady, before them, with much intrigue and curiosity. After introducing themselves, they asked Demeter where whe came from and tried to understand why a woman of her suspecting age, was alone, outside of the city center and not already employed as a nurse by a household. Demeter introduced herself as a woman from Crete, by the name of "Doso" and claimed to have escaped the capture of pirates, who were going to sell her off. She weaved a convincingly good, yet, sad tale that captured the sympathy of the King's children. The maiden, Callidice, who was described as the "godliest" in the Homeric Hymn, suggested that the old lady follow them home. She convinced Demeter that their father, the King, would surely welcome her services in their household and that their younger brother would benefit from a nurse of her caliber.

Upon meeting the disguised Demeter, the King Celeus, and his wife, sensed that indeed she would be a welcomed addition to their Kingdom and a fine nurse for their young son Demophoon, although in some text he was also known as Triptolemus. There is also some conflicting stories about Iambe as yet another daughter of the Queen or perhaps another name for the bawdy, jovial Baubo herself, who was the nursemaid that ultimately helped end Demeter's lament.

And thus Demeter, still in disguise, was employed by the Queen, Metaeira, to become nursemaid to the baby boy. She raised this baby as if he was her very own. Time spent with the boy employed her inherent divine matriarchal gifts and also became a diversion from the worries over her ubducted daughter. As time went on, she indeed grew quite fond of this child. In Demeter's care, Demophoon was raised like a God and her love for him, oneday inspired her to bless him with the fires of immortality.

The child was about to become immortal by her own making, as Demeter had the special fire rite of immortality prepared for Demophoon. His mother, the Queen, came upon them as it was about to take place and intercepted the frightful looking, fire ritual. Imagine her surprise to discover the old nursemaid they had hired, was actually the Goddess of the Grain, Demeter. Immediately, Demeter's divine luminescence manifested, upon being caught by the Queen in the midst of this rite. And, Metaneira was no sooner, harshly berated by the Fertile Grain Goddess for her interference in the will of the Gods. In her anger, the Goddess demanded that a temple be built in her honor there in the city of Eleusis, immediately.

Once the temple was built, the Goddess Demeter planted herself there until the return of her daughter. She vowed she would not step foot on Mount Olympus, or allow anything to grow or be born on the Earth, until her daughter was returned to her. And this was a most tragic state for the earth and humanity's wellbeing. Zeus tried to implore her to return to her post. Other Gods and Goddesses also came to her, bearing gifts and supplications. The people of the land also left numerous offerings to the Goddess to entreat her to return. Demeter was unmoved and refused to give into their demands. In one myth, Zeus finally sends the messenger God, Hermes, to retrieve Persephone from the underworld and bring her back to her mother. In another more accepted version, it is the Crone, Hekate that finally helps unite, Mother and daughter.

Their overdue reunion was full of intense heartwarming emotions but in the end, bittersweet. Demeter learns then that Persephone had eaten the fruit of the dead, pomegranate seeds, while in the underworld and must now come to accept that her daughter will only be with her part of the year and return to her husband, Hades, in the underworld, for the remainder of the year.

The Homeric Hymn to Demeter focused on Demeter's response to Persephone being abducted by Hades and this was the basis of the Eleusinian Mysteries - the most powerful religious and sacred rites of ancient Greece. Held in secret for over two thousand years, these sacred rites ended with the destruction of the Eleusis Temples by the Goths around fifth century A.D. More recently there has been a resurgeance and interest in ancient mythology, anthropology, Paganism and Goddess spirituality. Research into these archaic, longstanding Greek rites, reveal a great deal about our ancestors and their spiritual practices - knowledge that can enrich our own present day beliefs and religious practices.

In the Greek Goddess, Demeter we see another aspect of the Mother Archetype. We are introduced to a Mother deity that is passionately and wholly submersed in her role as Mother. She appears solely defined by her role as Persephone's mother. It is not only the land and the harvest that she is commited to but to her daughter, Kore. Demeter exemplifies for us what it means to be a fierce defender and protectress of our children and our creations. In Demeter we see a mother exercise her convictions and negotiating skills. She knows the power she has as a Mother and she wields this power for her child. Her great strength and determination to secure her daughter's wellbeing is evident in the myths and, with her energy, we traverse into the matriarchal realm where we find a love for our children so deep that we realize there is nothing we wouldn't do to protect and bless them.

*Greek Goddess of the grain, she is the benevolent Harvest Mother who supports, protects and nourishes her children. She comes into your life at this time to inaugurate the Mother within. She awakens in you a connection to all things that need nurturance and protection, including yourself. Like the immortal Goddess, who would not let the grain grow until her daughter's return, where are you being asked to put your foot down? Where are you being called to fully care for your needs and not compromise your dignity? Where will you utilize your own bargaining power? And where will you need to make some initial sacrifices to attain your goals? This Goddess asks, where in your life are you being called to be the Mother? It is a time of assessments and preparedness. Demeter invites us to consider our role as committed, nurturing mothers to our creative pursuits and take this brief pause in our journey to reflect, assess, review and nurture.

YEMAYA

Yemaya is also known as Yemonja, Yemoja, Yemanja, Yemaja, Iamanje, Imanje, Ymoja, and many other variations of this name. Yemaya is the Yoruban Orisha and Goddess of the great Ocean. She is a powerful matriarchal Goddess who is attributed to birthing many of the sacred Orishas in the Yoruban pantheon, including birthing the sun and the moon. She is widely embraced as the divine mother that hears the cries of her children. Her compassionate and nurturing attributes cannot be underestimated and her devotees know they are heard, supported, loved and well protected by this great Goddess. Hers are the gift of fertility, sexuality, love, feminine beauty, healing and mothering. She is very sympathetic to her devotees and is not known to anger quick, though, like most deities, she can express another aspect, if crossed.

Her worship can be traced back to West Africa and regions like Ghana, Benin and Nigeria, yet this beloved Orisha appears to be known worldwide. From Brazil, to Cuba, to Puerto Rico, and parts of the United States, to so many other countries, her worship has clearly grown and expanded throughout the years.

She is the Queen of the ocean, a matriarchal Goddess, a powerful Orisha in Lucumi, Umbanda, Macumba, Santeria and the Brazilian Candomble religion. As a mother archetype she is called upon for numerous healing rites and love workings. Annually by the sea, Yemaya is worshipped and honored in special rites in Brazil, and all across the globe, to commemorate her day on New Year's Eve (December 31st).

While Oshun is the Orisha or Goddess of rivers, Yemaya rules over all of the waters upon the Earth; saltwater, freshwaters (rivers, lakes, and oceans). Her name translates as mother of a multitude of fishes. It derives from the Yoruban word, "Yeye Omo eya," which translates as, mother of fishes or mother whose children are the Fish.

Often depicted in her shimmering blue and white colors, she has overflowing large breast to denote her powers of fecundity. You will often see images of her as a beautiful woman, crowned with long flowing dark hair, resembling a mermaid, with her mermaid's tail upon the foaming ocean waves. Statues of her resemble the Catholic Virgin Mary, donning a blue and white robe. In Cuba, they connect Yemaya with Our Lady of Regla.

As a great matriarchal deity she is attributed for birthing many of the Orishas (gods/goddesses) and because of her great matriarchal gifts, it is said she would often even take care of Oshun's children. Her strong maternal gifts, also links her with adoptions. According to folklore, she adopted Chango/Shango, the God of Thunder. His greatness as a leader and Lord of Thunder is mostly attributed to her nurturance and special guidance. They share a profound love and much, much later on, it is said, he becomes one of her great lovers. As can be expected with a beautiful water deity, she had numerous lovers. Her known accepted consorts were Olokun and Ogun. Ogun is the warrior God, the blacksmith and patron of civilization and human technological advancement. Olokun is the Orisha or God of the depth of the Ocean and consequently the depth of our unconscious; together they are a force to be reckoned with.

As a Goddess so intrinsically linked with women and the ocean, Yemaya is also very much connected with the moon. It is believed her mother is the Orisha, Odudua; the dark womb mother of all.

Yemaya's sacred number is 7 and altar offerings to her can include seashells and anything sweet: like chocolate, candy, coconut balls, syrup, honey, melons, watermelons, cakes and cookies. Even fried green plantains, hens and fried pork can be offered to her on her altars but never offer her fish, as she is the mother of fishes and will take great offense to this. There are some, however, that say you can offer her shrimp dishes, just not fish. Obviously any Altar to Yemaya would be incomplete without some type of chalice, bowl or vessel containing water. Altar candles to Yemaya can be blue, green, white and even better, seashell shaped candles, if you can find them.

Sometimes on her altar she is worshiped with her sister, Oshun, as both of these Goddesses were connected with the sacred element of water. Oshun is a love Goddess that shares many attributes with Yemaya. Oshun rules the rivers, while Yemaya rule's the oceans and essentially all waters upon the earth. Yemaya rules over all fluids; our tears, our amniotic fluids, our saliva, our womanly juices, waterfalls, showers, all expansive waters are her domain. When she rides or possesses her *servituer* in religious rites and ceremonies they often dance a sultry rhythmic dance that mimics the swaying ocean waves.

Yemaya is a beautiful, highly recognized Orisha that personifies the great expansive, sacred element of water. She is the compassionate mother that illustrates for us the gifts of nurturance, healing and love. Invoke her energy to explore self-love and acceptance, and to further learn ways to Mother yourself best.

KUAN –YIN/Quan Yin/ Guanyin/Kuanyin

Kuan-Yin is the Chinese Buddhist and Taoist Deity of Compassion and Mercy. Her full name is Kuan-shih-yin and it translates as, *"She Who Listens to the World's Sounds."* More specifically, it refers to, *"She, who hears the cries of humanity."* Kuan-Yin is by far one of the most recognized and embraced ancient deities across China. Her worship can be traced as far back as the first century and she continues to be a Goddess highly venerated today.

In ancient Sanskrit she is known as *Padma Pani*, which translates as, *"Born of the Lotus."* Early Sanskrit Buddhist scriptures speak of Kuan-Yin and the *Lotus-Sutra*, which was later translated into Chinese, delves into her worship and her illustrative myths. The section of the *Lotus –Sutra* that highlighted Kuan Yin's worship, was later re-titled and redistributed as, *Kuan-Yin-Sutra* by the Chinese. These scriptures along with many other writings helped to spread the worship of Kuan-Yin even further.

It is important, however, to recognize certain paramount observations about Kuan-Yin. She is renowned as the Chinese female Buddhist, Bodhisattva Avalokitesvara. In early Sanskrit Buddhism the Avalokitesvara is male but by the 11th century it is clear through many of the early writings of the time that this female deity was becoming more prevalent. Avalokitesvara incarnates in many forms but the distinct presence of Kuan-Yin as a Goddess reveals itself more definitively between the 10th and 11th century.

By the 11th century, Kuan-Yin becomes fully embraced as a female deity and a revered manifestation of Avalokitesvara. She is closely connected to the Tibetan White Tara. Tara is a Tibetan Buddhist Goddess who was believed to have been born from the tear shed for humanity's suffering, by the Buddha. She is the female Tibetan Buddha and Kuan-Yin shares many similar attributes to Tara. Both are recognized as female manifestations of the Avalokitesvara.

Kuan Yin is a Buddhist-Chinese deity. She is embraced as the archetypal Goddess of Mercy and Compassion. She is the Celestial one who hears the cries of humanity. As a beloved Matriarchal deity she is connected to the Sheng Mu, the Holy Mother, the Goddess of pregnancy and bringer of children. In this aspect she becomes a very personal deity that is welcomed and venerated by her devotee in their homes and businesses. Her connection to Buddhism is not as magnified in this aspect but her role as a Goddess of fertility, protector of women, mothers, and bringer of children is strongly highlighted.

Kuan-Yin is also association with the Goddess Matsu. Her connection to Matsu links her worship as that of a Goddess that protects fisherman and all who are connected to the sea. Hence her worship grew near coastal towns where she became a protector and patron Goddess for all who traveled by sea. There are numerous shrines and temples dedicated to Kuan-Yin. The island of P'u t'o loka was the place of her erected first temple, which became one of many shrines and temples created for her. Here, her worship exponentially propagated and eventually spread to nearby regions. It is clear her worship spread not only across China but eventually spread to the west. The plethora of images, sculptures, shrines, temples and personal home altars to Kuan-Yin only support and illustrates how widely embraced she has been throughout the years as a Goddess much revered.

DEPICTIONS

The myriad of diverse images of the Goddess, Kuan –Yin, makes her and her worship more accessible to us and helps us better understand this extraordinary, matriarchal deity. When we look closer at some of her depictions throughout the centuries we get a better glimpse into Chinese culture and this much revered ancient deity.

Often she is depicted dressed in a flowing white robe, to symbolize her unquestionable purity. She has a strong association with water and thus, she is often seen holding a slim vase/jug filled with her sacred restorative waters. It's interesting how water is typically seen as connected to the realm of emotions and so she is very much linked with this sacred component. She is the one who cries for humanity and feels deeply the struggles and pain of the human race. Her blessed waters are described as always offering transformation, rebirth and vitality. She is also seen holding a Willow tree branch which she uses to wet and sprinkle those she chooses to bless with healing. The Willow tree is known as the first tree to bloom in the spring and the last tree to give up its leaves in autumn and thus, its powerful symbolism is connected to Kuan Yin. This Goddess has also been illustrated holding a peach. The peach is a symbol connected to longevity and youthfulness. In one of her famous legends the peach was given to her so that she would not hunger or thirst during her long journey to P'u-t'o-Shan/ P'u t'o loka (a special island off the coast of Southeast China, this would become the site of her first sacred temple in 847AD). Kuan Yin has also been depicted on a white Lotus and ridding dragons and Tigers. In one of her myths she is transformed into a Tiger and rescued from harm.

Often Kuan –Yin is seen with two attendants by her side; a young male to her right and a young female to her left. Devotional piety is exemplified by her young male attendant, *Shen-ts'ai*; his name means Golden Youth. According to one legend, one day, he approached the Goddess vowing complete devotion. In an effort to test his devotion she staged her death; falling from a high cliff. He immediately and selflessly chased after her to try to rescue her but found his own demise instead. The Goddess was so moved by his bravery and devotion that she brought him back to life and made him her attendant.

The female figure to her left represents steadfast piety. Known as, Lung-nu, her name translates as *Jade Maiden*. She was the grand-daughter of the Naga King who was sent to deliver a special repayment gift to the Goddess at P'u -t'o- Shan. Kuan Yin had rescued the King's son and he wanted to show his gratitude by offering the Goddess a "luminous pearl." The young maiden presented the Goddess with this magickal pearl which facilitated her ability to read the scriptures in darkness, at night, and had many other magickal usages. Upon meeting the Goddess the young maiden felt so captivated and inspired that she begged to be accepted as a student of Buddhism. Kuan Yin placed her as one of her attendants, after she succeeded proving her devotion.

HER MYTH

As an ancient Chinese deity one can expect many stories and legends connected to this Goddess. One myth in particular, written in the 11th century, speaks of how she came to be and it is the story of a noble princess that lived in 700 B.C.

King Miao Chuang had three daughters. His youngest was named Miao Shan. They say that when she was born, they knew she was special because there were indications on her actual body that she was of noble blood and possibly the incarnation of a holy person. As she grew older she exemplified unusual traits not commonly regarded in a royal princess. She dressed in plain clothes and carried herself in a way that would prove she indeed was not your average young lady.

Her two older sisters married, as was the custom, but when it was time for Miao's wedding to be arranged, she protested. She wanted to renounce the world, much like the Buddha himself. She told her father that she did not wish to marry, instead she wanted to become a Buddhist nun but this did not sit well with her regal father, who had great expectations of her imperial wedding. His daughter appeared very rebellious in her protest, something eschewed in Chinese culture but after much resistance the King finally gives in. He sends her away to a special monastery. However, he arranges for his daughter's stay at this monastery to be nightmarish, in the hopes his daughter would give up the idea of becoming a Buddhist nun. He asks the attendants at the monastery to be extra harsh on Miao and overwhelm her with numerous tasks and harsh labor that she was not accustomed to doing. Miao Shan, however, took on all her responsibilities apparently with great joy. She was in her element being of service at the monastery. It appeared she was able to magickally accomplish all of the tasks she was given, even those that seem nearly impossible to do. Some say she had celestial aid intervening on her behalf to help her because it was the only way to explain how she was able to complete some of these arduous tasks. It seemed there was no way of discouraging Miao Shan from her devotion to her compassionate vocation. Upon hearing of his daughter's progress at the monastery her father became enraged. It is said he became so infuriated that he lashed out and killed his daughter or, according to one version of the story, had her executed. He was so enraged that he destroyed and burned down the monastery. As with most ancient myths there are varied versions to the ending of this tale. Some claim Miao manages to escape her father's execution, another version tells she is rescued by a spirit and turned into a tiger. And yet another version she is killed and actually descends to the land of the dead where she becomes much like the Greek Goddess Persephone; a compassionate attendant to the dead. In the realm of the dead, Miao devotes herself to caring for the sorrowful dead; nurturing them compassionately, serving them food, quenching their thirst and changing the entire energy of this darkened realm. Her light and compassion nearly eradicates the land of the dead. She eventually gets removed from this realm and gets sent back to earth to reenter her body and become the Goddess Kuan-Yin.

Meanwhile, the murderous king is not free from his atrocious crimes against his pious daughter. He finds himself battling with a deadly disease that is resistant to any medicinal cure. A monk finally exams him and prescribes an unusual cure that apparently can only be performed by the severed arms and eyes of a living person that is free of anger. The king resigns himself to never being cured because he doesn't believe such a person exists in the world but the monk assures him there is one person who can help. The king sends word out that he is in dire need of help. His daughter Miao Shan, hears of her father's terminal condition and in her usual compassionate nature, she willingly sacrifices her arms and eyes to help heal her father. As the tale continues, the king becomes healed and later learns that it was his daughter who helped him. They reunite and Miao Shan then is transformed into the thousand armed and thousand eyes, Beloved Chinese Deity of Mercy and Compassion. This becomes yet another popular image she is often depicted as; the multi-armed, multi-eyed Goddess.

In this story we can also see her important connection to the dead and the afterlife. She becomes known as a savioress, not just to the living, but to those suffering, lost souls, in this dark realm. She becomes like a mediator between the living and the dead, helping the deceased transition into the land of the dead. Chinese believed the living had an obligation to their deceased ancestors. Those living were supposed to perform rites and prayers to assure that their deceased ancestors would not suffer too much in the realm of the dead. The Goddess Kuan-Yin is called upon to help in theses distinct sacred rites and assure the nurturance of the beloved deceased ancestors.

The Buddha, initially in ancient Tibetan and Buddhist scriptures, was presented as a male figure and that was pretty consistent until about the middle of the 10th century, possibly even earlier. Little by little the presence of a female Buddha started to reveal itself in these early writings and by the 11th century it was clear there was a noteworthy change and an important addition to the pantheon of Chinese Gods. The female Buddha, Kuan-Yin, was now manifested as a highly revered matriarchal Goddess of Compassion. Her veneration was so great; it was believed that simply reciting her name, numerous times like in a mantra, would result in incredible miracles.

There are a plethora of personal accounts, documentations of devotees and their personal prayers answered by this great Goddess. Ancient Buddhist and Chinese scriptures reveal just how beloved and impactful this female deity became over time for the Chinese.

Part of her appeal for us as contemporary women, especially in the story about Miao Shan as Kuan-Yin, is her strong message about our own choice in the role we agree to play in society. For the Chinese, she is not only exemplary of a proper Buddhist in their culture; self-sacrificing, compassionate, renunciation of worldly possessions and merciful, but she exemplifies for us as women an admirable strength. In Miao Shan/Kuan-Yin, we see modeled for us great fortitude in standing our ground and a real examination of women's role in society. We see in Kuan-Yin not just a merciful, compassionate figure but also a rebellious, tenacious spirit that exercises her choice, which in ancient times women often didn't appear to have many choices. In Chinese culture, upon penalty of death, you were expected to obey your parents and then you were expected to obey your husband and it appeared you didn't have much of a choice in your role or the direction of your life, for all was decided for you. In the ancient scriptures, Kuan-Yin as Miao Shan, stood her ground and crafted for herself her divine choice. She saw, perhaps, a freedom from the oppressive role as a wife and mother and instead saw her inherent womanly gifts of nurturance and compassion as best, serving humanity. For Miao Shan, becoming a Buddhist nun was a more suited choice in alignment with who she was and what she strongly believed was her life purpose and this is incredibly empowering for women to witness. There is great power in recognizing our choice and exercising that power.

The legend of Miao Shan and Kuan-Yin's presence is also a powerful teacher about Justice, Karmic balance, temperance and forgiveness; which ultimately leads to our own inner liberation and enlightenment.

For a matriarchal, female Chinese deity to command such monumental veneration; beloved increasingly throughout the centuries, by not only the Chinese but across foreign lands as well, it's profoundly noteworthy. Her shrines and temples (both personal and public) were numerous in ancient times and they continue to flourish even now, centuries later. As in ancient times, Kuan-Yin is unquestionably a powerful deity for us to connect with as women and she awakens our own gifts of fortitude, compassion, nurturance and empowerment.

MAIA

Maia, is the Greek Goddess of Springtime. She who is bright joy, love, frivolity, fecundity, and blossoming flowers. She who is beautiful and maternal, nurturing and makes the flowers grow, in the spring. Maia is the patron Goddess of nursing mothers and a deity deeply connected to theme of mothering. In this chapter, Maia takes her rightful place among the many matriarchal deities we are exploring together as part of our journey.

She was the eldest daughter of the strong Titan, sky holder, Atlas, and the Oceanid, Pleione. She is one of the seven Pleiades sisters. They were known as Taygete, Elektra, Alcyone, Asterope, Kelaiono, Merope and Maia.

Her name is often linked with the word mother but for the ancient Greeks, her name meant, "She who is great." Maia was also connected with several other deities like Bona Dea and Magna Mater.

Upon deeper inspection of the name Maia, we can see evidence of her chthonic origins. Within her name we see "aia," a reference to the Earth; more specifically underneath the ancient Earth.

According to Greek mythology, Maia became one of many of Zeus' secret lovers. Together they birthed Hermes, the cunning God of travelers, boundaries, languages, eloquence, commerce and magick. Hermes was also known as Mercury, the emissary and messenger of the Gods. He had a reputation for being a trickster and was even known to be a God of thieves. Because he was attributed for discovering magick, Maia has often been given the title, Grandmother of magick.

Maia was known as a Mountain Nymph (nature spirit) and found herself living most of her life in Mount Cyllene in Arcadia. She gave birth in this region and remained there to protect herself, and her son, from Hera's jealous wrath. Maia's maternal nature is evident throughout the Greek myths. She was reported to have raised Arcas, the child Callisto had with Zeus, when her mother was turned into a Bear by the jealous Hera.

In Latin, Maius, was the month of May. As one can surmise by looking at her name, the month of May was sacred to her. The celebrations most Pagans revel in as part of their Beltane celebrations are connected to the Greek Goddess of May, Maia. Annually, a May Queen would be crowned at this lively ecstatic holiday. We also cannot dismiss how all Mothers are venerated in the U.S.A. on Mother's day in the month of May.

As you connect with the Goddess Maia, it is a perfect time to reflect on all the mothers you are blessed to know; Your mother, your grandmothers, and your Great-grandmothers, as well as your aunts and elder aunts. It is a good time to create an honoring rite to your matriarchal lineage by gathering photos of all the women in your family herstory and lighting a votive candle for each woman or offering a potted plant or flower to each. Contemplate on aspects of their lives and the impact its had on your own. You may be inspired to quietly gaze at the photos to receive spiritual messages from your maternal ancestors.

Take this moment to pause and reflect on your own personal journey towards Motherhood (whether you are a mother now or hope to be one someday). You can make a special pledge to yourself to nurture, love and mother yourself in the healthiest manner or you can send out Universal love to all mothers. As part of our theme in this chapter you are invited to explore and honor the Archetype of the Mother.

ASHERAH

We first learn about Asherah through the Ugaritic documented mythologies of the 14th century BCE but evidence of her existence can be traced three centuries before this time. Asherah is a Pre-biblical; Canaanite Goddess whose worshipped was tenaciously found throughout various tribes in ancient times as far back as 1750 BCE. The Creatress, known as the consort of the Canaanite Chief God of the heaven's, El, and later, controversially, coalesced and addressed as the wife of Yahweh, upon Christianity's inception, her worship was unquestionably cemented in the inhabitants of this land in the far and Middle East.

Some suspect that her numerous names in various regions were; Elath (meaning Goddess and the feminine aspect of the God, El), also Athirat, Atharat, Astarte, Ashtorah, Ashratum, Ashrurah. And there still exist confusion regarding her titles and attributes in various regions, as they are used interchangeably in the writings of the time. The bible also seems to indistinguishably address her as both Asherah and Ashtarte, Astarte. It is clear from archeological findings and writings of this period that Israelite, Perizzites, Hittites, Hivites, Jebusites, Amorites, shared in the Canaanite's love and veneration of this great mother Goddess and the cult of her son Ba'al.

In Southern Arabia she was known Atharath, in Egypt as Qudsu (meaning Holy One) and in Sumeria and Akkadia she was known as wife to the supreme chief God, Anu. There, she was more commonly known as, Ashratum, a specific name found on excavated 14th century BCE artifacts, supporting her importance in this region.

She was known as a fertility deity called upon by "cursed" barren women, as well as for agricultural blessings. She was creatress, mistress of sexual rejoicing and she who facilitated childbirth. As Qudsu, she was the revered Holy one. Asherah was considered Mother of all the Gods, princes and Kings, and as the one who suckled and nurtured both mortals and gods alike. In particular she was mother of the seventy deities in the Ugaritic pantheon, which included; Ba'al, her son, and Anath, her daughter.

As the supreme mother Deity and one of the first Goddesses worshipped and embraced by the Hebrews, who shared the land with the Canaanites, in the area of Palestine now, her worship was incised in the root of this region. At this time, numerous intermingling of marriages and religious practices was common, thus it was assumed that in marriage one naturally took on the gods of their marital partners.

In Judah, Rehoboam, the son of Naamah (an Ammonite and wife of King Solomon) marries Maacah, who helps spread the worship of Asherah in this region, as she was a known priestess of the Goddess. Another example of how the intermingling of marriages between different people of different tribes promulgated Asherah's worship is in the story of Jezebel and King Ahab. In Samaria, when the King Ahab, married Jezebel, yet another Sidonian Princess, the worship of Asherah again took center stage in this region. Jezebel ordered a more elaborate carved wood image of the Goddess (which it appears had been destroyed at an earlier date) and she had this sacred Goddess and her image placed in the center of Samaria- contributing even further to the growing popularity of this revered maternal Goddess. Another perfect example of the contribution of intermingling of tribes is found in the tales of King Solomon and his extraordinary First Temple of Jerusalem in the mid 1oth century BCE, documented in the bible and the writings of the time. This temple was dedicated to the monotheistic Israelite God, Yahweh, during King Judah's reign. Although the bible states Solomon loved Yahweh, it also claims that Solomon, was easily led astray by his old age and his many wives (700 wives and 300 concubines to be exact), in his controversial idolatry and polytheistic religious practices. King Solomon married numerous wives from various nations in his effort to gain power, wealth and allegiances. Naturally every one of his wives brought to their union, and consequently, their home in the temple, the worship of their respective gods. The Temple of Solomon had multiple sanctuaries and became known as the sacred place of worship, there were numerous deities from different pantheons who were being worshipped here, as this was Solomon's way of accommodating his numerous wives. In particular, he is credited for introducing the worship of Asherah to the people of Jerusalem, as his first wife (at the start of the building of the Temple) was a Sidonian princess, daughter of the Pharoah and a beloved priestess of Asherah. Clearly we see reflected here, the new religion of Yahweh being practiced among the existing and well established polytheistic religions of neighboring regions.

Solomon's father, King David, was attributed for unifying Israel and was to formulate the first house of Jerusalem for Yahweh but he was not able to complete this task and it was left up to his son to fully accomplish this ambitious feat. Most significantly, the Temple of Solomon was meant to house the treasured "Ark of the Covenant" and Mose's Ten Commandments, received on Mt. Sinai. It was Jerusalem's First temple reputed to exalt Yahweh, the tenets of this new monotheistic religion and unite Israel but this is in direct contrast to the numerous finding and writings about King Solomon's temple true function.

The temple itself shared many similarities to Pagan temples of old, in particular, its three section structure with; a Vestibule, Nave, Inner sanctuary was identical to a ninth century Pagan temple in Canaanite and Syria. King Solomon also used a Tyrian craftsman called Hiram Abif (tribe of Naphtali) to help build it, including the two distinguished Pillars made of brass, a common metal often incorporated in Pagan Temples, like the one in Hazor. It becomes quite evident that King Solomon's Grand Temple in Jerusalem, though initially built by Yahweh's command and counsel, was heavily inspired, influenced and created with Pagan polytheistic ideals.

Interesting to note, it was also documented that a King, in the land of Amorite (yet another region known for Asherah worship) was known as Abdu-Ashirta, which translates as "slave of Asherah" proof of his personal devotion to the great Goddess and an indication of her reverence and popularity in this region as well. In some of the writings, we also learn about Asherah's servant who was called, Qadesh wa-Amrur, which translates as, *"Fisherman of the Lady Asherah of the Sea."* This reveals a distinct connection this Goddess had with the Sea.

Some documents translate the name Asherah as meaning; *"She who walks on the Sea."* Her worship in the independent seaport towns of Tyre and Sidon, which were near the Mediterranean coastline, made the water's ocean a vital part of the people's wellbeing and garnered her the name, "Lady of the Sea." There are also many other indications of her strong prevalence at this time. There were towns and seaports with her name like, Elath (which is one of her many titles, the female aspect to her Consort El) it was in the south gulf of Aqaba and titles like, Elath of Sidon and Asherah of Tyre that also reflect the importance of this Goddess.

DEPICTIONS OF ASHERAH

There are some conflicting mysterious stories regarding Asherah's actual appearance. In the Hebrew Bible and the writings of the time, she was depicted as an actual wood pole, set up, planted in the ground near the altars to her son, Ba'al and she was often closely linked to his popular cult following. Yet, the altars to her son did not have the same weight or meaning as the actual planted sacred pole known as the Asherah herself. She was often depicted as a tree and or groves - sometimes addressed as singular and sometimes in the plural form. Most often she is described as a sacred carved elaborate wood pole, planted firm in the earth. Some say an obelisk represented her, as well as the Pagan, modern day phallic, Maypole.

Though the harsh rainy climate of Palestine was not conducive to preserving much archeological evidence of Asherah's sacred wood pole artifacts, we do find plenty of evidence in the writings of the time on clay tablets and even within the Hebrew bible. Numerous archeological evidence of Asherah's dominance in the polytheistic worship of ancient Israel and the whole of the far and Middle East is found in the survival of a multitude of naked female figurine statues made of clay. These were small figurines with large pronounced breast, protruding bellies and the hands upholding, cupping, the breasts in a sign of nurturance. And the most fascinating discovery was that these clay figure religious artifacts were found in archeological sites near and within residential homes, proof that Asherah was not only a Goddess revered in public, communal town rituals, but her worship extended privately and more intimately in the homes of ancient women. This was clearly indicative of a Goddess who was so revered and loved that she was worshipped in formal public rites, as well as in domestic religious practices of women at the time.

BIBLICAL EVIDENCE

Asherah is mentioned at least forty different times in the Hebrew's Bible. Several times in the Old Testament she is documented as the "Queen of heaven;" Jeremiah 44:17-21 and Jeremiah 7:17-18

*"The Children gathered wood, the fathers kindled fire
and the women knead the dough to make cakes to the Queen of heaven
and to pour out drink offerings unto gods..."*

An invocation to Asherah found on a 7th century BCE artifact tablet, invokes the Goddess for help with fertility and childbirth and it is believed that in the very early chapters of the Hebrew bible, (Genesis 30:10-13) we encounter Leah who actually names Zilpah's son, Asher. This is an obvious reference and namesake to the Goddess Asherah who was clearly invoked for childbirth blessings and highly venerated during this period. It also hints at the likelihood that the worship of Asherah was occurring simultaneously with other deities, including Yahweh.

The book of Judge (Judges 6:25-32) reveals yet again the worship of Asherah and the poor attempt to eradicate it by the son of the town Chieftain and devoted Priest of the Goddess -Joash the Abiezrite. In the town of Ofra, in the 12th century BCE, his son Gideo ends up destroying the town's beloved Asherah and altar to Ba'al and manages to escapes the town's persecution due to his father's prestigious position as the Priest of Asherah.

Another interesting set of passages in the Hebrew bible indicative of obstinate Pagan worship alongside Yahwenism is found in *Ezekiel 8*. The chapter begins with...

*"...and it came to pass in the sixth year,
in the sixth month in the fifth day of the month...."*

Perhaps this is the month of August, as August in Latin translates as Sextilis, the sixth month, and was considered the sixth month during Augustus Caesar's reign. This coincides with the Harvest and a time when the sun's strength was viewed as dying and waning.

One can only surmise that for people who depended on the fertility of their land, this was a time when they were more intimately invested in the nature deities that would assure their land's sustainable wellbeing and thus their own livelihood.

*Ezekiel 8:14- "Then he brought me to the door of the gate
of the Lord's house, which was towards the North;
and behold, there sat women weeping for Tammuz..."*

This passage reveals that the women worshipped **inside** the temple and clearly they were not worshipping Yahweh, but rather a highly venerated Pagan Sun God, Tammuz. They were described as loudly crying, mourning, wailing for Tammuz and this was viewed as normal. It was a common practice and not viewed as strange, as it was customary, at the time, to perform agricultural rites to manifest much needed rain for the land and they were doing this in the "house of Yahweh in Jerusalem." Women in their power, in ancient times, were the ones who **could** do this. Women, so closely linked to the Mother Goddess Asherah, were the ones that magickally bled once a month, connecting to the Divine Moon and evidently produced new life and gave birth. Women's power was clearly visible for ancient indigenous cultures and it is only later that it becomes perverse by patriarchy and monotheism; with lies, degradations, oppression and manipulations. And thus, at this time, women inside the holy temples actively involved in performing rituals to manifest rain, to help the crop of the land, by wailing and shedding their own tears (performing a type of sympathetic magick rite) for the Sun God Tammuz, is quite indicative of women's power at this time. It is in total contrast to what their role would develop years later at the hands of oppressive monotheistic religions. At the very least, this short passage reflects the acknowledgment, respect and power that women held as active participants in priestessing and worshipping the Gods of ancient times in Jerusalem.

*Ezekiel 8:16- "And he brought me into the inner court of the Lord's house,
and behold, between the porch and the altar,
were about 5 and 20 men, with their backs towards the Temple of the Lord,
and their faces towards the East; and they worshipped the Sun towards the East..."*

Again, this is reflecting the important worship of the Sun God/ the son of the Goddess, in the Temple. The Hebrew bible also reveals that women often weaved cloths for the Goddess Asherah **inside** the temple and they worked in the Holy Temples in numerous capacities, although they would essentially be described in the Hebrew bible as being temple prostitutes; a terminology also used very loosely for men employed in the temples as well. This was a debasing way to discredit women and the worship of the Goddess during a time when monotheism was trying to assert itself upon the people.

The most fascinating, controversial finding, relating the Goddess Asherah to the monotheistic God, Yahweh is discussed in *"The Biblical Archeology Review,"* Vol. 5, No.2 (March/April 1979), pp24ff. It shares a more recent discovery, an inscription dated from the 8-9th century BCE, found at Kuntillet Ajrud, in the North East Sinai Peninsula, South of Israeli and Egyptian border and it reveals a most telling inscription on large storage jars (*pithoi*) artifacts.

"May you be blessed by Yahweh and his Asherah."

This is a most illuminating inscription and some speculate that it reveals a special relationship between the new God, Yahweh and the established ancient Pagan mother Goddess, Asherah. There was another discovery on a tomb at Khirbet -El-Qom which was noted for having a similar inscription. These discovered inscriptions and blessings like; *"Yahweh of Samaria and his Asherah"* and *"Yahweh of Tenan and his Asherah...."* and *"May Uriyahu* (a governor at the time) *be blessed by Yahweh, my guardian and by his*

Asherah, save him Uriyahu.." an inscription dated from the 750-700BC *(Biblical Archeology Review, Vol. 10, No. 6 (Nov./Dec. 1984)pg. 42.)* indicates a possible connection between these two deities. And clearly the proselytized monotheistic initial views of Judaism and Christianity are highly challenged when we find these numerous findings connecting Asherah (a Pagan Goddess) to Yahweh (the new God claiming monotheism as the **only** way). Two Gods are clearly being venerated in these inscriptions and the presence of Asherah's name becomes quite intriguing, especially when we know her importance across numerous tribes in the far and Middle East.

These blessing inscriptions reveal the Goddess as Yahweh' right hand, worshipped simultaneously with the new, Hebrew God, contradicting the monotheistic claim of early Yahwenism. It is rather convoluted how Asherah is represented in the old testament of the bible. Sometimes she appears as a wood pole, sometimes as a place. In some other documents she is "*his Asherah,*" and then sometimes she is simply a sacred attribute. Some believe, this confusion was purposely created to diminish her importance and trivialize her great power and hold on the people. As one can surmise, the Bible, written exclusively by men in support of the new monotheistic, patriarchal religion, obviously fulfilled their agenda in maintaining the worship of the Feminine Divine veiled and behind the new God, named Yahweh. It helped implement and establish the supremacy of men over women. Anything that did not support their new patriarchal ideologies was omitted, altered or disregarded and purposely obscured. Yet, the great Goddess Asherah is actually mentioned forty times in the Hebrew bible, which reveals how powerful and prevalent her presence had to have been at this time in the ancient far and Middle East.

The people cleaved to Asherah, and her worship, for centuries even after the introduction of Yahweh and it wasn't until threats, violent manipulations and coercions and the risk of persecution did her worship begin to slowly wane, for as always, those with physically mightier armies and political influence, sadly have the power to oppress and eradicate a mass of people as we have seen throughout history.

HER CONECTION TO TREES

In researching, unearthing, learning and connecting to this great ancient Mother Goddess, I couldn't help but notice how often she was associated with trees, groves, high mountain tops and carved wood poles. Writings of the time actually reveal that the wooden pole was more than just a symbol of the Goddess; it was revered as the Goddess herself. As a result, it had more weight and value than the very altars created for her son, Ba'al, which lay beside her. The altars were a place of offering but the carved wooden pole was viewed as the Goddess herself. And ironically enough, while the altars to Pagan gods like Ba'al were quick to be destroyed by overzealous Yahwenist, the large Asherah poles that stood next to them and Asherah's strong worship was not so quick to be pulverized nor obliterated. Her worship, as is evident from excavated artifacts and the writings of the time, lingered, permeating several regions, long after the introduction of monotheism and it appeared her tenacious worship was coalesced with that of the new Yahweh.

Throughout the Hebrew bible there are numerous references and warnings about idolatry via the tree aka Asherah. And we must also remember in Genesis, the introduction of the tale of the forbidden fruit in the esteemed Tree of Knowledge, of which Adam and Eve were reputed to have eaten from before being cast out of the Garden of Eden. All this talk about trees made me wonder why the big taboo concerning trees and what could possibly be so threatening; within the tree, nature, the moon, the sun and stars and Asherah's worship, to this new monotheistic deity coming into the foreground.

     Then I began to muse on trees and how numerous cultures have important folklores related to trees. I started to take a closer look at women and how intimately similar our attributes can appear to that of actual trees but I suppose the same can be said for so much in nature divinely reflects woman; from the moon, the ocean, the yoni shaped flowers and sea shells, to the erupting cavernous volcanoes, thunder and rainstorms.

     Trees give forth life, sustain life and yet, in them, we see its cycles of life, death and rebirth; as it appears fruitless, leafless in the winter and then returns to its fullness, fruitfulness and splendor in the Spring and Summer. It nurtures and sustains humanity with oxygen and its fruits and thus, since the beginning of time, humanity has relied on its existence. Sacred regenerative principles are easily palpable in trees, the same regenerative qualities in "wombmyn"/woman's biological make up. I suppose this can be quite threatening to the rise of patriarchy.

     The veneration of trees has existed in numerous ancient cultures and religions since the beginning of time. In Scandinavian Norse Mythology there is the Ygdrasil tree, that connects the various nine worlds; from the underworld, axis, middle, halls of the gods, heavens etc... It is a pivotal vehicle for spiritual journeying. In Genesis, as already stated, the Tree of Knowledge had fruits that were forbidden due to its inherent ability to awaken truths and spiritual knowledge, but through the offer from Lilith (as the serpent) it brought about major shifts and an awakening to both Eve and Adam, that according to biblical scriptures changed the course of humanity forever. In Egypt there is reference to the Sycamore tree being utilized by the Goddess to feed the dead souls as they journey to the underworld. For Buddhist, it was the Bhodi tree that passed enlightenment and wisdom to the Buddha. In Jewish Mysticism, known as the practice of Kabbalah, the most hallowed tree was the Ash Tree, which connected the sacred realms. It is depicted as an upside down, inverted tree, in which the roots originate in the heavens and the branches reach down through the ethers, to the earth. The Goddess Shekhinah is believed to imbue this tree with her divine energy and light according to Cabbalistic lore. The special branches of this sacred tree are known as "emanations" or sephiroth, and there are believed to be ten, which humanity is behooved to journey and work through. Interesting to note this number ten, as the day of Ashurah (*Aashrurah*, *Ashurah*, *Aashoorah*) for Muslims it is considered the 10th day of Muharram and the word *Ashrurah* is interpreted in Arabic as "ten." According to Islamic lore, the beloved grandson of Muhammad, Husayn Bin Ali, was killed by Umayyard, at the battle of Karbala (Iraq) and this day commemorates the tragedy of this event with mourning. The name Ashurah is clearly connected to the name of our venerated ancient Tree Goddess, Asherah. There are some scholars that link the ancient worship of Asherah to one of the most venerated symbols for modern day Jewish people - the menorah. The menorah resembles her sacred tree with its branches as the seven, sometimes ten, candlestick arms, holding the sacred lights so powerfully symbolic for Jews.

     Women and trees share a similar embodiment of fertility and the divine, with its sacred cycle of; birth, life, death and rebirth in the outwardly appearance of fruition in the summer and spring and then the barrenness so apparent in the winter season. It is quite fascinating to consider that one of the most beloved ancient mother Goddesses, Asherah, still lives on today, right before our very eyes as a living breathing Goddess, still exemplified in the tall, sky reaching trees that surround us today. In this sense, Asherah reminds me of the primordial Greek Goddess Gaia, which seems to transcend all cultures and time and space and yet in her role as a Sea Mother Goddess, I can't help but think upon the Orisha, Yemaya. Asherah, and her tenacious worship, was deeply loved in ancient pre-biblical times, so much so that perhaps we can still see glimmers of her strong veneration being transferred and carried through in the discovery of many other nurturing mother deities. The supreme Mother Goddess archetype continues to prove itself to be an important force for all women to connect with regardless of time and place and I believe Asherah to be a most powerful immortal Goddess for modern women to invoke in their respective lives.

Hail to you Asherah!

*Asherah is the embodiment of the mother archetype and reflects our beauty, fertility, sovereignty and staying power as women. She is the grounded energy of the fertile earth and reflects the beauty found in nature. She is the Canaanite Goddess of the Tree and will ask you to embrace the distinct sacred aspect of Trees, as admirable reflections of your womanhood.

THEME WORK SUGGESTIONS
5. MOTHER ARCHETYPE

Light a pink candle
In a special rite, light some incense and sit down to pen a letter
to your mother or to your grandmothers (whether alive or dead).
Write a letter to your future children or to your existing children.
Commit to one weekend, when you will pamper and nurture yourself
with good experiences; healthy food, a bubble bath, manicure/pedicure,
a good book or a movie to watch, good conversation,
Delve into anything that will nurture you and bring you fulfillment.

HEALING & PROTECTION THEME WORK SUGGESTIONS

These suggestions are not limited to this chapter. They can be explored and revisited when working with other themes throughout this book.

1. Incorporate Prayers, Invocations, Altar creations, Lunar and Goddess Rituals as often as you see necessary. Spend time in nature and Draw down the energy of the Full Moon.
2. Creativity: Engage your inner Muse and connect to the power of birthing and creating something uniquely yours.
3. To clear negative energy from your space or your body, use the sacred smoke of a Smudge wand of White Sage and Copal.
4. Journaling is a powerful source for healing. Connect to the cathartic power of your written words expressed freely in your own handwriting upon your journal.
5. Nutritional Healing: Cook with a specific intention and dine on healthy foods; ingesting specially prepared meals with a positive intention.
6. Fasting periods (ex; fast from anything of significance; sweets, chatting, sex, alcohol, etc).
7. Incorporate a daily practice of Trance, Meditation or Channeling work.
8. Body Awakening. Connect to the power within our physical body; sweat producing magick, and physical ecstasy. Tap into the runner's high, increase serotonin levels.
9. Freely connect to the spiritual practice of Dancing frenetically as a form of worship. Bring healing and your own vibrational elevation through dance.
10. Embodying/Evoking. When connecting to a deity you may feel called to embody this Goddess. It is a powerful process of allowing your body to become her vessel in order to aspect the Goddess and garner deeper understanding of her gifts.
11. Usage of the Sacred element of Water; use church Holy water, Rose water or Florida water to cleanse and bless yourself or your space.
12. Infusions. Using charged herbs and crystals you can incorporate these into a glass of drinking water or hot teas. Drink it with the intention of offering yourself healing.
13. Egg Clearing. The egg is an ancient sacred symbol of the Goddess and rebirth. Use it to scourge and purify yourself by rubbing it over your body like a magnetic bar of soap, with the intention to clear yourself of all negativity.
14. Sound Healing. There are so many ways you can explore this healing modality. You can use; bells, rattle, drumming, mantras, singing, music, tone vibrations, singing bowls, crying, laughter and simply your own voice to manifest powerful shifts in energies and healing.
15. Use traditional Witch Bottles for Protection, Honey Bottles for Love or Prosperity Bottles for money. They are contained bottles with varied herbals ingredients, charged with a specific intent.
16. Herbal Salt Baths and Beer Baths are traditionally used to cleanse and purify ourselves from negative vibrations and manifest Spiritual Healing.
17. Working with Animal Energy. As it has been introduced throughout this book, incorporating our animal allies in our spiritual healing work is invaluable as they become our teachers and protectors.
18. Creating Talisman, Amulet, Poppets or Herbal plackets. Gather & create special objects with specific intention. Using these objects found in nature, keep them near for blessings.
19. Crystals and Gemstones can be incorporated in your healing work. Place moon-charged gemstones under your pillow, in your baths, even in your undergarments, and use them in various ways to heighten their healing attributes for you.
20. To release something toxic or bring about healing you may write it down or have a symbol of what you are releasing. Take this written paper or item and you may burn it, bury it in the earth, or to suspend something you may freeze it.
21. Certain vegetable and fruits have been traditionally used for their varied spiritual properties like; Limes, Lemons, Onions, Apples, Pomegranates, Bay leaves, etc... You can pin your written petition to these items with a specific healing intention.
22. Mirror Rites can be incorporated into our Self-Love Blessings but you can also use a charged mirror to deflect something you don't want in your life.

JOURNALING

What does the word Mother mean to you personally?
_____
_____

How do you personally define a good mother?
_____
_____

Who do I mother now?
_____
_____

Do you have any pets or plants or nieces or children of your own?
_____
_____

How do I feel about my own mother?
_____
_____

How do I feel about myself as a Mother or if I am not a mother, do I wish to be one in the future?
_____
_____

What feelings come up when I consider becoming a mother?
_____
_____

How often do I treat or pamper myself?
_____
_____

Describe how I will nurture myself?
_____
_____

INVOCATION & POETRY

CORN MOTHER
Corn Mother hearing,
Corn Mother nurturing,
Corn Mother sacrificing,
Returning again.

Corn Mother, feeding us Love
Corn Mother, pulsating in each stalk
Corn Mother, hearing the hungry child
Unearthing, ruminating,
from her human flesh, creating.

Daily in the hut, secretly you squat,
Bringing forth the grain, that they
Demanded and sought.
They could not believe,
Nor accept this way to feed,
Divine Mother forgave them and
Knew it was time to leave.

Corn Mother hearing
Corn Mother nurturing
Corn Mother sacrificing
Returning again.

Corn mother, shedding her blood,
Seeing past the present,
into the great beyond
Preservation of her people,
May the Corn help them live on.

Corn Mother's blood
in each kernel we eat,
May we embrace all her rainbow parts.
Preservation of her children,
May we all return to her,
through our own awakened sacred
heart.

Corn Mother hearing
Corn Mother nurturing
Corn Mother sacrificing
Returning again.

Page 39 from "Goddess Grimoire Journal, a Collection of Simple Prose and Spells" by B. Melusine Mihaltses (Isbn# 9780985138431)

INVOKING THE MOTHER
Steadfast Mother,
Show me the way,
Heal burnt bridges
That once caused me pain.

Be the antidote,
That brings me true light.
Mother Goddess,
Sculpt me in this fight.

Nurture and protect me,
Teach me your gifts,
Fertile Creatress,
I am yours to lift.

Higher and higher,
I rise with you,
All of your traits
My soul now imbues.

Herein I awaken,
To the Mother within me,
This I make true now,
So mote it be!!!

***You are now encouraged to create your own altar(s) & invocation(s).
)O(Blessings!

MAGICK RITES & TOOLS

This is your personal page to document your sacred rites and the tools you elected to use.

DECIDE WHERE TO SET UP AN ALTAR
Place an Altar Cloth in the Color of your choice.
Color: _____

GODDESS
Place an image of your Deity.
Goddess: _____
This image can be a Statue, handmade Sculpture or a simple Photo _____

FIRE REPRESENTATION
Place a blessed/charged Candle in the color of your choice.
Candle Type and color: _____

AIR REPRESENTATION
Light your Incense stick.
Incense Scent: _____

WATER REPRESENTATION
Place a Chalice of Water
Water Item: _____

EARTH REPRESENTATION
Place a Potted Plant or Fresh Flowers on your Altar
Add Salt or a plate of Dried Herbs
Herbs: _____
Chosen Gemstone: _____

YOUR WISH

_____

_____

_____

Place a symbol of your desire, if you have one available, and also write your wish out clearly, on a piece of parchment paper, or you can even use a cut up brown paper bag. These are the basics for a very simple altar & rite. Ultimately, your sacred space is only limited by your imagination. You can make your altar & rite as big or as small as you prefer and the addition of other personal items is really up to you.)o(Enjoy!

ALTAR PHOTOS

"A Woman is the Full Circle, within her is the power
to create, nurture and transform…" Diane Mariechild

CHAPTER SIX

"I raise up my voice not so I can shout but so that those without a voice can be heard, we cannot succeed when half of us are held back" Malala Yousafzai

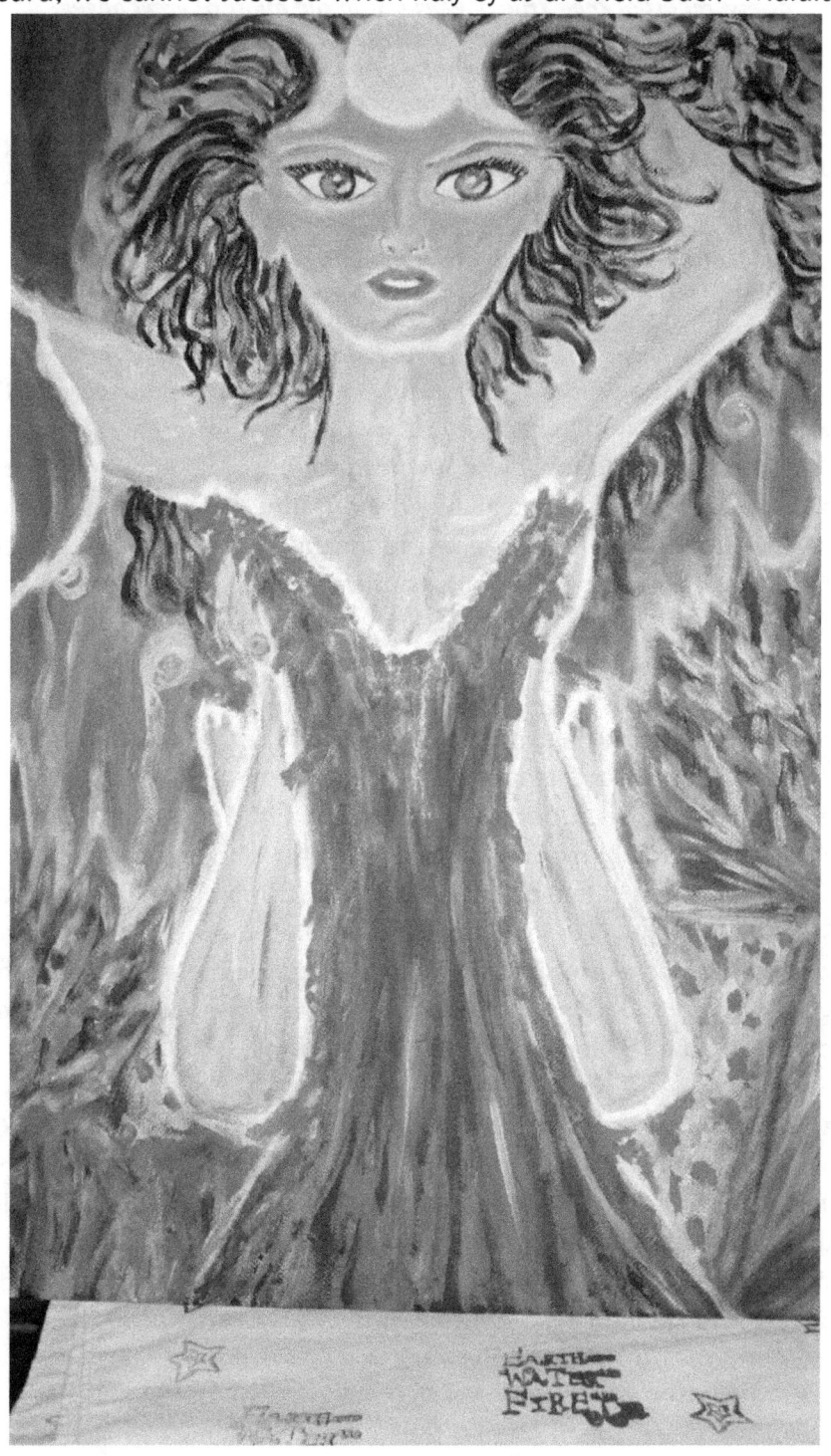

THEME: STRENGTH & RAGE

*I can tell you so much about anger and rage... how it has the
potential to deplete you of your true power or
lull you into a false sense of immediate supremacy.
I can tell you stories of witnessing those who had no knowledge
or awareness of their true power; lost in the midst of great anger
or sometimes unexpressed, buried rage....
I can tell you stories....through the eyesof a child witnessing rage,
from presumably responsible adults...
through the eyes of enablers, so blinded by the façade of love...
I can tell you stories of irresponsibly expressed anger, through the eyes of victims of abuse.
I can tell you stories of mothers & teachers witnessing
children sort and unravel their long entangled threads of fits of rage...
I can tell you stories...tales of raging storms within,
carefully suppressed and smothered into illnesses
and other toxic physical manifestations...
oh, the varied complex stories I can tell you of rage....*

We have reached the point in our journey where we are inducted into the powerful emotion of anger, and its capacity to awaken in us incredible strength, healing and massive transformation. No longer do we need to suppress, deny or hide our emotions for fear they go against societal expectations of us. We no longer have to fear feeling our powerful anger worried it might consume us in ways that are inconceivable and destructive. We can work to honor all of our emotions, including anger, and work with it; knowing it serves a higher purpose... knowing it can bring about productive changes and healing.

When we study various deities from different cultures we may be shocked to discover examples of Goddesses that are raw expressions of Rage and manifestations of a different face to empowerment. Goddesses like the Hindu Goddess, Kali who was born out of Durga's brow and the Egyptian Goddess, Sekhmet, who is another aspect of the benevolent Goddess, Hathor; these deities can sometimes intimidate a novice to the world of Goddess Spirituality. Yet these, sometimes gruesome looking, deities are powerful and much needed expressions of Women Empowerment. There are many throughout various ancient Goddess pantheons but in each one we see an expression of anger and how it is used to both destroy and create worlds.

As part of our work here, we meet with the archetypal energy of these Goddesses that speak to our souls about anger and its complexities; complexities that can have a significant affect our own spiritual journey. We see examples of how uncontrolled rage, unleashed out in the world, brings about destruction but it also can be a catalyst for healing and massive transformation. In other words; new worlds can be created if we hone into our rage and anger in a proper constructive way.

**"...Understanding has given us the power
to control the unconscious instincts represented by the lion.."...**

Page 190 Easy Tarot Guide by Marcia Masino copyrighted 1987

When I look at the Strength card in the Tarot deck it is a clear depiction of how the proper use of energy can subdue our inner lioness and put her energy to better use in a constructive manner rather than a destructive one. Our inner lioness is symbolic of our inner rage; anger that can be the much needed impetus for some massive powerful changes that sometimes cannot even commence without this catalyst. We reach a point in our journey where we touch upon the power of alchemy, where we allow anger and rage to be a transformative force used as our tool of empowerment.

As we have done before, in this chapter we will explore further our theme with the help of several resources. We will endeavor to connect with Goddesses Pele, Kali Ma, Sekhmet, Aine, Ereshkigal and the sacred animal energy of the Tiger. We will connect with our 3rd chakra, the Solar Plexus chakra, and gemstones that can help better facilitate this connection. We will also look at the corresponding Lunation and a Tarot card that is connected to our theme.

THE STRENGTH TAROT CARD

*"She uses her powers of
understanding to quiet the Lion – her desire nature;
no longer do her unconscious angers and phobias
dominate her attitudes and behavior..."*
Page 190 Easy Tarot Guide by Marcia Masino copyrighted 1987

The Strength card in traditional tarot decks often shows a beautiful woman in nature, dressed in white, stroking and calming the King of the Jungle; the most fearsome beast of all animals - a Lion. With her gentle touch she appears to subdue this ferocious creature and clearly has the skills to tame this beast. The card speaks of her ability to turn the natural primal rage of this powerful animal to work in her favor. It is a gift that we too can connect with if we consciously chose to.

We arrive at a pivotal point in our journey where we are asked to explore what is boiling within us, what is simmering with anger and how do we take that anger and use it in a constructive manner. How do we make sure that we're not being destroyed by our anger, or turning such a powerful emotion into self-sabotage or self-harm. Like the woman depicted in the Strength Tarot card, how do we utilize our primal attributes and transform them. For it is up to us to decide whether we want to be engulfed by this emotion or utilize it for something great. Like a magician, tapping into the power of Alchemy, we reach a point in our journey where we can decide how to utilize our emotions and transform them like gold to our spiritual growth. Our inner lioness can either engulf us into a destructive path or, if approached with reverence and awareness, can offer us a new reality.

MOON IN LEO FIRE/SUN

THEME: Strength & Rage

| **LEO** | **FIXED** | **FIRE** | **MASCULINE** | **LION** |

The Moon in Leo has garnered the reputation of being slightly dramatic. After all, when have we ever known, the renowned King of the Jungle, the Lion, to be unassuming or introverted? Lions command attention, don't they? With their flamboyant, long mane, unquestionable beauty and physical strength, and their brazen presence among the animal kingdom, it is no wonder why they command our admiration.

The astrological sign of Leo is actually a Fire sign and it is ruled by The Sun, the center of our Solar System. This fact alone explains why the Moon in Leo can be such a potent lunation for anything related to leadership, the entertainment industry and anything requiring great strength. When we combine the commanding energy of our Sun and the ferociously powerful symbol of the Lion, we can begin to understand the gifts this lunar transit can provide.

When working with this lunation, ask yourself where in your life can you use the spotlight that a moon in Leo will undoubtedly unveil. Where can you best use the lion's roar to command respect and attention? Often overlooked is how the Moon in Leo can awaken our voice and certain deep primal parts within us. A Leo moon is known to touch upon our inner child and any issues related to tending to it. This would include our creative impulses and our need for drama and attention.

Take a moment to reflect and consider where can its gifts of leadership, strength and showmanship support your own personal goals? Where do you need to connect with the strength of the Lion? Where can you utilize your inner roar to draw attention to something important in your life? And finally, what does your inner child require most of you? The moon in Leo can be indispensable and lends a most beneficent element to your determination, courage and powers of manifestation.

> *"Strength does not come from physical capacity,
> it comes from an indomitable will…"*
> *Mahatma Gandhi*

HERSTORY

A permanent scowl had imprinted itself on her once bright, naïve, smooth face…She knew she was no longer that gullible, hopeful, flawless face teen but it still shocked her, to be greeted, one morning, by the mirrored reflection of that angry scowl across her face. How long had that been there? She asked herself…. The question irrepressibly erupting only seemed to make her even angrier and the scowl… even deeper.

Yes, she was angry…there was much to be angry about in the world. I mean have you turned on the news lately? So many injustices in the world; governmental issues, gender equality, civil rights, human rights, animal right, so many issues that, if you're not angry, you must be asleep…. But she was fully awake and enraged by all she was seeing on a global scale.

On a personal level, well… that was a whole other *enchilada*… She had every reason to be enraged…her partner of over ten years was caught cheating on her with a saucy family member, the promotion at work she was promised was given to her nemesis, the rotten neighbor across the street keeps letting their dog poop on her front lawn and … well… shall we go on… She has much that is angering her these days but what she is doing with such a powerful emotion, like anger, is another subject all together that requires scrutiny.

She arrives at the unsuspecting, cathartic gate of Rage and Anger to learn that there is always a better choice in how we process such a cataclysmic emotion. Anger can either be a prison to misery, frustration, self-destruction and unresolved pain or it can be a powerful tool for radical change and even a great architect in our lives. She was ready to face her anger and utilize it to serve her as Strength….

********Take a moment to document here, or in your journal, your unique story.**
_____
_____

AFFIRMATION

**My strength comes from facing my anger
and using it to fuel change.**

**I recognize and honor my anger
and let it inspire my transformation.**

**There is strength in my roar: My voice HEARD becomes
my strongest weapon.
I wield my Anger as a tool of Empowerment and
allow it to fuel my inner strength**

CHAKRA & GEMSTONE WORK

3rd Chakra   **MANIPURA/NAVAL SOLAR PLEXUS CHAKRA**   **COLOR:** Yellow

Ego, willpower, impulses, anger, personal Power, our strength, desire, Confidence, interactions with others, realm of fire,

Mantra: I Am/ I Shine

)O(WORKING: Nurturance (emotional & Physical), Weight Loss Work

GEMSTONE CONNECTION: **Tiger's Eye** is a superb grounding gemstone of protection that enhances integrity, confidence, good fortune and strong will-power. It is a quartz stone, found in varying shades of light and dark brown. Sometimes referred to as, "Cats Eye," due to its appearance of a cat's pupil, it is reputed to help remove illusions, bring clarity and connect us with the proper use of power. It also has the ability to help us unearth, embrace and apply our hidden talents in a way that best serves our highest purpose. Tiger's Eye is known to promote wealth, happy travels and enhance good luck. There is also a belief that Tiger's Eye can bring to you just the right kinds of helpful people, at just the right time, thus, it is a most auspicious gemstone to work with. It has an obvious affinity to the element of earth.

GEMSTONE CHANNELING

We begin this work by first securing a safe place where our healing and meditation practice can occur without any interruptions or unnecessary stress. Find your sacred space to begin this work. If you can go outdoors in nature that would be most ideal but any place where you can relax, undisturbed, would be fine. The most important thing is to make sure you have a few free minutes of quiet and solitude to continue.

You are invited, to place yourself in a comfortable position; you may sit or lay down. If it is available to you, place in your hands the Tiger's Eye gemstone *that we are working with today. Take a moment to actually hold your* Tiger's Eye gemstone *and look at it carefully. Reflect on how it feels upon your hands. Does your gemstone feel hot or cold, rough or smooth? What thoughts are coming to mind as you hold this gemstone? (Pause) Hold your* Tiger's Eye gemstone *up and inspect it carefully for a few more minutes, in silence... Quietly, gaze upon it and make note of any thoughts or images that immediately start to unfold before you. (Pause)*

When you're ready, you may close your eyes now and begin this short meditation. As with all trance work, we begin with our breath. You are asked to take a deep breath, slowly filling up your lungs. Hold that inhalation for 3 seconds and then release it... Counting now at your own pace; breathe, 1, 2, 3, and exhale on 4....and again....breathe in, 1, 2, 3, and exhale on 4. Let's do this one more time and then quietly counting in your head.... Breathe 1, 2, 3...release on 4. (Pause) Breathe, trusting in the natural rhythm you have now established, of your relaxed inhalation and exhalation.

Tiger's Eye gemstone wishes to impart a special channeled message for you. See this gemstone in your mind's eye. See it shining brightly, embedded upon its dark, fertile, mother earth. Draw nearer to it and ask if it will allow you to pick it up. When permission is granted, gently gather it in your hands. (Pause) With your mind's eye, gaze upon it again; studying its various hues, its texture, its veins or any other specific details that captures your eyes.... Ask it to speak to you. (Pause)

Now visualize the top of your head opening. You may see it almost like a chalice; open and receptive to individual Spiritual messages that want to come through for you. Look for messages about how to unearth your inner strength and how to transform intense emotions for greater healing. You may envision your crown chakra now unveiling a magnetic Tiger's Eye Gemstone portal, allowing for this **Crystal Transmission** *to come through... (Pause)*

Bring your attention now, from your crown chakra to your belly area, near your Solar Plexus Chakra. Guide the energy of your Tiger's Eye Gemstone into your Solar Plexus chakra and see it cascading around this region. Continue to breathe. (Pause) When you feel you are ready, you may open your eyes and begin to write down any messages that came through for you. You may document them in the space provided below, or in your own personal journals.

TIGER PROTECTIVE ENERGY

The Tiger is respected as one of the most fierce, ferocious animals in the animal kingdom. They are popularly linked with courage, willpower, great passion, sovereignty, and inner strength. What greater ally and protector to have by our side as we delve deeper into this work?

Greatly revered in China, Africa, India and numerous other cultures, throughout history, tigers are attributed with the primal energy of the invincible warrior, the passionate fighter and the unstoppable victor. They are linked with the gift of leadership, courage, protection, tenacity, ambition, and confidence. For indigenous people and shamans, tigers are known as the walkers of the ancient path. They are the fearless, diviners of personal truths, beauty, grace and power; holding on to their strength and personal conviction. They are nocturnal beings that relish in their solitary freedom and unencumbered explorations. Their night vision is known to be six times better than any human. With their exceptionally keen sense of smell, hearing and sight, they are effective, silent hunters in the night; deliberately weighting carefully their strategy before an attack. Study a Tiger's approach to their prey and it will send shivers down your spine. They are invincible in combat and their powerful energy is unmatched.

Rests assure, when you are called by tiger's medicine, it will awaken your fiery courage and creativity, your inner and physical strength, and your ability to express your deepest feelings, with great passion. You will feel things at a heightened level. The Tiger is known as the awakener of our sensitivity. Because tigers are sensual beings; carrying themselves majestically in these sleek muscular bodies, they can awaken us to our own physicality and sensuality. We become more physically in tuned with our bodies and discover deeper levels to our senses.

Tiger's natural nocturnal tendency may find you being most productive and creative at night. And... suddenly all those things that you have been avoiding, due to fear or intimidation, become a welcomed challenge to exercise your new found courage.

Tiger energy offers a plethora of attributes worthy of further exploration. It offers us, willpower, in the face of adversity. It offers us passion, to pursue exactly what we desire. It also offers a fierce sense of focus, that is able to clear the mind of all distractions, and help us tap into the power of now.

The tiger loves to travel and roam the earth freely and typically alone. It has a curiosity and appetite for life that leads him to unexpected adventures and new terrains. For the most part, they are solitary beings that only come together with partners when they are ready to mate. Tigers will have a litter of cubs once, every three to four years, and their litter will vary, anywhere from a single birth, to six offspring. Mama tigers are known to be fiercely devoted mothers. Their baby cubs are born blind and thus, need to stay with their mother until around the age of two. It is not surprising that mothers keep a vigilant watch on their little ones for such a long time. Tigers also remind us of the value of our sanctuary to repose and gather our strength. After extraneous activities like hunting, fighting, birthing etc.... a tiger will require a period of rest and recuperation. It often has a den hidden in plain sight which no one will dare penetrate due to her ferocious protective nature. She is, after all, known to be very territorial and she knows her capacity to rest and recuperate will directly influence her success and survival in the wild. Among the numerous attributes already discussed here, Tiger energy also encourages you to spend time in complete solitude, in your personal lair or sanctuary, to luxuriate in your alone time and fully recharge yourself. Great courage and strength awaits you with the Tiger as your ally and protector.

THEME WORK SUGGESTIONS

Work with the Leo moon, symbolized by the Lion,
and work with The Tiger energy and the various
Goddesses offered here in this chapter.
Perform the Red Balloon Ritual offered in this chapter
or the Fire Purging Ritual.
Dance the expression of your anger.
Experiment with sound healing works like Mantras
and "breath work." Explore weather energies and connect
with the fierce energy of a Thunderous Rainstorm.

GODDESS EMPOWERMENT

KALI

The name, Kali comes from the word, *Kala*, which means, *time*. We quickly can see her divine connection to the element of time, space and the cosmos when viewing some of her myths. She is known both as a fierce Goddess in her own right and an aspect of the Hindu Matriarchal Goddess, Durga. Ancient text reveals that she was born from the powerful brow (third eye) of the Goddess Durga, in the midst of a gruesome war, fighting off an infinite number of the demons in the Universe. Durga's rage was so strong that she called forth the birth of Kali, to fight off demons and drink of their blood. According to the myth, each blood spilled by a slaughtered demon produced the birth of even more demons and thus, Kali's long red tongue was employed to prevent this vicious cycle and save the world.

Kali's depiction is one that not only raises eyebrows but is meant to evoke great fear in the uninitiated spectator. She is often depicted naked, with garlands of skulls and aprons of dead severed limbs on her black (or dark blue) colored flesh. She is as black as the infinite sky and her gruesome image is full of powerful symbolism. Four arms, sometimes even eight, are seen protruding from her dancing body. She holds swords, scythes, sharp cutting apparatuses and severed bloody skulls from these arms. How can this sight not induce fear? Her image is one that evokes nightmares for some yet not for others. She is clearly not a Deity for the faint of heart. Her very distinct, jaw dropping image reveals, she is Goddess of destruction, death courage, strength, transformation and rebirth.

Kali Ma, represents Energy, also known as Shakti, and many ancient texts speak of her well-known *Dance of Destruction*. Her disheveled black long tresses, in many of her depictions, reflect her untamable freedom and unstoppable energy. She was often seen dancing upon the body of her consort, Lord Shiva. According to the Hindu text, Lord Shiva placed his body under Kali's feet to get her to stop her feverish *Dance of Destruction*; a dance that was destined to bring about the end of humanity. She was in such a state of ecstasy through her wild, frenetic dance, while helping Durga destroy demons, that she got carried away and danced upon his corpse. It was only upon seeing his presence under her feet that she then realized what she was actually doing. It made her pause, snap out of her bloodthirsty trance, and this act put an end to the destruction of the world.

Kali can then be seen as the personification of anger and expressed rage, but she is so much more. You will find a plethora of books dedicated solely to her and her intriguing, ancient worship. She is Goddess of tantric practices and of deep states of divine ecstasy. She is patron Goddess of the purge, of clearing out what no longer serves our highest purpose and like the skulls on her garland, Goddess of severing and pruning. She is immeasurable strength and courage. She is Goddess of the fires and incinerators; connected to the crematory of India and therefore death and life. Many of the images we have of Kali serve to reveal her great strength and inspire our own courage.

Her frightful dark imagery is probably one of the most well-known across India and her numerous cults today are even more prevalent than in ancient times. Her devotees see her not as this frightful, calamitous, bloodthirsty Deity, but rather come to her, humbly, with great reverence and respect. For many, she is this extraordinary, unmatchable ancient deity that fiercely protects her devotees. In this way she is wholeheartedly embraced as a beloved Mother, defender, and protectress; and, one who inspires us to meet life with great strength and courage.

PELE

The Polynesian Volcanic Goddess, Pele, is a Fire Goddess known for her passionate, unpredictable, lava spewing insatiable ways. To the people of Hawaii, she is beloved "Tutu Pele" (Grandmother Pele), a demonstrative name revealing much respect and adoration. She is also known as Pele-honua-mea (Pele of the sacred land) and also as, Pele-ai-honua (Pele the devourer of land). This Hawaiian Goddess of beauty, anger and sexual liberation among her many other titles was also known as Ka-ula-o-ke-ahi, a reference to the redness of her fires.

According to Polynesian cosmology, in the beginning was pure darkness. There was formlessness, the infinite. Similar to the cosmology of numerous cultures, in this darkness we find the Earth's womb; the feminine, the Goddess- Papa. Then light was born and this light was the masculine, known as the Sky God –Wakea. When this union between light and darkness joined, the Universe was thus formed and first born. From this union of opposites, mother darkness and father light, emerged all the Gods and all of creation. The creator God, Kane came to be and numerous other important deities followed like Lono, the agricultural God and Kanaloa and Ku, to name a few. Pele is the daughter of the Earth Goddess, Haumea and holds the spirit of the Female Goddess, Hina; as all female deities were considered her direct descendants. In some legends her father was Kuwahailo, a sky God and brother to Hina.

There are many legends about Pele and her vast extended family. We know for example that she had numerous brothers and sisters, as can be expected from her fertile Mother, the Goddess of the Earth. Most notably, her sisters were the patron Goddesses of Hula dancing; Laka and Hiiaka. Laka was a fertility goddess but she was also known as Kapo, in another incarnation, the shape shifter Goddess of dark powers and sorcery. Pele's youngest sister, Hiiaka, was especially dear to her. Hiiaka was born in the shape of an egg and Pele assumed big sister duties by being in charge of caring for that beloved egg. In Hawaiian folklore, we learn of how Hiiaka was held by her sister, as an egg, close to her armpit during the journey to the island of Hawaii, until the egg one day changed into a beautiful little girl. Some of her other important siblings were; Komohoalii, a Shark God. He was her eldest brother and guarded the fiery Goddess often. In some legends he was the Sea God who provided the canoe for her journey to Hawaii. Kane-hekili was also her brother, the God of Thunder and Kauila-nui was yet another brother, the God of lightning. Namaka was her rivaling sister, the Goddess of the Sea, and they had numerous intense battles according to Polynesian folklore. The most famous of these had to do with Pele seducing her husband and Namaka chasing her sister, away from the rest of the family.

In ancient times, Pele was considered part of the Aumakua, family of lesser Gods, and thus her worship did not require the elaborate, formal structured rituals of the major Hawaiian Gods. Perhaps this is one reason why her myths and her worship have survived all this time among the Hawaiian people. Her worship and the practice of her rituals were very informal and individualize, allowing the average laymen the ability to connect with this Divine deity and call on her, in their own personal way. Pele remains one of four most powerful Hawaiian Goddesses still revered and worshipped by natives and non-natives alike on the island. A visit to modern day Hawaii will confirm her as one of the most well-known, venerated deities still commanding our attention today.

Often, Pele was described as beautiful, but easily angered, very volatile, impulsive and jealous. Depicted with long brown hair and sometimes just as an erupting volcano, her priestesses were not allowed to cut their hair, unless it was done so as an offering to the Goddess. Frequently, her priestesses, and those seeking to connect with the Goddess, would cut their long locks as an offering and place it at the edge of the volcanic craters, where many forms of rituals and gifts were offered to her. Gin bottles would be left at Halema'uma'u crater within Kilauea caldera, as well as baked pork, coffee, flowers, fruits and vegetables.

Pele's known home was in Mount Kilauea, Hawaii, but all volcanoes were sacred to her and thus viewed as her ruling domain. Not surprisingly, lava rocks are sacred to her, as well as natural glass. The gemstone Peridot was also linked to Pele. Her colors are the colors of fire; red, orange, yellow and black. The red Lehua flower, from the Ohi'a tree was also sacred to her. During childbirth it was a common practice to call on the midwife aspect of Pele. Polynesian women would invoke her strength and the esteemed Lehua flower was used to entreat her help and ease the pain in childbirth.

Legend tells of how often she would disguise herself as an old lady to test the loyalty of her people. As a crone, she would ask for a plate of food and bless those that complied. Conversely, she would curse with fire, those that were less than generous, as is evident in many of her known tales. Similar to the Greek Goddess Hekate, Pele was seen as a Triple goddess because sometimes she would appear as an old Crone woman, or sometimes as a child. And still at other times, she would appear as a beautiful, insatiable, passionate young maiden. There are myths that tell of Pele truly being an old Hag that reveals her true self, only in dreams.

The Goddess Pele garnered herself a reputation for being, strong tempered, passionate, lustful, wanton and free. As the Goddess of liberation she was a pleasure seeker, a sexual Goddess and what we might term as a minx. Living solely in the moment without thought to consequences, she pursued her passions. Whatever and whomever she wanted, she targeted, pursued and often achieved at attaining. She is a beautiful enchantress, few could resist her and, needless to say, she had many lovers. However, her volatile persona caused much problems within her family and all around the island of Hawaii. Her myths reveal she had many problems with her siblings and was known to have slept with her sisters' husbands. Pele had a rival in the Goddess of the snow-capped mountains-Poloahu. This rivalry is not surprising, due to the fact that Fire never gets along with ice or water.

Pele was known to have had a tumultuous relationship with the Demi Pig- God of agriculture, Kamapua'a. Together they were believed to have had one child who later becomes the ancestor of Polynesian chieftains, intimately connecting the people to their Gods. Kamapua'a appeared to the Fiery Goddess as a handsome chief, who could shapeshift into numerous images from a huge, eight eye boar, to plants and fishes. He was known to have had quite the sexual appetite which meant he pursued numerous dalliances. The first sight of Pele excited him greatly and although she had no interest in him, he pursued her relentlessly; causing the Hawaiian landscape some distress. When she finally surrendered to their union it was riddled with many battles for they were polar opposites. Even their home land had to be divided, as Pele required drier land for her lava to flow and Kamapua'a required verdant, moist and fertile land and thus the two could not live together. Yet interesting to note that although, Pele makes the land from her spewing Lava seemingly separated from her mate, evidence of his bountiful gifts are seen when seeds somehow take root upon the lava, eventually becoming fertile soil. According to author, Herb Kawainui Kane, in his book, *"Pele, Goddess of Hawaii's Volcanoes"* (pg 31), "...Pele may build the island with her lava, but it is the incessant attentions of Kamapua'a that makes it fertile."

There are numerous tales of Pele and her volatility causing much conflict and drama on the island of Hawaii. One tale in particular reveals much about this Goddess.

Pele was madly in love with her new lover, a mortal hula dancer named Lohiau, whom she had a passionate love affair with, when she visited the Earth. They were separated after she had decided to return to her realm in her moment of restlessness. But soon after leaving the earth, she began to long for him. She asked her little sister, Hiiaka, to retrieve him and brings him back to her. Her sister agreed, but only if Pele would tend to her beloved garden during the time she was away. Pele agreed. Hiiaka ran into some trouble however, in this endeavor, and could not bring Pele's lover back to her quickly enough. Lohiau had died from a broken heart during the journey and Hiiaka had to revive him.

Their journey back to Pele was full of challenges. Much time lapsed and Pele, being a jealous Goddess, assumed her sister had betrayed her by taking her lover for her own self. Pele angry, and in a fit of uncontrollable jealousy, destroyed her sister's garden in retaliation. When Hiiaka finally returned and saw what her sister had done to her garden, she in turn retaliated by giving in to her own suppressed desires for the mortal,

Lohiau. Throughout their journey, the two had fallen in love with one another, but resisted temptation. Lohiau had confessed, at this time, to loving Hiiaka more but the fear of Pele's retribution helped him resist his desirous impulses. The couple did not give in to their passions due to their vow to Pele but upon discovering Pele's betrayal, Hiiaka took Pele's lover to the sacred crater of the Volcano, where the Goddess could bear witness to what would unfold.

Hiiaka took Lohiau and there proceeded to make love to him. As you can surmised, this act angered Pele, the great Goddess of violence . She wasted no time in killing the mortal, sending him quickly to the land of the dead and making Hiiaka terribly distraught and heartbroken. The end of this tale reveals Pele's fickleness with lovers, as she later resurrects Lohiau from the land of the dead. She willingly gives him up to her sister in exchange for a new love found in the Hula dancer's best friend. Clearly, honesty was crucial to Pele and she did not hesitate to punish those that failed her. She was known to hurl Lava at her lovers when they would not meet her expectations.

Despite the introduction of Christianity by the missionaries in the 1700- 1800's Pele is one of the most well-known, venerated Polynesian deities today. As a Volcanic Goddess, Pele symbolized the internal fires found in the core of the Earth but also within womyn. She is the unbridled power of anger that moves us and becomes a catalyst for great change.

This Polynesian Goddess is a symbol of passion and perseverance and raw power. Pele is about asserting will and the expression of anger. She teaches us to honor our feelings and allow them to move us into courage and action. Pele teaches us to honor and embrace our deep rooted passions and allow them to surface, so that we can effectively pursue and attain our heart's desire. She teaches us how anger can be a catalyst for great change in our lives. She knows what she wants, is self-assured and may sometimes appear brat-like in her relentless pursuit of her desire, yet, this is a Goddess who will not allow you to become a victim or self -martyrdom, she has no patience for the weak. Like her, she expects you to be strong and passionate... And in Pele, we find the qualities of strong will, purposeful action, passion, strength and women's empowerment.

*Pele is one of the most well-known Goddesses in our modern times. She is the ancient Polynesian Volcanic Goddess, still very much venerated today in Hawaii. Her energy is palpable to us as women, when we are deeply connected to our emotions like, anger and our deep passions. The volcanic, uncontrollable, erupting, passionate Goddess awakens us to great strength, willpower, desires and insatiable energy. She awakens passion deep within and a relentlessness to pursue that which your heart desires. She inaugurates a type of boiling fire energy sweltering from deep within that needs to be approached with great awareness and reverence. She beckons you to give credence to your feelings, validate them, and give them strength. Pele demands that we give volume to our voice. *"Speak out, roar it out,"* she says. Like the rumbling of her volcanoes, she awakens in you the ability to acknowledge the sacred cathartic emotion of passion but also anger. Pele invites you at this time to banish complacency and get real with your true voice. Then let it be heard! Like the rumbling of her Volcanoes and the spewing of her scorching lavas, don't hold your true emotions inside, let them out... let it all out and let your passionate voice be heard.   Pele's energy encourages you to speak your mind, value your passion and emotions, express them openly and be like the volcano; let your voice be heard.

SEKHMET

By far, Sekhmet and her highly recognized image is one of the most widely venerated deities of ancient time. Sekhmet is the Egyptian Lion headed Goddess of Vengeance, Retribution, Anger and Destruction. She was viewed as both a destroyer and protector. She is often depicted sitting or standing, holding the ankh and sometimes a scepter, made of papyrus reed. On her head is a solar disk, reflecting her connection to the sun and she is sometimes seen with a serpent headdress as her crown. She is the woman with a fierce looking Lionhead, donning a red dress to denote her connection to blood, life and death.

To begin to understand this important Egyptian Solar Deity, let's first look at her name. The Egyptian word *"Sekhem"* translates as *"power," "might,"* or *"the powerful one,"* or *"she who is powerful."* As the ancient writings reveal, she was known then as *"Mistress of Dread," "Bringer of Plagues," "Lady of Slaughter," "The Red Lady,"* and *"The Lady of Pestilence,"* to name just a few of her known epithet. We know much of her because she was mentioned so often in many of the surviving text of the time and the myriad of statues representing and venerating her back then still remain today.

Her main Temple was found in Memphis and she was also worshipped with her consort at the temple of Leontopolis, at the Taremu.

Sekhmet is viewed as the personification of the destructive force in the universe. It is quite interesting because she is both worshipped as the "Lady of Life" but also "The Lady of Destruction and Terror." Ancient Egyptians believed it was her breath that formed the Egyptian desert and she was the Eye of Ra, the Egyptian God of the Sun. She was the protector of the Pharaohs and she was connected to the art of Medicine and Physicians. She could bring destruction, yes, but she could also help avert it and bring healing.

Although she may physically resemble the Egyptian Cat Goddess well known as Bast, there is no Familial relation between these two deities. Bast was viewed as a Goddess of the lower Egypt, while Sekhmet was viewed as a Deity of the upper region.

Sekhmet was an aspect of the benevolent Goddess of Joy, Pleasure, Sexuality, and Music, Hathor. Their father thus was the Sun God, Ra and Mut was considered Sekhmet's mother; although it is believed later on, Mut would absorb many of Sekhmet's attributes. There are many surviving myths connected to this Goddess and most will reveal different aspects and a deeper understanding of this astounding Goddess. For example, there is a well-known story that exemplifies best the ferocity of Sekhmet.

According to one legend, the Egyptian Sun God, Ra was growing old and weak and he believed his followers were beginning to lose faith in him. He started to feel like humanity was plotting against him; to dethrone him. This paranoia led him to make a journey into the desert and while there, he drew forth from his brow an aspect of his beloved daughter Hathor, as Sekhmet. He sent the Lion Goddess to humanity to devour and destroy all those who had betrayed him or showed no allegiance to him. As the ferocious Goddess started to slaughter and feed off the betrayers, the blood carnage grew bigger and bigger. Something strange started to happen with Sekhmet as she fell into this killing trance and delighted in the blood. The more blood was spilled the more bloodthirsty it seemed she became and she was consumed with blind rage. She fell deeper into this massacre rampage, devouring and delighting in the blood spillage. Her savagery escalated exponentially, and it appeared she would destroy ALL of humanity.

According to this famous myth, when the Sun God, Ra, beheld the sight of his Lioness daughter in the midst of this atrocious bloodbath he feared this would be the end of humanity and he panicked. Witnessing Sekhmet's bloodthirsty dance, he quickly got the idea of mixing pomegranates and beer to replicate the look of the blood that the Goddess appeared to be feeding off of in her rage. He poured the colored beer and Sekhmet continued to lap up what she believed to be blood, only to eventually find herself terribly intoxicated, by the beer. Inebriated, she stopped the carnage and found herself passed out, asleep. Upon awakening, it is said she returned to her Hathor aspect. In another version of the story, the Goddess Sekhmet passes out inebriated from the beer but when she awakes, her eyes set first upon, Ptah, the Creator and she falls in love. Thus, combining, Ptah (creation) and Sekhmet (destruction) results in her son, healing, Nefertum.

Sekhmet is a powerful Goddess to work with. Evidence of her existence is unquestionable due to the numerous statuary remnants that have been found throughout archeological excavations. Rituals and offerings would be made to petition the Goddess to avert calamities and bring protection to Egyptians. To appease this Goddess, it was well known that her priestesses performed rituals each day to a different sacred image of hers and thus, many statues were made of Sekhmet.

Recently there was an amazing discovery of numerous Temple statuaries of the lion headed warrior goddess. 66 well preserved statues were found in Luxor by archeologist, in what was the ancient city of Thebes. It is believed that there might have been as many as 700 statues of Sekhmet at this pharaoh's temple. Here at this newly excavated site, they discovered the burial temple of the ninth Pharaoh in the 18th dynasty, Amenhotep III, he ruled during a prosperous time in Egypt and was clearly devoted to the Goddess Sekhmet.

AINE

The Lady of the Lake, Aine is also known as Aine Marina, Aine Cliach, Cnoc Aine, Aine of Knockaine. She is a much beloved Celtic Goddess whose name appears throughout several regions in Ireland where she is most revered to this day. The Knock Aine of Ireland, Dun Aine and Aines Hills in the province of Munster are most reflective of the worship of this Goddess. Three miles South West of Lough Gur is the region of Cnoc Aine or KnockAiny and this is the reputed Hill of Aine. She is also most celebrated and revered in Dunany point, which is lovingly referred to as Dun Aine, in honor of the Goddess.

The etymology of her name reveals a lot about the character of this Goddess. Her name means; *delight, pleasure, agility and melody*. In Gaelic, Aine means "*radiance*" and this would be a fitting name for a Goddess believed to be both a Solar and a Lunar deity. The Celtic Goddess, Aine was also often known as the Irish Red Mare that no one could outrun, because this was her chosen form to shape shift. Like most ancient, Celtic Goddesses, there are a number of various attributes linked to her myths.

At some point she was solely revered as a Sun Goddess and held to high esteems during the holy day of Midsummer, Litha (or Summer Solstice, as is better known to some). Burnt offerings of straw and flowers were made to this Solar Goddess in order to insure favorable blessings on love, crops and homes. There are some documented prose and rituals that support this belief and reveal her significant worship at this time of the year, with torch-lit processions through-out the fields to insure a prosperous, fertile crop. Lughnasadh (August 1st) is also a holy day traditionally associated with this Solar Goddess and most notably sacred to her are the three days (Friday, Saturday, Sunday) following Lughnasadh.

Yet, the Goddess Aine, is also very much known as a legendary enchantress; a Moon Goddess and a Goddess of Love. She was known to have numerous divine, royal and human lovers, with a preference for the latter. In ancient times, she was a goddess called upon for fertility magick, whether it was fertility for a woman's womb or the Celtic land itself. She became a patron Goddess for women, agricultural magick and the proliferation of animals and crops. Most notably she is identified as the Faery Queen of Munster and she is an appropriate Goddess to call upon when working with Faery magick.

Aine is believed to be the Daughter of King Egobagal, one of the Tuatha de Danann and there is even some confusion regarding her possible assimilation with other Goddesses like Grainne and the Morrighan. There are some that sometimes view Aine as simply an aspect of Grainne, as both Solar Goddesses, respectively, reflected the waxing and waning Solar year. Still there are other myths that depict her as a Goddess and daughter, even possibly a wife, of the Sea God, Manannan. Thus here, we see a connection to the element of water, hence the South-West cardinal points are sacred to her, as they are to two other well-known Goddesses; Saraswati and Brigit.

There are some of the opinion that Aine was an absolutely beautiful, human woman, from the Leanan Sidhe, meaning, "*Sweetheart of the Sidhe*" and a direct connection to those people with the surname O'Corra. It was believed, she possessed a magickal ring that could unearth faeries and some alleged she became enchanted by the Fae, and taken in by this magickal realm. Subsequently, she became the Faery Queen of Munster and was forever connected, lovingly, with faeries. As a Faery Queen, she was very fond of mortal men, consorting and mating with numerous lovers. She is often attributed for creating a magickal Faery race, called the Dinnshenchas [Din- sheen-k'has]. These were believed to be, more specifically, shape shifting, fire dwarf faeries that came to strengthen and assist wommin in danger of being harmed by men and they undoubtedly served their Queen, Goddess Aine.

Many of the beloved Celtic myths that survive today reveal a great deal about Aine's character and her attributes. According to one Celtic story of the time, she once made a quirky, strange vow not to sleep with a gray-haired man and this tale exemplifies her serious commitment to promises and magickal vows. When Aine's lover, Fionnis, was sadly enchanted by her jealous sister-Miluchrach, and his hair turned gray, Aine kept her vow. In yet another infamous tale we see glimmers of the strong character of this beloved Irish Goddess as she is credited for killing The King of Munster, Aillil Olom, after he had attempted to rape her. In yet another revealing Irish tale of Aine we learn of a stone, known as Cathair Aine. It clearly was an enchanted stone that belonged to the Goddess and it was believed that anyone who sat on it was susceptible to losing their wits. If anyone dared sit on her rock for more than three times they were doomed to loose themselves forever. In this tale, we again see Aine's character as a Goddess not to offend, for her fiery, red wrath throughout various myths has proven to be severe. There are, however, also tales that reflect her generous powers of creativity bestowed upon bards and writer, yet if they failed to meet her high demands and expectations she would not hesitate to severely punish them.

Most of the myths agree that Aine became the wife of Gerald, The Earl of Desmond, although it is not clear how that union came about. There are numerous conflicting tales of how they first met and fell in love. According to some legends, The Earl of Desmond came across the enchanting beauty, while she bathed in a river and he was instantly smitten. He spied upon her magick cloak, the one that was so often used by Aine to enchant men into lovers, and he saw her scattered clothes set upon a nearby boulder. Essentially, he blackmailed her into matrimony, refusing to give back her prized possessions until she agreed to the union. Another version of this story, tells of how he saw her combing her hair by the river and upon discovering her unsupervised clothes, he stole her legendary magickal cloak. Wearing the enchanted cloak himself, he used her very own magick powers against her, to ensnare and enchant her into love and marriage. Still another version tells of how she herself, having a reputation for being a beautiful enchantress and acquiring numerous lovers, wore the magick cloak and ensnared The Earl of Desmond into marriage.

Married to the Earl of Desmond, together they had one known son; Geroid Iarla, Earl Fitzgerald; although here too there might be conflicting mysterious stories. In some of the writings of the time he is addressed as "The Magician." Some believed he is indeed Merlin or an archetype of Lancelot in Arthurian mythology. According to one famous tale, upon the birth of their son, Aine warned her husband not to ever be surprised at what their son could do. It was a type of taboo The Earl of Desmond needed to agree and adhere to. One day however, he witnessed his beloved flesh and blood, jump in and out of a tiny bottle, a very non-human act and the poor man could not contain his utter shock. This very act resulted in Geroid turning himself into a wild Goose and Aine fleeing her marriage and the husband who failed to keep his critical vow.

Some believe their son, the Magician, still lives today under the Lake, inside Lough Fur, in county Limerick and one myth claims that he will one day return to remove all foreigners from his beloved Ireland. The immortal Goddess Aine is still very much revered today by the Irish and the name itself is quite common in certain regions of Ireland. There is great pride in this beloved Goddess, some even feeling an ancestral connection to her. There are some that believe she still lives on today in Knock Aine, in a Faery Castle.

Call upon the Goddess Aine for Faery magick; solar and lunar spells, fertility and prosperity rituals, love magick, creativity workings - especially for writing. When making oaths and vows, it is Aine who can be beseeched on your behalf. She can also be called upon when needing to flee an unsuitable mate. When endeavoring to give birth to a wizard; magickal offspring or a creation, she is the Goddess to call upon. The Meadowsweet is associated with Aine but also the Yew tree, which reflects her connection to life and death. She will be very sympathetic and prove to be helpful when doing rites to punish rapist as well. The Red Mare (Lair Derg) as she was sometimes titled was often called upon when blessing cattles and herds. Rabbits and Swans are also her sacred animals, and she is still often invoked and honored during her feast day, on Midsummer's day.

*Irish Red Mare, Solar and Lunar Goddess, Aine, is the fiery enchantress who inspires the writer and the songstress. She is a Fierce Protectress of Women, especially those who have been mistreated, abused, lied to, molested or raped by men. An oath and vow guardian, she awakens in you a call to action, where action is needed. Defend yourself and unearth the confidence to utilize your own gifts of enchantments, when needed. Aine connects us with the energy of Fire, in her Solar aspect, although she was later similarly connected to the moon. With the Goddess, Aine, we hone in on the various wonderful gifts of the element of fire and how to best utilize it in our lives, channeling it into the manifestation of cherished goals. With Aine's fiery solar energy, we are blessed.

ERESHKIGAL

Ereshkigal is the Mesopotamian Goddess of the Underworld. She is reminiscent of the Greek God, Hades and even shares some connection to the ancient Goddess, Hecate/Hekate. She has full dominion over the land of the dead, known as Kur, and she is the omnipotent law and judgement in this dark realm. What makes her even more fascinating to us, as we study early Sumerian writings mentioning Ereshkigal, is that she appears to be the sole ruler of this realm. The underworld oftentimes, in later myths, was relegated to male deities, thus it's a powerful message to see a Goddess as the sole ruler of this very significant realm. Later, we see the introduction of her consort, sharing rulership with her, in the underworld, also known as Irkalla.

Her name literally translates as, "Queen of the vast Earth," more specifically, "Queen of the under earth." She is embraced as the Goddess of the Great Below.

As the older sister and aunt to the Queen of Heaven, the Goddess, Inanna, their brother was Utu, a Solar Deity. Their parents were Nanna, the Moon God and Ningal, the Moon Goddess. Ereshkigal had several consorts. Her First husband was Gugalanna, *the Bull of Heaven*, and with him she birthed Ninazu, who became another deity of the underworld. With the God of Air, Enlil, she birthed Namtar (meaning Fate /Destiny). Coincidentally, Enlil would be considered her grandfather, as he fathered the God, Nanna. She was later associated to the God of war, pestilence and plagues, known as Nergal, and together they had the Goddess, Nungal. Nungal was also known as Manungal and she too became a deity of the underworld like her mother. Later known as "Queen of the Ekur," she married the God, Birdu. Interesting to note, Nungal's role became the Judgement of the wicked in the underworld.

Ereshkigal's main temple was located in, Kutha, but she also had temples in Azzur and Umma, according to discovered tablet inscriptions and writings of the time. It is clear her worship was not limited to Mesopotamia as she was known in other lands. She was said to live in Ganzir, which was the entryway to her realm, the netherworld. Her worship and petitions by her devotees was meant to secure a comforting afterlife for she was the guardian of the dead and many feared they would be utterly lost in the underworld. The underworld in ancient times was seen as a dark, painful, muddy realm where the dead would suffer hunger and thirst, if neglected and forgotten by their loved ones remaining on earth. ...Hence the great emphasis on frequent food offerings, prayers, ritual and proper burials, regarding the dead. Ereshkigal, however, was not what you would consider the stereotypical evil view of a deity ruling the dead. Instead, in many of the remaining, early Sumerian writings you can easily empathize with her character and the many situations she found herself in. Yes, Ereshkigal is a strong, powerful deity and was prone to, anger easily and express quite a temper, but like most of us, she is multifaceted. As Goddess of the netherworld, it is believed her role was more significantly, the protection of the earth, and humanity, by creating a boundary and maintaining a final resting place for the dead. She was a patron Goddess for those inexplicably experiencing spiritual possession and thus, it was clear her role was to make sure the dead remained in her realm, behind the seven gates of Irkalla.

There is much reference to Ereshkigal's temper and jealousy of her younger sister, Inanna, and it is easy to understand why there would be such turmoil between the two. No matter what era we are in, it is not uncommon for siblings to struggle with such powerful emotions as jealousy and anger. Given how Inanna was deemed the Queen of Heaven and a beloved deity, gifted with great beauty and the realm of love; it is easy to empathize with Ereshkigal's plight. She was given the dark gloomy realm of the underworld and some have even suggested that Ereshkigal was actually tricked into being the Goddess of this realm. In the Sumerian poem, **"Gilgamesh Enkidu and the Netherworld,"** the Goddess Ereshkigal had been abducted in the same way Persephone, in Greek mythology, had been abducted by Hades. In this poem, Ereshkigal gets abducted and dragged into the underworld by a dragon named, Kur and she is forced to remain there in the netherworld and rule over this gloomy terrain.

In yet another interesting, ancient Sumerian myth, there is an example of her legitimate reaction when she feels disrespected. According to the legend, all the Gods had planned this great lavish banquet on earth and Ereshkigal, as a noteworthy Goddess, was of course invited. But, as a Deity of the underworld she could not depart her realm and the Gods could not bring the banquet to the Goddess because law stipulated that no one could leave the underworld once they arrived. Saddened to hear of the dilemma, the Gods encouraged her to send someone in her place to stop by, gather some of the feast, and return it to the Goddess for her enjoyment. Ereshkigal decided to send her trusted servant and son, Namtar. When he arrived to the Banquet as her representative, all the Gods stood in respect and honor of the Goddess, except for one...The God of Pestilence, Nergal. He showed great disrespect by not standing up and it was immediately noted. Namtar quickly wanted to defend his mom's honor by taking care of Nergal himself, but instead, he was convinced to share the details with Ereshkigal and let her deem the final, proper punishment.

There are many variations to this legend and how it ends, but essentially the God, Nergal is sent to the underworld to explain himself to the Goddess and receive his punishment. With the protection of fourteen beings (or demons) he ventures into the netherworld with the intention of breaking the rule and eventually getting out. He gets through all the gates and by the time he approaches the seventh gate he instructs two beings to leave the gate open behind him so that he may escape. Long story made short here, the God of war and pestilences is forced to stay in the underworld as her consort. There are other versions and interpretations of this legend. Some speculate that the Goddess managed to seduce him while in her realm and that together, they feasted and made wild, passionate love. Whether he was kept in the underworld as punishment for his disrespect or simly as her lover, his presence becomes evident. Nergal becomes the only other deity that is required to stay with the Goddess and co-partner with her as ruler of the underworld. In this way, a male deity is introduced as a co-ruler of the netherworld, sharing power with a female deity in this critical realm. His contractual presence in the underworld is reminiscent to Persephone's with Hades, as he, the God of war, is only required to stay with Ereshkigal for half of the year; returning to the earth the other half. It is demonstrative of the primeval idea that war (God of war, Nergal) could only be endured on earth for a part of the year.

Remnant of Sumerian and Akkadian writings found on tablets throughout the years by archeologist has fascinated many of us. They confirm an unquestionable truth, that the Sacred Feminine, in her numerous guises, was at the center of ancient civilization. When pieced together they reveal some of the most beautiful poems, stories and prayers (Hymns) to the numerous deities venerated long ago. They are also yet another reminder of how relevant the Goddess was then, as she still remains today.

By far one of the most impactful, beloved legends found among the early Sumerian writings was, **"The Descent of Inanna."** In this work we not only journey with Inanna into the underworld but also encounter her powerful sister, Ereshkigal.

Inanna makes her way to the entryway of the underworld. Her sister's husband, Gugalanna, *The Bull of Heaven*, has died and she wishes to pay her proper respects by attending his funeral rites. However, it's important to note that his death is partly due to her carelessness. In a previous story, it was Gilgamesh and Enkidu that slaughtered Gugalanna in a type of retaliatory act towards Inanna herself. The reality was that Inanna, shared blame for his death and her appearance at the gate of the netherworld was partly due to her own guilt.

Inanna prepares herself for the visit and the confrontation with her sister and dresses in her finest Royal adornments. She reaches the entryway and cries out to the gatekeeper, Neti, to let her inside. Neti quickly alerts Ereshkigal of this shocking visitor to her queendom and the news stirs all sorts of emotions and worries. Ereshkigal already has a tenuous relationship with her sister, the beloved Queen of Heaven, and she suspects that Inanna has come to try to lay claim to the underworld as her own, in order to expand her powers. She carefully contemplates the situation and then instructs Neti to *"bolt the seven gates of the underworld."* She tells Neti that in order for Inanna to be granted passage through each of the gates, she must surrender one of her Royal adornments and garments. These Royal adornments were closely linked with Inanna's Divine power. They were intimately connected to her supremacy as a Goddess.

Inanna humbly arrives at each of the gates of the underworld and she complies with each demand; sacrificing one of her adornments or clothing article at the entryway of each gate. By the time she arrives at the seventh gate, Inanna finds herself completely naked, stripped of all of her power as a Goddess, and weakened. Ereshkigal rises from her throne and faces her sister. Full of much intense bottled up emotions, Ereshkigal declares aloud all the offenses against Inanna and presents it to the, Annuna, the judges of the Underworld. She accuses the Goddess, Inanna, of trying to usurp her Queendom and of being directly responsible for the death of her husband, . The Annuna passes judgement against Inanna and she is given to Ereshkigal to put to death. The Goddess of the Underworld takes the naked body of Inanna and hangs her to die. Like a piece of rotting meat, for 3days and 3nights, the naked Inanna hung from a hook.

Now three days and three nights have passed and Inanna's servant, Ninshubur, is frantically worried. She goes to implore all the different Gods for their help but no one would dare. Finally she goes to the God of Wisdom, Enki, and after hearing the story he agrees to help. He fashions two genderless creatures from the dirt under his fingernails. He names them; *Kurgarra* and *Galatur*. He instructs them to fly into the underworld and rescue Inanna by giving her the food and drink of life. He warns them of Ereshkigal and the painful moaning she would emit and he instructs them on how to get the Queen of the Underworld to surrender Inanna's corpse.

The two creatures reach the throne of Ereshkigal and they find her moaning in agony. They begin to imitate her sounds and empathize with the pain she was feeling. Somehow it brought the Goddess so much comfort that she grants them a wish. Naturally they ask for the corpse of Inanna and Ereshkigal complies. They find Inanna lifeless and immediately offer her the bread and drink of life. Revitalized, they attempt to get Inanna out of there but as they were ascending out of this dark realm, the Annuna stopped them; reminding them of the law in the Netherworld. The only way Inanna could be escorted out of the Underworld is if she had someone to take her place. A multitude of demons from the underworld, called the Galla, attached themselves to Inanna. They harassed the Goddess, Inanna and would not leave her alone until she found her replacement for the underworld. They traveled upon the earth with her, as she was now resurrected from the dead. When Inanna returns to the Earth she finds that her death, while it was being mourned by so many, her beloved consort, Dumuzi, did not express a single sign of remorse for her death. He was found enjoying himself, dressed in his finest royal garment; unmoved by her absence. She confronts Dumuzi and seeing how he had not one shred of grief for her death, she offers him up to the Galla, in anger and disgust. He protested but the decision had been made. The Demons of the underworld gladly took him as a replacement for the Goddess, Inanna. In some text it is stated, his sister volunteered to accompany and console her brother to the underworld.

Ereshkigal is yet another powerful image of the Sacred Feminine. We meet in this Sumerian Goddess an image of great strength and autonomy, and a reminder to honor our emotions. She serves as a message to stand our ground, assert our voices and thus, our power. There is also an aspect regarding her domain and her domicile in the underworld. She encourages you to embrace and defend your own Queedom. Ereshkigal is the awakener of the voice necessary to defend ourselves from anyone that is disrespecting or disregard us. Her voice is ultimate authority, what she states is decree, and throughout the ancient texts, it's clear she is both feared and highly regarded. The autonomy of this Goddess becomes evident in every tale she's mentioned in and it serves to inspire our own journey.

THEME WORK SUGGESTIONS
6 STRENGTH AND RAGE

Light a black or red candle

Engage yourself in something physically arduous like; running, dancing, mountain climbing, cycling, cleaning your house, purging and organizing your closet, etc....

If you're in the right space, you may scream and yell out any pent up frustration and anger. You can also speak aloud or record your anger
in your journal or a recording device.

BALLOON RITE

Get a red balloon and blow into this balloon all of your anger. Then when you're ready, pop that balloon to surrender all of your pent up rage.

Commit to a greater cause; be an advocate for those that appear voiceless.

You can volunteer for organizations that help women and children in abusive situations.

Lend your voice to a good cause. Be the voice of the voiceless.

JOURNALING

How do you feel about anger and the demonstration of rage?
_____
_____

Ask yourself, "How do I express anger today?"
_____
_____

How has the emotion of anger been exemplified or expressed during your formative years?
_____
_____

How would you handle a child throwing a fiery tantrum?
_____
_____

Do you feel safe to express frustrations and all of your feelings?
_____
_____

What angers you most today?
_____
_____

Can you measure how often you get upset or angry in a day?
_____
_____

How can anger be a healthy expression and fuel for my strength?
_____
_____

INVOCATION & POETRY
UNLEASH YOUR ROAR
Tiger's Roar,
Rings in my ears
Louder and Louder
Banish all Fears…

Pouncing ferociously,
Demanding what it seeks,
Anger spilling over
Watch it now speak…

Listen to its potent Truth,
Things held tight
Now come unglued,

Bones dug deep,
Rise with her roar,
Rainbow only shines
After a rainstorm…

Honor Her Voice,
Honor her depth,
You inner Tiger,
Has now pounced and leapt.

A buried voice
Now makes her debut
Rise with the Tiger
At this Leo full moon.

Set the sacred platform,
Let Her take the stage,
Don't you know,
She's got something to say?

Listen, make note…
Use her potent force.
Hers is your strength,
Lock down no more…

*** You are now encouraged to create your own altar(s) & invocation(s).   )O(Blessings!

MAGICK RITES & TOOLS

This is your personal page to document your sacred rites and the tools you elected to use.

DECIDE WHERE TO SET UP AN ALTAR
Place an Altar Cloth in the Color of your choice.
Color: _____

GODDESS
Place an image of your Deity.
Goddess: _____
This image can be a Statue, handmade Sculpture or a simple Photo _____

FIRE REPRESENTATION
Place a blessed/charged Candle in the color of your choice.
Candle Type and color: _____

AIR REPRESENTATION
Light your Incense stick.
Incense Scent: _____

WATER REPRESENTATION
Place a Chalice of Water
Water Item: _____

EARTH REPRESENTATION
Place a Potted Plant or Fresh Flowers on your Altar
Add Salt or a plate of Dried Herbs
Herbs: _____
Chosen Gemstone: _____

YOUR WISH
_____

_____

_____

Place a symbol of your desire, if you have one available, and also write your wish out clearly, on a piece of parchment paper, or you can even use a cut up brown paper bag. These are the basics for a very simple altar & rite. Ultimately, your sacred space is only limited by your imagination. You can make your altar & rite as big or as small as you prefer and the addition of other personal items is really up to you.)o(Enjoy!

ALTAR PHOTOS

"The task ahead of you is never greater than the strength within you." Anonymous

CHAPTER SEVEN

"Take care of your Body. It's the only place you have to live…"
Jim Rohn

THEME: BODY & HEALTH

Our theme in this chapter is our health and our physical body. We've reached a point in our journey where we are being asked to recognize a powerful source that lies within our own physical form.

In pursuit of our personal development, so often we place an exorbitant amount of energy and emphasis on our emotional and spiritual growth, and throughout this process we can become neglectful and almost complacent about our earthly form. As a spiritual Goddess woman, I am, of course, a strong advocate for all spiritual, mental, emotional and psychic development. However, my own journey has revealed this undeniable truth that we are here on earth, in our earthly body, which is not something to be to be trivialized or dismissed. Our physical body is an integral part of our human existence and while many religious and spiritual practices promote the rejection of our flesh and bones it is important to recognize that there is value and purpose to our physical forms. Our body is meant to work in harmony with our spiritual, emotional, psychic and mental development. It is not something to be dismissed, cursed, burdened or be blocked by; it has the potential to be a great asset to our human experience and evolution. If we learn to honor it we can reach a point in our journey where we discover the wisdom and loyal companionship found within our physical body.

It is through our physical body that we receive intuitive and spiritual messages. It is our body that can warn us of impending dangers when we get that queasy spinning feeling in our gut that something is not right. It is through our body that we can experience great joy and ecstasy. It is through our body that we can get warning signs of imbalances and unaddressed emotional issues. It is through our physical body that we can sometimes tap into spirit on a complete different level; like for example when we invoke or aspect a deity, draw down the moon or a spirit, or offer a ritual or partake in an ecstatic dance as a form of reverence or prayer. Even in the seemingly mundane act of a daily physical fitness regime, we can cross into other realms of our psyche through our physical form. Ever heard of the runners high, spinning or dancing to connect with the Divine? There are levels of heightened awareness that are born out of those moments when we connect and honor our body.

There are treasures to be found in our earthly form that are indeed compatible to our spiritual growth. Our physical bodies can be a powerful tool to our existence and human development but only if we honor it and integrate its gifts with our other resources.

Like in previous chapters, to help us further explore our theme we will work with several helpful resources. We will endeavor to connect with the Goddesses Artemis, Skadi, Macha, Sunna, Uzume and the sacred animal energy of the Deer. We will connect with our 3rd chakra, the Solar Plexus, and gemstones that can help better facilitate this connection. We will also look at the corresponding Lunation and a Tarot card that is connected to our theme.

THE JUDGEMENT TAROT CARD

The Judgement card in the Tarot is often depicted, in traditional decks, with several people appearing to rise from their tombs. The Archangel Gabriel is seen blowing on his celestial trumpet, sending a wakeup call to all those who were slumbering in death. This is a tarot card about awakenings and rebirths. It tells of a dawning, an age of enlightenment, and a time of a potentially new phase in our lives. It is almost celebratory, like a time of harvest and reaping what you've sown. When we relate it to our theme, it invites us to consider a new way of honoring and working with our physical body. It speaks to us about a rebirth and an awakening to the potentiality of our earthly form. It also serves to remind us that we are here in this physical body for a limited time and thus, it behooves us to live consciously and honorably. Receive the wakeup call and vow to honor your health and physical form as we proceed in our work here.

MOON IN VIRGO   EARTH/MERCURY

THEME: Body & Health

| **VIRGO** | **MUTABLE** | **EARTH** | **FEMININE** | **THE VIRGIN** |

The Moon in Virgo is interesting. Virgo is the second astrological sign, ruled by the planet Mercury. However, the astrological sign of Virgo is quite different from its Sister-sharing sign of Gemini. Virgo is an earth sign, represented by the image of the Virgin, the Maiden aspect of the Goddess. Its energy concerns itself with matters of our health, hygiene, wellbeing and other earthly matters. Virgo's celebrated attributes are linked with service to humanity, efficiency and bringing order to all things. It is exceptionally gifted in its ability to analyze situations and solve complex undertakings. When the moon is in Virgo, it is not only a good time to clean and organize our lives but also to purge, both, our exterior and interior worlds, of things that are no longer serving our highest good. It is a time of assessments, careful planning and strategizing. As an earth sign, Virgo connects us with our physical body and thus, this lunation is ideal for any goals connected to fitness, health and overall wellbeing.

"If you can't fly, then run, if you can't run, then walk,
if you can't walk, then crawl,
but whatever you do, you have to keep moving forward..."
Martin Luther King Jr.

HERSTORY

Hers was an endless, painful struggle with her body and that fluctuating scale didn't help... It's not like she was ever planning to be as paper thin as a Victoria Secret Super model but she just longed for the day when she could feel comfortable in her own skin. It's what every human being probably secretly wants more than anything; to feel comfortable with the body they are in. Most of her youth and teen years, however, were spent in an unhealthy, vicious cycle of yo-yo dieting, body shaming and self-loathing. By the time she reached adulthood, she had given up, not only on her ideals but just on her own physical form and its capacity to work for her.

She had stopped hoping, trying and wishing and at some point just gave up caring. It was as if her body did not exist to her; her physical body no longer held her interest or concern. She unconsciously made a pact to divorce herself from her persistently disappointing body. She walked among her fellow humans as if separated from her own flesh and bone. Admittedly, she treated her body as the enemy and betrayer it appeared it had become to her and she no longer had a relationship with her body. That distinct deliberate abandonment of her own physical body, led her to abandon other parts of her beautiful self. Consequently, many unanticipated painful issues started to sneak up in her world...

A recent health scare found her shaken and dragged to this pivotal point in her life....would she be open to rebuilding and renewing her relationship with her physical body. Alas, divorcing and abandoning her body was no longer an option and she knew it was time to face the truth.... She is being awakened to the gifts inherent in our physical form...and the power and beauty that lies from within.

******Take a moment to document here, or in your journal, your unique story.

_____

_____

AFFIRMATION

When I move; dance, jump, run, and
just engage in my physical body,
I connect to deeper ecstatic levels of my existence.

**My physical body is
a vehicle for divine ecstasy.**

My Body is Sacred

I honor and strengthen my relationship with my sacred body...

CHAKRA & GEMSTONE WORK

3rd Chakra   **MANIPURA/NAVAL SOLAR PLEXUS CHAKRA**   **COLOR:** Yellow

Ego, willpower, impulses, anger, personal Power, our strength, desire, Confidence, interactions with others, realm of fire.

Mantra: I Am/ I Shine

)O(WORKING: Nurturance (emotional & Physical), Weight Loss Work

GEMSTONE CONNECTION: Yellow Jasper is a bright solar stone that benefits your endocrine glands. It is known as an emotional energizer. It gives you physical energy, which has a positive effect on our mental and emotional health. It is related to the third chakra, our Solar plexus, and helps us explore self-expression, while connecting us to our regenerative gifts. It also helps relieve stomach bloating and soothes digestive disorders.

Yellow Jade is a yellow opaque colored gemstone with a positive solar energy. It promotes personal growth, vitality and an optimistic perspective. Healers work with its peaceful energy to build self-confidence, help with self-expression and promote balanced digestive system.

Citrine is one of the best, all-around, beneficial gemstones you can work with. It can be found in different shades of translucent dark or light yellow. As you can imagine just by looking at it, it is closely linked with the Sun and the element of fire. It promotes confidence, joy, prosperity, accolades and helps attracts good friends. As a solar gemstone it exudes a positive warm energy that supports optimism, wellbeing, good fortune and inevitable success. Not surprising, it was also known as the lucky, "Merchant-stone," reputed to bring prosperity to businesses that kept citrine near their cash registers. It was also known as the, *"Stone of the Mind,"* and helps to promotes willpower, while clarifying and magnifying personal power and energy. Citrine helps relieve depression and heal digestive disorders. This makes it an ideal stone for healers working with the third chakra. It increases creativity and honesty and helps to eliminate fears of being judged by others, which is a personality trait most creative artist desire. Citrine is known to eliminate negativity but, unlike other stones, it does not absorb negativity from its surroundings, it simply transmutes it. This gives Citrine the very unique attribute of never needing to be energetically cleaned or cleared. It is able to regenerate and restore itself, autonomously. This is an interesting attribute that its wearer can explore further, as well.

GEMSTONE CHANNELING

    Greetings and welcome to this important point in our journey. As part of this work of love and self-care, you are invited now to find a comfortable place where you can be assured of your privacy, safety and comfort... We endeavor now to start our meditative journey. If you can go outdoors in nature that would be most ideal but any place where you can simply relax, undisturbed, would be fine.

    Place yourself in a comfortable meditation position; you may sit or lay down. If it is available to you, place in your hands one or all of the yellow gemstones we are working with today. You may hold a Yellow Jasper or Yellow Jade or Citrine Gemstone. These yellow colored gemstones are connected to our Solar Plexus and they are known to offer much healing, guidance and vitality.

    Hold your yellow gemstone in your hands and consider how it feels upon your skin... Do you sense heat from it or coldness? Does it feel smooth or rough? Reflect now on how your gemstone feels. Gaze upon its shape and its varying yellow hues. (Pause) Look at your Yellow Jasper or Yellow Jade or Citrine Gemstone more deeply and let your scrutiny unveil all of its precious details. Quietly, continue to study this gemstone and make note of any thoughts or vivid images that immediately start to unfold before you. (Pause) When you're ready, you may close your eyes and begin this short meditation.

    As with all trance work, we begin with our breath. You are asked now to take a deep cleansing breath; slowly filling up your lungs then release.... (Pause) Now let your next breath possess the element of this Yellow Gemstone. Feel the bright Yellow hues of your Yellow Jasper/Jade or Citrine Gemstone rise into the ethers and inhale this swirl of bright vitality and healing energy. Breathe in and exhale. (Pause) As you breathe in, direct the energy of your breath, from your crown chakra, all the way down to your belly region, near your Solar Plexus. Stay with this energy for as long as you need to. (Pause) Continue to breathe and hold this breath for 3 seconds and then release it... Counting now at your own pace; breathe, 1, 2, 3, and exhale on 4....and again....breathe in, 1, 2, 3, and exhale on 4. Let's do this one more time and then quietly counting in your head.... Breathe 1, 2, 3...release on 4. Breathe, trusting in the natural rhythm you have now established, of your relaxed inhalation and exhalation.

    Yellow Jasper/Yellow Jade/Citrine gemstone wishes to impart a special channeled message for you. See this brilliant, Solar colored, gemstone in your mind's eye. See it as the sun itself, shining brightly. See it now embedded upon the dark, fertile, mother earth. Draw nearer to it and ask if it will allow you to pick it up. When permission is granted, gently gather it in your hands. With your mind's eye, gaze upon it again; studying its color, its texture, and any inclusions or other details that captures your eyes.... Ask it to speak to you.

    Now with your next breath, place your attention on your crown chakra and imagine a lid being open. Allow your head or crown chakra to become almost like a chalice; receptive and open to any spiritual messages that may be unfolding for you now... Envision your crown chakra unveiling a magnetic Yellow Gemstone portal allowing for this **Crystal Transmission** *to come through... Gently guide this energy of the gemstone, again from your crown chakra, to your Solar Plexus, the place of your fire and strength ... (Pause)*

    Continue to inhale the bright yellow cathartic energy of this gemstone and then, exhale.... When you feel ready, you may open your eyes and prepare to document your experience. As you come out of this meditation, it is a perfect time for you to document any images or messages that came through for you. You may write them here, or in your personal journal.

DEER PROTECTION ENERGY

At this point in our journey, as we endeavor to explore the subject of our physical body, there are quite a few different animals that wish to serve as allies and protectors. What a beautiful blessing they allow themselves to be in our spiritual work? Connecting with animal energies has proven to be instrumental in my own personal journey and whenever I find myself at a crossroad with a decision, I invariably will find my answer when I connect with them and the Sacred Feminine. Today, I feel the presence of, not only forest animals, but the Greek Maiden Goddess, Artemis, who is offering us in this chapter, the sacred energy of the Deer.

The deer is one of the gentlest creatures in the forest. A beloved being of the Maiden Greek, Goddess, Artemis, deer exemplifies beauty, grace and gentleness. She is a prey animal and thus, lives most of her life in an alert, defensive mode; acutely aware of her surroundings. Perhaps some of us can identify with this alert, heightened way of living. She is able to camouflage with her environment and remain motionless when confronted with a threat, before swiftly running away. There is no question she is fast and her swift decisive action, when taken, can be the difference between life and death. She teaches us the art of being unseen and knowing when to stand still and when to act; to protect ourselves from predators.

In the wild, there is clearly a need to quiet down, connect to your body signals and trust your intuition; it is the only way to survive. The Deer reminds us of this precious gift. Our body and its many subtle, and not so subtle, ways of communicating with us is a gift too often overlooked. But Deer reminds us of our physical existence and the importance of our part in this Universal time and space. How do we move, on this earth? How do we honor our physical body and integrate it with our intuitive body? She almost becomes this iconic symbol for all those who are struggling with similar questions.

The athlete, the dancer, the runner; who delights in the sanctuary of the forest and nature, all find an ally in the Deer. Oftentimes, the unexpected discovery of a deer amidst my early morning, nature walks, has stopped me right in my tracks, leaving me transfixed and enchanted. I usually take that opportunity to quietly watch her beauty, in awe. There is no question; she can help you rediscover your inner child to begin exploring the world through innocent, deer wide-eyes. Considered one of the most docile, kind and compassionate animals, her gaze will leave you speechless and mesmerized. She is not the aggressor, nor the initiator of an attack; she approaches life with empathy and benevolence and serves to remind you to be gentle with yourself and others.

A Deer's horns or antlers are interesting because they are used to defend and protect themselves from predators but they possess a remarkable regenerative quality about them. When they fall off or break, they are able to grow back, much like the skin of a snake. The powerful imagery of their notable antlers reaching upward towards the heavens, from the crown chakra, is for us, an indicator of their connection to higher spiritual knowledge. Thus, the Deer, not only serves to remind us of the importance of our physical body, but also the integration of our intuitive gifts in conjunction with our physical existence. You will soon discover that the Deer is indeed a powerful ally and protector as we proceed in this transformative work.

THEME WORK SUGGESTIONS

Work with the Virgo moon, symbolized by the Maiden,
and work with The Deer energy and the
Deities offered in this chapter.
Make sure to start with your Doctor appointments;
Schedule your next wellness visit.
Get physically active and
commit to one fitness activity; Walking, Running,
Cycling, Dancing, Rock climbing, Skating or a Yoga Practice, etc.
Maintain a Nutritional Journal and consider
joining a Gym or even an aerobic or cardio class.
If you're facing some type of addiction, seek an outside
support group or a professional for added guidance.

GODDESS EMPOWERMENT

ARTEMIS

Virgin, maiden, whole unto herself, Artemis is the Greek Goddess of the Crescent New Moon. She is the Huntress, known in Rome as Diana-Artemis. She is Goddess of the wilderness, Goddess of Archery and the Hunt. Artemis was considered a leader to the Amazons and a patron Goddess to all wild animals, women and children. She is the immortal spirit of the wild, free maiden and her name is derived from the Greek word, "*Artemes*", which means, healthy and energetic and a reference to strength and vitality - all attributes she exemplifies.

As Lady of Ephesus, she was depicted with a multitude of breast and worshipped more as an ancient, pre-Olympian, Mother Goddess. In Rome she was known as Diana-Artemis, mother of Aradia, and thus, Goddess of the Witches, according to Charles Godfrey Leland.

The Greek Huntress Artemis is associated with the crescent new moon and was often depicted wearing a short tunic and a circlet of the crescent moon upon her brow. Artemis was sometimes viewed as the maiden aspect of Hekate. There are numerous variations of this trinity, but a common one makes Hekate, the crone, symbolized by the dark moon, Selene (a Titaness moon Goddess) as the mother, symbolized by the Full moon, while Diana-Artemis, as the maiden, was symbolized by the crescent.

As a lunar Goddess she shares some characteristics with Hekate and their connection is undeniable. Some text reveals that Hekate was actually a cousin of Artemis because her mother's sister, Asteria, was mother to Hekate. In this cosmology, their great grandmother was the primordial Goddess, Gaia, and their grandmother was the ancient Moon Goddess, the Titaness, Phoebe. Phoebe, interestingly enough, translates as *"light-*

bearer" and this is an attribute that all her familial descendants possess.

Artemis was the daughter of Zeus and the Goddess Leto and she was a twin to Apollo-The sun God. Though she herself, as a Virgin deity, never gave birth, she was considered the Goddess of Childbirth, and often called upon by women in the midst of labor. She was immortalized in the writings of her time as the young one who was immediately employed to be her mother's midwife, as the birth of her twin brother proved to be difficult.

According to the well-known myths, documented in the Callimachus, and the Homeric hymn, Artemis was born on the Greek Island of Delos, also known as Ortygia, Isle of Quails. Perhaps this is one reason why she is also known by the name of Cynthia, a reference to her birthplace on Mount Cynthus, in Delos. According to one account, her mother searched tirelessly to find a safe place to birth her children, away from Hera's jealous wrath. Zeus's wife, Hera, had decreed that Leto would not be allowed to give birth anywhere upon the earth, but with some divine intervention, the Greek island of Delos emerged from deep within the sea, as an enchanted island, immuned to Hera's curse. Although there are some variations to this story, Artemis was first born and witnessing her mother's distress and struggles to birth her twin brother. She wasted no time in immediately helping her beloved mother and easing her labor pains. This is one reason why she is so often associated with women and childbirth and the practice of midwifery. In this capacity she is known as, *Kourotrophos*, the nurse for the young and as *Locheia*, the Goddess of childbirth.

Throughout mythology, this maiden Goddess was often seen coming to her mother's aid and protecting various women in distress. She became known as the protector of the hopeless, the vulnerable and the defenseless, such were at the time; children, women, young girls, animals beast, babes. In the tale of Niobids, the Queen of Thebes made the grave mistake of boasting about her fourteen children and comparing her rather fertile birthing abilities, as more superior than that of the Goddess Leto, who had only given birth to one male and one female. For Artemis and Apollo, who loved their mother dearly, this was gravely offensive. They spared no time in defending their mother's honor and succeeded at killing the Queen's children by shooting at them with poisoned arrows. The father, Amphion, completely distraught, killed himself upon witnessing the tragic death of his sons. The Queen, Niobe, and her remaining children were quickly turned to stone by Artemis as they mourned the tragic, demise of their family. It becomes clear in this tragic tale, and numerous other Greek lore, that Artemis, while very protective of the vulnerable and defenseless, could also be just as fierce, unapologetic in her defense and quick to retaliate if offended. A Goddess of swift action, there were many men, as well as women, in Greek mythology that fell victim to her volatile wrath when they dared to fail her expectations.

The Cypress and Laurel wreath were sacred to her, as were the mountains, wilderness and the raw powers found in nature. Here is a Goddess who perfectly exemplified this wild, untamable, raw power. All wild beasts, in her beloved forest, fell under her love and care. Artemis was sometimes known as the stag lover and some of her sacred animals were the deer, bears, horses, hare, and like Hecate- the hounds. She was often associated with bears, perhaps because she too, exemplified the same fiercely, protective nature towards the young, as bears do with their cubs. In many artistic depictions of the Moon Goddess we see her holding her bow and arrows, surrounded by stags, hare, wild beast and dogs. She was indeed the huntress, but engaged in this sport with great reverence. The act of killing an animal, for mere pleasure, was sacrilegious to this Goddess and resulted in her unforgiving retaliation.

All forest animals were under her protective domain, as were young girls. Young maidens were expected to dedicate themselves to her. Traditionally, her devotees would spend a year in her service, prior to marriage. Some of the text of the time reveals interesting rituals young girls performed in her honor, like wearing yellow tunics and mimicking animals in a special bear dance. Numerous priestesses took vows of chastity and exemplified the virtues and attributes of Artemis in their service to her. She was depicted as pure and chaste and demanded her priestesses to also live their lives in the same manner, devoted to her. Her numerous temples were found in Sparta and the town of Brauron and the largest, in Delos, her birth place. At Ephesus in Ionia (Turkey) her temple became one of the Seven Wonders of the World. Her Temple of Ephesus was built around 323BC and therafter; updated and rebuilt numerous times throughout history.

Artemis is the Goddess of the Hunt. Her Archery skills were unmatched and her aim and focus unsurpassed. She did not back down to any man and proudly display her archery skills at every opportunity. It was also apparent, she preferred the company of women, over men. Greek lore reveal that she probably was once in love, with a mortal hunter named Orion, but she vowed never to love again when that love ended tragically and of course, there are various accounts of this tale. Her brother, who was also a fine, competitive archer, engaged her in a little competition one day, which subsequently resulted in her arrow killing the love of her life. According to one myth, Apollo loved his sister greatly and perhaps was jealous of the relationship she was forming with Orion, but some speculate, that he also wanted to protect his sister's chastity. One day he challenged his competitive sister to see if she could hit a shiny target, far away in the distance, near a lake. Artemis, lover of challenges and never one to miss her target, aimed... and unbeknownst to her, she shot the arrow that would inevitably kill Orion -the man she loved.

Although she interacted very little with men, she had an extremely close relationship with her brother, but it becomes apparent through some of the Greek literature of the time, that she also had a special relationship with her father, Zeus. Artemis was always confident, focus, strong willed and very decisive. She displayed these strong attributes at a very young age too. According to the popular Greek writings of the time, by her third birthday she already knew precisely what she wanted as a gift and made her request known to her beloved father, while sitting upon his lap. Without hesitation, Zeus conceded to his bold, confident birthday girl and provided her with the desired bow & arrows, sixty nymphs, as well as stags and hounds, just as she requested at age three. She wanted to be chaste and free of the confinements of marriage and she wanted a silver bow and arrow, like her twin brother. According to the legend, at this tender age, she let it be known that she wanted to reside among the wild, in the mountains and Zeus was only too pleased to comply. The Hellenic Goddess didn't want to wear the traditional attire that women of her time wore. She wanted a short tunic as her hunting attire, which gave her maiden legs freedom to run. She wanted to bring light into the world, in the same way her twin brother did, as God of the Sun, and she was not at all interested in the distractions of love and thus, she was given immunity from Aphrodite's charms.

In Artemis we see the roots of feminism, leadership, sisterhood and the spirit of independence. She embraced being a leader to her clan of nymphs and amazons, yet the young Artemis passionately valued her freedom and those moments of solitude. She fiercely defended her privacy and there are numerous tales of her retaliations on those who dared violate her privacy, especially if they were men.

Artemis was known as a maiden, virgin Goddess because she belonged to no one. The term Virgin, was a title in ancient time, referring to societal position - not necessarily sexual and more than anything it pointed to her autonomy. The Hellenic Goddess was never married and had no known children and thus, she was considered whole unto herself, belonging to no one. In mythology we see how she was fierce and impulsive, if pushed to anger. Often men and some women fell victim to her wrath, if they failed to meet her expectations. Still, this immortal Greek Maiden Goddess is a champion of women/wommin and exemplifies for us; autonomy, strength and the power inherent in our focus and passionate will. She awakens us to our inner confident maiden; embracing our physical strength, competitiveness, athelitism and the freedom to exist in the world, not by societal standards but by our very own defined tenets. Artemis demanded to live her life on her own terms, unconventionally, not conforming to the traditional roles of women of her time. She is quite a force of empowerment for today's modern women and feminist alike.

*The Greek Maiden Huntress, Artemis is the Goddess of our untamable, wild inner child. Artemis arrives to remind you of your effervescent youth, your inner maiden, running freely and the power intrinsic in youth's fearlessness. Do you remember running as a child, do you remember how it felt....? Artemis connects you to the value of your physical body and the joy of being in your earthly form.

The archer's supreme, intense focus begins to take hold now. She is the Divine huntress, whose archery skills and keen focus are unmatched. She also awakens in you the gifts of friendships, supportive sisterhood, and reminds you of the power inherent in your gender, when it partners with other like-minded beings. The Huntress awakens in you the gift of a Maiden's willpower and energy. She stirs your heart to a special connection to the beloved creatures that inhabit the forest. Connect to her exeburant leap, as she beckons you to move, run, jump, dance, engage in a comepetitive sport, and connect to your sacred body.

LESSON ON ARTEMIS

- **Known as:** The GreekVirgin Maiden Goddess Artemis
- Goddess of the Hunt, Goddess of Archery, Goddess of the New Moon, Goddess of the Amazons.
- Patron Goddess to Women, Children, Animals.
- Her name also translates as "protector/safety"
- Virgin meaning: whole unto herself and no one else. It was a word referring to a societal position -not sexuality. She was never married, no known children.
- She was also known in Rome as Diana, Diana Artemis, multi- breasted Lady of Ephesus.
- **Birthplace:** Born on the Greek Island of Delos, she was daughter of Zeus & Goddess Leto (Goddess of Child birthing). She was twin to Apollo-The Sun God. Thus she shares a lot of characteristics with her brother, such as being a light bearer. When she was born, as mythology reveals, she was immediately employed as midwife to assist her mother, who was having a difficult time birthing her twin brother. This is one reason why she is often associated with women and childbirth and is the Patroness of midwifery though she, herself, never had any known children.
- **Her Symbols:** Associated with the Crescent new moon and is often seen as the maiden aspect of Hekate and part of that trinity (maiden, mother, crone). Selene,

Hekate, Diana-Artemis many variations on this trinity like Demeter, Kore & Hekate etc... She is Light bearer sharing similar characteristics to Hekate.
- She became known as the protector of the hopeless and defenseless, which at the time were; children, women, young girls, animals beast, babes etc. Young girls would often dedicate themselves to Artemis and she had numerous priestesses and temples.
- Her sacred animals were the Stag, Rabbits, Bears, and like Hekate, Dogs, all wild beast and offspring were sacred in her beloved forest. The mountains and the wilderness were sacred to her. Perhaps because she was the known defender & protector of women and the defenseless, she became the Goddess of the Witches as her Roman counterpart, Diana.

- **Her Mythology/stories:** When her mother was ready to give birth she ran into trouble trying to find a safe place to deliver her twins due to Hera's wrath- no one dared assist the pregnant Leto. A magical island (the Greek island of Delos) was made available and there she was able to give birth to Artemis.
  - Through out mythology she was often seen coming to her mother's aid and defending and protecting her, along with other women.
  - Artemis was confident, even at the early age of three, she knew she wanted; her bow & arrow, sixty nymphs, hunting dogs. She wanted to reside among the wild in the mountains. She knew she didn't want to wear traditional dress and wanted her hunting costume as her attire; she wanted to bring light into the world. She did not want the distractions of love and thus she wanted immunity from Aphrodite's charms.
- **Her Gifts:** She was seen as pure and chaste and she expected her priestesses to live in the same way. Artemis valued her freedom and could be quite fierce if angered. She loved her time in solitude but also being a leader, to nymphs and to her clan of Amazons. She was very competitive and no one could match her aim & focus as an Archer; she backed down to no man. The beautiful Callisto was her known, beloved companion. Artemis was self-confident, strong, decisive and loved the company of women.

SKADI

Skadi is the Norse Goddess of Winter, mountains and wilderness. She is a Viking Goddess known by several other names like; Snowshoe Goddess, Ski Goddess, Skade, Skadhi, Skathi and Shinning Bride of the Gods. Interesting to note, her name bares a similar resemblance to the Hindu Goddess of Feminine energy, Shakti. Skadi is a Giantess and the beloved daughter of the Giant Thiassi/Thjazi and she became a Goddess through her union and marriage with the Gods of Aesir. She was described as a Jotunn and a fair maiden, in the Heimskringla book, Ynglinga saga. It is also widely believed that the country of Scandinavia received its name from this beloved Goddess and apparently her name, or derivations of her name, can be found throughout Scandinavia. She was also known as Ondurgodth, which means, "Ski God," and Ondurtis, which means "Ski Lady," both words come from the Old Norse language.

There are numerous conflicting stories about Skadi's etymology, but her name in Old High German is linked with the word, "Scato", which mean "*Shadow*". This may reflect an older, initial depiction of the Goddess as a bringer of death or a deity of the underworld. Along with the word shadow, her name has also been translated as meaning; "scathe", "damaged," or "harm".

In Norse mythology there were three known clans of Deities; the Aesir gods, who lived in Asgard and the Vanir gods, who lived in Anaheim. Eventually these two respective clans resolved their differences to join together and recognize Asgard as the hall and home of all the gods. The third clan of Norse deities was known as the Jotun, the wise, but malefic race of Giants and this is where we find Skadi's lineage. More specifically, she was believed to be part of the Frost Giant clan.

According to Norse cosmology, the sun was the first to exist in the world and from the sun came two beings; the great cow, Audhumla, and Ymir, a great giant. From the sweat of Ymir, during his sleep, his offspring were born and thus partheno-genetically, he gave birth to the race of giants. Creation of the earth and its inhabitant can be attributed to Ymir, who appears to be very much like Gaia in his role of populating the earth, as Norse cosmology reveals.

Ymir had a reputation for being extremely cruel and one day he met his fate by being killed by Odin and his brothers. The earth and its inhabitants were thus formed from pieces of his torn body. Subsequently, all giant descendants died with his blood being shed upon the earth, all except for two. Two giants, Bergelmir (mountain old) and his wife survived, by hiding in the great World-Mill. From these two giants the race of

Jotnar was born and thus, here we have Skadi's Great grandparents and her ancestral lineage traced.

In Norse mythology there are the Aesir, warrior deities and agricultural gods known as Vanir, The Jotnar/Jotun or Giants were viewed as primal, primitive, existing since the beginning of time and they seemed to be losing popularity next to the cultured more sophisticated Asa-gods (combination of Aesir & Vanir gods). It is reminiscent of the Greek battle between the old primordial Titans and their new descendant, the Olympians -the old gods vs the new ruling class.

As a giantess, Skadi makes her homes in Jotunheim [JO-tune-haym] meaning a cold cliff. The threshold to this realm was the wilderness, also known as Utgard [oot-guard] and this was Skadi's beloved realm. Not much is stated about Skadi's mother, but we know of her father and how close she was to him. He was the giant known as Thiazi/Thjatsi/Thiassi. Like most Giants in Norse mythology, he had the ability to shape shift and he would often manifest himself into an eagle. In chapter 56 of the Prose Edda book "Skaldskarparmal, Bragi tells Aegir the tale of how the giant Thjazi was killed.

The story begins with Odin (father of the Gods), Hoenir (a warrior, Asa-god, who lacked wit) and Loki, (the trickster God/giant, son of the giant Farbauti -Cruel Smiter). These three Gods were traveling through the realm of the giants. They stopped at Utgard and they failed to leave the expected traditional offering of respect as they passed into the Giant's realm. Skadi's father, Thjazi was watching the offenders very closely in his popular shape as an eagle. As the three Gods, later that day, hungrily tried to roast their dinner, Thjazi would not allow them to cook it. In the form of an eagle he kept grabbing their food and in frustration Loki tried to stop him, but ended up getting snatched up, along with the food, by the infuriated eagle. He was nearly killed but was spared upon agreeing to Thjazi's one demand.

Loki agreed and was then obligated to bring the beloved Goddess of youth, Idunna and the sacred golden apple, to the realm of the Giants. He fulfilled his promised to Thjazi but as a result, the gods of Vanir soon began to lose their strength, beauty and immortality, for it was Idunna who was solely responsible for keeping the gods youthfulness alive. And the longer the Goddess Idunna stayed in Jotunheim, the more desperate the gods became. Angered, they relentlessly molested Loki and demanded that he retrieve Idunna for the sake of all the gods in Asgard. Together the Gods desperately devised a plan and it started with the Goddess Freyja, lending Loki the Falcon shape form, so that he could remake the journey to Utgard and finally retrieve Idunna. When Loki arrived however, the Giant was nowhere to be found, so Loki turned Idunna into a small nut and quickly commenced his journey, with her, back to Asgard. Unbeknownst to Loki, Thjazi was flying about as an eagle and when he saw what had transpired he quickly gave chase to stop the abduction and reclaim Idunna. The gods of Asgard however, had prepared a large fire in anticipation of this and because Thjazi was flying so recklessly fast, he flew right into the blaze of fire and was tragically burnt to death.

This would seem like the end of the story but it doesn't end here. From across the snow covered, crystallized landscape comes a larger than life figure, donning a warrior's helmet, suit and armor and approaching Asgard, with much purpose and speed. It was Thjazi's orphaned daughter, Skadi. Enraged, fearlessly seeking to avenge her father's death without concern for her own safety, she arrived. She wanted justice and rightfully deserved it, as Norse tradition often provide great familial compensation when a Kinship had been unjustly killed and this was the case before them when she arrived to Asgard. She enters the hall of the Gods with much anger and conviction - determined to avenge her father's death with blood. She carries with her; sword, spears, arrows and war weapons prepared for retribution. Because she is primal, she is quite capable of taking on any of the gods and perhaps this is yet another reason why the Gods at Asgard avoided a confrontation with the Giantess and quickly conceded to her rightful demands. In some of the text, there is a reference to her breathtaking beauty which might have also contributing to their compliance of her demands.

At first, the father of all gods, Odin, tries to placate Skadi by offering her mounds of gold, but she is already full of riches, according to Norse mythology, due to all the pillaging of her clan and thus she is not interested in currency. Instead she proposes laughter (since, in her mourning, she has been grief stricken, unable to laugh and doubts anyone could make this happen) and since her kinship has been killed, she demands a spouse. Odin agrees with the stipulation that she must elect her spouse, blindfolded, looking solely at the feet of the gods to make her decision. She agrees, and the gods are lined up and covered, so that only their feet are exposed. Now, Skadi had hoped she could distinguish the feet of Baldur among the other gods, for she had secretly desired the god of Beauty and Light. When she spotted a pair of beautiful, clean white feet she automatically assumed they belonged to Baldur, but instead they belonged to the Vana God of the Sea, Njord. He was known to walk barefoot upon the sea quite often, making his feet appear supple and aesthetic pleasing. Imagine her disillusionment to learn that she would be partner with an older, wealthy, mediocre looking god. Still, oaths were sacred to her and she had agreed to the marital arrangement.

The next part of the agreement involved laughter and the trickster god, Loki, was only too eager to entertain. According to one story, Loki tied a string to his testicles and the other string to the beard of a goat (although some text state it was the horns of a live goat). The goat and Loki begin to engage in a weird dance, a tug and pull of buffoonery that ends with Loki clumsily falling backwards unto Skadi's lap. The entire hall of the gods was vibrating in their laughter, including Skadi and thus the second part of the agreed compensation had been fulfilled- they succeeded in making her laugh. Gratified, she had attained her compensation and a spouse in Njord.

Her marriage to Njord proved to be unfulfilling however and short lived, as neither could agree on a single place to live, simultaneously as husband and wife. Njord's beloved home was the seaside hall of Noatun, but after nine days of trying to adjust to this new abode, Skadi found the seaside home and the various sounds of this realm, aggravating. Together they tried Skadi's beloved home of Thrymheim, up in the snowy peak mountains of her father's old domicile. For nine nights Njord also tried to adjust to the new dwelling, but he complained of the wolf howlings and the sounds of the harsh winds. After eighteen nights they realized it was a hopeless, dreadful situation because Njord hated the mountain and the howlings and Skadi could not sleep with the sea birds screeching. They decided it was best to separate. Their separation, however seemed amicable and there appears to be no indication of an actual divorce but rather an understanding of their unconventional living arrangement.

It appears however, that Skadi was the model of an independent female, retaining her autonomy even in the midst of several relationships. One story tells that after Njord, she returned to her home in Thrymheim and found love with her soul mate, the God of Winter, archery and skis, Ulle. Together they appeared to share many characteristics and enjoyed their life amidst the snowy mountainous landscape- skiing and hunting. Other tales reveal that she actually married Odin, King of the Gods. Both Odin and Skadi share similar attributes, in their love of wolves and their love of fierce battles and thus, their union would seem quite natural. Although she never had any children with Njord, the myth of her time tell that she did bear Odin many sons, most notably, Saeminger, the

King of Norway and the first in the line of Jarls of Hladhir (this was a clan of fierce protectors of the Norse Ancient Religion).

We can learn a great deal about Skadi's character through some of her myths. Her role as one who seeks justice is reinforced when we learn of how she punished Loki for the wrongful death of two of her beloved kinsman. As with many of the multi dimensional Goddesses mentioned in this book, their numerous attributes can easily fit into themes found in other chapters of this book. Skadi is no different, and her energy can also be explored in the chapter of Justice, but I disgress. Loki, the trickster god of Aesir, who was also a giant and blood brother of Odin, was always causing mishap. In this tale, a mistletoe dart was thrown by the blind God, Hod, but guided by the trickster God Loki, it ends up wrongfully killing the young, beautiful son of Odin and Frigga - Baldur. Now Skadi was quite fond of Baldur, if you can recall the earlier tale, in the Prose Edda, when she secretly had hoped it was his feet she had chosen as a life mate. For Skadi, this was the second man she loved, killed by Loki, and his shenanigans. Naturally, it was she who was called upon to exercise retribution for the wrongful death of Baldur. According to the tale, she bounded him and placed a venomous snake above his face, and it remained there to burn him drop by drop, making him writhe so much so, that the earth trembled, as a result we have an explanation for earthquakes. We also learn of Skadi's kind nature in Norse mythology. For example we know that despite her failed marriage to Njord, she was an extremely caring guardian and step-mother to Njord's children; Freyr and Freyja and she took great interest in their lives.

Skadi is the Norse Goddess of snow, ice, mountains, hunting, archery, justice and fairness. She is a patron Goddess to independent women and those serving the military. She invites you to reclaim the wild maiden and live your life by your own rules, in your own unique, most beneficial way. It becomes clear from the Norse writing of the time that Skadi is a strong, confident Goddess that always seems to act from a place of truth, justice and righteousness. In this aspect she is reminiscent of the Goddess Themis in her pursuit for what is right and yet her love of the wilderness, archery, wolves and her uncompromising freedom, reminds me greatly of the Greek maiden Goddess, Artemis.

Skadi is described often as a beautiful giantess, with long flowing hair, courageous and clearly following her emotions and instincts. As a snowshoe, skiing Wintry Goddess, exploring the wilderness and delighting in the mountains, she is unquestionably a very physical Goddess who will expect you to also engage your physical body in your communion with her. She challenges you to confront fear and insecurities and is a good guide when you are ready to see how far you can go. She will test your strengths and boundaries. Don't be surprised if she, manifest herself in your body, inspiring you to take up extreme sports and a more adventuresome approach to life.

*Skadi is the Norse Giantess Goddess, who fiercely defends what she believes to be right. She is part of the ancient early tribe of Norse Gods. As the Snowshoe Maiden Goddess she is an archer, connected to the wilderness and the snowcapped mountaintops and she is known for her strength and her physicality. She awakens the Amazon woman within you and offers the gift of physical wellbeing, strength and perspective. How vastly different our challenges appear when we see them through the eyes of the Giantess, up high on the mountaintops? How vastly altered you would feel, to walk and act in the armored body of a Giantess, like the Norse Goddess, Skadi. Skadi's energy is proud and strong reminiscent of the Greek Maiden Goddess, Artemis. When she enters your realm you will feel her inviting you to honor your body. She calls you to tap into your inner & outer strengths. Unearth your convictions & righteousness and honor your body. You can manifest powerful changes now for Skadi, the Giantess Amazon, lives in every woman.

UZUME

Uzume is the Japanese Goddess of Dawn, revelry and joy. She quintessentially represents the cathartic power of laughter and is also depicted in Japanese Kyogen farce- as a woman who delights in her sensuality, called Okame.

Her full name is Ame –no-Uzume no Mikoto and it is quite intriguing to note that her name is sometimes interpreted as meaning *"The Terrible Female of Heaven."* In the Shinto religion, the name Uzume is linked to a "strong, brave woman." Today you might even hear the term "*osushi*," to refer to a Japanese woman, a modern reference to one who exemplifies Uzume herself and the attributes she blesses women with.

As a deity often associated with the springtime, Uzume is considered a patron Goddess of the Rice fields. She is also very much connected with trance drumming and Shamanic practices. And, as her most popular myth will reveal, she is a Goddess of revelry and dance, more specifically ritualistic, ecstatic dancing. She is known also, as the wild chaotic abandonment sometimes found amidst the powerful surge of creative energy. Uzume is embodied Shakti energy and she is a Goddess often linked with early forms of Divination and psychic powers. Though often portrayed as the maiden, there are some texts that suggest another aspect of hers, represented as the wise crone.

There is very limited scholarly research and information on this early Japanese deity but we can extrapolate much from the ancient writings found in the Japanese sacred texts of the Kojiiki and the Nihonghi. The Kojiiki (*The Japanese Records of Ancient Matters*), C712 C.E./712 A.D. is one of the oldest existing written record of Japanese myth, legends and historical narrative related to Japan's imperial family and its assertion of Divine connection. The Nihonghi, (*Chronicle of Japan from the Earliest Times*) AD 697 AD, also sheds a great deal of insight into Japanese mythology, its origins and the worship of deities in ancient times. In these early sacred texts, the Goddess Uzume, is known as "*The Heavenly Alarming Female*" as well as "*The Great Persuader*" and she is still very much worshipped today as a prominent Shinto deity.

Shinto comes from the Chinese word, "*Shen-tao*," meaning the way of the Gods. It is the indigenous, native religion of Japan that quite possibly has its roots in the Animist religions of Siberia. It is an ancient religion that lacks dogma yet practices the venerations of nature, spirits, ancestors and deities (referred to as Kami) and it pre-dates Buddhism. There is a strong belief in animated and unanimated objects and it is a Polytheistic religion that venerates a myriad of superior beings and spirits, known as Kami.

Interesting and most important to note, the Japanese name for Japan is Nippon, which literally means; Sun Origin and this is a direct reference to the highest venerated deity in Japan, the Sun Goddess, Amaterasu. Shintosim is a religion whose central deity is female unlike other World religions. And the Sun Goddess, Amaterasu, is of great significance because she is attributed for birthing Japan itself. Thus Shintoism is a spiritual practice intimately connected with Japan's divine origin and its people.

The Goddess Uzume is most often associated with the Japanese Sun Goddess, Amaterasu and she is attributed for playing a big part in tricking the Goddess out of her cave and self- imposed imprisonment. In the ancient myths, it was Uzume, with her ability to raise a ruckus that helped return Amaterasu back to her rightful place in the heavens, as the Sun Goddess and restore balance upon the earth.

According to Japanese lore, the Sun Goddess, Amaterasu O- Mikami, had retreated from the world when her volatile brother, the Storm God, Susano-O-no Kami, had defiled her sacred Temple. In one of his usual uncontrollable episodes he haphazardly tossed excrement and a colt (her sacred animal) unto the weavers of her holy temple. This vicious act singlehandedly caused great distress and misfortune to Amaterasu and her Priestesses. The benevolent Sun Goddess had tried many times before to reconcile with her brother, forgive him and somehow live peacefully in the world with him but this time he had gone too far. In his violently explosive behavior he had not only defiled Amaterasu's sacred temple but also injured many and killed one of her beloved priestesses. The Sun Goddess, saddened beyond measure, reached a monumental turning point and decided she could no longer shine her light for the world in his presence. Grief stricken, she retreated into the Heavenly Rock-Cave, where she removed her brilliant light from the world and stayed hidden, refusing to come out again. The earth, as a result, stood motionless and was needless to say negatively affected by the darkness that ensued. Nothing grew upon the earth without her divine light. There was famine, chaos and much calamity without the bright power of the sun. Both mortals and Gods alike were adversely affected by this indefinite Solar eclipse and they were greatly concerned about the state of the world, as the wild untamable, Susano-O- no Kami, now reigned freely. The ancient text found in the Kojiiki stated that the eight million Gods (or Kamis, as they are known in Japan) gathered to discuss a possible resolution and devise a plan to bring back the Sun Goddess. They too suffered gravely without her Divine light and the Kamis were desperate to restore balance and world order. The Japanese God, Takami-Musubi-no-Kami, called upon the council of Gods and they gathered on the Eight-sand-Bank River, in the heavens, according to Shinto lore and they began to brainstorm. The craftsman God, Ishiko-ritome-no-Kami was to build a great big mirror made out of copper, brought from the Heavenly mount Kagu and it was their hope that if Amaterasu caught a glimpse of her own Divine reflection in this sacred mirror she would enchant her own self with her brilliance and finally return to her post as the venerated Sun Goddess. The deity, Kushi-Akarutama-no-Kami was in charge of creating yet another magickal tool of enchanting distraction- sparkling jewelry. It was their hope the sparkling brilliance of these divinely crafted jewels would entice the Sun Goddess to come out further for a better look and hopefully remain in the world, out of her dark cave. Woven white cloths, made from mulberry paper, were also among the many items made and hung by the sacred trees surrounding the cave entrance all in an effort to entice the Sun Goddess. Ame-no-Mahitotsu-no-Kami crafted and offered swords, axes and tinkling bells of iron as well. The Sakaki tree from the Heavenly mount of Kagu, with its multitude of braches, was carried by the Gods. It was decorated with all the bright jewels, reflective items and finely woven cloths and streamers in an effort to lure the Goddess even further out of her cave. The God, Futotama-no-Mikoto held the sacred Sakaki tree while he began to eulogize the Sun Goddess and Ame-no-Koyane-no-Mikoto recited invocations to Amaterasu... still the Goddess would not come out of her cave.

Our Goddess here, the spring maiden, Ame-no-Uzume-no-Mikoto then took center stage. Uzume wore a scarf made of club moss around her shoulders and a wreath. And while holding a tinkle belled crafted spear and bamboo grass and leaves, she lit the sacred bonfires before the Heavenly rock-cave. With all the Kamis surrounding the area, intensely waiting for a sign from the Sun Goddess, Uzume jumped on top of an overturned bath tub and began a silly, almost burlesque-like, dance. This wild dance was steeped in licentiousness and it stirred up the audience of tense Japanese deities. The laughter that ensued from Uzume's bawdy striptease created quite a commotion and it, unsuspectedly, also stirred Amaterasu's curiosity from behind the dark, blocked caved. She wondered how there could be any laughter or joy upon the earth in her absence. Hearing all the laughter and frivolity, she wondered if they had forgotten her or had somehow replaced her with another deity. These gnawing, uncomfortable doubts motivated her to investigate even further and so, she proceeded to crack open the entry of her cave, just enough to get a peek at what was going on outside. Naturally when she took her first glimpse outside of the cave she caught sight of all the brilliant sparkling jewels hanging from the trees and its beauty moved her to come out even further. Then she caught sight of her own divine reflection. Needless to say she was enamored by the golden luminescence of her own reflection. The surrounding Gods seized that very moment to quickly close off the cave entrance behind her to secure Amaterasu's staying presence in the world. She then discovered that it was Uzume's dance that had inspired such a wonderfully loud, joyful noise outside of her cave. Thus, Uzume and her bawdy, sexually liberating dance is attributed for pulling the Sun Goddess out of her grief and self-imposed exile, in the same way as the old nurse maid, Baubo, in Greek Mythology, helped awaken the Grain Goddess, Demeter, from her own despondency. Just as it was Baubo's bawdy lifting of the skirt, exposing her genitalia that snapped the Greek Grain Goddess out of her depressive hopeless state, so it was the Japanese Goddess Uzume who achieved the same feat. With her licentious, frenzied dance, lifting her kimono, she roused up not only the eight million Kamis but the dark grieving earth itself. And their collective joy and laughter over what they witnessed in Uzume, eradicated the darkness and brought forth the rebirth of the great Sun, Amaterasu. It becomes clear that Uzume is a Goddess who speaks to women on the power of laughter and the unabashed joys found when one embraces their sexuality. Yet, Uzume also speaks to us about the incredibly cathartic powers found in our physical body, Shakti energy, our body's rhythm and our personal dance.

There is another tale in the ancient Japanese text found in the Kojiiki and the Nihonghi that allows us yet an additional alternative glimpse into the beloved Goddess, Uzume.

When the Sun Goddess was ready to send to earth her beloved grandson, Ninigi, the August Child, to rule the people of Japan and proselytize her divine teachings, there was conflict. The heavens were divided, as some supported Amaterasu's decision, while other Gods were not happy to see Ninigi as first Japanese emperor to establish the first Imperial family. According to the Kojiiki, as he was about to descend upon the earth he noticed something blocking his entry way. It was a huge, monstrous looking creature that was described in great detail in the ancient Japanese text. This deity blocking the pathway for Ninigi was a frightful sight. It had a nose seven hands in length and glowing fiery eyes according to text found in the Kojiiki. This being was huge in size and was fiercely intimidating to Amaterasu's divine grandchild. Desperate, Ninigi called upon the Goddess Uzume who had acquired the powerful reputation for being the one who could always be relied upon to help the Gods.

The August Child called upon the Goddess Uzume, explaining his plight and asking for her assistance in this matter. She quickly descended to the heaven and earth threshold to confront the blocking monster. With her pushed down band across her navel and her exposed pendulum bare breast she confronted the monster and asked what business he had to be there. The monster was taken aback by her nakedness and bold candor. Bewildered by her appearance he introduced himself as Saruta-Hiko-no-Oho-Kami and then inquired about her reasons for this unconventional approach. He proceeded to tell her that upon hearing the Heavenly Grandson was about to descend to the earth he wanted to make himself available to the Future First Emperor of Japan. He was there waiting for Ninigi, not as an enemy, but to offer his assistance in whichever way served the Heavenly grandchild best. Thus, Uzume's bold confrontation births knowledge of Ninigi's true ally, unblocking the pathway to his destiny and it becomes the vehicle for the first Imperial family to be born. Ninigi was too frightened to see for himself who or what was blocking his destiny but it was Uzume's typical bold feat that resolved the paralyzing standstill and allowed the Sun Goddess's Grandchild to take his rightful place upon the earth. Again Uzume is called upon and acts as an intermediary so that the Gods are able to take their rightful place upon the heavens and the earth.

Known as the Crossroad God, Saruta Hiko or Sarutahiko-Okami as he is sometime known, was to guide the heavenly Grandson from the plains of high heaven to the wondrous peak of Takachiho in Hyuga, Tsukushi and then, thereafter, Saruta Hiko would leave to the river, Isuzu at Sanagata, in Ise. He was so impressed by the bold Goddess that he invited Uzume to join him in this journey and she did, becoming later on, his wife according to Japanese ancient text.

Saruta-Hiko-no-Oho-Kami, is venerated as the God of the Crossroads and he is paired with the Goddess Uzume as her consort. There is something to note when we consider that Uzume is joy, ecstasy, magick and trance dancing. When she is paired with her consort (a monstruous deity connected with the crossroads) it adds another dimension to our understanding of this ancient Japanese deity. It is as if she invites us to the edge; the mysterious, pivotal crossroads of magick and ecstasy.

Together, Uzume and Saruta Hiko are credited for both accompanying, the Heavenly Grandson throughout his journey to become the First Emperor of Japan and build the first Imperial family. It is this reason why Uzume and Saruta Hiko are considered the ancestors of Japan's sacred Imperial family.

Consequently, Ninigi held the Goddess, Uzume with great honor for her help in facilitating his Imperial journey. She was made the founder of the Sarume Order and the patron Goddess for the ritual dancers who perform in annual Sacred Festivals. These were mostly women and their dances take on a comical appearance which is valued as divine and necessary, in most traditional Japanese religious ceremonies. At the First Fruit Festival, Japanese perform the Saru-Mahi, a monkey dance. The word Sarume actually means *"She-Monkey,"* thus, it is clear Uzume's sacred dance is a primal one, wildly connected to a monkey's movement. Many Shinto ceremonies incorporate other Uzume dances like the Nakatomi and the Imbe. These are the origins of the Kagura (a ritualistic dance-mime). Uzume's dance upon the overturned bathtub during the ancient myth related to the return of the Sun Goddess is still venerated and widely performed today in many Shinto ceremonies. These dances were often associated with early forms of medium possession, trance and shamanistic practice.

It is clear the Japanese Goddess Uzume played an important role in ancient women's lives and her significance for contemporary women needs to be highly considered. This is a sacred feminine, immortal Goddess whose spirit and energy is still very much venerated today in Shinto religious ceremonies just as it has been for hundreds of years. For those in the Goddess community, seeking to unearth, connect and worship the multitude of ways the Feminine Divine appears to us, Uzume is yet another wonderful expression of womanhood (*wombmynhood*) and thus, another sacred aspect of Goddess.

*The Japanese Goddess of merriment, Uzume, is often closely connected with the Sun Goddess, Amaterasu; much the same way as the Goddess Baubo is forever immortalized with the Greek Grain Goddess, Demeter. She is boldness and merriment all contained and reflected in the physical body and she introduces us to the powerful art form of the Burlesque. Uzume exemplifies for us the power and magick, found in our beautiful physical body and the gift of dance. She also awakens us to ecstatic trancing and the value of shamanistic practices. Uzume's silliness and buoyant laughter helped eradicate darkness on the earth and return the Sun Goddess to her rightful place in the heavens. She is thus, the cathartic power of laughter, ecstasy and the joys found in our physical body.

MACHA

Macha is an Irish and Scotland Goddess of War, Protection, Victory and Sovereignty. She is particularly connected with land and the province of Ulster, in ancient Ireland. She is also connected to fertility, strength and childbirth. Often depicted wearing the color red, with distinctly red long tresses, she is connected to horses and fire.

The Celtic Goddess, Macha, is also considered an aspect of the Triple Warrior and Death Goddess, Morrighan. There are many varied opinions on this subject because there were many different Machas mentioned in various Celtic and Scottish folklores yet her veneration cannot be underestimated. As part of the trinity connected to the triple Goddess Morrighan, there was; "Badb" (Scald Crow), "Nemain" (Battle Fury) and "Macha" (the Raven One).

According to one of many folklores connected to Macha, there was a story about a grieving farmer in the land of Ulster who was alone in his remote distant home, his name was Cruinniuc. He had recently lost his wife and in his grief his entire household was falling apart without the loving touch of a wife and mother for his son. One day, out of the blue, a lady is seen approaching his castle. She enters his home and quite inexplicably, begins to fix things and brings order into the neglected home. She is said to lie in bed with him that night, thus inferring her acceptance as his new bride. In her presence all things that were chaotic, uncared for and neglected became organized and well-tended to. She was his savioress. For Cruinniuc, there was nothing she couldn't do as she brought so much love, healing and order into his life. Together they built their home and family, and life was good.

One day, Cruinniuc decides he want to attend the annual fair held by the prideful king of Ulster. The lady of the house was now pregnant and much too far advance in her pregnancy to accompany her husband to the fair. She gives her blessings for him to go alone and enjoy himself at the fair but only if her promises not to speak of her existence to anyone. Well, Cruinniuc agrees and when he arrives at the fair, he begins to enjoy himself a bit too much and partakes of many libations. He then breaks his promise to his wife and begins to boast to everyone about his wife's many gifts.

After watching the chariot races, he brags to the king's men that his wife is so powerful that she can even outrun the kings' horses. Well, upon hearing his assertion this did not sit well with the prideful king and he angrily detained Cruinniuc until his men could fetch the wife and personally attest to the claim. When they met her they explained the situation and warned her that her husband's life was in jeopardy if she did not come with them to prove the claim that her husband drunkenly made. She was obviously very pregnant and tried to implore for their compassion but they refused to reason with her. She assured them that she could partake in the race with the horses if they would simply allow her to give birth first but the King would not hear of it. To save her husband's life, the very pregnant Macha was forced to partake in the grueling race against the king's Horses.

As the legend goes, it is said she painfully gave birth to her twins in that Chariot Race, in the midst of childbirth. Her great strength unmatched, she not only gave birth to twins but she won the race against the King's horses and proved her husband right. The story however did not end there. Upon her victory she cursed all the men of Ulster, for the next nine generations that they too shall know the great pains and suffering that she was, unsympathetically, forced to endure. The cursed of pain and agony would last for 5 days and nights annually for descendants of Ulster. Consequently, the place where she was victorious and where she gave birth to her twins was then known as "Emain Macha" meaning, Macha's Twins.

SUNNA

Sunna is the benevolent Goddess of the sun in Norse mythology. She is seen by Scandinavians as holding a maternal role due to her nature as a sun deity. Known as the daughter of Mundilfaeri (his name means, axis mover), her brother, Mani, is known as the Moon God.

According to the myths, Mundilfaeri gave birth to two children and was so enamored by their beauty and light that he named them, the Moon and the Sun, respectively. Upon hearing of this, the Gods were not pleased and so they took his offspring and sent them up to the sky, to represent the Moon and Sun. These deities are often depicted, driving their chariot. Sunna drives a chariot of the Sun, while her brother drives the chariot of the Moon.

In ancient Norse mythology there are of two noteworthy wolves, named Skoll to and Hati. It was a common belief that these two wolves run after the chariot of the Sun and the chariot of Moon, always in an infinite attempt to devour these principal celestial bodies. Lunar and Solar Eclipses were often seen as the wolves actually succeeding at taking a bite out of the Sun or the Moon. According to Norse cosmology, the much feared end of the world, known as, Ragnarok, would one day manifest the moment these two wolves successfully devour the Sun and the Moon. There is an indication that the Goddess Sunna, will give birth to a daughter who is expected to take on her mother's role after the destruction of the world.

Most of what we known about Sunna comes from the Prose Edda, by Snorri Sturluson. In his 13th century writings he includes Sunna among the revered Norse Gods. As a Sun Goddess she is view as having healing attributes. She gives the earth much needed light and warmth, in the North, where the frigid climate is brutally endured. Her healing aspects can also be seen in Ragnarok, when she intentionally births a daughter, which she offers up to the Universe in order to sustain humanity after destruction.

While Egypt, Greece, and the Middle East region viewed the burning bright sun as both a destroyer and protector, in the north, it did not hold the same perspective. The sun did not have the same destructive, warrior like qualities, in the North. There were no consistent worries about rivers, or water sources, drying up, or crops being burnt and destroyed by the scorching hot sun. In Norse mythology, the sun was appreciated as a nourishing entity; melting away the icebergs, warming the bitter cold air and helping inhabitant of this icy terrain withstand the usual frigid temperatures. It is thus easy to understand how Scandinavia, Britain, Ireland and the Northern region could view the sun as a nourishing healing, Benevolent Goddess, like Sunna.

JOURNALING

How do I genuinely feel about my body at the present moment?
_____

_____

Are there any pressing health issues that I am facing?
_____

_____

Is there anything in particular that is really concerning you with regards to your physical body?
_____

_____

Can you personally define what a healthy, fit body is?
_____

_____

What were the messages you received as a young child regarding your body and health?
_____

_____

If my body could speak to me right now, and it can, what exactly would it say to me personally?
_____

_____

Do you have or plan to get any tattoos or other body modifications?
_____

_____

What color or art message would you paint across your body?
_____

How do I build a positive healthy relationship with my body?
_____

_____

THEME WORK SUGGESTIONS
7. BODY & HEALTH

Light a Green or Brown candle
Use daily affirmations and journal writing to explore issues
related to your body and your health.
Arrange for a wellness checkup and attend any follow up appointments necessary.
Explore different nutritional options and ways to improve your daily eating habits.
Acquire a food journal and notate your daily meals to keep track of your calorie intake.
Make a vow to improve your diet by adding more nutritional foods and learn new ways of preparing tasty meals. Commit to engaging in one physical activity daily, whether it is
walking for 30 minutes a day, or cycling. Do some research to join your local gym, a YMCA or a Yoga or Zumba dance class. Commit to spending some time outdoors in nature.

INVOCATION & POETRY

A CALL TO HEALTH
Amazon Sister,
Deity of the wild,
Join me in this Journey
Guide my inner child.

Maiden Huntress,
Awakener of my Strength,
Goddess Artemis,
Be my Defense...

Teacher of my Body
And all it can do,
Run with me, Huntress,
Be my Sacred Fuel.

Teach me your ways,
To connect me with the Earth,
To Listen to my Body
And heal what may hurt.

To Listen to the Moon
And other signs I receive,
Communicate and Honor
My Sacred Body...

Devoted to good Health,
I invoke your energy,
Fuel my every step,
As I will it,
so mote it be...

*** You are now invited to create
your own altar(s) & invocation(s).
)O(Blessings!

MAGICK RITES & TOOLS

This is your personal page to document your sacred rites and the tools you elected to use.

DECIDE WHERE TO SET UP AN ALTAR
Place an Altar Cloth in the Color of your choice.
Color: _____

GODDESS
Place an image of your Deity.
Goddess: _____
This image can be a Statue, handmade Sculpture or a simple Photo _____

FIRE REPRESENTATION
Place a blessed/charged Candle in the color of your choice.
Candle Type and color: _____

AIR REPRESENTATION
Light your Incense stick.
Incense Scent: _____

WATER REPRESENTATION
Place a Chalice of Water
Water Item: _____

EARTH REPRESENTATION
Place a Potted Plant or Fresh Flowers on your Altar
Add Salt or a plate of Dried Herbs
Herbs: _____
Chosen Gemstone: _____

YOUR WISH
_____
_____

_____

Place a symbol of your desire, if you have one available, and also write your wish out clearly, on a piece of parchment paper, or you can even use a cut up brown paper bag. These are the basics for a very simple altar & rite. Ultimately, your sacred space is only limited by your imagination. You can make your altar & rite as big or as small as you prefer and the addition of other personal items is really up to you.)o(Enjoy!

ALTAR PHOTO

CHAPTER EIGHT

"How people treat you is their karma; how you react, is yours..."
Wayne Dyer

THEME: JUSTICE

In this chapter we brace ourselves to enter the righteous realm of Justice, Karma and Balance. Our journey together leads us to yet another pivotal point in our spiritual growth. We are met by the theme of Balance and Karma and it leads us to, She who holds the sacred scales, the power of discernment and the ultimate executioner of justice.

There is a situation in our lives that requires us to scrutinize our world and look deeper at something that appears to be unfair, imbalanced or requiring a higher jurisdiction. We arrive at a point in our journey that asks us to step up to the cosmic scales of justice and consider what is right and what is wrong in our personal situation. In this sense we are almost beckoned to invoke or become our own inner Goddess of Justice and cultivate our sovereign powers of discernment. We are asked to pause for a moment, to take a much needed step back to see the whole of a situation and bring balance where there appears to be none. Admittedly, it is not a lighthearted task to engage in. Most people would rather runaway and avoid facing any judge in a Court of Law and thus, confrontations related to what is fair and righteous might stir great anxieties within us. However, it should go without saying that there are some situations in our lives that require the sacred hands of Justice to execute proper mandate. And, even within our own personal realms we are called upon to sometimes fulfill this role of executioner of Justice.

At this point in our work, we are asked to be the peace maker and balancer in our lives and tap into our inner magistrate, to bring about some form of harmony, justice, balance and karmic resolution.

As we have done before, in this chapter we will explore further our theme with the help of several resources. We will endeavor to connect with the Goddesses Ma'at, Rhiannon, Astraea, Tara, Sedna, Themis, Irene, and the sacred animal energy of the Ostrich. We will connect with our 7th chakra, the crown chakra, and gemstones that can help better facilitate this connection. We will also look at the corresponding Lunation and a Tarot card that is connected to our theme.

THE JUSTICE TAROT CARD

The Justice card in the Tarot is often depicted, in traditional decks, by a Woman seated between two pillars. She is typically crowned, holding a large intimidating, double edged sword, which is considered the sword of truth. Wearing a long cascading robe, her ensemble would be incomplete without her sacred scales, which she holds prominently in her hand. Her sovereignty cannot be underestimated in this image. She is Karma and the ultimate executioner of what is just. It might not make complete sense to you but her decision is just and fair. Her meaning in the tarot speaks to us about proper action, fair judgement and bringing some type of stability and balance in our lives. It also augurs of a legal situation that may involve the judicial system; whether it is a literal or a metaphorically one.

MOON IN LIBRA — AIR/VENUS

THEME: Justice

| LIBRA | CARDINAL | AIR | MASCULINE | SCALES |

The astrological sign of Libra is known as a peacemaker and a seeker of balance. It is quite interesting to note but Libra is the only astrological sign that has an inanimate object, the scales, as its sacred symbol. Thus, when we consider a Moon in Libra we can naturally conclude that its energy is going to be related to Justice, the Courts, Karma and anything connected to bringing upon balance.

The combination of its sacred symbol, the scale, and the fact that it is known as an air sign contributes to its cool, almost aloof, detached veneer. However, it is interesting to note that, just like Taurus, Libra is a sign ruled by the Deity and planet, Venus. Yes, this air sign is also ruled by the Roman Goddess of Love and Beauty but her Venusian gifts reveal themselves very differently in Libra, when compared to the earth sign of Taurus.

In an astrological sign like Taurus, those Venusian aspects are quite physical, very connected to our earthly forms and lives. In Libra, I believe, they transcend the physical and move up to the ethers; Spirit, Universal Law, Soulmate connections, Divine contracts, Karma etc... Because Libra is ruled by Venus we can still expect a Libra Lunation to be ideal for anything related to love, beauty, harmony, partnerships, and prosperity. But with this air sign, it offers up another level to these Venusian gifts. Moon in Libra can be ideal for works related to contracts and Legal issues that include marriages, work partnerships and all types of harmonious alliances. It strives to bring the proper balance necessary for these well-known, beloved, Venusian ideals.

Moon in Libra is perfect for any work having to do with cooperation, peace, the judicial system, bringing balance and harmony into various situations and the creation of proper partnerships; not limited to romantic types. When reflecting on this lunation we might ask ourselves, where is something out of balance in our lives? Where is there an injustice? What can best utilize the gifts of the balancer and peacemaker?

THEME WORK SUGGESTIONS

Work with the Libra moon, symbolized by the Scale, and work with The Ostrich energy and the Goddesses presented in this chapter.
Commit to a daily meditation practice to help you ground and center.
Perform the Water Purge Rite offered in this chapter.
Spiritually cleanse yourself, your home, and work area regularly with a smudge wand of Copal and White Sage

> *"Every action has equal and opposite reaction.*
> *This is the law of the universe*
> *and it spares none.*
> *Wrong done, and injustices inflicted,*
> *is paid back in the same coin.*
> *No one has escaped Justice of the universe.*
> *It is only a matter of time... "*
>
> Anil Sinha

HERSTORY

She was scared; there was no question about it! The thought of facing, some bigger than life, authoritative figure intimidated the hell out of her, and it was what kept her on the straight and narrow path all of her blessed life. Let's face it, she was a good person, at least that's how she always felt about herself. She made sure to never find herself in trouble with the law or any person of authority. Maybe it was her strict upbringing but she learned quite early on in her life to just keep her head down, fulfill tasks at hand, be responsible, follow rules, and do good to garner a good life.... Oh, if only the rest of the world had read the same instructional manual, but alas, they didn't.

She assumed others would adhere to the same "good behavior, good life" motto that she was raised with, until the day she discovered the truth. Her rude awakening had her contemplating on justice, questioning Karma and preparing to meet in court, the "Balancer of Scales…"

********Take a moment to document here, or in your journal, your unique story.**

_____
_____
_____
_____

AFFIRMATION

They say Karma is a Bitch, but I need not worry,
I have a good relationship with Her.

In all things I strive for balance and justice.

I am Balanced

There is nothing that can remain hidden
in the light of spirit.
All is seen and I trust in
Karmic law to guide, protect and reward my path…

CHAKRA & GEMSTONE WORK

<u>**7th Chakra**</u>   **SAHASRARA/CROWN CHAKRA**   **COLOR:** White

Enlightenment, Ascension, Wisdom, Divine connection, integration, receiving Divine insight.

Mantra: I Know

<u>**)O(WORKING:**</u> Awareness, Insight, Ancestral Work, Knowledge, Spiritual Communication

GEMSTONE CONNECTION: Charoite is a beautiful, purple to violet, colored stone, with some indigo veining patterns adding to its beauty. It is a fairly new stone, alleged to be founded only in one region of the world; Siberia and Russia. It is a stone of high vibration, known to enhance one's psychic powers and opens up channels within the individual, to receive divine messages. It facilitates communications between spirit and our higher self. It balances our crown chakra and helps to ground and clear the energy of all chakras. This is why it is known as the *"soul-stone."* Charoite is a very protective spiritual stone that dispels anger, negativity, fears and chaos. It can even help those struggling with migraines and obsessive-compulsive disorders. It is a stone with a high love frequency that helps promotes peace and harmony and supports those who are suffering with pain and major life transitions. If you feel like someone is draining your energy, this gemstone can intervene to help you better assess the situation and gain deeper rooted insight. It shields the wearer from psychic vampires and negativity, making it a perfect stone for naturally empathic individuals. It is a good gemstone to sleep with, under your pillow, to ensure deep sleep and prophetic dreams. It encourages lucid dreaming and helps to integrate both the head and the heart. Charoite has an affinity to the element of water and it is ruled by the planet of illusion and enlightenment, Neptune. It would come as no surprise then, that this prized gemstone is most connected with both the heart and crown chakra.

GEMSTONE CHANNELING

Greetings and blessings upon your journey towards love, self-care, healing and empowerment. Today, as part of our work, you are asked to find a comfortable spot where you can find a few moments of peace, solitude and tranquility. Finding the right space and time to engage in this practice, on a regular basis, can prove to be invaluable for our stability and our continual evolution. If you can go outdoors in nature that would be most ideal but any place where you can relax, undisturbed, would be fine for this work.

You are invited to place yourself in a comfortable meditation position; you may sit or lay down. If it is available to you, place in your hands the Charoite Gemstone that we are working with today. Take a moment to actually look at your Charoite Gemstone. Notice how it feels in your hands. Does it feel rough or smooth, cold or hot? Make note of its various purple, lilac hues and the different shapes and images it might create. Hold your Charoite Gemstone up and study it carefully for a few minutes, in silence... Quietly, gaze upon it and make note of any thoughts or visions that immediately start to unfold before you. (Pause)

When you are ready, you may close your eyes now and begin this short meditation. As with all trance work, we begin with our breath. You are asked to take a deep breath. (Pause) Let your first inhalation take on the purple hues of your gemstone. See your breath in the purple hue, as if it was the Charoite Gemstone itself, transformed into ether. Breathe, slowly fill your lungs up now with this purple hue of enlightenment, for 3 seconds and then release it... Counting now at your own pace; breathe, 1, 2, 3, and exhale on 4....and again....breathe in, 1, 2, 3, and exhale on 4. Let's do this one more time and then quietly counting in your head.... Breathe 1, 2, 3, and release on 4. Breathe, trusting in the natural rhythm you have now established, of your relaxed inhalation and exhalation.

This Charoite gemstone wishes to impart a special channeled message for you. See this gemstone in your mind's eye. See it shining brightly, embedded upon its dark, fertile, mother earth. Draw nearer to it and ask if it will allow you to pick it up. When permission is granted, gently gather it in your hands. With your mind's eye, gaze upon it again; studying its varying purple colors, its texture, the veins or other details that captures your mind's eye.... Ask it to speak to you. (Pause)

With your next breath, visualize now, the top of your head opening up like a window. Your crown chakra is open and receptive now to receive any spiritual messages that may be developing... (Pause) You may envision your crown chakra unveiling a magnetic purple Charoite Gemstone portal, allowing for this **Crystal Transmission** *to come through... Continue to breathe and exhale... (Pause) Stay with this energy for as long as you need to. When you feel ready, you may open your eyes and document your meditative experience. You may write down your messages here, in the space provided for you or in your personal journals.*

_____
_____
_____

OSTRICH PROTECTION ENERGY

One of the largest living birds in the animal Queendom, that does not fly, Ostrich is a symbol of purity and truth. Ostriches can stand as tall as 8 feet and weigh as much as 300 pounds. The head and neck of this majestic bird have short feathers but their bare legs and thighs do not. It will eat just about anything and with its super speed capabilities; it can outrace its enemies.

As an ally, protector and spiritual guide, the Ostrich is not recognized by Native American traditions, but it is still a worthy animal to explore & work with. As one of the tallest birds, with its long, outstretched neck reaching for the heavens, it is often connected with Divine knowledge; more specifically, the desire to attain ethereal esoteric insight. It's also strongly connected with the earth and grounding our energy to its fertile life source. An ostrich's feet are flanked, big and rooted on the earth; therefore we can call on ostrich when we are in need of grounding ourselves to mother earth. It becomes clear that ostrich energy has an affinity to the elements of both earth & air, and it speaks to us about taking ethereal knowledge and applying it to our earthly, everyday life. With ostrich, we can stand tall and proud. We can also connect with its protective powers that can help us sort out what is no longer needed and what must be surrendered in our lives. It is therefore connected with exorcism, psychic protection and truth.

The Ostrich was linked with the dark Goddess in Semitic and Babylonian cultures, known as Tiamat. Here her animal energy might have been viewed differently than in other cultures. However, we can probably learn most about Ostrich and its prized attributes through Egyptian scriptures and mythologies.

In Egypt, the Ostrich was intimately connected with the Goddess of Truth and Justice, Ma'at. She is the Goddess who meets you in the underworld to judge the whole of your life against her divine virtues and tenets of morality. Upon her golden sacred scales she takes your heart and weights it against the light Ostrich feather. If your heart is heavy, it will outweigh the feather, and you will be judged harshly. A heavy heart revealed a life that did not measure up to the ideals represented by that ostrich feather and thus, the heart would meet its fate, devoured by the awaiting jackal-headed deity, Annubis. If your heart weights lighter than the feather then you have lived a good life and are welcomed into her graces. It is a most revealing example of how important the Ostrich, more specifically her feather, was deemed in ancient Egyptian culture. Some of the writings of the time even go as far as to name the ostrich feather as the Goddess herself. Clearly the ostrich was considered a symbol of truth and thus, her feathers were a sacred symbol of the Goddess of Justice.

Ostrich energy can be invaluable to explore. It is a powerful symbol of truth and integrity. It is also a protector against harmful psychic or spiritual invasions. It can tell you when to stand tall and be seen or when to lay low and become invisible. It is an energy that allows us to seek spiritual knowledge and ascension, while also remaining rooted upon the earth.

GODDESS EMPOWERMENT

MA'AT

Ma'at is probably one of the oldest, most recognized deities in the Egyptian pantheon. She stems from the Old Kingdom (c.2680-2190 BCE) and the earliest mention of this Goddess can be found on the Pyramid text of King Unas in the 5th Dynasty (around CA 2375 BCE - 2345 BCE). *"Egyptian religion" by Siegfried Morenz, translated by Ann E. Keep page 275, 1992 Cornell University Press.*

Most of what we know about Ma'at is derived from the Egyptian *"Book of the Dead,"* a collection of funerary text, religious and magickal rites. Composed mostly in hieroglyphics or hieratic script, its original Egyptian title translated as, *"Book of Coming Forth by Day"* or *"Book Emerging Forth into the Light."* Its origins come from the Egyptian city of Thebes and can be traced to the first pyramid text of the 5th Dynasty (around 2400 BC). Kings and Pharaohs would often commission their own personal version of *"The Book of the Dead,"* later this practice was taken over by nobilities and those with status and the financial means to commission a personal funerary text rite. This text served as a guide for the dead transitioning into the afterlife via the journey through the Duat (the underworld). The numerous spells found in these writings were often painted and engraved on coffins, tomb walls, pyramids, and sarcophagi. Some of these funerary text, the more traditional ones, date as far back as the 3rd millennium BC but new Egyptian spells and writings were created as time went by and it was not uncommon to also reuse well established older, funerary text from this period. *"The Book of the Dead"* is an extremely invaluable source for those seeking to understand funerary practices and beliefs, related to death and the afterlife in ancient Egyptian culture. In early times it was a text well consulted by many and today continues to provide much insight on a mysterious subject that still eludes so many of us.

Ma'at, or Mayet as she is endearingly called, is the Goddess of Truth, Justice, the Law and Divine Order. She is Goddess of Moral Integrity and a primordial Goddess of Righteousness. She is the judge of the dead in the halls of Duat, in the underworld. She is the personification of order and the law. Because she is considered a primeval deity, some debate whether she is a Goddess in actual human formed or simply the concept or female principle of order in the universe. She epitomizes the importance of justice for a thriving society, the importance of proper behavior, and fairness for the disadvantaged. She is in essence, truth embodied but she is more than the legislative; she is the cosmic law of the universe.

Her name in Egypt is synonymous with the word truth. Some scholars translate her name as literally meaning, *"that which is straight,"* a reference to her abilities to create order from chaos and provide the straight foundations necessary for the world to be built upon and exist in harmony. Even her hieroglyphics, an Ostrich feather, depicts this important aspect of the Goddess, with its straight lines, the hieroglyphics represents the Goddess of Justice.

Lady of Heaven, Mistress of the Underworld, Ma'at was often depicted with wings and this connected her to the pre-dynastic vulture deity of Upper Egypt; Nekhbet. Whether sitting, kneeling or standing, she is often shown dressed in the traditional Egyptian close fitted dress, in the color red or gold with a feather protruding from her head of solid black straight stresses. On one hand she holds the Ankhs, an ancient symbol of peace and on the other hand she holds a scepter, a symbol of power. Though many Egyptian deities are often linked with animals and are sometimes even depicted with an animal's head form, you will not find this to be the case for Ma'at. She is often represented as a beautiful woman, or an Ostrich feather or simply the very scales she would employed as she judged the dead.

As with most ancient deities there is some confusion regarding her parentage but we do know, from the ancient texts, her strong connection to Ra. The Egyptian Sun God, Ra, originally had two known daughters; Hathor-Sekhmet and Tefnut-Ma'at. The beloved Ma'at was considered the eye of Ra but also the heart, for it is the heart where moral judgment is made and this was her domain. Today, she continues to be the one who steers his boat, as he flies across the sky. It is Ma'at who guides the sun to set at night and rise every morning. She is the Goddess who controls the motions and patterns of nature in the Universe. She regulates the seasons, the stars, the planets and the waters upon the earth. Even the inundation of the Nile River, which was so important for Egyptians, falls under her domain. Ancient Egypt and its prosperous growth was heavily dependent on the water of the Nile river and naturally a Goddess who rules over the progression of the season and its sacred patterns found in the universe, would be responsible for these vital waters as well.

Ma'at existed since the beginning of time, according to Egyptian mythos, and cosmology. In the beginning there was darkness, the void, formlessness and chaos, as numerous cultures confirm and support in agreement in their respective folklores. In this chaotic, abysmal, boundlessness, which is found in so many varying myths explaining the earth's beginnings, there was also water and a cosmic egg floating upon the shapeless world. In the cosmic egg was the Kephera, the light, which remained hidden inside the darkness of the egg, until one day it was cracked open and unleashed upon the formless universe. In that very moment the world began to take shape; Shu, the atmosphere, manifested and soon thereafter Tefnut, as moisture, emerged, and through the space between these two, emerged the Sun God, Ra. According to Egyptian writings one of the first deities to manifest was the Sun God, Ra. Ra emerged from the Nun, the primordial waters and subsequently right then, the straightness to set the orderly foundation of the world was immediately necessary and thus, the Goddess Ma'at was called upon and she too emerged with Ra. Some scholars believe Ma'at gave birth to Ra, making her his mother, but more often she is considered one of his beloved daughters. Upon creation she is the one who organizes chaos and brings cosmic order into the universe. In this respect she is very similar to the Chinese Goddess, Nukua. In Ma'at's presence the natural laws of the universe exist and are enforced. She rules the movement of the stars and planets, the rising and setting of sun and the ebb and flow of the waters.

According to Egyptian cosmology, at this auspicious moment in the creation of the universe, there existed three Gods alone on the Solar Barque; the Sun God, Ra, Ma'at, Goddess of Divine order and her consort, the God of Wisdom, Throth. Ma'at was to eventually replace the God of Chaos and destruction, Set, and she becomes his antithesis. And this reminds me of the Japanese myth related to Amaterasu, the Sun Goddess, and her struggles to eradicate the chaos of her brother, Susano-0, but I digress. These three primordial Egyptian Gods emerged and rode on the sacred *"Boat of a Million Years"* and together they helped to tame "Chaos." They organize the universe, bring balance, cosmic harmony, order and form into the world.

On a coffin inscription it states: **"Tefnut is my living daughter and she shall be together with her brother, Shu; his name is life and her name is Ma'at...."**

Ma'at is sometimes associated with other Goddesses and Gods. She was considered an aspect of the parthenogenetically birthed Tefnut, the lion headed Goddess of Moisture, Dew and Rain. Tefnut was linked with Throth as his partner but so was Ma'at. The God of Wisdom and Knowledge, Throth, or Tehuti as he is also known, was considered Ma'at's consort. It is important to look at her spouse because in understanding him we can begin to understand parts of her. Some say they share similar attributes and they complement one another, as can be expected when two powerful deities are joined. Lord of Time, Throth was a Lunar Egyptian deity, attributed for inventing speech and writing. He reflects Ma'at's ideals and her finest qualities. In the *Papyrus Nebseni*, he is quoted as declaring that he brings Ma'at and her gifts to those who love her. His role as "bequeather" of Ma'at's most precious gifts becomes indisputable. It's important to note that Throth, the Lord of Wisdom, is also the patron God of Scribes. In ancient Egypt, scribes were exceptionally important. They were the ones that documented in writing; religious, political and social events of great significance to world history. In the *"Instruction of Amenemope,"* Egyptian scribes are encouraged to follow the ways of their Goddess, Ma'at, in their work but also in their personal lives.

The Ibis headed, Throth, who is credited for having invented Hieroglyphics, and also rules over learning and sciences (involving measuring and counting) reflects the best of her laws. She becomes known as his counterpart. In their unified light, all darkness is eradicated. Together they were credited for creating eight children, Amon, being the most famous of all of them. These offspring became known as the Chief Gods and Goddesses of Hermopolis. Thus, Maat and Throth became known as the ancestor Gods of Hermopolis and respectively mother and father of the Ogdoad.

"She adorns the breast of Throth"

Just as it is stated, Throth carries her on his chest with great love, the Kings and the Pharaohs of Egypt also held the Goddess Ma'at with the highest esteem. The Pharaohs were known as priest of Ma'at. She was their mystic sister and they too wore emblems, and personal symbols of the Goddess. They also carried with them ostrich feathers, to symbolize their commitment to represent her cosmic laws when asked to judge. Everyone, from the lowest of slaves, to the Pharaohs and Kings, all were considered instrumental for cosmic order and harmony, by the Goddess Ma'at. For Egyptians, there was a particularly strong belief that, lack of integrity caused disharmony not just in their personal lives but they also believed it had the power to reverberate into the cosmos; directly affecting nature, potentially causing global disasters; like plagues, earthquakes, droughts and famine upon the land.

Egyptian Kings were also zealously devoted to Ma'at and her tenets of truth and justice. Some would even add her name to their title to suggest an even stronger allegiance and devotion to the great Goddess, Ma'at. A King's decision always rested on Ma'at and her Divine righteousness and laws. In Egyptian theology there is a belief in a reciprocal relationship to deity, that as they give and provide to you, the devotee, so must you also give back to them; via offerings, worship, ritual, and songs etc.. Humans and the Divine cooperate and help one another exist in the universe and this is the balance and harmony of Ma'at.

"Lady of Heaven, Queen of the Earth, Mistress of the Underworld' E.A. Wallis Budge....

Another very important function of the Goddess Ma'at is to judge the dead. The *"Egyptian Book of the Dead"* reveals the Goddess Ma'at is met by every person who has transitioned to death. She waits at Duat, the underworld, where the Jackal headed God, Annubis, leads the dead to meet their fate on her scales. In Ma'at's Hall it will be determined if the deceased person's soul may continue onward to meet the God Osiris and join the other Gods and Spirits into eternity.

With Throth by her side and the 42 Assessors of Ma'at, a life review for the deceased is inevitable in her Judgment hall. This is the moment of her truth, when the true heart of a person will be examined and weight. Ma'at, sometimes known as the scale herself, will weight a person's heart against her sacred Ostrich feather. A scale is presented and on one side rest Ma'at's ostrich feather and on the other side the deceased person's heart. All in Ma'at's Hall will watch as the scale will go back and forth trying to find its equilibrium and then in the end, reveal the deceased person's fate in the afterlife. If it is a balanced scale or if the heart appears lighter than Ma'at's ostrich feather, then that person will be met and embraced into the Hall of the Gods and immortality. They will go on to meet with Osiris, the Egyptian God of the Dead and the Afterlife. However, if the heart of the deceased person is heavy and out weights the feather, then the deceased person will have much explaining to do, for this will reveal a life lived poorly and sins, much too many, to be welcomed into the Hall of the Gods. The God, Ammit, the devourer, will ghastly lick her choppers in anticipation for what's to come next, as the deceased person will be sent to the deep recesses of the underworld, while its heavy heart gets hungrily devoured by hideously looking Ammit. Ammit, who was a smorgasbord grisly looking deity beholding the menacing snout of a crocodile, the mane of a lion and the body of a Hippopotamus, fed on those heavy sinful hearts of man. But before giving Ammit the satisfaction of a juicy meal, the deceased person will have a chance to come before the 42 deities of Duat, known as the "Assessors of Ma'at," to plead their case and recite the "42 Denials of Sins," also known as the "Negative Confessions." These writings derived from the *Papyrus Ani* found in chapter 125, of the "*Book of the Dead.*" Below they are listed. *(Wikipedia.com)*

The "Forty Two Declarations of Purity" or "Negative Confessions"
1. I have not committed sin.
2. I have not committed robbery with violence.
3. I have not stolen.
4. I have not slain men or women.
5. I have not stolen grain.
6. I have not purloined offerings.
7. I have not stolen the property of the Gods.
8. I have not uttered lies.
9. I have not carried away food.
10. I have not uttered curses.
11. I have not committed adultery; I have not lain with men.
12. I have made none weep.
13. I have not eaten the heart.
14. I have not attacked any man.
15. I am not a man of deceit.
16. I have not stolen cultivated land.

17. I have not been an eavesdropper.
18. I have not slandered no man.
19. I have not been angry without just cause.
20. I have not been debauched the wife of any man, or God.
21. I have not debauched the wife of any man,(repeated addressed a god)
22. I have not polluted myself.
23. I have terrorized none
24. I have not transgressed the law.
25. I have not been wroth.
26. I have not shut my ears to the words of truth.
27. I have not blasphemed.
28. I am not a man of violence.
29. I am not a stirrer up of strife or disturber of peace
30. I have not acted or judged with undue haste
31. I have not pried into matters.
32. I have not multiplied my words in speaking.
33. I have wronged none, and done no evil.
34. I have not worked witchcraft against the King nor blaspheme.
35. I have never stopped the flow of water.
36. I have never raised my voice, spoken arrogantly or in anger.
37. I have not cursed or blasphemed the Gods.
38. I have not acted with evil rage.
39. I have not stolen the bread of the Gods.
40. I have not carried away the Khenfu cakes from the spirit of the dead.
41. I have not snatched away the bread of the child, nor treated with contempt the God of my City.
42. I have not slain the cattle belonging to the Gods.

From http://en.wikepedia.org/wiki/Maat--

Before Throth, Ma'at and the 42 deities, known as the "Assessors of Maat," (Their names listed in the Papyrus of Nebseni), the deceased person will have a chance to address his or her sins and hopefully, save him/herself from remaining in the darkest, place of the underworld, tragically ending his journey in the afterlife.

From the earliest of dynasties it was the Goddess, Ma'at who was well worshipped and today continues to reign powerfully in our collective consciousness. Ma'at is the standard by which we measure ourselves from. The heart must be free of weight for you to enter the hall of the Gods in the afterlife. Living by her laws of truth and justice, helped manifest an orderly thriving universe.

Though some compare Ma'at to the Hindu concept of Karma this is erroneous, as Karma implies that negativity is simply punishment for something done in a previous life. Early Egyptian doctrines would not have agreed in this belief, instead viewing the exact same negativity as proof of Ma'at's absence and indicating the need to supplicate her presence in order to make things fair and right. Early Egyptians and worshippers of Ma'at viewed misfortunes and catastrophic disasters as being caused by demons or spirits of the dead or being a direct result of falsities and inauthentic, unbalanced living, not by Ma'at herself. She was not viewed as a vindictive Goddess but rather as one who made things right, straight, fair and just. In this case she does not resemble the Hindu concept of Karma.

Recognized from the middle of the third millennium even earlier, Ma'at had many known Temples dedicated to her worship but today only one still survives. Her Temple in the city of Thebes, in Karnak (Carnac) lies in ruins as an open air museum in Egypt today. Some parts of it were believed to be originally built by the pharaoh, Queen Hatsheput. Later when it had been destroyed by invaders it was commissioned to be rebuilt again by Amenhotpe. Many Egyptian Pharaohs had a part in constructing this Temple throughout the years and part of its renowned reputation comes from the fact that it was started in the Middle Kingdom and continued to be rebuild and expanded upon through into the Ptolemaic period.

Over three millennia, whether as a concept or an actual Goddess in human form, Ma'at, the Goddess of Truth, Justice and Divine Order has reign in our lives, making herself and her laws and principles prevalent in our lives. Invoke her when you are facing anything related to the law, our judicial system or when trying to correct a wrong done unto you. Before invoking her in your workings, be sure you examine your motives and assess your own life, to make sure you are living in the most authentic, righteous and Ma'at pleasing way. She is also a powerful Goddess to connect with when you are approaching death (whether literal or figuratively). She will help you dig deep to intimately connect with you, the genuine you, and offer memories of those times when you best exemplified her attributes of truth, order and justice. She will force you to be honest with yourself and look at the many ways you can lighten your heart so that it will match the lightness of her ostrich feather. Her presence in your life will bring a greater awareness of your authenticity, righteousness, justice and a deeper contemplation on matters of the heart.

*The highly esteemed, Egyptian Goddess of Truth, Ma'at is cosmic law. She is the Divine being we expect to greet, in the golden hall of the Afterlife, where the Celestial Scales are presented before us. These sacred scales weigh our heart against Ma'at's ostrich feather, which determines our fate in the afterlife. Ma'at is an ancient, highly venerated Egyptian Deity that some believe existed before time itself. She is the personification of truth and the power of final judgment. She beckons you today to take an honest look at your whole life. It is time for some serious assessment of your soul, your heart, and the choices you are making in this lifetime. She lays down the invitation to closely inspect your heart to unearth what weights it down now and offers you the cathartic gift of an unburdened soul. She invites you to seek balance and truth in your world.

TARA

The name *Tara* translates as, "*star or planet*" and it begins to paint a picture of this Universal, feminine deity. Tara is the Tibetan Buddhist Goddess of Compassion. She is a Goddess of immortality, physical prowess, benevolence, liberation, hope and a fierce protector and savioress of humanity. She is Mother of all the Buddhas and Mother of Liberation. Part of her name in Sanskrit means, "*to traverse or to cross,*" which speaks of crossing the stream of suffering or struggles. The Goddess Tara is also known as Arya Tara and Jetsun Dolma, in the Tibetan language. She is embraced by both Hinduism and Buddhism.

Her worship can be found and traced back to Bengal, Tibet, some parts of China and India, more specifically Aboriginal India and Hindu Jain. When we work with this Goddess we have to consider the two different regions she is associated most with and her distinct venerations in these cultures.

Tara is a Tantric Goddess in the Buddhist Tantric Religion. She is also venerated as a protectress and savioress of Humanity and a beloved Mother deity. As a Tantric deity, Tara is known to have five main forms represented by five different colors; although there are quite a few other aspects to Tara; in a Mandala she's depicted with 21 forms.

SITATARA	White Tara	**Compassion, Serenity, Healing**
SYAMATARA	Green Tara	**Peaceful, Protection, Enlightenment**
EKAJATA	Blue Tara	**Wrathful, Transmutation of Anger**
BHRKUTI	Yellow Tara	**Prosperity, Wealth, Wish Granter**
KURUKULLA	Red Tara	**Heroic, Swift, the Magnetizer**

The earliest mention of the Goddess Tara can be found in the middle of the 7th century. Her name is found amidst a Buddhist prayer in the *Subandhu's Vasavadatta*. She is described as the Lady Twilight, donning a red garment, devoted to the stars. Today Tibetan nuns and monks wear multi-layered robes made of this color red or deep maroon, mustard yellow/saffron and white.

The Goddess Tara belongs to the family of *Dhyani Buddha Amoghasiddhi, according to Buddhism*, and she is also more popularly linked with Bodhisattva Avalokitesvara. According to the well-known Tantric scriptures, Avalokitesvara heard the distress and lamentation of all the beings upon the earth. Humanity was beginning to mourn his imminent departure, as he journeyed towards nirvana. Upon hearing of mankind's pain, this Avalokitesvara sheds a tear of great compassion for all those he would leave behind suffering; from his tear, the Goddess Tara was born. It is stated she manifested from his tear and committed to staying upon the earth to serve humanity in all of their needs. Tara thus becomes the compassionate one and the savioress of humanity; who stays on earth to answer the prayers of her devotees. She is the Female Bodhisattva, viewed as the Mother of all Buddhas but in some traditions viewed as both offspring and companion of the Avalokitesvara.

For Tibetans, the Goddess Tara is seen as both queen and mother. She is the one born from a tear of compassion, highly revered as the Feminine Avalokitesvara. It is clear she is the beloved deity dedicated to answering the desperate prayers of humankind. Like the Chinese Goddess, Kwan yin, she is highly sympathetic and compassionate to her devotees. She is known as the "cheater of death" and can bestow a long life to her followers. There have been a plethora of writings exalting her answered prayers and documenting the numerous times she has intervened and helped her devotees.

She is known as the bringer of longevity, the rescuer of humanity and a Goddess deeply connected to life. She is not particularly called upon as a Goddess of fertility, although it is in her power to bless those who ask for that type of blessing. As a Goddess primarily connected with life and immortality, she is the one who preserves and guards our lives. Therefore she earned the titled, "cheater of death," and "prolonger of life."

In some parts of India, she was seen as the wife of *Brhaspati* who was abducted by Soma. In this context, she later gives birth to the Buddha, thus becoming Mother of all Buddhas. In Bengal, *Ramprasad Sen* (an 18th century devotee of Kali) wrote about Tara as a Hindu Goddess, almost synonymous with his beloved fierce patron Goddess, Kali.

In Hinduism, Tara is viewed very distinctly. She is indeed one of the *Mahavidyas;* the beloved Matriarchal deities and sacred mothers of humanity. Her appearance in descriptive Hindu sacred text and her rendered illustrations, reveals a Goddess that shares many of Kali's prominent characteristics. Tara is described in Hinduism as dark, wearing a necklace of head skulls, while Kali wears a garland of freshly chopped-off, gruesome, bloody heads. Tara is described with her disheveled braided hair, standing with one foot over a corpse, near a funeral pyre. Kali is described as naked, dark as night, hair disheveled as well, and standing over the corpse of Shiva. Kali is also near a crematory ground similar to the depiction of Tara. In this respect here, the Goddess Tara is embraced in Hinduism in her *Blue aspect as*, Ekajata or Ugra-Tara. You may also see her form as Red Tara, known as *Kurukulla*. Interesting to note, in Nepal she is embraced as Green Tara, better known as, *Khadiravani* Tara.

TARA'S HINDU & BUDDHIST SACRED MANTRA
"Om Tare tuttare ture svaha (or soha)..."
Translation: Om Tara, I pray, Oh swift one, so be it....

TIBETAN BUDDHISM

The introduction of Buddhism came to Tibet via India around the seventh century. Chinese Buddhism eventually also influenced Tibet later on between the 9th and 10th century. Buddhism and possibly the worship of the Goddess Tara, however, is believed to have started around 641CE. The Tibetan King Songstsen Gampo married two wives that same year and this helped unified Tibet. His brides were the princess Bhrikuti of Nepal and the princess, Wen Chang from China. Together they were credited for introducing the first king of Tibet to their spiritual practice of Buddhism. The king embraced Buddhism and had ancient Sanskrit scriptures translated and soon thereafter, Buddhist temples built. There are some writings of the time that claim the King's wives were different incarnated aspects of the Goddess Tara: Bhrikuti of Nepal was linked with Green Tara and Wen Chang of China, was linked with White Tara.

DEPICTIONS

Depictions of the Goddess Tara show her as a slim, energetic, playful and very beautiful young woman. She is almost always depicted in a happy, jovial disposition, wearing a royal crown on her head and dressed in regal garments. Upon one of her hands she will often hold a lotus flower and express a mudra with the other hand. As a benevolent deity she is always glowing in gold shimmering light and sometimes, you may even see her depicted sitting on the crescent moon or upon the sacred lotus. Obviously, her depictions are quite extensively varied and dependent on her exact aspect. It is of interest to note that her image is one that emits peace, joy, hope and vitality to her followers.

SACRED TEXTS

"The Homages to the Twenty -One Taras," and *"Tantra which is the Source for All the Functions of Tara, Mother of all Talhagatas,"* are among some of the many texts revealing many of Tara's hymns; giving us a deeper glimpse into the many aspects and attributes of this beloved Female Bodhisattva.

HER RELEVANCE & OUR WORK

The Buddhist Tantric Goddess, Tara, also has a form known as Black Tara, Ugra-Tara, which is an aspect connected to power and mantra emanation. Our universe manifested from sacred sound, the Om, therefore this aspect of Tara is highly linked with divine creation and power. By far her most commonly known aspect is Green Tara. In this form she is known as Khadiravani. As Green Tara she gives courage to face our inner demons and fears. She helps us accept the truth of all matters and liberates us from delusions.

As Green Tara she protects us from Mara (the evil one/the Devil Tempter) and helps us transcend fears. It is Tara that gives us swift courage and helps us balance and differentiate what is real from the unreal. She clears our path from illusions and fortifies us on our spiritual journey. She helps us cross the stream of pain & struggle towards freedom.

Tara inspires us to live virtuously and pursue the attainment of the seven treasures or jewels in Buddhism. With Tara we pursue mastery of the seven virtues known as:
1. **Faith**
2. **Morality**
3. **Consciousness**
4. **Consideration**
5. **Learning**
6. **Generosity**
7. **Wisdom**

The Goddess Tara is beloved as "Mother Liberator," the one that helps us transcend all things. She frees us from the eight types of dangers or eight fears. According to Buddhist tenet, these eight dangers are:

1. **Pride** — represented by the Lion
2. **Ignorance and Delusion** — represented by the Elephant
3. **Anger and Hatred** — represented by Fire
4. **Envy and jealousy** — represented by the Snake or Serpent
5. **Fanatical, Wrong Views** — represented by Robbers
6. **Avarice** — represented by Fear of Imprisonment
7. **Lust, Desire, Attachment** — represented by Floods
8. **Doubt** — represented by Demons or Ghost

She is titled as *Arya-Tara* which means, Noble being. Clearly this Goddess has many attributes that we can further delve into. And, she could've easily been included in the chapter of Mothers and in the Chapter of Liberation but her message to us related to balance needed to be explored here. One of the reasons why she is included in this chapter is her message to us regarding our heart, the center of our being. Our heart is our treasure; within it we can find our point of balance and our personal altar. Therefore we walk with our sacred sanctuary contained, intact within our heart. The Goddess Tara reminds us to honor our hearts and live from this sacred place. She is yet another beautiful reflection of Goddess; exemplifying a powerful expression of the Divine Feminine for us women to draw our inspiration and strength from.

Today, the Goddess Tara continues to be a highly venerated deity across numerous countries, not limited to her initial birth place. She is yet another prominent example of how the Sacred Feminine is still very much alive and vitally present in our modern world.

ASTRAEA

Astraea is the Greek Maiden Goddess of innocence, purity, Justice, knowledge, astronomy and learning. She is intimately linked with the star constellation of Virgo. Her name is derived from the Greek word "*Aster*," which means Star. Her name is often interpreted as "*Star Maiden*" or interpreted to mean, "*Those Who Shine like the Stars.*" During Queen Elizabeth's reign, she was often believed to be the incarnation of the Virgin Goddess, Astraea.

Homer declared her to be the daughter of Zeus and the Goddess, Themis. Others believe she was the daughter of Eos and Astraeus. She was often connected with Dike/Dyke, the Goddess of Justice, and even the Goddess Nemesis, known as rightful indignation. Writings of the time refer to her as, "*...the Virgin of the Stars, Astraea, nurse of law abiding man...*"

Long ago on the Earth, Gods and Goddesses walked among human beings. This time period was often referred to as the Golden Age. As time went on the introduction of the Iron Age and the Bronze Age brought about wickedness, massive changes in the collective consciousness and destructive changes to human behavior. Man, little by little, turned away from righteousness and turned towards greed and evil. As humans started to express these negative destructive attributes, the Gods one by one began to depart the earth, opting to dwell in the heavens. The Goddess Astraea was purported to be one of the last deities left on the earth, who finally departed but with the intention of one day returning when a revival of the Golden age commenced. Until that day, she remains in the sky as the star to the constellation known as Virgo.

Astraea is often depicted as a winged, beautiful woman, holding a flaming torch in one hand and the balancing scales of justice on the other. She is even sometimes illustrated holding Zeus' sacred thunderbolt to denote her power over, Divine Justice.

We call on the Star maiden, Astraea, to support us in our studies, especially if those include; astronomy, astrology or any studies related to constellations or the Law. We can invoke The Virgin Goddess, Astraea, much like the Egyptian Goddess of Truth, Ma'at, to seek balance or divine justice in our lives. She can also help us bring order into our lives and sometimes offer us a different approach to an unfair situation. Anything that may seem unfair; requiring truth and justice, will benefit greatly by this Star Maiden. Call on this ancient Goddess by setting up an altar with a blue or white candle, a chalice of water, her image, and scales of Justice, along with your petition. Let the Goddess Astraea bring truth, righteousness and Justice into our lives when we call on her.

RHIANNON

Rhiannon is the Beautiful Lunar Goddess in Welsh mythology, who later becomes known as a Fairy Queen. Her name literally translates as, *"Divine Queen"* and she was known to have a beautiful singing voice. She is most popularly known as the Welsh Mare Goddess, sometimes depicted as a beautiful long haired woman, dressed in gold, ridding her white mare sidesaddle and sometimes, she is depicted as the horse itself. She is closely linked with fertility, freedom, creativity and maternal concerns, typical attributes of a Lunar deity, but she was also protector of horses, animals and the stable.

As the horse was a very important, sacred animal to ancient cultures and held a great deal of esteem and veneration, there are a number of Goddesses all closely associated with horses, like Rhiannon. In Celtic mythology there is the Goddess Epona, who had a great cult following there and when she was brought over to Rome, they named her Rigantona or Rig Antonia which translates as, *"Great Queen."* For the Irish she was sometimes known as Macha and for the Gaulic, Edain.

According to one of her folklores, Rhiannon was being pressured to follow her family vows and marry an older God who was more suited to their Divine family lineage, but she refused. Instead she sought after a mortal prince by the name of Pwyll (also known in English as Paul).

In Welsh mythology there was often an enchanted small mound in various distinct sacred areas on the land, known as a "tor." This tor was believed to be a portal for the Divine to interact and sometimes even enchant mortals. One day, the handsome mortal prince, Pwyll, found himself standing on one of these very sacred mounds. His accompanying entourage saw him and fearing the legendary tales warned him not to stay but quite unexpectedly, while standing there, he witnessed a beautiful white mare, galloping quickly right passed him. A woman with long tresses, dressed in gold, rode on this white horse and he instinctively was captivated. The next day he decided to try his luck again and see if, perchance, he can actually catch up with this beautiful maiden.

The next day, he approached the same "tor" and waited well prepared. Within minutes she appeared again, only this time she galloped even faster and his attempt to catch up with her failed miserably. On the third day, he was more determined than ever to catch up with this fast paced white mare but when, defeated and out of breath, he failed again, he finally just called out to her in desperation to please wait and stop. To his surprise, she did, and when they met, eye to eye, they were immediately enamored with one another. He asked her what she was doing there and her answer was simply that she was there to acquire his love. From the very first day he saw her, he admitted, she indeed had acquired his devotion. Rhiannon then tells him to return to the same sacred mound, a year and a day later, and promises him that if he does, they will be married on that day. And so a year and a day later, the mortal prince returns to the same "tor" to claim his beautiful Lunar Goddess as his bride and future Queen.

As promised by the Goddess, their beautiful marriage ceremony took place that very day, in the enchanted forest, with all of nature supporting their union, all except for one very angry ex-suitor. The old, resentful man she had been promised to in marriage made unwarranted scandalous advances to the new bride and in her effort not to draw too much attention to the situation and ruin their special wedding ceremony; she converted the harasser into a badger. She then placed the badger into a sack and tossed it into the ocean, but the bag became undone and he managed to sneak himself back into the Prince's entourage as they were heading back home. Later on in this tale, this would prove to be a most dreadful calculating occurrence, as he vowed to have his revenge for being rejected by the Goddess.

The wedding took place but soon thereafter, the mortal prince and his new bride returned to his kingdom, where she was greeted as a stranger with much suspicion surrounding her qualifications as a Queen, for she was not like them. She was a Lunar Goddess, of divine lineage and now she was among humans. They did not easily embrace her and she quickly became the subject of many rumors, gossips and distant mistreatment.   Finding fault with her at every bend, they wondered why after a few years of marriage she had not provided a proper heir, with a baby. By the third year of marriage, however, Rhiannon finally did give birth. She gave birth to a beautiful baby boy and the entire kingdom seemed overjoyed with their celebrations.

As was the custom back then, the Queen had several attendants especially with a newborn. The attendants were all required to help in keeping a close watch over the baby while the new mother would catch up with her sleep and recuperate from the strenuous birthing experience. On one particular night, as Rhiannon slept, in confident that the baby was well cared for, all six maid attendant inexplicably fell asleep simultaneously and it was then that her beloved newborn tragically disappeared. Much chaos ensued but it appeared the baby was kidnapped. When all her maid attendants woke up and, to their mortified surprise, could not locate the royal baby, they feared their own fate and knew they would be executed for child neglect. In their desperation to save their own lives they immediately sought to blamed the Queen, Rhiannon, who was already subject to much suspicion and prejudice. Frantically, they located and killed a nearby puppy, smeared its blood and bones across the slumbering Queen and prepared to plot and accuse Rhiannon of the unthinkable. They accused her of eating her own child in a moment of insanity. All in the kingdom already disliked Rhiannon for her unusual Divine blood lineage and so it was not a particularly demanding task to convince everyone that indeed the Goddess/Queen had gone mad and done this horrific, unthinkable act.

Traumatized by this horrific crime, both she and her husband reacted in the way that most people would react to traumatic news regarding their own child. Rhiannon started to question herself; guilt-ridden and traumatized she blamed herself. Her husband didn't know who to believe. He too was distraught and could not defend his wife but he neither wanted to divorce her nor have his wife executed. He beseeched the courts to spare her life and rule for clemency. He implored the courts to have mercy and find another form of punishment besides the death sentence she was expected to receive for such a heinous crime.

In the end, they allowed her to live and stipulated her punishment would be to forever greet all visitors to the kingdom with the sad, horrific tale of the death of her son. She would then be required to offer them her back, as a mare, and carry them all the way into the castle. Most people who heard her story did not take advantage of her offer to ride on her back but many came from far and wide to hear her tell this very ghastly, tragic personal story.

The years went by and Rhiannon, in her numbed state, accepted her fate. One day, a couple with a young child arrived at the entryway and as Rhiannon had done for the last seven years, she resigned herself to tell the sad tale once more and then offer her back to carry them into the castle. When she finished telling her story, she looked into the young boy's eyes and noted a familiarity within his gaze; it stunned her to the bones. He was the spitting image of her husband, the King Pwyll and it was in that very moment that the old couple admitted they had found the baby seven years ago, abandoned in a field, and since they had no children of their own, they raised him as if he was their very own. They now believed him to be the King and Queen's royal son. Immediately the news spread of the young boy's return and when pressed, the maid attendants from that horrid fateful night finally confessed to what they had done. Later, it was revealed that the badger, Rhiannon's resentful old suitor, had kidnapped the child that night, seven years ago while everyone slept.

When the story spread quickly of this injustice and Rhiannon's innocence, they quickly restored her to her throne and re-embraced her as their Queen. She was more loved and respected than ever before because she had endured so much unjust pain and suffering in this entire cruel misunderstanding and yet, she exemplified such strength and dignity in the way she handled herself and the way she accepted her wrongful punishment for the last seven years.

Despite the horrific accusations and the loss of her child for seven years, she remained steadfast in her truth, believing one day the real story would be revealed and justice would prevail. The Goddess impressed the people of her land even further when she expressed great compassion and forgiveness to those who had placed her in such a dreadful position with their false accusations. She understood full well why her maid attendants did what they did and, despite the great loss and pain it caused her, she extended boundless compassion, understanding and forgiveness to her accusers in the end. This is the gift of this Welsh Lunar Goddess, for she teaches us to remain steadfast in the face of great chaos and crisis and above all, she exemplifies the healing gift of forgiveness and compassion.

RHIANNON MUSING

Rhiannon is a Goddess of truth and integrity and the strong belief that justice will prevail no matter what. There seems to be hints of the Justice deity, Themis, in this Goddess but more than anything, while working with this deity, I was most struck by her similarities to Goddesses like Kwan Yin, the Virgin Mary and Corn Mother, Selu, in her ability to withstand so much sadness and heartache and yet, be able to trust that in the end, everything would work itself out. There is an aspect of Rhiannon that wholly exemplifies the cathartic gift of compassion and the power of forgiveness, for despite everything that she was put though, she was able to look into the heart of the situation, face the truth and move on. In her ability to endure the loss of her newborn and then survive with dignity, the cruel accusations that she had eaten and killed her very own son is demonstrative of a Goddess who knows great inner strength. She exemplifies the art of holding onto one's truth in the mist of horrific chaos and calamities.

Throughout her myths she appears misunderstood and always going against the grain by exclusively following her heart. From the moment she refused to marry her family's first choice for a husband, rejecting the old man's advances, to her unwelcomed arrival in her mate's mortal realm and kingdom, she follows her heart. Despite surrounding pressures and great discomfort in her life, she is true to her heart. Yet, she displays great conviction and steadfasness that all will work itself out. In this case she appears to consistently refuse to play the role of victim and is continually illustrating for us inner strength and faithfulness.

These attributes; strength and steadfastness, are closely linked to her totem animal, the mare; for indeed horses are powerful, strong, grounded animals that exemplify stamina, loyalty, devotion and an uncanny ability to overcome obstacles. The Horse is also a warrior spirit; safeguarding its master. A lover of freedom and travel, the horse is, most interestingly, faithful to its master at all cost. And these are transferable qualities palpable in the Goddess Rhiannon. It is these very significant attributes that we see revealed to us in her myths.

I think for those of us who have been wronged in our lives or erroneously accused of things that go so against our very nature. Rhiannon can offer us solace and is quite a powerful message to help us sojourn to inner healing. This is Goddess work! She invites you to step back into your own power and not necessarily fight fire with fire, nor gets entangled in *he said, she said* games but rather moves beyond the drama and trust that the truth will eventually prevail. Now this is easier said than done, and it takes a great deal of patience, maturity and divine wisdom to be able to rise above certain situations and release negative events in our lives, like she so illustrated for us in her myths. In meditating on Rhiannon, I contemplate on those who are victims of gossip and lies; whether it's in a scholastic environment, religious, labor or residential community, it is an excruciating thing to have to deal with and our natural inclination might be to fight back with our own set of nasty lies and rumors or worse... but Rhiannon opens the door to yet another way of handling the situation, one where you will not lose your heart and soul in the battlefield.

With her, I also contemplate on those who at this very moment are incarcerated and are wrongly accused of crimes they could not have possibly committed but... because of gender or race or social status or any of the other ridiculous prejudicial reasons, except for the facts, must endure our flawed judicial system. Rhiannon is not very well received by her husband's kingdom, they hold prejudice views against her, right from the start and it's clear no matter what she does or doesn't do, she will not have a chance to have a fair trial. And sadly this tragedy happens too often on so many different levels in our own lives. The unfairness of judgment exercised, simply based on something other than the facts is routine in our modern day society and it is wrong... Yet, on every level from job applications, politics, to popularity contest in schools and Universities, to actual crime investigations, people are subject to unproven accusations that can negatively, destroy lives.

Rhiannon does not allow herself to be destroyed by the horrific loss of her son nor by the damaging, erroneous accusations that she was entangled in, instead she anchors herself in the truth. She accepts her punishment and remains strong, knowing that the Universe will always return to balance after periods of chaos... and truth, no matter how long it may take, will always prevail.

"Only what is true will remain because what is true doesn't need anybody to believe it..." Don Miguel Ruiz

There is great wisdom, maturity and trust that we so often fail to have naturally within us, but with Rhiannon as our guide, we can begin to consciously practice these attributes and tap into those helpful traits, applying them to our own personal lives. She gives us the strength when strength is needed... and she helps us to stand in our truth amidst chaos and insurmountable crisis.

*The Welsh Mare Goddess, Rhiannon, is a symbol of steadfastness and forgiveness. Her story is one that classically depicts the struggles of woman as maiden, as bride and then as sacrificial mother, who mysteriously loses her child and a part of herself in the process. She teaches us the importance of balance and the cathartic powers, of releasing the painful suffocating chains of the past and allowing forgiveness to heal our hearts when tragedy has ensued. She exemplifies for us how to persevere despite tragedies and represents the strength and unwavering faith in the face of adversity, prejudices and injustices. When we feel unsupported and marginalized by our situation or a community or when we are being accused of some horrific act, we can find comfort in the messages the Mare Goddess presents to us. Karma is real and the Universe has a way of rewarding our temperance and understanding, during some of the most challenging situations in our lives.

SEDNA

Sedna is the Inuit Goddess of the Deep Sea and all the sea creatures inhabiting this realm. She was also known as Nuliayuk or Taluliyuk; a half woman, half fish deity of the waters. Inuit are the indigenous people of the Alaskan region and their ancient shamanistic beliefs are deeply intertwined in their way of life and very evident in their surviving folklore. Eskimos or Inuit believe in Animism, where all things are deemed to have vital life force and valued as spiritual beings. Humans, animals, all of nature, and all objects are animated with spirit and vital life force, according to their ancient shamanistic religion. Sedna's tale on the surface reveals how whales, seals, polar bears, fishes and sea creatures came to be but as a Goddess folklore, she has much more to reveal to us.

The story begins by a sea port, where a young beautiful maiden is admiring her reflection upon the frozen water. She is enamored by her own beauty and it is said, she spends most of her days submersed in her vanity, admiring her reflection upon the icy waters. Her father just lost his wife and he's a widower struggling to financially support himself and his young daughter. Because of her great beauty there were a plethora of suitors that came offering marriage to Sedna, but she did not find any of them appealing enough to pull her away from her own beautiful reflection on the water. Some time passes and her father becomes increasingly frustrated with his daughter. Unable to financially support them any longer, he forces his daughter to marry the next suitor that approaches their home. Sedna reluctantly agrees and when a dark, mysterious cloaked man approaches them, proposing marriage and promising Sedna a better life, she is forced to accept.

Now, as with all ancient folklores, there are often many different versions or alterations to the story. Some tales speak of the cloaked man giving her a sleeping potion to disorient her; others say she was blindfolded on their journey to their new home. In any event, when Sedna arrives at her new marital abode, she finds herself in a nightmarish predicament. Her husband is not who he claimed to be and she soon learns all of his promises were meant to deceive her into this marriage.

She discovers underneath his dark cloak, he is really a nasty vile Raven. He traps her high up on the mountains, isolated, totally dependent on him for her survival. She is forced to sleep in the cold, on a filthy floor, with no tent of her own, and she is fed the raw, putrid carcasses he gathers from his vile beak. Daily he mistreats her and her hope and beauty slowly begin to fade in that miserable existence.

Sedna finds herself in a dark place, alone and brokenhearted. Nightly she sends a desperate call out to the winds in the hopes that her father could hear her and come to her rescue. Eventually, her father does rescue her, and they set out to run towards the waters, to escape in a kayak.

They begin to feel hopeful in their escape plan but all of a sudden the Black Raven and his family of wild birds are spotted nearby. The monsoon of black birds targeted their kayak, rocking it back and forth, and they start to stir the waters wildly to create a much frightening turbulence. The old man panics, fearing for his life. He cries out, repentedly to the Raven, to let him live and take back his daughter as a bride. Fearing he would not survive, he tosses Sedna out, into the stormy waters. Sedna is utterly devastated and hurt by her father's betrayal but she is also determined to fight for her survival. Her fingers claw the edge of the Kayak, holding on to it for dear life but her selfish, frazzled father takes an ax and chops off her fingers; destroying any chance of her survival.

Those severed fingers become seals, whales, fishes, and the sea creatures that bless the ocean, according to Inuit. Sedna drops to the bottom of the sea and there her sacrificial blood; the betrayal and tragedy she endured, transforms her into the much revere Goddess of the sea and its sea-life creatures. Today she is a highly revered Goddess of the waters and its sea life. She is reverently petitioned by all those who depend on the waters and sea life for their sustenance and survival. Fishermen and all those who work or travel by water, make earnest offerings to appease her. She remains a very important deity for many.

SEDNA MUSING

For a few weeks I was reflecting on the Goddess Olwen, the Goddess Hina, and the Goddess Sedna, and how they reveal the thread of a common theme. Their stories reveal what happens when we find ourselves in oppressive situations or relationships, where our light or our "mere" existence literally is a threat to the oppressor and forces them to either control or get rid of us entirely.

In the case of Olwen, her father knows that if she finds love and happiness and goes off to marry her husband, it will result in his very own death. In the case of Hina, she is about to traverse into the moon. She has awakened and finally endeavors to follow her heart; she knows that it belongs in that celestial light. She knows she must follow her bliss and that she no longer belongs to the pain and the heartache of her earthly family situation. Her husband immediately recognizes this (her awakening) as a threat and goes after her; he ends up violently severing her leg in his effort to stop her.

Hina's pursuit of her divine light is a threat to him, much like Olwen's love becomes a threat to her father and in the case of Sedna (a very tragic story) we see a similar theme. Her husband ends up being yet another unveiled oppressor, trying to destroy Sedna's core being but it's her father who actually delivers the final blow.

In the beginning her widowed father is trying to get rid of her because she's a financial burden, so he forces her to find a husband. Towards the end of the story, her very existence becomes a threat to his own. In the stormy, turbulent waters, she holds on to the kayak, trying to survive. And yet, in his panic, confronted by his own mortality, he betrays her to free himself from death, by cutting off her fingers.

The question that I keep hearing in my head is; how many of us have had Sedna's experience? How many countless women, have had their fingers chopped off; metaphorically chopped off, by the one person we never in a million years thought could betray us in such a vile, gruesome way....? The one person who we thought would protect us, love us, prioritize us, ends up literally killing us with their betrayal... The question becomes do we allow them to fully kill us or do we take power into our own hands and allow ourselves to be forever transformed.... dare I say, deified by such tragedies... And by deified, I mean; reclaiming our inherent powers as Goddess women and transforming our tragedies into our strength. And lastly, allowing the death of our old selves to compost into our inner Goddess. We come out of our chrysalis to finally, fly freely, in our majestic beauty and strength - changed forever. This is the collective message of Sedna, and many of the Goddesses presented in this book.

MUSING ON DEATH

Connecting to the image of the chrysalis and how it becomes a butterfly, I realized, even the Egyptians understood this concept of death. They, like many ancient cultures, understood that death was never seen as finality but rather a process of transformation and preparation for the next stage in our soul's journey. Egyptians mummified the dead, taking great care in this delicate process of wrapping the body, much like a chrysalis. They understood that once the chrysalis was ready, it would awaken in a new realm, transformed, as a beautiful majestic, colorful, liberated butterfly. From chrysalis to a new life; wrapped & mummified, in preparation for the realm, the afterlife with Ma'at. Sedna does not die in the ocean but is transformed into the Great Goddess she becomes for the Inuit.

MUSING ON HER WATERS

At the beginning of Sedna's story, you may note the young maiden is in the realm of the water's surface; admiring her beauty reflected on the surface of the water. She is in this "superficial" realm, on the surface of this frozen water, admiring herself, yet by the end of her story, she finds herself transformed. By the end of the tale she is sunken in the deepest part of the sea, at the bottom of the water. We're talking about the most profound part of the ocean, the deep subconscious waters. These are clearly not Aphrosinian top layered, foamy, surfaced waters. This is not the bubbly, effervescent, romantic, sensual, giggling realm we so often associate with, when it comes to other Ocean deities; like Yemaya and Aphrodite. The Goddess Sedna ends up at the bottom of the water, at the darkest base of the ocean realm of our subconscious; intense emotions and mysterious, great powers are anchored here. According to some legends, Sedna is purported to be given dominion over the deep hallowed waters; connected to where the souls go after their death on earth. The realization that she rules over life and death through the sacred element of water makes her that much more important.

SURVIVAL

Sedna has every right to be angry as some have speculated she was and still is. When there are powerful storms, sea life tragedies or deadly water turbulence, it is considered an expression of Sedna. Often Inuit shamans (better known as Angakoks) perform rituals to appease her. Within some of her folklore it is evident she was terribly abused and betrayed at various times on different levels before becoming a Goddess. First, she loses her mother at a young age and is left with her widower father. Then she begins to sort of lose her father as he makes it clear he is not able to care for her alone any longer. He tries to pass her up to her potential new husband. It appears he is eager to surrender his paternal duties over to her spouse. When she finds herself in the horrible predicament of an abusive marriage, she calls out to; the only one a child can call out to, her sole parent. Her father does come and rescues her but only if it does not involve sacrificing his own life.

There is an uncomfortable aspect I felt channeled through as I worked with Sedna; a painful message about child abuse and neglect. Sedna speaks to me about parental betrayal, deep horrific parental betrayal and one that I could partly channel due to my own childhood experiences.

The loss of her mother at such an early age can be viewed as one betrayal, for mothers are supposed to live a long time to love, guide, teach, protect and be there for their children...but she dies. As a result Sedna is left alone, motherless, and with a neglectful father.

The next betrayal comes when her widowed father was no longer willing to prioritize his daughter. He pushes her to become someone else's responsibility. Again we have a parental betrayal. As a father, he is supposed to love, support, and protect his daughter but he's unwilling to do that any longer; it is reminiscent of parents who do not prioritize their children or abandon them.

He pushes her out the door to find a husband and it leads her into a most horrific situation where she is at the hands of an abuser, yet another betrayal. When she calls out for help, to the only one she can call on, her father, he does come. He witnesses her situation and attempts to rescue her but here is the ultimate betrayal.....because he's only willing to rescue her, as long as it does not inconvenience him or require his own life..... And this is the pinnacle of parental neglect and abuse. Placing conditions on your love, protection and overall parental responsibility for your children is just wrong. As her sole parent, he is the one that is supposed to protect her, prioritize her, support, love and sacrifice for her, but he doesn't. He only meets his parental obligation as long as it doesn't inconvenience him or require his own life and this is the route of child negligence & abuse.

As a parent, when we don't prioritize our children, when we don't protect them, and look out for their wellbeing first and foremost, when we surrender them consciously to negative situations, we tread on dangerous ground. The cycle of child abuse and neglect is a horrible, devastating pestilence and it plagues our society in more ways than we realize, and on so many various levels.

Sedna's story speaks to me about this delicate subject. It is not just the obvious betrayal and victimization that so many women have been subjected to in their most intimate relationships but also the taboo topic of child abuse and neglect. Her story speaks to me about the tenacious survival amidst abuse, abandonment, isolation, and the effects on our emotional terrain; the deep waters of our subconscious. Yet, her story touches me on so many levels. It speaks to me about our great strength as women and our determination in the face of trauma, and consequently illustrates the potential birth of our inner Goddess through it all.

IRENE

Irene is the Greek Goddess of Peace. She is the patron Goddess of Divine Order and Justice. According to the writings of the time, she was considered one of the Horae and a daughter of Zeus. She and her sisters were guardians of the entrance at Mount Olympus and it was their duty to make sure all who entered through the gates of this sacred place had the best of intentions. A Goddess as benevolent as Irene required no blood sacrifice as was customary for other deities.

THEMIS

Themis is the Ancient Greek Goddess of Justice. She is the personification of Divine Law, Social Order, Natural Law and Truth. The scales and the tripod are her sacred emblems and therefore she is known as the Goddess of fairness, order and balance.

It is important to note that she was a daughter of Gaia and Uranus and thus, she is considered one of the Titaness. Mentioned in many of the ancient writings of the time by Homer and Ovid, she is the personification of the law and divine order.

The Greek word "*Tithemi*" means "to put," as in, to put in order or to put in place. In ancient times, Greek judges were known as servants of the Goddess, Themis, and they were given the name, "*Themistopoloi.*"

Her image is sometimes depicted holding a sword, which is known as the sword of truth and also always holding the Scales. Images of the Themis as the Lady of Justice wearing a blindfold is considered a modern rendering not recognized in ancient times. As Goddess of the foreseer, she was attributed for building the Oracle of Delphi, which was given to her by Gaia and, according to one mythology, later then offered to the Goddess, Phoebe. She was also believed to have birthed, with Zeus, the Moirai; also known as the Three Fates. These two examples are indicative of how she was also connected to Foresight and Karma.

Justice was seen as quintessentially critical to moral living, religious and cosmic order, survival of traditions and even connected to proper relationship between a man and a woman. Her existence was at the core of an effective, evolving civilized society. There is no question, Themis was an important deity for the Ancient Greeks but her veneration and her indisputable significance to our world still reverberates greatly today. We see her in everything connected to our legal system as the Lady of Justice; holding up the sacred scales that champion's truth, fairness, balance, justice and the law.

THEME WORK SUGGESTIONS
8. JUSTICE

Light a white or gold candle

Commit to a daily meditation practice, if you don't meditate you can simply pray. You can also use Mantras or daily affirmations. This is all in an effort to ground yourself and connect to your center, to your heart. If you have in pending court cases take the time to investigate and find the right lawyers and mediators for your situation. Research and acquire the right council for your personal situation and gather whatever documents will be needed. Armor yourself with self-education and the tools needed to go into a court of law. If an injustice was done on to you or you witness injustices in the world consider one altruistic action on your part that may alleviate or help the situation.

Perform a Burning Rite. Take a piece of paper, write down the injustice that was done to you (or the injustice that you have witnessed) take this piece of paper,

Place it in a cauldron or fire resistance bowl/plate, and burn this paper.

As you burn this paper see yourself releasing any negative or toxic connection to this situation.

See yourself releasing within the flames the pain and injustice, as your paper Burns.

JOURNALING

Do you feel you have obtained stability in your life?

_____

_____

How do I define Balance in my life? What appears out of equilibrium?

_____

_____

If Ma'at would weight your heart right now, would it be balanced with her Sacred ostrich feather?

_____

_____

What seems unfair in your world?

_____

_____

Where is there an injustice that you feel requires a remedy?

_____

_____

Additional Thoughts......

_____

_____

INVOCATION & POETRY

A CALL TO MA'AT
Golden Goddess,
Ancient as Time,
Holder of Secrets,
Judge of our lives.

Ma'at, I call you,
With my words,
Knowing each one of them
Is vitally heard.

You are the Balancer
Of Sacred Scales,
Correcting all wrongs
Where Justice has failed...

Weighting our Hearts,
Against thy Sacred Plume,
Awakening us
From Self-imposed tombs

Karma igniter,
Bestower of the Law,
Righteous, with Honor,
Heal what is raw.

Bring the Balance needed
Let the Karma be set,
I call on you, Egyptian Goddess,
Let thy Justice manifest.

A BETTER DAY
Prep for the Rainbow,
And the bright Sun,
"Cuz whatcha gonna do,
When the rainstorm is done?"

All this crying and sorrow,
And unneeded pain,
You know the situation
Will eventually change.

See Your tomorrow,
In love with your life,
See your World turning,
From darkness, to bright lights.

See the toxicity,
Get washed far, far away.
By will and by word,
All that had me trapped,
Will now finally wane.

***You are now encouraged to create your own altar(s) & invocation(s).)O(Blessings!

MAGICK RITES & TOOLS

This is your personal page to document your sacred rites and the tools you elected to use.

DECIDE WHERE TO SET UP AN ALTAR
Place an Altar Cloth in the Color of your choice.
Color: _____

GODDESS
Place an image of your Deity.
Goddess: _____
This image can be a Statue, handmade Sculpture or a simple Photo _____

FIRE REPRESENTATION
Place a blessed/charged Candle in the color of your choice.
Candle Type and color: _____

AIR REPRESENTATION
Light your Incense stick.
Incense Scent: _____

WATER REPRESENTATION
Place a Chalice of Water
Water Item: _____

EARTH REPRESENTATION
Place a Potted Plant or Fresh Flowers on your Altar
Add Salt or a plate of Dried Herbs
Herbs: _____
Chosen Gemstone: _____

YOUR WISH
_____
_____
_____

Place a symbol of your desire, if you have one available, and also write your wish out clearly, on a piece of parchment paper, or you can even use a cut up brown paper bag. These are the basics for a very simple altar & rite. Ultimately, your sacred space is only limited by your imagination. You can make your altar & rite as big or as small as you prefer and the addition of other personal items is really up to you.)o(Enjoy!

ALTAR PHOTOS

CHAPTER NINE

"The behavior of a human being in sexual matters is often a prototype for the whole of his other modes of reaction in life." Sigmund Freud, *Sexuality and the Psychology of Love*

THEME: SEXUALITY, POWER & DEATH

Here we reach a point in our journey where we are confronted with our Primal selves and issues connected to our power. When we reach this stage in our spiritual journey we are invited to explore our hidden secrets and taboos and bravely consider who holds power in our lives. For if we are scared or unwilling to talk about something, then we need to consider who or what has silenced us and who we have relinquished our power to. We are invited to delve into parts of ourselves that perhaps we are ashamed of, or have suppressed, for whatever reason; whether it's societally not acceptable or whether it's not tolerable in our families or religious affiliations. We've clearly now entered a dark realm, full of shadows and ambiguities, and lines that are easily blurred with questionable edges that dare us to walk brazenly on.

What is it that you secretly desire or are secretly dealing with that you're scared to address or don't want anyone else to know? The Devil card, which is connected to our theme in this chapter, confronts us and asks, "What has your throat in its grip, choking you, dominating you? What is enslaving you…? What is the thing that you have surrendered your power to, and what has you in a state of disempowerment?

Our themes in this chapter are Sexuality, Power & Death. It may seem like a strange combination but upon closer inspection you will understand why it's part of our journey, especially as women. The subject of sex has always been entangled in issues of shame, power, appropriateness, and secrecy; among many other issues. Yet power is something that all too often we willingly surrender without much consciousness or awareness. And the power that we can access when we embrace our own sexuality and abandon all reservations of our primal selves is transformative. In other words, reclaiming our sexuality is a form of also reclaiming our power. It is a profound lesson all too clear when we delve deeper into the Sumerian Goddess, Lilith.

The subject of Death conjures up many uncomfortable feelings for most people in our western culture. It is sometimes stragely wrapped in taboo and secrecy, or simply, avoidance. It's not a subject most people care to deeply engage in, nowadays. However, this wasn't always the case and our indigenous brothers and sisters had a different opinion and approach to the subject of Death, in earlier times. Perhaps the acknowledgement and honoring of death in earlier civilizations had an impact on human evolution that is clearly now lacking in our world. Together, in this chapter, we will journey towards this taboo subject.

As we have done before, in this chapter we will explore further our theme with the help of several resources. We will endeavor to connect with the Goddesses Lilith, Blodeuwedd, Inanna, Ichtar, Grande Maman Brigitte, BabaYaga and the sacred animal energy of the Snake. We will connect with our Root chakra, the first chakra, and gemstones that can help better facilitate this connection. We will also look at the corresponding Lunation and a Tarot card that is connected to our theme.

"Sex is always about emotions. Good sex is about Free emotions, Bad sex is about blocked emotions." Deepak Chopra

THE DEVIL TAROT CARD

The Devil card depiction in most traditional Tarot deck can make many people feel uncomfortable, fearsome and awkward but while on the surface it's meant to do this, it has a deeper meaning to explore here. It's not necessarily an image of the devil that the Christian religion has depicted for our collective consciousness but rather a depiction of the horned one; the Pagan Deity that lives deep in the dark woods, connected with its primal powers.

When we look at the traditional image of the Devil card, it is usually a very dark image of a horned, gruesome, hairy beast that is holding a naked man and a naked woman, with chains around their necks. It is clear through this depiction that this horned, beastly creature is in total control over these two beings; as if he is the charioteer and they are his obedient horses. And, the couple does not seem at all bothered by these devil chains. As a matter of fact, in their nakedness they appear unaware, open and willing to surrender all authority to this beast.

It is an interesting card that speaks to us not only about power and who we surrender our power to but also about those unseemly things we'd rather not openly disclose. As a side note, I can see how The Devil card might be linked closely with the 8th house, in astrology, because here too, we are delving into secret taboos, other people's resources and power, sex, death and all things that we'd prefer not to openly talk about. So it becomes very obvious that we have now entered this very dark, shadowy realm of the devil, where we might not fully feel comfortable visiting but where we know there is much transformative work to explore.

MOON IN SCORPIO   WATER/MARS & PLUTO
THEME: Sexuality, Power & Death

SCORPIO	FIXED	WATER	FEMININE	SCORPION

The astrological sign of Scorpio has deservedly garnered its reputation as being this massively secretive, esoteric, dark, taboo sign. Perhaps what contributes to its ominous reputation is its association with the distant, now declared dwarf planet, Pluto. Pluto, who is also known, in Greek mythology, as Hades, the God of the underworld, does not offer us bright pink, sweet images of unicorns and rainbows. Let's be honest! When we think about Hades/Pluto and the underworld we can only see images of a dark, possibly painful, mysterious, unknown realm of the dead. It is a realm found deep below our earthly plains and metaphorically speaks of the deep recesses of our own subconsciousness. But these places; whether we are speaking of Pluto's realm of the dead, or our own subconsciousness, offer us something that we cannot obtain if we are not willing to face our fears and commit to diving deep. For you must believe there is indeed something of great value to be obtain when we dive into deep depths that few dare to even approach. It is by diving into the mysteries of life and death, and all in-between that is the hidden, that we gain true wisdom.

It should go without saying that the Moon in Scorpio offers each of us a journey that promises to be very personalized by its very nature. A Moon in Scorpio touches upon so many different aspects but they all share a common thread regarding depth and topics that are often approached with some level of fear or dread. This lunation seeks to enlighten us, uncover dark secrets, and explore our shadows. It touches upon issues of our subconsciousness and taboos; sex is included in this equation, as is death, the occult and all manner of the hidden realms.

When the moon is in Scorpio this is a perfect lunation for any works having to do with transformation, death, the occult, uncovering secrets and of course anything related to sex, power and taboos.

> *"I am tough, I am ambitious and I know exactly what I want. If that makes me a bitch, okay."*
> — *Madonna*

HERSTORY

Miss Prim and Proper, not a hair out of place...You can spot her from a mile away. She is dressed modestly, in neutral colors and takes great care not to speak too loudly or take up too much space, wherever she is. She takes great pride in her meticulous, sanitized life and her appropriateness for every occasion is met with her own comfort and much appreciation by most. It's as if everyone always knows what to expect of her. What would happen if she changed her routine or broke a few rules? What if she let all those nocturnal visions and hidden fantasies come out? However, what became just her normal predictable way of being has admittedly become almost like a prison sentence that she cannot seem to shake off.

Everyone assumes who she is by her proper exterior façades, never questioning if there is more underneath her prim and proper ways. Even she failed to question if there was more to her persona...that is, until one day when life tore away all of her precious façades, and her pristine edifices were detonated by her own sexual awakening... Her "nice girls' dos and don'ts" list gets singes in the fires of Divine Sexual Awakenings and Goddess Empowerment.

********Take a moment to document here, or in your journal, your unique story.**

_____
_____
_____

AFFIRMATION

There is great power in a woman's Orgasm.
I tap into my Divine Primal Self.

Within me are treasures
to be explored.

I connect to the sacred powers of my orgasm.
My Climax is a gift to myself and a potent tool of Empowerment.

Pleasure is a gift to myself, first and foremost,
and this is my power!

Sex is a natural expression of Love
and that includes, Self-Love.

CHAKRA & GEMSTONE WORK

<u>2nd Chakra</u>   SAVADISTHANA/SACRAL CHAKRA   **COLOR:** Orange

Sacral realm, sex chakra for women, womb, water realm, creative expression, self-worth, emotions, energy.

Mantra: I Delight/I Am a Sexual Being

)O(**WORKING:** Honoring Your Physical Body, Fertility, Sexuality, Courage, Energy & Sexual vitality

GEMSTONE CONNECTION: Serpentine is considered a new type of Jade. It is can be found in subtle varying shades of light and dark olive green. It is a gemstone of peace. As a heart-chakra gemstone, it helps with fidelity, peace, compassion, love and the realization of one's true potential. It emits a calming energy and supports positive experiences during trance meditations. Placed under the pillow, it can help with dreams but also, aid a woman's sexual climax. It is known to help nursing mothers produce more milk and can ease menstrual symptoms, thus making it a wonderful gemstone for women to explore further. It is ruled by the planet Saturn and the element of fire and it promotes resourcefulness, prosperity and the gift of attracting happy clients & customers for your business.

Sunstone is a dark to light orange colored stone that helps stimulate the sacral chakra. It is related to masculine energy and it is ruled by the sun. Naturally, it is affiliated with the element of fire and it is a wonderful stone to explore your sacral chakra. It emits warm energy and encourages good health and vitality. This stone helps the wearer tap into their ambition and also has a protective quality regarding health and safe pregnancies. It is an excellent stone to help you develop better leadership skills and unearth the courage to move forward. It is also reputed for igniting and balancing sexual desires.

GEMSTONE CHANNELING

As part of this important work of self-empowerment, assessment and self-directed transformation, you are invited now to find a comfortable place where you can be assured of your privacy, safety and comfort... We endeavor now to start our Chakra meditation in a safe space that is conducive to our healing work. If you can go outdoors in nature that would be most ideal but any place where you can simply relax, undisturbed, would be fine.

Get yourself into a comfortable meditation position; you may sit or lay down. If it is available to you, place in your hands the Sunstone or Serpentine gemstone we are working with today. These gemstones are connected to our Sacral Chakra which is located in your lower abdomen, beneath your belly button. This is the sacred portal of our sexuality as women. It is also the place connected to our desire and ambition.

Hold your Sunstone or Serpentine gemstone in your hands and consider how it feels upon your skin... Reflect now on what energies you can detect from these specific gemstones. Do they feel rough or smooth? Do you sense heat from the gemstone or coldness? Gaze deeply upon your Sunstone or Serpentine gemstone and make note of its shape and color. (Pause) Look at your stone and let your scrutiny unveil all of its precious details. Quietly, continue to study this Sunstone or Serpentine gemstone and make note of any thoughts or vivid images that immediately start to unfold before you. (Pause) When you are ready, you may close your eyes and begin this short meditation.

As with all trance work, we begin with our breath. You are asked now to take a deep cleansing breath; slowly filling up your lungs, then releasing it.... (Pause) Reflect now on your gemstone and let your next breath possess the element of your Sunstone or Serpentine gemstone. Serpentine can be found in varying shades of Olive green, while Sunstone is typically a peach to deep orange hue. Utilize the corresponding color of the stone you are working with today and envision that color becoming vaporous and part of the ether. Breathe in this powerful gemstone energy... As you breathe in, direct the energy of your breath, from your crown chakra, all the way down to your lower abdomen region, near your Sacral Chakra. Stay with this energy for as long as you need to. (Pause) Continue to breathe and hold this breath for 3 seconds and then release it... Counting now at your own pace; breathe, 1, 2, 3, and exhale on 4....and again....breathe in, 1, 2, 3, and exhale on 4. Let's do this one more time and then quietly counting in your head.... Breathe 1, 2, 3...release on 4. Breathe, trusting in the natural rhythm you have now established, of your relaxed inhalation and exhalation.

Your Sunstone or Serpentine gemstone wishes to impart a special channeled message just for you. See this vibrant gemstone in your mind's eye. See it now embedded upon the dark, fertile, mother earth. Draw nearer to it; ask if it will allow you to pick it up. When permission is granted, gently gather it in your hands. With your mind's eye look for any messages it may have for you.

Now with your next breath, place your attention on the top of your head; your crown chakra. See this area as a large, open chalice, ready to receive any spiritual messages that may be unfolding for you now... Envision your crown chakra unveiling a magnetic Sunstone or Serpentine gemstone portal, allowing for this **Crystal Transmission** *to come through... Gently guide the energy of the gemstone, again from your crown chakra, all the way down to your Sacral Chakra, the place of sexuality, desire and ambition... (Pause) Continue to inhale the energy of the Sunstone or Serpentine gemstone. When you feel ready, you may open your eyes and prepare to document your experience. As you come out of this meditation, it is an ideal time for you to document any images or messages that came through for you. You may write them here, or in your personal journal.*_____

SNAKE PROTECTION ENERGY

There are over 2,700 different species of snakes around the world today. Apart from dinosaurs, I don't know of any other animal more ancient in stature than the snake. Scriptures and early writings, document the existence of snakes, present at the inception of the earth, possibly even before humanity. Myths and folklores from across the globe, throughout the ages reflect different tales about the snake and its importance in our cosmology. It helps us to understand a little better this slithering ancestor.

Admittedly, the subject of snakes would be a vast, ambitious undertaking for me to take on in this book and while I am quite passionate about my love and reverence for snakes, I will try to keep this chapter as concise as possible.

Snakes are known as cold-blooded, reptiles. They cannot regulate their own body temperature and thus, require an external source of heat to keep them active and alive. They enjoy a diet of mammals; mostly rodents. Of course, in the wild, they will consume just about anything that can fit into their unhinged jaw. They can be found in different lengths and different colors and for the most part, they are covered with small scales and the most intriguing patterns across their bodies. Many of them have lethal venom that makes them poisonous, others are known as powerful constrictors that will choke their prey to death before consuming. Today, much like in ancient times, some snake species are enjoyed as household pets. I myself have had a corn snake from the time she could fit snuggly in the palm of my hands, at 3 months of age. She has been a wonderful teacher and companion.

Since the earliest of times snakes have, almost exclusively, been associated with the Sacred Feminine. They are a symbol of the earth but also of healing and balancing of polarities. The snake's ability to shed its skin and re-grow new one on a consistent level, makes her relatable to women. Its regenerative skills mimics those found in a woman's reproductive system. As a woman bleeds and sheds her uterine lining approximately every 28-30 days, when it has not been fertilized, so too is the snake able to shed its skin lining and start anew. It is a physical reflection of a more monumental, ethereal concept in mysticism. The snake is a symbol of transformation, reincarnation and immortality. It has always, for the most part, been linked with the Goddess and for humanity it serves as an intermediary between the worlds; being both a spiritual and an earth creature. It represents deep ancient wisdom and mystical knowledge. The snake, therefore, can become for us a powerful ally and protector in our spiritual work.

Snakes were embraced and exalted in Mediterranean & European myths, much more than in the near-eastern and Indo-European region. The snake in Roman, Greek and Cretan households was well regarded. Here they were linked with the present day cults; like the Mystery cults and deities associated with healing. The Greek God of the Sun, Apollo had two offspring, Hygeia, the Goddess of Woman's healing and Aesclepius /Asclepius, the God of Medicine.

They were both often depicted holding snakes and their worshipping temples often maintained snakes for rites. The symbol of two intertwining snakes on a rod, often associated with Aesclepius/Asclepius is known as the Caduceus; a healing emblem that continues to be recognized today.

Before the Sun God, Apollo, took over the Delphic Oracle, we must remember it was first maintained and founded by the Greek Goddess of the Earth, Gaia. Gaia at that time was referred to as "Gaea Pelope," which means, "female serpent." Interesting to note the priestesses that served at this temple were known as serpent priestesses, named, Pythonesses. In Greek mythology, the Goddess Hera was reputed to have had a gigantic snake named, Ladon, which protected the apple tree of life. A snake guarded the temple for the beloved Goddess of Wisdom, Athena, in Athens. And of course, we cannot forget the foreboding image of the serpent headed Goddess, Medusa, so often linked with the myths of the Goddess, Athena.

In Northern India, a rainbow is called, *Budhi Nagin*, which, interestingly enough means, "old female snake." The Sanskrit word for snake is "Naga." In India the Nagas are a special group of female, rain deities with the body of a snake and the head of a human or simply depicted as a full snake. They were guardians of the riches of the world, namely material and spiritual riches. They resided in the underworld with all the rich minerals of the earth, surrounded by extravagance and they symbolized Shakti and cosmic power. The Nagas had dominion over rainclouds and rainbows and they were keepers of the ancient mysteries. The mother of the Nagas is the Indian serpent Goddess; Kadru. The Nagas appear reminiscent of the Mayan Goddess of the Moon, Ix Chel, as she too had dominion over rainclouds and rainbows. She is also linked with a multitude of serpents adorning her skull. This correlation between serpent deities, water, rain, the moon and women seems to be compulsory throughout early writings.

For most Native Americans, they believed snakes had great power and was a potent teacher. For the Celts, snake is connected with the healing Goddess, Brigit. According to Celtic mythology there was an Imbolc tradition that involves the search for the Goddess, embodied as a slithering snake, coming down from the mountains to announce the early arrival of spring on Imbolc. This is a rite reminiscent of our U.S.A. Ground Hog day. Nordic tradition spoke of the Midgard serpent, also known as the World serpent that swallows its tail to create a whole circle and reflect the infinity of life. In Greece this serpent was known as Oceanos. In Japan the Oceanic God of turbulence, Susano-O, was sometimes depicted as a snake and although modern Chinese view serpents as destructive and deceitful, ancient Chinese tradition did not. The Goddess of Creation, Nu-Kua and her mate/brother Fu-Xi are both depicted as half human and half serpent. In ancient Chinese tradition, this half serpent Goddess is recognized as the Creatrix, responsible for birthing humanity upon the earth.

Unquestionably, one of the most powerful symbols of transformation and regeneration is this reptile; the snake. Often associated with healing and esoteric knowledge it is the earliest animal mentioned and documented as existing upon the inception of humanity. It is one of the oldest beings mentioned in early scriptures and well documented in the earliest of folklores and mythologies. The Snake connects us to ancient wisdom, the sacred feminine, birth, rebirth, transformation and regeneration. One can see it as spiral energy, related to healing waters, the moon, and infinity. The Snake connects us to Kundalini energy, varying levels of consciousness, and esoteric knowledge. It is death and rebirth, surrendering and shedding our skin to let new growth take place. It is an ancient animal with so many conflicting stories, irrational fears and taboos connected to it. However, if we delve deeper into this powerful animal we will find a most powerful protector, teacher and ally to our transformational work. Snake is one of the oldest spiritual teachers available to us. It connects us to the Goddess, our Feminine Intuition, and our womanly gifts of transformation. We are reminded that we are descendants of the Sacred Feminine, embodying this ancient snake energy.

THEME WORK SUGGESTIONS

Work with the Scorpio moon, symbolized by the Scorpion, and work with The Snake energy, as well as the many Goddesses offered in this book. Spend time exploring your female genitalia and create your own personal Yoni Ritual. Work with gemstone crystals placed in your underwear pocket to clear away any unwanted energy. You may also burn a vagina shaped candle to ignite healing and balance in this region. When delving on the theme of death, visit a cemetery and explore ancestor worship.

GODDESS EMPOWERMENT

LILITH

"...Once women are free to bestow their favours and affections where they will, the whole structure of patriarchal society starts to crumble..."

The Cult of the Black Virgin," by Ean Begg, Page 137,
Chiron Publications, Wilmette, Illinois 2006

    Probably one of the most controversial Pagan deities and one full of conflicting, yet intriguing mythologies is the Sumerian Goddess Lilith. Lilith is a powerful archetype for any women to unearth and work with.

    The Goddess, Lilith today is viewed as a Goddess of the night, Goddess of Sexual Liberation, a Goddess of revenge and retribution and anger. According to a collection of ancient writings, she could not be wild and free in God's heavenly presence in the Garden of Eden and she would not subordinate herself to her spouse, Adam. Thus, she's a Goddess that represents independence among many other feminist ideals. She is the liberated woman who does not compromise herself and she answers to no one. She is the one who embraces the pain of solitude rather than relinquish her power to any man. Lilith represents the autonomous woman who refuses to subordinate herself or lay down beneath her oppressor. She is the women who reclaims her powers and reclaims her authentic self in a world that so persistently, only wants to control and oppress her. She is the rebellious one who refuses to play societal stereotypical roles. She is sexual liberation, delighting in her unbridled sexuality and enchanting beauty. She is flight of spirit that comes and goes as she pleases. Lilith is the opposite of the nurturing maternal Goddess, even though she is attributed for birthing a race of demonic beings; she is far from the coddling mother archetype. She is considered the shadow side of Eve; that part of her she has yet to embrace or discover, for Eve only appears to accept her limiting role as Adams' rib, created inferior to him.

We claim Lilith now as a powerful Goddess for we see her significant value and cathartic importance for modern day women, especially with the rise of Feminism, but when researching Lilith you will soon discover ancient text that reveal she was not initially viewed as a Goddess but rather as a very much feared She-Demon. Perhaps, as many Dianics claim, she was indeed initially a Goddess a long time ago, who was stripped of her crown and demoted with the rise of patriarchy. One will never really know. Despite limited resources, remnant scriptures, actual sacred text scattered about mentioning her numerous different names and a plethora of mixed, conflicting tales, she has survived into the 21st century, which is astounding, when you really think about it. Consider that her oral traditions remained strong throughout the ages and sustained her in our auric "herstory."

Lilith has often been viewed by Wiccan Feminist as a Goddess who was simply demoted, vilified as a demon because, in a patriarchal society, that is the ultimate way to control and oppress a woman; vilify her, make such a scandalous rebellious Goddess, evil, to discourage any other woman from reclaiming her own powers or even slightly considering how vastly different her world might be, if she stood up as well. Lilith's claws or talon represents her tenacity; digging her heels, refusing to surrender her ideals. Her wings represent her freedom and her red eyes represent anger of those who tried to restrain and oppress her. She is often depicted with wings, owl talon as claws for her feet, and hairy legs (for in ancient times, a hirsute woman was considered a sign of demonic association). Suspecting that Queen of Sheba was demonic, King Solomon asked to see her legs and behold he discovered that she was indeed very hairy and this led him to conclude that she was the embodiment of Lilith.

Some symbols linked to Lilith are the flower lily and the lotus as well as gemstones like the Garnet and Bloodstone. Her depictions with animals indicate that she had an affinity to wild creatures. Animals like the owl, wolves, the lion, scorpions and the serpent were accepted as her symbols and the screeching owl, a name so often used in the bible, to refer to her. The serpent in particular, was often representative of the Goddess herself. She has also been associated with harpies, sirens, mermaids, undines, nymphs and melusines, perhaps due to her close connection with water and the sea. French poet and novelist, Victor Hugo (1802-1885) even claims Lilith as Satan's eldest daughter and as a succubus, she was attributed for creating a race of vampires.

The name Lilith, which translates in the Semetic language as "Night," is also associated with the wind and the breeze. The word "Lil" or "Lilitu," meant ghost, spirit breath, wind and storm demon. What is remarkable is that the name Lilith and various derivations of her name appear throughout history in Sumerian, Kabbalistic writings and Jewish mysticism and yet, it's quite interesting that according to Kabbalah scriptures, she was the first woman God created; Lilith (night) and yet, the next woman created for Adam was consequently named Eve (again a reference to night), reaffirming a connection between woman and the night.

According to Raphael Patai, in his book, *"The Hebrew Goddess,"* he states that **Lilith or Lillu** was actually one of Four Demons, belonging to the vampire or incubi-succubae class.

Lilitu and **Lillu** (Lilith) believed to be a She-Demon
Ardat Lili (Lilith's Hand maiden) who visited men at night to procreate offspring.
Irdu Lili (male counterpart) who visited women to also proliferate, impregnate and further expand the race of Demons.

The Goddess, Lilith was originally considered to be a part of a clan of Storm Demons, due to some confusion with the origins of her name, which sometimes refers to wind, breeze, ghost and spirit of the dead. There was also around the third Dynasty of Ur, another documented Sumerian Goddess, by a similar sounding name, Ninlil. Ninlil was a known Babylonian - Sumerian Goddess of the Wind and she was also known as the Avenging Bride, perhaps there was some confusion regarding these two feminine figures or perhaps they are one the same. Clearly the myths and attributes of Ninlil and Lilith are intriguingly similar and there is no question they crossed path at some point.

Lilith was known by many names and interestingly enough, sometimes, she was referred to in the singular form as well as in the plural. She was known as Lilin, Abito, Abizo, Amo(z)rpho, Haqash, Odam, Kephido, Ailo, Tatrota, Abniqta, Shatrina, Kalubtza, Tiltoi, Pirtsha.

By far one of the most controversial Feminine figures in ancient mythology is Lilith. There are numerous conflicting and controversial references to this ancient deity. We find references to her in Jewish mysticism; Kabbalah, the Talmudic, the Zohar, even the Bible, in Isaiah 34:14. Some early writings revealed she manifested when, on the fifth day of creation, God created the Sea creatures and she was among them. Other text, like the one found in the Zohar, claims she was a soul lodged in the Abyss that finally was called down upon, to descend, only after Yahweh had created Adam. Notice in this myth she was already present before Adam's manifestation.

In the lost Midrash Abkir, Kabbalistic writings of the 10th century, Lilith, who was also named, Pizna was actually viewed as two spirits in one. She is considered Lilith and Naamah. According to this text, Adam's beauty was so radiant and irresistible that they were both enchanted by him as he slept and they mated with him, unable to restrain themselves. Together they procreate the "plagues of mankind," the demonic race of Lilim. And the name Naamah, translates as the **"charmer"** and she is known as a high ranking demon that often accompanies Lilith. In Talmudic- Midrashic mythology, Naamah is actually depicted as a human being, a beautiful enchantress, daughter of Lamech and Zillah and sister of Tubal Cain. She is clearly a descendant of Cain and in her great beauty; she is a deadly enchantress, as sadly, all dangerously, magnetic women tend to be ironically portrayed. It is believed she then becomes Noah's wife, that is according to Abba bar Kahana. However, later, in the Kabbalah she was transformed into semi-human, demonic stature and thus, an aspect or a type of Lilith.

Barely mentioned in the Bible, most of what we know today about this enigmatic female figure, Lilith, can be extrapolated from pre-Biblical writings, Jewish Mysticism, oral traditions passed down and documented in many scriptures, as well as Kabbalistic writings, preserved in the Midrashic, the Zohar and Talmudic works of Sages and Rabbis throughout history. Perhaps it's best to start from the beginning with one version of her birth and manifestation but as can be expected with such an ancient figure, there are numerous versions and theories related to her birth.

"*The Alphabet of Ben Sira*," written in German between the 8th and 10th century gives a complete narrative and description of one version of Lilith's manifestation and perhaps it came about to explain the confusing Biblical lore found in Genesis, which upon closer inspection does not make much sense. "*The Alphabet of Ben Sira*" was considered a satire but in reality it was more likely a surviving oral tradition that sustained itself through the ages to explain the existence of Adam's first wife. According to "*The Alphabet of Ben Sira*," Lilith was the first woman created by God, not Eve. Although some authors like, Janet and Stewart Farrar in their book, "*The Witches' Goddess*," suggests that Eve and Lilith are really one the same and thus Lilith is the shadow aspect of Eve.

> *"Truths banished to the unconscious do acquire talons –*
> *representing both our fear of them and their ability to tear away*
> *through the veils of hypocrisy and distortion*
> *with which we have tried to surround them.*
> *Only when we come to terms with them and*
> *integrate them with consciousness is their loveliness restored,*
> *so that their talons become feet again.*
> *Only when the night-owl is admitted to the sunlight*
> *can we appreciate the beauty of her plumage.*
> *Lilith the true Mother of All living, must be re-acknowledge –*
> *so that She and Eve can become One again*
> *For without that One, Adam is only half man..."*
>
> (The Witches' Goddess," Janet and Stewart Farrar page 133)

In "*The Alphabet of Ben Sira*," Lilith was created at the same time as Adam, on the fifth or sixth day of creation. And God had fashioned Adam from the earth and he used the same raw material to create Lilith probably before or at the exact same time. There are other conflicting works that claim that God picked up, not the clean earth as he did for Adam, but the filth and impurities or sediments from the earth to form woman and thus it was to be expected that she was to have an impure, evil spirit, this was according to some very patriarchal Talmudic writings. Clearly a poor attempt by patriarchy to pollute our entire gender right at the start of humanity by claiming woman is destined to be evil, since she was created from impure soil and sediment. There is yet another version of Lilith's manifestation which claims that she manifested not from God himself but from the spontaneous great supernal abyss and out of the power aspects of God; the Din and the Gevurah. God was believed to have ten mystical attributes, Serifot, and his lowest kinship with the realm of evil was referred to as the, "*dreg of wines*" and this is where both, Lilith and Samuel or Satan originated from, according to these early Talmudic writings.

Lilith and Adam were created equally from the earth as written in *"The Alphabet of Ben Sira."* One day Adam desiring to have sexual relations with his mate demanded that she lay down underneath him but Lilith, viewing this position as subordinate, refused. She demanded to know why she should lay beneath when they had both been created as equal. *"Why should I lower myself, surrender my power to you when we have been created equally?"* I imagine her asking. Adam would not have it any other way and neither would Lilith. A huge argument ensued and in this contemptuous, stressful, highly emotional moment, Lilith utters the unspeakable secret name of God, something that was forbidden in the Garden of Eden and she then flies away. Although, there are variant versions that reveal she actually lulled Adam to sleep, enchanted God to reveal his secret powerful name to her and then, she went ahead and uttered it to manifest the wings that would inevitably get her out of the Garden of Eden. Be that as it may, in this power struggle with Adam she uttered the unspeakable, effable name of God, which was not viewed favorably and upon doing this she grew the wings that would allowed her to flee her oppressors and escape from the Garden of Eden. And Lilith flew away from the light of God, paradise, and Adam and chose the notorious Red Sea; a place scandalously known for harboring fallen angels, demons and evil spirits. There is a connection at this time between the waters and demons, especially the waters of the Red Sea and it's attraction to malign entities, and evil spirits. It is stated that Lilith upon the edge of the Red Sea delighted in numerous sexual relations and she fornicated and took to unbridle promiscuity; having intercourse with a multitude of demons daily and procreating a myriads of children, a race of demons called Lilim. Three days later, Adam finally begs God to bring her back to the Garden of Eden and so God sent three angels to lure and fetch her from the Red Sea. He sent the angels; Senoy, Sansenoy and Semangelof.

When the three angels arrived they found her copulating; indulging in various sexual dalliances with numerous demons and giving birth to many offspring. According to early scripture interpretations, the angels approached her and asked her to return with them to the Garden of Eden and she refused. They threatened to drown her in the Red Sea and she seemed un-moved, almost bothered by their angelic presences and demands. The angels threatened to kill off One Hundred of her very own offspring daily and she retorted she would do the same to any children born to Eve. All of these threats and the presence of these three angels were beginning to bore her and in her efforts to get rid of them, she finally agrees to not kill any future babies that have the inscribed names of the three angels, Senoy, Sansenoy and Semangel, upon them.

"..... Let me be for I was created in order to weaken the babes:
if he is a male, I have power over him from the moment of his birth until the eighth day
of his life, that is when he is circumcised and
thereby protected, and if a girl, until the Twentieth day..."

Pg 224, The Hebrew Goddess by Raphael Patai,-Alpha Beta di Ben Sira, ed. Einstein, Otzar Midrashim, pg.47

Interestingly enough, there are other tales found in the Zohar that reveal the first humans created by God were Hemaphrodites or Androgynes, attached to each other by their backside initially. All creations were created in the image of God, according to Biblical scriptures, and thus, all contained both male and female attributes, how this later changed, remains a mystery but there is a belief that Lilith was joined with the King of demons (Samuel, Satan or Ashmodai etc..) and they were created in the exact mirror image of Adam and Eve to represent the synchronicity of, as above so below. Adam and Eve were also alleged to be Hemaphrodites or Androgynes and this couple, mirrored Lilith and Samuel, but I digress.

As was her custom, Lilith was known to tickle newborns (which explains why babies have these random, spontaneous smiles while they sleep) and she is credited for leading them to their deaths but in this myth she agreed to allow One Hundred of her own demon offspring to be killed daily by God and she makes an oath to not harm any babies that revealed the names of the three angels upon them. Much controversy surrounds Lilith as a SheDemon that kills and even cannibalistically devours children's blood and bones. There was no other way of explaining such horrific tragedies as stillborn and mysterious infant deaths except to blame a demoted deity and contribute to her fabricated, growing negative reputation. Stillbirths, miscarriages, children that mysteriously died in infancy and spontaneous abortions were all attributed to her. A plethora of artifacts found with incantations to her, supplicating her to keep away from newborns, supports this connection.

Returning to the tale of Lilith's manifestation from "*The Alphabet of Ben Sira*," the angels left Lilith to live in a cave by the Red Sea and now Adam, in the Garden of Eden, required a new mate and here is where the Bible begins its tale. Adam now required a new spouse and from the hidden part of Adam, his rib, Eve was crafted by Yahweh. She was to be more obedient and subservient to Adam, always beneath him, complacent, accommodating and she was to reflect the nurturing maternal attributes that Lilith so lacked. Now here is where we get some conflicting stories because according to one tale, Lilith was matched to the King of demons, Samuel, Satan, Ashmodai, Lucifer but according to other scriptures, God, fearing these two (Lilith and Samuel) would populate the earth with a powerful breed of demons, castrated Samuel, in his effort to control their proliferation of children. And because licentious Lilith was now in need of a sexual partner, she chose to sneak back into the Garden of Eden from time to time to have relations with Adam while he slept, through nocturnal emissions. The conflicting part is that some say Lilith would inevitably return to the Garden of Eden as the Serpent and in her wrath and jealousy, would eventually lead Adam and Eve into sin, by offering them the fruit from the forbidden Tree of Knowledge. There is some text however, that reveals the Serpent was really Samuel/Satan, the King of Demons himself. Samuel, exercising retribution, since his wife was taking on Adam as her nightly lover, he felt justified in now seducing Eve in the same manner. Nonetheless, both Adam and Eve had tasted of the forbidden fruit, from the Tree of Knowledge, according to Biblical lore and as a result there immortality was taken from them. They were expelled from the Garden of Eden, as we all have learned through popular Biblical interpretations.

In his remorse and disgust, Adam vowed 130 years of celibacy and self- imposed punishment, fasting and self-denial. Both he and Eve roamed the earth during this time and according to the numerous mystical writings. It was during this 130 year sojourn and because of his sin, that Lilith now had even more access to him. His very sinful nature made him vulnerable to her presence according to the writings of this time. She frequented him nightly, having sexual intercourse with him through nocturnal emissions, aka wet dreams. Eve was not spared of this either, as she too was visited nightly by the King of Demons and was impregnated daily so that she would give birth to half human and half demon, light and dark beings, just as Lilith would give birth to Adam's half demon, half human children. It is believed that through these unions between Lilith and Adam, and Samuel and Eve that the descendants of Cain, Tubal-Cain and his sister Naamah, manifested. It is also believed that when Cain, after Abel's murder, was banished by God, Lilith took him on as her lover and together they too populated the earth with the first demonic vampiric race this is according to these early Kabbalistic writings. Researching these ancient scriptures, it would appear to me that the whole of humanity is somehow connected to Lilith, Adam, Eve and Samuel as direct descendants of both human and demonic lineage.

Even older than *"The Alphabet of Ben Sira"* are the numerous artifacts found displaying Lilith's name, function and revealing how she was truly viewed in ancient time by the Sumerian people. One of the earliest mentions of Lilith is found in 2000 B.C.E. on a clay tablet in which we have the Mesopotamian Epic tale of Gilgamesh, Inanna and the Huluppu (Willow) tree.

According to the Gilgamesh epic, Huluppu tree lore, the great Goddess, Queen of Heaven, Inanna, discovered the tree in the sea and brought it to her garden, planting it near the Euphrates River, where she tended to its growth and nurturance. The tree grew nice and strong and one day, lamenting that she did not have a personal throne, she saw the tree as the perfect material to make her divine throne from but when she approached the tree, she learned that it was already inhabited. There was a fierce serpent, a special serpent-dragon that could not be charmed, living at the base of this tree. She also discovered a Zu bird which had built a nest way up above, at the crown of the tree and much to her surprise, the Dark Maiden Lilith, had made her home in the trunk of this Huluppu tree. And these three obstacles sadly prevented Inanna from reclaiming her tree and thus creating her divine throne. In the tale, she calls on Gilgamesh and he's able to chop down this tree with a special Bronze axe and he saves the day by removing all the obstacles and Lilith as a result of this, abandons the tree and flies into the wilderness, the desert. Interesting to note Gilgamesh's father, a Sumerian king was known as a Lilludemon, a reference to Lilith and her Clan of demons. This epic tale reveals Lilith's early myths and her connection to the Queen of Heaven, as she was sometimes known as Inanna's Hand-maiden and some tales reveal Lilith in "Erecht", as one who gathered men from the streets, with her beauty, to come enter the Goddess Temple for ritual sex offerings.

> **Isaiah 34:14 "The wild –cat shall meet with the jackals and the satyr shall cry to his fellow, Yea, Lilith shall repose there, and find her rest…"**

And here we have one of the only mentions of her name in the bible and it supports the Gilgamesh Huluppu tree Epic, which claims Lilith flew away to live in the desert.

In Nippur Babylonia, modern day Hilla in Iraq, there were many discovered bowl artifacts with carvings and inscriptions referring to her name. These bowls, from about 600 B.C.E., with their inscriptions, revealed how Lilith was viewed by the locals and how her myths still survived outside of academia and the scholastic researcher's domain. Sacred scriptures found in the Zohar and Talmudic writings revealed how the elite and the educated viewed Lilith and her myths but via these excavated artifacts we get a glimpse into the most precious and intimate views on this iconic female figure by the everyday people amidst their residential communities. Many of them had inscriptions, invocations with protective charms and incantations to keep Lilith away and to safeguard their offspring. In Mesopotamia and North Syria, by the eighth century B.C.E., she was clearly already known as a She-Demon in Israel. A 7th century B.C.E, clay tablet found in Northern Syria depicts her as a sphinx with an inscription…

> **"O, flyer in the darkness, Go away at once, O Lili…"**

pg 222 The Hebrew Goddess, by Raphael Patai.

There is a medieval story preserved in Hebrew and Arabic which tells of a youth who marries the daughter of Ashmodai. He later decides he wants to be free of her and gives her a "*Get*" which is a kind of letter of divorce required back then when one intended to separate from their demonic spouse. Seems strange but this tale supports the notion that demons, in ancient times, married and intermingled with humans. It is quite a curious bizarre tale and reflective of a time when the belief of Demon attachments was so prevalent. The result of this was even more enthralling. As planned, the letter is finally delivered and as documented, the daughter of Ashmodai responds to it with a kiss of death.

Rabbi Joshua Ben Perahia, and the names of other rabbis are invoked several times and found, documented on these excavated Nippur bowls. Rabbi Joshua Ben Perahia, was a first century B.C.E. sage who was believed, by the sixth century CE, to have been a powerful exorcist of demons and often called upon with regards to exorcising a Lilith. First century teacher, Rabbi Hanina stresses the importance for man not to sleep alone in his home, less Lilith gets a hold of him via nocturnal emissions, revealing she is a Goddess men should fear because, remember, it was during Adams' 130 years of solitude and self-imposed punishment that Lilith had her way with him nightly, through these nocturnal emissions. The Rabbi warns men not to sleep alone as it will invite her presence and this caution for Jews still survives to this very day.

Early 14th century Kabbalist writer, Bahya ben Asheribn Halawa, (death-1340) reveals in his biblical commentaries that Lilith was one of four known Mother Demons. Lilith, Naamah, Igrath and Mahalath were the four wives of Esau's divine patron, aka

Samuel, Ashmodai, Satan. These four women, each ruled their respective Tequfot (Winter Solstice, Summer Solstice, Vernal Equinox, Autumnal equinox). The writer Halawa also claims King Solomon had rule over them and they were considered his slave-women aka his Liliths, which he manipulated for his personal gains and invoked freely as needed.

Another tale reveals an encounter between the Prophet Elijah, Lilith and her Clan or band. The Prophet Elijah, saw Lilith and asked her where she was going and she boasted that she was going to the house of a woman in the middle of childbirth, Mercada daughter of Donna. ***"....to give her the sleep of death and to take her child, which is being born to her, to suck its blood, and to suck the marrow of its bones and to seal its flesh..."*** *(Page 227 "The Hebrew Goddess" by Raphael Patai.)* The prophet then recited a curse to restrain Lilith, " *with a ban from the name Yahweh, Blessed be He, be you restrained, be restrained and Be you like unto a stone.....*" and she recites back and asks to be released of the restrained placed upon her and promises not to harm them. Lilith gives a list of her sacred names and her various titles, that if she is called by these names or if she sees these names in print, she will do no harm and she will be rendered powerless. These are the names she recited to him that day; Lilith, Abitar, Abiqar, Amorpho, Hakash, Odam, Kephido, Ailo, Matrota, Abnukta, Shatriha, Kali, Taltui, Kitsha.

Hayyim Vital (1543-1620) a Safed Kabbalist, explains in his writings that there was a fallen angel, known as *"the flame of the revolving sword."* This angel was sometimes referred to as a demon called Lilith and thus it would appear that Lilith and this fallen angel are regarded interchangeably and as being one the same. According to one tale in the Zohar, when Lilith first manifested she sought companionship immediately, and soaring up high she rose to attach herself to the small boy faces of the Cherubim, which she saw surrounding God's throne. When God created man, with Adam, he detached her from the Cherubim and ordered Lilith to descend to earth. Upon seeing Adam with Eve, she felt displaced and immediately sought to return to the Cherubim but by then, they knew what she was up to and barred her from heavens, banishing her to the Sea. *Which begs the question, why is she banished to the Sea? It appears that Biblical scriptures always view the sea as containing evil and water as a place for the uncontrollable, the volatile, evil spirits, and the wicked. Yet water is closely related to the Moon and therefore to Night and somehow Woman has always been linked with these realms. I find this fascinating and it conjures up all kinds of musings, but I digress.*

Visual Depictions:

Lilith has often been depicted in numerous conflicting ways. Some claim she is wind, just a breath, nonhuman in form and yet others depict her as a woman with her lower half enflamed with roaring fires. In connection with one of her totems, the Owl, she is depicted as a screeching Owl, a winged creature in nocturnal flight. She has also been portrayed as a wise calculating Serpent, with a woman's head and a snake's slithering body. As an incubus succubus and Mother of Vampires she has been depicted as an enchanting, blood thirsty vampire. During the age of Enlightenment many artist and poets, like Dante Gabriel Rossetti, romanticized her image, depicting her as an exquisite beautiful misunderstood woman. The 1889, "*La Fille de Lilith*" by Rossetti, tells her tale of retribution. Goethe includes her in "*Walpurgisnacht*" and her likeness appears in Shaw's "*Back to Methuselah*" as well as Thornton Wilder's "*The Skin of Our Teeth.*" Writer, Anais Nin, dedicated the Erotic poem, "*Delta of Venus*" to Lilith and there is no question that many stories and images of Lilith have inspired many artist and writers throughout the ages. Depicted in a way that our human eyes can comprehend, an old Babylonian Terra cotta, Burney relief, remains now in a British Museum and here is a visual description of this image of her;

"She is slender well shaped, beautiful and nude with wings and owl feet. She stands erect on two reclining lions, which are turned away from each other and are flanked by owls. On her head she wears a cap embellished by several pairs of horns. In her hand, she holds a ring and rod combination."

(Emil G.H. Kraeling, Bulletin of the American Schools of Oriental Research 67 (Oct.1937), pages 16-18)

As an enchantress she is often describes with long flowing red hair, pale skin and red lips and blushing cheeks. Sexually inviting, her beauty is unmatched and she is so captivating that she leads men to their own death. She is often adorned with ornaments as described in the passage below.

"Her ornaments for the seduction of the sons of man are: her hair is long and red like the rose, Her cheeks are white and red, from her ears hang six ornaments, Egyptian Cords and all ornaments of the land of the East hang from her nape, Her mouth is set like a narrow door, comely in its décor; her tongue is sharp like a sword, her words smooth like oil, her lips red like a rose and sweetened by all the sweetness of the world. She is dressed in scarlet and adorned with 40 ornaments less one."

Raphael Patai's, The Hebrew Goddess,pg 233

Today Lilith is embraced by most modern day Pagans and Goddess worshipping women as a Goddess of the Night and Sexual freedom, who initially debuted as a vilified, much feared She-Demon. Lilith is understandably the saboteur of patriarchy, the one who will NOT go with the flow, will not succumb nor lay down to be ruled over. She is the rebellious one who will create her own rules to live by. Demonized by a patriarchal society, Lilith represents the most frightening aspect of femininity. She represents what patriarchy wants to control, rule over and oppress. She can be seen as the hidden subconscious, as she's connected with night, the Moon, and the Moon is connected with waters, emotions, deep hidden emotions of the murky waters. In patriarchal writings, she is classified as a harlot, a vampire, a hag, a witch, an enchantress, seductress, barren one, child killer, insatiable, blood thirsty and most of all misunderstood. She is one with no milk upon her breasts as described in ancient texts and yet, she is also considered the mother of a race of Demons and equally referred to as a maiden in her epithet. She is a virgin archetype -for she belongs to no one and experiences life by her own rules.

Lilith and even Eve, perhaps share in the traits of another deity known as Blodeuwedd, as their most negative attributes seem to have been created by men's vision and fantasy, created to serve patriarchy; to be obedient, subordinate, unrealized, disempowered, sexually confined and restricted, only to serve the "master." And yet, both (Lilith and Blodeuwedd) appear to be "punished" into Owl-hood, banished into the night for their divine awakening and refusal to play by the oppressor's rules. Representing the dark side of the unconscious, the night and the shadow, they become the scariest threat to patriarchy, and must then be ostracized, relegated, demonized into the night. How frightening must it be to a nation of self-proclaim masters to confront the true all-powerful strength of Goddess; reflected in the maiden, mother, crone, the bitch, the harlot, the warrior, the protectress mother, the seductress, sex loving, pleasure seeker, commanding, demanding, sea lover, compassionate, wise, strategic, intelligent, competent, beast lover, cave dweller, howler of the night......in each and every awakened woman/Wombmyn upon this earth!

She is Goddess and a model for those who have opened themselves up to their autonomy, great beauty, sexuality and their self-reliant strength. For those who gladly surrender the suffocating chains of complacency and stereotypical female "nice-a-ties" of a life played under the thumbs of patriarchy, she is a powerful force to unearth. Yes, she is a She-Demon, just as todays' powerful, no nonsense, feminist is classified as "the bitch" and both are... in my opinion, **Goddess.** There is no debate, in my mind, whether she is a She-Demon or Goddess, for in Lilith we come to yet another sacred aspect of the Divine Feminine. A thunderstorm, with its massive pouring of rain, can neither be classified as good or bad for in the dry desert she is everything connected to good and in the marshland she is everything connected to bad. Thus, a thunderstorm, much like the Feminine Divine, and all of Nature, is neither good nor bad.... **it just is!!!** And to deny one aspect is to only embrace and comprehend half of Goddess. Hail to you most powerful beautiful Liliatu!!!!

*The Sumerian Goddess, Lilith, is a most fascinating, yet controversial Goddess. She enters your life in a most distinctly irrefutable fashion and her influence is probably one of the most impactful on a women's life. She is the Dark Goddess that rises from the depths of our subconscious and provokes you into your own powers. When the Goddess Lilith asserts herself in your life you will feel the depths of her intense strength, energy and her intolerance for women's suppression and inequality. She is the adamant voice that will not be victimized, oppressed nor engaged in patriarchal rules. Lilith is autonomy and freedom and she will not succumb to societal pressures, no matter what names are flung at her. You can call her demon, bitch, cunt, dyke, witch, monster, whatever... but she WILL remain whole and authentically true to herself, for she will not lay herself down, beneath anyone. She will not subordinate herself for man's pathetic, sick ideologies and she soars in flight with her autonomous woman power intact throughout the ages because of it. She is brazen pleasure seeker, whole unto herself and epitomizes woman's sexual liberation and a powerful representation of Feminism.

BLODEUWEDD

Blodeuwedd, pronounced [blow-dai-weth] is the maiden, Welsh, flower Goddess who was magickally created by two very powerful wizards. Her name is translated as "Born of Flowers" or "Flower face." Often labeled as the Goddess of Betrayal, and one who reflects both dark and light aspects, she is known by many other titles. She is recognized as the maiden Goddess of love and beauty, a Goddess of secret lovers and the archetype of women awakening to her desires. She is sometimes viewed as the maiden part of the trinity of Welsh Goddesses, with Arianrhod, considered the Mother and Cerridwen, the Crone. Although, I have also seen her classified as the Lover archetype, while Arianrhod was deemed the virgin.

Although we learn about Blodeuwedd in Robert Graves' *"The White Goddess"* We first encounter Blodeuwedd and her myths in an ancient text called *"The Mabinogion,"* of the 13th century. Some Welsh scholars, however, believe this text was in existence long before the time of Christ and throughout long standing Pagan traditions.

According to *"The Mabinogion,"* the Moon Goddess Arianrhod's second son, Llew Llaw Gyffes (or Llew as he is sometimes referred to) was cursed by his own mother due to a humiliating incident regarding his uncles and her chastity and reputation. As Arianrhod's curse stipulated, Llew was to never bear a sword or arms, he would never have a name and would never be allowed to marry a woman of this earth and this itself would preclude him of ever holding any rank or kingdom. This was a most dreadful way to assure her son's failure, for at this time in Welsh history these were the prerequisite and the only means by which a man could acquire power. The boy's crafty uncles, Gwydion & Math ap Mathonwy, however, had a plan to circumvent this powerful, wretched curse.

Map and Gwydion, who had become almost like beloved foster fathers to Llew, were two of the most powerful wizards in the land and they decided that since their nephew could not marry a real woman of the earth, they would then craft one magickally from flower blossoms. Some text state that Blodeuwedd manifested from simply three powerful blossoms but a more commonly accepted tale, confirms Graves', writings in, *"The White Goddess."* This breathtaking, beautiful woman, meant solely for Llew's pleasure, was created by layering together nine enchanted blossoms; oak, broom, meadowsweet, cockle, bean, nettle, chestnut, primrose and hawthorn. And thus, this non-human, magickal Flower woman manifested and was properly named, Flower-face, Blodeuwedd. With her as his bride, Llew (or Lugh as he was sometimes called) was able to rise to power and assert his basic privileges and civil rights as a Welsh deity. And as Blodeuwedd was created by these powerful men, one can only surmise she was breathtakingly beautiful, sexual and born fully as a grown woman. Yet it's important to note that some believed she lacked the faculties of an adult, for she was made solely to give pleasure to her husband and expected to think, act, and feel as she was dictated; never once having to unearth her own thoughts, emotions or opinions on anything. Some might say although she was unquestionably a woman, her mind and her life experiences, up to that point, were reminiscent of a child but this did not grieve anyone for many years.

Llew and his new bride lived happily for many years in their castle at, Tomen Y Mur. Blodeuwedd, who always had a pleasant disposition, had many maid attendants but very little contact with the outside world and not many opportunities to meet others. As was his custom, one day Llew left his bride alone in their castle, while visiting with his beloved Uncles in the far off distance.

During this trip away, Blodeuwedd, as always, endeavored to remain in her castle with her attendants and one day she heard the raucous sounds of people nearby the royal grounds. She looked out the window and spied several hunting hounds and a group of Hunters coming towards her direction. To her surprise this greatly excited her and the prospect of meeting new people enthralled her in ways she had not anticipated. She watched them for many hours and learned that Gronw Pebr, Lord of Penllyn, was in charge of the hunting excursion. As it was getting later into the evening, she sent one of her attendants to extend a hospitable invitation to the group for a late night dinner in her lonely abode and they gladly accepted. There are some conflicting tales that state, Lord of Penllyn actually left with his group when they were done but he later return to the castle alone to take her up on her offer for a late meal. Whichever version you accept, it is clear the two came together on this fated night and unbeknownst to both, they would be swept up in a tumultuous passionate love affair that would alter their lives forever.

According to the Welsh mythology, they talked for hours on this night and had a real soul connection. That night (and many others that followed) they gave into their strong desires for one another and surrendered to their carnal lust. They made passionate love and remained inseparable....that is until her husband's return. It grieved them terribly to think they could never be together again for they knew they belonged together. And as Blodeuwedd had a rather childlike mind and had never experienced such overwhelming emotions like desire, love and passion, she was probably beside herself. After a few days of torrid love making they decided they could not be apart and together they devised a plan to bring that to fruition by killing Llew. However, as the Sun

God, he was not human and not so easy to destroy. There was a list of configurations and prerequisites before her husband could be successfully killed and Blodeuwedd had no idea what they were. She promised she would let Gronw know, as soon as she was privy to this information and the two lovers sadly prepared to say goodbye before Llew's arrival.

When Blodeuwedd's husband arrived, he noticed immediately something different about his flowered bride. She blamed it on her great love and concern for him and a gnawing worry for his life. He explained she had nothing to worry about but Blodeuwedd having ulterior motives insisted she needed to be reassured with great details. So unsuspecting Llew explained to his wife the impossible coincidences that had to be in place in order for his death to occur and gosh... were there many.

According to Welsh mythology, Lugh's death could only happen with a spear (prepared a year and a day in advance) and this would be needed to execute the final blow. Lugh continued to explain to his seemingly worried wife that there should be a thatched roof, built over a cauldron and he would need to be in a bath, by the side of the river Cynvael and somehow have one foot on the back of a deer and the other foot on the edge of the Cauldron in order for him to be successfully killed. Blodeuwedd made special note of all the preposterous, overwhelming details and sent word to her lover.

Over a year passed and just as the two lovers had planned, they managed to have all the right circumstances before Gronw attacked and pierced her husband, the Sun God, to his death. However, he managed to shape-shift into an eagle and although quite injured, still managed to fly away. For Blodeuwedd and Gronw this was enough to allow them to fulfill their dream and together they took residence in the castle for quite some time as lovers.

After Llew flew away as an eagle, the Goddess and her new love felt safe enough to set up their love nest and fufill their heart's desires. And since the Sun King had abandoned his post as the ruler of Dinodia, Gronw was now the successor and ruler to both Penllyn and Dinodia.

However, the injured Llew did not perish entirely. He remained high above a tree slowly dying in his eagle form. His beloved uncles started to worry, for they had not heard from their nephew in a long time and they suspected something was wrong. It was Gwydion who one day spied an injured, sickly looking eagle, high on a tree top and after several enchanting melodies, he managed to coaxed the bird to descend for a closer look. With a swish of his wand, Gwydion unearthed his nephew in the eagle, who at this point was seriously expiring. His uncle rescues him and takes him to the best physicians in Caer Dathyl to help him fully mend and it is then that the men devise a plan for revenge and retribution.

Perhaps word quickly spread of Llews recovery for when the magician Gwydion returned to Mur-y-castle, he discovered Blodeuwedd, already trying to escape off into the mountains with her maidens. But while crossing the river Cynvael all her attendants inexplicably drowned. Blodeuwedd, alone, in the middle of the river, was then cursed by the great magician to never see the light of day and she was converted into an Owl. The myth ends when we also learn that her lover suffered a greater fate when caught by Llew

Llaw Gyffes and his magician, uncles. Although Gronw, in desperation for his life, offered a number of things including his own kingdom, Llew was not impressed and wasted no time in striking his rival dead. Thus ends the tragic Welsh tale in *"The Mabinogion"* and where our initial inquisition of this great Goddess begins.

BLODEUWEDD MUSING

The Welsh Goddess Blodeuwedd had been lingering in my psyche for a few years, actually two years to be exact. I kept seeing images of her and hearing her name mentioned every now and then, even though I had no idea who this Goddess was at the time. And so I started doing some preliminary research on her, first out of curiosity and then… I just stopped and turned my attention to other things in my life. The ebb and flow of my life was such that every once in a while I would have an experience or a vision that would bring her surging back into my life with intense relevance and necessity, but then, distraction would veer its ugly head. Finally, I found myself at a crossing point in my life and lo and behold found her there. She was there at this threshold, smirking at me, kind of saying, *"What took you so damn long?"* It was and is a question I still can't fully answer.

Blodeuwedd is a powerful Goddess for wommin to connect with. She is richer and so much more complex than what you might initially believe. The thought of her just being a Goddess of Betrayal does not sit well with me as there is more to this Goddess than meets the eye.

The first thing that jumps out at me in her myths is how she came to be through the element of earth via the transient, impermanence of flowers. Born of nine powerful, enchanted blossoms, she was magickally manifested by two gifted wizards. She is born and created by these men (the patriarchs in the family) solely for the purpose and pleasure of the Sun God, Llew Llaw Gyffes. She is made to be breathtakingly beautiful and sexually gratifying for Llew. She comes into being as a fully grown woman and comes into the world with no life experiences, no history, no lineage, no family, no thoughts nor emotions of her very own. Everything she is to feel, do or think, is provided for her by these men, her creators…and this for me, appears reminiscent of the modern day Stepford wives.

She appears to be created to have no desire of her own, except to please her husband and she has no existence before her manifestation; no interest or purpose besides being her husband's adored wife. And yet, because this is all she knows, she gladly accepts this way of life without any question. But lo, how one day everything changed. For in an instance, she opens up the floodgates of repressed emotions and discovers an almost undetectable buried voice of her own and it made itself known in one night…a voice she did not even know existed…. And it clamored for love and desire and engulfed her in a passion she had never known was possible. A passion so consuming and so rapturous, shockingly presented itself and quickly altered her self-image and life's purpose. Prior to the arrival of Gronw, she did know what lurked in the dark corners of her heart, yet, once this shadow and desire made itself known in her life, through this masculine catalyst, her life would never be the same.

It reminds me a little of the Abrahamic scriptural tales of Adam and Eve found in the old testament, for once Eve had tasted of the forbidden fruit offered to her by the serpent, her eyes were awakened to truths beyond what she could comprehend prior to that moment in time. Life is never the same when we are offered knowledge and experience an inner awakening. I muse and think on an extreme level, about women who find themselves in oppressive marriages. Many wives, especially prior to the 1970s, had their own voices stiffled and some perhaps even abused so continuously, that they lose the power of their own voice, that is, until one day when something happens to awaken them to reclaim their own power. Upon unearthing that repressed inner voice, life is never the same. I think of a woman who might never have climaxed, a non-orgasmic woman, who after finally experiencing the first orgasm, is awakened to her sexual nature and her life from that point on takes on a different hue. I think of a heterosexual woman who has been comfortable in her traditional role as wife and mother and quite shockingly discovers a tiny voice from within that unearths a sexual desire for her same gender. I think of women who have committed themselves, all of their lives, to being "*good girls*," following rules and expectations placed on them since birth and somehow, despite the loud external voices from society they have this one experience that allows them to finally break free and hear their long repressed inner desires and emotions. The common thread here is that in each one of these examples there is a discovery of a shocking, repressed emotion, an awakening to something we never suspected of housing within us. This is Blodeuwedd's realm. This is her potency and great relevance to us as wommin... We quit being the pretty flower (who really has no shelf life when you think about it). The flower who lives solely for adoration, causing no conflict with patriarchy and we then awaken to our deep, inner authentic desires. And it is this desire that shifts and reshapes the landscape of the remainder of our lives.

And so, with Blodeuwedd, she is an imperative Goddess for modern day wommin to connect with, for she is more than the Flower Goddess of Betrayal, she is the Goddess of Awakenings. She is the archetype that introduces us to long repressed or unknown emotions, longings and our authentic voice. She is the Goddess who awakens us to those emotions that might have seemed foreign to us or maybe even slightly taboo. And it is not just any old awakening; it is usually a dark, deep awakening because it is something that she would never have suspected of harboring within. The discovery of such strong dark emotions, like passionate desire, can catapult us causing great upheaval in our world and can take us to a very dark place in our psyche. Just look at how this great passion and love for Gronw makes her deceitfully scheme a most horrific crime to kill her husband. Prior to unearthing these emotions she was a flower Goddess; simply pretty and bright, purely happy just being adored, and now, this was no longer satisfying. It reminds me of those in our modern world still suffering in the same scenarios, overtaken by lust and desire, engaging in extramarital affairs or addictions (drugs, alcohol, food or sexual in nature) and how these dark longing lead to dramatic, sometimes deadly, life altering experiences.

It's very interesting that in the end, Blodeuwedd was not killed but instead was converted into a nocturnal animal, the owl. A winged creature that holds so much controversy because in some indigenous cultures the owl was seen as a harbinger of death, while in others, the owl was seen as wise, all-seeing, mysterious, coolheaded, reserved, cunning and highly cerebral.

For the Greeks, the Goddess of Wisdom, Athena, was often represented by an Owl and the Sumerian Goddess, Lilith also has deep connections with this night creature. It's interesting that the beautiful, earth ruled, flower Goddess would then be given dominion over the element of air and night, as an Owl. As patriarchal punishment for her earthly sins or moral crimes of the flesh, she is sent to the realm of this controversial bird, where perhaps her mind and intellect take precedence over her flesh. She's punished by removing the earthly daylight passions, first experienced and discovered through the flesh, and it is replaced now with the cool calm, intellectual qualities of the night owl. We come to realized that Blodeuwedd is the Goddess of really two opposing realms, for as a flower Goddess she delights in the brightness of the Sunlight, yet later, as an Owl, she delight in the solitude of night.

This too reminds me of the Greek maiden Goddess Persephone, because she is a bright flower Goddess. As the Sun god's wife, and a flower bride she is in her element in the light of day but once she enters the realm of desire and all-consuming passion for her lover, she begins to descend and journey into a darker realm. And I say journey because it was a year and a day of her planning and scheming with her lover to kill her husband and I'm sure during that time an array of emotions were experienced. So this Welsh Goddess begins her journey and her descent, as a result of this initial awakening. When towards the end, she is converted into an owl; she is no longer in the light of day but rather in the nocturnal dark world. As an Owl, she is now a part of night and it reminds me of Persephone because she too ruled over two opposing realms. She also has this experience of transitioning from a fertile daylight Goddess, as Kore, belonging to her mother, then to a night Goddess and Queen of the underworld; challenged and perchance conflicted in her new role in this darker realm. She too has this familiar journey, one we can surely identify with as wommin. She too has an awakening to emotions that a maiden would never suspect from within. And she too has this experience of going from one element; daytime, sunshine, brightness, happiness even ignorance, to this other side; around this dark realm of questionable shadows. It is the confrontation of night and day, ignorance and wisdom, slumber and an awakening and both maiden deities; Persephone and Blodeuwedd exemplify these traits for us as women.

I know many immediately relegate this Welsh deity simply as a Goddess of deception and lies or a deity of love and beauty and it's very easy to just pick one aspect of this deity and run with it but I personally feel this particular Goddess has a number of layers for us to study and really connect with as wommin. Blodeuwedd can be any one of us, whether in the 21st century or the first century. The inaugurated gifts, wisdom and insight that this Goddess presents to us women are timeless and invaluable for our gender.

*Blodeuwedd is the awakener of our dark shadowy places, our taboos and subconsciousness. She stirs the deep suppressed longings that society has forbidden. She is the awakener of your own personal truths. Blodeuwedd is the Welsh Flower Goddess of exceptional beauty and allure. She knows all too well the two realms of night and day; of shadow and wakefulness. She is the encased beautiful flower who becomes the free flying, night owl. She is the one who reflect the dichotomy our gender so often is subjected to; that of living in two realms. She reveals the sins of patriarchy and our gender's need to be awake and alert as the owl, in a world that would rather contain us as simply beautiful, voiceless flowers. She is both the shadow or secrets and the awakener to our inner power.

ISHTAR

Ishtar is the ancient Akkadian, Assyrian Goddess of Love, Sexuality, Fertility, War, and unbridled Passion. For her devoted followers, Ishtar was and continues to be a supreme ancient Goddess that rules over all areas connected to a Woman's life. Some might even consider her one of the first known, Goddesses of Love. Her presence was well documented as early as the first millennia and her worshipped crossed numerous regions and survived throughout the centuries.

Known also as; Ishara, Istar, Istara, the name Ishtar is considered a Semitic or an Akkadian name related to star. It should therefore come as no surprise that one of her sacred symbols is the eight pointed star. In Babylonian astrology, Ishtar was deemed as the personification of the planet Venus; the morning & evening star. She is also considered to be an important part to the celestial Triad representing, Life force. In this triad, she joins the Sun God, Shamash (who represents justice) and the Moon God, Sin (who represents wisdom).

Ancient Babylonian scriptures refer to the Goddess, Ishtar as, *"The Opener of Wombs," The Righteous Judge,"* and the *"Exalted Light of Heaven,"* among her numerous titles. They are indicative of a highly venerated Goddess who remains linked to our gender's progress and empowerment. In ancient times she had numerous temples build in her honor and she was also embraced as a patron Goddess of prostitutes; again reflecting her powerful sexual attributes. Often depicted nude to denote her unquestionable connection to beauty and sexuality, Ishtar was also shown in robes and war armour. Holding a bow and arrow, and other weapons of war to reveal her warrior aspect; her fierceness was also symbolized by the Lion. Other symbols connected to Ishtar include, the dove, the owl, the snake, and gemstones like Lapis Lazuli and Carnelian.

As with most ancient deities there are some conflicting stories related to genealogy and because she is so often assimilated with other deities, like the Sumerian Goddess, Inanna, it's hard to know for certain. She is considered a daughter of the Uruk deities; Moon Goddess, Ningal and Moon God, Sin (Suen) but also known as daughter to Anu and the Sky god, An. She is believed to be assimilated with the Goddesses; Astarte, Lilith, Isis and of course Inanna. Most historians connect her numerous myths and depictions to be a surviving aspect of the Sumerian Goddess Inanna and later as the Semitic Goddess,

Astarte. She and the Goddess, Inanna share many similarities and myths. Most noteworthy are the collection of passionate illustrative scriptures about her beloved consort, Tammuz, who appears to be similar to Inanna's consort, Dumuzi. Throughout Mesopotamia (the region mostly known today as Iraq, Syria, Kuwait, Turkey) Ishtar was exalted as one of the earliest, most important deities among the pantheon of Gods across this regions and within this beloved deity we are gifted with a supreme symbol of woman empowerment.

INANNA

By far, one of the most treasured Deities found throughout Ancient Mesopotamia is the Goddess, Inanna. Known as the Queen of Heaven, she is the Goddess of Love, Sexuality, War, Leadership, Supremacy and all aspects of Femininity. She embodies all the attributes of an ancient Goddess that is of monumental importance to women. And, her prominent worship in ancient times reveals how vastly different women's role and value were then, compared to various other times in history.

She was often depicted as young, strong, assertive, independent, beautiful, very sexual, and in tuned with her gender's inherent powers. In ancient times there were many depictions of this Goddess with a lion or riding a lion to show her supremacy. It was also not uncommon to see images of Inanna with quiver and bow, or suited up in armor, to reflect her attributes connected to war. Statues of Inanna show her cupping her breast with her hands possibly also elucidating her sexual attributes, very similar to Ishtar.

Her temples and shrines were numerous in ancient Mesopotamia. Her main cult center was located at Uruk, where she was even revered among the sacred prostitutes of the temples. Many writing of the time describe explicitly her great powers of sexuality and the many rites & invocations her worshippers engaged in. At the Akitu annual Festival in Babylon, the king and queen, as well as its citizens, would re-enact the sacred union between the Goddess Inanna and her beloved consort, Dumuzi. In this common ritualistic sexual act, they believed they could help guaranteed the land's fertility.

Early Sumerian writings included Inanna as one of the seven primordial entities that would later become the foundation of other developed deities. Inanna was among, Anu, Enlil, Enki, Ninhursag, Nanna, and Utu. There are varied stories connected to her parentage as one would expect from such an ancient deity. She is believed to be daughter of the Moon God, Nanna and Ningal but also as possible daughter of the Supreme God, Anu. But she is also linked to being fathered by the God Enki, and the Air God, Enlil. Her connection to Ereshkigal, the Goddess of the Underworld, is illustrated best in the story of, "The Descent of Inanna." One of the most beloved remaining poems, illustrative of Inanna and her relationship to her sister, the Goddess of the underworld, Ereshkigal, is, "The Descent of Inanna" (c.1900-1600BCE). It is the powerful story of survival, inner journeys & transformations, similar to that of the Greek Goddess, Persephone and her descent into the underworld. Another well-known work that speaks of Inanna, among many is found In the Epic of Gilgamesh (C2700-1400BCE). Here in this well-known, Sumerian Babylonian poem, the Goddess Inanna is spoken of as the Goddess Ishtar.

GRANDE MAMAN BRIGITTE

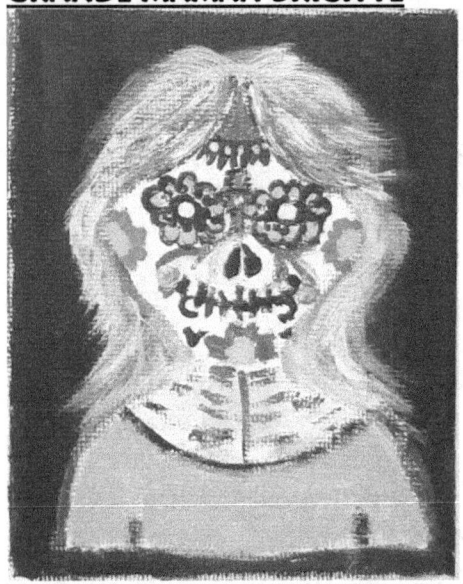

Maman Brigitte is a Voodoo Loa who comes to us from New Orleans, though her origins surely begin in Haiti and quite possibly Africa. She is often referred to as a new World Loa/Goddess (I mean no disrespect to the culture, but I will use the term Goddess which is so ingrained in my own personal vernacular when referring to this beloved Voodoo loa). In Voodoo, as is in most spiritual theologies fully submersed in ancient indigenous practices, the Loa is more than just an archetype or lofty deity but a personification of a living breathing spirit. Since this too is my own personal definition of a Goddess I will respectively, use both terms interchangeably.

Maman Brigitte is born as a result of the merging African slave and European influence in New Orleans, but most important to note is that she is born, like most Loa, out of a need. With the brutal rise of the African and Haitian slaves came the increase in senseless horrifying deaths. A multitude of vagrant, unidentified, displaced cadavers abound and for a people who venerated their land and their ancestors, this was a most tragic experience, to say the least. Back home, when death arrived, they were comforted in the knowledge that they would be bury in their homeland and reunited with their beloved sacred ancestors. Dragged to this new land, they couldn't even hope for this, as their customs and spiritual beliefs were challenged and nearly eradicated through the vile practice of slavery and assimilation. Clearly the need for a loa, like Maman Brigitte, becomes imperative... a fiercely protective mother who assures you, your death will not be in vain, your bones will be properly cared for upon your death and your spirit will be led to your homeland to reconnect with your sacred ancestors where you belong. This is the very least you can hope for and Maman Brigitte takes on this critical role for a people stripped of everything else.

There is clear evidence that there was a lot of mingling of cultures in this new land, and the Irish and English undoubtedly influenced the manifestation of this Voodoo loa. Grande Maman Brigit (as she is also sometimes called) is often linked to the Celtic Goddess Brigit, who was attributed to inventing the art of keening (a special funerary howl of grief), hence the similarity in their names and attributes. There are some that believe Maman Brigitte is known as a healing, matron smith Goddess, just like St. Brigit. Sometimes this Loa is even depicted as being very light skin, possibly blue eyed with reddish or white hair- the obvious genetic attributes of someone from European descent.

In some of the writings I have read about this Voodoo Loa there is sometimes reference to Maman Brigitte, as just being another aspect of the Yoruban African Goddess, Oya. I don't see this at all... I feel her in my body vastly different than Oya. I love both Goddesses and worked with Oya exclusively a few years ago and can honestly say that these two are respectively different deities. They might share in some of their well-known attributes like; being strong willed, ruling over the cemetery, and patron Goddesses to our female gender, being particularly sympathetic to women's issues, but they must be respected and worshipped as two very distinctly different deities.

Oya is a Yoruban African Orisha, an ancient Goddess very much connected to the Niger river. She is most known as a fierce elemental Goddess of drastic Change, thunderstorms, high winds, tornadoes, cyclones and the Elements; Air, Earth, Fire and Water are associated with her. She is a warrior Goddess, who often will join her consort, Chango, in battles. She appears to me very physical, willful and strong, dare I say lots of testosterone energy in a feminine package. Yet even with noted connections to various lovers and husbands, she is not terribly tied into them for she is known as fiercely independent, intelligent, autonomous, a shrewd business feminine leader and an inspirer to women to share in her gifts.

Grande Maman Brigitte, for me personally, comes as a sort of Corpse Bride. It is not surprising the Celtic Goddess Brigit (whom she is so often associated with) also has a connection with this aspect and was known as St. Bride. Maman Brigitte clearly has this very strong linked to her Spouse, Baron Samedi, together they rule the cemetery. Respectively, they are both known as father and mother to the (Ghede) dead and share many similar qualities. Writings, documenting spiritual possessions, claim that when she arrives, although she can first appear very proper, she will sometimes take on some of Baron Samedi's eccentricities. She might even choose to wear his black top hat and match his level of vulgarity with her own bawdiness and potty mouth.

For Maman Brigitte, the cemetery alone is her beloved realm. Unlike the Orisha Oya, who had originally been given dominion over the Oceans and who (as some myths reveal) through trickery, was given the cemetery to tend to forever after, (a duty she rightfully might not fully embrace). Maman Brigitte appears quite comfortable as Mistress of the Cemetery. This is in total contrast to Oya and Maman Brigitte happily appears to reside over bones and claims the cemetery as her home and here too, is another reason why I strongly believe Oya and Maman Brigitte are two very distinct deities.

I don't recall reading anything that connects Maman Brigitte to Elemental energy like; Winds, Fire and Water, unlike the Orisha, Oya. I don't see Maman Brigitte having any link or correlations to fighting wars or wielding a "machete" or sword... but maybe a long phallic shaped wand or pole to ride on during her licentious banda dancing. To me she appears so much more bawdy and lighter, it seems, in her derelict humorous nature and much too interested in getting a good chuckle than in fighting wars. Perhaps after a life of various stressors and "war- like" challenges, battled in the flesh, while living on this earth, it is in death that we can finally be liberated from such nuisances. Maman Brigitte makes it a point to remind you of the liberating freedom from these human, earthly, trifling concerns. She is not a war deity perhaps, because in death the battle is already over and done with and all that remains is a resignation to tend to your spiritual peace and happiness.

Another interesting observation is that Oya is known as the mother of Nine but it is Maman Brigitte who is known as the mother of the Dead. With all the dead being her children, (an obvious multitude) you can imagine she is a fiercely strong Goddess with some amazing matriarchal skills and when someone needs the guidance and ardent protection of a mother, she becomes the best one to invoke.

Some of the writing reveals that there is also a connection to Maman Brigitte invoked by her worshippers as a judge, like the Egyptian Goddess Ma'at. She is called upon when there are extraneous, unfair circumstances that need to be mediated and here too the loving, righteous, protective nature of a mother is almost compulsory.

To me, Maman Brigitte is indeed a New World (U.S.A.) Goddess of the Cemetery, with origins from Africa and Europe. For practitioners of Voodoo, she is the Loa of the dead, mother of the Ghede, Corpse Bride wife to Baron Samedi. She is keeper of the bones and the one who greets you upon your awakening. The first female buried in a cemetery is sacred to her and you will find Maman Brigitte near this tomb. It is my belief that she is not a Goddess of the underworld like Persephone, Ma'at, Erishgigal or so many other underworld Deities like Hades/Pluto, but rather she is ruler of entryway, doorways, and transitions. Here she resembles the ancient Greek Goddess Hekate, in this role as gatekeeper and as the one who dwells in those sacred transitory junctures. Her home IS the cemetery and her role is to help you understand you are no longer in the flesh, but of bones and then, soon enough.... of ether. It is with her help that we transition from one realm to the next and the next.

Lover of Bones, she is the gate keeper of the Cemetery and this is her realm NOT the underworld, not what I envision to be the forever after. To me, and of course this is just my personal opinion, when we first die, there might be lots of confusion and an obvious period of adjustment. For some...that period might be longer than others, but this period of adjustment is where Maman Brigitte is most needed and called upon. I suppose that is why she is known as the Mother of the dead. When you die or... find yourself in a strange, unfamiliar place, in a uniquely different circumstances and situation and lacking all that was, previously, familiar to your personhood, it is precisely at this moment when we most need "Mother." It happens upon our birth, as it happens upon our death. Maman Brigitte is the Mother who helps and guides us as we figure out how to maneuver our way in this new realm and with these new, vastly different skills.

As a growing embryo, floating and merging with uterine water, was your specialty. Upon leaving that realm, to enter into the living, you encounter a vast set of circumstances that require the nurturance and guidance of mother for your very own survival; such is the inception of every human's life. As a Corpse, I suspect you'll have a similar experience as you find yourself exiting one familiar realm to enter another, quite mysterious, perhaps just as daunting, and scary of a place, as this living realm first appeared to you. And with death comes different skills to experiment and familiarize yourself with; a metamorphosis, new form of being, a vast set of circumstances that, again, require the nurturance and guide of mother for your very own survival. It is Maman Brigitte who, according to popular Voodoo tenets, will be waiting there to help in this role.

You've probably never actually watched a human body decompose. The concept of death and its grueling intricate process in our modern day society seems so shrouded in mystery. I think in particular, in the U.S.A. now, death is more often than not, handled very privately, almost concealed and beautified for us. The old and sick, nearing death, are separated by sterile hospitals and old age homes, sometimes devalued, pushed away from society long before their actual deaths takes place. Cadavers receive beautifications via the practice of embalming and then there are some funerals that opt for a closed casket. No one appears to want to talk about it and for many Westerners, it is either not given much thought or it is simply feared. Perhaps what makes it so frightening is the inexperience and lack of knowledge of what actually happens to us when we die. And so it seems, that the process of rigamortis appears hidden from us... and most of us go to our own graves never knowing what to expect at this junction in our journey.

Unless you are in the medical field, mortuary business or a forensic scientist, you probably have little experience and knowledge in the process of a decomposing body or the process of death. Ignorance in the process of dying might make it easier to trivialize its value and sacredness, unlike in centuries past and in those indigenous cultures, where death was and still is exalted and commemorated on the same stratum, echelon as birth. I muse and wonder how vastly different our present day society would be, if there was more reverence and respect, expressed and understood, towards the process of death. Living and dying are so intrinsically linked that I imagine, a reverence for death, would naturally result in a more heightened way of living in harmony with nature and a deep rooted respect and need to live every minute aware of the Divine within and all around...

When the "Tomb" is honored, the sacred "Womb" is honored and everything in between falls harmoniously into place.

For indigenous cultures, their religion and spiritual practices are linked to the "old ways." Death and its sacred process is highly esteemed and venerated and thus, merits a Goddess dedicated dutifully to its provision. Voodoo loa, Maman Brigitte fits that role perfectly as Mistress of the cemetery, guardian of the bones and Mother to the dead.

Long may she be respected, loved and worshipped...
Hail Grande Maman Brigitte!!!

*The Voodoo Loa Maman Brigitte is the gatekeeper, threshold guardian and beloved Ghede Mother of Bones and the dead. In the darkness of the unknown, on the threshold of life and death, we must all eventually pass through these realms; here she makes herself known to us. Maman Brigitte arrives with a rather unusual sass, lightheartedness and humor about death. Rather taboo and unconventional, she reminds us, death is not a finality but a transition and one that should be approached with love, not fear or trepidation. *"What are you afraid of, death is simply a transition and if you are free of this fear, there is very little else to be afraid of in life...."* *"After all, there is no death, only transformations, my little ones..."* She draws near and the hairs on the back of your neck are felt rising. In her bawdy style, she jokes and dances for you, while daring you to enter her realm of cemeteries. We begin to consider our very own mortality and the content of our lifetime now. She comes to remind you that your time here on earth is very limited; unlike your infinite spirit, she dares you to face this fact. And your life's purpose must be met within those physical time restraints. She arrives as a wake-up call, announcing death's unpredictability, as never too far away. Whether young or old, she awaits to reclaim your sacred bones when that time does come. *Will you be ready to relinquish your bones to her, upon your death? Will you be ready to surrender all that you've known in this physical life to enter the next stage in your development, with a Mother who will lovingly and humorously guide you into the next phase? Are you living your life mindful of the expiration of your flesh and the infinity of your spirit?* Maman Brigitte is the crone that prepares you for death and transitions, whether metaphorically or in actuality. Her energy however, is not one of doom and gloom but rather celebratory.

BABA YAGA

"But Baba Yaga does not merely stand for the end of the cycle; She is the Cycle, the black earth that closes over dead bones yet also is the fertile womb for seedlings in Spring. Her hut turning on its chicken legs is the turning of seasons, the endless motion of the Universe..." Rebecca Vassey, writer for SageWoman Magazine

Her imageries conjure up all sorts of frightening stereotypical, old images of the Witch, the Hag, the decrepit wicked and the near dead. With her long bony fingers and limbs, and her oversized long nose with hairy warts decorating its edge, she can appear quite frightful to our inner child. Her hunched back and the appearance of her menacing gnawing iron clad black teeth is enough to make you run for the hills. She triggers our earliest memories and terrors of heart stopping childhood fairytales that warned us about the unknown and kept us from going into secluded, distant places, like the woods. We didn't ever want to meet the child-eating witch out there and so these infantile fairy tales, with their ghastly painted pictures, certainly made us cognizant of the possible dangers in the worlds but also fed our consciousness, tenacious prejudices and negative views on the unknown, the different and the old.

Baba Yaga is the Slavic Crone. Her origins come from the Baltic region and there are hints of her in Ukrainian and Polish folklore as well. She is found in numerous fairy tales as the wicked terror-striking Hag and although there is some conflict regarding her deity status, many myth scholars and Goddess worshippers exalt her as the quintessential, and misunderstood, Crone. She is elevated from this fairytale folklore dark fearsome character, to the Black Goddess we unearth her to be, after years of patriarchal suppression. Baba Yaga, like many powerful, ancient female deities that can threaten patriarchal growing societies, has been vilified and pushed out into the outskirts of civilization, far out into the uncultivated woods. Those who are researching "herstory," connecting to the Divine in her numerous guises and seeking to reclaim lost forgotten heritage are finding it in the tales orally passed down and later documented; patriarchally altered and revised and modified to hide the sacred feminine. We are finding her again and Baba Yaga is yet another reflection of Goddess in her Crone aspect; as Grandmother Moon, as Dark Mother, as the Black Goddess. And again I must stress, as I have in my previous books, that the color Black is not viewed as negative, at least not in Goddess Spirituality. Black, the Crone and Dark Goddesses in general are not viewed as negative or something evil or bad, on the contrary, they are very strong and powerful... and necessary. Black connotes the mysteries yet discovered, like our dark womb, it is a term used to define the hidden, the shadow that which is misunderstood, what is prime and awaiting fertilization, There is much power in this.

Baba Yaga is a Goddess of death, and regeneration. She is a Goddess of monumental transformations and courageously facing our biggest fears. As her myths will reveal, she is a Goddess of initiatory characteristics, for she inaugurates for us, change that comes from knowledge and facing our truths. She is the Grandmother archetype, the wise, all knowing Crone. A Deity of prophecy and bringer of psychic and intuitive gifts, she is Goddess of our intuition and the primordial mysteries found in nature and her cyclical continuous patterns. Though her image might be frightening and at times down right gruesome, she beckons us to take courage and lift the façade, to unveil considerable wisdom and power that can positively transform our lives.

Perhaps it is best to begin by examining her name. In Russia the word for Grandmother is *Babushka*. Not surprising, some believed the name *"Baba Yaga"* originates from this sweet affectionate appellation. However when we look at the word *"Baba"* it has not only a different feel but also a slightly different meaning. In Russia the term *"Baba"* was used to describe an old woman, more specifically it was a term meant to describe a woman who is or was married and therefore non-virginal. Listening to the sound of the word *"Baba,"* it has a harsher phonetic feel, as this was a deprecating term, meant to infer the whining wife. *Baba* meant the complaining, constant yelling and nagging woman. It is a word to connote that women, once they become wives or mothers, are witch-like, hags, complainers and naggers. Therefore, the first part of her name in our modern language suggests a rather whining, bothersome, unpleasant woman and old, certainly not virginal or maiden-like. Another indication of her association as a crone deity is her nicknames. Baba Yaga was also called "Blue-nosed" and "Bony-legged" Her full name was accepted as, *"Baba Yaga Kostianaya Noga,"* which means "Baba Yaga Boney Legs" and this confirms even further her elderly status.

Connected as a Goddess of Cycles and Life and Death, it is not surprising she is Goddess of Bones but also a Goddess very much linked with the Harvest. For it is believed she plants us, fertilizes us, then prunes us and (throughout the cold Winter months) keeps us safe until we are ready to be replanted again, to bloom in the spring. Baba Yaga is the cycles of nature and the cycles of birth, life and death and rebirth, we personally experience at various points in our lives.

Described as a bony, hunchback, with numerous warts covering her face, disheveled silver hair and a bent crooked, long nose, that could reach the underside of her chin, she was meant to conjure fear in you. Baba Yaga was a frightening sight. As frail and bony as she appeared, she was a ferociously strong force to be reckoned with and she delighted in the nightly rides inside her spinning iron mortar and pestle. She would steer her pestle across the sky and make the howling sound of the fierce nightly breeze and if you listened closely enough you could hear her cackles amidst the orchestra of night. Yet it is important to note that it is our fears of the unknown; of death, of the old, that makes Baba Yaga so fearsome and ugly in our collective consciousness.

Gruesomely depicted as an ogre and known as a Hag, it is very important to understand that the term Hag had a very different meaning in olden times than it does today. In the Middle-Ages, the word Hag was often associated with nature Fairies. The word Hag often connoted something holy. It is derived from the Greek word *Hadia* or *Hagiolatry*, which means the worship of Saints. Considering this definition and Baba Yaga so often being referred to as a hag, her numerous names and titles already begin to reflect a different perception of this Dark Goddess, when we endeavor to study her more closely.

To be sent to Baba Yaga was to be sent on a journey to death but courageously facing this fact manifested into an unfathomable freedom and liberation from all things fearsome. As a Goddess of death she was known to be the Guardian of the Waters of life and death. It was believed, corpses were brought back to life with a mere sprinkled of these waters, of life-powers, to be reborn again. Baba Yaga is best viewed as a Goddess of initiation and transitions. As the midwife of death she is the sacred portals we must all bravely pass through.

The brick oven, which plays a prominent role in her Baltic myths as the place where she lures and bakes her victims before devouring them, has often long been associated with the sacred womb. In its capacity to heat up and transform grains into nurturing bread, it is reminiscent of the pregnant Mother/Goddess birthing new life. In this same manner we are invited to consider that Baba Yaga's myth reveals her powers of actually taking us through this process of womb-like transformation, as we face our biggest fears, allow them to be devoured, buried, then transformed and reborn again. She is thus, in this way, a midwife of death and powerful initiations.

Often we think of three archetypal stages for women but really one may consider there to be four and the fourth one can be viewed as the afterlife or what appears after death. Baba Yaga precedes this stage and prepares us for the next, whether it does come to pass or whether a slight of hands changes our fate unexpectedly. As the Maiden precedes the Mother and the Mother precedes the Crone, it seems likely that the crone prepares and precedes what comes next, until the cycle is repeated once more. This is Baba Yaga's domain. They say she eats humans, especially children but it is really our inner child that she devours and transmutes in preparation for the next stage of life. In this way she is indeed the perpetual alchemist who transforms our fears and pain into our ultimate strengths. She leads women into transformational states, into this sort of new, second stage; a new age of Woman, one in which she is no longer suffocatingly bonded to the role of maiden (daughter to her parents) nor mother to her offspring. In this new stage of her life, her new role affords her to taste freedom and this allows her to better serve her community and herself. As with other ancient deities presented in this book, it becomes clear that Baba Yag, with her numerous divine attributes can offer us many different themes to explore. She could have easily been included in the chapter on leadership and community, as well as, the chapter on Liberation. Here, she is offered in a chapter that touches upon the subject of taboo and included in that theme are the issues related to sex, death, fear and power.

The crone is ultimately the one who births herself and, as a wise-woman, she offers the opportunity to receive and re-view the world through different eyes; wiser, all knowing eyes, that can reflect back to a long life filled with experiences and monumental reference points that shed invaluable spirit filled wisdom. Yes, she is indeed a midwife and the real labor unfolds as she reflects back at the culmination of her life experiences and looks forward to birthing the space for this new era as she enters into herself and the archetype of the Crone.

More of Baba Yaga and her Dark Goddess stature is memorialized in the famous popular Russian tale of **"Vasilisa the Beautiful"** There are numerous versions of this Russian tale that introduces us to Vasilisa and Baba Yaga. The story of Hansel and Gretel also comes to mind as well as a Spanish folktale named, *"Don Octavio"* and "Pedro and the Witch," coming from the Philippines. Below I will try to capture one version of the famous Russian tale as best I can.

"Vasilisa the Beautiful"

Most of the various versions of her tale begin in the same way...

There was once a man and his lovely wife who lived together in a home with their exquisite child, named Vasilisa but one day the wife became very ill and unexpectedly died leaving the man a mournful widower. On her death bed, right before dying, the mother asked to see her daughter. She handed her daughter a tiny wooden magickal doll. She spoke to her daughter about the importance of this doll imbued with love and how it had been passed down to her from her mother. She instructed Vasilisa that the doll would protect and help her in times of need and that she should keep it safe and hidden. In times of distress, she should feed the doll and heed its counsel. The crying Vasilisa took the doll with both hands, trying to logically comprehend her mother's last words. She then embraced her dying mother for the last time before death snatched her away. Many mournful years passed for her before Vasilisa even remembered the doll, her mother's instructions or the doll's intended purpose.

Life without his wife became very difficult for Vasilisa's father. He was required to make numerous business trips and eventually he realized he needed to find a new wife to help with the maintenance of his home and rearing his beloved only daughter. At the time, there weren't too many available women in their village. He didn't have much of a selection to choose from, but he took on a widower who already had two daughters that were older than Vasilisa. The news of her father's engagement was dreadful to Vasilisa, especially because he would be marrying the well-known village's shrew, named Lilya, but she tried to accept this turn of events. In time her father remarried Lilya and brought the daughters along with his new bride to move into their home with Vasilisa. Life changed drastically for Vasilisa as a result of this marriage. This new wife did not look too kindly to her stepdaughter, as Vasilisa was beautiful and well-loved by everyone in the community. It was hard to find potential suitors for Lilya's aging daughters, as every young man that came by the home only wished to see and court the young and beautiful Vasilisa. As time progressed the stepmother grew more frustrated, resentful and intolerable of her stepdaughter. Daily she showed preference for her own children while slowly denying her stepdaughter a mother's care and affection. Often she would yell at her and order her around the house to do various harsh and laborious chores but Vasilisa, with her blessed wooden doll, was well protected. This doll, when petitioned with a small morsel of food, would often comfort her and magickally do the entire chores for Vasilisa. When Vasilisa felt alone and mistreated, she often found comfort in the little wooden doll her mother gave her. It repeatedly made things right and assured her she was truly still loved.

Resentment and disdain for her stepdaughter grew as Lilya could not compete with Vasilisa's beauty and popularity. The thought of getting rid of her became ever more prevalent in Lilya's wicked heart and one day she crafted a plan that would surely get rid of the child.

Vasilisa's father was often absent from the household, away on long business trips and one day he had to take an exceptionally long trip away from home. When Vasilisa was told of this impending trip she begged her father to stay and tried to convince him of the cruelty she was experiencing in the hands of her stepmother and stepsisters but the father had to meet his work obligations. He assured his beautiful daughter that all would be right and perhaps it was all in her mind and that she needed to try to get along with everyone. Despondently, she accepted her father's request and watched as he left. As one would have expected, the abusive cruelty towards Vasilisa escalated as soon as her father left. Even the nosy neighbors now made notice of how cruel Lilya and her daughters were treating the beautiful Vasilisa. And though they tried to intervene to help the young maiden it only made matters worse as the stepmother began to lie and publicize that Vasilisa's father had abandoned them and would never returned.

Unbeknownst to anyone, the stepmother decided that they would move to the countryside in the middle of the night. She had hoped they would move close enough to the forest, where the infamous old hag, who loved to kidnap and eat children, would surely catch and devour the young Vasilisa. Lilya's plan was revealing itself, as she had hoped to feed her to the old Hag of the Forest, Baba Yaga.

Vasilisa during this painfully abysmal time relied on her magick wooden doll and it reassured her that her father loved her and had not abandoned her at all and thus she stayed hopeful and happy. Although she was sent often to work and fetch things in the deep frightening forest, she always returned safe and sound, much to her stepfamily's chagrin. Unbeknownst to anyone, the wooden doll her mother gave her, kept her well protected and safe during these frightening sojourns. One night however, the wicked stepmother and stepsisters orchestrated a plan to get Vasilisa eaten by the ill-reputed Baba Yaga once and for all. Late at night, when the last candle had been blown out in the household, the sisters sent Vasilisa out to the nearest neighbor, to Baby Yaga's hut, claiming a need for a source of light (candle) so that they may fulfill their mother's wishes and chores. Vasilisa was frightened but as always, she found comfort and strength in her mother's wooden doll. Close to her heart she carried it and asked for its counsel and guidance. She was assured that all would be well on the journey, so she continued onward towards the forest.

Vasilisa headed out into the deep dark forest and she walked for what seemed like eternity until she felt hopeless and lost. There was nothing in sight, except for darkness and she began to feel a gripping terror. She walked further deep into the forest and then discovered the house, passed a clearing. It was a wooden hut strangely elevated on chicken legs, with eyes for windows, and a mouth as its door. It was a house strangely animated; appearing as if it had its very own personal soul and entity. The frightened Vasilisa looked around and spied a plethora of scary bones and bright red eyed skulls all around the property and the fence that was made up of corpses. There were animals too; a black cat, vicious geese-swan and a hungry looking dog. Then all of a sudden, she heard the thundering hooves of a horse approaching, it was getting louder, then flying above her, as it went passed Baba Yaga's entryway. She saw the Black Horseman disappearing into thin air as he entered the hut. Eventually she would also see a Red Horseman flying through Baba Yaga's entryway and in the morning she would again hear the hooves of horsemen and watch as a White Horseman would appear to fly into her hut and disappeared into thin air. Vasilisa would later learn that these were Baba Yaga's servants. They were her brightest Dawn, her Red Sun and her Black Dark Night. Vasilisa would also learn that Baba Yaga shared her home with her "Soul friends" and "trusty servants," the herdsman named Koshchey and three magickal hands that would grind the grain for her breads and press the oil from her Poppy seeds.

Standing in the dark of night, Vasilisa finally encounters the bony, hideous looking Baba Yaga as she flew in her spinning mortar and pestle, back to the elevated chicken leg held hut. She utters an incantation to make the hut turned to her, lowered itself, and welcome the hag inside but not before smelling the scent of a Russian nearby. Baba Yaga smelled the child near and confronted her. Terrified at the numerous ghastly sights before her, Vasilisa finds the strength to speak to Baba Yaga and tells her why she is there. Baba Yaga immediately puts the child to work, telling her she will get what she needs and will not get devoured by her, if she completes a number of tasks. Secretly, with her doll in hand, Vasilisa is again comforted and protected by her mother's blessing, as all the daunting tasks the hag had demanded from her were magickally completed by nightfall. Baba Yaga returned from her daily rides on her spinning mortar and pestle to find her house had been cleaned and a large meal prepared for her by the young girl. The old Hag devoured the meal, fit for ten men and laid herself out, dissatisfied that she had nothing to complain about. She gave Vasilisa another series of task for the next day with the same threat, that if she wanted to survive in her hut, she needed to complete these tasks. Baba Yaga indicated that her Poppy seeds needed to be cleared of any signs of the earth and Vasilisa was again required to complete some of the most hideously daunting tasks to gain her freedom. With her wooden doll however, she was able to magickally complete these demands. The poppy seeds were cleaned and now pressed by Baba Yaga's trusty servants, the three magickal hands that had prepared the grain for bread the night before.

When all was done and Baba Yaga had finished her colossal feast she asked the child to finally speak. Vasilisa asked the crone about the three different horsemen she had seen outside. Then Baba Yaga asked how she managed to get these impossible tasks done and the intimidated girl replied simply, with her mother's blessing. This revelation of Vasilisa's mother's blessing sent Baba Yaga into a tiff. *"I cannot have a child blessed by her Mother in my home, away with you..."* I imagine her saying. Baba Yaga claimed that Vasilisa's mother's blessing was actually hurting her bones and she needed to swiftly get out of her hut. Vasilisa hastily tried to get out of the house as quickly as possible but she had not yet received the source of light she was obligated to bring back home. Quickly Baba Yaga pulled one of her red-eyed glowing skulls, propped it on a stick and gave it to the child to give to her stepmother and stepsister for light. Then swiftly the young girl proceeded to get herself out of there and, in darkness, find her way back to the house.

Vasilisa tried to hurry as fast as she could but the journey was long and arduous. She walked for eternity it seemed without any clue or evidence if she was even on the right path but she persevered. The red glowing eyes of the skull, given to her by Baba Yaga, helped shine a light for her but its light went out a few time throughout the long journey, only to come back on as she finally arrived to the doorsteps of the house. When she arrived back home, she found her stepmother and stepsisters looking rather sickly, crouched in a corner in the dark. They had not eaten nor had any form of light since Vasilisa had first left on her journey. Somehow they were unable to maintain a consistent source of light in their house in her absence and they looked horrible. When Vasilisa presented them with Baba Yaga's gift they dismissed and ridiculed it. They poked fun at the maiden for taking so long to return. Then, unexpectedly, the red eyes of the eerie looking skull began to glow brightly and it stared right back at the ungrateful women. Within minutes Lilya and her two daughters caught sight of the skull's enchanted stare and they quickly burned; disintegrating into ashes. Vasilisa, with her pure heart and protected by her mother's love was unscathed by Baba Yaga's final tool of enchantment.

The Russian tale ends with Vasilisa returning to her old home in the village and happily finding her father there awaiting her return. Some claim she would become the love target of the Tzar and later agree to become his loving bride but that goes into yet another fascinating Russian folk tale.

BABA YAGA MUSING & MEDITATION

*"...She has a way of showing certain mountains up
for the relatively insignificant molehills they often are..."*

Rebecca Vassey, writer for SageWoman Magazine

The Dark Goddess, Baba Yaga, is the shadowy, hidden ugliness that one must admit to before arriving at our destination. She is the test! The painful confrontation of all that paralyzes and scares you is encapsulated in her frightful cackles. She is a mirror to our deepest fears and reluctancies. In the end, she reveals and exemplifies a fearlessness and courage based on simply her truths, for she doesn't sugar coat the battle scars we are expected to courageously endure, if we dare. She is the old crone who has earned the right to tell it like it is without any filters, fears or concerns and this is very scary for most in our society; as the unpleasant is always disguised and relegated to the far off regions of mainstream society. Our fears of the unknown; of death, monstrocities, the sick and the old, is what makes Baba Yaga so fearsome and ugly in our collective consciousness. Her ways are viewed as harshly abrasive or negative, even evil, to those uninitiated, because she doesn't have to make her message pretty, nor acceptable to our esthetic. Our modern day society, that so often likes messages to be delivered neatly in veiled illusions, is ill-equipped to handle the uncensored power of the bold, fearless Crone, who is untamed and immuned to societal manipulations. She stands in her truth, unadorned, alone and sovereign, for she has lived a long life that has garnered her unfathomable gifts. Her eyes pierce through all realms and her lips reveal truths marinated in her oozing rawness and timelessness. She does not need to be ornamented, laced up in pretty pinks or enchanting youthfulness, for those days of endured entrapment have long gone.

Baba Yaga has lived, it seems many lives and played many conventional and unconventional roles and I bet she has also sacrificed a lot in her lifetime in order to survive for so long. And Baba Yaga has seen, experienced and witnessed much in her unnaturally long life. Unnatural...for how many people are able to live many years and outlive their families, communities and even survive being marginalized and relegated to the irrelevant and invisible realm of the near silence.

Her bony, disheveled, hunchback physique is a testament to all she has endured in her lifetime and her frightfully mangled body reflects numerous wounds (emotional, mental, spiritual and physical) as well as the years of battle scars that have rewarded her with wisdom. She has earned the right to be...simply be, in her truth; whether nice or gruesome, clean or disheveled, unadorned, alone and in rags. She is not invested in impressing you or society at large. She simply is and this state of being intimidates many who are unaware, unconsciously living, and many who dare not dream of unearthing their own authentic voice.

You need to meet her to confront that which appears ugly, threatening and downright frightening.... Let the rest of the world stay in sad states of delusions, self-deceptions, states of unconsciousness, complacency and ignorance and paralyzing fears.... You know your life is a Soul journey, cyclical and ever evolving. You have embraced that your life is approaching a major turning point and these are the fires you must now confront to proceed forward. This is the dark forest you must travel through. She is your test and passage of initiation, for you have arrived at the sacred threshold, the edge of her forest. You are ready to be free of all hindrance. And in her spinning mortar and pestle you will find the liberation to just be and fly. Her wisdom expands far beyond your self-imposed limited reality and she will not save you, nor spare you of the truth. Heed her tasks, heed her counsel and she will lead you though the labyrinth of darkness, pain, destruction, rebirth and ultimately into the conquerable. Be prepared to know, what it is you seek and why you must stand before her now.

The journey to her chicken leg elevated, wooden hut is monumental. Beginning the journey alone through this dark forest is an admirable feat, in and of itself, but it is not enough. Arriving at her door steps and courageously demanding to be let in, to face her and your deep rooted fears, is only the beginning of this journey. Come face to face with Baba Yaga and bring your purest of hearts encased within. Come with your sincerest endeavor to know, to heal, to unearth truth, her wisdom, to be guided and to somehow find the spark of light within the darkness. Meet her eye to eye and come with reverence for the one who has immeasurable wisdom and insight to guide you through even the darkest of Labyrinths. Come and confront the archetype of the Crone and welcome Baba Yaga's ancient wisdom.

"Why do you come here?
What do you seek to know from me?" you hear her ask.

"….. Baba Yaga, I am scared… I am scared of failing but most of all, I am scared of succeeding. Oh my… oh dear…I am scared of actually succeeding, it hadn't dawned on me but I am scared of actually achieving my biggest brightest childhood dreams. I am scared of being fully fulfilled, happy and completed. I am scared of meeting myself as this brilliant, talented, well-loved being. It has been such a long time on this expansive, self-defeating road. I've gotten so accustomed to feeling loneliness and failure that they have become comforting familiar friends. Anything else to feel and experience would send me to a frightful place and awaken the intense anxiety so entangled in my self-worth. And I fear the self-sabotaging entity that always seems to creep up at the most expertly orchestrated moments. I need to say goodbye to past failures and ideals that no longer serve me and release the comfort of the painfully outworn. I wish to singe the scripts of the past so that I may be liberated to rewrite new ones…"

"How do you prepare your bones for death, most holy, old wise one? I fear I will die…I will surely die. I know I will… She who has placed herself in the hermitage coffin, the orphaned, the isolated island, the frightened, secluded, lonely one will die and I fear her death. I fear the consequences of her death. I fear the metamorphosis in her absence… I fear what she will demand of me next…I will have nothing to hold on to, nothing to blame for this life and the choices I've made and the ones I was too scared to make. I will have nothing holding me back….no more excuses, for the wings will be exposed and Baba Yaga will say…."**Fly!!!!**" And I will say, "**but…I, I have no wings**" and she will point to the ones that have always been on my shoulders; dusty, neglected, abandoned so long ago. "**FLY!!!!!**" she commands, as she pushes me off her spinning mortar and cackles away…" "**Fly….**"

*She is the archetype of the old, wise crone. She is the Slavic hag and Dark Goddess, who frightens our inner child with her distinctly, gruesome appearance. Her bony hunchback body, her wild silver hair and long warty nose and her shrieking cackles are a frightening depiction of our worst nightmare. She is not someone we typically want to encounter, not the way patriarchy has defined her but she is a force to be reckoned with. Baba Yaga is the crone, a most imperative, crucial invaluable aspect of the Goddess. She is meant to dare you to take a daunting step towards growth and transformation, by initially first confronting her nightmarish appearance. She represents that which is frightening and unknown, as the start of the winter months so often brings a tangible fear of what the frigid weather may bring. We wonder if our harvest will last throughout the next four months and will we confront death and survive. All that we fear but must confront is represented in the hag and she comes into our realm to challenge and build up our courage.

JOURNALING

How would you personally define Power?
_____
_____

Do you feel powerful in your life right at this moment?
_____
_____

Do you feel like others hold power over you?
_____
_____
_____

Is there a situation in your life that leaves you feeling disempowered?
_____
_____
_____

What are your personal feelings about sexuality?
_____
_____
_____

Are you sexually active right now?
_____
_____

At what age did you first become sexually active?
_____
_____

Do you feel satisfied and fulfilled in this arena?
_____
_____

What animal do you feel most connected to and which could best describes you? _____

INVOCATION & POETRY

INVOKING LILITH

Temptress Snake, Eve Awakener,
Coiled inside every Womb.
Dark aspect unearth,
Deep within me, she must be searched,
She who makes up her own rules...

Because you would not lay underneath,
Refused to play the role of the weak
Angered Adam in pursuit of equality,
You garnered a reputation unfairly
bequeath.

Misunderstood Lilith,
Labeled Demon and ill,
Goddess, You were first created
And your name is worshipped still.

First of the Feminist,
Demanding Equal respect,
Sexually free, fierce and strong,
Nocturnal and Independent.

They said you thrived
On Blood of babes,
And Men, in dreams,
Aroused with your gaze.

Oh Beautiful Lilith,
Insatiable and free,
Herein this ritual,
I call upon thee....

Hail and Welcome Lilith.....

EMPOWERED

Slither and Spiral
Into my core,
Fearlessly open
All those locked doors.

Light of this moon,
Pierce through the dark,
Bring to the surface,
What hides in my Heart.

Fuel me with strength,
As I embrace my gifts,
Cleaning and purging
All Karmic rifts...

Freedom to stand now,
In my true light,
Goddess within me,
Empowered to fight.

Fearless I go,
Awakened and free,
Reclaiming my Power now,
So Mote it Be!!!

Page 59 from "Goddess Grimoire Journal,
a Collection of Simple Prose and Spells"
by B. Melusine Mihaltses (Isbn# 9780985138431)

***You are now encouraged to create
your own altar(s) & invocation(s).
)O(Blessings!

MAGICK RITES & TOOLS

 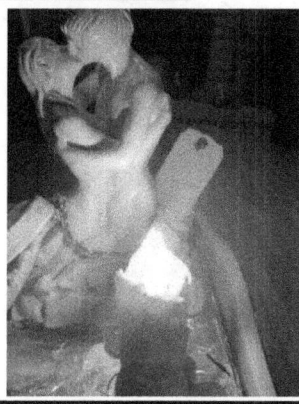

This is your personal page to document your sacred rites and the tools you elected to use.

DECIDE WHERE TO SET UP AN ALTAR
Place an Altar Cloth in the Color of your choice.

Color: _____

GODDESS
Place an image of your Deity.

Goddess: _____

This image can be a Statue, handmade Sculpture or a simple Photo _____

FIRE REPRESENTATION
Place a blessed/charged Candle in the color of your choice.

Candle Type and color: _____

AIR REPRESENTATION
Light your Incense stick.

Incense Scent: _____

WATER REPRESENTATION
Place a Chalice of Water

Water Item: _____

EARTH REPRESENTATION
Place a Potted Plant or Fresh Flowers on your Altar

Add Salt or a plate of Dried Herbs

Herbs: _____

Chosen Gemstone: _____

YOUR WISH
_____
_____
_____

Place a symbol of your desire, if you have one available, and also write your wish out clearly, on a piece of parchment paper, or you can even use a cut up brown paper bag. These are the basics for a very simple altar & rite. Ultimately, your sacred space is only limited by your imagination. You can make your altar & rite as big or as small as you prefer and the addition of other personal items is really up to you.)o(Enjoy!

THEME WORK SUGGESTIONS
9. SEXUALITY, POWER AND DEATH

Light a black or red candle

It should go without saying when working with this theme you should explore your sexuality in the safest healthiest manner. You may journal your most intimate thoughts. Consider visiting a hypnotherapist or past-life regression expert.

Take the time to journal any memories or issues that come up afterwards.

Reflect on whom or what you feel is disempowering. Create a ritual where you are able to release that in your life. You can do The Burning Ritual from the previous chapter or The Drowning Rite. Write down who or what is disempowering you with a black or red marker, then take this paper and submerse it in a prepared herbal bowl of water. The prepared water can be rain water, moon-charged or sunbathed water, or a bowl of water with various crystals. Envision the disempowerment dissolving as the ink of your writing dissolves in the water.

One of the most powerful rituals you can do, in regards to the theme of death, is writing your own obituary. Consider writing your obituary or a farewell letter to your loved ones. Working with your ancestors is also a very powerful ritual. Create an altar for your ancestors with pictures candles and items they would enjoy; like their favorite foods. If you feel called, you may also consider a trip to the cemetery to visit your ancestors or a beloved family member that has passed. Take the time to connect with those that are across the veil and reflect on your future role as an ancestress.

ALTAR PHOTO

CHAPTER TEN

"There is a powerful driving force inside every human being that, once unleashed, can make any vision, dream, or desire, a reality." Anthony Robbins

THEME: AMBITION

It's very interesting that the week I started working on this chapter, I was wrestling with my own deadlines and numerous responsibilities and I found myself having a slight, stressful meltdown. I picked up my Tarot Deck, as I sometimes do when I am in need of some guidance and comfort, and low and behold the Chariot card presented itself to me. I laughed because I immediately understood its message to me and it feels only appropriate to share that message here.

The Chariot Tarot card, as we will learn more later on, is connected to drive, ambition and our asserted focus. It is precisely the theme we will be exploring in this chapter. Our work together has brought us to this pivotal point, to connect us to our Ambition, unearth our powers of concentration and manifestation.

You will note that throughout this book we have already been tapping into the skills and resources needed to sharpen our powers of manifestations but also to create magick, protection, and empowerment for ourselves. We've arrived at a point in our journey where we are being asked to find our inner drive and our inner vision to bring opposing forces together and wield them to our desire.

The Chariot card in the tarot is traditionally a card of travel but more importantly, it delivers a message about the need for our strong will to be applied strategically and skillfully to bring opposing forces together. It is a card typically depicted with a Charioteer asserting control over two opposing animals. It depicts two contrasting animals, usually a black and white pair of horses or a black and white set of Sphinxes. In this card we see this charioteer, the driver, having to assert great strength and skills to wield these two divergent forces and make them work for him. This is the energy and theme for this chapter. We've arrived at a point in our journey where we have to bring two or more opposing forces and make use of them in a way that will serve us best. These sometimes conflicting forces presumably can mean the death of us but if we engage our minds and our powers of manifestation we can convert and utilize that which seemed against us and use it to fulfill our desire. The first step however, is mastery of the mind and the ability to clarify and decide where you want to go. That is the first step for the Charioteer; she must decide, first and foremost, what is her destination. She must get very clear in her mind and decide what she wants and where she wants to go before she can take these two contrasting animals and steer them in the right direction. If she doesn't take the time to sort these details first, she not only risk never going anywhere but possibly her own death; as opposing animals have a way of pulling us, literally and figuratively, apart.

This is where we are in our journey today, we will explore what it is that we want, where it is that we want to go and get very clear about the resources that are before us and the opposing forces that we will need to subdue and perhaps manipulate to get to where we want to go.

Like in previous chapters, to help us further explore our theme we will work with several helpful tools. We will endeavor to connect with the Goddesses Durga, Mauve, IxChel, Nike, Freyja and the sacred animal energy of the Eagle. We will connect with our 2nd chakra, the Sacral Chakra, and gemstones that can help better facilitate this connection. We will also look at the corresponding Lunation and a Tarot card that is connected to our theme.

*"We are what we repeatedly do,
Excellence, then, is not an act, but a habit..."* Aristotle

THE CHARIOT TAROT CARD

The Chariot card reminds me very much of the Magician card in the Tarot because it is very similar with its message about connecting to the power of our mind, honing into our resources and connecting to our ambition. It really speaks of the mastery of our mind and the effort needed to create what we desire by applying just the right vision and willpower. We've already discussed the Chariot card in the Tarot and its depiction in most traditional tarot decks. We see the two divergent beasts potentially pulling the chariot into two different directions and yet it is the skill of the Charioteer that is able to take their great energy and make these two animals work in harmony to fulfill his desire. This tarot card encapsulates the theme we are working on in this chapter; sharpening our inner Charioteer.

MOON IN SAGITTARIUS   FIRE/JUPITER

THEME: Ambition

SAGITTARIUS   MUTABLE   FIRE   MASCULINE   CENTAUR

     In my opinion, a Sagittarius Moon is probably one of the most energized lunation. Sagittarius Moon is very distinctly optimistic. Perhaps this noticeable shift in energy becomes more palpable when we consider where the moon was last transiting before coming to the astrological sign of Sagittarius. After leaving the intense dark realm of Scorpio, the moon now transits into Sagittarius and everything changes. I mean, everything becomes clearer when we consider that Sagittarius is ruled by the planet, Jupiter, which is known to bestow its expansive, benevolent energy to whatever it touches. Therefore, it should go without saying that a moon in Sagittarius has a feeling of expansion, freedom, benevolence and optimism. It is also often connected to higher education and spiritual pursuits. Sometimes it is even seen as a higher dimension of the travel and communication energy of Mercury.
     The astrological sign of Sagittarius is symbolized by The Centaur, the Archer. This half horse, half human, mythical creature exemplifies the energy of Sagittarius. It seeks freedom, illustrated by the horse, yet with its focused arrow as the archer, it is determine to achieve whatever it places its focus on. These are phenomenal energies that we can connect to when the moon is transiting the astrological sign of the archer, Sagittarius.

*"If one is lucky, a solitary fantasy
can transform one million realities "*
Maya Angelou

HERSTORY

She came from modest means and watched her family work and struggle to make ends meet. She also remembered being raised to believe that an education would be the key to success and prosperity; the same one that had eluded her throughout her life. But, as it turned out, life pulled her in so many conflicting directions throughout the years that she barely could think straight, let alone put a plan into motion. Yes, at times she felt overwhelmed by her numerous obligations but she also had a gnawing feeling of her unfinished work and potential life purpose. The palpable stirring of desire and ambition were simmering from within and she knew her life could be different if only she could narrow in on her goals and take the measured steps necessary to achieve them. She had her education to complete, life experiences to gain and suppressed desires to finally fulfill.

********Take a moment to document here, or in your journal, your unique story.**

_____

_____

_____

_____

AFFIRMATION

**My reality is built upon my vision,
clarify my vision
and it becomes a road map to success.**

I manifest what I envision

**My visions help to clarify my desire
and fuel my powers of manifestation.**

**What I place my focus on
receives my energy for manifestation.**

CHAKRA & GEMSTONE WORK

2nd Chakra   **SAVADISTHANA/SACRAL CHAKRA**   **COLOR:** Orange
Sacral realm, Helps Clarifies Desires, Ignites Bravery and Courage to Act, Enhances Self-Worth, Motivation, Womb & Women's Sexuality.
Mantra: I Achieve
)O(WORKING: Honoring Your Desires, Amplifies our Ambitious & Focus, Augments Courage, Increases Sexual vitality, Energy & Fertility

GEMSTONE CONNECTION: Carnelian is an orange to red colored Agate (chalcedony) stone. It is a powerful, fiery stone that excites and helps one attain good health and vitality. It has an affinity with the Sun and the element of Fire and thus, it is a stone that inspires creativity. It is quite the motivating stone that helps stir ambition and the self-confidence to get things done. The gemstone, Carnelian, has long been associated with courage and it is believed warriors, in ancient times, would wear it upon their breastplates before going into battles to assure their success and bravery. It is a stone reputed to keep evil away. It is also alleged to strengthen the voice of the timid and weak. This stone is known to help the reproductive organs and therefore it is seen as the magick stone of fertility. It is an ideal stone for large families and groups settings because it helps stimulate a cooperative, joyful energy among groups. Known as the radiant stone to inspire and motivate its wearer, it can help manifest great creative achievements and financial success.

GEMSTONE CHANNELING

     I will admit it; life sometimes has a way of pulling us into too many conflicting directions. Finding that one tiny moment for ourselves can be challenging but you are encouraged now to prioritize this task. Make a concerted effort to find that place where you will be safe and undisturbed for at least a few minutes to devote yourself to this work of self-care and healing. The importance and revelatory value of this daily habit cannot be overstated enough. As part of this work you are invited now to find a comfortable place where you can be assured of your privacy, safety and comfort… If you can go outdoors in nature that would be most ideal but any place where you can relax, undisturbed, would be fine.

     Place yourself in a comfortable position for our meditation to begin; you may sit or lay down. If it is available to you, place in your hands the Carnelian gemstone that we are working with today. This Carnelian gemstone is connected to our Sacral Chakra which is located in your lower abdomen, beneath your belly button. This is the sacred portal of our courage and self-worth as women. It is also the place connected to our desire and ambition. Hold your Carnelian gemstone in your hands; reflect now on what specific energies you can detect from this gemstone. (Pause)Gaze upon this orange colored gemstone and let your scrutiny unveil all of its precious details. Quietly, continue to study this gemstone and make note of any thoughts or vivid images that immediately start to unfold before you. (Pause) When you're ready, you may close your eyes and begin this short meditation.

     As with all trance work, we begin with our breath. You are asked now to take a deep cleansing breath; slowly filling up your lungs…. Now let your next breath possess the element of this Carnelian gemstone. Feel the deep orange hues of your Carnelian gemstone rise vaporously into the ethers and inhale the swirl of orange vitality it emits. Direct this breath from your crown chakra all the way down to your sacral chakra. Stay with this energy for as long as you need to. (Pause) Continue to breathe and hold this inhalation for 3 seconds and then release it… Counting now at your own pace; breathe, 1, 2, 3, and exhale on 4….Breathe, trusting in the natural rhythm you have now established, of your relaxed inhalation and exhalation.

     Your Carnelian gemstone wishes to impart a special channeled message just for you about courage. It has a message about finding your place in the world, tapping into your life's purpose and finding the passion necessary to follow through on your vision. Give yourself a moment to connect with any other messages coming through. In your mind's eye, see this Carnelian gemstone shining brightly, embedded upon its dark, fertile, mother earth. Draw nearer to it and ask if it will allow you to pick it up. When permission is granted, gently gather it in your hands. With your mind's eye, gaze upon it again; studying its color, its texture, its cloudy formations or inclusions or any other details that captures your eyes…. Ask it to speak to you.

     Now imagine the top of your head opening like a window, this is your crown chakra. Let it become almost like a cauldron; receptive and open to any spiritual messages that may be unfolding for you now… You may envision your crown chakra now unveiling a magnetic Carnelian gemstone portal allowing for this **Crystal Transmission** *to come through… Gently guide this energy of the Carnelian gemstone from your crown chakra to your Sacral Chakra, the sacred place of Courage, ambition and self-worth… (Pause) Continue to breathe in the energy of your Carnelian.(Pause)*

     *When you are ready, you may begin to open your eyes and prepare to document your meditation experience. As you come out of this meditation, it is a good time to document any images or messages that came through for you. You may write them here, or in your personal journal.*_____

_____

EAGLE PROTECTION ENERGY

The Eagle is a majestic bird in the sky and by far, one of the most highly revered animals for Native Americans. They are connected with the Great Spirit and are a powerful ally and protector for all forms of spiritual work and manifestation. The Eagle is the Spirit keeper of the Eastern direction or Air quadrant, in the Native American medicine wheel. They are teachers of vision, discernment and clarity. Ever heard of the aphorism, *"He has an eagle's eye"*? From extraordinary distances the eagle is able to spot his prey and at great velocity, fly to attain it. It is a study, for us, on the effectiveness of great vision and laser beam focus; which happens to be the theme in this chapter. The energy of the Eagle serves to remind us to connect with the power of now and learn how to get clear on what we truly desire most. The Eagle is a strong teacher and ally that can offer us keen insight, visionary gifts, clairvoyant abilities and spiritual growth. It becomes clear that the Eagle is an invaluable guide to those learning how to harness their powers, in alignment, with the law of attraction.

With their impressive, expansive wing span they are rulers of the sky. The eagle can fly to great heights, higher than any other creature and thus, they are intimately linked with the element of air. They are also connected with the element of earth in their ability to feed off the land. The Eagle teaches us to be able to live in the spirit realm and still maintain connection and balance with Mother Earth.

Eagles are traditionally connected to freedom and new explorations. When we connect with Eagle it is able to take us to new journeys, whether physical or metaphorically; to offer new insight and new vistas of perception. The Eagle's long talons and its ability to effortlessly grab what it needs, is yet another exemplary gift it offers us. Eagle carefully advises us to grab opportunities while we can; while they are within our grasp, for they can slip away from us, just as quickly as they came. When we chose to connect with Eagle we learn to harness our courage to soar above the mundane levels of life and engage our inner vision to truly see the truth in all situations. As we delve into this chapter we will come to appreciate the relevant gifts, Eagle offers us in connection to our theme.

As many Americans probably already know, the bald eagle is a symbol of truth and justice, and has been embraced by the United States of America to represent our devotion to freedom, honor, respect and dignity. These are all commendable attributes connected to the Eagle and thus, exalted by the United States of America. Eagle's spiritual message is to be victorious, proud and strong but also to show humility in the process. As a powerful ally and protector, Eagle encourages us to use our gift of sight to discern the truth in all situations and to courageously fly to new heights of awareness. They become then, the most ideal animal to connect with as we delve deeper into the subject of clarity, keen focus and ambition.

GODDESS EMPOWERMENT

"Om Dum Durgayei, Namaha..."

Om and Salutations to that Feminine energy which protects from all manner of negative influence and for which dum, is the seed.

DURGA

Durga is one of the most beloved and widely embraced Hindu Goddesses. She is often considered the supreme Goddess (Mahadevi) and a Universal Mother credited for protecting the world from demons in Hindu religion and Mythology. She is the warrior Goddess who combats anything that threatens the stability of the cosmos and is devoted to fighting the evil and negativity afflicting the world. Her numerous aspects and incarnations makes her one of the most multi-dimensional deities and by far one of the most intriguing.

Most of what we know today about Durga and her worship can be extrapolated from the puranas, the agamas (ancient Hindu texts) and the ancient Vedic text of around 4th century A.D. The Yajur Veda, Vajasaneyi Samhita, Taittareya and the Devi-Mahatmya all reveal a great deal about this well esteemed Goddess. We know that, although her worship can be traced to the 4th century B.C.E. and during the Harappan period, her worship became more prevalent after the 6th century. There are several puranas (sacred text) ranging from the third and fifteenth century, that mention her and several are even dedicated exclusively to her. The Devibhagavatan is one such purana, as well as the very similar, Durgasaptasti, better known as the Devi-Mahatmya. This seventh century text dedicated to Durga can be found in the Markandeyapurana also known as Chandi Mahatmya. It is one of the most highly recognized and venerated text to Durga and it is even often used as a mantra dedicated to the Goddess. There are also many Hymns like the Narayanistuti, which describes Durga as the mother of all creations and the physical embodiment of the earth. The Aparajitstotra Hymn praises Durga for her unconquerable abilities to defeat the demons; Sumbha and Nisumbha. Further research into this Goddess reveals there is no other deity among the vast impressive Hindu pantheon that comes close to exemplifying all that Durga does.

Her name is often translated as *"a Fort"* or *"One who is unreachable"* or *"difficult to know."* Sanskrit interprets her name as *"invincible"* and already, these combined translations of her name begin to paint a perfect picture of this ancient deity. Some scholars believe the name Durga is actually an abbreviation for Durgatinashini, which translates as, *"the one who eliminates suffering"* and this definition probably describes this Goddess best. It is interesting to note that **"Du"** represents, in Hinduism, the four devils; poverty, suffering, famine, evil habits, while the **"r"** represents diseases and the **"ga"** in her name represents, destroyer of sins, injustices, cruelty, laziness. *(Source from kalikraft.com)*

Durga protects mankind from misery and evil by destroying the demons known to man as selfishness, jealousy, prejudice, hatred, anger, and most of all, ego. Some of her incarnations are known as Kali, Bhagvati, Ambika, Lalita, Gauri, Kandalini, Kaushiki, Chamunda, Parvati, Java, Rajeswari, to name a few. Sometimes she is referred to as "Triyambake" meaning, Three eyes. Her left eye is representative of "desire," connected to the Moon. Her right eye is "action," connected to the Sun and the middle or center eye is "knowledge," linked with Fire. (www.Hinduism .Com, KOAUSA .org/ gods/goddess Durga)

Durga has numerous Feminine cosmic powers and aspects and I will mention a few of her most known aspects here. She is known as Kali (power of eternity and infinite night) and as Tara (void and night of anger). She is Chinnamasta (sacrifice and night of courage) and Kamalatmika (perfect happiness, night of paradise). Durga is also known as Dhumavati (deprivation and night of frustration) and as Tripura Bhairavi (death and the night of destiny) as well as Matangi (domination and night of illusion).

As her numerous myths, found in the sacred Hindu text, will reveal, Durga is the defender and protector of the Universe. She is slayer of numerous demons like; Sumbha,

Nisumbha, Raktabija and Mahisura and she is the one who eradicates all the demons that plague humanity, represented in ego, lust, hatred, jealousy and greed.

The Goddess Durga is the embodied strength of the Gods. The Hindu Scriptures note she was born from the assemblage of all the angered and infuriated male deities who had gathered on one fated night to express their collective rage. Long ago there was a demon who was threatening to destroy the world and because this demon appeared to be succeeding in his venomous endeavor, it angered the Hindu pantheon. The story begins with the sly, demon Mahisa (Mahishasura). He was born to a Goddess who bestowed on him great powers. One day his mother approached the creator God, Brahma, and asked him to make her son immortal but the God refused, believing every man that is born must eventually meet his own death. Mahisa, trying to outsmart Brahma, asked, *"Then, let me meet my death in the sole hands of a woman."* He secretly thought, surely this would render him immortal, for what woman could possibly defeat this powerful demon to death? Women in India at this point in time, just didn't engage in wars and battles. Unsuspecting Brahma agreed to the wish and granted Mahisa his desire, never considering the consequences of his action. Soon thereafter Mahisa, believing he would live forever, gathered an army of demons and marched to the capital of heaven, the home of the Gods, known as Amarapur, to make his demands and claim the heavens for himself as Lord of all the worlds. On the turf of the Gods a horrific battle thus began between the King of Heaven, Indra, his league of Gods and the army of demons, led by Mahisa. This terrible battle would last for hundreds of years, according to Hindu writings.

Eventually, the Hindu pantheon of Gods was defeated. Angered and hopeless, they were removed from their home by the demon Mahisa. They did not know how to reclaim their sacred realm and overthrow Mahisa and his Demon army and they felt disheartened. Desperate, the Gods consulted Brahma but when he realized his part in this disaster, since it was he who granted the demon his wish, he suggested they all consult Lord Shiva. Then utterly frustrated and hopeless after speaking with Lord Shiva, together they traveled to Lord Vishnu to see what he might have to say about the situation. The three fuming Gods; Vishnu, Shiva and Brahma were beside themselves in complete rage that they would lose their sacred abode to the deceitful demon, Mahisa. The more they talked about it, the more their anger grew and grew. Their collective rage grew until it literally created a piercing bright light that first emanated from their mouths and grew brighter, until the form of a women's body, brighter than a million suns, appeared before them. As they expressed their anger it spilled forth, creating a powerful energy and this energy transformed itself into the great Goddess, Durga.

According to Hindu scriptures, Durga's body was formed by these male Gods. They also equipped her with copies of their own powerful weapons. Hindu scriptures state her face was fashioned by the light of the God Shiva. Durga's ten arms were formed by the light of Lord Vishnu, while her feet were formed by Lord Brahma. Her beautiful long hair came from the light of Yama, the God of Death; although some text claims it was Brahma who created her hair. From the King of Gods, Indra, her waist was formed.

Her breasts were created by the Moon God, Somanath, while her toes were created by the light of the Sun God, Surya. Varun, God of the Oceans, gifted her with her legs and thighs and her swaying hips came from the light of the God of the earth, Bhoodev. It was the light of Prajapati, the Lord of creatures, that created her teeth and the light of the Fire God, Agni, is credited for manifesting her three eyes. Her ears were fashioned by the light of Vayu, the God of the Winds and the two Sandhyas, known as sunrise and sunset, created her eyebrows. *(source; www.dollsforindia.com)* It is clear Durga embodies the sacred Hindu Gods with every fiber of her being and she is their great anger and fury personified. This indeed makes her a powerful force to be reckoned with and evidently, she could've been included in our chapter exploring rage or a number of other chapter themes in this Goddess empowerment book. All of the Goddessess presented throughout this book have a plethora of attributes that can be explored in various chapters.

Upon her magnificent birth, Durga was gifted with the most treasured weapon possessions and many other powerful tools from these Gods, all in an effort to equip her with the necessary tools for victory in battle. Lord Shiva surrendered a Trident to her and Lord Vishnu presented her with a discus. Her spear was given to her by the God Agni and Vayu gave her the arrows. The Thunderbolt was given to her by the King of the Gods, Indra, as well as his white skinned elephant. The God Varuna gave her the sacred conch and a noose she would later use on Mahisa. Yama surrendered his sword and shield to the Goddess. From Vishwakarma, Durga received the axe and armor, while the God of the mountains, Himavat, gave to her, jewels and the magnificent Lion/Tiger as her sacred vehicle. Many other Gods bedecked her with numerous other gifts and weapons to arm her for full battle with the demon, Mahisa. *(Source;www.dollsforindia.com)* There are also many variations to this tale as can be expected with ancient deities and myths. Some, for example, claim it was Brahmna who bestowed to her the bow and arrow.

Although she was created by the Hindu male deities, the Goddess Durga is known to be fully autonomous, never requiring their direct aid in battle and never producing male helpers, instead opting to manifest female, bloodthirsty, helpers in battles, like Kali. Her ravenous female helpers are known as "Matrikas," which interestingly enough means, mother. Durga does indeed fight for her male creators when invoked and she defends them without their assistance, one of the only deities in Hindu mythology who can boast this attribute. She also does not lend her (Sakti/Shakti) powers to the Gods, unlike many other Hindu Goddesses but she is known to seize their powers and their fires for battles. And their inner strength is quite often surrendered to her freely. Vishnu for example is made to sleep and is rendered powerless and helpless in her presence. She causes him to be unconscious and he is thus, disempowered in her presence. In this aspect she is Mahamaya, the supreme creator of illusion and the one who puts powerful spells that even Gods, like Vishnu, cannot escape. She bestows the Yoganidra (meditation and deep sleep) the power of sleep, cosmic slumber unto Vishnu at the inception of the Universe according to some text.

This brings us to her connection with the God Vishnu. Durga is personified Maya, also recognized as the mysteries power of Lord Vishnu. Some texts refer to her as the female version of Lord Vishnu, because of her recognized ability to create, sustain and destroy the world and yet, repeat the sacred cycle numerous times. She intervenes on a grand cosmic scale, to rid the world of anything that threatens its balance and equilibrium. She becomes not only a sheroe/saviouress of the Universe but also a personal saviouress for her children and devotees. Durga is known to come to the aid of her worshippers during times of great calamity. She is personified power and strength and when invoked by her devotees, she proves to be most helpful in battling both inner and outer demons. Forest fires, imprisonment, robberies, attacks, executions and even threats from wild animals also fall under her protective domain.

The Great Mother Goddess, Durga, personifies Maya, that which deludes individuals into thinking they are the center of the universe. Maya is ego, individualism, personal identity and a delusion according to Hindu tenet. Yet creation and delusion fall under this domain and are under her jurisdiction. She is known by many names and each name describes an attribute or prominent role she plays. As Raktadanta, she is the one with red teeth. As Sataksi she is the one with one hundred eyes. As Bhima, she is the terrible one and as Simhavahini, she is the rider of Lions. One of Durga's epitet is "Mardini" the slayer of the demon Mahisa (Mahishasura).

As Durga's famous legend continues on, upon her birth she was immediately dressed in the weapons of the Gods and sent to the Vindhya Mountains where she would meet and confront the demon, Mahisa. She is known in this aspect as Mahisasura-mardini. The demon, upon hearing of this brilliant beautiful mysterious woman arriving at the sacred mountain was smitten and he sent a personal message to the Goddess, that he had every intention to claim her as his bride, since he was now the Lord of the Worlds, but Durga had other intentions. *"I can only marry a man who can defeat me in battle,"* she said to him and he took this as an invitation for battle. He brought his army of demons with him to claim her and what ensued was a gruesome, catastrophic battle that is forever memorialized in the sacred Hindu text.

Upon meeting the beautiful Battle Queen, the demon was greeted with a proper introduction to his destined killer but he didn't believe it to be so. Durga reminded him of the wish Brahma had granted to him and with great confident, she engaged him in battle. Mahisa was a known shape shifter and when he saw how great Durga's strength was, he changed himself into his true form, a black buffalo. He charged at her but he was of no threat to the great multi-armed Goddess who was riding her fierce lion and wielding her multitude of arms with commanding weapons. She is destined to be victorious in all battles. Durga relishes in the bloody battle as if it was a game for her (Lila aspect). The gruesome harsh battle continued with no end in sight and Mahisa was astounded at Durga's great strength. Many demons died by her hands and despite Mahisa's numerous animal shape shiftings, he could not defeat the Great Durga. In one version of the story, Durga pins him down with her trident and kills him but in another version of the story Mahisa, desperate to be the victor, cast a spell to make every droplet of his blood spilled on the ground, manifest into new fiercer demons. In this way, his army would only multiply and grow in power with every drop of his spilt blood on the earth. The Goddess

Durga, for a temporary moment, found herself overwhelmed by the sheer multitude of demons springing to life and in her rage and supreme powers she manifested the Blue/Black bloodthirsty Goddess, Kali from her brow. She would then become the embodied manifestation of Durga's wrath and great fury. Kali thus, sprang forth from Durga's furrowed brow and with her long darting, magnificent tongue; she immediately began lapping up every droplet of blood preventing it from spilling onto the ground, lessening the volume of demons on the battlefield. With Kali, Mahisa and his army of demons were finally defeated by the Goddess.

This aspect of Durga, ferociously helped defeat the demon Mahisa and restored harmony and dharma upon the earth once more but it was not the only time Durga battled demons with her fierce bloodthirsty helper, Kali. There is another tale of Durga fighting the Demon brothers; Sumbha and Nisumbha and their generals; Canda, Munda and Raktabija. These demon brothers drove the Gods out of heaven and again, Durga comes to their aid, in her form as Mahatmaya (mother Goddess). The Devi-Mahatmya text reveals it was the demon, Raktabija, whose spilt blood on the earth continued to birth even more demons and it was Kali who emerged from an aspect of Durga as Kaushiki, to lick up this blood, again, preventing any more blood to fall on the earth. Ultimately Kali swallows Raktabija whole and the battle against the myriads of demons is won once again.

Durga is described as exceptionally beautiful but her beauty lacks its normal function according to Hindu text, for it is an exquisite beauty that is not meant to attract a spouse but rather to lure her victims into fierce battles. And while it was most common to depict women in relation to men, as daughters, sisters, mothers, wives, lovers, Durga's appearance breaks with these conventionalities. She is depicted autonomously and without significant reference to a consort. She simply is and stands on her own in the bloody battlefield fighting without the aid of male Gods. There is no man coming to her rescue but on the contrary, it is Durga who is invoked to come to man's rescue. It is interesting that while she is worshipped as a Matriarchal Goddess who cares and protects the world and her children, Durga's image in these early writings is quite the contrary. She quintessentially appears as a maiden, unwilling to marry any of her numerous embattled suitors and she appears to take great pleasure in her freedom and her ability to defeat any man who thinks he might be worthy of her hand in marriage.

"In many respects Durga violates the model of the Hindu woman.
She is not submissive; she is not subordinate to a male deity,
she does not fulfill household duties and she excels at what is
traditionally a male function, fighting in battle.
As an independent warrior who can hold her own
against any male on the battlefield,
she reverses the normal role for females
and therefore stands outside of normal society..."

Page 97 -Hindu Goddesses, Visions of the Divine Feminine in the Hindu Religious Tradition, by David R. Kinsley, University of California Press, Berkeley and Los Angeles California, 1988

In one of her festivals, held during the Autumnal Harvest, she is worshipped as the returning daughter, which contradicts her role as a matriarchal deity. And here we start to see a resemblance to that other highly venerated daughter archetypal energy, the Greek Maiden, the Goddess Persephone.

A closer look at this fierce, multi-armed, Goddess and how she is portrayed both in Hindu art and ancient writings reveals a wild ferociousness unlike any other Hindu deity ever seen. She is a warrior Goddess who delights in the flesh and blood of the battlefield, as well as on her altar offerings. It was customary to petition the Goddess Durga with offerings of flesh meat, alcohol and blood sacrifices in ancient times. There are still hidden, far away parts of this world that continue to worship her in this manner. It becomes clear that she is a power that stands outside of what we deem as societally acceptable and civilized. One look at Kali, Durga's most well-known aspect, will convince you of this, as this aspect of hers appears, wild, primal, dark, untamable, violently bloodthirsty, gruesome and strong beyond belief but this is just proof of Durga's very well known, liminal nature.

Durga was known as Vindhyavasini (she who dwells in the mountains) and Tribal people on the outskirts of civilization, like the Sabaras, venerated her and held her up to high esteem, offering flesh and blood sacrifices. It is for this reason why one may conclude that her worship originates with non-Aryan or pre-Aryan people, for the Aryan would have considered this type of worship unthinkable as they viewed wine, flesh meat and blood as pollutants to religious rites. In the Devi-Mahatmya her devotees are even encouraged to offer their own flesh and blood as offering to the Goddess Durga.

When we consider the harsh terrains of the Himalayas and the Vyndhya mountains and its geographical location, outside and far away from civilization and city centers, we begin to understand Durga in a different context. Also keep in mind the frightening, hostile appearance of tribal people and how they would've been viewed by Aryan society, yet this is where Durga's worship manifested and flourished most. She has a liminal nature that almost requires her worship to take place outside of understood civilized edifices and confinements. This is what makes Durga's presence only found when we step outside of orthodoxies. She can only be understood in this way.

HER DEPICTIONS

Durga is often depicted dressed in the color red, which symbolizes both death and birth, our blood, action, war and the victor in battle. She appears standing next to or ridding a tiger/lion to denote her supreme powers, although it may also denote her ability to control and have power over others. She is also sometimes depicted riding a Buffalo, representing her defeat of the Buffalo-demon, Mahisa. The Goddess is often depicted with a multitude of arms; sometimes, four, eight, ten, eighteen, or even twenty arms. Each hand from her arm always holds a significant weapon, the various tools necessary to combat the numerous kinds of evil that plague humanity. Displayed in her many hands are the Trident, Bow and Arrow, sword, discuss, mace, spear, rosary (mala beads), bell, conch and wine-cup, to name just a few of her most common Divine tools.

The conch shell she carries is used as a musical instrument to make the primordial sound of creation, "aum." The bow and arrow represents the energy of the thunderbolt. The lotus, also known as Pankaja (and born of mud) is a symbol of steadfastness amidst the obstinate obstacles of the world. The sword represents knowledge and the discus instrument, which she spins on her finger, represents the unfailing weapon that destroys evil. The Trident or trishul, a gift from Shiva (Siva) represents three qualities; Satwa (inactivity), Rajas (activities), and Tamas (non-activity). As fighter of evil, negativity and injustices, she stands in "Abhay Mudra" to guarantee freedom of fear.

In a rarer, domesticated role, there is an aspect of Durga as the wife of Shiva, she is known as Parvati. In the "Skana Purana" she is the demon that threatens the world, Lord Shiva calls on the Goddess Parvati, who then becomes Durga herself, fighting this demon also named Durga. Seems rather confusing but it is important to note that when Parvati endeavors to fight this demon she sheds her outer sheath and it is thus the great warrior Goddess Durga that arises.

Durga was also connected to Lord Shiva in yet another aspect, as the Goddess Sati. As Sati, she was the first born daughter of King Daksha. From an early age Sati showed exemplary devotion to the God Shiva and thus, upon learning of her great devotion to him, Lord Shiva sought to have her as his bride. The King however, did not approve of such a match for his daughter but despite his disapproval the two got married. Later the story reveals the eventual demise of Shiva's beloved bride. After the union, the King arranged for his daughter, a Yagna, which is a kind of penance ceremony in which offerings were made to a fire deity. Lord Shiva was not invited to this event but he attended it anyway and was subjected to a multitude of grave insults and humiliation by the King. His daughter was so distraught by the entire incident that she sacrificed herself within the sacrificial altar fires. The grief-stricken, enraged Shiva picked up the body of his deceased beloved and there commenced his violent dance of destruction upon the earth, known as the Tandava. The witnessing Gods were frightened as the earth shook terribly in response to his powerful dance. The only thing that finally pacified Shiva was Vishnu's successful attempt to cut up Sati's body, while being held up by Shiva, into little pieces that were scattered about the earth. When the last piece of Sati's fragmented body fell, Lord Shiva was placated and now it is believed the land known as Shaktipeeth holds her scattered sacrificial body parts. This was one know aspect of the Goddess Durga as wife to Lord Shiva.

There are also three important elements Durga illustrates; Sakti, Moksa and Prakrti.
Sakti/Shakti: It is the creative, powerful force of the Divine. It is the underlying power or source of the Gods. Sakti is different from the term **Tejas,** which is understood as the energy or fire of the Gods; the power and source of the Divine.
Moksa: In this element, she is protectress of the cosmos and destroyer of demons. Created by the male gods, she acts on their behalf and defends them, as well as transcends them. She restores harmony in the cosmos. She births, destroys and rebirths again in continuous sacred cycles.

Prakrti: In this element she is the actual physical world. Durga is the embodiment of the earth, and the rhythm of the Universe. Durga sustains and protects the world and its inhabitants. As **"Sakambhari"** she provides the world with food and sustenance from her very own body and this is very reminiscent of the indigenous Goddess of the Americas; Selu/Corn Mother but also resembles the Greek Goddess Demeter and the primordial Goddess, Gaia, as an actual embodiment of the earth.

Durga is the personification of knowledge, memory and wisdom in this aspect she is Aparavidya (knowledge of secular Sciences). As Paravidya, she is linked with higher knowledge concerning spiritual matters. She is Tamasi (darkness) and she is the great delusion as Mahamoha. She descends from time to time to defend the earth. She helps the Gods and humanity, and restores the earth's harmony; in this way she resembles the Chinese Goddess, Nu Kua, who was also a creatress and saviouress of ancient China.

FESTIVALS

There are numerous Festivals associated with the Goddess Durga and her worship but there are two that are universally, well known; the Navaratra (Durga Puja) and the Dasara. It is also important to note that her worship in the North of India varies from the South.

Durga Puja is her annual festival held for nine days near the Autumnal harvest, it is also known as Navaratra. This festival is held during the lunar month of Asvin and it is a splendor to behold. During the Durga Puja she is often depicted with four other deities considered her children; Sarsawati, Lakshmi, Ganesa, Karttikeya. Other texts, however, reveal she is the mother of Jyoti as well. The altars for Durga during the Navaratra festival are often elaborate with numerous offerings and larger than life images of the multi-armed Goddess, made out of Clay but also made of many other interesting materials like; fibers and food. Durga's many appellations are commemorated for each of the nine days of Durga Puja, they are listed below.

DURGA PUJA AND HER NINE APPELLATIONS, mentioned in the Devi Kavacha of the Chadipatha scriptures...

DAY 1.Shailaputri, This word means daughter (Putri); daughter of the mountains (Shaila). She is worshipped on the first day of the festival and she embodies Brahma, Vishnu and Shiva. She rides a bowl and carries a trident and a Lotus in her two hands. Also known as Parvati, Sati, Hemavati, daughter of the Hemava/Himalayan.

DAY 2.Brahmacharini, (meaning unmarried) In her second form as mother goddess she is worshipped on the second day of the Navaratra festival. Her name means one who practices devout austerity. This was Parvati during her period of great devotion waiting for Lord Shiva to recognize her as his destined bride. She holds a rosary on her right hand and water utensil or a Kumbha, which is a water pot, in her left hand. She is blissfully happy and peaceful and is the way to emancipation. She bestows prosperity and grace upon all her devotees who worship her. This aspect of Durga is the holder of knowledge and wisdom. Divine grace is gifted to us in her presence.

DAY 3.Chandraghanta, The third form of the Goddess and worshipped on the third day of the festival, she brings peace, tranquility and prosperity in the life of those who invoke her. She has a Chandra or half Moon on her forehead in the shape of a bell. This form of Durga is depicted with ten hands, each holding a powerful weapon and three eyes. She is a disciple of bravery and possesses great strength to fight in the battle against demons. She is giver of knowledge and bliss.

DAY 4.Kusumanda, (Kushumanda) The fourth form of the Goddess, worshipped on the fourth day. "Ku" means a little, "ushma" means warmth, and means the cosmic egg. In this form she is considered the creator of the universe and she holds weapons in her eight hands and a rosary while she rides the lion/tiger.

DAY 5.Skondamata, (Skanda mata) Her name means the mother of Skanda. Notice similarity to the Norse Giantess named Skadi. In Hindu mythology, Skanda was the son of Lord Shiva and Parvati, He was a commander in chief of the Gods, to fight the demon. In this appellation, she is worshipped on the fifth day, accompanied by Lord Skanda, in his infant form. She has a bright complexion and she sits on a Lotus. She is depicted with four arms and three eyes while holding a Lotus in her hands.

DAY 6.Katyayani, The sixth form, worshipped on the six day of the festival. She is an avatar of Durga. There was once a sage named Kata or Katyayan, who had a son named Katya and according to one legend, Kata, prayed for a daughter like a Goddess and his wish was granted when Katyayani was born as an avatar of Durga.

DAY 7.Kaalratri, Her name represents the enemy of darkness and ignorance. She is the seventh form of Durga, worshipped on the seventh day of the Navaratra festival. She is dark skinned, disheveled hair, in a fearless posture and wearing a necklace, flashing around her neck. She has three eyes, flames from her breath and her vehicle is a donkey. On her upper left hand she holds a thorn like weapon, made of iron. She is also known as, Shubhamkari, the one who does good. She resembles Kali in her midnight hue and she holds a sparkling sword in her right hand, ready for battle.

DAY 8.Maha Gauri, her name means "Fair." She is exalted and worshipped on the eighth day of the Navaratra festival. The sins of the pass, present and future get washed away and purified in her presence. She is intelligent, peaceful and calm. She wears white clothes and displays four arms while riding a bull. Her right lower hand holds a trident. Her left upper hand holds a damaru. She expresses unfailing and fruitful attributes for her devotees.

DAY 9.Siddhidatri, The name means the giver of siddhis (magical or spiritual powers to control the self and others and the forces of nature) This is Durga in her ninth form and the most powerful form. She is worshipped on the ninth day of the Navaratra Harvest festival where she exemplifies supernatural healing powers. She has four arms, holding a club, a lotus and a conch shell. She is always happy. She rides on a lion/tiger as her sacred vehicle, displaying great powers and she blesses the entire Universe.

DASARA

Durga's second festival, held after the Navaratra, is the Dasara. The Dasara festival is much more connected to military feats and the impactful influence of the powerful Goddess, Durga and her ability to bless military weapons and grant victory in the battlefield to her worshippers. She is exalted as Abita, Ambika or Aparajita, as the one who blesses the military and its soldiers, but she is also directly connected with the fruitfulness of the Harvest as we will see in her other Festival.

Returning to Durga Puja, it is celebrated during the lunar month of Asvin, which coincides with the Autumnal Harvest in North India. During this festival, Durga is the power inherent in all vegetation. Nine different plants are bundled together, they create a Navapattrika, which is a bundle of different plants worshipped and venerated as the Goddess herself. Durga is associated with the successful growing, fertile crops. She is the sacred crops and frequently, as an offering, worshippers will bring to her altars, sugar cane juice and sesame seed oil. Durga in this aspect is unquestionably connected to the fecundity of crops. There is also another ritual during this festival in which a priest takes five grains, scattered firmly on the dough, rice wheat and barley, the burghii, also known as "mas." The sesame is placed on the dough as the priest says the invocation that alludes to the Goddess actually being these grains.

Durga is the power of life which the Gods utilize to achieve immortality. She is the one who appeases the hunger of the world and protects her worshippers from the numerous demons plaguing society. At these Festivals, blood sacrifices are common and an intrinsic part of the ceremonies to reenact her ancient myths, connected to the buffalo demon and the blood that was shed. Goats and sheep are also sacrificed and sometimes, to quench Durga's thirst for blood, worshippers would even sacrifice their own blood as offerings to her. This was done to replenish her powers, to invigorate the Goddess and give her back life force, now contained in the form of blood and animal sacrifices. Blood was seen as a recharger and re-awakener needed to refuel the strength of the mighty protectress Goddess.

"Om, you are the rice, Om, you are the life,
you are the life of the Gods, you are our life, you are our internal life,
you are long life, you give life, Om, the Sun with his rays
gives you the milk of life and Varuna nourishes you with water…"

pg 111-112 Hindu Goddesses, Visions of the Divine Feminine in the Hindu Religious Tradition, by David R. Kinsley, University of California Press, Berkeley and Los Angeles California, 1988

The interdependence of human sexuality with fertility and the success of harvest crops are evident in the worship and rituals of many different cultures and this extends to India as well. Particularly, when such a wild, primal powerful deity, like the one who lives outside of the boundaries of civilizations, is propitiated, one can expect an intense experience. It is to be expected, that Durga's worship might take on a boisterous, wild, rambunctiously liberating and even pleasurable undertone. It would not be unlikely to see couples, copulate in the field of India, just like in many other cultures during this time of the year, believing that their copulation and the spilt secretion of their lovemaking would result in a more prosperous harvest. This is a form of giving back vitality and energy to the spirit underlining the crops. Semen and sexual fluids were believed to have great fertilizing powers, powers that were necessary to fertilize the field and manifest a prosperous harvest.

NORTH INDIA -DURGA PUJA

However, in North India, we are privy to an alternate approach to her worship. It was almost compulsory for girls to be married at an early age, and as was expected they would leave their family to join their husband's clan. This was not a transition most found easy, on the contrary, young brides would suffer much separation anxiety during those early honeymoon years of marriage. In Bengal however, daughters were allowed to happily return to their home villages once a year during Durga Puja and this was often a highly emotionally charged event for young brides, who were probably deeply missing their home and family of origins. This returning home theme is why Durga herself is sometimes perceived as the returning daughter, during this Harvest festival. Many chants sung during the Durga Puja Festival support this belief. Songs with the theme of welcoming back, farewells and the difficult life of a daughter, when she is in her husband's home (in contrast to her loving parent's home) are a prevalent theme. In these documented songs Durga is identify with the Goddess Parvati, wife of Shiva, daughter of Himalaya and his wife Mena and she is the perpetual sacred daughter returning home before having to sadly depart once more.

Many worshippers during this festival view Durga as the beloved daughter returning home and it's a very intimate experience, as worshippers' commune and connect with their beloved Goddess. A clay image of the multi-armed Goddess is often found on her altar and it is worshipped as the Goddess herself. Worshippers caress affectionately and highly venerate the image of their beloved Goddess as if she indeed is an intimate family member. She is depicted triumphing over a powerful demon but many worshippers in this part of the world simply see her as – sacred Daughter, returning home for her annual Autumnal visit. It is also a time when worshipper will consider the returning daughter, Durga, as an actual family member and lavish onto her all the love, attention and adoration to her image. It seems almost as if their Goddess becomes Persephone, returning home to help the crops grow and to share her powers of fecundity upon the land. The devotees then appear to take on the role of the Mother, like Demeter welcoming back Kore. *"We become the mothers that are welcoming back the daughter, the Persephone, during this festival..."* When this festival comes to a close, everyone prepares to bid her adieu at the waters; Durga, as the daughter, is bid adieu. This returning daughter archetype in this Autumnal Harvest festival will often find women gathering around the representative images of Durga; weeping, mourning, crying as an expression of the melancholy they feel over the daughter preparing to leave and her inevitable departure during the Dark season.

SOUTHERN INDIA - DURGA PUJA

In the South there is a vastly contrasting approach to the worship of this great Goddess in the Navaratra Festival. There is a wild, untamable, almost sexual tension that is highlighted between Durga and the buffalo demon, Mahisa. A Buffalo is sometimes sacrificed on the altar to Durga and blood is significantly featured during ceremonial rites to represent the blood many shed in battle with the Goddess. This demon is viewed as her suitor who she ultimately engages in battle, defeats and refuses to submit to. Her untamable sexual energy is indisputably dangerous and almost deadly to any man who dares to approach her. There is an implication that one must submit to Durga before engaging in any safe sexual encounter with her. Mahisa loses the battle and is unable to do so, but other myths reveal that Lord Shiva becomes her consort, yet, this is only as the aspect of Parvati and Sati. Durga is a fatal threat to those who try to conquer her or approach her sexually. In the South, Durga Puja festival gives more credence to Durga's role as a determined, fierce independent and untamable Goddess, whose origins are found among tribal people, in the far off distant mountains. Her worship in these southern regions are considerably more wild, free and more ecstatic than in the North.

In conclusion, it is important to note the slight difference in her worship, for in Northern Indian traditions, Durga is viewed more prominently as the returning daughter (or young bride) in need of family tenderness and adoration. She is viewed as the returning daughter, suggesting a shift in season, while in the South; she is seen as wild, untamable, strong independent, and an unmarried Goddess; delighting in her liminal aspect.

*Multi-armed, Hindu Goddess, Durga, is the ferocious tiger. She is the fierce warrior maiden but also the protectress guardian Mother of humanity. She is compassionate towards her devotees, and she's called upon for help, like the Goddess Kwan Yin and many other Mother Archetypes, but she is a fighter. In the Hindu Goddess Durga we find a warrior who will fiercely fight to protect humanity from all kinds of maladies in the world. Durga is anger manifested and employed into action. She was born from the collective emotion of anger that stemmed from the Gods. This anger is not held within to self-destruct, no, she uses that anger as a vehicle of action for her victory, while defeating those who are trying to destroy her. She is the embodiment of sovereign autonomy and awakens us to our own potential for victory.

Durga is the Goddess, embodying supreme strength and power. When presented with demons and threats to her world, she fights and she delights in that combat. She takes great pleasure in the act of this battle and she is always guaranteed victory. With her numerous arms there is nothing she cannot tackle and her wielding arms are so reminiscent and symbolic of our gender's numerous roles and obligations. It is her Divine energy that helps us connect to our ambition and powers of manifestations. Multi-armed to denote her supreme powers and capabilities, she is a Goddess that juggles numerous tasks with great ease and success. Her ability to achieve her heart's desire is evident and an inspiration for us to emulate. She is the charioterer able to tap into her powers of concentration, to drive and get much accomplished. Durga is the embodiment of sovereign autonomy and she awakens us to our great strength when pursuing our dreams or facing adversity.

MAUVE

Mauve is a Celtic Goddess intrinsically connected with the land of Ireland. Like most ancient Goddesses there are numerous early writings and tales, as early as the first century AD, that reveal various elements connected to the Sacred Feminine and her worship.

In early times she was known as Medb/Mebhdb and these names are connected to "Mead," a beloved beverage for the Irish. Her name, Mauve, is known to translate as *"intoxication"* and this might reveal her importance as a Goddess who offers libation and, in so doing divinely elects the proper King to rule the land. This was considered a very sacred rite, only through this Goddess chalice offering could the next King be chosen. May Day, a well-known Pagan Holiday celebrated with much libations and merry making, was oftentimes the season when new rulers were selected. It is precisely why Mauve is associated with Beltane and May Day Rites.

Mauve is a beautiful, passionate, Celtic Goddess of Sovereignty and the Irish land. She is a fierce warrior and a Sovereign Queen. Daughter of the King, *Eochalb Feidlech*, she was gifted the land of Connaught. Her most famous Celtic story, *"Tain Bo Cuailing"* or "Cattle Raid Cooley," is a rather interesting one, and reflective of this Goddess and her notable attributes.

Long ago Queen Mauve, who was known to have many lovers, was married to King Ailill mac Mata, in the land of Connaught. The King and Queen one day were cuddled up in bed, as lovers sometimes do, reminiscing and chatting. Well, King Ailill mac Mata, feeling prideful and good about himself begins to boast about how lucky Mauve should feel to be married to someone as rich and powerful as he is. He claims that she should be grateful to have such a rich accomplished, fine specimen. Well, she hears him and does not share in his sentiment. Actually, Mauve becomes very offended.

Her immediate response to him was to begin listing all of her own numerous accolades, riches and great attributes. She painstakingly reminds him of how many battles she had fought and won by his side and how she has proven that she is just as strong and just as rich. It is the King that should be counting his blessings with her as his bride. The two begin to banter back and forth about who's better, who's richer who's luckier...

It's important to note that in Ireland at this point, women were viewed very differently than they have been viewed in previous times in history. Women were often viewed as possessors of magick, connected to the Goddess, responsible for the fecundity of the Irish land and some were indeed considered sovereign and land owners. Irish women as Goddesses were seen as powerful and just as strong in combat as men; even depicted in the grueling bloody Battlefields. But what is most interesting to note is that there was a strong belief that your wealth and the amount of abundance you owned determine the amount of power you could wield. The richer you were whether you were a man or woman, the more power you held. Therefore this argument between the King and the Queen was a valid one. The King was trying to assert his dominion over the Queen by touting all of his riches and fine attributes but the Queen, not only disagreed with him but felt that she was the one who had more resources and therefore, more power.

As the story continues they both become so enraged and determined to prove their case that they summoned their respective servants to gather and reveal all of their personal resources. Each of their servants gathered up all of the animals they owned, all the gold and all of the proof of their abundance. As it turned out they did have equal amounts in everything. The King then brings up his prized possession, his magick bull. He claims it is the finest and the strongest and the only one owned by him alone in all the land of Connaught. He declares that ownership of this bull basically makes him the richest and therefore, more powerful. Well, it is at this moment that Queen Mauve becomes even more infuriated because she reminds him that the bull was once, owned solely by her but because the bull did not want to be owned by a woman it was given to the king. He knew she was correct and seeing how the argument had now dangerously escalated, he agreed they were thus equal. He conceded that they were equal, claiming that indeed the Bull belonged to both of them. At this point King Ailill mac Mata, just wanted to call it a truce, however, that response was not good enough for the Queen. This did not sit well with Mauve and she was determined to acquire her own bull to prove her superiority over the King.

The story then gets lengthy and more complicated with diverse versions of it, but essentially the Queen implements a plan to retrieve a famous Red Bull named, Donn Cuailnge. This bull was in Ulster, owned by Daire mac Fiochna. After numerous unsuccessful offers to acquire the Bull, she decides to take matters into her own hands and kidnap it. She rallies her numerous supporters in Connaught and gathers an army to go to Ulster to retrieve this massive, prized Bull. At Ulster, the army was led by the young, Cuchulainn, son of the God Lugh. Cuchulainn had garnered a reputation as being a fiercely, unstoppable warrior and leader of the army at Ulster. However, the men at the time were spellbound and rendered weak by the Goddess Morrigan, due to an offense towards the warrior Goddess at the hands of Cuchulainn. When faced with Mauve and her army he made a deal with them that he would fight them one by one since his army was inaccessible. Cuchulainn put up a good fight and was almost successful but eventually, succumbed by his injuries, was defeated. Had it not been for the healing restorative gifts of his father, Lugh, he would have perished entirely.

As the great legend continues, Mauve and her army were able to fight and claim the prized Bull, Donn Cuailnge. In this version, they manage to bring the bull back to Connaught to prove to the King that she was indeed superior. It was undoubtedly a long, arduous trip back and the bull suffered for it but they made it back. When the bull arrived before the King Ailill, it was immediately greeted and challenged by the King's existing bull. According to the literature of the time, the two Bulls confronted each other and engaged in a fierce battle. They eventually tore each other up and some tales state they fought each other to their deaths. Other versions speak of Mauve's Bull defeating the king's bull but later on collapsing to his own death due to the enormous strain and injuries.

Mauve is an important Goddess for us to connect with and her story almost reminds me of the Sumerian Goddess, Lilith, because here again we have a Goddess needing to defend herself and prove why she is, not only equal to man, but moreover, superior. In the case of the Sumerian Goddess, Lilith, she refused to lie underneath Adam during sex. As supreme Deities, both she and Mauve are not only demanding equality but demanding that their superiority and their sovereignty be acknowledged and honored. This is extremely important for modern women today. We are so often overly concerned about the subject of equality that we fail to see beyond it and consider that maybe, in some circumstances, it is not equality we should strive for but the recognition of our supremacy and authority.

Celtic mythology often reveals an understanding and an acceptance that women were intrinsically linked with the sacred feminine and that they were indeed equal and more often than not, superior to men. The Goddess Mauve is in this chapter about ambition and focus because this Sovereign Queen reminds us that sometimes we too have to make an argument for our own supremacy and authority. We too have to acknowledge our own gifts, gather our own resources & attributes, and let our light shine even if it blinds others. In this Irish Goddess we are also reminded to set our sights on what we want and commit to doing whatever it takes to accomplish it. A Goddess so connected to sovereignty is a beautiful reminder and an example of what we can aspire to be.

FREYJA (FREYA, FREIJA, FREYIA, FREJA)

Freyja is the Norse Goddess of beauty, love, sexuality, fertility freedom and independence. She is also known as the Goddess of war, death, travel, gold, and sorcery. It is clear, like with many ancient Goddesses, Freyja is an all-encompassing Goddess that was and still remains today an important representation of the Sacred Feminine.

Her name translates as, *"Lady"* or *"Mistress"* and she was part of the Vanir Tribe. The Vanir were much older and came before the Aesir. They were focused on nature, animals, the wild, and even the unseen realm. It is only after the war between these two tribes, when the Aesir also came to claim Freyja as one of their own.

Freyja is believed to be very much a shaman Goddess and even had the ability to shapeshift. As a Goddess of Magick and Divination, she was attributed for introducing the Gods and Humanity with a special type of Norse magick, known as Seidr. She also had the special proclivity to connect worshippers to their Female ancestors and divine the future with their help. She could travel through all nine realms and is connected to the Valkyries; known to travel at night with them as their leader.

Her name appears numerous times in ancient writings and her image can also be found in various sources. Often depicted as the Fair one, with blue eyes and long flowing or braided blonde hair, she was known to ride a chariot led by two black cats. Theses cats were gifted to her by Thor but she was also connected with a Boar, named Hildisvini. When she wasn't using her cat led chariot she would ride this Battle Boar, who was secretly known as her human lover. Freyja also had a connection with raven and falcon. Her magickal cloak was made of Falcon feathers and with it she could fly to great heights. Many other deities borrowed her magickal cloak whenever they needed the gift of flight.

Her father is Njoror and his sister, the Earth Goddess, Nerthus, is her mother. She is a twin to her brother, Freyr. The question of her husband stirs some variations in stories. Early writings reveal she is married to Odr but this name eventually disappear in the writings and it leaves many to speculate that it is an older version of the name Odin. Either way Odin which is a derivative of Odr means ecstasy, furor, frenzy, inspiration. Most of the early writings of the time reveal that Freyja had two beautiful daughters with Odr. They were known as Hnoss and Gersemi.

Freyja, as the Norse Goddess of Love and Beauty, commands great powers of attraction. Her beauty was unmatched and it was a known fact that no man could resist her advances. Despite being married she had numerous lovers and lived her life quite independently. She is known to pursue her desires regardless of consequences or other's opinions, as is evident in many of her myths. Her connection to beautiful objects like jewelry, gemstones and gold becomes apparent when you learn through her myths that her very own tears would become amber when they fell upon water and gold, when they fell upon stones. And of course, there is the famous story about how she acquired her legendary, magickal gold necklace, *Brisingamen*, meaning fire.

One day Freyja passed by four busy dwarves, that were working on an exquisite golden necklace. She caught a glimpse of this brilliant work of art and admired aloud its beauty. The dwarves replied with an admiration of her Divine beauty but no matter, because she had already set her sights on possessing this necklace. She offered to buy it from them. She negotiated with them, proposing all sorts of gold and silver but the dwarves were not interested in these things. They felt they already had enough gold and silver in the lives but they lacked something that they knew only the Goddess of Love could offer them. They each wanted to lay with the Divine Goddess. They agreed to surrender the exquisite necklace to her only if she agreed to have sex with each of them. Her expression of love and sexual gifts were more precious to these dwarves and thus, she used her sexuality as currency to get what she wanted most, at that very moment. It would not be the first nor the last time this type of negotiation is made by this Divine Goddess.

As a Goddess of War, she and Odin shared the brave lost souls that died in the battlefield. She had the honors of gathering first, before Odin, and she delivers her half of these brave beings to Folkvangr, the heavenly field, where they are to find their final resting place. Immortal Freyja lives among the Norse Gods in Asgard and her own house is known as Sessrumnir, located near Folkvangr, where her first choice slain warriors enjoy the afterlife.

IX CHEL

The Goddess Ix Chel [Pronounced: *ee shEll*] is the ancient Mayan Goddess of the Moon. Also known as "Lady Rainbow," due to her association with moisture and rain, she rules over the various phases of the moon and thus, a woman life. Ix Chel is a Goddess that rules; fertility, creativity, sexuality, intuition, and childbirth. Known also as a patron Goddess of expectant mothers and the healing and medicinal arts, she is the Goddess of artisans and weavers. Textiles, decorative cloths and weaving were sacred women's handicraft, considered very important in many cultures, including Central and South America. Ix Chel was called upon to bless young girls with this vital and prosperous skill.

As Goddess of the Moon, which rules over the ebb and flow of the ocean waters, it is not surprising, all waters are her domain. She is the patron Goddess of intuition which also falls under the Moon's realm. This Lunar Deity was in charge of regulating the waters that can bestow fertility onto the land or great destruction, with her uncontrollable floods. In this respect, she is seen as a Goddess of abundance and fruitfulness, in the same way that Demeter and Gaia (Earth Goddesses) are seen as bringer of abundance and fruitfulness to their native land.

According to some mythologies it is believed that the well documented (Haiyococab) flooding of the Earth, many years ago, was attributed to Ix Chel who unleashed her sacred waters from a giant earthen vessel. As the legends describe it in this part of Mayan cosmology, she poured out her waters upon the earth to cleanse it and revitalize new growth. In this depiction we see her great powers as a water deity providing nurturance and quenching the earth's thirst. But here, we also see her potentially destructive nature if she inundates us, pouring forth an inordinate amount of water with the potential to destroy.

As a water deity she was also regarded as a Goddess of medicine and healing. In ancient times, it was believed she would approach and tend to the sick. If proper supplications and offerings are made, some claim to see her shadow, as a crone, by the foot of the bedridden and it was believed she could heal, as well as make the transition smoother for those who would need to cross over into the realm of the dead. The rising smoke from a smudge of Copal and tobacco would draw her near, as well as other offerings like; guava tips, sap of a rubber tree, turkey broth, haaz papaya and pulverized crab powder. Here was a Goddess who unquestionably ruled over the realms of life and death for Mayan people.

Ix Chel also has been seen as Goddess of creativity and commerce in her ability to inspire and teach wommin to provide for themselves by way of their handicrafts and creative arts. A Goddess of wommin who need autonomy and financially independent, She thus became a patron Goddess of weaving and textile because these were the skills and trade accessible for wommin to excel in. One myth tells of her intense concentration upon a spider weaving her web and from this act, she was able to pass on this critical knowledge and imperative skill (which would prove to be profitable) to wommin on earth. Textile knowledge, like how to work with looms, spinning cotton, and how to dye cotton in various colors, were examples of her Divine gifts to wommin. Most importantly she championed wommin's use of their sacred hands in various hand-crafts, artistry and numerous creative and profitable outlets.

She was sometimes depicted holding a sacred urn (vase) upside down, which was a symbol of her watery wombs being released upon the earth. Water lilies were also sacred to her. This Mayan Goddess of the Moon was most beloved by wommin because of her well documented ability to impart fertility and ease in child birthing. It was a custom, in ancient times, for all pregnant wommin or those wanting to conceive, to make the journey to her famous Shrines in Cozumel or "Isla de Mujeres," for it was believed that in these sacred waters, fertility and her blessings were guaranteed.

As a Moon Goddess, she unquestionably rules over all the waters; including the waters of our womanhood, our blood, our urine, our moisture, sexuality, amniotic fluids and childbirth. Her Shrines can still be found today on the island of Cozumel, near the Yucatan Peninsula... just to the northeastern coast of the Peninsula. A quick Google search on the internet will provide a list of numerous tour companies eager to share Ix Chel's Temples, waters, caves and ruins, still accessible today.

As an ancient deity, Ix Chel was known as a triple Goddess that could take the form of a beautiful young maiden, brushing her long hair upon the moon, or as a nurturing mother helping her people or as a crone; a hag with a skirt of bones. Other popular images show her with a crown of snakes upon her head, pouring water from an earthen vessel. Still other depictions show her as a voluptuous, naked, sensual enchantress alongside her totem animals; the hare, the snake or the jaguar. Sometimes she is depicted with eagle feathers and was known also as "Eagle Woman" because the eagle was known as a messenger of the Moon. For the people of Guatemala, Campeche and the Yucatan region she was considered the First woman of the world, and thus, a mother deity who gave birth to all succeeding women and Goddesses.

THE STORY OF IX CHEL and THE SUN

According to Mayan cosmology, the earth began with two very bright, luminous beings in the sky; the Sun and the Moon. The Moon, Ix Chel, was known to be the most beautiful enchantress, but she had a notoriously jealous grandfather who guarded her carefully and as her numerous tales reveal, her life was plagued by this theme of jealous, oppressive beings, trying to control her. The Sun God, was in love with Ix Chel and he infatuatedly watched her daily, although in some tales it is Ix Chel who is greatly enamored by the Sun God, Kinich Ahau. While she was actively pursued by numerous deities, she only had eyes for the great Sun God and she tries to attract his attention, despite her vicious, jealous grandfather's threats.

One Mayan Tale, reveals that Kinich Ahau, the Sun, endeavoring to endear Ix Chel and get closer to her, disguised himself as a Hummingbird. In his Hummingbird form he flew to her home and as a bird he was quite welcomed by the Goddess. She offered him honey from the tobacco flower and as they were sharing a quiet moment, the hummingbird fell down, wounded by a fierce clay pellet that had been shot and aimed at him by her jealous grandfather. With great empathy, she quickly safeguarded the helpless bird and nursed him to health in the privacy of her room. According to folklore, this very act awakened and stirred in her, deep, unknown affections for him. When he recovered and flew robust and full of life again, he revealed his true identity and convinced her to leave her home and her monstrously, oppressive grandfather and so... they fled together.

When Ix Chel's grandfather caught sight of the two luminous divine lights escaping, he became greatly infuriated and in his raged he called upon the assistance of Chac, the one who controlled lightning and the storms. According to this tale Chac hurled lightning bolts to both the Sun and the Moon deity as instructed by her grandfather. Although they appeared to be able to retreat momentarily into the water, Ix Chel as a crab and the Sun as a turtle, the Moon Goddess was not able to escape. She was eventually killed by the lightning bolt. In another tale, it is Ix Chel's grandfather himself that aims and shoots the lightning directly at Ix Chel, killing her instantaneously.

The next part of this ancient tale is retold differently by various accounts, but they all reveal a great deal about Ix Chel's sacred symbols and her connection to dragon flies, the number thirteen, death and resurrection and snakes. Some tales tell that while she lay lifeless, thirteen dragonflies sung to her and brought her back to life. Another story tells of how her lifeless body was nursed for thirteen days by a multitude of celestial dragonflies, that sang to revive her. And in this particular story we learn of how the dragonflies created thirteen hollow logs and on the thirteenth night, twelve logs broke open to reveal twelve divine snakes -while the thirteenth log, broke open to reveal the Goddess Ix Chel, alive, resurrected and brilliant, once more. The Sun God, who had been mourning her death up to that moment, rejoiced to see her come back to life, bright and whole. He immediately proposed marriage to his beloved and she agreed. Together they set up their home in the heavens, side by side, they were also believed to have given birth to the four Jaguars Gods, who became the guardians of the four corners of the world. But alas, married life soon proved to be very difficult and more challenging than anticipated for the Moon Goddess.

The Sun's brother, the morning Star, Chac Noh Eck, was known to visit their marital abode much too often and apparently he appeared to be quite fond of the Moon too, lingering closer to her than to the Sun himself. This made the already hot tempered, volatile Sun, extremely jealous. He accused the brilliant Ix Chel of unthinkable infidelities with his brother, Chac Noh Eck. Lashing out cruel words and false accusations, he refused to hear her defense, and the Sun God, violently expelled her from the heavens.

Banished from the heaven, she landed near a volcano, not far from Lake of Atilan and there she contemplated this horrible turn of events. She was angered at the unjust accusations made by her husband and was of course saddened by his abuse. A vulture appeared nearby and having sympathy, offered her a ride to his home, way up high in the mountains. Here she met the King of Vultures and together they took residence in the mountains, where they also became lovers.

When the remorseful Sun God learned of this amicable union, it did not sit well with him and he soon struggled to devise a scheme to entreat his wife once more to forgive his brute ways and return to the heavens. One story tells that he hid himself in the hide of a dead deer and waited for the predictable vultures to approach the carcass. Unsuspectingly, he jumped on the vultures back and was flown to Ix Chel's new abode. When he arrived, he managed to corner Ix Chel and pleaded with her to give him another chance and to recall all the wonderful moments they had shared as young lovers. Tugging at her heartstring, she allowed his words to move her and... sadly prepared to leave the home she and her Vulture lover had so successfully created. She returned to her throne in the heavens, but the story does not end here.

No sooner had she returned to the heavens, when the jealousy and volatile accusations of her husband started up again. According to some tales there was incessant verbal abuse but also physical abuse, as the Sun God tried to destroy her beauty and disfigure her with scars, to lessen her enchanting nature. They say this is why the moon has visible carved craters on its surface.

One night, the Moon Goddess had endured enough and with all of her willpower and strength, she left into the night. Some say she shapeshifted into a Jaguar, vowing to stay away from the Sun for eternity. She is known to hide in the day when he is awake and wanders through the dark of the night. And although her beauty made many lovers propose marriage to her, she opted to embrace her freedom, belonging to no one, but herself. Ix Chel was known to truly relish her freedom after the torment she endured with the Sun God and she vowed never to dim her light or become owned by anyone else again. It was believed that she retreated to her Island in Cozumel, where she could enjoy her freedom and delight in assisting women in child labor and all aspects of feminine activities.

In this myth we see her as a champion for the oppressed and a Goddess of bold action, who teaches us as women not to become victims of abuse. She teaches us to assert ourselves and not allow ourselves to be emotionally, nor physically victimized. Anything that negatively affects our soul and wellbeing must be eradicated in order for our inner light to shine. Much like many other Lunar Goddesses from various cultures and throughout the ages, she exemplifies the independent spirit of a woman with no ties to any man. Some believe she was touched by the cries of myriads of struggling women everywhere on earth, but especially those making offerings, prayers and supplications at her shrines on the island of Cozumel. She proudly devotes herself to women, their struggles, answering prayers and being an advocate for women's freedom, strength and creativity.

*Ancient Mayan Lunar Goddess, Ix Chel, rules over the waters, our intuitive gifts, the moon and our gender's emotions. With Ix Chel we begin to open ourselves up to the gifts of our gender; reflected in her watery realm and the sacred Moon. This Mayan Goddess has a story to tell and it echoes the story of so many women throughout "Herstory." She empowers us to forge our own paths and like many lunar deities, she encourages our independence and autonomy. Ix Chel is the inspirer of our creative gifts and the profitable handcrafted skills needed to assure our autonomy and financial success. She is the awakeners of our internal unique voices and advocates shinning our own light brightly, despite those who would prefer us hidden and unnoticed. She imbues us with the courage to follow our path, and embrace our ancestral, matriarchal lineage. As divine Creatress, she reminds you of your own fertile, luminescent gifts. No matter, if you are a spicy-wild maiden, nurturing mother or a wise old crone, all of these archetypes reside within you and all are sacred reflections of Creatrix Lunar Goddess, Ix Chel.

NIKE

Nike is the immortal spirit of triumph, the Greek Goddess of victory and success. In Rome she was better known as Victoria. Often depicted standing on a globe with wings, and holding palm and Laurel wreath, she was described as quite beautiful by most of the ancient literature of her time. It appeared she was desired by everyone, for, of course, victory is that prized attribute longed for by, men and women, mortal and immortal alike. That perpetual spirit of victory is present in all wars, competitions, award ceremonies and athletic events today, as it was in ancient times and thus, her immortal presence can still be felt today.

Perhaps this is why the very successful American athletic shoe company (which began in Oregon, in 1962) adopted its name, Nike. In doing so it honors one of the most beloved Champion Goddesses in Greek mythology. Today, it is one of the most prosperous conglomerate corporations in the world; doing its part to campaign for this highly cherished Greek Goddess, sustaining her name alive in our vernacular.

In Greek mythology she is the winged daughter of the dark River Styx and the Giant Titan Pallas. Her siblings, interestingly enough, were "Cratos," which means Strength, "Bia," which means Force and "Zelus," which mean Rivalry, an indication that all three attributes were ever present, when Victory was invoked.

In Rome, as Victoria, she was worshipped quite early on and was considered the divine protector of the senate. There isn't a whole lot of detailed information on the Greek Goddess, Nike. Most of what we do know about her is extracted and derived from mere mentions, every now and then, in various ancient Greek writings. There are no long epic myths associated with her, nor any indication that she had conflict with anyone in particular. And although she was desired and welcomed by all, there is no indication of any romantic liaisons with Gods, nor with any humans.

Although, in Greece, she had no known cult following, nor any special festivals or temples, as many of the other Greek Goddesses did, she was often associated with both Zeus and Athena. Most art and sculptures of her time depicted her as a small figure held in the hands of Athena, the Greek Goddess of War and Wisdom. There is even some literature that alleged, Nike was simply another aspect of the beloved Athenian Goddess. However, more evidence reveals that indeed they were two separate deities, with many impressive similar attributes, which would explain the conflicting tales. Athena, being a Goddess of Wisdom, debates and war, would certainly want near her, the continuous blessings from the Goddess of Victory. They were considered as having a close alliance and there is even some contention in the Greek myths that directly connects Athena with the death of Nike's father, but she apparently, suffered no grave punishment due to their close relationship.

Nike's worship would have been compulsory on the battlefield, pageantries, athletic events and numerous other competitive situations for both mortals and immortals alike; with libations, offerings and sacrifices. The patriarchal Olympian head God, Zeus, cherished Nike immensely due to her help in attaining victory in the battle of the Titans. It is perhaps this reason why Zeus appointed Nike as his official charioteer and employed her family as attendants; allowing them, the rare privilege, to reside with him in the royal palace among the divine Gods.

Her most famous depiction is found in *"Nike of Samothrace"* a sculpture by Paeonius (c.424 B.C.) which was discovered on Samothrace in 1863. Presently this illustrious creation is contained at the Louvre Museum in Paris, France.

Wherever victory and success is, Nike is there too, immortal, ever present as the spirit of Victory, a pure ambitious drive, ready to award you with success. She is forever the Maiden archetype and a wonderful Goddess for modern wommin to connect with, when we are ready to tap into our fierce competitive spirit. As the Divine Charioteer, she is also an excellent Goddess to call upon for, not only Victory, but also in driving and travel rites. Invoke her when you wish to succeed in a personal endeavor or anything requiring ambition and drive. She is the energy of the marathon runner, reaching the finish line, hands outstretched towards the heavens, in pure elation and accomplishment..... This is Nike... the Goddess of Victory!

Times are indeed changing but previous studies have shown that as women, we tend to be inclusive and less competitive than our male counterparts. Oftentimes, even in our youth, as young girls, we may have been discouraged from being, *"too aggressive"* or *"too competitive"* or *"too bossy,"* etc... Admittedly, even as adult women in various different communities (work, collegiate, religious) I notice we are often still made to feel self-conscious about how aggressive or competitive we are coming across to others. If we appear too ambitious or too competitive we are easily labeled *"the bitch"* or *"the one who has an attitude"* or *"the ugly one,"* because apparently there are some blind people in this world that cannot see the beauty of every diverse Goddess roaming this earth, but I digress.

Now, I know times are changing and we are indeed in the midst of human evolution here. I strongly believed that times have changed much and it is my hope that today, we are raisng our daughters to shine their own unique light, without any preconceived prejudices on what is proper male or female behavior. Yes, inclusivity, compassion, nurturance and all the numerous gifts we possess as women should be embraced and encouraged in ourselves and the next generation. But the notion of telling another human being that they cannot aspire for greatness (their definition of greatness) is preposterous, no matter what your gender may be.

Nike is the Goddess of greatness, of supreme successs... every girl (and for that matter, every boy) should indeed be allowed and encouraged to pursue their own well defined level of greatness. Let the Goddess of Victory inspire us to unleash our inner competitive maiden, to thrive in this world with the best of them, uninfluenced by preconceived ideas of what is proper, or not, within our gender. Let Nike be our armour of inspiration and defense against those who would try to snuff out our unique, divine flames. And may we be sparked by her immortal essence to thrive and fearlessly pursue our heart's desire regardless of the naysayers and dream killers.

*Nike is the Greek Goddess of Victory. The laurel wreathed maiden Goddess of Triumph, rewards generously for works accomplished, this is her sweet domain. She anxiously awaits your success and stirs within you a healthy dose of competition and ambition. Our laurel wreath is awaiting and she stirs in you a desire for her presence –a desire for success. *Do we enter it victoriously; projecting a sense of ordained achievement? Or have we already failed before we have even begun?*

The Goddess Nike invites you to celebrate the small and large accomplishments in your life, knowing that this acknowledgement will positively influence future ones. With Nike, we celebrate our great drive and ambition and we take bold steps towards monumental victories; carving out our own unique path to successs.

THEME WORK SUGGESTIONS

Work with the Sagittarius moon, symbolized by the Centaur,
and work with The Eagle energy and the deities presented in this chapter.
In a previous chapter you were encouraged to create a collage or vision board,
you are encouraged to expand on it or create a new one.
Engage in a regular Meditation and visualization practice.
Acquire a journal and begin a regular writing practice.

JOURNALING

What is your greatest accomplishment at this date?
_____
_____

What would you say is your greatest failure or regret at this date?
_____
_____

When you were a child, what did you dream of becoming?
_____
_____

Have you fulfilled most of your childhood dreams?
_____
_____

What goals still feel a long distant away from being reached?
_____
_____

How do you approach goal setting?
_____
_____

Do you have a 5-10 year wish list?
_____
_____

Who, in your personal life exemplifies success?
_____
_____

What celebrity or historical person do you admire most and why?
_____
_____

If you could do anything in the world, and YOU CAN, what would it be?

_____

_____

What are your immediate goals and your long distant goals?

_____

_____

How do you define the attainment of success?

_____

_____

THEME WORK SUGGESTIONS
10. AMBITION
Light and Orange candle

Consider where you may need more education or skills and gather some books and resources to acquire new skills. Engage in a daily meditation practice, to help sharpen your focus and to help you clarify what you want in this life.

Experiment and create a mandala or some type of work of art as a form of clarifying modality. Find a few people (celebrity or historical or within your own community) that will become your model of inspiration. Let their story serve to motivate the development of your story. Explore the Abraham Hicks, Law of Attraction Tenets. Ask yourself what is the very first step I need to take, in order to achieve the very last step I hope to attain. Explore Visualization techniques.

INVOCATION & POETRY

A CALL TO OUR FIRES
Bow and Arrow
In my hand,
I awake
to all I have

Gifts and skills
Received right now
Sight to See
Answers to How

Freyja's Fire
Stir in me
I can manifest
all I need…

Road maps open
In my heart
Clearly speak
And bless this start

Hail to you Goddess
And all that is Divine
Hear this prayer
on this Lunar night.

*** You are now encouraged to create
your own altar(s) & invocation(s).
)O(Blessings!

MAGICK RITES & TOOLS

This is your personal page to document your sacred rites and the tools you elected to use.

DECIDE WHERE TO SET UP AN ALTAR
Place an Altar Cloth in the Color of your choice.
Color: _____

GODDESS
Place an image of your Deity.
Goddess: _____
This image can be a Statue, handmade Sculpture or a simple Photo _____

FIRE REPRESENTATION
Place a blessed/charged Candle in the color of your choice.
Candle Type and color: _____

AIR REPRESENTATION
Light your Incense stick.
Incense Scent: _____

WATER REPRESENTATION
Place a Chalice of Water
Water Item: _____

EARTH REPRESENTATION
Place a Potted Plant or Fresh Flowers on your Altar
Add Salt or a plate of Dried Herbs
Herbs: _____
Chosen Gemstone: _____

YOUR WISH
_____
_____

_____

Place a symbol of your desire, if you have one available, and also write your wish out clearly, on a piece of parchment paper, or you can even use a cut up brown paper bag. These are the basics for a very simple altar & rite. Ultimately, your sacred space is only limited by your imagination. You can make your altar & rite as big or as small as you prefer and the addition of other personal items is really up to you.)o(Enjoy!

ALTAR PHOTOS

CHAPTER ELEVEN

"Money is only a tool. It will take you wherever you wish, but it will not replace you as the driver..."
Ayn Rand

THEME: WORK & PROSPERITY

Our work and finding the necessary resources to exist comfortably in the world is a common concern and quest many of us have here on planet earth. Even those fortunate enough to be born into great wealth still have the encumbrance of finding fulfilling work that connects them to their passion, their life's purpose and an incentive to wake up every morning. Yes, there are bills and taxes to be paid, bellies to feed, homes to be bought, medical expenses to tend to and so many more financial obligations pulling at our wallets on a daily basis. It is all a part of the contract we agree to as responsible adults playing our part in our species' theater masterpiece on earth. It goes without saying but securing the proper type of fulfilling work that will provide the resources we require for our day to day expenses becomes almost compulsory in our lives.

It is clear that this dynamic subject is not one that can be avoided and therefore it behooves us to arrive at this crossroad, in our journey, with a willingness to receive its life affirming lesson.

There's a difference between this chapter and the previous chapter which touched upon our resolve, ambition, visualization and powers of manifestation; while also addressing how to wield two opposing forces to get to our ultimate destination. We arrive at this chapter having clarified our goals and desires and having attained a level of mastery of our drive. In this chapter we have reached a pivotal point where we are called upon to bring commitment and hard work towards the fulfilment of our dream; especially one related to work, finances and our vocation.

We've reached a point in our journey where we are actively pursuing this Golden goblet and feel ready to taste victory. The World card, which is the last card of the Major Arcana in traditional Tarot decks, is a perfect companion to our theme for this chapter. With its message about completion of cycles, and victorious achievements seized, it illustrates beautifully where we find ourselves at this point in our journey. There is a great desire to roll up our sleeves and get to work. The theme of this chapter is clearly about work; a maturity and readiness to put in whatever great effort is necessary to achieve our goals in the world we live in. As part of this process we will explore the animal energy of the Horse, which exemplifies so poignantly our theme. It's also important to note that the hard working, tenacious mountain goat, which is connected to the astrological sign of Capricorn, is also very demonstrative of our theme here. The astrological sign of Capricorn, which is the lunation we are working with in this chapter, is ruled by the elder, taskmaster, Saturn and thus, we can see how all of these elements lend support to our theme in this chapter.

Throughout our journey, we have been challenged with numerous lessons and have stayed the course to grasp mastery of many. As a result we arrive at this pivotal point in our work where we are offered a glimpse into our potential reward if we continue onward.

As we have done before, in this chapter we will explore further our theme with the help of several resources. We will endeavor to connect with the Goddesses Athena, Sri Lakshmi, Benten, Fortuna, Tyche, Gefjun and the sacred animal energy of the Horse. We will connect with our Root chakra, the 1st chakra, and gemstones that can help better facilitate this connection. We will also look at the corresponding Lunation and a Tarot card that is connected to our theme.

THE WORLD TAROT CARD

The World card in the Tarot is often depicted, in traditional decks, with the formation of a circle by the Ouroboros; the snake consuming its tail. It is a powerful, alchemical symbol of infinity and wholeness. In some tarot decks there is an image of a wreath, which is also a symbol of victory and the four sacred elements are often represented in this card's imagery.

The serpent's image found in the Word card speaks of completion and powerful journeys coming to an end. There is a great victory being bestowed upon the Fool, who had started his journey, at the beginning of the Major Arcana, with nothing more than his satchel, curiosity, naïveté and great enthusiasm. The Fool embarked on this journey not knowing what he/she would encounter. After many adventures and numerous challenging lessons, the Fool arrives at a pivotal milestone. The World Card in the Tarot is that moment of mastery and fulfilment of our dreams. Hard work and effort has been applied to our journey and it leads us to the completion of one cycle and the inauguration of a new realm, dressed in victory.

MOON IN CAPRICORN   EARTH/SATURN

THEME: Work & Prosperity

CAPRICORN   CARDINAL   EARTH   FEMININE   MOUNTAIN GOAT

The moon in Capricorn tends to lend an atmosphere of getting down to business and fulfilling obligations. Capricorn is an earth sign and by its very nature concerns itself with earthly matters. The Mountain Goat that represents the astrological sign of Capricorn reveals some of this sign's most dominant attributes and characteristics that are highlighted when the moon is transiting this earth sign. It is tenacious, methodical and known to be a hard worker; this too is the nature of Capricorn.

What adds an even greater emphasis on hard work, responsibility and tenacity is the fact that the sign of Capricorn is ruled by the planet Saturn. Saturn, also known in Greek mythology as Cronos, is the Old God of Father Time. He is the authoritative energy of the patriarch; the sometimes oppressive systems put in place, to rule. He is restrictions and the obligations we must all, at some point or another, carry forward to fulfill our destiny.

When the moon is in Capricorn you can best employ this energy by considering where you might need more structure, discipline and hard work to attain a goal. This lunation makes it ideal for anything related to job searches, career advancement and meeting personal obligations. It can also help with issues related to discipline and strategizing each carved out step that can potentially bring you closer to your dreams. In the same way the Mountain Goat, very stubbornly and judiciously, charts out each step it will take to get to the top of the mountain, we too can follow its example.

The energy of the Moon in Capricorn can help awaken us to the best roadmap for success, discipline, maturity and eventually mastery of our craft. Capricorn Moon can help us unearth our determination to manifest our goals; especially as they relate to career goals and prosperity building.

> *"Opportunity is missed by most
> people because it is dressed
> in overalls and looks like work..."*
> *Thomas Edison*

HERSTORY

She found herself unexpectedly out of a job and she knew time was of essence. No one was going to rescue her now from this predicament and she needed to make money fast. Bills were piling up; demands on her time and energy were escalating. She was solely responsible for getting herself out of this mess. Her livelihood was dependent on her level of ambition now. It was time for her to roll up her sleeves and take her career goals and aspirations more seriously. She had procrastinated long enough and now it was time to commit to her career goals if she was ever going to change her financial situation.

**Take a moment to document here, or in your journal, your unique story.

_____
_____
_____
_____
_____
_____
_____

AFFIRMATION

**My sovereignty is born
out of my determination to work.
I become queen of my domain
the moment I roll up my sleeves.**

I work

**My skills & talents magnetize
the ideal work/career**

CHAKRA & GEMSTONE WORK

1st Chakra　　　　**MULADHARA/ROOT CHAKRA**　　**COLOR** Red/Black/Burgundy

Security, physical existence, stability, the self, earth grounding, home, basic human needs, sexuality, it is considered the sex chakra for men.

Mantra: I Am Primal/I Am Rooted

)O(WORKING: Totem Work, Protective Work, Home and Family Roots, Grounding, Kundalini, Fear Security issues

GEMSTONE CONNECTION: Bloodstone is a type of opaque, green colored, quartz. It is known also as Heliotrope. It is dark green with tiny flecks of red, which symbolizes blood, hence the name. There are some gem folklores connecting it to the crucifixion and the blood that possibly splattered on the ground to create this stone. It is clear from this tale alone; the stone is highly linked with blood, vitality and life-force. Most gemstone literature asserts that Bloodstone is a known blood purifier and was believed to detoxify the spleen, liver and kidneys. It was also beneficial to other parts of the body like the heart and the reproductive system. Healers use it to remove energy blocks and treat different types of blood disorders. Bloodstone is best known for its gift of strength and increasing courage to its wearer. In ancient times it was believed to be a powerful, protective stone that removed all obstacles and kept its wearer safe, thus it could always be found on the breastplates of warriors before going into battle. In ancient Egypt, Bloodstone was used for tumors and abnormal growths and it was believed to bring blessings of auspicious strength. Soldier believed it could help stop bleeding and stimulate fearlessness, thus, it became known as, *"The Hero's Stone."* Bloodstone is a grounding stone that balances our root chakra, with an affinity to the element of earth. It is reputed to bring abundance and success to its wearer and was known to strengthen all relations. Today it can also be used to help build successful enterprises, invite more prosperity into our life, and help us conquer all fears of the unknown.

Smokey Quartz is a highly protective stone that transmutes negative energy; it is a type of crystal quartz that can be found in different shades of translucent brown and greys, possibly due to carbon, iron, titanium impurities or decaying radium within the crystal itself. Smokey Quartz is therefore a good stone for those exposed to radiation or chemotherapy treatment. Traditionally it was a stone used for scrying, crystal gazing and the psychic arts. Connected to the root chakra, it has the capacity to bring wisdom and financial success. It helps you balance and prioritize things in your life to reach your most cherished personal or career goals. It also encourages inner strength, stamina and courage. It is considered a highly protective stone that acts as a physical and psychic shield. It enhances organizational skills and our receptiveness to acquire new knowledge. Placed around a workplace or home, it can foster cooperative feelings from the group and neutralize the energy. This grounding stone is linked with the astrological signs of Capricorn and Sagittarius and it is known to help with insomnia, hyperactivity, depression, stress, jealousy and anger. Smokey Quartz is used to cleanse auras and has the unique ability to connect us with prophetic sounds, including telepathic resonances. It is also reputed to connect one with the sacred reverberations of the Universe.

GEMSTONE CHANNELING

     As part of our work today, you are asked to find a safe place where you will not be disturbed for a few minutes. Life in our modern era is rife with so many distractions, demands and incessant clatter that a few moments of silence seem nearly impossible to attain. However, the effort put forth to carve out this almost illusive yet prized period, becomes even more valuable in our hectic lives. You are asked to find a comfortable place where you can be assured your privacy, safety and comfort... If you can go outdoors in nature that would be most ideal but any place where you can fully relax would be fine.

     Place yourself in a comfortable meditation position; you may sit or lay down. If it is available to you, place in your hands the Bloodstone gemstone or the Smokey Quartz Crystal that we are working with today. Take a moment to actually look at your gemstone. Whether you are holding a Bloodstone or a Smokey Quartz you want to now look deeply at its form and begin connecting with its energy. (Pause)Take a deep look at the different hues and patterns found within your gemstones. Bloodstone is a green stone yet if you look closer you might find lots of little specks of red. Smokey Quartz can possess numerous inclusions and reveal all sorts of interesting patterns when we scry into it. Take this moment to fully examine your crystal or gemstone. (Pause) Hold your Smokey Quartz crystal or your Bloodstone and silently study it carefully for a few more minute... While gazing upon it, make note of any thoughts that immediately start to unfold before you.

     When you are ready, you may close your eyes now and begin this short meditation. As with all trance work, we begin with our breath. You are asked now to take a deep breath; slowly filling your lungs up and then releasing the breath. With your next inhalation, breathe in the energy of your gemstone. (Pause)Take a breath and hold it for 3 seconds, then release it... Counting now at your own pace; breathe, 1, 2, 3, and exhale on 4....and again....breathe in, 1, 2, 3, and exhale on 4. Let's do this one more time and then quietly counting in your head.... Breathe 1, 2, 3...release on 4. Breathe, trusting in the natural rhythm you have now established, of your relaxed inhalation and exhalation.

     Your Smokey Quartz Crystal or Bloodstone wishes to impart a special channeled message just for you. You are invited now to view this gemstone in your mind's eye. See it shining brightly, embedded upon its dark, fertile, mother earth. Draw nearer to it and ask if it will allow you to pick it up. When permission is granted, gently gather it in your hands. With your mind's eye, look at it; studying its color, its texture, its inclusions or any other specific details that captures your eyes.... Ask it to speak to you. (Pause)

     Now with your next breath, visualize the top of your head, as it opens. Let it become almost like a chamber; open, ready and receptive to receive any spiritual data that draws near. You may envision your crown chakra now revealing a Smokey Quartz Crystal or a Bloodstone magnetic portal, allowing for this **Crystal Transmission** to come through... Continue to breathe and let the potent energy of your gemstone travel from your crown chakra all the way down to your Root chakra now. Let it nourish, energize and serve your Root Chakra in the best way possible. (Pause) You are welcomed to stay connected to this process for as long as you'd like.

     When you feel you are ready, open your eyes and be prepared to document your meditation experience. You may write them down here, or any other place you wish to write them.

_____
_____
_____

HORSE PROTECTION ENERGY

As we delve deeper into our transformative journey, we encounter now one of the most significant animals to exemplify our theme of work. By far one of the biggest contributors to humanities' evolution and advancement has been the horse. Consider that prior to the use of horses, people were stuck in their birth place or resigned to either, taking long journeys by foot or by water. The horse, across all cultures, is highly respected and well regarded for literally advancing civilization. It allowed for travel and thus, discovery of new terrains, new cultures and a new way of life. It expanded our world exponentially and radicalized our former primitive way of living. Our land could be tilled easier with Horses, as they were easily domesticated, and it had a positive effect on our agricultural advancement. Horses allowed for transporting items and it inaugurated commerce. They were so valuable, that horses were eventually seen as currency. Their very existence in our household was just as treasured as another member in our family or our workforce. Horses, as you can see, have always been a trustworthy, welcomed ally to humanity. For our spiritual work here, they continue to be an ally and protector.

When we think about it, horse energy becomes almost compulsory to explore our potential industrious nature. Throughout the ages, Horses have tirelessly helped us, humans, by carrying our burdens and even fighting our wars. They are known for their great speed, stamina, strength, devotion and their cooperative spirit. They are deeply loved by their owners' today, as they have been since the beginning of time. They are freedom lovers but also work well within the herd to help advance their owners' lot. Horses are adventuresome, extremely tenacious and hardworking. Ever heard the saying, *"they are working him like a horse...?"* Horses are known to get things done and their spirit can be relentless once they have a goal set in motion. Horse energy therefore, is invaluable for overcoming obstacles. It can help us better direct our energy. As a powerful, protective, spirit guide, they can help us with all types of travels; physical or spiritual.

Shamans believed the horse to be a Spirit guide that could travel through different realms; helping the soul travel from life to death. The Horse therefore can be used for astral travels and other shamanic spiritual journeys. For Native Americans, horses were connected to the element of air, due to the fact that riding a horse speedily, literally felt like you were flying in the air. The introduction of horses to Native Americans was reputed to have come from the Spaniards, when they first came to this new land.

Horses have long been associated with various deities in numerous cultures; like the Norse God, Odin and the Greek Goddess of the Hunt, Artemis. The Middle Eastern Goddess, Anahit, rode a chariot of Horses and the Greek Sun God, Apollo, was also depicted riding a chariot of horses. Kwan Yin, the Buddhist Goddess of Compassion, was sometimes symbolized as a white horse, as was the Welsh Goddess, Rhiannon. The Hindu deity, Vishnu, was purported to one day incarnate as a white horse and in India, the Sun God, Surya, was also connected with horses. Roman and Celtic myths connected the horse with the Goddesses; Epona, Macha, Edain and Rigatonia.

For those of us who work with Horse energy, we value them as an excellent ally to travel through different realms with because of their swift movement. Horse energy is often associated with the element of air but also with the element of the earth, as it is solely responsible for advancing our agrarian society. Horse energy connects us to the gifts of faithfulness, loyalty and trustworthiness. It is an industrious, hard-working energy that can be harnessed to help us grow and prosper in our personal lives. It can help us unearth the physical prowess and powerful energy to get things done and that's exactly what we need, as we explore this particular theme in this chapter. Horse medicine helps us attract the right friends and group alliances. It is considered both solar and lunar and it represents completed life cycles; birth death and rebirth. Horse has always been an ally; unconditionally offering itself in service to humanity's prosperous growth. Among the numerous attributes it offers, it will awaken the spirit of servitude, devotion and hard work. Many may not know that Horses are herbivores and they are recognized for their physical prowess and their immeasurable energy. Their personality tends to be compassionate, forgiving, kind-hearted, and socially oriented. It should go without saying; the Horse has incredible stamina. As a matter of fact, with their natural stamina and their need for little sleep, they are representative of the hard workers and an example for us to follow as we endeavor to pursue our own work goals.

THEME WORK SUGGESTIONS
Work with the Capricorn moon, symbolized by the Goat, and work with The Horse energy and the Goddesses shown in this chapter.
Perform a Money Spell.
Create an Herbal Green packets (recipe offered in this chapter).

GODDESS EMPOWERMENT

ATHENA

The Greek, Maiden Goddess of Wisdom, intellect and war-craft was often referred to as Grey-eyed Athena in the writings of her time. She was described as bright eye, wide eye and often depicted with her totem animal, the Owl. The Owl is a perfect representation of her wisdom and this common reference to her piercing eyes. Athena was reminiscent of the Goddesses found in ancient Minoan and Mycenaean Culture, in that these earlier deities had snakes as their sacred symbols and were regarded as protectors of cities and palaces - the way Athena was regarded as the protector of the city of Athens. On the Acropolis, the olive tree was considered Athena herself because of its ability to recover quickly from any damages and thus it was seen as a perfect symbol for this resilient Goddess. Athenians believed their Greek Goddess also took the form of her many sacred totem animals; the snake, birds and the revered owl. The more we learn of this Greek beloved Goddess, the more we see her correlation to ancient deities and how her existence and her worship goes back a lot further than originally believed.

According to Greek mythology (most of it written by men) Athena was born parthenogenesis, out of Zeus' head. As the well-known Greek mythology reveals, Zeus had been suffering from a horrible headache for days. He called on Hephaestus, the Smith God, to split his head open hoping to attain some relief from the pain. When Zeus' head was cut open, out sprang Athena. She was born fully armored, with her spear, and shield, a popular depiction of this Goddess that has survived throughout the ages. Important to note that she was born not as a child, but already as a full grown woman, ready for battle.

Athena's Mother was an ocean deity, the Goddess Metis. Not much is known or written about her mother for most literature connects Athena primarily with her father. We do know that Metis was the first consort of Zeus. We also know that she herself was the Goddess of wisdom and intelligence because her name translates as such. As can be surmised, Athena's own wisdom and great intelligence can be attributed to being born from Zeus' head but most importantly, her gifts should be attributed to having the lineage of a mother who was known as the Goddess of intelligence and wisdom. It is important to note that her intellect was not of the mystical kind. Athena was not about other-worldly wisdom or esoteric, spiritual knowledge. She was pragmatic and cherished practical, useful knowledge, cultural and historical knowledge. She was also a lover of all skills and art forms. In the myths of her time, we also learn of her impressive skills in handiworks, dressmaking, embroidery, pottery and needlecrafts among her many skills and gifts bestowed to her devotees.

In her mythologies we learn that Zeus, after being warned by oracle seer, feared that an offspring with the Goddess Metis would produce a child more powerful than himself. He tried to remedy this situation by swallowing Metis whole. However, she was already pregnant with their child. Athena thus, continued to grow and live on (now) inside of her father, Zeus. A headache soon began to overtake Zeus and when his head was cut open, out came the strong and wise Athena. Zeus fell instantly in love with his daughter and throughout literature we also see her great devotion to her father.

Athena is the beloved Goddess of the Greek city of Athens. There, she is the personification of civic law. The story of how she came to be the patron Goddess for Athens reflects her popularity and early examples of democracy. Athenians had to participate in a democratic vote to decide who would be the patron God/Goddess for the city. The choices were the God of the Sea -Poseidon or Athena, the Goddess of Wisdom and War-craft. When the ballots were counted, they discovered that all the male citizens voted for the male God, Poseidon and all the female votes were given to Athena. Because there were more female citizens at the time in Athens, Athena was the natural winner. As can be expected, the men of Athens did not like this turn of events and displayed much resistance. As a result, they imposed a series of new laws that would need to be implemented, if they were to accept a Female Deity as leader of their beloved City. The most significant new laws that manifested from this election was the replacement of matriarchal lineage by the patriarch. It meant that a child would now carry on the father's last name, instead of the traditional mother's name, according to the writings of this time.

Eventually Athena was fully embraced as the patron Goddess of Athens by both, men and women.

This beloved Greek Goddess also has an ancestral connection to her people through the first King of Athens -Erichthonius. This myth is very similar to the Sun Goddess, Amaterasu and the first Imperial family of Japan. According to one myth, Athena was seduced by Hephaestus. As a virgin deity, she refused him, but interestingly enough, Hephaestus' semen falls upon her thigh. In total disgust, she takes a rag and wipes it off. She throw the rag upon the Earth and from this action a child is produced. The Earth (Gaia) then gives birth to a child, which Athena then nurtures and raises as her own. In this story we see the preservation of her status as Virgin Goddess, adopted mother and teacher. She names the boy, Erichthonius and teaches him everything, including the worship of Gods. In him she creates one of Athens' first leaders. Erichthonius fulfills her vision for Athens and succeeds in establishing civic law and governmental structure and thus Athena is directly responsible for Athens' growth and civilization as a prosperous city. There is also a direct connection between the Goddess and her ruling class descendants. Today, a trip to modern day Greece will reveal Athena is still honored and revered in her famous temple - the Parthenon, in Athens, Greece. Images of her are sold in every neighboring Greek tourist kiosk surrounding the still commanding nearby ruins and the Parthenon is an amazing site to behold.

As a Virgin deity she was never married, nor did she ever actually give birth to a child. According to Jean Shinoda Bolen, M.D. in her book *"Goddess in Everywoman, A New Psychology of Women,"* Athena perhaps refused to be linked romantically with a man for fear this would restrict her active participation and involvement with politics, war and her public life image. However, unlike other Virgin Goddesses, she does not appear to have any animosity towards the opposite sex. Quite the contrary, she seems to have great love and adoration for men and clearly uplifts, inspires and supports numerous men throughout Greek mythology. She was born from her father and clearly had a strong bond solely with him. Throughout Greek mythology she is always surrounded by various men and sometimes even disguises herself as one. She appears to be a defender and cheerleader of men in her efforts to empower them for battles. She does not express any romantic feelings, nor sexual liaisons with men for fear it would demean her or make her seem subordinate to men. In the writings of her time, she appears to enjoy competition with men and her virginity strictly assures her independence and her status as their equal. She is almost unapproachable sexually by men and her virginity and chastity, maintain her platonic camaraderie relations with men. Reckless emotions left one vulnerable in times of war and thus she was an advocate of moderating ones' emotions... something quite difficult to do in the throes of a passionate love affair.

Athena was most concerned with order, socialization, culture and institutions - Marriages falls under this category. Though she herself never married and while she was not an advocate for romantic or sexual unions, she was a promoter and protector of marriages. Marriages are social institutions and promote a valued structure and order in society, according to her specific ideologies. Athena is not a Goddess to be called upon for fertility or child birthing skills, as she never actually gave birth to a child, nor does she appear to concern herself with these things. Learning of her connection to Erichthonius, we can surmise her attributes regarding children. With children, she is more concern with their education and their socialization as future citizens and leaders of her beloved city.

As a Goddess of War-craft, she was a prudent Commander and had the gift of strategizing war. She was responsible for the skills and the weapons of war in ancient times.

Athena is about courage and inspiring that courage in Heroes and their companions on the battlefield. She encourages willingness, intelligence, and control of emotions, boldness and a will to victory. Athena was known for her cunningness and her ability to use words and her intellect in battles and debates. She was more about calm emotions, restraint, clear thinking, and not resorting to brute violence. Mindless killings did not appeal to her. This Goddess was not an advocate of killings just for the sake of the sport. In contrast to the other Gods of war, like Ares, who fights in an emotional frenzy and fury, Athena's approach to war in battle fields was calm, methodical and controlled and she always tempered her emotions. She despised anything crude, wild, barbaric, uncivilized. This Virgin Goddess does not use Aphrodite's physical, sexual charms to win, nor does she use the violent, brute force like Ares. She uses intellect to win all her battles. For Athena, war is more than just a battle of strength; it is part of what's necessary to attain specific goal or higher ideals. She was defender of social order and the prosperity of civilization. Anything that deviated from these ideals inspired her to battle. She represents rational, practicalities, democracy, and administration of justice, rhetoric and the art of persuasion. Athena is the personification of a cultured society and she was victorious in wars because of these honorable attributes.

*Greek Goddess of wisdom, skills, war-craft and intelligence. She is the embodiment of a strong mind, tempered heart and fierce leadership. She inspires greatness in all your undertakings and blesses all hand crafted projects. She is the teacher and awakens in you a drive for excellence and competence. If magick is to be defined as, changing consciousness at will, then indeed aligning our mind with our will makes perfect sense, and Athena would be a great catalyst for this procedure. All things we wish to bring to fruition must first begin with a thought, an initial vision, a plan, and the engagement of the mind, this is Athena's realm. She comes into your life now to teach you that wishes and goals are best met, first and foremost in our initial imagining and strategizing. She beckons you to tap into the power of your mind; plan, strategize, organize to achieve your goals, for this can be much stronger than sheer brute force.

GEFJUN

Also known as; Gefyun, Gefyon, Gefn, Gefiun, Gefion, Gefjun, is an ancient agricultural Norse Goddess of Prosperity, Fertility, Magick, Wellbeing and Protection. She was beloved to the Norse-Germanic people as a Goddess of field ploughing, and connected to manifesting the Danish Island of Zealand. Known as, "The Generous one," her name is associated with the verb, "*gefa*" which means to give. It is therefore indicative of her connection to abundance and generosity.

Our knowledge of this beloved ancient deity comes from the writings of the 13th century acclaimed historian, Snorri Sturluson. He shares a story in his writings about a woman that comes before the King, Gylfi, in Sweeden asking for land. Not suspecting her gifts and unaware of her Goddess status, the charitable king offers her, *"as much land as 4 oxen can plough in one day…"* Well, Gefjun invokes her four sons, which were fathered by a giant and she turns them into these four strong oxen. With their help, she successfully ploughs the land in one day and manages to connect the terrains and forms the Danish Island of Zealand. Today this land is known as Copenhagen.

FORTUNA

Fortuna is the Roman Goddess of Good Fortune. Her name mean, "*she who brings…*" Her role is therefore that of one who brings to us prosperity and abundance. As a Goddess of the Abundance, she is often portrayed holding an overflowing cornucopia. She rules over our fates and good fortune.

BENTEN/BENZAITEN

Benten is the Japanese, Shinto Goddess of Good Fortune and Prosperity, one of the few Japanese Goddesses connected to Prosperity. She is connected to white serpents and is often depicted riding a serpent or a dragon. In Japan, Benten is also known as Queen of the Sea and many portrayals of this Goddess reveal her connection to the element of water. It is interesting to note that there is also a strong similarity to the Hindu Goddess Saraswati, as both are often portrayed playing a stringed instrument; Benten plays the "*biwa.*"

TYCHE

Tyche is the ancient Greek Goddess of Good Fortune, Fate and Prosperity. She is worshipped in this aspect as the Goddess, Eutychia. Her name translates as "luck," "chance" or "fortune."

She is often depicted, just like her Roman counterpart, Fortuna, holding a cornucopia. However, in some statuary depictions she is seen wearing a crown made up of the walls of a city, to denote her connection to a city's success. Sometimes she is portrayed with a blindfold over her eyes to indicate her title as the blind Mistress of Fortune, and the unpredictable nature of blind fate, blind justice, and blind luck and the game of chance. Some mediaeval art shows her with wings, holding a ship rudder (often two) or a ball to signify the up and down unpredictability of fortune. She is illustrated with a Wheel of Fortune, indicative of her powers over our changeable fate. It's important to know she also appears on many Hellenistic coins that existed before the Christian era. These coins attest to her prominence as a Goddess of good fortune.

Tyche had many known Temples in Constantinople, Alexandria, and Maritima to name just a few. In Crete, she was highly venerated at Itanos.

She is mentioned in numerous writings of the time, including, Hesiod's works. He noted that she was the daughter of the Titans; Oceanus and Tethys. This genealogy was later disputed, connecting her with Zeus. According to other Greek mythology she is daughter of Aphrodite and Hermes, making the Goddess of Good Fortune the result of unifying love and intellect.

SRI LAKSHMI

The name Lakshmi in the Hindu language denotes "Good luck." In Sanskrit text it comes from the word, "Laksya" which loosely means "a goal" or "an aim." In yet another text, the name Lakshmi has been interpreted to mean; a sign, an omen (good or bad). The first part of her name, "Lakh" means, a "hundred thousand," that is to say, a multitude and this supports the understanding that Lakshmi is a Goddess who bestows abundance, a multitude of blessings and prosperity.

Lakshmi or Sri Lakshmi, as she is best known in later Vedict text, is the Hindu Goddess of wealth, well-being and prosperity. Known by over one hundred eight different names, she is the radiant, golden one. She is known as Padma, Kamala in this role as the beautiful one who bestows riches, great fame and beauty. She is also the embodiment of the ideal wife in Hindu culture, as she exemplifies; chastity, truth and righteousness.

It is believed that Sri Lakshmi is actually the amalgamation of two Goddesses, for in the early Hindu sacred text we learn only of the Goddess Sri and this name, later in the Vedas, becomes appended to the name Lakshmi, evolving to Sri Lakshmi. These two respective Hindu deities hold numerous identical attributes that makes it nearly impossible to separate the two. To get a clearer insight into who we worship today as Lakshmi, it helps us to begin, by first taking a closer look and researching further this earlier version or aspect of her.

Scholars note that we don't even begin to see the name Sri Lakshmi in early Vedic text but we do find the isolated name Sri. Later, during the Upanishad period, we begin to unearth the acknowledgement and amalgamation of Sri Lakshmi as the supreme Hindu Goddess of wealth.

Sri is possibly a Pre-Vedic fertility Goddess possessing many of the same attributes as Lakshmi. A bringer of wealth, fortune, fertility, power and beauty, she was sought after by many, including those pursuing positions within royalty. According to author Carl Olson in his book, *"The Book of the Goddess, Past and Present,"* Sri might have been a pre-Aryan Goddess and possibly considered a Yakshinis, which were the feminine aspect of the Yakshas. Yakshas were semi-divine chthonic spirits and known to be guardians of wealth. In particular, Yakshinis, as feminine spirits, were guardians of the root of trees, as one can surmise the roots of trees and its overall good health and wellbeing, determine the potentiality for fruits, sustenance and richness upon the land and its inhabitants. It is the source for humanities nurturance and prosperity and a logical place for these beloved prosperity spirits to tend to. Yakshas were also known to be shape-shifters and they were attendants to another great, well known Hindu deity of wealth, Kubera. Interesting to note, much like Lakshmi, the Yakshinis were often linked with the waters of life.

"I invoke Sri Lakshmi who has a line of horses in her front, a series of chariots in the middle, who is being awakened by the trumpeting elephants, who is divinely resplendent. May that divine Lakshmi grace me. I hereby invoke Sri Lakshmi who is embodiment of absolute bliss; Lakshmi who is of pleasant smile on her face; whose luster is that of burnished gold; who is wet as it were, (just from the milky ocean) who is blazing with splendor and is the embodiment of the fulfillment of all wishes; who satisfied the desire of her votaries; who is seated on the Lotus and is beautiful like the Lotus..." *(a excerpt from the Hymn to Sri in the Sri Sukta)*

More can be learned of Lakshmi through Sri when we look at early Hindu text. There is an appendix to the later Rig Veda text, which is the Sri-Sukuta hymn of praise to Sri. She is considered bountiful, giver of fame; abundance, gold, cattle, horses, food, prosperity and riches of all kinds. And she is said to eradicate her sister, Alakshmi, who is bringer of misfortune. Sri is described as radiant as gold, illustrious as the moon and wearer of both gold and silver necklaces. She is depicted as shinning like the sun; like fire, which is a most sacred, divine element for Hindu Spirituality. The Hymn of the Sri-Sukuta which pre-dates Buddhism, reveals her powers of fertility in the description of her scented moistness and as dwelling (as described) amidst cow dung and bringing an abundant harvest, for she was also associated with the plentitude of grains and rice. She is even attributed for having a son called, Kardama and this name translates as; mud, mire, slime. This links her closely to the rich soil of the dark, moist earth. Ancient worshippers of Sri Lakshmi are known to even anoint their foreheads with cow dung as well, during the Nilamata Purana festival. Another example of her fertile, moist attribute can be found in the Pancaratra text. There is a Lakshmi tantra in the Pancaratra, in which she is quoted saying, *"Like the fat that keeps a lamp burning, I lubricate the senses of living beings, with my own sap of consciousness (50:110)"*

In the Mahabhrarata (300 B.C.E. and 300 C.E.), Sri Lakshmi is considered the daughter of Brahma, though the God Brahma is often associated with another great Hindu Matriarch, the Goddess Saraswati. In one tale she has two brothers; Dhatr and Vidhatr and she is one of ten daughters of Daksha. In this particular myth she is given in marriage to the God, Dharma. Later, Sri Lakshmi becomes associated with the special attribute of Dharma (righteousness) as one of her many aspects and names.

In the Vaishnava texts, of the late fifth to sixth century C.E., Sri Lakshmi appears as the creative power of the God, Vishnu and she is the prakriti (life force) of the Universe itself.

In the Mahabhrarata, it is stated that she is born out of the sacred golden lotus that came forth from the brow or forehead of the God Vishnu, the preserver. And here again we have what appears to be a common tenet in Hindu mythology, that of the Goddess being both bride and daughter, much like Saraswati is considered daughter and bride to the God, Brahma. It wasn't until late 400 C.E. that we see a consistent connection to Sri Lakshmi and her steadfastness devotion and inseparability to the God Vishnu, whom she lives with in Vai Kuntha.

Some of Sri Lakshmi's symbols are the lotus, pouring water, vessels, gold, the owl, elephants and the colors; pink, dark gold, yellow, white. Sometimes she appears as golden as the sun or as yellow as the corn, which was an important food stable for Hindus. She might appear glowing white as a symbol of purity, the moon, the milky waters she is born from and her Divine righteousness. In her aspect as the dutiful loving wife she would appear in pink and rose hues. In the Mahabharata she is shown as wearing white robes and white clothing, emerging from the churning white, milky sea. When she is shown with her four hands she is holding;
1. Padma,
2. Sankha,
3. Amrtakalasa,
4. Bilva, a Fruit or a more citrusy fruit, Mahalinga.

When Sri Lakshmi is shown with eight hands it is a reference to the supreme Hindu Mother Goddess, Durga. In this aspect, she usually holds in her hands; a discus, mace, bow and arrow and the additional attributes of;
5. Dharma –righteousness,
6. Artha –wealth,
7. Kama- pleasure of flesh,
8. Moksa –beautitude.

One popular image of Sri Lakshmi is of her rising from a vessel, or also, rising from a lotus flower that is in a vessel. Like the Japanese Sun Goddess, Amatersu's association with the mirror, Lakshmi is distinctly linked with vessels. They are known for their receptacle, womblike quality, succinctly resembling the Yoni and their feminine qualities of containment, openness and universal receptivity. The Goddess of wealth is the ultimate sacred vessel and the Divine cornucopia; with its food association of nurturance and its open shape, it is a perfect example of her many gifts and relevance to women.

The Lotus is an extremely powerful ancient symbol in Hindu mythology. Often Sri Lakshmi is shown holding a lotus in each hand or sometimes holding her sacred fruit, the Bilva. The Bilva, much like the pomegranate, was a citrusy, sometimes bitter fruit associated with longevity and the removal of illusion (Maya) and misfortune. Lakshmi was known as, Mahamaya, as the Goddess who removed illusions and blessed women's womb.

According to the Brihadharma Purana, Lakshmi in her devout worship offered one thousand lotuses to the God Shiva daily. When one day she noticed she was missing one, she quickly offered, in its place, her breast and this was transformed into the sacred Bilva fruit.

Lakshmi is almost always adorned with lotus garlands and some text describes her adorned with gold and silver necklaces around her neck. Standing or sitting on a lotus, Lakshmi is often in yellow to represent her association with Gold, the sun and even the yellow nurturing corn. She was sometimes known as Gauri, linking her to these essential foods and grains in Hindu culture.

Another popular image of the Goddess Lakshmi can even be seen in the royal coinage of ancient times. One image found in the early coins of India, reveals Sri Lakshmi being showered by two elephants, one on her left and one on her right and these elephants are holding her sacred vessels, pouring or spraying her with water, as a sign of her fecundity. This popular image, known as Gaja Lakshmi, represents her fertilization gifts of wellbeing and earthly Goddess attributes.

There are eight known forms of Lakshmi and they are known as the Astamahalaksmi. Some of her most popular forms are mentioned below.

- Gaja Lakshmi -this most popular image of her found on door frames, and royal coinage, shows her seated on an eight petal lotus. She has four hands and a conch, framed by two elephants. They are shown pouring water over her.
- SamanyaLakshmi or Indra Laksmi, Here she is depicted with two hands in this role.
- Varalaksmi, holding two lotus in two hands and mudras in her other two hands she is known as Varalaksmi.

Other Sacred Names Sri Lakshmi is known by are;
1. Adi Lakshmi - here in this aspect known as Rama (bringer of happiness to humanity), and also known here as Indira (holder of lotus of purity) servant of the whole of creation via her consort. She resides with Lord Narayana/Vishnu in Vaikuntha. She is Shakti, energy and the source and power of Narayana.

2. Dhanya Lakshmi – Harvest aspect as Dhanya means grains. In this aspect she is the guarantor of good Harvest.
3. Dhairya Lakshmi – infinite Courage and strength are her gifts in this aspect. She grants patience and inner stability.
4. Gaja Lakshmi – daughter of the Ocean-a most common depiction of the Goddess being born from the churning ocean like the Greek Goddess Aphrodite. She is seated or standing from a Lotus flower, surrounded by two elephants on either side of her pouring water on her, from her sacred vessels. This most popular aspect of Lakshmi is even captured in the coinage of the time and can even be seen on entryways carvings and temples.
5. Santan Lakshmi -children and family blessings, in this aspect she blesses your family with many desirable healthy children and long life.
6. Vijay Lakshmi – Vijay is Victory and in this aspect Lakshmi presents the victory in all areas of your life.
7. Dhana Lakshmi – Dhana means wealth. In this aspect she imparts wealth in its numerous guises; love, health, intellect, prosperity, food, land etc…
8. Vidya Lakshmi - Vidya means education, thus in this aspect she imparts the numerous blessing that come from education including but not limited to sincerity, equanimity, adaptability, tenacity, generosity, purity, humility etc..

MORE OF HER SACRED SYMBOLS

Sri Lakshmi has a strong association with elephants, who are also sacred to the remover of obstacles, the God Ganesh. It makes sense that a Goddess so attached to the manifestation of prosperity would also be linked to the elephant God who removes obstacles and thus, elephants would play an important part in her own mythologies.

Long ago, it was believed that elephants had wings, and lived in the sky. Ancient Hindu mythology reveals that elephants were the clouds themselves, regulating rain showers upon the earth. The elephants lost their flying privileges and cloud connection when, according to one Hindu folklore, a Sage, one day, meditating under a tree was disrupted by the fall of one elephant. He cursed all elephants as a result, stripping them all of their wings and flying capabilities. Today, they still retain their great value to the Hindu culture, as we see them so often incorporated in marriage nuptials and other important Hindu ceremonies.

In ancient times, elephants were extremely important to Hindu Culture, as war artillery. They were considered weapons in wars, as valuable vehicles for the King to ride and as a sacred symbol of Royalty. The King always owned several of them and, as royalty, he was only fit to ride on the massive regal looking, elephants. Even the Rajasuya, a royal consecration ceremony, involved the abhisekha ritual in which the king would be blessed with the pouring waters from elephants to validate his Divine rights. This royal ritual mimicked the popular image of the Goddess herself being divinely showered by the elephant's pouring waters in the Gaja Lakshmi portrayals.

> *"There is a Goddess who possesses eyes like a Lotus flower (Padma, Kamala), her thighs are like the Lotus, she possesses a Lotus face and her skin is the color of the lotus. She dwells in this aquatic flower, sometimes envisioned as standing erect on the lotus and often holding the lovely flower in her hands. Once upon a time she was born from the lotus, her ears delighting to the trumpeting sounds of elephants...."*
>
> "The Book of the Goddess, Past and Present" by Carl Olsom, Chapt 10 page 125.

The Lotus is an aquatic, sacred flower born and rooted in the muddy waters, yet miraculously able to blossom and shine in its exquisite beauty, uncontaminated by the mud. It is one of the most recognized, venerated symbols of transcendence for Hindu and Buddhists, as it connotes spiritual authority. In this flower's wholeness and its ability to hold, nurture and water its own seeds, there is a divine reflection of the Universe itself and this links it to the Gods of the Hindu pantheon. We see the Lotus associated with many other deities, like Saraswati. It is also shown growing from Vishnu's navel as well as his forehead, where it is believed to have birthed the Goddess Lakshmi herself. Thus, the symbols of Divine source, purity, spiritual authority and the nectar of all creations, is represented in the Goddess Lakshmi through the Lotus flower.

Of all the creatures to be associated with the Goddess Lakshmi, it seems, at first glance, odd that the Owl would be one of them. The Owl, however, has often been associated with various deities from different pantheons; like the Greek Goddess of Wisdom, Athena, the Sumerian ancient Goddess, Lilith and the Welsh Flower-born Goddess, Blodeuwedd. The Owl is a sacred symbol of wisdom and divine insight and in Hindu mythology it is depicted as Lakshmi's vehicle. Known as an Uluka, in the Hindu language, the owl was also another name for Indra, the King of the Gods. One can only surmise that Lakshmi ridding an owl, or the King of the Gods, is a reference to her powers over anything connected with Kings and royalty. It is Sri Lakshmi who can bestow fame and fortune, fertility, longevity and success and thus, her blessings are sought after by all, especially those seeking sovereignty.

ROYALTY & COINAGE

We first see images of Sri Lakshmi appearing in coins during the Gupta Dynasty (320-540 C.E.) During the Samudragupta (ca.335-376), her image in the coinage is now seen on a throne with a lotus to hold her divine feet. And in the Chandragupta II (ca. 376-415) period we begin to see the King now portrayed on the opposite side of the coin holding a lotus in his hand, while Sri Lakshmi's image, an exact pose with the lotus, is revealed in support of the king, on the other side of the coin. By the Skandagupta period (ca. 454-467) Lakshmi is shown on the same side of the coin, standing right next to the King, who is holding a bowl. This is remarkable evidence of the King's Divine right to rule and Lakshmi's blessings on his kingdom. It was believed that only through her blessings of wealth, fame, longevity and wellbeing, could any King rule with much success and thus it is Lakshmi who blesses and ordains sovereignty. Sri was so valuable to a King that it was considered the actual cushion which the King must sit upon, for she bestowed not only prosperity and success but also physical health, longevity, beauty, and special blessings to the ruling Kingdom.

HER BIRTH

The Hindu Holy book of Srimad Bhaganata tells the story of Lakshmi's birth, known as Samudra Manthan. According to this sacred text, one day there was a battle between Demons and the Devas (minor Gods), and they both wanted the nectar of immortality, also known as Amrit. *(This story already sounds familiar, reminding me of the Norse tales of the Goddess, Idunna and the Apple of immortality for the Gods of Asgard, but I digress…..)* Desperate, the Devas consulted the God, Vishnu, who was now in the form of Kurma, the wise tortoise. Vishnu instructed them to churn the ocean floor; churn it and while they churned, the wise tortoise would endeavor to maintained and hold up the mount of Mandara on his back. Thus the Devas churned the ocean into a frothy milk and there unearthed Amrit, the Elixir of immortality, in the birth of Sri Lakshmi herself. Then as she appeared, Sri Lakshmi elected to reside in Vishnu's chest, his heart, making this her beloved dwelling place.

HER CONSORT

Most of Hindu mythology connects Sri Lakshmi to the God, Vishnu, also known as Narayana, among his numerous incarnations. She is inseparable from her consort and the sacred text of ancient times reveals that however Vishnu incarnates, Lakshmi is always there by his side; whether he appears as human or as creature; she too, almost always appears in a complimentary aspect to her consort. They have a relationship of supreme, tender love and for Hindus, an aspiring model of an ideal marriage. Lakshmi is viewed as the ideal dutiful wife, always tending to her partner's needs and comfort. She exemplifies devotion and self-surrendering to her husband and the embodiment of "Prema," an ideal love that rises above carnal desire. One common depiction of the Goddess by the feet of her reclining consort expresses their relationship best. In this image, Vishnu has one foot resting on the Divine Serpent, Sesha, and the other foot is upon his adoring dutiful wife, who appears to be massaging his foot, catering to his comfort.

Sri Lakshmi is held in high esteem as the model of a Hindu devoted wife, exemplifying chastity, beauty and controlled proper sexuality. Their marriage appears to be the personification of pure love, tenderness and profound fondness for one another, according to Hindu culture. The numerous depictions of the two together, gazing lovingly into each other's eyes, supports this conclusion, as well as the images of the two deities exchanging lower body parts, revealing their supreme unity.

Lakshmi is considered to be the energy or Shakti of Vishnu. Sometimes Vishnu is depicted with other wives like Sri and Pusti (prosperity) or Sri and Bhu (earth Goddess) but Sri Lakshmi herself always appears on his right side, denoting supremacy.

Interesting to note, when depicted with her husband, Sri Lakshmi only appears to have two arms, unlike the four arms she is typically attributed with, when depicted alone. She also sometimes appears diminutive in size compared to Vishnu and some believe this is yet another patriarchal representation of her subordination to her husband. I would like to think that perhaps with a loving strong spouse by her side the need for four hands becomes superfluous –maybe… or maybe her powers are so great that displaying them all at once on the table could threaten the patriarch, represented by the God Vishnu. Despite some of the interpretations of Hindu sacred text I've encountered, it is hard for me to view a Goddess, especially one of her great caliber, to be subordinate to anyone, let alone her mate but perhaps what we as humans interpret as lowly or subordination is really, in actuality, something effable and completely beyond our understanding in relation to ancient deities and spiritual beings.

She is known as the dispenser of grace. She grants all desires and salvation and she is the bestower of liberation. Lakshmi's worship has withstood the test of time. She is a Goddess still worshipped today much like in ancient times but it's important to note here her worship in relation to her consort, as she was widely worshipped both alone and in succinct connection to her husband. In the Maharashtra region of India, in the city of Pandharpur, there is a temple dedicated to the Divine Couple but interestingly enough, the shrine for Lakshmi is found in the Southern region of this temple, which, according to some Hindu scholars, was typically considered the region associated with dark, esoteric or demonic forces and the dead. Some might view this shrine's positioning, again, as a reflection of Lakshmi's subordination but remember, she was called upon to remove evil with her golden light, as well as to keep the dead at bay, so this placement makes perfect sense not as a place of subordination but as a critically compulsory and valuable for any temple.

As protecting powers of Vishnu, Lakshmi is known as;
- Sridevi- Goddess of wealth and fortune
- Bhudevi – earth representation
- Sridevi – again but as junior sort of consort Vishnu, symbol of sovereignty over the earth
- Saraswati- Mother of Learning
- Priti – Love personified
- Kriti and Santi – Fame and peace
- Tusti and Pusti – grants pleasure and strength
- When propitiated, she can dispel evil and bring prosperity –She eradicates Alaksmi, the opposite of Laksmi, a goddess of misfortune…

RELATING TO OTHER GODS

In some sacred text Sri Lakshmi is the wife of Dharma and her father is Daksa, the Virtuous conductor. Some other Hindu text reveals that she resided in Prahlada with the Demon God, Bali, when he succeeded in defeating the God Indra. And here we have a reflection of her attraction to the energy of Success and Victory, for she only draws near him due to his great achievement. Later on she withdraws from him when Vishnu intercedes on behalf of Indra to reclaim his power.

To the male rain God of Indra, who becomes the King of the Gods, she bestows Royal authority and powers. And there are images of the Goddess ridding Indra as an Owl. She appears and blesses the God Soma; Lord of plants, vegetation, associated with saps, when he performs a sacrifice in her honor. And as already mentioned, she is often associated with the God of Wealth, Kubera. Kubera is known as the Lord of Yakshas, the race of supernatural beings who dwell in uncivilized areas; like the wilderness and forest. They are guardians and distributors of wealth, and are linked with her early incarnation as the Goddess Sri. In Prajapati, it states that all the gods having witness Sri and her gifts of fortune, fame and prosperity, desired with all their heart to be blessed by her presence. The Gods, seeking the Elixir of Immortality, found it in her and thus, sought after her continuous blessings forever more, thereafter.

FESTIVALS

Lakshmi is a Goddess who has transcended all time as she is very much venerated today as in ages past. Her known month is October and coincidentally, her festival Dipavali (Diwali) is usually held in late autumn. Lakshmi's birth and wedding day are commemorated at this time, for three days, during Navarathri. And Friday is also a very special day for Lakshmi's celebrations. The Friday before the Full moon, of the month of Sraavan, is of great significance to her worship. Known as a festival of light, lamps are lit in her honor and there is merry making and lots of great celebratory noises to drive out any maladies or signs of her sister, Alaksmi. Merchants use this time to bless their financial documents, accounting logs and businesses plans. Sheep and goats are sacrificed and offered to the Goddess during some festival ceremonies and there is also cow dung veneration, for this is how the ancient sacred text depicts her; as the moist, fertileness of her sacred animal's dung. Her close associated with cows, due to their nurturing attributes, is very reminiscent of the Egyptian Divine Bovine, the Goddess Hathor.

Lakshmi Puja is celebrated, again, on the Full moon night of the Kojagari Purnima. At this time of the year, in late autumn, she is also called upon to keep the ghost of the dead away from the living. It is not surprising that this festival coincides with the ancient Pagan/Druid holiday of Samhain and the themes of the final harvest, surviving the darkness and the propitiating of the dead, as these are the prevalent theme at this time of year.

Kaumundi Purnima Festival -In this festival, women honor her in the mounds of seeds and grains and together they recollect the ancient tales, quite similar to the Greek Goddess Demeter, in which Lakshmi had temporarily disappeared from the Earth taking away her gifts of prosperity from the land. They pay homage to her gifts in the hopes of never experiencing her devastating withdrawal from the world.

Caitra-Gauri Festval -Held during the second month of spring. Here in this festival Lakshmi is celebrated for her vegetative attributes to the land.

Durga Puja-Here in this festival, Lakshmi is also celebrated as another aspect of the divine mother and in her agricultural association. She is supplicated to bring back the crops, make them abundant and fertile. This festival takes place at the Full-Moon following the Durga Puja.

Pujabi Festival-In this festival Lakshmi is exalted with gratitude for her fertile, womb blessings. Women celebrated her with colored cord representing each child they were able to conceive and offering these cords in gratitude to Sri Lakshmi's blessings.

There is also a festival in the **Summer** time that honors both Sri Lakshmi and Vishnu in their role as the ideal Divine couple. In this festival sometimes Vishnu is known to take on a second wife or he is believed to hibernate and fall asleep for a long period, either way, he will not be available to his beloved Lakshmi. At this time, worshippers call upon the Goddess and her gifts of steadfastness, loyalty, truthfulness, and strength within all relationships.

Gobardhan Puja - In this festival Lakshmi is celebrated as the fertile, prosperous giving mother and exalted as an incarnate Bovine.

The Goddess of abundance, beauty, royalty and prosperity is very much alive and worshipped today as she was in years past. She has transcended time and has remained a beloved immortal Hindu Goddess that speaks to our gender on the exclusively unique gifts of the Feminine Divine. She introduces yet another important aspect of the sacred feminine, one that is sought after by both men and women who seek to know success, victory, beauty and abundance.

SOME MANTRAS DEDICATED TO LAKSHMI AND MANIFESTING ABUNDANCE

1. *Om Shreem Mahalakshmiyei Namaha*
    Salutations to that heart centered and great Lakshmi....

2. Kubera Yantra, for the Banker of Heaven
Chant:
Om Brezee Namaha (108x)
**27, 20, 25
22, 24, 26
23, 28, 21**

3. *Om Brzee Namaha Dattatreya*

4. *Om Shreem brezee namaha*

5. *Om Shreem, Om Hreem, Shreem, Hreem,
Kleem, Shreem, Kleem, Vitteswarei (continuous repetition of her seed mantra)*

6. *Shreem, Shreem, Shreem.....*
    Reciting her seed chant 108x daily also is very effective.

7. *Om Shreem Hreem Shreem Kamale Kamalaleyi
Praseed Praseed, om Shreem Hreem Shreem MahaLaxmiyei Namaha....*

   Translation: Underlying vibration of all creation, abundance please, cherishing your lotus feet, be pleased Great Lakshmi Goddess, I bow to You. *Youtube,*

Lilasakura, Recording sung by Shri Anandi Ma's group and Dileepji, from CD "Mantra for Abundance." Published by Sounds True also see Youtube by Lilasakura

8. Om Kleem, Shreem Lakshmi (another popular mantra exalting the Goddess, Lakshmi)
9. Om Hrim Shri Lakshmi Bhyo Namaha
Check out, Youtube by Sainath459

10. Om Shreem MahaLakshmiyei Swaha

<u>Om</u> seed sound for the 6th chakra that commences most mantras, where the masculine and the feminine meet in the brow.

<u>Shrim</u> second seed sound for the principle of abundance

<u>Maha</u> means "great all" referring to quality and quantity

<u>Lakshmi</u> is Sanskrit word meaning the energy of abundance

<u>Swaha</u> new levels of energy rise uttering this simple principle of abundance.
For more info see, Youtube by wealthful

<u>*11. Lakshmi Gayatri*</u>:
"Om Mahalakshmyaye cha Vidmahe, Vishnu patnyai cha dhi-Mahi, Tanno Lakshmihi prachodayat.."
Translation: Om. Let us meditate on the Great Goddess Sri Lakshmi, the consort of Sri Maha Vishnu. May that effulgent Maha Lakshmi Devi, inspire and illuminate our minds with understanding.

12. Om Hreem, Shreem, Lakshmi Bhyo Namaha...
Translation: Om, Goddess Lakshmi, resides in me and bestow sthy abundance on all aspects of my existence...   Source: www.freemeditationinfo.com

*The Hindu Goddess of Prosperity, Beauty and Love has garnered quite the reputation throughout the years and as one can surmise, she has a myriad of devout worshippers. The beautiful, Sri Lakshmi, is often depicted in gold, bejeweled from head to toe, accompanied by the elephant God, Ganesh. She represents our feminine beauty, fecundity and prosperity. She enters our realm to make us aware of our many riches and our potential to maintain and manifest even more. She is the abundant golden Harvest itself with her great beauty and palpable ripeness and she beckons you to embrace, with gratitude, the gifts of abundance, love and beauty.

JOURNALING

What do you feel you excel in, what are you exceptionally good at?
_____

_____

Can you list all of your skills and talents as well as past work experiences?
_____

_____

Do you have an updated resume?
_____

_____

Are you presently working and what do you do?
_____

_____

Are your skills and talents being properly compensated?
_____

_____

Do you feel you are getting paid the right salary?
_____

_____

What career aspirations do you hold? Where do you see yourself in five years?
_____

_____

Can you become prosperous, happy and successful if you remain where you are right now?
_____

_____

Do you feel you have the potential to be rich and happy?

_____

_____

What did your parents do for a living?

_____

_____

As a child, reflect back on the messages you received regarding work. What were the messages you received regarding the pursuit of a job?

_____

_____

Can you personally define what an ideal work day looks like to you?

_____

_____

Additional Thoughts....

_____

_____

_____

_____

INVOCATION & POETRY

SEDUCING PROSPERITY

Today I invite,
Prosperity into my life,
I set out our Altar,
To welcome it, just right.

I make a spread,
of all our favorite foods;
Wine and sweets
To make us both swoon.

Flowers and pretty things,
That Sparkle with joy...
Bells and Music,
Happily, here, employed.

I cast this circle space,
Imbue it with light,
May I be Blessed
With your presence here tonight...

May you come Quickly,
And easily find me...
Place on my crown,
Your warm cloak of security,

Waken me to pleasures,
And so much ease...
No more doubts or Fears
Or Insecurities.

Comforts and dreams,
Experienced firsthand,
Gone are the days,
When I was poor and sad.

Kiss me to seal,
Our magickal, Sacred pact,
And may the scent of your presence,
linger now and last.....
so Mote it be.....)O(

PROSPERITY

Capricorn New Moon,
I draw upon you,
Prosperity, Abundance,
and New Blessings to bloom...
    I light the wick,
    and invoke the flame,
    for prosperity and riches,
    to now be claimed...
The gold of this candle,
to represent riches...
the "Nine of Pentacle" and "World card"
and the green of my stitches...
    Desire of my heart,
    my will and my word,
    I call and conjure now,
    as the Magick now stirs...
Come with ease,
and overflow,
U.S. currency
to buy my own home,
    Come to heal,
    And the erase all debt,
    College education,
    for my kids, all the very best
Autonomous Woman,
I embrace now my worth,
I am a magnet now
for prosperities births!
    Tune into my powers,
    And strength to manifest,
    Money comes with ease,
    My creations and I are blessed.
The scent and these words,
Candles and New Moon rite,
The Goddess invoked,
Witnesses this spell tonight.
    I invoke money -Lotto wins...
    Well-being, success now comes
    And by my will and word
    it is done, done, done....
This spell bound round and it shall be,
These things or better,
So mote it be...

THEME WORK SUGGESTIONS
11. WORK AND PROSPERITY

Light a green or gold or yellow candle light

Pull out your resume and update it. Search through classified ads, register with an online employment agency and connect with a Temp agency to help advance your employment search. Practice how you will communicate and interact with your future employer and get comfortable with the interviewing process.

WALLET/CHECKBOOK BLESSING RITE

Place a few drops of cinnamon or bayberry or mint oil on your purse or checkbook.

PROSPERITY RITUAL

Write yourself a check in the amount of money you wish to receive from the universe.

HERBAL GREEN PLACKET

Make a green herbal placket. Take a green felt cloth, place inside of it some dried herbs like; chamomile, mint, clove, ginger, and cinnamon sticks. Place a few drops of scented oils like patchouli, add a piece of a magnet and sprinkle some gold glitter. Gather all of your ingredients inside the green felt fabric and sew it up with a green or white threaded needle. As your sew it shut, envision the prosperity you wish to manifest. When you're done charge it under the full moon before sleeping with it under your bed for a few nights. Carry this herbal placket in your purse, near your money, until your wish is manifested.

MAGICK RITES & TOOLS

This is your personal page to document your sacred rites and the tools you elected to use.

DECIDE WHERE TO SET UP AN ALTAR
Place an Altar Cloth in the Color of your choice.
Color: _____

GODDESS
Place an image of your Deity.
Goddess: _____
This image can be a Statue, handmade Sculpture or a simple Photo _____

FIRE REPRESENTATION
Place a blessed/charged Candle in the color of your choice.
Candle Type and color: _____

AIR REPRESENTATION
Light your Incense stick.
Incense Scent: _____

WATER REPRESENTATION
Place a Chalice of Water
Water Item: _____

EARTH REPRESENTATION
Place a Potted Plant or Fresh Flowers on your Altar
Add Salt or a plate of Dried Herbs
Herbs: _____
Chosen Gemstone: _____

YOUR WISH
_____
_____

Place a symbol of your desire, if you have one available, and also write your wish out clearly, on a piece of parchment paper, or you can even use a cut up brown paper bag. These are the basics for a very simple altar & rite. Ultimately, your sacred space is only limited by your imagination. You can make your altar & rite as big or as small as you prefer and the addition of other personal items is really up to you.)o(Enjoy!

ALTAR PHOTOS

***You are now invited to create your own altar(s) & invocation(s).
)O(Blessings!

CHAPTER TWELVE

"Authentic freedom is actually the freedom of knowing who you are, why you are here, your purpose in life, and where you are going when you leave here…"
Wayne Dyer

THEME: LIBERATION

If you've been diligently working through the lessons found in each chapter of this book, then the arrival to this final chapter should bring with it a level of pride and accomplishment. I would moreover hope that at this point you've also achieved a level of enlightenment, healing and much progress in your spiritual growth.

Our journey together has touched upon several key lessons that are pertinent for a woman's path to empowerment, magick and protection. We started this journey exploring and honoring our intuition, and then examining our communities and the many ways we can better serve and develop our leadership skills. We then connected to our heart to explore our powers of creation, what we love and how we love. It led us to the next lesson in which we explored the Mother archetype and how we nurture ourselves. We then traversed into the gift of our voices and our emotions; like the power found in our anger and how we can use it as a catalyst for building great strength. We were awakened to the power of our physical body and the need to cultivate balance and Justice in our world. In chapter 9, we acknowledged and explored the empowerment found within our sexuality and we them sharpened our vision and ambition, in chapter 10, to help us clarify our powers of manifestation. Our journey together then led us to chapter 11, where we rolled up our sleeves and invited work and prosperity into our lives. And now these last eleven Lunations collectively usher us into this new chapter.

Our beautiful journey together leads us now to explore this chapter's theme connected to, Freedom. It is our inherent human right to be free yet, so many of us are in bondage and find ourselves in various types of prisons. Whether these prisons are metaphorical, imagined, and only in our minds or whether they are literal. Either way, when we are wrestling with a prison in our midst, it will have a massive impact on how we carry forth in our lives.

We've reach a point in our journey where we might sense walls caving in on us and an uncomfortable desperation for new air, new space, and a new life. We might all of a sudden find that all the things we sought to attain and achieve might no longer serve us the way it used to. Perhaps we've simply grown and things that might have felt comfortable before, and almost necessary to wear as our exterior façade, no longer feels the same. But, even potentially more poignant in our unique journeys is the possibility that something out of the blue has struck our world; causing a bewildering theft of all we had grown accustomed to; offering in its place, Freedom. How do we react to such an enormous gift from the Universe?

All the lessons in the world, all the gifts and experiences we've garnered throughout our numerous lifetimes can have very little significance, if we don't have the one thing every creature on this planet longs for; Freedom.

Freedom is found first and foremost within our mind and our attitude. Freedom and the beliefs we attach to our liberation inaugurates adventure and a willingness and openness to experience all the gifts that life has to offer us in the form of challenges and lessons before us. This sets up a platform for all that is about to transpire in our lives and

makes a way for a path, for our journey, to begin once more. Because, it is important to note that our growth and evolution is a spiral journey. It goes forward and returns only to move us further up in the celestial sphere of our ascension. Thus, this may appear to be our final chapter in this book but it is not the end of our spiritual journey. We can begin again with new levels of understanding and bring newly acquired skills to seemingly repeated lessons that only call for new levels of mastery.
***

I've been personally contemplating on why this chapter and the subject of freedom has been approached so differently than the way I had first imagined. Initially I thought of this chapter as being about getting free from toxic people or toxic situations and possibly finding our inner roar. But, I found that these issues were already touched upon in the chapter of Karma and Justice, and in the chapter of Rage and Strength. It appears to me that we reach this ultimate chapter with an awareness of how important it is to really gather all of the lessons we've learned and apply them to this pivotal point in our journey.

This chapter is about true freedom, true liberation! It is the Fool in the Major Arcana of the Tarot deck. It is walking away freely without encumbrances or heavy baggage, like he exemplifies so impeccably. There are no heavy emotions or obstacles for him. He surrenders their oppressive impact. He is joyful, enthusiastic, animated and ready for anything. This chapter is about this type of freedom, The Fool's adventure.
The Fool is awakened to his gifts, his autonomy, his confidence, strength and his enthusiasm. He is ready to take with him his hope, joy, certain life experiences and move onward. He takes his love and all aspects of his whole self on this journey as an asset not a burden. The dog often illustrated by his side is perhaps a primal aspect of himself that is also traveling within him, but it's clear he hasn't a care in the world because he's rooted in himself. In his satchel one can surmise that he has some additional prized possessions but the Fool is rooted in the knowledge that he has all that he'll need within himself. That's Freedom! That's the kind of freedom we are exploring here.

Oftentimes, the Fool is considered naïve or impetuous, young and inexperienced. But upon closer inspection we can ask ourselves how many times has the Fool embarked on this journey? It is a spiral Journey, after all, so how many times has he packed up his satchel, ready to go off into the world? How many times have WE been the Fool; packed up our bags and started anew? How many times have we gathered our lessons, our pain, our joys, our knowledge and our experiences (whether negative or positive) and wrap them up in our bag, to walk out into the world, with a distinctly new willingness to savor freedom? How many times have we packed up ourselves, invoked freedom, to start anew? This is where we are in our journey; this is the point where we explore the gifts of Freedom.

As we have done before, in this chapter we will explore further our theme with the help of several resources. We will endeavor to connect with the Voodoo Lwa and Goddess Erzulie Dantor, Goddesses Feronia, Shina Tsu Hime, Hina, Iris and the sacred animal energy of the Wolf. We will connect with our Root chakra, the 1st chakra, and gemstones that can help better facilitate this connection. We will also look at the corresponding Lunation and a Tarot card that is connected to our theme.

THE FOOL TAROT CARD

The Fool card in the Tarot is often depicted, in traditional decks, as a young man, dressed in very unusual, unconventional attire, carrying a long stick with a satchel attached to its end. One is to assume that all of his precious belongings fit neatly in that one satchel. He happily carries it across his back and with the other hand he holds a white rose. The Rose can be seen as a symbol of love and passion but the fact that it is white denotes a connection to naïveté, purity of Love, and his freedom from lower levels of desire.

In the traditional Rider Waite Tarot deck The Fool is often considered a card similar to The Joker card in a regular, card playing deck, due to its wild, jester-like energy. It is an intriguing card perhaps because it's so colorful; evoking so much joy, enthusiasm, freedom and inspiring a number of questions about the main character. For starters, the number assigned to the Fool card is 0. Some see this card as the first card in the Major Arcana and some have argued that it should be considered the last. Because it has the number zero assigned to it, it really can be considered as both; the first card and the last. Either way it's a fascinating card. It shows a youthful person dressed in very colorful artistic attire or sometimes, in what appears to be rags, but he doesn't appear to care what he's wearing. He is depicted in the middle of his adventure so there is great momentum in this card. There's a level of action portrayed in this card that contrast the number of sedentary figures encountered throughout the tarot. Often there is a dog accompanying him on his journey and both are portrayed approaching the edge of a cliff. They are exuberant, happy and naïvely unaware of how close they are to falling off that cliff. The question becomes, is it really that dangerous or it simply an illusion. The shining bright Sun is also very prevalent in this card, as are the cliffs and mountain peaks. The sun is very much indicative of the positivity, wellbeing and youthfulness of this card and nature is in harmony with him.

The Fool is a message about freedom and adventure. It is a card that denotes not having a care in the world or at least, not letting the cares of the world burden or dictate our path in life. The character of the Fool travels light, meaning; he's not overwhelmed by negativity, excess baggage or superfluous things. He really appears not to have a care in the world. He and his dog companion are looking upward in a state of bliss. Some might say he's in such a blissful state that he's not fully aware of the potential dangers around him. And the little dog nearby appears just as animated and just as impetuous as the character of the Fool.

The Fool is a card about Liberation. It speaks to us about letting go, releasing concerns, fears, negativity and anything that weights us down. It entices us to join him in this quest and savor the joys of existing on this earth, liberated. It speaks of letting go of unnecessary things that no longer serve our highest purpose. It is a message about moving forward in life; freely embarking on our true bliss. It is a card that ignites our inner youth and desire, for new adventures. As a result, this card can also encourage us to take on new travels and explore new terrains; whether they are metaphorical or literal. It is a perfect card to explore, in conjunction with our theme in this chapter. The Fool is quintessentially the personification of freedom and it becomes a perfect card to work with as we further explore our theme of Freedom.

MOON IN AQUARIUS   AIR/URANUS

THEME: Liberation

AQUARIUS   FIXED   AIR   MASCULINE   THE WATER BEARER

The Moon in the astrological sign of Aquarius is a rebel. Aquarius, in my humble opinion, has an almost fiery energy to it, but it is symbolized by "The Water Bearer" and yet, this is considered an Air sign. The rebellious energy of Aquarius is probably mostly attributed to Uranus, the planet it is ruled by.

Uranus is known as the global agent of change. It considers the microcosm and the macrocosm and seeks to cause global transformations by any means necessary. It is a dedicated humanitarian, seeking to evolve our species and tending to the radical shifts in our auric realm.

The astrological sign of Aquarius offers us many gifts. It has been known to be eccentric, a pioneer and an innovator. Its energy seeks to embrace and assert its uniqueness, without conforming to status norms. Yes, the Moon in the astrological sign of Aquarius holds a poignant radical energy that can be best harnessed for works connected to personal liberation and anything connected to drastic change. It is the Moon in Aquarius that can help us break stalwart bad habits, negative situations and relationships, to help us finally attain our freedom.

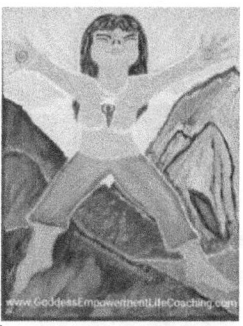

THEME WORK SUGGESTIONS

Work with the Aquarius moon, symbolized by the Water Bearer,
and work with The Wolf energy and
the Deities found throughout this book.
Work exclusively with your chakras.
Perform a Cord Cutting Rite.
Consider doing a massive cleaning and
purging of your physical home
and of your internal body.
Do an inventory of your life and release
what is no longer serving your highest good;
that includes people, relationships and situations.
If you can, plan to relocate, or switch up the rooms in your home.
Take a long distant voyage.

> *"There's no greater freedom
> then the freedom to be yourself.
> Give yourself that gifts and
> choose to surround yourself
> with those who appreciate you
> exactly as you truly are..."*
> — *Doe Zantamata*

HERSTORY

After years of tolerating certain toxic aspects in her life she was done and ready for a massive change. She had been in an abusive relationship for far too long and had reached a new level of rock bottom when authorities were called to her chaotic home. Things were not good in her world and she knew it was time to fight back and surrender to transformation. She was done with her old life and was ready to liberate herself and transform her life.

**Take a moment to document here, or in your journal, your unique story.

_____
_____
_____

_____

_____

AFFIRMATION

I walk this earth
rooted in the certainty of
who I am; an empowered, free woman.

I am Free

Every Revolution of great change
begins with the slaughtering,
tenacious fight for Freedom...
it is our inherent human desire to know this freedom.

I welcome my emancipation to enter the realm of Liberty

CHAKRA & GEMSTONE WORK

1st Chakra   **MULADHARA/ROOT CHAKRA**   **COLOR** Red/Black/Burgundy
Security, physical existence, stability, the self, earth grounding, home, basic human needs, sexuality, it is considered the sex chakra for men.
Mantra: I Am Primal/I Am Rooted
)O(WORKING: Totem Work, Protective Work, Home and Family Roots, Grounding, Kundalini, Fear Security issues

GEMSTONE CONNECTION: Red Coral is known as the Garden of the Sea. It is a stone created naturally from the accumulated skeletal masses from the once living sea polyp organisms. We are focusing here on the red corals but they can be found in other hues. In ancient times there was a belief that our beloved red planet, Mars, was composed of red coral. Today it is an excellent stone to help us visualize and unearth our motivation and personal sense of direction. Red Coral symbolizes life and blood force energy and makes an excellent stone for our root chakra. It is reputed to cure sterility, lethargy and depression. It was believed to prevent illnesses and, if kept in the home, it protects the house from theft or lightning storms. Years ago it was worn around the neck to help with skin disorders and it was also given to malnutrition children to help them balance any nutritional deficiencies. The red coral was grounded up and made into a fine powder, then mixed and served in a liquid, like honey or milk. It was believed to stimulate the digestive system, heal and nourish blood cells and regenerate our body tissues. Red Coral incites potent passions, ambition and strong powerful emotions. Interestingly enough, the gemstone displays a lot of the attributes it shares with its planet of affiliation, Mars. It can encourage, within the wearer, anger, determination, stamina, independence and great strength. It facilitates the attainment and transfer of new knowledge and can bring honor, success and fame.

GEMSTONE CHANNELING

There is no question that many of us live multifaceted, busy lives but making the time for this type of work is invaluable to our continued growth and self-actualization. You are applauded for the dedication and commitment you've expressed towards your healing, spiritual connection and self-empowerment. Today you are asked to locate a quiet place, where you will feel safe and where you will not be distracted by the mundane. The importance and revelatory value of finding the time and space for a daily meditative practice cannot be overstated enough. If you can go outdoors in nature that would be most ideal but any place where you can relax, undisturbed, would be fine.

As part of this work you are invited now to place yourself in a comfortable meditation position; you may sit or lay down. If it is available to you, place in your hands the Red Coral gemstone that we are working with today. This Red Coral gemstone is connected to our Root chakra; the place of our foundation and basic human needs. Hold this Red Coral gemstone in your hands. Consider how it feels upon your skin... What shape is it in? Does it feel hot or cold against your flesh? Is it a rough or smooth gemstone? (Pause) Gaze deeply upon this Red Coral gemstone and let your scrutiny unveil all of its precious details. Quietly, continue to study this gemstone and make note of any thoughts or vivid images that immediately start to unfold before you. (Pause)

When you're ready, you may close your eyes and begin this short meditation. As with all trance work, we begin with our breath. You are asked now to take a deep cleansing breath; slowly filling your lungs up and then releasing it.... Now, let your next breath possess the powerful element of this Red Coral gemstone. (Pause) Feel the potent red color of this coral gemstone rise into the ethers and breathe in the energy of its essence. Breathe in and exhale.... Now, direct this next breath all the way down to your lower spine. (Pause) Consider the importance of your spine and your root chakra; the way a root on a plant is so distinctly monumental to its overall wellbeing. Breathe and stay with this energy for as long as you need to. (Pause)

Continue to inhale and exhale, and hold this inhalation for 3 seconds and then release it... Counting now at your own pace; breathe, 1, 2, 3, and exhale on 4....and again....breathe in, 1, 2, 3, and exhale on 4. Let's do this one more time and then quietly counting in your head.... Breathe 1, 2, 3...release on 4. Breathe, trusting in the natural rhythm you have now established, of your relaxed inhalation and exhalation.

The Red Coral gemstone has much to express to you. It has a special channeled message waiting just for you. See this Red Coral in your mind's eye. See it now embedded upon its dark, fertile, mother earth underneath the sea. Draw nearer to it and ask if it will allow you to pick it up. When permission is granted, gently gather it in your hands. With your mind's eye, gaze upon it; studying its color, its texture, and any other details that capture your eyes.... Ask it to speak to you.

Now imagine the top of your head opening up, as if the lid of a box was removed. Let your Crown chakra become almost like a chalice; receptive and open to any spiritual messages that may be unfolding for you now... You may envision your crown chakra now unveiling a magnetic Red Coral gemstone portal allowing for this **Crystal Transmission** to come through... Breathe and with your next breath, gently guide this energy of the Red Coral gemstone, from your crown chakra all the way down to your root chakra. Feel it pulsating and energizing this sacred region in your body. (Pause)

Continue to breathe in the energy of the Red Coral gemstone. When you are ready, you may begin to open your eyes and prepare to document your experience. As you come out of this meditation, it is a perfect time for you to document any images or messages that came through for you. You may write them here, or in your personal journal. _____

_____

WOLF PROTECTION ENERGY

Wolf is a Great Spirit teacher that awakens our intuition and our primal senses. Known as a path finder, it will help us locate the right path to our true destiny. They have a strong connection with the Moon and are known as shape-shifters; adapting and melding into the environment. Wolves are teachers that show us when we need to be more resourceful and how to find the right resources when we need them most. It is easy to see how the Wolf becomes an invaluable asset to us in our spiritual work, especially when connected to the theme of this chapter.

Wolf is related to strength, cunningness, endurance, courage and independence. It awakens our self-confidence and self-reliance. Wolf is also a staunch lover of his freedom; freedom to roam the earth to find new adventures and this too makes it an ideal animal to connect with as we explore the theme of freedom.

The Wolf as a spirit guide encourages us to move forward; assessing and adapting to each situation individually, helping us find what we are searching for. As a pathfinder, Wolf is important when you feel lost because it is his energy that will always guide you in the right direction. A loyal, protector of the family, Wolf also reminds us of the importance of our tribe.

It is interesting to note that Wolves have inhabited almost every continent (except extreme dry desert planes) and their inevitable paths crossings with human beings, have allowed us to learn from them. Wolves are part of the canine family known as "*Cani Lupus.*" They are highly intelligent, freedom loving, wanderers of the earth. They are also devoted tribe members, seen traveling with other wolves in small to medium packs. They display a strong sense of allegiance to their wolf family and are fiercely protective of them. They are travelers that move about in search for food and new adventures but they are never far from their tribe.

Known as "Howlers of the Moon," they use their distinct howling to communicate at great distance with their clan. Much scientific research has been done regarding this phenomenon, but there has been no concrete proven evidence that wolves actually howl at the moon. There are however, a number of observations and logical conclusions to this intriguing phenomenon. Some might say, Wolves are always howling. This is how they communicate with one another. They are nocturnal creatures and thus, you will naturally find them awake, active and communicative at night. The presence of the Moon can only be spied in the dark of night; therefore it would make sense to connect wolves with the moon. The fact that, since Neolithic times, wolves have always been connected with the moon is evident in early cave drawing and documents of the time. This only anchored further the association between the two. Wolves howl for many different reasons and as mentioned before, it is their most effective form of long distance communication. Wolf Medicine should then be viewed as an awakener to more effective communication skills, as well.

Wolves howl to assemble the pack and warn them of impending danger. Wolves howl to alert the tribe of his whereabouts, to scare off their enemies and to signal an alarm. Funnily enough, wolves are known to howl when they simply get together as a way to reaffirming their bonds to one another. They also howl to mark their territory and attract potential mates. During a time of courtship, usually peaking in the winter months, from about December to January, you will hear many wolves howling as a mating call. Perhaps this is one reason why the month of January has a Full Moon that was given the name, "Wolf Moon." For indigenous cultures that lived so intensely aware of nature and its cycles, they would have noticed the increase in the wolves' nightly song. It is easy to see how the wolf and his distinct howl would've been linked to the Full Moon, especially at this time.

There is also an ancient belief that a wolf could hear and communicate with the spirits of the dead. And because a Full Moon has esoteric links with spirits and the deities from the underworld, it is very easy to link the two together. Traditionally the Full Moon was believed to open the gates of the underworld, inviting the presence of spirits and wolves howling were simply seen as communicating with the dead. For the Native Americans, more specifically the Seneca tribe, there is a belief that the wolf's song, or howl, helped to actually manifest the Moon into existence.

Wolves were also often associated with numerous deities like Apollo, Aries, Mars and Silvanus. Descendants of the Trickster God, Loki, in Norse mythology, are believed to be wolves. The God Cernunnos, was often depicted with a wolf and in Ireland, the King Cormac, was pictured accompanied by wolves. The Egyptian God, Wepwawet, whose image was revered and publicized openly during celebratory processionals among the pharaohs, was often depicted as a wolf or with a wolf head. In Norse mythology, the Moon and the Sun are chased by two wolves. They are known as Skoll (repulsion) and Hati (hatred). They are purported to beckon the night and day that arrives daily. When there was an eclipse, in ancient times, it was alleged the wolves had temporarily swallowed the sun. There is an ancient theory that one day they will fully devour the sun and the moon and fulfill the doomsday prophesy. The God Odin was believed to enjoy the loyal companionship of two wolves, known as Geri and Freki. They may have been the offspring of Hel's mother. Wolves were sacrificed and sometimes eaten at the Temple of Arcadia, where there existed a well-known Wolf cult that worshipped Zeus Lycaeus. Here the initiates would call themselves, Lukoi. The Goddess, in early Rome was known as Lupa or Feronia, meaning the great "*she wolf.*" Here she was worshipped and honored in the legendary Lupercalia festivals, known as the festival of the "*she wolf.*" In this aspect, the Great Goddess was celebrated as the mother of Roman ancestors.

The energy of the Wolf helps us face our deepest fears and in shamanic trance journeys, they will offer themselves as invaluable spirit guides. Indigenous cultures consider wolf to be an instrumental teacher. Highly revered for their strength and confidence, they can help you come to conclusive decisions. Wolf energy helps you trust your instincts and your inner voice. This beloved animal helps you balance friends & family and find time for yourself. They have this impressive ability to maintain autonomy and individuality, while still being a part of a tribe. For our transformative work, we can extract much wisdom from this gift.

The Wolf is connected with intelligence; invisibility, endurance, courage, and outwitting those who want to harm us and avoiding our enemies. For Native Americans, the Wolf is a powerful spirit teacher that offers us wisdom, protection, introspection, and guidance; in dreams, meditation and trance journeys. They are invaluable teachers for us as we learn to balance our own freedom and autonomy with our family and friend obligations. You are encouraged to work with Wolf energy to unearth a remarkable spiritual resource and a powerful partner in your transformational work.

THEME WORK SUGGESTIONS
12 LIBERATION
Light a white or black candle

Endeavor to purge and cleanse yourself with a smudge-wand of White Sage or ritually cut your hair and engage in meditation and focused breath work. Explore the element of air. You can study and contemplate the flight of butterflies and consider flying a kite. Let this kite represent what you are releasing; let the wind take it away & let it go. Perform a cord cutting ritual or a Prayer Flag Rite (instructions provided below). Engage in the Ho'oponopono; reciting this powerful Hawaiian prayer of reconciliation and forgiveness (information found in this chapter).

PRAYER FLAG RITE

For the theme of liberation & freedom in this chapter, it is recommended to work with the element of air. Performing a ritual, working with Prayer Flags can prove to be very effective. We begin by gathering 4 to 6 square pieces of a torn fabric, preferably in different colors. Upon each piece of tattered cloth use a marker and write on it, a word or a symbol that represents what you are liberating yourself from. Have a long piece of string that will serve as your main cord, in which you will fasten these colored, cloth pieces to. Attach your square pieces of cloth to the one long cord with shorter strings. You may sew or simply make a small puncture into these cloths pieces so that you can loop the shorter strings inside of it. Now, attach these labeled square pieces of fabric unto the main long cord. Finally, you should have a long cord with your 4 to 6 square, labeled cloth pieces tied to the main chord. Take this long cord outdoors on a windy day and hang it on the highest branch you can find, on a tree. As the wind blows your newly crafted prayer flag, send an intention that the wind will blow away those things you have specified and in return offer you the freedom from those things you wish to be free from. That is how you do one simple version of a prayer flag ritual. Prayer Flag rituals were initially very common in indigenous cultures and they continue to be an effective powerful ritual for releasing what is no longer serving our highest good.

HO' OPONOPONO PRAYER was first introduced by the Kahuna (Spiritual Healer) Morrnah Nalamaku Simeona in the mid-1970s. Originally used by the venerated elders to resolve disputes within family tribes, its effectiveness to manifest peace in the world became obvious to Simeona. Her first Ho'oponopono seminar was offered in Germany and after her death in 1992, her administrator and dedicated pupil continued her legacy. Ihaleakala Hew Len, PhD, was one of her devoted students and he simplified and expanded the work she had started.   As a psychologist and a shamanic practitioner he coauthored a book titled, "Zero Limits," which delved deeper into Ho'oponopono tenets. When asked about his work at the Hawaii State Hospital and miraculously healing the criminally insane, he was quoted as stating, **"...I did not heal them, I healed part of myself that created them..."** This simple statement encapsulates how Ho'oponopono works.

In Hawaii, Ho'oponopono, means, "to make it right." It is a type of mantra or prayer recited continuously to help us forgive and release what is not in our highest good. Because it is strongly believed that our unconscious mind carries all of our significant relationships, experiences, and people throughout our lifetime (some might even say throughout many past lives), when we offer forgiveness to others, we are essentially offering forgiveness to ourselves.
The Ho'oponopono prayer facilitates this process of liberation from all source of negativity.
"The process of Ho'oponopono is to align with and clean up our genealogy as well as to clean up our relationships with other people in our lives..." Source from; www.ancient huna.com

There are four important elements as part of this powerful forgiveness prayer, they are:
1. **Repentance: When we recite, "I'm sorry"**
2. **Forgiveness: When we recite, "Please forgive me"**
3. **Gratitude: When we recite "Thank you and**
4. **Love: When we recite, "I love you..."**

The Ho'oponopono is practiced first by connecting with your breath. Take several slow deep breaths. When you are calmed and centered bring to mind a person, an emotion, a challenge, a relationship or a situation that you are ready to release in your life. Then when you feel ready, begin repeating these four phrases continuously.

*Repeatedly recite, *"I am sorry, please forgive me, thank you, I love you, *I'm sorry, please forgive me, thank you, I love you, *I'm sorry, please forgive me, thank you, I Love...* etc." Continue to recite these words until you feel called to stop. Practice this ritual as often as needed, until you can honestly feel the freedom from that taxing situation. You know you've prompted a change and healing, when the thought of the person or situation no longer has the same distressing burden on you, as it did before; thus, achieving liberation.

GODDESS EMPOWERMENT

"As the spirit of light in darkness she comes to break the chains of those who live in the prison of unconsciousness and restores them to their true home...

"The Cult of the Black Virgin, by Ean Begg." Page 134,

ERZULIE-DANTOR

Erzulie-Dantor is part of an assemblage of powerful iconic Voodoo Lwa, known as Erzulies. They are loa, also known as Mysteres that dedicate themselves to the realm of love, sex and the arts. There are numerous Erzulies in Haitian Voodoo but for the time being we will focus on Erzulie-Dantor and occasionally make mention of her sister Erzulie-Freda who is very much a part of her history and folklore.

In Voodoo, there are the Loas, spirits, Gods, (and forgive me for I will tend to use these term interchangeably, as I address loa as Gods and mean no disrespect by doing this). I understand the Loa in Voodoo are viewed as mysteres and living spirits and since this too is my definition of Goddess and Gods I will often use the term in regards to loas. The loa are divided into nanchons (nations) or groups. There are several Voodoo nanchons like the Ghede, Nago, Djab and the two we'll speak about here are the Rada Loa and the Petwo or Petro Loa. Some make the mistake of viewing these two nanchons as good and evil or light and dark but (according to author and Houngan, Kevin Filan) it is probably most effective to view them as Hot and Cold spirits or pantheons.

The Rada, which contains the loa; Erzulie-Freda, La Sirene, Atibon Legba, Dambhala Wedo, Agwe Tawayo are considered cold, balanced, stable and beneficent. They are sometimes related to royalty and are familiar in nature. Their lineage is traced to West Africa; sometimes Dahomey, which is now considered Benin, Africa. The Petwo Loa are considered hot, spicy, volatile, warrior-like, and become aggressive and quick to take actions. They are connected to military and also foreigners. Erzulie-Dantor, Ogou, Maynette and Ti-Jean loa fall under this nanchons. Red is their color and there is no question of their mars-like intensity. They are even honored on a day ruled by Mars, Tuesday. The Petwo loa's origins are found in some parts of Africa, like the Congo, and the New World (Americas), which is why so many of them retain some of their slavery attributes. Erzulie Dantor's origins would therefore be linked to Africa but more obvious is her connection to the new World, in Haiti.

Erzulie Dantor (Dantor, Danto, Ezili-Danthor, Ezili-Dantor etc...) is embraced as the Patron Loa/Goddess of New Orleans and the one who protects the newly initiated Priest/Priestess (Mambo and Houngan) in Voodoo. She is also considered to be a part of the Orthodox practice of Voodoo. She is a Warrioress, fierce Mother, protectress of women and children. As a Loa of the Petwo type, she is so strong and aggressive, sometimes even feared for her boldness, that some have even labeled her as a loa from the "Djab," which translates as Devilish or connected with sorcery and magick. Others can view this reference to her as simply that she is a fierce loa/Goddess, who exemplifies the "bitch" and is not one to be trifled with or approached haphazardly. She is known to exercise retribution when supplicated by her worshippers and she is a great defender of those women who have been abused or betrayed by their lover.

Erzulie Dantor's manifestation is linked and attributed to a very important historical period in Haitian history, as has been documented by numerous sources. It is believed that the Haitian Revolution began with Erzulie Dantor's manifestation at a Voodoo ceremony taking place in Bwa Cayman (Bois Cainman), Cainman Forest in 1871. There are some minor conflicting tales regarding the details of this night, for some say it was the spirit of Ogou that manifested, but a more popularly accepted belief among Voodoo practitioners is that Dantor was the spirit that made herself known on that fateful night.

At this particular time in Haiti there was much political unrest, resentment and anger among the citizens of the French Colony, known then as Saint-Domingue before the revolution. The land was one full of riches; producing sugar, coffee, cocoa, tobacco, indigo, cotton, sisal, fruits and vegetable to its mother land, France. Although it was a rich, fertile land, it was France and its greedy royalty that was benefitting distastefully due to Slavery. Citizens of Saint-Domingue were white, European, black African slaves, mulattoes, maroons (escaped slave blacks), free blacks, white slave owners as well as blacks and there was a lot of anguish and hostilities towards Europe's control on this rich land and its multi-raced people. It is important to note that the French Revolution (1789) and the dethroning of Marie Antoinette and Louis XVI must have also influenced this capricious, turbulent period in Haitian history.

These were unpredictably volatile and unstable times. Many Haitian slaves of African descent were being abused and even killed by their masters without any retribution or just consequence. There was mounting frustration, anger and resentment by the growing number of Blacks who were actually beginning to outnumber white citizens. It would not take much effort to push something that was clearly already on the edge of transpiring. Although the Haitian Revolution is documented as occurring from 1791 till 1804, its inception clearly began much earlier, but one particular documented event, catapulted Haiti's metamorphosis and eventual liberation.

Many disgruntled citizens; blacks, African descendants, slaves and maroons, were already gathering regularly trying to organize themselves but with little success. The evening of August 14, 1791, a Petwo loa Voodoo ceremony was taking place at Bois Caiman, (Alligator woods) led by the maroon Houngan, Dutty Boukman. At this particular ceremony, according to legend, a priestess drew down the spirit of Erzulie-Dantor. As Dantor rode her serviteur she took her favorite form of offering, a Black pig, slit its throat and proceeded to have all participants' drink of its blood, while simultaneously inciting courage and the warrior's energy and confidence to these otherwise oppressed citizens of Saint-Domingue. Most present at this ceremony were of African descent, brutally suffering at the hands of European enslavement and Erzulie-Dantor ridding her serviteur rallied them to fight...fight for their freedom, fight for their humanity, banish the French and establish for themselves, the "Free Black Republic of Haiti." A week later, on August 21st, 1791, the Haitian Revolution had begun with unspeakable acts of courage and violence, massive killings, incineration of Haiti's lush land and a horrific revolution that would last for thirteen years before Haiti could declare itself the victor and finally free of France. It is only the second colony, next to the U.S.A. that was able to successfully free itself from the tyrannical, oppressive restraints and enslavement of a European country; its connection to Erzulie-Dantor is considerably monumental. Dantor can be seen as the liberator and mother of the "Free Black Republic of Haiti."

> *"...Wisdom has always cried on the rooftops or at the street corners, and the spirit of this world always punishes those who buy her wares. The great age of the Black Virgin is the 12th century, but the legends about her hark back to the dawn of Christianity, the dynasty of the Merovingians and the age of Charlemagne..."*
>
> The Cult of the Black Virgin, by Ean Begg" Page 133
> www.webster.edu/-corbetre/haiti/history/revolution/revolution1.htm,
> http://www.travelinghaiti.com/history_of_haiti/slave_rebellion.asp, http://wikipedia.org/wiki/Haitian_Revolution

The Revolution is also attributed to Dantor being mute. There are two different stories explaining how she became a mute. One claims that her own people cut out her tongue in fear that she would divulge their secrets if caught, captured and tortured to speak up by the enemy and it was a necessary sacrifice to protect and maintain their spiritual practices. Others say that she was indeed a victim of the Revolution and that the opposition abducted her and she was brutally tortured by these soldiers. They mutilated her by chopping off her tongue for being a part of that ceremony and instigating this civil war. The "Ke, ke, ke, ke, ke, ke, ke," clicking of her tongue is the only sound you'll hear from her when she rides her serviteur nowadays in Voodoo rites. She is also known to spit out and vomit blood from her mouth, when she is in possession of her horse, her serviteur. This can be quite frightening for the uninitiated to witness but there is an explanation for it.

According to one Haitian Lore, Dantor was a savvy Business woman who actually sold Black Pigs (native to Haiti) at the marketplace in Port-Au-Prince. One day, she was attacked by a man and legend has it she was stabbed seven times, which is why you will find references to her being stabbed seven times in many of her songs, invocations and poetry. There is also a belief that her spitting or vomiting of blood is, again, related to the torture she underwent by the hands of the French. For each of the seven stabs she endured by the hands of her captors, she spat blood at them.

Set kout kouto, set kout pwenya,
Prete m dedin a pou m al vomi sang mwen,
Set kout kouto, set kout pwenya,
Prete m dedin a pou m al vomi sang mwen,
Sang mwen ape koule.

Seven stabs of the knife, seven stabs of the dagger,
Lend me the basin, so I can vomit my blood,
Seven stabs of the knife, seven stabs of the dagger,
Lend me the basin, so I can vomit my blood,
My blood is pouring down...

This very revealing and well known Haitian song is about the Petwo Iwa, Dantor and it is included in VoodooMystic's website page created by Bon Mambo Racine Sans Bout Sa Te La Daginen as well as the Book, "Mama Lola: A Vodou Priestess in Brooklyn," by Karen McCarthy Brown, University of California, 2001

Despite the numerous tragedies surrounding her manifestation and her life, she is far from being a victim and instead is worshipped as someone who exemplifies strength and opens the gateway to our own inner strength and endurance capabilities. She awakens in us the fighter, the warrioress, the survivor that she herself is. In such an impoverished country, where daily living presents so many obstacles and challenges to ones very own precious livelihood, Erzulie-Dantor is a remarkable loa/Goddess of fierce hope, determination and strength. Many say that she is a mystere who will fight for you with all her heart and soul and that she doesn't require much in exchange, unlike other loa. She only requires that you not pity yourself and crawl away in fear but rather, to take action, when action is needed, and value yourself enough to fight... fight for what is yours... just as she incited Haitians to fight for their country and re-claim it as theirs. She want you to embrace your worth and take action. She is a fierce mother, a warrioress and protectress, who is particularly protective of all women and children; especially women who have been raped, violated and abused by men and single mothers trying to provide for their children.

Impoverished conditions in Haiti requires many men to travel far to find work, sometimes even forced to leave the country (going to U.S.A. and the adjoining country Dominican Republic) to find ways to generate income. This creates a society brimming with numerous abandoned wives (or mates, as actual marriage ceremonies were not as popular, nor necessary in Haiti). This creates a society filled with single mothers left alone with their children, having to find a way to carry on and feed their kids during their father's absence. Erzulie-Dantor is therefore one who is very sympathetic to the struggles of woman, especially financial and she is quite moved to defend women and become invested in women's issues, especially those unique issues plaguing mothers and their children in today's day and age.

Erzulie-Dantor herself is known to have seven children. One of her daughter's, "Anais," is her personal translator and interpreter since she is mute. Anais is often depicted being carried in her mother's arms, holding a book, in a very popular Black Madonna depiction. Erzulie-Dantor also has a son, named Ti-Jan with one of her spouses, Ti-Jean. And some within Voodoo make her and her husband, Ti-Jean, the beloved respective mother and Father of the Petwo Loa nation. She actually had two known husbands; however, they were Simbi Makaya (a Magician) and Ti-Jean (the Herbal magician). Baron Samedi the Lord of the dead and cemeteries and Ogou, the warrior, are also two other lovers, Erzulie-Dantor is often linked with.

Some say she is a Patron Goddess of Lesbians, though there is no mention of her being one, except that she is very bold, strong, aggressive and, again, exclusively very sympathetic to women's struggles and issues. I suppose these can be viewed as the perfect marker for a Goddess embraced by the Lesbian community, but certainly it is not a requirement to worship her.

In contrast to her sister Erzulie-Freda, Erzulie-Dantor is not as Frilly in pink, ultra-feminine nor overtly romantics. She is a warrior Goddess, loa, mystere, who concerns herself with survival, strength, passion, sex, and the empowerment of women. You will find her dressed, not in the pink lace Chantilly that her Sister Erzulie-Freda donnes, but in the blue denim dresses (known as karabel in Haiti) of the common folks. She will also sport on her head a calico "moushwa" (headscarf) or a red handkerchief and always carries a dagger, as she has a great passion for knives, swords and daggers. Any altar dedicated to her would not be complete without displaying some sort of dagger for her.

Images of Erzulie-Dantor always reveal her cheeks scarred with two slashes, also known as "Twa mark" (three marks) even though only two slashes are visible. There are some conflicting stories behind these noticeable brutal scars on her face. Some say they are probably just indicative of the common sacred scarification that identifies certain African tribes and these scars might connect her to her roots in the Congo. Others note how similar these scars are to the warrior face painting that most indigenous tribes, like the Tainos, would wear prior to going into battle and since she is a warrioress this makes perfect sense. However, a more common explanation for these scars can be found in Haitian folklore that would also explain the rivalry between her sister, Erzulie-Freda.

According to one lore, Erzulie-Dantor and Erzulie-Freda both fell head over heels in love with the charismatic warrior Loa, Ogou. These scars are the result of an intense fight where Erzulie-Dantor took her dagger and stabbed her sister through the heart (which explains Freda's popular image as the Mater Delarosa) and Erzulie-Freda in turn then took her dagger and slashed her sister's face a few times. This fight would also explain why many Voodoo Priest, Houngan/Mambo stress the importance of having separate peristyle (ritual spaces or rooms) for these two powerful loa. It is not wise to serve or worship these two Sisters together, as they do not get along and your wanga (magick) will suffer as a result, according to Voodoo practitioners. Their respective Veve are also reflective of this connection with swords and daggers and the heart. One of Dantor's veve is a Heart with two daggers piercing through it.

Regarding the origins of the scars there is also a legend related to the original icon of the Black Madonna of Czestochowa, which is one of the most popular depictions of Erzulie-Dantor. It is alleged that a while back, in Poland, where this venerated icon was maintained, vandals caused damaged to the face of the painting of the Black Madonna and it resulted in these noticeable slashes upon the holy image of her right cheek. Despite numerous restorations the scars would always miraculously reappear and so to this day, when her image is reinterpreted and recreated authentically, those slashes are always revealed for they are a part of her lore and history.

While Erzulie Freda is often depicted as white or light skinned, Dantor, however, was often depicted darker; either as a mulatto woman or black, as in the numerous Black Madonnas, found scattered throughout history. Commonly accepted images of her can be found in the Mater Salvatoris, Our Lady of Perpetual Help, Santa Barbara Africana, Our Lady of Mount Carmel and Our Lady of Czestochowa. Erzulie Dantor as a patron Loa of New Orleans is also connected to Our Lady of Lourdes, since she too, is patron Saint of New Orleans in the U.S.A. There are some lore that also connects her to heavy rainstorms, hurricanes and natural disasters and this is slightly reminiscent of the Orisha, Oya, worshipped in Santeria.

The Black Madonna of Our Lady of Czestochowa is a beloved image often associated with Erzulie-Dantor. It reveals a dark skinned woman dressed in a dark blue robe, crowned as the Virgin Mary along with her child. She is holding her baby who has a book in her left arm. This image of the Virgin holding baby Jesus is believed to be Erzulie-Dantor with her daughter, not the baby Jesus so evangelized by Christians. And this image has been highly venerated in Poland since the late 1300's. Perhaps this holy image arrived to Haiti's shores when Polish soldiers came to fight with and against the French, alongside with the Haitians during the Revolution. Haitians immediately recognized in this image their beloved Loa, mama Dantor.

> *"It is, however, no longer shocking, to suggest that the images represent a continuation of Pagan Goddess- worship, and that some may have once been idol concentrated to Isis or other deities. It is also undeniable that a remarkably high proportion of Madonnas over 200 years old, that are credited with miraculous powers, are Black, as are the traditional patronesses of nations provinces and cities."*
> "The Cult of the Black Virgin, by Ean Begg" Page 130

August 15th is the Asumption day-The Virgin Mary is celebrated and
July 16th is Erzulie-Dantor's Feast Day
The Black Madonna of Czestochowa's feast day is on August 26th

The origins of this famous icon are mysterious but according to several sources the Byzantine icon was originally painted by St. Luke the Evangelist, who lived during the same time period as the Christian, Virgin Mary. He painted her likeness on a cypress table top alleged to have been owned by the holy family and handcrafted by Jesus himself when he was a carpenter and an apprentice to Saint Joseph.

Research reveals that the icon was kept hidden in Jerusalem by the disciples during the Roman's reign, fearing it would be destroyed but around 326 A.D. the icon was found again by St. Helena, mother of Constantine the Great, who took it to Constantinople. She then either gives it to her son or delivers it herself to Constantinople, where a special shrine is built for it among several other relics. It eventually went through various different owners and was housed by many, including the prince of Ladislaus of Opole. When his fortress was invaded by Tartars and their arrows had pierced and damaged the throat region of the painting, he sought to save and preserve it immediately. Some even claim he was guided by angels in dreams to have the precious icon safely sent to Czestochowa, Poland. He surrendered the painting to the Pauline monks and had it moved to Czestochowa, where it arrived on August of 1382 and remains to this day in Jasna Gora (translated as Bright Hills). In 1383 the Jasna Gora monastery was created by Pauline monks, who had originally hailed from Hungary, and had been invited to create this special monastery by Wladyslaw, Duke of Opole.

In 1430, when the church of Czestochowa was invaded by looters, although many sources claims it was the Hussites that ransacked the Pauline monastery where the holy icon was being stored, the painting received more damage. According to one legend, the thieves ended up slashing the cheek region on this painting twice and there is a renowned folklore that tells of the severe punishment they experienced, as they tried to steal this icon and further damaged it with an unsuccessful third slash. According to popular folklore, the robbers fell to the ground, writhe in severe agony and quickly met their death. Another legend tells that the painting of the Madonna started to bleed actual blood at the place where the gashes had been executed. It was enough to scare the robbers and eventually spread the word of her great powers.

The icon of the Black Madonna of Czestochowa, is so often associated with Erzulie-Dantor, has garnered a reputation throughout the centuries for performing all kinds of miracles. To this day people make holy pilgrimages to visit and view this icon reputed to answer prayers and bring about all kinds of documented miracles.

In 1656, after frightening the Saracens from invading the land, Poland finally declared the Black Madonna as their Queen. In a ceremony held at the Cathedral of Lviv, the Black Madonna was there finally crowned and formally declared as Queen protectress of Poland, on April 1, 1656, by the King of Poland, Jan Kazimiertz.

The Song; Black Madonna,

There is a recess on this earth,
Where everybody wants to come back,
Where reigns Her face,
On the face – two cut scratches,
Eyesight has sorrowful, anxious,
Like She wanted to ask you,
You to entrust yourself to Her Protection.

Madonna, Black Madonna,
How it is good to be Your child,
O, allow, Black Madonna,
To be hidden in Your arms.

In Her arms you will find peace
And you will be protected from evil,
Because for all of Her children,
She has loving heart and she will protect you,
When you give Her your heart,
When you will repeat these words:

Madonna, Black Madonna,
How it is good to be Your child,
O allow, Black Madonna,
To be hidden in Your arms.

Today, when trouble is around us,
Where a person can hide herself,
Where a person should go,
If not to the Mother,

who will give consolation.
So, we are beseeching , O, Madonna,
Direct eyesight on Your children
And hear, when we are singing , asking you:

Madonna, Black Madonna,
How it is good to be your child,
O allow, Black Madonna,
To be hidden in Your arms.

From: www.catholicculture.org/culture/library/view.cfm?recnun2996, www.marypages.com/czestochowa.htm, www.Czestochowa.pl/welcome *and*
www.jasnagora.com, www.enwikipedia.org/wiki/Black_Madonna _of Czestochowa,

(I don't know the original author of this poem to the Black Madonna but it fits perfectly for Dantor....It was attained from http://www.Marypages.com/Czestochowa*)*

Her Worship, Offerings and Altar Set Up

Serving Erzulie-Dantor is quite simple as she is a Loa that welcomes her vodouisant/worshippers and, unlike her sister Ezulie-Freda, who loves all things pink; her preferred colors are Navy Blue and Gold or yellow. Sometimes red is added because, after all, she is a Petwo Loa. Her colors reflect her beloved connection to the Revolution and to Haiti's independence and thus, she shares in their flag color of blue, red and gold. And because she is a hot Petwo loa, it is suggested to first begin all workings for her with a goblet of cool water to keep her from getting too hot. An altar decorated with her sacred colors, via various altar cloths, flowers, candles, even the food (like the icing on a cake offering) can display her favorite colors. Practitioners of Voodoo spare no expense when it comes to their exquisite altars and rites and they really lay out ostentatious spreads for their loas. Erzulie Dantor's altars should have daggers as these are sacred to her, as well as maraccas or calabash, dolls and silver jewelry, as this is her preferred metal of choice. She also enjoys the perfume Reve D'Or and Kleren or Aguardiente. And of course, no Voodoo altar would be complete without some Florida water on hand, as this is reputed to bring on spiritual possessions.

Food offerings, which are an important part of Voodoo rites, are also offered to Erzulie-Dantor. She is particularly fond of cane liquor, sweet potatoes and among her preferred offerings are the Griyo (fried pork). She loves unfiltered cigarettes, grilled pork, and rice, red or black beans. Cakes, with blue and yellow frostings, would also be appropriate on an altar dedicated to her. Black pigs are incorporated in rituals to her in Haiti, perhaps due to her folklore connection to this animal and the tales surrounding that infamous Voodoo Rite that started the Haitian Revolution. She is also noted for appreciating the offering of a spicy Haitian Dish made with marinated fried Pork cubes. Other common offerings to her are pan fried corn with pepper, fried bananas, black rice made with mushroom (also known as Riz Djon-Djon). And of course, serve her rum, red wine or honey with cinnamon and pepper, for as you can see, a hot Petwo loa requires hot spicy food offerings. Brown Grain Breads can be used in place of animal offerings if you are a vegan and opposed to these meat offerings according author and Houngan, Kevin Filan and Sallie Ann Glassman but I feel it's best to respect the culture and their lore and serve the loa what they would appreciate regardless of your own personal dietary preferences.

When preparing your food offerings for the Loa it is suggested to first lift up the food (or food dish) over your head in a sign of offering, then lower it to your lips, breathe on the actual food, pouring your essences over it. Then elevate it to your forehead, then to your heart chakra and finally to your root chakra or pubic region to bless it. Next, one should pour three drops of crème de cacao on the ground and then place your food offerings to Erzulie-Dantor and verbalize your gift to her. Light your Voodoo candles around these food offerings. Allow your offering to surround your Voodoo candles and let it melt over it, burning all night if possible. The next day gather all remnants and these should be disposed of at a crossroad or wilderness, where hopefully it will not be disturbed by humans and will become compost for the earth.

Interesting to note, early Voodoo ceremonies allowed food offerings to be given to the animals whose blood would eventually be sacrificed to the Gods. This prepared and consecrated the animals for the Divine.

To begin your Voodoo rite to Erzulie-Dantor, begin by calling on your highest Divine deity. Most in Voodoo will begin by reciting the Lords' prayer (the Our Father) and the Hail Mary. Afterwards, as no loa can cross the threshold into this realm without the help of Legba, the guardian of the Crossroads, you would be wise to invoke him and respectfully ask him to open the gates so that spiritual communion may take place. Be sincere in your petition and present an offering to him on the earth. Papa Legba will open the gates and allow for divine interaction to bless your rite from this moment onward.

The center of the peristyle (the Voodoo ritual room) holds a large erect pole at the very center. It is considered a Divine axis, the sacred pole, which is reminiscent of the ancient Canaanite Asherah; this center pole is the axis. It is through this pole that heaven and earth meet and we can begin to have access to the spirits/Loa, for it is believed they travel through this pole to grace worshippers (vodouisants) with their presence. Spiritual possession, which is a common occurrence in Voodoo, is encouraged and very much a part of all Voodoo rites.

Erzulie Dantor, as a patron and protectress of those first initiated into Voodoo, is often invoked during a Kanzo, this is a special Petwo rite of initiation. She is also the patron of the "paket," which is a special power object made under the guidance of the Hougan/Mambo for the newly initiated Voodoo Priest/Priestess. "Bat guerre" or "Bat Ge" is the ceremony that comes before the initiation or Kanzo Ritual and it is the opening ceremony of a Voodoo initiation rite. All these rites fall under her domain as a Petwo Loa and this also includes the creation of the "paket."

Other Rituals for Erzulie Dantor

For a Voodoo money ritual, a website called "Roots without End" suggests putting your candle within a boiled sweet potato, pour Crème de Cacao and let it burn. It is also suggested to offer frenetic dances to Dantor, as she greatly appreciates movement and dance as a form of worship. There is another simple ritual incorporating a request to the Warrioress loa, written on a sheet of blue and gold decorated paper. Fold this paper with your written wishes and then, with your dagger or special knife, stab it seven times in her name and declare your wish done!

Musing

Erzulie-Dantor exemplifies for us the spirit of the true protectress and fierce warrior. She elevates the spirit of humanity with inspiration and confidence to go into battle, wherever those battles may be; whether in a country facing turmoil and fighting for its independence or in the privacy of ones' home, while asserting liberties and basic human rights. Her validity and importance for us today, is just as relevant as it was centuries ago and yet, her aggressive, "hot" energy is so often feared by women who have yet to unearth this aspect within themselves.

Some that may fear her but remember she is a fierce protective mother, first and foremost, to her vodouisant and worshippers, who so often even endearingly refer to her as Mama Dantor. Consider the nature of a Mama bear with her cub, consider your own interactions with those you most love and cherish, what wouldn't you do for them....? Approach her with this view as a protectress mama bear and you will see your fears turn into reverence, great love and appreciation for someone so lovingly invested in your own wellbeing. You are her cub. She would rather bestow to you magickal abilities and wealth but not the lavish, superfluous riches that her sister Freda is so often connected with. She rather bestow to those who serve her, the many opportunities to create riches of all kinds, through jobs and other means. Dantor opens the way to help you make your own fortunes and resolve challenges in unexpected fashion. In this way, she is loa, and yes, a Goddess, who opens the way to reveal opportunities, liberation, strength, courage and confidence to do more than survive but to thrive in pursuit of your most cherished goals.

> *"Our ancient, battered, much –loved, little –understood, Black Virgins are a still-living archetypal image that lies at the heart of our civilization and has a message for us. The Feminine Principle is not a theory but real and it has a will of its own which we ignore at our peril..."*
>
> The Cult of the Black Virgin, Ean Begg page 134

*Liberator, Erzulie-Dantor, is the awakener of our desire for freedom. In Voodoo, Dantor is the spirit of the revolutionist who incites our courage to stand for what is right and just. She is the Voodoo Loa Mother, who defends her offspring at all cost. She is the fierce, machete/dagger wielding energy of the Dark Goddess. Protectress and defender of women and children, she will go into battle when the only way to be emancipated is to finally fight back. When wars need to be fought she incites the heart with strength and when we must face our abusers and oppressors, she equips us with the courage. Yes, she is a love Goddess like her sister Erzulie-Freda but her energy has a ferocious passion that will bring about monumental changes. She is an advocate for your emancipation and lures you into a transformative journey towards true freedom.

FERONIA

Feronia is the ancient Roman Goddess of Abundance, Fertility, Wilderness, Vitality, and Freedom. In ancient times she was petitioned to grant freedom to slaves most notably during her annual festival, the **Feroniae Festival,** held November 13th.

In Latin, the word, *"Ferus"* means the untamed, crude or, of the field, and uncultured. It is interesting to note that many of her ancient shrines were found in places that would've been considered away from the general population and in the wild, untamed remote parts in nature. Therefore, it is not difficult to see her connection to the wilderness.

As a Harvest Goddess, she received the first fruits in order to guarantee an abundant crop for the year; this was customary for most Harvest deities in ancient times. She had one Temple at the base of Mount Soracte, near Capena and many others near water springs, which is indicative of the types of rites offered to her. She had many known cults and shrines, many of them found near groves and remote areas. Two notable Temples of Feronia were in Aquileia and in Terracina.

Beloved by Plebeians and Freedmen, a surviving inscription at one of her sanctuaries indicates why she is a patron Goddess for Civil Rights and the enslaved. It is said that there is a surviving stone at her Temple in Terracina which states, *"Let deserving slaves sit down so that they may stand up free..."* this according to Roman historian, Titus Livius Patavinus.*wikipedia* There is also a reference by an ancient writer, Servius, who documents that there was a Roman Goddess of Liberty named, Feronia or Fidonia. Here we find several supporting evidence that connects Feronia as a Patron Goddess of Freedom. The Roman Goddess Feronia thus becomes a wonderful deity to work with in this chapter as we explore the theme of liberation.

SHINA TSU HIME

Shina Tsu Hime is a Japanese Shinto Goddess connected to the winds and sailing ships. She is the Goddess of Freedom, Movement, Playfulness, and the Fulfillment of Wishes. Her connection to playfulness and the wind explains why rituals involving kite flying are performed in her honor.

Sailors have been known to petition her protection and blessings upon their voyages and because of her many known gifts. Farmers called upon her to bring rain and blow fertile seeds upon their land. She is also known to thwart negative winds and blow away evil. She can almost be seen as the personification of the morning breeze or the one that parts the clouds and scatters the morning fog away. In this way, we see her as the one who allows the light into our world; the bringer of the morning sun. She liberates the sky of darkness so that the light comes forth. It is a beautiful metaphor for our exploration of freedom in this chapter.

Partnered with her consort, Shina Tsu Hiko, she is venerated at the Shinto Temple of Ise Jingu but their main temple can be found in the small Japanese town called, Yamamoto.

IRIS

Iris is the Greek messenger for the Gods, similar to Hermes and Mercury. The Goddess Iris traveled between the earth and the other realms freely to execute her role as Divine messenger. She was often depicted as a winged young maiden. Rainbows are particularly of great significance to her and she is known as a patron Goddess of protection, peace and freedom. Connect to the Goddess Iris to awaken your inner freedom loving, adventuresome, youthful spirit. Delve into your inner maiden with Iris and consider taking a trip to a far off land. The rainbow is a powerful symbol of hope, after surviving dark turbulent storms. Spend some time reflecting on the imagery of a colorful bright rainbow (you may even paint one) and note what emotions it conjures up. The Goddess Iris can sometimes be seen as the personification of the rainbow; bringing us hope, freedom and peace.

HINA

Hina is the Hawaiian Goddess of the Moon. Her name, translates as "girl" or "woman" and sometimes even more precisely as "woman in the moon." Hina, in Polynesian and Tahitian cultures, connotes the feminine spirit. According to Hawaiian cosmology, the first Gods to step foot on the great Island of Hawaii were Ku and Hina; respectively, male and female. Ku was viewed as the rising Sun, the East and Hina his opposite, the west and the setting sun. This links her directly to the Moon. Hina embodied all the attributes of a Moon Goddess. She ruled over Fertility and intuition and she ruled over the waters; the ebb and flow of life and procreation. Hina also reigned over planting, agriculture and the fishing cycle.

As the first female Goddess of Hawaii, she ruled over the procreation and population of her people. Much like the Greek Goddess Gaia, Hina is seen as the great Mother of the Polynesian people. She created a number of impressive descendants, like the Pig God, Kamapua'a and Maui, the demigod. Hyphened and variations of her name can be found in several other Goddesses throughout Hawaiian mythology. There are also some references to Hina as a triple Goddess, much like many significant, ancient Goddesses throughout mythologies of various cultures. She was attributed for bringing numerous gifts to the Hawaiian people including the revered coconut.

According to one myth, Hina, in the heavens, was so enamored by the lush landscape of Hawaii that she decides to descend upon it and make it her temporary home. Hina came down from the cosmos and made the island of Maui her abode and there, she fell in love with a mortal. She married a man known as a great warrior. Together they lived in Ka'uiki, under the volcano called, Haleakala. As the Hawaiian lore reveals, most of her days were spent working hard, pounding the Kapa board to make fine craftsmanship textile and clothing. She was known to make magic with her extraordinary Tapa cloth and her contribution to Hawaiian Textile was significant.

Once married, she gave birth to two half-human, half-deified children. Everyday Hina worked very hard, fetching water and fresh shrimp for her family. She also worked hard on her Tapa cloths but as time went on, her husband became very lazy, expecting her to do everything because, after all, she was a Divine Goddess. Her half-blood children, also became too much to handle, as they too adopted their father's laziness and arrogance. They were known to be quite mischievous and extremely demanding of their mother.

According to a popular Hawaiian lore, one day, when Hina was out by the river working, she caught sight of the most beautiful rainbow (although in some stories they say she had the ability to manifest rainbows herself). In this story she tried to climb up the rainbow to join the brilliant light of the Sun that called, but the heat of the mid-day sun was too much for her to handle and she could not bear it. After exhaustibly trying to climb it, she fell and slipped off the rainbow. Then, over heated and weakened, she fainted and passed out. Some time passed by before she finally woke up in the early evening hours. Frantically worried for her family, she got up quickly and rushed back home. As one would suspect, when she returned home, her abusive husband, needless to say, was furious. He berated her stronger than usual. The children also added insults to their mother, angered that their precious dinner had not been prepared.

Late at night, when they had all fallen fast asleep, Hina longingly stared out at the window and there presented before her, was another brilliant light that once again captivated her heart- the light of the Full moon. She remembered the light of the sun beckoning her in the day time and yet, here was another brilliant light strongly urging her to come again. It was then that her heart stirred and she felt the strong urging to leave her misery behind and unite with the familiar divine light before her. She wasted no time and immediately packed her bag with her prized calabash and tapa cloth. Hina endeavor to take only her most cherished possessions with her. One look at the brilliant light of the moon and she was enamored by its comforting light. She knew there was peace and harmony within the moon.

Enchanted by the glow, she was determined, more than ever, to leave her painful situation on earth; to go and join this beloved light, now beaming from the moon. This light was a spark of remembrance, a familiarity she had long forgotten that was now being restored to her via, the Moon.

A rainbow appeared, as if by magic, she manifested this sacred vehicle to lead her to her Divine destination. As she began her climb, she was invigorated and felt a renewed determination to reach the moon. Alas, she was getting closer, when all of a sudden; she felt the sensation of her leg being pulled. It was him…her abusive, earthly husband. He caught sight of her trying to escape and he violently tugged and pulled on her leg. He threatened her and screamed at her, not to go...but this only made her more determined to leave. With all of her Divine strength she pushed onward, towards the Moon. But he was strong and had the strength of a warrior. He pulled and pulled and with a mighty force he yanked her foot right off. He severed Hina's foot and, simultaneously, fell down to the ground, while she managed to muster up enough strength to continue onward on her journey, until she made it safely inside the moon.

Within the moon Hina found rest, peace and eventually was able to heal, recuperate and grow a new foot. Legend says she still feels throbbing in her foot as a reminder of what she endured and left behind on earth. Hawaiians today still worship Hina and seek her reflection in the full moon. She continues to be revered as the beautiful Lady of the Rainbow-Beloved Feminine Goddess of the Moon.

Hina Musing -Creating Sanctuaries

Our beloved Polynesian Goddess of the moon and her legends can be seen as a metaphor for women in need of safety. Whether it is a safe place, in our own individual mind/soul, or an actual physical place or room. Our safe space can be found in a number of places, like rituals (whether solitary or within a group) or a special meditation that transcends and transports us there. Even a simple prayer (as one envisions Hina reciting to the light of the moon she saw from her window) can bless us with a sanctuary. In times of stress, we can utilize our imagination and simply visualize this sacred temple or we can actually create it physically. Either way, Hina and her most popular myth, teaches us the importance of this sacred space for women and encourages us to find our freedom.

When we are feeling hopeless, overwhelmed and confused in our daily living or when sadly, our own lives are compromised and threatened, a personal sanctuary becomes absolutely invaluable. It allows us a chance to regroup and rethink our personal situation. It allows us an opportunity to find healing and renew our sense of self-worth. Sometimes this sacred sanctuary, whether real or imagine, can make the difference between life and death for some women.

Having endured so much abuse on earth, Hina reaches that pivotal point when she begins to long for freedom and an exodus from the pain. Hina's escape into the divine Moon and the very act of selecting it as her new home is symbolic of this transformative phase in her life. The moon, which has always been a symbol of intuition and feminine spirituality, becomes her sanctuary and she looks upon it now, as her way out of her unhappiness –the Moon thus becomes her "savioress." Herein the Moon is Hina's safe place, to retreat from her troubles -in this case, her lazy human husband and half blood, mischievous children.

Inside the Moon, she endeavors to heal, regroup, regain her sense of self and reconnect with something that goes so deep, far deeper into her lineage and ancestry than she could possibly begin to understand intellectually. But she comprehends it intuitively, and the call is to her soul, which has no boundaries, or timelines and unquestionably, she can no longer deny the call. Hina follows her intuition and goes inside the nurturing, grandmother moon that calls unto her, leaving behind her stressors and those painful earthly trials and tribulations. She finds her liberation within the moon.

It is also quite a powerful metaphor is when we get to the part of the lore when her leg is severed. At the most pivotal point, when she was approaching her sacred place, her scoundrel of a husband grabbed her leg, pulling and violently yanking it- not letting her go, not letting her take care of herself. He pulled her so hard that her foot breaks off. Yet the Goddess perseveres, abandons her severed, bloody foot and continues on her journey towards the moon. She knows then the value of her freedom and is willing to sacrifice even her foot, to attain it. There is a powerful message here, for we learn that, sometimes, there are parts of us that must be cut off and severed, before beginning any journey of self-healing and self-discovery. As the cutting off of a foot is bloody and violently painful, it is what Hina must face and endure before reaching her sacred sanctuary within the Moon.

The husband tugging at her foot can be seen as a symbol of our obligations and our roles, making every effort to tug, break and defeat us. And sometimes this gruesome act, being fueled by selfishness, anger and volatility, is so intense, that indeed, parts of us are broken in the process of our healing. The husband, in this case, is that which keeps us in the perpetual state of hopelessness, bondage, paralysis, keeping us where we are or where we have always been.

Sometimes our obligations and responsibilities keep us stagnant and, in the only place we've probably ever known, thus blocking us from any further growth. Opportunity for change and transformation are stunted. That tugging of the leg is symbolic of being blocked from what could essentially transform us... improve us and give us wings. Her foot is tugged and ripped like the clipping of a bird's wings (or an attempt to do so) right at the critical moment it's about to take flight. In this case, Hina did not let this sabotage her flight and, with mutilated "wings" (aka leg) she continued on her journey.

Oftentimes, those you least expect, those you believe love you the most, are the ones that can impede your progress in life. Those beloved people or situations can try to stunt our own personal growth and transformation, like Hina's husband and family. It can be a brother or sister, a mother, father, relative, lover, boyfriend, girl-friend, professor, boss, even a mere acquaintance. Sometimes it's a deliberate action and sometimes it's on another unconscious level or even a dark part of our own psyche, but the intent remains the same, to keep you in your place.

In Hina's tales we learn of the importance to care for our own selves as womyn and the value in finding our own personal sanctuary, whether it's *Calgon moment*" in our sudsy bathtubs, an elaborate candle light ritual or trance meditation or in severe cases, a woman's shelter or friend's home. Our sacred sanctuaries are important to define and possess, as we go through life's numerous trials and tribulations and endeavor to grow spiritually. She is symbolic of women awakening to their need for freedom, independence, self-care, and safe sanctuaries in their lives. In Hina, we find a brilliant Goddess that, according to her lore, recognized her need for freedom from those who had tried to oppress or control her. She is beckoned by the rainbow and the divine light of the moon and instinctively recognizes the value of this peaceful sactuary. Hina invites us to seek and embrace those journeys that will inevitably bring peace, freedom and great transformation.

*Hina is the primordial Polynesian rainbow Goddess, who makes the ancient Moon her home. She comes into your life to remind you of the sacredness and necessity of your freedom and the need to create your personal sanctuary. She arrives at this point in your life to ask you, *"Do you have a personal space that nourishes and heals you and keeps you protected?"* Where can we retreat to regain ourselves? Physical vacations are common and act as our temporary escape where we may touch upon a certain type of freedom but, what if we have available to us, a mental and spiritual place to retreat to, whenever situations require an escape? The question she now presents to you is, *"Can you find your freedom?"* *"When confronted with toxic situations or people and negative relationships, are you able to find a sacred space (within) to guard and recharge yourself? Are you able to manifest safety, serenity; a liberated peace of mind?* She enters your life at this time and beckons you to erect your core spiritual home and unearth a place of peace. With the Goddess Hina you are invited to live your life authentically and free.

JOURNALING

What does it mean to you to be Free?
_____
_____

Can you recall a time in your life when you were restricted or bound?
_____
_____

**Can you recall a time in your youth when you felt free?
Describe this feeling...?**
_____
_____

Who or what demands most of you today?
_____
_____

Is there anything right now that is restricting you or oppressing you?
_____
_____

Is there anyone or any situation causing you to dim your light?
_____
_____

What does Freedom feel like to you?
_____
_____

Can you paint a picture or attach a color to the word, Liberation?
_____
_____

Is there something in your world that you wish to break free from?
_____
_____

Can you name or personify what this is?
_____
_____

How would your life be enhanced by this feeling of liberation? What would you do with this freedom and what would you do to attain it? _____
_____

Do you feel many people are living in this world with all of their freedom? _____
_____

What feelings or images are conjured at the thought of a caged Lion in a zoo? _____
_____

What small step can you take today to progress towards your freedom or the freedom of others who might be oppressed and silenced in the world at large? _____
_____

THEME WORK SUGGESTIONS
GRAIN & WIND WORK:

Holding Grains in your hands (you can use wheat or rice or Farina or flour...) hold it tightly in your hands and imbue it with the energy of all you are surrendering in your life now. Let this grain represent what you are releasing in your life. Take this grain to an open field and on a windy day, while opening up your hands, spin your body 3x times as you release the grains to the winds with the intention of attaining your freedom from those things that no longer serve your highest good... End this rite, like many others, by declaring, *"It is done for the greater good, so mote it be!"*

INVOCATION & POETRY

LIBERATION GRASP

Age of Aquarius,
Let Freedom Ring,
Embers are burning,
Stirring from within…

Every soul is seeking,
To fly and to soar,
Breaking all shackles,
Opening all doors…

I am autonomous,
Blessed and Free,
Spark of Divinity
Birthed within me

Dantor, Goddess
Voodoo Loa Divine
Let my prayers
Reach you now in time

Grant me the strength
To attain what I seek.
Liberate me,
From all that makes me weak.

Herein accept,
This offering to you,
Goddess, Liberator,
Help my wish come true.

*** You are now encouraged to create
your own altar(s) & invocation(s).
)O(Blessings!

MAGICK RITES AND TOOLS

This is your personal page to document your sacred rites and the tools you elected to use.

DECIDE WHERE TO SET UP AN ALTAR
Place an Altar Cloth in the Color of your choice.
Color: _____

GODDESS
Place an image of your Deity.
Goddess: _____
This image can be a Statue, handmade Sculpture or a simple Photo _____

FIRE REPRESENTATION
Place a blessed/charged Candle in the color of your choice.
Candle Type and color: _____

AIR REPRESENTATION
Light your Incense stick.
Incense Scent: _____

WATER REPRESENTATION
Place a Chalice of Water
Water Item: _____

EARTH REPRESENTATION
Place a Potted Plant or Fresh Flowers on your Altar
Add Salt or a plate of Dried Herbs
Herbs: _____
Chosen Gemstone: _____

YOUR WISH
_____
_____

Place a symbol of your desire, if you have one available, and also write your wish out clearly, on a piece of parchment paper, or you can even use a cut up brown paper bag. These are the basics for a very simple altar & rite. Ultimately, your sacred space is only limited by your imagination. You can make your altar & rite as big or as small as you prefer and the addition of other personal items is really up to you.)o(Enjoy!

ALTAR PHOTOS

******

CHAPTER THIRTEEN

"Character cannot be developed in ease and quiet. Only through experience of trial and suffering can the soul be strengthened, ambition inspired and success achieved…" Helen Keller

"The World is round and the place which may seem like the end may also be only the beginning." Rebecca West

There are traditionally 13 Lunations in a year and the number 13 has always had a deep esoteric connection with the Sacred Feminine. It is therefore, only logical to come to the end of our journey in this book at chapter 13.

The Wheel of Fortune card from the tarot deck presents itself in our lives today. We've reached a pivotal turning point in our journey. The wheel turns once more. It is yet another noteworthy Crossroad in our pathwork together. Like most sacred crossroads, it brings us to a moment of deep contemplation and an examination of our past experiences and the lessons attached to them.

Together, in this book, we traversed many milestones and worked through various themes.
1. Intuition
2. Leadership
3. Creation & Birth
4. Love & Joy
5. Mother Archetype
6. Strength & Rage
7. Body & Health
8. Justice
9. Sexuality, Power & Death
10. Ambition
11. Work & Prosperity
12. Liberation

We encountered these themes in our lives as important lessons and faced the challenges and gifts they offered us. In so doing, we carved out our own growth and spiritual journey. As we reach chapter 13, the final chapter of this book, it's important to note that this is not the final stage of our journey. It not just one journey we embark on in life, it is often, many. And, spiritual growth and our personal human evolution is a Spiral path. When we reach a level of mastery it often leads us to yet another portal to begin a higher level of existence. Thus, the Fool that we encountered in the previous chapter now leads us into the beginning of a new cycle; and a new adventure begins. Only now the character of the Fool takes with her, all the priceless, unique lessons learned from the previous cycle. She may face similar situations only now with new skills, new tools to reach new levels of proficiency.... to finally master what could not be mastered previously.

We may come to the final stage of this book but it is not the final stage of our journey. We move onward now, like in the Death card in the Major Arcana of the Tarot deck, ending one cycle to begin anew.

I wish to thank you for joining me on this journey. For all those who have been long supporters of my work and read and purchased many of my creations, I send my deepest love and sincerest gratitude, for you have been an integral part of my own journey as a Goddess woman, a writer, an artist and a priestess.... As you continue on your personal journey, I wish you much love, success, and happiness. May all your Collective Journeys in the spiral dance continue to bring you Magick, Protection, and Empowerment.   )O(**Blessed Be!**

A PLACE TO DOCUMENT FINAL THOUGHTS.....

_____

_____

_____

_____

RESOURCES & BIBLIOGRAPHY

CHAPTER 1
PERSEPHONE
Circle Round, Raising Children in Goddess Tradition by Starhawk, Diane Baker and Anne Hill
Goddess in Every Woman, a New Psychology of women by Jean Shinoda Bolen, MD.
Greek Goddess of innocence and Queen of the underworld. http://www.goddessgift.com/goddess-myhths/greek-goddess-peresphone.htm
Persephone Unveiled, Seeing the Goddess and Freeing Your Soul by Charles Stein
The Goddess Path, Myths, Invocations and Rituals by Patricia Monaghan
The Meaning of Persephone's name-m.anthony, http://quantum-witch.com/theos/w/p-name.htm
The Myth of Persephone- Greek Goddess of the Underworld by Laura Strong, PhD., http://www.mythicarts.com/writing/persephone.html
The Mythic Tarot, a New approach to the Tarot Cards by Juliet Sharman-Burke and Liz Greene
The Witches 'Goddess, The Feminine Principle of Divinity by Janet and Stewart Farrar
Wikipedia.com a free Encyclopedia

ARADIA
Aradia; The Gospel of the Witches by Charles Godfrey Leland
Grandmother Moon, Lunar Magic in our lives by Zsuzsanna E. Budapest
Hereditary Witchcraft, Secrets of an Old Religion by Raven Grimassi
Italian Witchcraft -the old religion of Southern Europe by Raven Grimassi
The Book of the Holy Strega by Raven Grimassi
The Holy Book of Women's Mysteries by Zsuzsanna E. Budapest
The Witches 'Goddess, The Feminine Principle of Divinity by Janet and Stewart Farrar
Stregherie.com
Witchcraft for Tomorrow by Doreen Valiente

HEKATE
Pagan Anger Magic, Positive Transformations From Negative Energies by Tammy Sullivan
The Witches' Goddess, The Feminine Principle of Divinity by Janet and Stewart Farrar
The Theogony by Hesiod
Homeric Hymn
Grandmother of Time by Zsuzsanna E. Budapest
The Holy Book of Women's Mysteries by Zsuzsanna E. Budapest
Hekate Soteira, a Study of Hekate's Role in the Chaldean Oracles by S.I. Johnston
Who is Hekate? from WitchVox.com by Helena Domenic
SageWoman No.# 39 Autumn 1997, One of Ten Thousand; Goddess Lore and Ritual Article by Diana L. Paxson Hekate Guide of the Soul

ISIS
Egyptian Gods and Goddess- 4 from Ellie Cystalinks.com
Egyptian Mythology by Veronica Irons
Goddesses in World Mythology, a Biographical Dictionary, Martha Ann and Dorothy Myers Imel, Oxford
The Book of the Goddess Past and Present, An introduction to Her Religion, edited by Carl Olson, The Crossroad Publishing Company, New York NY, 1987
The Goddesses' Mirror, Visions of the Divine from East and West, by David R. Kinsley, State University of New York Press, Albany New York, 1989

CIRCE
Pagan Anger Magic, Positive Transformations From Negative Energies by Tammy Sullivan
Goddesses in World Mythology, a Biographical Dictionary, Martha Ann and Dorothy Myers Imel, Oxford
INTERNET: Http: www.Maicar.com/GML/CIRCE.HTML
INTERNET: Http: www.Greekmythologydotcom
INTERNET: Http: www.Theoi.com/Titan/Kirke

CHAPTER 2
OYA YANSA
A Ritual For Change, The tribal tradition Omnipresent Oya.com By Heathwitch
Carnival of the Spirit, Seasonal Celebrations and Rites of Passage by Luisah Teish
Jambalaya, The Natural Woman's Book of Personal Charms and Pracitical Rituals by Luisah Teish
Oya; in Praise of the African Goddess by Judith Gleason
Powers of the Orishas by Migenes Gonzalez-Wippler
The Blue Roebuck.com and A Primer in Dianic Witchcraft by Bendis also known as Deanne Quarrie founder of the Apple Branch
The Goddess Oracle, A Way to Wholeness Through The Goddess and Ritual by Amy Sophia Marashinsky and Hrana Janto
The New Book of Goddesses and Heroines by Patricia Monaghan
Paganwiki.com
SageWoman No. #47 Autumn 1999, Petition to Oya, a letter offering from a reader by Juniper in Colorado
SageWoman No.#55 Autumn 2001, One of Ten Thousand: Goddess Lore and Ritual article- Oya, Lady of Change by Diana L. Paxson
SageWoman No. #65 Truth and Beauty, Masks for the Goddess by Lauren Raine
Santeria, the Religion by Wippler, Migenes Gonzalez

SIF
Dictionary of Northern Mythology, byRudolf Simek
Goddess Afoot, practicing Magic with Celtic and Norse Goddesses by Michelle Skye, Llewellyn Worldwide Publishing, Woodbury, Minnesota, 2008
Myth and Religion of the North, by Turville-Petre
Norse Magic by D.J. Conway, Llewellyn Publications, St. Paul Minnesota, 1997
Northern Mysteries and Magick: Runes and Feminine Powers by Freya Aswynn, published in 1998 by Llewellyn

Poems of the Elder Edda, Trans. P Terry
Poetic Edda. Snorri Sturluson, Trans A. Faulkes
Sagewoman Magazine, Issue 62, Courage, A Circle is Cast, Column, by Sage women readers. Autumn Equinox Ritual by Gallina Krasskova page 73-76
Scandinavian Mythology, by H R Ellis Davidson
The Cassell Dictionary of Norse Myth and Legend by Andy Orchard
The Goddess Oracle, a Way to Wholeness through the Goddess and Ritual, by Amy Sophia Marashinsky, Massachusetts, Element Books, 1997
The Rites of Odin by Ed Fitch 1990, Llewellyn
365 Goddess, a Daily Guide to the Magic and Inspiration of the Goddess by Patricia Telesco, HarperSanFrancisco, a Division of Harper Collins Publishing, 1998
Internet: http://www.sodahead.com/unitedstates/sif-norse-goddess-of-the-grain/question-1596611
Internet: http://www.mysticwicks.com
Internet: http://www.thorshof.org/sif.htm.
Internet: http://ancienthistory.about.com/od/norsemyth/a/aa081799Norse.htm
Internet: en.wikipedia.org/wiki/sif
Internet: http://www.Valkyrie tower.html.com/sif
Internet: http://www.Mistress of EnchantmentBlog.com:Sif- 2010

HESTIA
Ancient Mirrors of Womanhood, A Treasury of Goddess and Heroine Lore from Around the World by Merlin Stone
Goddess in Every Woman, a New Psychology of women by Jean Shinoda Bolen, MD.
Goddess In World Mythology, a Biography Dictionary by Dorothy Myers Imel and Martha Ann
The Goddess Oracle, A Way to Wholeness through The Goddess and Ritual by Amy Sophia Marashinsky and Hrana Janto
365 Goddess, a daily guide to the magic and inspiration of the Goddess by Patricia Telesco
Wikipedia.com free Encyclopedia

AMATERASU
Circle Round, Raising Children in Goddess Tradition by Starhawk, Diane Baker and Anne Hill
Goddess Mirror, Visions of the Divine From East and West by David Kinsley
The Book of Goddesses, Past and Present: An Introduction to her Religion by Carl Olson
The Goddess Path, myths, invocations and rituals by Patricia Monaghan
The Goddess Oracle, A Way to Wholeness Through The Goddess and Ritual by Amy Sophia Marashinsky and Hrana Janto
Nihonghi -translated by W.G. Aston
SageWoman No.# 54 Summer 2001, Reclaim Your Power...and Find inner Peace, Too! by Lady Moondance
SageWoman No. #65 Truth and Beauty, Calligraphy lessons by Kela Vaeltaja
Wikipedia internet free encyclopedia

ODUDUA
Jambalaya, the Natural Woman's Book of Personal Charms and Practical Rituals by Luisah Teish
Ritual and Spells of Santeria, by Migene Gonzalez-Wippler
The Handbook of Yoruba Religious Concepts, by Baba Ifa Karade
Goddesses in World Mythology, a Biographical Dictionary, Martha Ann and Dorothy Myers Imel, Oxford
Mama Lola: A Vodou Priestess in Brooklyn, by Karen McCarthy Brown, University of California, 2001
Secrets of Voodoo by Milo Rigaud, City Lights Books, San Francisco, CA 1969, 1985
The Cult of the Black Virgin, by Ean Begg Chiron Publishing, Wilmette, Illinois 2006
INTERNET: Http: www.Awonifadotcom/orishas
INTERNET: www.the Yoruba.com
INTERNET: www.theOrisha.com
YouTube: Moses781 Youtube
YouTube: Orisha Yoruba, Chief Yuya Vlog

CHAPTER 3
GAIA
Ancient Mirrors of Womanhood, A Treasury of Goddess and Heroine Lore from Around the World by Merlin Stone
Circle Magazine, Celebrating Nature, Spirit and Magic Issue 87 Spring 2003 Earth and Spirit: Mother Gaia by Jesse Wolf Hardin
Gaia; A New Look At Life on Earth by J.E. Lovelock
Goddess In World Mythology, a Biography Dictionary by Dorothy Myers Imel and Martha Ann
Green Egg a Journal of the Awakening Earth Vol. 30 No #125 November-December 1998, Gaian Ministry; Reclaiming Earth and Spirit by Jesse Wolf Hardin
People of the Earth, The New Pagans Speak Out by Ellen Evert Hope and Lawrence Bond
Persephone Unveiled, Seeing the Goddess and Freeing Your Soul by Charles Stein
The Book Of Goddesses, Past and Present: An Introduction to her Religion by Carl Olson
The Goddess Path, myths, invocations and rituals by Patricia Monaghan
The Encyclopedia of Magical Herbs by Scott Cunningham
Wikipedia.com a free Encyclopedia

BRIGID
Circle Round, Raising Children in Goddess Tradition by Starhawk, Diane Baker and Anne Hill
The Goddess Path, Myths, Invocations and Rituals by Patricia Monaghan
The Wheel of The Celtic Year.com chalice centre.net/imbolc
The Witches ' Goddess, The Feminine Principle of Divinity by Janet and Stewart Farrar
Pan Gaia Exploring the Pagan World No #20 Summer 1999, Brigid in Ireland; Discovering the Magic by Diane Conn Darling
SageWoman No.#46 Summer 1999, One of Ten Thousand: Goddess Lore and Ritual article -Brigit, Inspiration Upwelling by Diana L. Paxson
Wikipedia.com a free Encyclopedia

SARASWASTI
Chakra Workout, Balancing your Energy with Yoga and Meditation by Mary Horsley

Goddess In World Mythology, a Biography Dictionary by Dorothy Myers Imel and Martha Ann

Grandmother Moon, Lunar Magic in our lives by Zsuzsanna E. Budapest

Healing Mantras, by Thomas Ashley-Farrand

Hindu Gods and Goddess by Swami Harshananda

SageWoman No.#46 Summer 1999, The Great Goddess Saraswati; Flowing River of Creativity, Inspiration and Joy by Suzin Green

SageWoman No. #64 Prayer and Invocation, One of Ten Thousand: Goddess Lore and Ritual- Article, Sarasvati, Word of Wisdom by Diana L. Paxson

The Book of Goddesses, Invoke the Powers of the Goddess to Improve Your Life by Roni Jay

365 Goddess, a daily guide to the magic and inspiration of the Goddess by Patricia Telesco

NU-KUA

Chinese Mythology, Irene Dea Collier, Enslow Publishers, Inc. 2001

Chinese Mythology: An Introduction by Anne Birrell

Goddesses in World Mythology, a Biographical Dictionary, Martha Ann and Dorothy Myers Imel, Oxford University Press, New York 1993

Handbook of Chinese Mythology (Handbook of World Mythology) Lihui Yang, Deming An, with Jessica Anderson Turner, Oxford University Press, 2005

The Goddess Oracle, a Way to Wholeness Through the Goddess and Ritual, Amy Sophia Marashinsky, Illustrated by Hrana Janto,Element Books, Inc, Rockport, MA, 1997

365 Goddesses, a Daily guide to the magic and inspiration of the Goddess, Patricia Telesco, Harper SanFrancisco,1998, Nu Kwa- Feb 13

Internet: www.Mysticwicks.com

Internet: www.Wikipedia.org/wiki/N%C3BCwa

Internet: www.chinavoc.com/history/ancient/myth_nw.htm

Internet: www.squidoo.com/nukuagoddess

Internet: From WIKI http://en.wikipedia.org/wiki/N%C3%BCwa

Internet: http://www.Chinavoc.com/history/ancient/myth-nw.htm

Internet: http://www.thaliatook.com/AMGG/nukua.html)

OLWEN

Goddess Afoot, practicing Magic with Celtic and Norse Goddesses by Michelle Skye, Llewellyn Worldwide Publishing, Woodbury, Minnesota, 2008

Goddess In World Mythology, a Biography Dictionary by Dorothy Myers Imel and Martha Ann

The Goddess Oracle, A Way to Wholeness Through The Goddess and Ritual by Amy Sophia Marashinsky and Hrana Janto

365 Goddess, a daily guide to the magic and inspiration of the Goddess by Patricia Telesco

https://www.Wikipedia.org-Olwen

CHAPTER 4

HATHOR

Ancient Mirrors of Womanhood, A Treasury of Goddess and Heroine Lore from Around the World by Merlin Stone

Egyptian Gods and Goddess- 4 from Ellie Cystalinks.com

Egyptian Mythology by Veronica Irons

Grandmother Moon, Lunar Magic in our lives by Zsuzsanna E. Budapest

Hathor, the Goddess of Love, Music, Beauty.com by Caroline Seawright

The Book Of Goddesses, Past and Present: An Introduction to her Religion by Carl Olson

The Goddess Oracle, A Way to Wholeness Through The Goddess and Ritual by Amy Sophia Marashinsky and Hrana Janto

The Goddess Path, myths, invocations and rituals by Patricia Monaghan

365 Goddess, a daily guide to the magic and inspiration of the Goddess by Patricia Telesco

Who is the Goddess Hathor? Pyramidcompany.com On the Internet by Rhiannon Barkemeijer de Wit

Wikipedia.com free Encyclppedia

BAUBO

Goddess In World Mythology, a Biography Dictionary by Dorothy Myers Imel and Martha Ann

Goddessgift.com Article on the Greek Goddess of Mirth- Baubo

365 Goddess, a daily guide to the magic and inspiration of the Goddess by Patricia Telesco

Reconnect With Your Inner Goddess.com byAnita Ryan Revel-2000

The Yoni, Sacred Symbol of female creative Power by Rufus C. Camphausen

Wikipedia.com Free Encyclopedia

ERZULIE-FREDA

Erzulie, Everyday better living.com by Judi Singleton

Pan Gaia, A Pagan Journal for Thinking People No. #36 Summer 2003 Erzulie Freda,

Mistress of Love by Kevin Filan

Rituals and Spells of Santeria by Migenez, Gonzalez-Wippler

Secrets of Voodoo by Milo Rigaud

Spellmakererzulie.love.com

The Book of Goddesses, Invoke the Powers of the Goddess to Improve Your Life by Roni Jay

The Book of Goddesses, Past and Present: An Introduction to her Religion by Carl Olson

The Haitian Voodoo Handbook, Protocols for Ridding with the Lwa by Kevin Filan

365 Goddess, a daily guide to the magic and inspiration of the Goddess by Patricia Telesco

APHRODITE

Ancient Mirrors of Womanhood, A Treasury of Goddess and Heroine Lore from Around the World by Merlin Stone

Ariadne's Thread, a Workbook of Goddess Magic by Shekhinah Mountainwater

Goddess in Every Woman, a New Psychology of women by Jean Shinoda Bolen, MD.

Goddess Mirror, Visions of the Divine from East and West by David Kinsley

Grandmother Moon, Lunar Magic in our Lives by Zsuzsanna E. Budapest

Grandmother of Time by Zsuzsanna E. Budapest

The Goddess Path, myths, invocations and rituals by Patricia Monaghan

The Witches' Goddess, The Feminine Principle of Divinity by Janet and Stewart Farrar

Wikipedia.com

FLORA
Goddesses in World Mythology, a Biographical Dictionary, Martha Ann and Dorothy Myers Imel, Oxford

365 Goddess, a daily guide to the magic and inspiration of the Goddess by Patricia Telesco

https://www.Britannica.com -Flora-Roman Mythology

https://www.thaliatook.com —Flora, Roman Goddess of Flowers

OSHUN
Mama Lola: A Vodou Priestess in Brooklyn, by Karen McCarthy Brown, University of California, 2001

Secrets of Voodoo by Milo Rigaud, City Lights Books, San Francisco, CA 1969, 1985

The Cult of the Black Virgin, by Ean Begg Chiron Publishing, Wilmette, Illinois 2006

The Haitian Vodou Handbook, Protocols for Ridding with the Lwa by Kenaz Filan (Houngan Coquille du Mer), Destiny Books, Rochester, Vermont, 2007

Vodou Love Magic, A Practical Guide to Love, Sex, and Relationships by Kenaz Filan), Destiny Books, Rochester, Vermont, 2009

CHAPTER 5
CORN MOTHER
365 Goddess, a daily guide to the magic and inspiration of the Goddess by Patricia Telesco

The Goddess Oracle, A Way to Wholeness Through The Goddess and Ritual by Amy Sophia Marashinsky and Hrana Janto

http://www.michellemays.com

Song: "Selu awa do li"

Corn - myth encyclopedia-mythology , god, story, names, world, creation, people, children, fire

http://www.mythencyclopedia.com/corn

http://www.abaxion.com/sz02.jpg

http://www.dovercards.com

http://www.rainewalker.com/selu.htm

Corn mother's gift by Chrity Salo

The story of Corn-History detective-in the beginning

http://www.campsilos.org/mod3/students/c-history.shtml

http://www.witcvox.com/music/bardic Circle-Michelle Mays;

The story of Selu, Michelle Mays

ASHERAH
Ancient Mirrors of Womanhood, a Treasure of Goddess and Heroine Lore from around the World, by Merlin Stone, Beacon Press, Boston, Massachusetts, 1979

Goddesses in World Mythology, a Biographical Dictionary, Martha Ann and Dorothy Myers Imel, Oxford University Press, New York 1993

The Book of the Goddess Past and Present, an introduction to Her Religion edited Carl Olson, The Cross Road Publishing Company, New York, New York, 1987

The Hebrew Goddess by Raphael Patai, Wayne State University Press, Detroit Michigan,1990-third enlarged Edition Internet: http://en.wikipedia.org/wiki/Asherah

Internet: "Asherah, the Tree of Life and the Menorah" http://wwww.asphodel-long.com/htm1/Asherah.html

Internet: The Goddess in Judaism www.asphodel-long.com/htm4goddess

Internet: "Asherah, the tree of Life" http://www.asphodel-long.com/htm1/asherah.html

Internet: Classical Hebrew.com - http://blog-en.classicalhebrew.com/tag/asherah

DEMETER
Ancient Mirrors of Womanhood, A Treasury of Goddess and Heroine Lore from Around the World by Merlin Stone

Circle Round, Raising Children in Goddess Tradition by Starhawk, Diane Baker and Anne Hill

Goddess in Every Woman, a New Psychology of women by Jean Shinoda Bolen, MD.

The Goddess Path, Myths, Invocations and Rituals by Patricia Monaghan

The Mythic Tarot, a New approach to the Tarot Cards by Juliet Sharman-Burke and Liz Greene

The Witches 'Goddess, The Feminine Principle of Divinity by Janet and Stewart Farrar

MAIA
Goddesses in World Mythology, a Biographical Dictionary, Martha Ann and Dorothy Myers Imel, Oxford

365 Goddess, a daily guide to the magic and inspiration of the Goddess by Patricia Telesco

YEMAJA
Goddesses in World Mythology, a Biographical Dictionary, Martha Ann and Dorothy Myers Imel, Oxford

Jambalaya, The Natural Woman's Book of Personal Charms and Pracitical Rituals by Luisah Teish

Powers of the Orishas by Migenes Gonzalez-Wippler

365 Goddess, a daily guide to the magic and inspiration of the Goddess by Patricia Telesco

KUAN-YIN
Goddesses in World Mythology, a Biographical Dictionary, Martha Ann and Dorothy Myers Imel, Oxford

The Goddesses' Mirror, Visions of the Divine from East and West, by David R. Kinsley, State University of New York Press, Albany New York, 1989

Https://www.Holymtn.com-Legend of Quan Yin

https://www.Goddess.ws

CHAPTER 6
PELE
Cofeetime.com by Betty Fullard-Leo

Goddess Mirror, Visions of the Divine From East and West by David Kinsley

MythicRealm.com

Pagan Anger Magic, Positive Transformations From Negative Energies by Tammy Sullivan

SageWoman No.# 54 Summer 2001, Reclaim Your Power...and Find inner Peace, Too! by Lady Moondance

Tales of Hina Online By Lana's Aumakua

The Goddess Oracle, A Way to Wholeness Through The Goddess and Ritual by Amy Sophia Marashinsky and Hrana Janto

365 Goddess, a daily guide to the magic and inspiration of the Goddess by Patricia Telesco

White Moon Gallery.com

Wikipedia.com free Encyclopedia

AINE
Aine - Wikipedia.com Free Encyclopedia
Ancient Mirrors of Womanhood, a Treasury of Goddess and Heroine Lore from Around the World by Merlin Stone
Love Magic, The Way To Love through Rituals, Spells, and the Magical life by Laurie Cabot
Goddess In World Mythology, a Biography Dictionary by Dorothy Myers Imel and Martha Ann
365 Goddess, a daily guide to the magic and inspiration of the Goddess by Patricia Telesco

KALI
Pagan Anger Magic, Positive Transformations From Negative Energies by Tammy Sullivan
The Goddess Oracle, A Way to Wholeness Through The Goddess and Ritual by Amy Sophia Marashinsky and Hrana Janto
365 Goddess, a daily guide to the magic and inspiration of the Goddess by Patricia Telesco
The Cult of the Black Virgin, by Ean Begg Chiron Publishing, Wilmette, Illinois 2006
Goddess Grimoire Journal, a Collection of Simple Prose and Spells, by B. Melusine Mihaltses, Publisher; Feminine Divine Works, Schertz, Texas, 2012
Hindu Goddesses, Visions of the Divine Feminine in the Hindu Religious Tradition, by David R. Kinsley,University of California Press, Berkeley and Los Angeles California, 1988
Hindu Gods and Goddesses by Swami Harshananda, The President, Sri Ramakrishna Math, Mylapore, Madras
Pagan Anger Magic, Positive Transformations from Negative Energiesby Tammy Sullivan, Citadel Press, Kensington Publishing Corp. New York, NY 2005
Twenty-Four Aspects of Mother Kali by Babaji Bob Kindler, SEV Associations, Honoka'a, Hawaii, 1996

SEKHMET
Egyptian Paganism for Beginners, bring the Gods and Goddesses of Ancient Egypt into Daily Life by Jocelyn Almond and Keith Seddon, Llewellyn Publications, St.Paul, Minnesota, 2004
Pagan Anger Magic, Positive Transformations From Negative Energies by Tammy Sullivan
The Goddess Oracle, A Way to Wholeness Through The Goddess and Ritual by Amy Sophia Marashinsky and Hrana Janto
365 Goddess, a daily guide to the magic and inspiration of the Goddess by Patricia Telesco
The Cult of the Black Virgin, by Ean Begg Chiron Publishing, Wilmette, Illinois 2006

ERESHKIGAL
Inanna, Queen of Heaven and Earth, Her Stories and Hymns from Sumer by Diane Wolkstein and Samuel Noah Kramer, 1983 First Edition
Goddess In World Mythology, a Biography Dictionary by Dorothy Myers Imel and Martha Ann
Goddess Grimoire Journal, a Collection of Simple Prose and Spells, by B. Melusine Mihaltses, Publisher; Feminine Divine Works, Schertz, Texas, 2012
Pagan Anger Magic, Positive Transformations from Negative Energiesby Tammy Sullivan, Citadel Press, Kensington Publishing Corp. New York, NY 2005
The Book of the Goddess Past and Present, An introduction to Her Religion, edited by Carl Olson, The Crossroad Publishing Company, New York NY, 1987
INTERNET: Http: www.Ancient pagesdotcom
INTERNET: Http: www.Ancient dot eu by Joshua J. Mark
INTERNET: Http: www.Mrpsmythopediadotwikispacesdotcom/Ereshkigal

CHAPTER 7

ARTEMIS
An ABC of Witchcraft from Past and Present by Doreen Valiente
Ancient Mirrors of Womanhood, A Treasury of Goddess and Heroine Lore from Around the World by Merlin Stone
Ariadne's Thread, a workbook of Goddess Magic by Shekhinah Mountainwater
Goddess in Every Woman, a New Psychology of Women by Jean Shinoda Bolen, MD.
Grandmother Moon, Lunar Magic in our Lives by Zsuzsanna E. Budapest
Grandmother of Time by by Zsuzsanna E. Budapest
SageWoman No.#57 Spring 2002, One of Then Thousand: Goddess Lore and Ritual article-Artemis, Hunting The Moon by Diana L. Paxson
The GoddessGift.com Artemis
The Holy Book of Women's Mysteries by Zsuzsanna E. Budapest
The Mythic Image Moon Maiden: Young Diana by Wynter Rose Stiles
The Goddess Path, Myths, Invocations and Rituals by Patricia Monaghan
Witches, Investigating an Ancient Religion by T.C.Lethridge
Women's Mysteries Ancient and Modern by M. Esther Harding

SKADI
Ancient Mirrors of Womanhood, a Treasury of Goddess and Heroine Lore from Around the World by Merlin Stone
Llewellyn's 2005 Magical Almanac; Article; "Skadi, Norse Goddess of Winter" by Lily Gardner
pg 64-65 St. Paul Minnesota, Llewellyn Worldwide 2005
Norse Magic, by D.J. Conway, Llewellyn Publications
The Elder Edda, translated by Lee Hollander, Texas, USA, University of Texas, 1986
Skadi - Wikipedia.com free encyclopedia

UZUME
Ancient Mirror of Womanhood, a Treasury of Goddess and Heroine Lore from around the World, by Merlin Stone, Beacon Press, Boston 1984 edition
Gathering for Goddess, a Manual for Priestessing Women's Circles, by B. Melusine Mihaltses.Publisher; Feminine Divine Works, Schertz, Texas, 2012
Handbook of Today's Religions- by Josh McDowell & Don Stewart
The Book of the Goddess Past and Present, an Introduction to Her Religion Edited by Carl Olson, The Crossroad Publishing Company, New York 1987
The Goddess Oracle, a Way to Wholeness Through the Goddess and Ritual, Amy Sophia Marashinsky, Illustrated by Hrana Janto,Element Books, Inc, Rockport, MA, 1997
365 Goddesses, a Daily guide to the magic and inspiration of the Goddess, Patricia Telesco, Harper SanFrancisco,1998, Nu Kwa- Feb 13
Shinto, a Celebration of Life by Aidan Rankin, OBooks, Winchester UK, Washington, USA, 2010
Internet: www.uwec,edu/philrel/shimbutsudo/uzume.html
Internet: www.greenshinto.com
Internet: Kojiki Records of Ancient Matters transl. B.H. Chamberlain
Internet: Religion in Japanese History, Joseph M. Kitagawa
Internet: www.1000questions.net/en/religion/shinto.html

Internet: en.wikipedia.org/wiki/Ame-no-Uzume-no-Mikoto

Internet: www.Goddessgift.com/goddess/Japanese_goddess_Amaterasu.htm

Internet: www.Pantheon.org.>Areas>Mythology>Asia>Japanese mythology

Internet: www.Bukisa.comReligion & Spirituality

Internet: www.Ancient history.about.com/od/uzumemyth/

Internet: www.Land of wisdom.com

MACHA
Goddess Afoot, practicing Magic with Celtic and Norse Goddesses by Michelle Skye, Llewellyn Worldwide Publishing, Woodbury, Minnesota, 2008

Goddess In World Mythology, a Biography Dictionary by Dorothy Myers Imel and Martha Ann

The Goddess Oracle, A Way to Wholeness Through The Goddess and Ritual by Amy Sophia Marashinsky and Hrana Janto

365 Goddess, a daily guide to the magic and inspiration of the Goddess by Patricia Telesco

Whitemoondotcom/goddess/Macha

SUNNA
Goddess Afoot, practicing Magic with Celtic and Norse Goddesses by Michelle Skye, Llewellyn Worldwide Publishing, Woodbury, Minnesota, 2008

Goddess In World Mythology, a Biography Dictionary by Dorothy Myers Imel and Martha Ann

The Goddess Oracle, A Way to Wholeness Through The Goddess and Ritual by Amy Sophia Marashinsky and Hrana Janto

365 Goddess, a daily guide to the magic and inspiration of the Goddess by Patricia Telesco

Scandinavian Mythology, by H R Ellis Davidson

The Cassell Dictionary of Norse Myth and Legend by Andy Orchard

CHAPTER 8
MA'AT
Ancient Mirrors of Womanhood, a Treasure of Goddess and Heroine Lore from around the World, by Merlin Stone, Beacon Press,Boston, Massachusetts, 1979

Egyptian Paganism for Beginners, bring the Gods and Goddesses of Ancient Egypt into Daily Life by Jocelyn Almond and Keith Seddon, Llewellyn Publications, St.Paul, Minnesota, 2004

The Book of Goddesses, Invoke the Powers of the Goddess to Improve Your Life by Roni Jay, A Quarto Book, Baron's Educational Series, Inc. Hauppauge, New York, 2000

The Gods of the Egyptians; studies in Egyptian mythology- Vol.I, by E.A. Wallis Budge, Dover publ.1969

The Goddess Oracle, a Way to Wholeness through the Goddess and Ritual, by Amy Sophia Marashinsky, Massachusetts, Element Books, 1997

The Witches' Goddess, the Principle of Divinity by Janet and Stewart Farrar, Phoenix Publishing Inc. Custer Washington, 1987

365 Goddess, a Daily Guide to the Magic and Inspiration of the Goddess by Patricia Telesco, HarperSanFrancisco, a Division of Harper Collins Publishing, 1998

Internet: Themystica.org/mythical-folk/articles/maat.html

Internet: From http://en.wikipedia.org/wiki/Maat

Internet: Egypt.idolhands/maat/intro.html

Internet: Crystalvaults.com/pages/goddess_maat.php

Internet: Paganwicca.about.com/od/egyptiandeities/p/maatprofile.htn

Internet: www.Daughterofmaat.hubpage

Internet: www.touregypt.net/godsofegypt/maat2.htmCaroline Seawright

Internet: ancient-egypt.info/2012/03/maat-egyptian-goddess-and-blinding-of.htm

Internet: In existence since the old kingdom, pyramid text of Unas (CA2375 BCE and2345 BCE)

Egyptian religion by Siegfried Morenz, translated by Ann E. Keep page 275, 1992

Cornell University Press, l

SageWoman Magazine no. #78, Spring 2010- Finding our Balance,

"One of Ten Thousand: Goddess Lore and Ritual' by Diana L. Paxson page 36-42

RHIANNON
Ancient Mirrors of Womanhood, a Treasure of Goddess and Heroine Lore from around the World, by Merlin Stone, Beacon Press,Boston, Massachusetts, 1979

Goddesses in World Mythology, a Biographical Dictionary, Martha Ann and Dorothy Myers Imel, Oxford University Press, New York 1993

365 Goddess, a Daily Guide to the Magic and Inspiration of the Goddess by Patricia Telesco, HarperSanFrancisco, a Division of Harper Collins Publishing, 1998

The Goddess Oracle, a Way to Wholeness through the Goddess and Ritual, by Amy Sophia Marashinsky, Massachusetts, Element Books, 1997

The (Mabignon) Mabinogi translated by Patrick K. Ford, Berkeley: University of California Press. 1977

Internet: www.mabinogion.info/Rhiannon.htm

Internet: www.paganwiccan.about.com

Internet: www.goddessgift.com/goddessgallery/Rhiannon.html

Sagewoman Magazine, Issue 73. Rhiannon the Mare Mother, One of Ten Thousand: Goddess Lore and Ritual regular Column by Diana Paxson (pages25-33)

ASTRAEA
Goddesses in World Mythology, a Biographical Dictionary, Martha Ann and Dorothy Myers Imel, Oxford

The Goddess Oracle, A Way to Wholeness Through The Goddess and Ritual by Amy Sophia Marashinsky and Hrana Janto

365 Goddess, a daily guide to the magic and inspiration of the Goddess by Patricia Telesco

TARA
INTERNET: www.Crystallinks.com> Tara

INTERNET: www.En.m.wikipedia.org> Tara

INTERNET: www.Religionfacts.com>Tara

INTERNET: www.Sacredwind.com>Tara

INTERNET: www.Hologramthoughts.com>Buddhism

Goddess in World Mythology, a Biographical Dictionary by Martha Ann Dorothy Myers Imel

Hindu Goddesses, Visions of the Divine Feminine in the Hindu Religious Tradition by David R. Kinsley

Hindu Gods and Goddeses by Swami Harshananda

Siddhartha by Hermann Hesse

The Book of Goddesses, Invoke the Powers of the Goddess to Improve Your Life by Roni Jay, A Quarto

The Goddess Oracle, A Way to Wholeness Through The Goddess and Ritual by Amy Sophia Marashinsky and Hrana Janto

Twenty –Four Aspects of Mother Kali by Babaji Bob Kindler

365 Goddess, a daily guide to the magic and inspiration of the Goddess by Patricia Telesco

SEDNA

365 Goddess, a daily guide to the magic and inspiration of the Goddess by Patricia Telesco

The Goddess Oracle, A Way to Wholeness Through The Goddess and Ritual by Amy Sophia Marashinsky and Hrana Janto

Goddesses in World Mythology, a Biographical Dictionary, Martha Ann and Dorothy Myers Imel, Oxford University Press, New York 1993

INTERNET: www.polarlife.ca>traditional

INTERNET: www.Goddessgift.com>goddess-myths

INTERNET: www.dltk-teach.com

INTERNET: www.wikipedia>wiki>Sedna_(mythology)

INTERNET: Franz Boas' (1888, Monograph)"The Central Eskimo"

IRENE

Goddess In World Mythology, a Biography Dictionary by Dorothy Myers Imel and Martha Ann

INTERNET: Http: www.Theoigreekmythologydotcom

INTERNET: Http: www.Goddessguidedotcom

INTERNET: Http: www.Greekmythologydotcom

INTERNET: Http: www.Wikipediadotorg

THEMIS

Goddess In World Mythology, a Biography Dictionary by Dorothy Myers Imel and Martha Ann

INTERNET: Http: www.Theoigreekmythologydotcom

INTERNET: Http: www.Goddessguidedotcom

INTERNET: Http: www.Greekmythologydotcom

INTERNET: Http: www.Wikipediadotorg

CHAPTER 9

LILITH

Ancient Mirrors of Womanhood, a Treasure of Goddess and Heroine Lore from around the World, by Merlin Stone, Beacon Press, Boston, Massachusetts, 1979

Goddess Grimoire Journal, a Collection of Simple Prose and Spells, by B. Melusine Mihaltses, Publisher; Feminine Divine Works, Schertz, Texas, 2012

Inanna Queen of Heaven and Earth, Her Stories and Hymns from Sumer, by Diane Wolstein and Samuel Noah Kramer, Harper and Row Publishers, New York, New York, 1983

Pagan Anger Magic, positive Transformations from Negative Energies, by Tammy Sullivan, Citadel Press, Kensington Publishing Corp. New York, New York, 2005

The Case of Lilith, 23 Biblical Evidences, identifying the Serpent as Adam's first failed wife in Genesis, by Mark Wayne Biggs, Published by ReligionBookMix, 2012

The Cult of the Black Virgin, by Ean Begg Chiron Publishing, Wilmette, Illinois 2006

The Goddess Oracle, a Way to Wholeness through the Goddess and Ritual, by Amy Sophia Marashinsky, Massachusetts, Element Books, 1997

The Hebrew Goddess by Raphael Patai, Wayne State University Press, Detroit Michigan,1990, -third enlarged Edition

The Witches' Goddess, the Principle of Divinity by Janet and Stewart Farrar, Phoenix Publishing Inc. Custer Washington, 1987

Internet:Embracing the Dark Goddess by Dominae

Internet:www.flutterbywings.com/goddess /Lilith.htm, "I am Goddess, Worship me" Nov. 2008

Internet:Sumerian Legend of Lilith, translated by Charles Alexander Moffat from The Lilith Gallery

Internet:An Order of the White Moon, "Lilith –Child of Light, Daughter of Darkness

Internet:Lilith; A Romance by George MacDonald, 1985

Internet:The Lilith Shrine by Dante Gabriel Rosetti, "Collected Poems," London 1906

BLODEUWEDD

Goddess Afoot, practicing Magic with Celtic and Norse Goddesses by Michelle Skye, Llewellyn Worldwide Publishing, Woodbury, Minnesota, 2008

Goddesses in World Mythology, a Biographical Dictionary, Martha Ann and Dorothy Myers Imel, Oxford University Press, New York 1993

The Goddess Oracle, a Way to Wholeness through the Goddess and Ritual, by Amy Sophia Marashinsky, Massachusetts, Element Books, 1997

The White Goddess, a Historical grammar of Poetic myth, by Robert Graves, International Authors, N.V. Farrar, Straus And Giroux, New York1948

365 Goddess, a Daily Guide to the Magic and Inspiration of the Goddess by Patricia Telesco, HarperSanFrancisco, a Division of Harper Collins Publishing, 1998

Internet: www.orderwhitemoon.org/goddess/Blodeuwedd2.html

Internet: www.goddessrealm.com/goddess-of-the-moment/16

Internet:: www.mysticwicks.com

Internet:www.paganpages.org/contenttag/blodeuwedd

BABA YAGA

Baba Yaga – The Ambiguous Mother of the Russian Folktale by Andreas John ($28) 2004, Isbn#13-9780820467696

Balkan Traditional Witchcraft by Radomir Ristic

The Goddess Oracle, a Way to Wholeness Through the Goddess and Ritual, Amy Sophia Marashinsky, Illustrated by Hrana Janto, Element Books, Inc, Rockport, MA, 1997

365 Goddess, a Daily Guide to the Magic and Inspiration of the Goddess by Patricia Telesco, HarperSanFrancisco, a Division of Harper Collins Publishing, 1998

Internet: www.realmagick.com/700 BabaYaga article by Freya

Internet: www.examiner.com/article by Juliet Friette

Internet: www.matrifocus.com/ SAMO/BabaYaga,Susun Weed Article

Internet: www.orderwhitemoon.org

Internet: www.healingwayofrabbit/BabaYaga Part I and Part II

Internet: www.helium.com

Internet: wwww.Blueroebuck.com

Internet: www.7yearoldwitch.blogspot, BabaYaga 2009

Internet: www.Mythling.com

MAMAN BRIGITTE

http://members.aol.com/racine125/index1.html website by Bon Mambo Racine Sans Bout Sa Te La Daginen internet

www.Meta-Religion.com world religions/voodoo/ancestors.htm internet

SageWoman Magazine, Autumn 2008- issue 75 -Surrendering and Awakening-One of Ten Thousand; Goddess Lore and Ritual (page 31-37) Article- Maman Brigitte, Priestess of the Tomb, by Diana L. Paxson

www. Sosyetedumarche.com/html/b...te.html -internet

www.Thaliatook.com/AMGG/mamanbrijit- Thalia Took Oracle website

The magical buffet.com/blog½...cemetery internet

Secrets of Voodoo by Milo Rigaud

Wikipedia.com free Encyclopedia internet

INANNA & ICHTAR

Inanna, Queen of Heaven and Earth, Her Stories and Hymns from Sumer by Diane Wolkstein and Samuel Noah Kramer, 1983 First Edition

Goddesses in World Mythology, a Biographical Dictionary, Martha Ann and Dorothy Myers Imel, Oxford

Goddess Grimoire Journal, a Collection of Simple Prose and Spells, by B. Melusine Mihaltses, Publisher; Feminine Divine Works, Schertz, Texas, 2012

Pagan Anger Magic, Positive Transformations from Negative Energiesby Tammy Sullivan, Citadel Press, Kensington Publishing Corp. New York, NY 2005

The Book of the Goddess Past and Present, An introduction to Her Religion, edited by Carl Olson, The Crossroad Publishing Company, New York NY, 1987

The Goddesses' Mirror, Visions of the Divine from East and West, by David R. Kinsley, State University of New York Press, Albany New York, 1989

CHAPTER 10

DURGA

Goddess Grimoire Journal, a Collection of Simple Prose and Spells, by B. Melusine Mihaltses, Publisher; Feminine Divine Works, Schertz, Texas, 2012

Hindu Goddesses, Visions of the Divine Feminine in the Hindu Religious Tradition, by David R. Kinsley,University of California Press, Berkeley and Los Angeles California, 1988

Hindu Gods and Goddesses by Swami Harshananda, The President, Sri Ramakrishna Math, Mylapore, Madras

Pagan Anger Magic, Positive Transformations from Negative Energiesby Tammy Sullivan, Citadel Press, Kensington Publishing Corp. New York, NY 2005

The Book of the Goddess Past and Present, An introduction to Her Religion, edited by Carl Olson, The Crossroad Publishing Company, New York NY, 1987

The Goddesses' Mirror, Visions of the Divine from East and West, by David R. Kinsley, State University of New York Press, Albany New York, 1989

Twenty-Four Aspects of Mother Kali by Babaji Bob Kindler, SEV Associations, Honoka'a, Hawaii, 1996

Internet: www.philhine.org/uk/wrting

Internet: www.Dollsofindia.com

Internet: lotussculpture.com/Durga.htm

Internet: www.Womeninworldhistory.com

Internet: www.srimatham.com/storage/docs/arjunas-hymn-to-durga

Internet: www.dipika.org.za/index.php?option...hymn...durga

Internet: www.shivashakti.com/durga.htm

Internet: www.hinduism.com

IX CHEL

Ancient Mirrors of Womanhood, A Treasury of Goddess and Heroine Lore from Around the World by Merlin Stone

Grandmother Moon, Lunar Magic in our lives by Zsuzsanna E. Budapest

Librarythinkquest.org

Ix Chel Wisdom, Seven Teachings from the Mayan Sacred Feminine by Shonagh Home

Mayan Healers-Daughters of Ix Chel by Rozanna Herrera

365 Goddess, a daily guide to the magic and inspiration of the Goddess by Patricia Telesco

The Goddess Oracle, A Way to Wholeness Through The Goddess and Ritual by Amy Sophia Marashinsky and Hrana Janto

SageWoman No. #57 Spring 2002, Coming across The Great Goddess Ix Chel by Bethany Walsh Smith

Wikipedia.com the free Encyclopedia

NIKE

GoddessGift.net

Hesiod's Theogony

Homeric Hymns

Loggia.com

Orphic Hymn 33 to Nike Translated by Taylor (Greek Hymns C3^{rd} B.C. to 2nd A.D.)

Theoi.com Project

Wikipedia.com free encyclopedia

MAUVE

Goddesses in World Mythology, a Biographical Dictionary, Martha Ann and Dorothy Myers Imel, Oxford

365 Goddess, a daily guide to the magic and inspiration of the Goddess by Patricia Telesco

The Goddess Oracle, A Way to Wholeness Through The Goddess and Ritual by Amy Sophia Marashinsky and Hrana Janto

INTERNET: Http: www.celticlifedotcom

YouTube Channel: Society of Antiquaries of Scotland, Lecture 5, the Goddess of Sovereignty

YouTube Channel: 3rd Coast Celtic, Beyond Green Beer

YouTube Channel: Celtic Notes, Ronnie Drew – Mauve & the Bull of Cooley

FREYJA

Goddesses in World Mythology, a Biographical Dictionary, Martha Ann and Dorothy Myers Imel, Oxford

365 Goddess, a daily guide to the magic and inspiration of the Goddess by Patricia Telesco

The Goddess Oracle, A Way to Wholeness Through The Goddess and Ritual by Amy Sophia Marashinsky and Hrana Janto

Norse-mythologydotnet/Freya-goddess-of-love

Northernpaganismdotorg/shrines/Freya/who-is-freya

Scandinavian Mythology, by H R Ellis Davidson

The Cassell Dictionary of Norse Myth and Legend by Andy Orchard

Poems of the Elder Edda, Trans. P Terry

Poetic Edda, Snorri Sturluson, Trans A. Faulkes

CHAPTER 11
ATHENA
Ancient Mirrors of Womanhood, A Treasury of Goddess and Heroine Lore from Around the World by Merlin Stone

Grandmother of Time by Zsuzsanna E. Budapest

Goddess in Every Woman, a New Psychology of Women by Jean Shinoda Bolen, MD.

Goddess Mirror, Visions of the Divine From East and West by David Kinsley

SageWoman No.# 35 Autumn 1996, 10th Anniversary, One of Ten Thousand; Goddess Lore and Ritual- Athene, The Reconciler of Opposites, Article by Diana L. Paxson

The Goddess Path, Myths, Invocations and Rituals by Patricia Monaghan

The Holy Book of Women's Mysteries by Zsuzsanna E. Budapest

Wikipedia.com a free Encyclopedia

LAKSHMI
Healing Mantras, Using Sound Affirmations for Personal Power, Creativity and Healing, by Thomas Ashley-Farrand, A Ballantine Wellspring Book- The Ballantine Publishing Group, New York, New York, 1999

Hindu Gods and Goddess by Swami Harshananda, printed in India; Sri Ramakrishna Math Printing Press, Mylapore, Madras

The Book of Goddesses, Invoke the Powers of the Goddess to Improve Your Life by Roni Jay, A Quarto Book, Baron's Educational Series, Inc. Hauppauge, New York, 2000

The Book of the Goddess Past and Present, an introduction to Her Religion edited Carl Olson, The Cross Road Publishing Company, New York, New York 1987

The Goddesses' Mirror, Visions of the Divine from East to West by David Kinsley, State University of New York Press, Albany, New York 1989

The Goddess Oracle, a Way to Wholeness through the Goddess and Ritual, by Amy Sophia Marashinsky, Massachusetts, Element Books, 1997

Internet: Goddess Lakshmi by Bansi Pandit at wwwkousa.org/Gods/God6.html

Internet: Lakshmi Goddess of Wealth and Beauty, by Subhamoy Das, About.com

Internet: www.freemeditationinfo.com

BENTEN
Goddesses in World Mythology, a Biographical Dictionary, Martha Ann and Dorothy Myers Imel, Oxford

365 Goddess, a daily guide to the magic and inspiration of the Goddess by Patricia Telesco

FORTUNA
Gathering for Goddess, a Manual for Priestessing Women's Circles, by B. Melusine Mihaltses.Publisher; Feminine Divine Works, Schertz, Texas, 2012

Goddesses in World Mythology, a Biographical Dictionary, Martha Ann and Dorothy Myers Imel, Oxford

365 Goddess, a daily guide to the magic and inspiration of the Goddess by Patricia Telesco

TYCHE
Goddesses in World Mythology, a Biographical Dictionary, Martha Ann and Dorothy Myers Imel, Oxford

365 Goddess, a daily guide to the magic and inspiration of the Goddess by Patricia Telesco

GEFJUN
Goddesses in World Mythology, a Biographical Dictionary, Martha Ann and Dorothy Myers Imel, Oxford

365 Goddess, a daily guide to the magic and inspiration of the Goddess by Patricia Telesco

Scandinavian Mythology, by H R Ellis Davidson

The Cassell Dictionary of Norse Myth and Legend by Andy Orchard

Poems of the Elder Edda, Trans. P Terry

Poetic Edda, Snorri Sturluson, Trans A. Faulkes

INTERNET: Http: www.Norsemythologydot org

CHAPTER 12
DANTOR (ERZULIE-DANTOR)
Gathering for Goddess, a Manual for Priestessing Women's Circles, by B. Melusine Mihaltses.Publisher; Feminine Divine Works, Schertz, Texas, 2012

Mama Lola: A Vodou Priestess in Brooklyn, by Karen McCarthy Brown, University of California, 2001

Secrets of Voodoo by Milo Rigaud, City Lights Books, San Francisco, CA 1969, 1985

The Cult of the Black Virgin, by Ean Begg Chiron Publishing, Wilmette, Illinois 2006

The Haitian Vodou Handbook, Protocols for Ridding with the Lwa by Kenaz Filan (Houngan Coquille du Mer), Destiny Books, Rochester, Vermont, 2007

Vodou Love Magic, A Practical Guide to Love, Sex, and Relationships by Kenaz Filan), Destiny Books, Rochester, Vermont, 2009

Internet:www.Voodoomystic.com, website page created by Bon Mambo Racine Sans Bout Sa Te La Daginen

Internet:www.squidoo.com

Internet:www.widdershins.org

Internet:www.Mysticvoodoo.com

Internet:www.rootswithoutend.com

Internet:www.vodoureligion.com

Internet:www.Qualiafolk.com

Internet:www.webster.edu/-corbetre/haiti/history/revolution/revolution1.htm,

Internet:http://www.travelinghaiti.com/history_of_haiti/slave_rebellion.asp,

Internet:http://wikipedia.org/wiki/Haitian_Revolution

Internet:www.catholicculture.org/culture/library/view.cfm?recnun2996,

Internet:www.marypages.com/czestochowa.htm, www.Czestochowa.pl/welcome

Internet:www.jasnagora.com, www.enwikipedia.org/wiki/Black_Madonna_of Czestochowa,

HINA

Goddess In World Mythology, a Biography Dictionary by Dorothy Myers Imel and Martha Ann

Hawaiian Mythology by Martha Berkwith

Hina Adventures.com

Hina, the Woman in the Moon from Legends of Maui, a Demi-God of Polynesia

by W.D. Westervelt also on Sacred text.com

Many Moons, the Myth and Magic, Fact and Fantasy of our Nearest Heavenly Body,

by Diana Brueton

The Order of White Moon Gallery.com presents, The Goddess Hina by Leigh Hall

365 Goddess, a daily guide to the magic and inspiration of the Goddess by Patricia Telesco

The Hawaiian Oracle, Animal Spirit Guide from the Land of Light, by Rima A Morrell, PhD

FERONIA

Goddesses in World Mythology, a Biographical Dictionary, Martha Ann and Dorothy Myers Imel, Oxford

365 Goddess, a daily guide to the magic and inspiration of the Goddess by Patricia Telesco

INTERNET: Http: www.wikipediadotorg

SHINA TSU HIME

Gathering for Goddess, a Manual for Priestessing Women's Circles, by B. Melusine Mihaltses. Publisher; Feminine Divine Works, Schertz, Texas, 2012

Goddesses in World Mythology, a Biographical Dictionary, Martha Ann and Dorothy Myers Imel, Oxford

365 Goddess, a daily guide to the magic and inspiration of the Goddess by Patricia Telesco

IRIS

Goddesses in World Mythology, a Biographical Dictionary, Martha Ann and Dorothy Myers Imel, Oxford

365 Goddess, a daily guide to the magic and inspiration of the Goddess by Patricia Telesco

OTHER RESOURCES

A Guide to Mystic Faerie Tarot by Barbara Moore

Easy Tarot Guide by Marcia Masino

Feminine Divine Works Intuitive Oracle, A Powerful Tool for Daily Insight and Inspiration by B. Melusine Mihaltses ISBN#978-0-9851384-9-3

Feminine Divine Works Intuitive 70x Oracle Deck

Gathering for Goddess, A Complete Manual for Priestessing Women's Circles by B. Melusine Mihaltses ISBN#978-0-9851384-4-8

Goddess Grimoire Journal, A Collection of Simple Prose and Spells by B. Melusine Mihaltses ISBN# 978-0-9851384-3-1

Living Goddess Spirituality, A Feminine Divine Priestessing Handbook by B. Melusine Mihaltses ISBN#978-0-9851384-7-9

Major Arcana Goddess Living Tarot, A Feminine Divine Works Creation by B. Melusine Mihaltses ISBN#978-0-9851384-8-6

The Mystical Tarot, a Step-by-Step Guide to the Tarot's Ancient and Mysterious Symbols by Roasemary Ellen Guiley

The Mythic Tarot, a New Approach to The tarot Cards by Juliet Sharman-Burke and Liz Greene

The Morgan –Greer Tarot Deck

The Spellcrafting Coach, A Metaphysical Guide to Revamp your Life by B. Melusine Mihaltses ISBN#978-0-9851384-0-0

The Tarot, Art, Mysticism, and Divination by Sylvie Simon

INTERNET: www.presentlove.com

INTERNET: www.laughteronlineuniversity.com

INTERNET: www.ancienthuna.com

**** For a more comprehensive Reference and Bibliography of helpful Goddess books check out the author's first book; "Gathering for Goddess, A Complete Manual for Priestessing Women's Circles," -Isbn#978-0-9851384-4-8

B. Melusine Mihaltses is a Certified life coach, a Published author, intuit artist, Priestess, writer and a Woman's group facilitator. She is also a classically trained singer, holding both a Bachelors and a Masters of Music in Vocal Pedagogy. From an early age she expressed and exemplified a passionate creative, artistic soul and her spirituality has always been steeped and deeply intertwined in her numerous creative expressions. She is a Goddess priestess, dedicated to the intense study of various goddesses from around the world and her commitment to understanding their positive influence on women is undeniable. As founder and priestess of, **Grove of the Feminine Divine**, one of the few all-women's Goddess group in Texas, she has been an active promoter of woman's empowerment and an advocate for women reclaiming their power and returning to their Goddess gifts. She Coaches her private clients weekly and monthly, she organizes beautiful gatherings in her home temple to encourage sisterhood, commemorate the changing seasons and honor various notable deities significant in every woman's journey. These celebratory gatherings are a testament of her love and devotion to her gender's empowerment and the immortal Sacred Feminine. Her first book, **"Gatherings for Goddess, a Complete Manual for Priestessing Women's Circles,"** holds her priestessing journey, invaluable lessons and precious experiences throughout the creation, nurturance and sustenance of this group. It is a treasure trove of insight for anyone heeding the call to promote community, wommin's Circles and Goddess Spirituality. In her other published books; **Goddess Grimoire Journal, a Collection of Simple Prose and Spells,"** and **"Living Goddess Spirituality, a Feminine Divine Priestessing Handbook,"** and **"The Spellcrafting Coach, A Metaphysical Guide to Revamp your Life,"** she continues to share her vast research on Goddess mythologies, Metaphysical tools, artistic creative expressions, inspiring words and her unique journey as a *GoddessWomyn*. She is also the creator of a beautiful 70x card Oracle deck and guidebook that features her own unique artworks titled, **"Feminine Divine Works Intuitive Oracle,"** and she also created the **"Major Arcana Goddess Living Tarot"** with its accompanied colored guidebook. All of her creations are available on Amazon, her FeminineDivineWorks Etsy page and you can also learn more at her website, **http://www.femininedivineworks.com**

As a Goddess Gathering Women's group Facilitator and a private life coach, she incorporates her training as a Certified Life Coach to empower women. Her mission in life is to fully co-create with women and help them reshape their lives and reclaim their inherent gifts through a more Feminine exalting tradition found in Goddess Spirituality. You can learn more about her Life Coaching Practice at www.Goddessempowermentlifecoaching.com.

Growing up in New York City afforded her many opportunities for Spiritual growth and knowledge. She was exposed to numerous learning venues, women's circles and greater opportunities to further her Metaphysical studies. In these numerous women circles, B. Melusine unearth great magick, empowerment, healing, sisterhood and an ancient way of being that resonated deeply with her core beliefs. A student at The Source of Life and at the New York Open Center, she studied tarot with renowned psychic/tarot reader Patti Canova. She also participated in numerous seminars on spiritual matters, drumming circles and rituals. She participated in open Sabbat rituals held by thealogian Susan Marie Hellerer, DMIV, lectures by Margot Adler, author of *"Drawing Down the Moon"* and Phyllis Currott, author of *"Book of Shadows"* & *"Witch Crafting"* and HP of Temple of Ara. At the Learning Annex she took classes on traditional magick, tarot and participated in lectures and rituals held by Donna Limoge, coauthor of *"Sexual Bewitchery and other Ancient Feminine Wiles."* She was part of a yearlong Pagan Grove study, at New York City's emblematic "Enchantments, Inc." and at the Zodiac Lounge, on the upper Westside, she was a member of The Zodiac Lounge Women's Circle, an all-female Goddess centered group led by High Priestess Jezibell. At "Crystal Quilt," in Manhattan,N.Y.C. She participated in a weekly, all female circle, advocating the tradition of – "Wise-Woman Healing Ways" and it was facilitated by Robin Rose Bennett; a well-known Herbologist, student of Susun Weed, Green-Witch and author of *"Healing Magic; A Greenwitch's Guidebook."* It was in these early precious Women's circles, amongst some of the most amazing powerful teachers and sisters (*"all of us were hungry for wisdom, healing and knowledge,"* she remembers) that her life started to shift in ways she had not anticipated. These circles along with the numerous female centered Goddess literatures she was being exposed to like; Shekhinah Mountainwater, Z. Budapest, Marion Weinstein, Ffiona Morgan, Diane Stein, all sparked a greater interest in Women's spirituality. These early Goddess and women centered groups enriched her life greatly and in the presence of such great teachers, facilitators and priestesses, she was privileged to learn a great deal about how to formulate groups and circles that nurture Women's spirituality.

Mrs. Mihaltses also participated in several Goddess Gatherings sojourns; traveling to San Jose California, to attend the 2008 Goddess Gathering, where she finally met and was initiated by beloved founder of the Feminist Dianic Wiccan tradition, Z. Budapest. The following year, she traveled to Madison, Wisconsin to attend yet another important Dianic event.This time B.Melusine partook of Dianic Author and songstress, Ruth Barrett's Daughter of Diana Festival. She attended this annual Goddess Gathering and here, she continued to expand her ritual experiences and knowledge of Goddess Spirituality.

In the autumn of 2013, B. Melusine Mihaltses was a presenter of workshops at the first, Goddess Spirit Rising International Goddess Conference, held in Malibu, California along with giving lecures at local events, introducing some of her works. Early summer of 2013, B. Melusine Mihaltses was the recipient of "The Shift Network Team Scholarship" for additional studies on Women Leadership and Spirituality. This scholarship was offered to her for participation and further course studies in the, *"Soulful Women Rising, Living your Soul's calling to Co-create a New World,"* taught by Devaa Haley Mitchell and Elayne Kalila Doughty, the founders of, "Inspiring Women Summit." With this training she intends to enhance her work as a Priestess, writer and Life coach for women and hopes to be of greater service to her Spiritual community.

A native New Yorker, B. Melusine is mother of three, handfasted and married for over eighteen years and is now making her home in the south of Texas. Currently she is working on the release of her debut recording of original Pagan Goddess chants and her seventh book, **"Goddess Coaching Companion."** Along with her published books, you can also find her unique creations, her special Oracle card decks and her Intuit-Goddess-Art on canvases at, **http://www.femininedivineworks.com**. Information on her Life Coaching services can be found at **http://www.Goddessempowermentlifecoaching.com.**

Author, B. Melusine Mihaltses, c.l.c., m.m., b.m.

FEMININE DIVINE WORKS
COMPANY ORDER FORM

www.Femininedivineworks.com

We are a Woman affirming, Goddess exalting company, dedicated to the Sacred Feminine and all works created with a Goddess, Feminist Wiccan message. We offer heart & hand-birthed creations that promote Goddess and Women Spirituality. Our mission is to support and awaken women to their own inner Goddess and empower them to embrace their inherent gifts through our numerous offerings.

Dear friends,

Thank you for your interest in our growing company and our various tools that facilitate spiritual growth. We have many more helpful products available for our wonderful patrons. Below we have provided an order form with some of our current offerings for sale. Please feel free to utilize this form to place orders or contact us; either by email, social networks, our blog or website, mailing address or Phone. Thank you again for your support, we look forward to being of service to you.

ORDER FORM

1. Living Goddess Spirituality, retail $19.99 $18.00 qty___ _____
2. Goddess Grimoire Journal, retail $16.99 $15.00 qty___ _____
3. Gathering for Goddess Manual, retail $26.99 $25.00 qty___ _____
4. Feminine Divine Works Intuitive Oracle BOOK retail $20.99 $20.00 qty___ _____
5. Feminine Divine Works Intuitive Oracle **70x CARD DECK** $50.00 qty___ _____
6. Goddess Gathering T-Shirts (s, m, l) retail $15.99 $11.00 qty___ _____
7. ****Original Artwork by the Author *(Please contact, price varies)*

8. The SpellCrafting Coach, retail $19.99 $18.00 qty___ _____
9. Goddess Songs Music CD Recording, retail $15.99 $11.00 qty-n/n _____
10. The Major Arcana Goddess Living Tarot BOOK, retail $24.99 $20.00 qty___ _____
11. The Major Arcana Goddess Living Tarot 25Card DECK only $30.00 qty___ _____

SPECIAL COUPON CODES FOR DISCOUNTS   Code____ _____
20% discount for purchases of 3 or more items: Disc____ _____
Shipping and Handling ($3.95 per item):   qty___ _____

Shipping:_____

SHIPPING TO:
_____

_____   ORDER TOTAL:_____

Please enclose Payment and this Order form in an envelope.

PAYMENT ENCLOSED_____

ORDER STATUS:_____

FEMININE DIVINE WORKS
P.O. Box 114, Schertz, Texas 78154-0114
Femininedivineworks@gmail.com
Visit our WEBSITE at: http://www.Femininedivineworks.com

www.ingramcontent.com/pod-product-compliance
Lightning Source LLC
Chambersburg PA
CBHW082033230426
43670CB00016B/2639

"Andrew Hampton has crafted a book that does exactly what it says on the cover. He has synthesised his years of Headship experience, knowledge and skill into this accessible yet erudite text. Highly recommended for those aspiring to Headship and those already there."

Dr David Paterson, *Assistant Head*

"A great read whether you are new to headship or have been in headship for some time. Andrew's thoughts make you reflect and challenge your own practice."

Emma Stanhope, *Vice Principal*

"Clear, well-written, and frank, Andrew Hampton's new book provokes reflection and constructive debate, both of which are extremely useful."

Dr Jill Berry, *Consultant in Educational Leadership*

"This easy-to-read guide has helped me step into the shoes of a new headteacher, offering a fresh perspective on leading and guiding a team of staff and children. It's honest and realistic view is incredibly refreshing, with a touch of humour that makes it even more engaging. A must read for SLT (Senior Leadership Team) members and any aspiring headteacher."

Azmina Hansraj, *Deputy Headteacher*

"As an experienced Deputy Head and Designated Safeguarding Lead, I thought I knew what it took to run a school – but after reading this book, I now realise there is so much more that goes on behind the scenes. If you are aspiring to become a member of SLT or a Head at some point in your career, I strongly suggest you read this book."

Jane Banks, *former Deputy Head*

"As a serving Headteacher and someone who appreciates advice that is embedded in research and referenced to 'gurus', I loved this book. Once I had started, I couldn't put it down as I wanted to find out more – especially to find out if there were any 'quick wins' I could employ. (Spoiler alert – there are!)"

Nicola Griffiths, *Headteacher*

TEN YEARS' CAPTIVITY
IN THE
MAHDI'S CAMP
1882–1892

FROM THE ORIGINAL MANUSCRIPTS OF
FATHER JOSEPH OHRWALDER
LATE PRIEST OF THE AUSTRIAN MISSION STATION AT DELEN, IN KORDOFAN

BY
COLONEL SIR FRANCIS WINGATE,
K.C.M.G., C.B., D.S.O., &c.
DIRECTOR OF MILITARY INTELLIGENCE, EGYPTIAN ARMY; AUTHOR OF 'MAHDIISM AND THE EGYPTIAN SUDAN'

*WITH ILLUSTRATIONS
BY WALTER C. HORSLEY AND A PLAN*

FOURTEENTH EDITION, REVISED AND ABRIDGED

The Naval & Military Press Ltd
in association with
The National Army Museum, London

Published jointly by

The Naval & Military Press Ltd
Unit 10 Ridgewood Industrial Park,
Uckfield, East Sussex,
TN22 5QE England

Tel: +44 (0) 1825 749494
Fax: +44 (0) 1825 765701

www.naval-military-press.com
www.military-genealogy.com
www.militarymaproom.com

and

The National Army Museum, London
www.national-army-museum.ac.uk

In reprinting in facsimile from the original, any imperfections are inevitably reproduced and the quality may fall short of modern type and cartographic standards.